Religion ⟨barcode⟩ *tics*

Religion and American Politics

FROM THE COLONIAL PERIOD TO THE PRESENT

Second Edition

Edited by
MARK A. NOLL AND LUKE E. HARLOW

OXFORD
UNIVERSITY PRESS
2007

OXFORD
UNIVERSITY PRESS

Oxford University Press, Inc., publishes works that further
Oxford University's objective of excellence
in research, scholarship, and education.

Oxford   New York
Auckland   Cape Town   Dar es Salaam   Hong Kong   Karachi
Kuala Lumpur   Madrid   Melbourne   Mexico City   Nairobi
New Delhi   Shanghai   Taipei   Toronto

With offices in
Argentina   Austria   Brazil   Chile   Czech Republic   France   Greece
Guatemala   Hungary   Italy   Japan   Poland   Portugal   Singapore
South Korea   Switzerland   Thailand   Turkey   Ukraine   Vietnam

Copyright © 1990, 2007 by Oxford University Press, Inc.

Published by Oxford University Press, Inc.
198 Madison Avenue, New York, New York 10016

www.oup.com

Oxford is a registered trademark of Oxford University Press

Library of Congress Cataloging-in-Publication Data
Religion and American politics : from the colonial
period to the present / edited by Mark A. Noll
and Luke E. Harlow.—2nd ed.
    p.   cm.
Includes bibliographical references and index.
ISBN 978-0-19-531714-5; 978-0-19-531715-2 (pbk.)
1. Christianity and politics—United States—History.
2. United States—Church history.   I. Noll, Mark A., 1946–
II. Harlow, Luke E.
BR516.R34 2007
322'.10973–dc22   2006100381

9 8 7 6 5 4 3 2 1

Printed in the United States of America
on acid-free paper

To Robert W. Lynn

Acknowledgments

THE FIRST EDITION of this book was made possible by a generous grant from the Pew Charitable Trusts, which funded a conference on the book's theme hosted by the Institute for the Study of American Evangelicals (ISAE) at Wheaton College. This second edition has been supported by funds from the Francis A. McAnaney Chair of History at the University of Notre Dame. It is a privilege to thank Wheaton, the ISAE, Notre Dame, and the Pew Trusts for their help.

Special thanks are also due to Margaret Bendroth, Richard Carwardine, Bente Clausen, Darren Dochuk, Michael Emerson, Sébastien Fath, J. Russell Hawkins, Mark Hutchinson, Lyman Kellstedt, Massimo Rubboli, Manfred Siebald, and Peter Steinfels for their willingness to contribute freshly written material to this book; and to George Marsden and Robert Wuthnow for updating what they contributed to the first edition.

It is also our pleasure to acknowledge our spouses, Maggie and Amber, for their faithful encouragement. Their support for our work on this project was essential, and we are most grateful.

The first edition was dedicated to Robert Lynn as a token of appreciation for a long history of cheerful assistance to scholars of American religious history. It is a privilege to repeat that dedication for this second edition.

Contents

MARGARET BENDROTH, the librarian and executive director of the American Congregational Association in Boston, is the author of *Fundamentalism and Gender, 1875 to the Present* (1993) and *Fundamentalists in the City: Conflict and Division in Boston Churches, 1885–1950* (2005); with Virginia Lieson Brereton she has edited *Women and Twentieth-Century Protestantism* (2002).

RUTH H. BLOCH has written *Gender and Morality in Anglo-American Culture, 1650–1800* (2003) and *Visionary Republic: Millennial Themes in American Thought, 1756–1800* (1985). She is a professor of history at UCLA.

RICHARD CARWARDINE, the Rhodes Professor of American History at the University of Oxford, is the author of *Evangelicals and Politics in Antebellum America* (1993) and *Lincoln: A Life of Purpose and Power* (2003), which was awarded the Lincoln Prize in 2004.

BENTE CLAUSEN is a journalist at the Danish newspaper *Kristeligt Dagblad* [Christian Daily], where she regularly writes on Islam, Judaism, church-state relations, and religion in the United States. Her book *For Guds skyld: Om protestantisme og politik i USA* [For God's Sake: Protestantism and Politics in the USA] was published in 2004. She has also worked for the Danish Ministry of Interior and contributed to the prime minister's Commission on Media and Minorities.

DARREN DOCHUK, who is an assistant professor of history at Purdue University, in 2006 won the Allen Nevins Prize for the best dissertation in American history for "From Bible Belt to Sunbelt: Plain Folk Religion, Grassroots Politics, and the Southernization of Southern California, 1939–1969" (University of Notre Dame).

MICHAEL O. EMERSON is the principal author of *Divided by Faith: Evangelical Religion and the Problem of Race in America*, with Christian Smith (2000), and *People of the Dream: Multiracial Congregations in the United States* (2006), with Rodney Woo. He is professor of sociology and director of the Center on Race, Religion, and Urban Life at Rice University.

SÉBASTIEN FATH, who is a member of the Groupe Sociétés Religions Laïcités, is one of France's most respected students of both Protestantism in French history and religion in the contemporary United States. His many books include *Du ghetto au réseau: Le protestantisme évangélique en France, 1800–2005* [From Ghetto to Network: Evangelical Protestantism in France, 1800–2005] (2005), *Billy Graham: Pape protestant?* [Billy Graham: A Protestant Pope?] (2002), and as editor, *Le protestantisme évangélique: Un christianisme de conversion* [Evangelical Protestantism: A Christianity of Conversion] (2004).

JOHN GREEN, the author and editor of many books on American politics, including (as co-editor) *The Values Campaign? The Christian Right and the 2004 Elections* (2006), is Distinguished Professor of political science and director of the Ray C. Bliss Institute of Applied Politics at the University of Akron as well as Senior Fellow in religion and American politics at the Pew Forum on Religion and Public Life in Washington, D.C.

JAMES GUTH, the William R. Keenan Professor of Political Science at Furman University and the 2005 South Carolina Distinguished Professor, has written several books with John Green, Lyman Kellstedt, and Corwin Smidt, including *The Bully Pulpit: The Politics of Protestant Clergy* (1997).

ROBERT T. HANDY is Henry Sloane Coffin Professor of Church History emeritus at the Union Theological Seminary in New York. He is the author of many works in American religious history, including *Undermined Establishment: Church-State Relations in America, 1880–1920* (1991) and *A Christian America: Protestant Hopes and Historical Realities* (rev. ed., 1984).

LUKE E. HARLOW, a Ph.D. candidate in history at Rice University, has published articles on antebellum controversies over slavery and religion in *Slavery & Abolition* and *Ohio Valley History*.

NATHAN O. HATCH became the president of Wake Forest University in 2005. His books include *The Democratization of American Christianity* (1989) and *Methodism and the Shaping of American Culture* (co-editor, 2001).

J. RUSSELL HAWKINS is a Ph.D. candidate in history at Rice University.

JAMES HENNESEY, S.J., who died in 2001 at age seventy-five, taught at several Jesuit colleges and seminaries and enjoyed a long relationship with Canisius College. He was the author of *American Catholics* (1981) and *The First Council of the Vatican: The American Experience* (1963).

DANIEL WALKER HOWE, who is a retired professor of history at UCLA and the former Rhodes Professor of American History, Oxford University, is the author of *The Political Culture of the American Whigs* (1979) and *Making the American Self: Jonathan Edwards to Abraham Lincoln* (1997). His volume on the 1815–1848 period has just appeared in *The Oxford History of the United States*.

MARK HUTCHINSON is dean of graduate studies at the Southern Cross College of the Assemblies of God in Sydney, Australia. He has published books and articles on many topics in Australian religious history, including several that trace Australian links with the United States, Canada, and the European continent. He is also the editor of several books, including *A Global Faith: Essays on Evangelicalism and Globalization* (1998).

LYMAN KELLSTEDT is emeritus professor of political science at Wheaton College. He has coauthored (with David C. Leege) *Rediscovering the Religious Factor in American Politics* (1993) as well as many works with John Green, James Guth, and Corwin Smidt, including *Religion and the Culture Wars* (1996).

GEORGE M. MARSDEN, the Francis A. McAnaney Professor of History at the University of Notre Dame, has written *Jonathan Edwards: A Life* (2003), which was co-winner of the Bancroft Prize and winner of the Grawmeyer Award in 2004; among his other books is *Fundamentalism and American Culture* (rev. ed., 2006).

JOHN M. MURRIN, professor emeritus of history at Princeton University, is the co-editor of *Saints and Revolutionaries: Essays on Early American History* (1984) and the author of essays on nearly every phase of American life in the colonial and revolutionary periods.

MARK A. NOLL, who teaches in the history department at the University of Notre Dame, is the author of *America's God: From Jonathan Edwards to Abraham Lincoln* (2002) and *The Civil War as a Theological Crisis* (2006).

MASSIMO RUBBOLI is a professor of North American history at the University of Genoa, Italy. He has published many books and articles on Canadian and American history, with a special focus on the connections of religion and politics. His works include *Politica e religione negli USA: Reinhold Niebuhr e il suo tempo, 1892–1971* [Politics and Religion in the USA: Reinhold Niebuhr and His Times, 1892–1971] (1986) and *Religione alle urne: Gli "evangelicals" e le elezione presidenziel negli Stati Uniti* [Religion at the Ballot Box: The "Evangelicals" and Presidential Elections in the United States] (1988).

MANFRED SIEBALD is a professor of American studies at the Johannes Gutenberg University of Mainz, Germany, who has often visited the United States, including visiting appointments at Wheaton College, Illinois, and Georgia State University. His published works include his dissertation on Herman Melville and *Der verlorene Sohn in der Amerikanischen Literatur* [The Prodigal Son in American Literature] (2003). He has also enjoyed a successful second vocation as a widely traveled singer-songwriter and acoustic guitarist.

CORWIN SMIDT is the editor of *Religion as Social Capital: Producing the Common Good* (2003) and coauthor (with James M. Penning) of *Evangelicalism: The Next Generation* (2002). He is the Paul B. Henry Professor of Christianity and Politics at Calvin College and has authored many works with John Green, James Guth, and Lyman Kellstedt.

PETER STEINFELS, who writes the "Beliefs" column for the *New York Times*, is co-director of the Fordham University Center on Religion and Culture. He is the author of *A People Adrift: The Crisis of the Roman Catholic Church in America* (2003).

HARRY S. STOUT is the Jonathan Edwards Professor of American Religious History and general editor of the *Works of Jonathan Edwards* at Yale University. His books include *Upon the Altar of the Nation: A Moral History of the Civil War* (2006) and *The Divine Dramatist: George Whitefield and the Rise of Modern Evangelicalism* (1991).

ROBERT P. SWIERENGA, professor of history emeritus at Kent State University and A. C. Van Raalte Research Professor at the Van Raalte Institute of Hope

College, is the author of *Faith and Family: Dutch Immigrants and Settlement in the United States, 1820–1920* (2000) and *Elim: Chicago's Christian School and Life Training Center for the Disabled* (2006).

JOHN F. WILSON is the editor of *The History of the Work of Redemption* (1989) in the Yale edition of the *Works of Jonathan Edwards* and co-editor (with Donald L. Drakeman) of *Church and State in American History: Key Documents, Decisions, and Commentary from the Past Three Centuries* (3rd ed., 2003). He is the Agate Brown and George L. Collard Professor of Religion emeritus and former dean of the graduate school at Princeton University.

ROBERT WUTHNOW is Adlinger Professor of Sociology, director of the Center for the Study of Religion, and chair of the Sociology Department at Princeton University. His many books include *American Mythos: Why Our Best Efforts to Be a Better Nation Fall Short* (2006), *America and the Challenges of Religious Diversity* (2005), and *The Restructuring of American Religion* (1988). He has also edited *The Encyclopedia of Politics and Religion* (2nd ed., 2006).

Religion and American Politics

*T*HE FIRST EDITION of this book was mostly made up of chapters presented at a conference in the spring of 1988. In that year's presidential primaries, which were about at their midpoint when the conference took place, two clergymen-candidates were still in the hunt, the Reverend Jesse Jackson as a contender for the Democratic nomination and the Reverend Pat Robertson for the Republican. At the time, the overt religious energy that Jackson and Robertson were injecting into the campaigns was the object of considerable media attention. By advocating a values-based agenda, Robertson was trying to mobilize his fellow Protestant Pentecostals, who had hitherto been relatively inactive politically, and also to find support beyond Pentecostals and the viewers of his television programming. Jackson's use of moral argumentation moved in a different direction as he sought to register black Americans, mobilize them as a voting bloc, and force the Democrats to strengthen their commitment to urban economic development. In the end, neither campaign was successful, for the Republican nomination went easily to George H. W. Bush, who was finishing his second term as Ronald Reagan's vice president, and the Democratic nod to Governor Michael Dukakis of Massachusetts.

In the fall presidential campaign of 1988, religion remained in the background. Observers did note something new/something old in the religious adherence of the candidates, with Dukakis as the first Greek Orthodox to stand for national office and Vice President Bush an Episcopalian, like so many presidents stretching all the way back to George Washington. Earlier in the Democratic primaries, character issues had sidelined Senator Gary Hart of Colorado (after a charge concerning an extramarital affair) and Senator Joseph Biden of Delaware (after a charge of plagiarism). During the national campaign, one or two reports circulated about the connections of Marilyn Quayle, wife of Republican vice presidential candidate Dan Quayle, to a Texas-based preacher of militaristic fundamentalism, Colonel R. B. Thieme. And after the November elections, a few perceptive observers did notice that a religiously motivated shift toward the Republican Party was continuing to strengthen among white conservative Protestants and white Catholics who were active in their parishes. But for the election season of 1988 as a whole, the most salient matters were questions concerning the candidates' competence, the legacy of Ronald Reagan, the dangers posed by the Soviet Union, and proper management of the economy. Religion did not feature as a major factor in explaining George Bush's comfortable victory in the popular vote (53 percent) or his broader margin in the electoral college (426–111).

In this climate, the first edition of *Religion and American Politics* was eager to offer an argument as well as simply present its historical findings. The argument concerned the enduring importance of religion in American political life and the necessity of understanding that significance with sophistication. The authors wanted to show that almost always, when researchers studied the history of American politics seriously, religion rose as a vitally important matter—but in complex and sometimes ironical ways. For instance, on the most famous church-state question, as shown in the chapters by John Murrin and John Wilson that are retained in this edition, the country's founding fathers testified to the importance of religion in the new nation by neutralizing it in the Constitution.

More generally, the authors were documenting that "religion" has never been a simple constant in American history. Catholics have indeed often acted differently than Protestants in politics, but sometimes Irish Catholics have acted differently than Hispanic Catholics, and sometimes being Catholic has meant one thing in Boston and another in the upper Midwest. By the same token, Baptists in the South have been associated with several different political philosophies and several different sorts of political behavior, depending on time, place, and circumstances. Moreover, denominational allegiance has often not meant as much politically as have styles of worship, levels of education, or attitudes toward moral absolutes—and this is as true today for the United States' growing populations of Muslims, Hindus, and Sikhs as it has always been for the country's many varieties of Christians.

The first edition also recorded how the very understanding of "American religion" has changed over time—from a branch of British Protestantism, through a broader, more indigenously American Protestantism, which then yielded cultural space (often grudgingly) to Roman Catholics, followed by a pluralism of "Protestant-Catholic-Jew," and then an even more pluralistic stage marked by divides between secularists and believers of all sorts, as well as between Christians and members of other faiths, and—continually—between Christians of different sorts.

In 1988, quite a few scholars and media pundits seemed to be concluding that, in an increasingly secular and diverse nation, religion was fading as a central political factor. In retrospect, it is now clear that this perception was misguided, even for 1988. One chapter in the original edition, by sociologist Robert Wuthnow, pointed to clearly discernible signs of growing religious-political salience along a broad liberal-conservative divide that Wuthnow had only shortly before detailed in a thoroughly researched book.[1] The recently named "new Christian Right" had, in fact, established itself as a fixture in the political landscape—even though an otherwise perceptive book growing out of the 1988 election season had just announced the demise of conservative Protestant political influence.[2] And careful attention to the presidential returns in 1988 would have shown that while the votes of white evangelical Protestants and white Roman Catholics for the Republican candidate were close to historic highs, the Republican vote of those who practiced no organized religion was dropping fast from what it had been in the two Reagan elections.[3] Yet in 1988 and into 1990, when this book first appeared, a case needed to be made that religion still counted in American politics.

Today, of course, things are dramatically different. Every presidential election since 1992, and most off-year congressional elections as well, have prominently featured religion in one form or another. The fall of the Berlin Wall in 1989 and the collapse of the Soviet Union in 1991 became, perhaps ironically, the occasion for fresh religious emphases in American politics. With "godless communism" removed as an overriding external foe, internal religious differences that had been muted in the face of external threat now broke into open combat. The intrusion onto American public consciousness of a very different sort of religion in a very disturbing manner on September 11, 2001, refocused and also reenergized all manner of religious issues in public debate: from questions about the separation of church and state and the free exercise of religion to whether the United States' conventions of Protestant-Catholic-Jew could be broadened to include "Muslim" and whether American actions in the Middle East were working for or against the root causes of sectarian strife.

Then, in 2004, "values voting" was widely held to have produced the reelection of Republican George W. Bush over his Democratic opponent, Senator John Kerry from Massachusetts. So impressed—or disconcerted, or amazed, or panicked—was the nation's intellectual sector with the results of this election and the deepening religious influences it was thought to reflect that publishers rushed entire subgenres of books into print—one set to explain (and usually to combat) the regrettable political consequences of the Bush campaign's successful appeal to white evangelical Protestants,[4] another to probe the character of these same evangelical Protestants,[5] and a third to revisit questions about the role of religion in the nation's past, which in this climate had again become controversial.[6]

Given the intense interest in contemporary religious-political connections, this second edition of *Religion and American Politics* does not need to make the argument of its predecessor for the enduring importance of religion in American public life. Yet collections like this are rarely indifferent to contemporary conditions, and along with its historical investigations this new edition is presenting a different sort of argument. This time, the argument concerns the need for contemporaries to lighten up, to incorporate a little bit of historical distance when tempted to extremes of approbation, condemnation, or bewilderment in the face of current events. The religious-political agitations of the recent past are, in fact, far from novel. Beginning with the Civil Rights movement of the 1950s and 1960s and going on to the rise of politically conservative evangelical Protestantism, American politics has returned to the normative situation that prevailed for most of American history.

To be sure, if the baseline for comparison is the period 1929–1954, then recent developments look like an anomaly. During those years, the overwhelming effects of the Depression, World War II, and the Cold War did defuse religious controversy in American political life, but only as an exception compared to what had gone before. By contrast, against the fuller sweep of American history, the political-religious interactions of the last few decades represent no new thing. From arguments over religious freedom during the Constitutional Convention and antebellum sectional division accompanied by learned public debates from Scripture about the morality of slavery, through religion-infused experiences on the home front and with the armies during the Civil War, the imposition of racial segregation after the end of Reconstruction, the rise of populism, the national campaign for prohibition, and the arguments used for entrance into World War I (and against entering that war), to the presidential election of 1928, when the Catholic faith of Democratic candidate Al Smith loomed large, religion was an ever-present if also constantly evolving fixture in American politics.[7] Attention to this longer history shows, for instance, that religious vitriol was spread around more widely during the Thomas Jefferson–John Adams presidential race of 1800 than with Bush versus Kerry in 2004; that public debate over the morality of slavery reached a depth and intensity beyond what has been experienced in debates over, first, African-American civil rights and then abortion and gay marriage; and that Jews and Catholics experienced levels of discrimination into the twentieth century that far exceed the discrimination against Muslims that has been documented for the early twenty-first century.

The point about such comparisons is not to dismiss the seriousness of contemporary religious-political controversies. Nor is it to make a statement in favor of or against any contemporary position. It is rather to suggest that the history of American politics is, for almost all of American history, also significantly a history of American religion, and that attention to this longer history would impart the illumination of perspective to the tangled, urgent—but in virtually no case unprecedented—contentions of recent political-religious engagement.

As with the original publication, this edition of *Religion and American Politics* strives for judicious and soundly researched accounts of major historical themes and periods. It includes nine chapters reprinted without change from the original (except for minor editorial corrections); two that have been revised for this edition; eight that appear here for the first time (with seven of those prepared expressly for this volume); and a collection of briefer comments from foreign observers on the current state of American religion and politics.

As was the first edition, this volume is the product of the recent flourishing of American religious history and the growing willingness of sociologists and political scientists to extend the insights of historians into the present.[8] That flourishing has come about for several reasons, apart from the recent attention to religion fueled by political events. More and more secular academics are acknowledging the importance of religion in the nation's past and present; at the same time, believing scholars show a greater willingness to set religious events into broader contexts of social, economic, intellectual, and cultural developments. The result has been an explosion in the quantity and quality of instructive writing on religion in the American experience.[9]

Religion and American Politics takes stock of existing historical knowledge concerning the relations of religion and politics in the United States from the colonial settlements to the present. The scholars who have contributed to this book are accomplished authorities, well positioned to summarize the most important recent conclusions for their periods or special subjects, even as they share the results of their own research. The notes, sometimes amounting to major bibliographies, suggest the wealth of literature available on almost all aspects of the political-religious relationship. In addition, a bibliographical supplement for the chapters that appear here as they did in the first edition—which follows at the end of this introduction—indicates some of the onward sweep of the scholarship.

In their chronological arrangement, the chapters treat many of the important developments in the history of religion and politics in the United States. But since they are diverse in their methodologies and themes, the chapters also suggest some of the richness—as well as some of the unexpected twists and turns—to be discovered in the subject in general.

THE BOOK BEGINS with John Murrin's overview of the striking circumstances that led from America's colonization by religious monopolists to the creation of constitutional freedom of religion in the early United States. Included in his study is a description of many roads not taken, like the Puritan effort to restrict (not expand) religious freedom, the Quaker experiment of government by pacifists in colonial Pennsylvania, and the religious anarchy of early Rhode Island. Murrin also ponders the network of events that led from the writing of the Constitution, with its largely secular intentions shaped by its largely secular authors, to the flourishing of religion in the new nation, where Americans were soon looking back with holy gratitude upon the work of those founders.

Four chapters follow on critical developments in the founding period and immediately thereafter. Ruth Bloch shows how important religious conceptions were, especially in New England, to the inspiration of the American Revolution and also how religious sensibilities evolved as the ideological excitement of the war gave way to the urgent necessities of nation building. Harry Stout looks at the way elite clergymen in New England found themselves unable to control, or even to understand, the course of politics from the Revolution (which they thought *they* had sponsored as a product of orthodox Christian convictions) to the realities of the democratic new nation (which they regarded as far along the road to godless dissipation and excess). John Wilson's tight focus on the place of religion at the Constitutional Convention and in the passage of the First Amendment is fraught with implications for the present. He argues that the needs of the political moment—specifically, the desire to create a national government from fragmented states jealous of their own prerogatives—dictated the constitutional provisions concerning religion. Along the way, Wilson administers a much-needed application of history to the present. Nathan Hatch, who returns from more narrowly political debates to broader cultural questions, takes democratization as his theme. His chapter testifies to the incompleteness of any historical view that leaves out the achievements of lower-order, dissenting Protestants who, as they drank deeply from the wellsprings of revolutionary rhetoric, greatly advanced the democratization of American religion and, in so doing, the democratization of American society and politics.

Three chapters then treat the dynamic contribution of religion in shaping regional identities during the antebellum period and along the road to war. Daniel Walker Howe, Robert Swierenga, and Richard Carwardine all make full use of a mature, respected body of ethnoreligious research, which demonstrates that religion was the single most important long-term factor in the political alignments of the period. Howe's chapter features an extended discussion of the evangelical contribution to antebellum intellectual and social life, a contribution that everywhere influenced more overt political behavior. Swierenga, a social-scientific historian at home with the techniques of statistical analysis, presents in accessible general terms the results of exacting quantifiable research into the complex, but regular, connections among voting, party affiliation, and religious allegiance. In large part, these connections characterized American politics from 1828 through the 1896 contest between William McKinley (a devout, Bible-reading Methodist friend of business) and William Jennings Bryan (a devout, Bible-reading Presbyterian populist). Richard Carwardine's case study of Methodist politics leading to the Civil War rescues the nation's largest religious movement from the lack of attention that scholars had paid to its large political significance. What Carwardine shows is a shifting set of political allegiances very much constrained by regional locations, but also a constant movement away from the Methodists' early efforts to steer clear of political partisanship.[10]

The chapters featuring developments from the time of the Civil War into the mid-twentieth century begin with Luke Harlow's effort to answer a straightforward question, but one that has not been diligently pursued by historians: if religious support was such a critical factor in the proslavery ideology that led to the Confederacy, what happened to that support when the North vanquished the South? Harlow's answer delves deeply into the tangled racial-religious connections that have been preeminent in American political history and provides, in effect, a bridge from what Carwardine documents to the later considerations of Darren Dochuk and Michael Emerson with J. Russell Hawkins. Robert Handy's chapter shows how closely religious expectations fit with major political developments during the Progressive Era. His account of American religion at the turn of the twentieth century serves also as a summary of ecclesiastical developments to that time and as a base from which to interpret the startling changes of the twentieth century. The chapter by James Hennesey treats Roman Catholics in the period between 1900 (when the Catholic church had clearly emerged as a major force in American life) and 1960 (when the election of John F. Kennedy as president marked a climactic Catholic breakthrough). At the same time, by ranging backward in time through the preceding centuries and with fleeting but telling comments on more recent history, Hennesey shows how central the experiences of Roman Catholics have become for recording and, even more, for interpreting American politics.

The next set of chapters takes the measure of the tumults and realignments since the Second World War. It begins with a magisterial summary of voting behavior and religious allegiance since the Great Depression. Lyman Kellstedt and his colleagues have pioneered in specifying connections between political and religious allegiances in the modern period. They do for these connections what historians like Swierenga have done in the antebellum period—only now with the advantage of mass public polling. The broad political patterns that Kellstedt and his colleagues document for the major religious groups over the last several decades serve as an indispensable social scientific infrastructure for understanding the landscape of contemporary politics and religion.

The chapters by Darren Dochuk and by Michael Emerson and J. Russell Hawkins offer explanations for the shifting allegiances documented by Kellstedt and his coauthors. Dochuk's close-grained study of southern evangelicals who moved to points farther west shows how the spread of a distinctly southern religious flavor also left in its wake a distinctly southern tone for politics. While Dochuk provides indispensable deep background for the political proclivities of white evangelicals, Emerson and Hawkins do the same for the striking differences between black and white conservative Protestants. Among the major religious segments in American public life, no two are closer together in doctrinal and ethical beliefs than black Protestants and white evangelicals—and no two are further apart in voting behavior and political attitudes. Emerson and Hawkins explain why.

Then follow chapters that explore two of the groups that were once marginal in American political life but which over the course of the twentieth century have become central. Peter Steinfels' account details some of the extraordinary range of critical political issues and some of the remarkable figures in the divergent cast of characters found in recent Catholic history. The complexity, ambiguities, and deep engagement with American culture, which Hennesey stressed, turn out to have been only the prelude to much, much more of the same in recent decades. Margaret Bendroth explores how the emergence of women as voters—which did not happen nationally until 1920—has intersected with the importance of women as religious actors. Her sensitive account of countervailing impulses active in mainline Protestantism, feminism, and the culture wars of recent years demonstrates that her subject is one of the most important but also one of the most complicated in contemporary public life.

The book's final section offers broader perspectives. It begins with short commentaries from five non-Americans who have traveled extensively in the United States and studied American history comparatively alongside their own national histories and who as a result are able to offer unusually farsighted assessments of recent American developments. Not surprisingly, these authors—from Germany, France, Italy, Denmark, and Australia—reflect sharper political (and religious) judgments about contemporary issues and individuals than are found in the book's other chapters. Mark Noll then tracks long-standing differences between religious-political connections in Canada and in the United States, but also shows that the most recent Canadian federal elections seem to be moving closer to American patterns. The larger purpose of these chapters is to remind readers that American configurations for religion and politics do not necessarily translate easily throughout the rest of the world.[11]

The book's last two chapters present reflections from two unusually capable observers. Robert Wuthnow's far-ranging general account of religion and politics since World War II explores the hidden chasm stretching across the contemporary religious landscape, a chasm not between denominations but between more basic attitudes concerning the place of religion in both private and public life. Wuthnow describes the development of the new divide with respect to religious divisions, but also with respect to fundamental recent changes in American society and political expectations. The book closes with George Marsden's equally far-ranging overview of the whole course of religion and politics in America. While much can be gained from the particular conclusions of the book's earlier sections, much can also be learned from an effort to view the picture whole. Marsden holds that it is possible to regard American history as a painful struggle to achieve religious consensus on political matters, a struggle that may have witnessed both its culmination and dissolution since the 1960s. These contributions by Wuthnow and Marsden were included in the book's first edition, but have been significantly revised here.

OF COURSE, EVEN a fairly substantial volume like this one cannot be comprehensive, even for its limited themes. So vast is the general subject that many important issues, incidents, and groups receive only passing attention or none at all. Were this an encyclopedia instead of a single book, it would include extensive treatment of Jews, Native Americans, the small sects that often become focal points for sensitive church-state problems, and the non-Christian faiths that now are found in abundance. Many telling episodes would also receive extended treatment, like the establishment of public schools as an extension of the Protestant "benevolent empire" before the Civil War, the crisis of Mormon self-definition when Utah sought statehood, the religious controversies played out in state capitals and local school boards, and the many-faceted role of religious groups in the history of the nation's wars. Still other topics that deserve more attention include religious lobbying for legislation in state capitals and in Washington, the religious convictions of leading politicians, and the symbolism of the country's mottos ("In God We Trust," "One Nation under God"), which in turn broaches the protean subject of civil religion.

Although *Religion and American Politics* does not consider all of these important and worthy subjects, it nonetheless still ranges widely over a broad terrain. In recent years, books and articles on questions across a vast range of the subjects grouped under "religion and politics" have poured forth in an ever-increasing cascade. Much of this published material is superficial or tendentious; much has been intellectually superb. Outstanding reference works now exist that digest and synthesize this flood of words.[12] Particularly innovative work has recently appeared on the regional configuration of religion, which regularly connects religion and politics.[13] And the drumbeat of serious historical scholarship on all aspects of church-state issues only grows with each passing Supreme Court season.[14]

This flood of books follows a path well marked by classic studies, the most provocative of which remains Alexis de Tocqueville's *Democracy in America*. De Tocqueville's specific judgments may have been constrained by the American conditions he observed in the 1830s, but his skill at recording the intimate connections among political culture, political behavior, and church-state circumstances remains unsurpassed, as in this assessment of religion's influence on American public life:

> I have remarked that the members of the American clergy in general, without even excepting those who do not admit religious liberty, are all in favour of civil freedom; but they do not support any particular political system. They keep aloof from parties, and from public affairs. In the United States religion exercises but little influence upon the laws, and upon the details of public opinions, but it directs the manners of the community, and by regulating domestic life, it regulates the state.[15]

After de Tocqueville, other foreign visitors materially advanced the discussion,[16] and they were joined by a number of Americans whose pioneering studies laid the foundation for the great edifices of sophisticated publication in recent decades.[17]

Times have changed considerably since the 1830s, as is evident in how the foreign observers recruited for this book write about the current landscape. They see, for example, much more direct religious involvement in politics than de Tocqueville observed, but also the same strong sweep of influences from the public sphere to religion and back again that he documented. Sorting out the continuities and discontinuities of American religious-political history is, in fact, one of the main goals of this volume.

Its chapters pay rigorous attention to the historical circumstances of America's different eras and so make it possible to address questions about singularity and continuity. Taken together, they represent an exercise in testing the limits, as well as the wisdom, of de Tocqueville's cryptic observation that "religion in America takes no direct part in the government of society, but it must nevertheless be regarded as the foremost of the political institutions of the country."[18]

BIBLIOGRAPHICAL SUPPLEMENT

This short bibliography is intended to suggest a few of the many scholarly resources published since the late 1980s that deal with subjects treated in the chapters from this book's first edition that have not been altered here.

1. John M. Murrin, "Religion and Politics in America from the First Settlements to the Civil War"

Butler, Jon. *Awash in a Sea of Faith: Christianizing the American People*. Cambridge, Mass.: Harvard University Press, 1990.

Hutson, James H. *Religion and the Founding of the American Republic*. Washington, D.C.: Library of Congress, 1998.

Hutson, James H., ed. *Religion and the New Republic: Faith in the Founding of America*. Lanham, Md.: Rowman and Littlefield, 2000.

Matthews, Richard K., ed. *Virtue, Corruption, and Self-Interest: Political Values in the Eighteenth Century*. Bethlehem, Pa.: Lehigh University Press, 1994.

Phillips, Kevin. *The Cousins' Wars: Religion, Politics, and the Triumph of Anglo-America*. New York: Basic, 1999.

West, John G. *The Politics of Revelation and Reason: Religion and Civic Life in the New Nation*. Lawrence: University Press of Kansas, 1996.

2. Ruth H. Bloch, "Religion and Ideological Change in the American Revolution"

Davis, Derek H. *Religion and the Continental Congress, 1774–1789: Contribution to Original Intent*. New York: Oxford University Press, 2000.

Engeman, Thomas S., and Michael P. Zuckert, eds. *Protestantism and the American Founding*. Notre Dame, Ind.: University of Notre Dame Press, 2004.

Hanson, Charles B. *Necessary Virtue: The Pragmatic Origins of Religious Liberty in New England*. Charlottesville: University of Virginia Press, 1998.

Hoffman, Ronald, and Peter J. Albert, eds., *Religion in a Revolutionary Age*. Charlottesville: University of Virginia Press, 1994.

Sandoz, Ellis, ed. *Political Sermons of the American Founding Era, 1730–1805*. Indianapolis, Ind.: Liberty, 1991.

Shain, Barry. *The Myth of American Individualism: The Protestant Origins of American Political Thought*. Princeton, N.J.: Princeton University Press, 1994.

3. Harry S. Stout, "Rhetoric and Reality in the Early Republic: The Case of the Federalist Clergy"

Den Hartog, Jonathan. "Patriotism and Piety: Orthodox Religion and Federalist Political Culture." Ph.D. diss., University of Notre Dame, 2006.

Grasso, Christopher. *A Speaking Aristocracy: Transforming Public Discourse in Eighteenth-Century Connecticut.* Chapel Hill: University of North Carolina Press, 1999.

Noll, Mark A. *Princeton and the Republic, 1768–1822: The Search for a Christian Enlightenment in the Era of Samuel Stanhope Smith.* Princeton, N.J.: Princeton University Press, 1989.

Sassi, Jonathan. *A Republic of Righteousness: The Public Christianity of the Post-Revolutionary New England Clergy.* New York: Oxford University Press, 2001.

4. John F. Wilson, "Religion, Government, and Power in the New American Nation"

Dreisbach, Daniel L. *Thomas Jefferson and the Wall of Separation between Church and State.* New York: New York University Press, 2002.

"Forum on Thomas Jefferson and the Danbury Baptists," *William and Mary Quarterly*, 3rd ser., 56 (Oct. 1999): 775–824.

Hitchcock, James. *The Supreme Court and Religion in American Life*, vol. 1: *The Odyssey of the Religion Clauses.* Princeton, N.J.: Princeton University Press, 2004.

Kurland, Philip B., and Ralph Lerner, eds. *The Founders' Constitution.* 5 vols. Chicago: University of Chicago Press, 1987.

Wilson, John F., and Donald L. Drakeman, eds., *Church and State in American History: Key Documents, Decisions, and Commentary from the Past Three Centuries*, 3rd ed. Boulder, Colo.: Westview, 2003.

Witte, John, Jr. *Religion and the American Constitutional Experiment*, 2nd ed. Boulder, Colo.: Westview, 2005.

5. Nathan O. Hatch, "The Democratization of Christianity and the Character of American Politics"

Hatch, Nathan O. *The Democratization of American Christianity.* New Haven, Conn.: Yale University Press, 1989.

Heyrman, Christine Leigh. *Southern Cross: The Beginning of the Bible Belt.* New York: Knopf, 1997.

Lazerow, Jama. *Religion and the Working Class in Antebellum America.* Washington, D.C.: Smithsonian Institution Press, 1995.

Lyerly, Cynthia Lynn. *Methodism and the Southern Mind, 1770–1810.* New York: Oxford University Press, 1998.

Sutton, William R. *Journeymen for Jesus: Evangelical Artisans Confront Capitalism in Jacksonian Baltimore.* University Park: Pennsylvania State University Press, 1998.

Wigger, John H. *Taking Heaven by Storm: Methodism and the Rise of Popular Christianity in America.* New York: Oxford University Press, 1998.

Wood, Gordon S. *The Radicalism of the American Revolution.* New York: Vintage, 1991.

6. Daniel Walker Howe, "Religion and Politics in the Antebellum North"

Carwardine, Richard. *Evangelicals and Politics in Antebellum America*. New Haven, Conn.: Yale University Press, 1993.

Hanley, Mark Y. *Beyond a Christian Commonwealth: The Protestant Quarrel with the American Republic, 1830–1860*. Chapel Hill: University of North Carolina Press, 1994.

Howe, Daniel Walker. *Making the American Self: Jonathan Edwards to Abraham Lincoln*. Cambridge, Mass.: Harvard University Press, 1997.

Johnson, Curtis. *Redeeming America: Evangelicals and the Road to the Civil War*. Chicago: Dee, 1993.

Matthews, Jean V. *Toward a New Society: American Thought and Culture, 1800–1830*. Boston: Twayne, 1991.

7. Robert P. Swierenga, "Ethnoreligious Political Behavior in the Mid-Nineteenth Century: Voting, Values, Cultures"

Holt, Michael F. *The Rise and Fall of the American Whig Party: Jacksonian Politics and the Onset of the Civil War*. New York: Oxford University Press, 1999.

McKivigan, John R., and Mitchell Snay, eds. *Religion and the Antebellum Debate over Slavery*. Athens: University of Georgia Press, 1998.

Miller, Randall M., Harry S. Stout, and Charles Reagan Wilson, eds. *Religion and the American Civil War*. New York: Oxford University Press, 1998.

Stokes, Melvyn, and Stephen Conway, eds. *The Market Revolution in America: Social, Political, and Religious Expressions, 1800–1880*. Charlottesville: University Press of Virginia, 1996.

10. Robert T. Handy, "Protestant Theological Tensions and Political Styles in the Progressive Period"

Handy, Robert T. *Undermined Establishment: Church-State Relations in America, 1880–1920*. Princeton, N.J.: Princeton University Press, 1991.

Higginbotham, Evelyn Brooks. *Righteous Discontent: The Women's Movement in the Black Baptist Church, 1880–1920*. Cambridge, Mass.: Harvard University Press, 1993.

Hutchison, William R., ed. *Between the Times: The Travail of the Protestant Establishment in America, 1900–1960*. New York: Cambridge University Press, 1989.

Kazin, Michael. *A Godly Hero: The Life of William Jennings Bryan*. New York: Knopf, 2006.

Luker, Ralph. *The Social Gospel in Black and White: American Racial Reform, 1885–1912*. Chapel Hill: University of North Carolina Press, 1991.

11. James Hennesey, S.J., "Roman Catholics and American Politics, 1900–1960: Altered Circumstances, Continuing Patterns"

D'Agostino, Peter R. *Rome in America: Transnational Catholic Ideology from the Risorgimento to Fascism*. Chapel Hill: University of North Carolina Press, 2004.

Dolan, Jay. *In Search of an American Catholicism: A History of Religion and Culture in Tension*. New York: Oxford University Press, 2002.

McGreevy, John T. *Parish Boundaries: The Catholic Encounter with Race in the Twentieth-Century Urban North.* Chicago: University of Chicago Press, 1997.

McGreevy, John T. *Catholicism and American Freedom: A History.* New York: Norton, 2003.

O'Brien, David. *Public Catholicism*, 2nd ed. Maryknoll, N.Y.: Orbis, 1996.

Steinfels, Margaret O'Brien, Peter Steinfels, and Peter Royal, eds. *American Catholics in the Public Square*, vol. 1: *American Catholics and Civic Engagement: A Distinctive Voice*; vol. 2: *American Catholics, American Culture: Tradition and Resistance.* Lanham, Md.: Rowman and Littlefield, 2003, 2004.

NOTES

1. Robert Wuthnow, *The Restructuring of American Religion: Society and Faith since World War II* (Princeton, N.J.: Princeton University Press, 1988). A revised version of the original contribution appears below as chapter 19.

2. Steve Bruce, *The Rise and Fall of the New Christian Right: Conservative Protestant Politics in America, 1978–1988* (New York: Oxford University Press, 1990).

3. For an account of these trends over time, see chapter 12 below, pp. 269–95.

4. As a partial list, see Randall Balmer, *Thy Kingdom Come: How the Religious Right Distorts the Faith and Threatens America: An Evangelical Lament* (New York: Basic, 2006); Greg Boyd, *The Myth of a Christian Nation: How the Quest for Political Power Is Destroying the Church* (Grand Rapids, Mich.: Zondervan, 2006); Monique El-Faizy, *God and Country: How Evangelicals Became America's New Mainstream* (New York: Bloomsbury, 2006); Michelle Goldberg, *Kingdom Coming: The Rise of Christian Nationalism* (New York: Norton, 2006); David Ray Griffin, John B. Cobb, Jr., Richard Falk, and Catherine Keller, *American Empire and the Commonwealth of God: A Political, Economic, and Religious Statement* (Louisville: Westminster John Knox, 2006); Sam Harris, *Letter to a Christian Nation* (New York: Knopf, 2006); George G. Hunter III, *Christian, Evangelical, and . . . Democrat?* (Nashville: Abingdon, 2006); Patrick Hynes, *In Defense of the Religious Right: Why Conservative Christians Are the Life-blood of the Republican Party and Why That Terrifies the Democrats* (Nashville: Nelson Current, 2006); Jan G. Linn, *Big Christianity: What's Right with the Religious Left* (Louisville: Westminster John Knox, 2006); Kevin Phillips, *American Theocracy: The Peril and Politics of Radical Religion, Oil, and Borrowed Money in the 21st Century* (New York: Viking, 2006); Jim Wallis, *God's Politics: Why the Right Gets It Wrong and the Left Doesn't Get It* (San Francisco: HarperSanFrancisco, 2005); and Mel White, *Religion Gone Bad: The Hidden Dangers of the Religious Right* (New York: Penguin/Tarcher, 2006).

5. Again, as only samples, see Richard Kyle, *Evangelicalism: An Americanized Christianity* (New Brunswick, N.J.: Transaction, 2006); Mark I. Pinsky, *A Jew among the Evangelicals: A Guide for the Perplexed* (Louisville: Westminster John Knox, 2006); Lauren Sandler, *Righteous: Dispatches from the Evangelical Youth Movement* (New York: Viking, 2006); Jeffrey L. Sheler, *Believers: A Journey into Evangelical America* (New York:

Viking Penguin, 2006); and Douglas A. Sweeney, *The American Evangelical Story: A History of the Movement* (Grand Rapids, Mich.: Baker, 2005).

6. For example, David L. Holmes, *The Faiths of the Founding Fathers* (New York: Oxford University Press, 2006); James H. Hutson, *The Founders on Religion: A Book of Quotations* (Princeton, N.J.: Princeton University Press, 2005); Isaac Kramnick and R. Laurence Moore, *The Godless Constitution: A Moral Defense of the Secular State*, 2nd ed. (New York: Norton, 2005); Jon Meacham, *American Gospel: God, the Founding Fathers, and the Making of a Nation* (New York: Random House, 2006); James P. Moore, Jr., *One Nation under God: The History of Prayer in America* (Garden City, N.Y.: Doubleday, 2005); Michael Novak and Jana Novak, *Washington's God* (New York: Basic, 2006); Donald W. Shriver, *Honest Patriots: Loving a Country Enough to Remember Its Misdeeds* (New York: Oxford University Press, 2005); Gary Scott Smith, *Faith and the Presidency: From George Washington to George W. Bush* (New York: Oxford University Press, 2006); and Thomas Wang, ed., *America, Return to God* (Sunnyvale, Calif.: Great Commission Center International, 2006).

7. See, as examples of a rich historical literature, the following books on these periods or subjects: Derek H. Davis, *Religion and the Continental Congress, 1774–1789: Contribution to Original Intent* (New York: Oxford University Press, 2000); Richard J. Carwardine, *Evangelicals and Politics in Antebellum America* (New Haven, Conn.: Yale University Press, 1993); Elizabeth Fox-Genovese and Eugene Genovese, *The Mind of the Master Class* (New York: Cambridge University Press, 2005); Harry S. Stout, *Upon the Altar of the Nation: A Moral History of the Civil War* (New York: Viking, 2006); Edward J. Blum, *Reforging the White Republic: Race, Religion, and American Nationalism, 1865–1898* (Baton Rouge: Louisiana State University Press, 2005); Michael Kazin, *A Godly Hero: The Life of William Jennings Bryan* (New York: Knopf, 2006); Richard M. Gamble, *The War for Righteousness: Progressive Christianity, the Great War, and the Rise of the Messianic Nation* (Wilmington, Del.: ISI, 2003); and Robert A. Slayton, *Empire Statesman: The Rise and Redemption of Al Smith* (New York: Free Press, 2001).

8. As examples of such contributions from social scientists, see chapters 12 and 14 below, and for one more outstanding recent example, see R. Stephen Warner, *A Church of Our Own: Disestablishment and Diversity in American Religion* (New Brunswick, N.J.: Rutgers University Press, 2005).

9. As just one survey of that scholarly explosion, see the 500 or so titles listed in Mark A. Noll, *The Old Religion in a New World: The History of North American Christianity* (Grand Rapids, Mich.: Eerdmans, 2002), 300–326.

10. This essay first appeared in *Church History* 69:3 (Sept. 2000): 578–609; it is reprinted in this volume with the permission of the American Society of Church History.

11. This salutary note is the theme of two illuminating books by Paul Freston, *Evangelicals and Politics in Asia, Africa, and Latin America* (Cambridge: Cambridge University Press, 2001) and *Protestant Political Parties: A Global Survey* (Burlington, Vt.: Ashgate, 2004).

12. See especially Robert Wuthnow, ed., *The Encyclopedia of Politics and Religion*, 2nd ed., 2 vols. (Washington, D.C.: Congressional Quarterly Books, 2006). The most useful of earlier reference volumes, with a coverage broader than the title indicates, continues to

be John F. Wilson, ed., *Church and State in America: A Bibliographical Guide*, 2 vols. (Westport, Conn.: Greenwood, 1986, 1987).

13. As building blocks, see Edwin Scott Gaustad and Philip L. Barlow, *New Historical Atlas of Religion in America* (New York: Oxford University Press, 2001); Dale E. Jones et al., *Religious Congregations and Membership in the United States: 2000* (Nashville: Glenmary Research Center, 2002); and Barry A. Kosmin and Ariela Keysar, *Religion in a Free Market: Religious and Non-Religious Americans—Who, What, Why, Where* (Ithaca, N.Y.: Paramount Market Publishing, 2006). The Religion by Region Project under the direction of Mark Silk and Andrew Walsh has made particularly good use of the materials gathered in these reference works and much more; see *Religion and Public Life in the Pacific Northwest: The None Zone*, ed. Patricia O'Connell and Mark Silk (2004); *Religion and Public Life in the Mountain West: Sacred Landscapes in Transition*, ed. Jan Shipps and Mark Silk (2004); *Religion and Public Life in the Midwest: Heartland as Common Denominator*, ed. Philip Barlow and Mark Silk (2004); *Religion and Public Life in New England: Steady Habits Changing Slowly*, ed. Andrew Walsh and Mark Silk (2004); *Religion and Public Life in the Southern Crossroads Region: Showdown States*, ed. William Lindsey and Mark Silk (2004); *Religion and Public Life in the South: In the Evangelical Mode*, ed. Charles Reagan Wilson and Mark Silk (2005); *Religion and Public Life in the Pacific Region: Fluid Identities*, ed. Wade Clark Roof and Mark Silk; *Religion and Public Life in the Middle Atlantic Region*, ed. Randall Balmer and Mark Silk (2006); and Mark Silk and Andrew Walsh, *One Nation Divisible: Religion and Region in the United States* (2007)—all Blue Ridge Summit, Pa.: AltaMira.

14. Again, as only examples from a vast literature, see John T. Noonan, *The Lustre of Our Country: The American Experience of Religious Freedom* (Berkeley: University of California Press, 1998); Philip Hamburger, *Separation of Church and State* (Cambridge, Mass.: Harvard University Press, 2002); James Hitchcock, *The Supreme Court and Religion in American Life*, vol. 1: *The Odyssey of the Religion Clause*; vol. 2: *From "Higher Law" to "Sectarian Scriptures"* (Princeton, N.J.: Princeton University Press, 2004); John Witte, Jr., *Religion and the American Constitutional Experiment*, 2nd ed. (Boulder, Colo.: Westview, 2005); and Noah Feldman, *Divided by God: America's Church-State Problem—and What We Should Do about It* (New York: Farrar, Straus & Giroux, 2005). For an outstanding collection of documents, see John F. Wilson and Donald L. Drakeman, eds., *Church and State in American History: Key Documents, Decisions, and Commentary from the Past Three Centuries*, 3rd ed. (Boulder, Colo.: Westview, 2003).

15. Alexis de Tocqueville, *Democracy in America*, 7th ed., trans. Henry Reeve (New York: Edward Walker, 1847), 332.

16. Andrew Reed, *A Narrative of the Visit to the American Churches by the Deputation from the Congregational Union of England and Wales* (New York: Harper, 1835); Philip Schaff, *America: A Sketch of Its Political, Social, and Religious Character*, trans. from German (New York: Scribner, 1855); James Bryce, *The American Commonwealth*, 3rd ed., 2 vols. (New York: Macmillan, 1895); André Siegfried, *America Comes of Age: A French Analysis* (New York: Harcourt, Brace, 1927).

17. Prime examples include Robert Baird, *Religion in America* (New York: Harper, 1844); H. Richard Niebuhr, *The Kingdom of God in America* (New York: Harper, 1935); Anson Phelps Stokes, *Church and State in the United States* (New York: Harper, 1950);

Winthrop S. Hudson, *The Great Tradition of the American Churches* (New York: Harper, 1953); Leo Pfeffer, *Church, State, and Freedom* (Boston: Beacon, 1953); John Courtney Murray, S.J., *We Hold These Truths: Catholic Reflections on the American Proposition* (New York: Sheed and Ward, 1960); Sidney E. Mead, *The Lively Experiment: The Shaping of Christianity in America* (New York: Harper & Row, 1963); Cushing Strout, *The New Heavens and the New Earth: Political Religion in America* (New York: Harper & Row, 1974); Martin E. Marty, *A Nation of Behavers* (Chicago: University of Chicago Press, 1980); and Marty, *Religion and Republic: The American Circumstance* (Boston: Beacon, 1987).

18. De Tocqueville, *Democracy in America*, 334.

A Protestant Era

Colonial Era to the Civil War

RELIGION AND POLITICS IN AMERICA FROM THE FIRST SETTLEMENTS TO THE CIVIL WAR

John M. Murrin

RELIGION IN AMERICA, we like to believe, is not only freer than in Europe and the rest of the world, but has always been so—or nearly always. One of the most enduring American myths—I intend nothing pejorative by this term, which I use in the anthropological sense of a body of folklore or a series of stories that organizes the way a particular culture tries to understand the world—remains the belief that this country was peopled largely by settlers fleeing religious persecution and yearning for the opportunity to worship openly and without fear. It was never that simple. At one level even popular culture provides a corrective in the equally persistent stereotype of the Puritan as cold, hard, bigoted, unimaginative, humorless—terrified by human sexuality and the enemy of all fun. "The Puritans hated bearbaiting," Thomas Babington Macaulay once remarked, "not because it gave pain to the bear, but because it gave pleasure to the spectators."[1] American undergraduates still respond warmly to this quotation. Like their elders, they prefer to believe both clichés about religion in early America.

I
_____

Of course, neither stereotype does justice to the religious complexity of early New England, much less colonial America as a whole. Most New England Puritans came to these shores not to establish religious liberty, but to practice their own form of orthodoxy. They experienced moments of tension and open conflict when they discovered that John Winthrop's orthodoxy was not Roger Williams's or Anne Hutchinson's. Perhaps Thomas Hooker's was not even John Cotton's. They spent much of the 1630s and 1640s trying to agree on what their orthodoxy was, a process that achieved institutional expression in the Cambridge Platform of 1648, bolstered on the civil side by the Body of Liberties of 1641 as it transformed itself into the law code of 1648. By 1648 most had made compromises that few had anticipated in 1630, but beyond any doubt they meant to narrow, not expand, the religious options available to people in seventeenth-century England.[2]

They succeeded. Outside of Rhode Island, religious belief and practice became far more uniform in early New England than in the mother country at the same time. Bishops, altars, vestments, choirs, the liturgical calendar, and the *Book of Common Prayer* all failed to survive this particular Atlantic crossing, but persecution did in a limited form. Puritans used the law courts to harass and punish the small number of Quakers and Baptists who remained among them. But even though they hanged four Quakers around 1660, few Puritans were comfortable with this behavior. They preferred to cope with dissent by shunning the dissenters. Advocates of severe repression always spoke in the name of a larger religious unity, but serious efforts to implement their program ended by dividing the community, not uniting it.[3]

Something analogous happened in seventeenth-century Virginia. The options available in England diminished sharply in the colony, but in this case dissent, not the establishment, failed to win a secure place in the new settlement. Governor Sir William Berkeley was delighted. "I thank God *there are no free schools* nor *printing*, and I hope we shall not have [either] these hundred years," he exulted, "for *learning* has brought disobedience, and heresy, and sects into the world; and *printing* has divulged them, and libels against the best government. God keep us from both."[4] Although Virginia never obtained its own bishop in the colonial era and clergymen were usually in short supply, the colony managed fairly well as a low-key, very Low Church Anglican establishment. It kept most dissenters far away even during the turbulent 1640s and 1650s, when the Church of England collapsed at home. During the last quarter of the seventeenth century and the first quarter of the eighteenth, the church made striking institutional gains in Virginia just when dissenting energies seemed to be flagging elsewhere. Few planters lamented these restrictions on their choices.[5]

Maryland, of course, began very differently. Although planned by the Calverts as a refuge for persecuted Roman Catholics, the proprietary family always encouraged a high degree of toleration and welcomed Presbyterian and Quaker dissenters to the province. But the hostility between Catholic and Protestant would not disappear. In the wake of the Glorious Revolution of 1688–1689, Catholics were disfranchised and the Church of England became established by law. When a large majority of planters rapidly accepted the new order, dissent in all forms, Protestant or Catholic, became increasingly marginalized. The religious complexion of Maryland began to resemble that of Virginia ever more closely. Partly because they had experienced directly the bitter conflict that religious choice could foster, most Marylanders seemed relieved to be delivered from the anguish of this particular liberty. They, too, were content to enjoy fewer options than those who had remained in England.[6]

In 1740 about 63 percent of the people of British North America lived in the New England or Chesapeake colonies under a Congregational or Anglican establishment with few real religious choices.[7] Some dissent did exist, of course, but for the most part it was stagnant or declining. Baptists and Quakers had ceased to grow in New England before the end of the seventeenth century; in that region only Anglicans were still expanding at Congregational expense, and their numbers were still very small.[8] Dissent had been shrinking rapidly in Maryland since the 1690s and had never achieved significance in Virginia. In both regions, the clergy worried more about popular indifference and laxity than about overt denominational challenges to the established order. More than a century after the first settlements, most of the people in British America lived within a narrower band of religious choices than fellow subjects enjoyed in England. A mere half-century before the drafting of the Bill of Rights, a well-informed observer could not easily have detected in most of the American colonies much of a popular base for the active separation of church and state as proclaimed in the First Amendment.

II

But the Chesapeake and New England were not the whole story. What was happening among the other third of the colonial population would help to shatter this older pattern and would eventually characterize all of nineteenth-century America.

Religion in the Middle Atlantic colonies marked the most striking departure from the European norm of an established church. In New Netherland, the Dutch Reformed church was actively supported by the government, and Peter Stuyvesant grimly persecuted Quakers and other dissenters. But the church lost its privileges after the English conquest of 1664, and the Church of England never came close to providing a substitute. No regular Anglican parish was established anywhere in the colony before the 1690s. The vast bulk of the English-speaking population consisted of dissenters, mostly New Englanders with little affection for formal Anglican ways. Few settlers from non-English backgrounds would support an Anglican establishment. Even though the legislature did establish the church in the four southern counties of the province in the 1690s, the institution remained weak, incapable of attracting the loyalties of most colonists. Toleration vanquished establishment if only because even those who favored establishment were divided over which church to support. The established churches of England, Scotland, and the Netherlands all had committed adherents by the eighteenth century. None could win preeminence in either New York or neighboring New Jersey.[9]

In Pennsylvania and Delaware, toleration became much more the preferred choice of the community as a whole. Lutheran, German Reformed, and Presbyterian clergymen lamented the "disorder" they detected all around them and sometimes all but despaired of bringing the proper worship of God to the American wilderness. But, beginning in the 1680s, the Quakers had set the tone for the Delaware Valley. At no point thereafter did an established church seem even a remotely viable option. Churches became voluntary societies that people joined only if they so desired and then supported through private contributions. They had to compete with one another for members, and they received no special privileges from the government.[10] Within its small corner of New England, Rhode Island had already moved in this direction beginning in the 1630s.[11] Somewhat less directly, North Carolina stumbled in the same direction in the colonial South. The Church of England was established there by law shortly after 1700, but most settlers seldom saw an Anglican clergyman. Dissent became the norm despite the law.[12]

III

Before 1740 the Chesapeake and New England colonies narrowed the religious choices that had been generally available in England. The Middle Atlantic colonies along with Rhode Island and North Carolina expanded them. Were these trends utterly contradictory or can we find any underlying uniformities between them?

Two points seem relevant here: the institutional possibilities that America created and the potential for sustained and effective governmental coercion.

Colonial North America was not a place where everyone was "doomed" to be free. It was an institutional void. Because it lacked the fixed structures of European societies, people could try out in the wilderness a whole range of ideas and experiments impossible to attempt in Europe. Some had a liberating vision that we still find bracing. The Quakers of West New Jersey drafted and implemented a constitutional system that was as radical as anything yet tried by Europeans. Other novelties could be extremely repressive. The Americas, not Europe, witnessed the resurrection of chattel slavery on a gigantic scale.[13]

Puritans erected their godly commonwealth in New England because the English Crown would not let them do so in England. To be sure, those who had remained behind overturned the monarchy and established their own Puritan regime, but it collapsed much more quickly than the one in America. Unlike Oliver Cromwell's Protectorate, the New England Way survived long enough to expose the tensions and contradictions inherent within the Puritan vision itself.[14] So did William Penn's Holy Experiment. Only in America did pacifists have three fourths of a century to demonstrate whether they could or could not govern a complex society in a world often at war.[15] Even Lord Baltimore's Maryland, too often dismissed as a stodgy anachronism, embodied an equally bold vision. Where else did a Catholic elite try to rule a Protestant majority through toleration, disestablishment, and broad political participation? To the Calverts, the emphasis on feudal hierarchy probably seemed a necessary cement for an otherwise fragile structure. The manorial system had little impact after the first decade or two, but the rest of the experiment lasted more than a half-century. After 1660 it was getting stronger, not weaker, until it was undermined by the Glorious Revolution in England.[16]

America may be, as Daniel Boorstin once argued, the burial ground for Europe's utopias. More important, it was the only place where these experiments could receive a serious trial. All were doomed to failure in Europe. In America, they got the chance to prove what they could accomplish. Only in America did several of them survive long enough to expose their inherent contradictions and to fail, not primarily because of conflict with outsiders, but through their own momentum or social dynamic. This pattern has long been clear for the New England Way and the Holy Experiment, but the logic even applies to the Church of England in colonial Virginia.[17]

Well into the first quarter of the eighteenth century, the planters seemed quite content to remain a colonial outpost of the mother church. Then this aspiration began to collide with the underlying demographic realities of North America, which affected even public worship in profound ways. Few planters hoped to become clergymen or to have their sons ordained. William and Mary

College, organized around the turn of the century, did little to change this situation. The Anglican church had to import clergy to survive. Just after 1700, the Society for the Propagation of the Gospel in Foreign Parts (SPG) made concerted efforts to send Oxford and Cambridge graduates into the colonies. In the Chesapeake, the ratio of clergy to settlers reached its highest point in the 1710s. But the population of the colonies doubled every twenty-five years. Oxford and Cambridge were stagnant. Even by sustaining its efforts, the SPG could not hope to keep pace with the demand in North America. It too would have had to double its efforts every generation. Although it did draw increasingly upon more dynamic universities in Scotland and Ireland, it was already losing the struggle by the 1720s. Especially in the Piedmont, the Southside, and the Valley, many of the laity were slipping out of touch with the established church. The Great Awakening would soon give them a chance to improvise their own solutions to this religious dilemma.[18]

In other societies, governmental coercion might succeed in imposing orthodoxy despite these difficulties, but in all of the colonies these instruments were weak. No governor commanded a permanent military force of any significant size. No reliable hierarchy of social and economic clientage or patronage helped to ensure that lesser people would accept the religious judgments of their social superiors. To an extraordinary degree, government relied instead on voluntary cooperation to be effective. The results could be quite authoritarian when the broader population accepted such goals, as New Haven's rigid Puritan regime well illustrates.[19] But when any sizable portion of the population rejected the values of those in office, government had little chance of securing broad compliance.[20] The Quaker magistrates of West Jersey could not surmount the open defiance of non-Quaker settlers by the 1690s.[21] When the justices of Albany County, New York, summoned individuals to court in the eighteenth century, a large majority never bothered to appear.[22] If any one feature of early America tells us how settlers who did not deliberately choose religious freedom got it anyway, the weakness of government is that factor.

IV

For most people during the first century of settlement and beyond, religious choice remained narrower, not greater, than what England allowed. After 1740, that pattern changed irreversibly. The reasons are not hard to find: the First and Second Great Awakenings with the Revolution sandwiched between them.

Together, these events generated the most important denominational reshuffling in American history. Into the 1730s, the prevailing denominations were

Congregationalist in New England, Anglican in the South, and—somewhat less firmly—the Quakers and their sectarian German allies in the Delaware Valley. New York and New Jersey were already a mosaic of competing denominations that no one group could dominate, a pattern that also characterized Rhode Island and North Carolina. But Congregationalists, Anglicans, and Quakers remained far more influential than all other rivals. The First Great Awakening, a series of intense revivals concentrated in the 1730s and 1740s, made New England and Virginia far more pluralistic than they had ever been before. The Revolution disestablished the Church of England from Maryland through Georgia. The Second Great Awakening, which spread throughout the continent after 1800, captured the religious loyalties of most settlers in the South and West and also disestablished the Congregational church in the New England states. By the 1820s, religious pluralism, the lack of an establishment, and full toleration had become the traditional pattern. It prevailed everywhere but in Massachusetts, which finally came into line by 1833. By then, even most clergymen considered the transformation a good thing. They believed that voluntaristic religion produced healthier varieties of Christian commitment than any form of state support could generate.[23]

In denominational terms, this shift meant that the three prevailing faiths prior to 1740 would lose influence and adherents to three newcomers by 1820. Baptists and Methodists vied for the largest membership in the United States, a contest that Methodists would win by a narrow margin before the Civil War. A distant third, but well ahead of all other rivals, were the Presbyterians. These three denominations shared one major feature: all had embraced evangelical piety in the eighteenth century. Anglicans and Quakers had rejected the Awakenings.[24] Congregationalists in New England were divided fiercely over the revivals. Old Lights generally prevailed in eastern Massachusetts and western Connecticut, the traditional heart of each colony; New Light strength was greatest on the periphery of each.[25] In the Middle Atlantic, the revivals also split the young Presbyterian church by 1741. Because Old Side antirevivalists outnumbered New Side awakeners at that point, the revivalists seceded from the Philadelphia Synod and organized their own synod in New York City by 1745, with the most dynamic leadership coming from the Tennent family in New Jersey and Jonathan Dickinson on Long Island. By the time this rift was healed in 1758, the New Side clergy had become far more numerous than their opponents simply because—first at the Log College in Neshaminy, Pennsylvania, and later at the College of New Jersey, finally located at Nassau Hall in Princeton in the 1750s—the New Side had acquired the means to train its own clergy. Old Side Presbyterians still relied on Ulster and Scotland as their source of ministers.[26]

Methodists and Baptists had even greater advantages in this respect. By not insisting on a college education and by emphasizing charismatic qualities over formal learning, they could train men quickly and were ideally situated to conquer the West. The three denominations that had dominated the colonies before 1740 never made much headway in the West. Anglican settlers who crossed the mountains almost never brought the Church of England with them, although many may have preferred Methodism to other evangelical faiths because it was an offshoot of Anglicanism. Similarly, New Englanders loyal to their ancestral faith rarely remained Congregationalists when they moved west. They were much more likely to become Presbyterians. Except for a few pockets in Indiana and elsewhere, Quakers made almost no headway in the West. From the 1750s through the War of 1812, the American frontier was an exceptionally violent place, as the Iroquois, Delawares, Shawnees, Creeks, Cherokees, and Seminoles organized the last heroic phase of their resistance to settler encroachment. Quaker pacifism did not thrive in this environment.[27]

V

The Revolution brought another momentous change to North America. By the late eighteenth century, the churches were no longer the only official representatives for public values. They had rivals. Today, many Americans like to think of the revolutionary generation as quiet and confident custodians of our fundamental values. They were less confused by their world than we are by ours. When we get into trouble, we can always turn to them to regain our moral bearings.[28]

This vision has a fatal weakness. The revolutionary generation never shared a single set of fundamental values. Then, as now, people had to decide which of a half-dozen sets of competing fundamental values they wished to uphold. These choices became urgent, even agonizing, as the century roared to its passionate conclusion in the violence of the French Revolution, an upheaval that shook America almost as profoundly as it did Europe. At least six discernible value systems competed for the allegiance of Americans: Calvinist orthodoxy, Anglican moralism, civic humanism, classical liberalism, Tom Paine radicalism, and Scottish moral sense and commonsense philosophy. They did not exhaust the possibilities. For example, Roman Catholics and Jews affirmed very different constellations of values, but far into the nineteenth century both groups still remained well on the margins of American life.

The prevailing six differed dramatically. While some of their emphases could be reconciled with one another, many could not. Calvinist orthodoxy achieved its most systematic and eloquent statement in America in the writings of

Jonathan Edwards and his students. It was no anachronism in the age of the Revolution. Edwardsians insisted on predestination, the inerrancy of scripture, and the centrality of the conversion experience in the life of a Christian. To be converted, a person must first recognize his or her utter lack of merit in the eyes of God. Only then would God bestow saving grace on someone to whom he owed nothing whatever.[29] Anglican moralists, by contrast, rejected the necessity of a conversion experience and emphasized the need to lead an ethical life in this world. This tradition left few systematic expressions in eighteenth-century America, but it undoubtedly made a deep impact on gentlemen planters and other elite groups.[30] Civic humanism went even further in its concentration upon this-worldly activities. The fullest life, its apologists insisted, is that of the citizen who must always be willing to sacrifice self-interest for the common good.[31] Civic humanists gloried in their own rectitude and incorruptibility. Although many evangelical Calvinists could embrace the ethic of sacrifice that civic humanists demanded, few people who began as civic humanists could ever become evangelical Calvinists. They could not persuade themselves that their best deeds stank in the nostrils of the Lord. They could not achieve the humility essential to an orthodox conversion experience.[32]

Classical liberalism—the philosophy that society will be much better off if individuals are left free to pursue their self-interest with minimal governmental restraint—clashed with all three of the older value systems. In many ways, it grew out of the natural rights philosophy of John Locke, a Socinian (or proto-unitarian) in theology. Its principal European spokesmen after 1740—David Hume, Adam Smith, Jeremy Bentham, and, later, John Stuart Mill—were all atheists, although Smith never advertised his loss of faith. Liberalism seemed to transform the Christian sin of greed into a civic virtue. It seemed to mock the civic humanist commitment to disinterested patriotism.[33] Tom Paine's admirers posed equally dramatic challenges. Many were deists rather than unbelievers, but their challenge to Protestant orthodoxy drove many clergymen close to panic in the 1790s.[34] Radicals also challenged an assumption common among moderate and conservative civic humanists, that gentlemen of leisure made the best citizens and officeholders. To radicals, this claim was but a disguised assertion of aristocratic privilege. Only men who worked for a living deserved the confidence of other citizens.[35]

Scottish moral sense philosophy derived mostly from Francis Hutcheson of Glasgow and from the Edinburgh literati, a remarkably talented group that made important contributions to most fields of knowledge in the last half of the eighteenth century. The Scots tried to synthesize the best of existing knowledge. Moral sense philosophy tried to find a more compelling basis for human ethics than John Locke's highly cerebral reliance upon explicit understanding of natural law among people living in the state of nature. The Scots, whose curiosity drove them to read much of the descriptive literature about American Indians, had difficulty imagining the Iroquois, for example, rationally deducing the laws of nature in their longhouses before embarking on moral behavior. Instead, the Scots endowed every human with a moral sense, an ingrained and instantaneous response to external stimuli. Until corrupted by their cultures or by habit, people react positively to benevolent actions (for example, a mother nursing her infant) and negatively to malevolence (for instance, teenagers clubbing a grandmother). Commonsense philosophy provided an antidote to the skepticism of Hume by, first, trying to establish what people can take for granted and then by building larger philosophical systems upon this foundation. At first, many Calvinists regarded moral sense philosophy as a challenge to the doctrine of original sin, but by the end of the century Scottish learning had triumphed almost completely in American academic life. Scottish commonsense philosophy is still taught today in fundamentalist schools. Its original enemies have become its warmest advocates.[36]

VI

Partly because disestablishment took government out of the business of proclaiming and defending fundamental values, the struggle among these systems was passionate but seldom violent. The state did not execute nonjuring clergymen—unlike the government of revolutionary France, which brought many priests to the guillotine. Although the officeholding class in the United States was probably no more orthodox than its counterparts in Britain and France, nearly all public officials deliberately minimized rather than emphasized how far they had strayed from ancestral beliefs. Thomas Jefferson and James Madison cooperated actively with Baptists and Presbyterians in Virginia politics to disestablish the Protestant Episcopal church, but to the dismay of many Presbyterians they also refused to sanction tax support for any other denomination or combination of denominations.[37] Jefferson and Madison along with George Washington, John Adams, Benjamin Franklin, and nearly all of the founding fathers claimed to be Christians; but, by virtually any standard of doctrinal orthodoxy, hardly any of them was. They demanded the right to think for themselves on the most sensitive questions of faith, doctrine, and morals, but they did not try to impose their conclusions on others by force.

Yet these were precisely the men who led the way in drafting the nation's fundamental laws—its most admired constitutions, state and national, and its bills of rights at both levels. The first state constitutions usually invoked God somewhere in the text. "The People of this State, being by the Providence of God, free and independent," declared Connecticut in converting its royal charter into a constitution in 1776, "have the sole and exclusive Right of governing themselves as a free, sovereign, and independent State."[38] The preamble of the Massachusetts Constitution of 1780 explicitly recognized the providence of God while "imploring His direction" in framing a government derived from the people.[39] New Hampshire in 1784 based all "due subjection" to government upon "morality and piety, rightly grounded on evangelical principles."[40]

The explicit theism of these pronouncements made them exceptional at the time. Other constitutions were more perfunctory, or they used the language of the Enlightenment rather than scripture or the ritual phrases of any of the Protestant churches. The preamble to the Pennsylvania Constitution, for instance, proclaimed that government exists to protect natural rights "and the other blessings which the Author of existence has bestowed upon man" and acknowledged "the goodness of the great Governour of the universe" for the people's opportunity "to form for themselves such just rules as they shall think best for governing their future society."[41] Even Massachusetts, while explicitly invoking providence, avoided the word "God." Instead the drafters acknowledged "with grateful hearts, the goodness of the Great Legislator of the Universe" in permitting the people of the commonwealth to assemble peaceably and create their own "original, explicit and solemn compact with each other."[42] The preamble to the Vermont Constitution of 1777 saluted natural rights "and the other blessings which the Author of existence has bestowed upon man."[43] Neither Pennsylvania nor Vermont joined Massachusetts in recognizing divine providence. Both assumed that the people had to make their political decisions for themselves. Even the Articles of Confederation, something less than a full organic document, explicitly invoked God, "the Great Governor of the world," who, however, assumed something more than a deistic role when he "incline[d] the hearts of the legislatures we represent in Congress, to approve of . . . the said articles of confederation and perpetual union."[44]

In some states, the reference to God was casual and incidental, but it did reveal something about popular expectations. Virginia mentioned God only in the last clause of the Declaration of Rights, which guaranteed full religious freedom because "Religion, or the duty which we owe to our Creator, and the manner of discharging it, can be directed only by reason and conviction, not by force or violence."[45] The New Jersey Constitution closely followed this model. Georgia acknowledged a deity only in prescribing specific texts for several oaths. Maryland made no explicit mention of God's blessings, but in requiring all officeholders to be Christians, its constitution was in fact far more traditional than most others of the period. In a slightly weaker clause, North Carolina, after barring all clergymen from public office (as did several other states), required all officeholders to believe in God, an afterlife, the truth of the Protestant religion, and the divine authority of both the Old and New Testaments.[46]

In the light of this pattern, the failure of the federal Constitution to mention God becomes all the more significant. The delegates to the Philadelphia Convention must have realized that they were doing something singular in this respect. They used the text of the Articles of Confederation quite often for specific clauses of the Constitution, but they omitted the passage that invoked God. They were used to seeing chaplains in their state legislatures and in the Continental Congress, but they invited none to participate in their deliberations. This choice was no mere oversight. When disagreements became particularly ferocious in late June 1787, Franklin moved to invite one or more clergymen to lead them in prayer at the beginning of each day. Hamilton objected on grounds of realpolitik. The delegates had sent for no chaplain until then; to do so at that moment could only inform the world how badly at odds they were. Edmund Randolph countered with the shrewd suggestion that they first invite a minister for the Fourth of July celebration and then continue the practice thereafter. The public would not realize that a transition had occurred. But the resolution won little support in either form—four votes, in all probability with only Roger Sherman and Jonathan Dayton joining Franklin and Randolph. Yet even in a convention closed to the public, the majority was much too prudent to vote directly against God. Instead, Hamilton and Madison carried a motion to adjourn.[47]

The federal Constitution was, in short, the eighteenth-century equivalent of a secular humanist text.[48] The delegates were not a very orthodox group of men in any doctrinal sense. The only born-again Christian among them was probably Richard Bassett of Delaware, a Methodist who generously supported the labors of Francis Asbury and other missionaries but who said nothing at the convention.[49] Roger Sherman may have been another, but his advocacy of New Light causes in Connecticut seems more political than religious.[50] One cliche often applied to the Constitution is not correct in any literal sense—that the founders, unlike the wildly optimistic French, believed in original sin and its implications for government and politics.

Quite possibly not a single delegate accepted Calvinist orthodoxy on original sin—that humankind is irretrievably corrupted and damned unless redeemed from outside. Washington, Franklin, Madison, Hamilton, James Wilson, and Gouverneur Morris gave no sign of such a belief at this phase of their lives. As a Methodist, even Bassett was probably an Arminian in theology, willing—like John Wesley—to give individuals some effective agency in their own salvation.

But if the delegates did not think that humanity is irrevocably corrupted, they did believe that humankind is highly corruptible and that a surrender to corruption had destroyed nearly every republic before their day. When combined with the vestige of aristocratic honor that most founders shared, this fear came to mean something rather different: a conviction that *other* people are corrupt. The typical founding father repeatedly insisted that *his* motives were pure, disinterested, patriotic—a judgment often extended to his close friends in public life as well. Jefferson had no higher praise for Madison, but he always suspected Hamilton of sinister designs.[51]

Although the dread of corruption had a genuine affinity for orthodox Christian values, it drew far more directly from civic humanist sources, the effort by the seventeenth and eighteenth centuries to understand why republics had failed in the past and how they could be constructed to endure. The convention's answer to this problem, although not always civic humanist in content and emphasis, came very close in most particulars to what today's evangelicals mean by secular humanism.[52]

Present-day conservative evangelicals usually define three components as the essential ingredients of secular humanism. First is the willingness to elevate human reason above divine revelation whenever a conflict appears between them. Beyond any doubt, nearly all of the founders qualify on this score. Jefferson and Adams certainly fit that description.[53] Madison, although he probably contemplated entering the ministry as a young college graduate and affirmed some basic Calvinist tenets as late as 1778, seemed much more comfortable with nature's supreme being than with the God of revelation by the 1780s. He looked increasingly to history, not to the Bible, for political guidance.[54] James Wilson also believed that the Bible usefully reinforced moral precepts that we learn through our moral sense and reason, not the other way around.[55]

As a group, the founders took Protestant private judgment a step beyond earlier eras and used it to evaluate the plausibility of scripture itself. Most of them were extremely reluctant to use the word "God" or "Christ." They flatly rejected miracles, whether attested by scripture or not. As Jefferson advised his nephew, one should read the Bible as one would any other book, accepting what is edifying and rejecting what is fantastic. He chose a sensitive issue on which to make his point. The virgin birth being impossible, Jesus of Nazareth must have been a bastard. "And the day will come," he assured John Adams several decades later, "when the mystical generation of Jesus by the supreme being as his father in the womb of a virgin will be classed with the fable of the generation of Minerva in the brain of Jupiter."[56]

A second criterion of secular humanism is the conviction that human solutions are adequate for human problems. Politicians need not invoke God or providence. At the Philadelphia convention, a large majority explicitly refused to do so, as we have seen, and they proceeded to devise a constitution that, in the words of one nineteenth-century admirer, became "a machine that would go of itself." Built-in checks and balances pitted one human passion against another. The separation of powers kept Congress, the president, and the courts warily watching one another. The House and Senate likewise checked each other and, within the broader federal system, so did the state and national governments as a whole. Madison hoped that he had created a political system that would routinely produce leaders who could identify and pursue the common good above narrow and selfish interests. In this respect, he left little to chance—or providence. Instead, he put his confidence in the structure of the constitutional system as a whole.[57]

Ethical relativism has become the third component of secular humanism, at least as defined by certain popular evangelical leaders. In the modern sense of a truly relative or situational ethics, the term does not apply to the founders. But while they admired the moral precepts of Jesus of Nazareth, virtually all of them also believed that humanity can do better than what the Bible prescribes. Anticlerical in a rather gentle way, they were extremely reluctant to let any minister or church define their moral priorities for them. They believed that man was still making tremendous improvements in the moral character of public life, which, on the whole, they valued above traditional private morality. The churches, they noted quietly from time to time, had contributed much misery to the world through internal conflict and persecution. Rational man, they assumed, ought to do better. They aspired, in short, to something more perfect than the organized Christianity of their own day. They differed from ethical relativists of today in their expectation that reasonable people would someday find a loftier moral code that all could affirm and implement. When Jefferson predicted shortly before he died that most American youths would enter adulthood as Unitarians, he proved to be a terrible prophet. But what he really meant is that he expected them to embody a stronger morality than traditional churches had espoused.[58]

On all of these grounds, the founders meet the definition of secular humanism. If it is now ruining the republic, they started the process. At a minimum, they expanded the content of American pluralism. Secular values became so prominent in the overall revolutionary achievement that, fully as much as the

Puritan vision of an earlier age, they emerged as an essential part of the American experience. Of course, the two systems of thought overlapped at many points. Defenders of the Puritan tradition were already recasting its original emphasis on religious and civil liberty (which in 1630 had meant the political freedom to practice religious orthodoxy unrestrained from abroad) into a new hierarchy that valued civil over religious liberty. Secular apologists for the republic, if they had a taste for historical precedents, usually learned to admire Roger Williams and Anne Hutchinson, George Fox and William Penn. Yet, despite genuine similarities, the underlying motivations between seventeenth-century religious radicals and eighteenth-century revolutionaries were quite different. Williams and the Quakers favored a sharp separation of church and state because they were convinced that, in any formal union, the state will always corrupt the church. Jefferson and Madison also favored rigid separation, but for the opposite reason. They believed that when any church is established by law, it will corrupt the polity.[59]

VII

The potential for conflict between secular leaders and the defenders of orthodoxy remained quite strong throughout the era of the Revolution and the early republic. At times, clerical denunciations of the new godlessness became shrill and even hysterical, particularly in the assault in 1798 upon the Bavarian Illuminati, a secret and conspiratorial group credited with the destruction of religion in France and who were now, supposedly, trying to repeat that triumph in America. When Jefferson ran for president in 1800, his religious convictions—or lack thereof—became a major campaign issue in New England.[60]

And yet the truly remarkable feature about the age as a whole is how contained this struggle was. About half of the clergy of France could not accept the Civil Constitution of the Clergy and became enemies of the revolutionary regime. In the United States, nearly all of the clergy (including even a majority of Anglicans) supported the Revolution, the Constitution, and later the War of 1812. Some of them perfectly understood the secular vision of the founding fathers. "We formed our Constitution without any acknowledgment of God," reflected Timothy Dwight as the War of 1812 threatened to engulf the land in a new calamity. "The Convention, by which it was formed, never asked, even once, his direction, or his blessing upon their labours. Thus we commenced our national existence under the present system, without God."[61] But this tone was never the predominant one even among the clergy, most of whom greatly preferred the Constitution to the Articles of Confederation in 1788 and never saw reason to change their mind.[62]

How can we explain this conflict that never quite happened? Several reasons come to mind. One is the most obvious contrast between religion and revolution in France and in America. France's radical republicans gloried in their assault upon orthodoxy, while the founding fathers all claimed to be "Christians." They used the word in a way that aroused the suspicions of numerous ministers, but in doing so they also signaled their unwillingness to fight, at least in public, about such issues. New England Federalists denounced Jefferson's godlessness in 1800. He never replied. Madison kept his religious opinions very much to himself as he drifted away from orthodoxy. Second, although the Constitution was in no explicit way a religious text, it was also not antireligious. It provided no overt threat to anybody's doctrinal convictions. Firm believers in original sin could find much to admire in it even if its drafters did not share their conviction. Finally, the secular humanists of 1787 eventually had to confront Madison's own logic about how things really worked in America. By 1798, as part of his own defense of the states' rights position of the Jeffersonian opposition, Madison insisted that the Philadelphia convention never had the power to implement and therefore define the meaning of the Constitution. That act took place through the process of ratification. Only the people in their separate state conventions had the power to put the Constitution into practice. Through the same process, only they could decide what it means.[63]

In the nineteenth century, the American public sacralized the Constitution. The extreme case is the Mormon church, which still teaches that the convention was inspired by God, that the Constitution is thus the product of explicit divine intervention in history. Others did not go that far, but by the 1820s, mostly because of Jonathan Dayton's garbled recollections, they were quite happy to believe that Franklin's prayer motion at the Convention not only carried but was passed with at most a single dissent and that it also marked the turning point in the debates. Soon after sending for a minister, according to Dayton's version, the large and small states agreed upon the Great Compromise, and the republic was saved. No effective answer to this claim was available until 1840, when Madison's notes were finally published. By then, the public's eagerness to sanctify the secular had probably gone too far to reverse.[64]

VIII

Americans are indeed a peculiar people. The enormous range of religious choice available to the public since the late eighteenth century has generally favored evangelical Protestants over more traditional ones, but it has also energized Roman Catholics to a startling degree. While Catholicism faced a serious threat of decline nearly everywhere in nineteenth-century Europe, it built a larger and more faithful base of communicants in the United States than anywhere else in the world. American Catholics were also less inclined to heresy and more loyal to the pope than just about any other large body of Catholics in the world. Somehow, the most traditional as well as the most evangelical of Christian churches were able to thrive in America. The land foreordained nobody's success, but it did provide amazing opportunities that groups and institutions could learn to use if they had sufficient energy and imagination.

The Revolution also liberated an important group of gentlemen from the constraints of orthodoxy long enough for them to draft the constitutions and bills of rights at both the state and federal levels. Major elements of the broader public have been trying to Christianize these texts ever since.

The real meaning of America and the American Revolution is not in one alternative rather than the other, but in their continuing and dramatic interaction. Neither the orthodox nor the skeptics have ever been able to destroy one another. Neither can they do so without drastically redefining the whole of the American experience. At some periods, such as the New Deal era, this tension has been very muted. At other times, it has come close to defining the central issues of the age. Without the northern evangelical assault upon slavery, there would have been no Civil War. Without the evangelical resurgence in the United States from the 1960s to the present, there probably would have been no Reagan revolution, nor the conservative political resurgence that has followed it—a lesser matter, to be sure, but hardly a trivial one.

The tension between secular humanist and orthodox or evangelical values has been an active part of American public life for more than two centuries. It shows no sign of abating.

Notes

1. Thomas Babington Macaulay, *The History of England from the Accession of James II*, 5 vols. (London: Longmans, 1849–1861), 1:161.
2. Puritans objected strenuously to the most recent contributors to religious diversity in the New England of 1630, namely, the Arminians. See Nicholas Tyacke, *Anti-Calvinists: The Rise of English Arminianism, c. 1590–1640* (Oxford: Oxford University Press, 1987). On the growth and acceptance of religious pluralism in Restoration England, see the essays by Geoffrey F. Nuttall, Anne Whiteman, and Roger Thomas in *From Uniformity to Unity 1662–1962*, ed. Nuttall and Owen Chadwick (London: SPCK, 1962).
3. Perry Miller, *Orthodoxy in Massachusetts, 1630–1650* (Cambridge, Mass.: Harvard University Press, 1933); David D. Hall, *The Faithful Shepherd: A History of the New*

England Ministry in the Seventeenth Century (Chapel Hill: University of North Carolina Press, 1972); William G. McLoughlin, *New England Dissent, 1630–1833: The Baptists and the Separation of Church and State*, 2 vols. (Cambridge, Mass.: Harvard University Press, 1971), 1:3–90; Jonathan Chu, *Neighbors, Friends, or Madmen: The Puritan Adjustment to Quakerism in Seventeenth-Century Massachusetts Bay* (Westport, Conn.: Greenwood, 1985).

4. William Waller Hening, ed., *The Statutes at Large: Being a Collection of All the Laws of Virginia from the First Session of the Legislature, in the Year 1619*, 13 vols. (New York: Bartow, 1809–1923), 2:517.

5. George M. Brydon's *Virginia's Mother Church and the Political Conditions under Which It Grew* (Richmond: Virginia Historical Society, 1947–1952) remains the standard history.

6. Russell R. Menard, "Economy and Society in Early Colonial Maryland" (Ph.D. diss., University of Iowa, 1975); Michael Graham, "Lord Baltimore's Pious Enterprise: Toleration and Community in Colonial Maryland" (Ph.D. diss., University of Michigan, 1983); Lois Green Carr, "Sources of Political Stability and Upheaval in Seventeenth-Century Maryland, 1634–1692," *Maryland Historical Magazine* 79 (1984): 44–70; John D. Krugler, " 'With Promise of Liberty in Religion': The Catholic Lords Baltimore and Toleration in Seventeenth-Century Maryland, 1634–1692," *Maryland Historical Magazine* 79 (1984): 21–43; Lois Green Carr and David W. Jordan, *Maryland's Revolution of Government, 1689–1692* (Ithaca, N.Y.: Cornell University Press, 1974).

7. Population estimates are calculated from U.S. Bureau of the Census, *Historical Statistics of the United States, Colonial Times to 1970*, 2 vols. (Washington, D.C.: U.S. Government Printing Office, 1975), 2:1168.

8. Susan M. Reed, *Church and State in Massachusetts, 1691–1740* (Urbana: University of Illinois Press, 1914), is still very useful although superseded for the Baptists by McLoughlin's *New England Dissent*. See also Bruce E. Steiner, *Samuel Seabury: A Study in the High Church Tradition* (Athens: Ohio University Press, 1971), although the primary focus of this book is on Connecticut after the Great Awakening.

9. Frederick J. Zwierlein, *Religion in New Netherland, 1623–1664* (1910; rpt., New York: Da Capo, 1971); George L. Smith, *Religion and Trade in New Netherland: Dutch Origins and American Development* (Ithaca, N.Y.: Cornell University Press, 1973); Randall H. Balmer, "The Social Roots of Dutch Pietism in the Middle Colonies," *Church History* 53 (1984): 187–99.

10. Edwin B. Bronner, *William Penn's "Holy Experiment": The Founding of Pennsylvania, 1682–1701* (New York: Columbia University Press, 1962); Gary B. Nash, *Quakers and Politics: Pennsylvania, 1681–1726* (Princeton, N.J.: Princeton University Press, 1968); John E. Pomfret, *The Province of West New Jersey, 1609–1702* (Princeton, N.J.: Princeton University Press, 1956); Pomfret, *The Province of East New Jersey, 1609–1702* (Princeton, N.J.: Princeton University Press, 1962); Jon Butler, *Power, Authority, and the Origins of American Denominational Order: The English Churches in the Delaware Valley, 1660–1730*, Transactions of the American Philosophical Society, No. 68 (Philadelphia: American Philosophical Society, 1978); Martin E. Lodge, "The Crisis of the Churches in the Middle Colonies, 1720–1750," *Pennsylvania Magazine of History and Biography* 95 (1971): 195–220.

11. Sydney V. James, *Colonial Rhode Island: A History* (New York: Scribner's, 1975).

12. No full-scale study of religion yet exists for colonial North Carolina, but in no year prior to 1750 were there more than three Anglican clergymen in the colony. Only for the three-year period 1768 through 1770 were there ten or more, the peak being sixteen. By contrast, the Baptists alone had thirty ministers in 1770, and other Dissenters, fourteen. Calculated from Frederick Lewis Weis, *The Colonial Clergy of Virginia, North Carolina, and South Carolina* (Boston: Society of the Descendants of the Colonial Clergy, 1955), 58–70.

13. For the extremes of West Jersey liberty and New World slavery, see *The West Jersey Concessions and Agreements of 1676/77: A Round Table of Historians*, Occasional Papers No. 1 (Trenton: New Jersey Historical Commission, 1979); Edmund S. Morgan, *American Slavery, American Freedom: The Ordeal of Colonial Virginia* (New York: Norton, 1975).

14. Perry Miller, *The New England Mind: From Colony to Province* (Cambridge, Mass.: Harvard University Press, 1953), is a brilliant exposition of this argument.

15. In addition to works already cited, see Alan Tully, *William Penn's Legacy: Politics and Social Structure in Provincial Pennsylvania, 1726–1755* (Baltimore, Md.: Johns Hopkins University Press, 1977); Ralph L. Ketcham, "Conscience, War, and Politics, 1755–1757," *William and Mary Quarterly*, 3rd ser., 20 (1963): 416–39.

16. See above, n. 6.

17. Daniel J. Boorstin, *The Americans: The Colonial Experience* (New York: Random House, 1958), 1.

18. Joan R. Gundersen, "The Anglican Ministry in Virginia, 1723–1776: A Study of Social Class" (Ph.D. diss., University of Notre Dame, 1972); Carol Van Voorst, "The Anglican Clergy in Maryland, 1692–1776" (Ph.D. diss., Princeton University, 1978). In the Chesapeake as a whole, the number of Anglican ministers did not reach twenty until 1680. It hovered around twenty-five for the next decade, rose dramatically to sixty or more by 1714, and then stagnated. Only in 1741 did it permanently exceed seventy. Calculated from Weis, *Colonial Clergy of Virginia, North Carolina, and South Carolina*, 1–57. For the Great Awakening in Virginia, see especially Rhys Isaac, *The Transformation of Virginia, 1740–1790* (Chapel Hill: University of North Carolina Press, 1982).

19. On New Haven, see the essays by Gail Sussman Marcus and John M. Murrin in *Saints & Revolutionaries: Essays on Early American History*, ed. David D. Hall, John M. Murrin, and Thad W. Tate (New York: Norton, 1984), 99–137, 152–206.

20. I develop this argument more systematically in "Colonial Government," in *Encyclopedia of American Political History: Studies of the Principal Movements and Ideas*, ed. Jack P. Greene (New York: Scribner's, 1984), 1:293–315.

21. This process can best be followed in Henry Clay Reed, ed., *The Burlington Court Book: A Record of Quaker Jurisprudence in West New Jersey, 1680–1709* (Washington, D.C.: American Historical Association, 1944).

22. Douglas Greenberg, *Crime and Law Enforcement in the Colony of New York, 1691–1776* (Ithaca, N.Y.: Cornell University Press, 1976), 87–88, 193.

23. William G. McLoughlin, "The Role of Religion in the Revolution: Liberty of Conscience and Cultural Cohesion in the New Nation," in *Essays on the American*

Revolution, ed. Stephen G. Kurtz and James H. Hutson (Chapel Hill: University of North Carolina Press, 1973), 197–255; Sidney Mead, *The Lively Experiment: The Shaping of Christianity in America* (New York: Harper & Row, 1963).

24. Gerald L. Goodwin, "The Anglican Response to the Great Awakening," *Historical Magazine of the Protestant Episcopal Church* 35 (1966): 343–71; Frederick B. Tolles, "Quietism versus Enthusiasm: The Philadelphia Quakers and the Great Awakening," in his *Quakers and the Atlantic Culture* (New York: Macmillan, 1960), 91–113.

25. C. C. Goen, *Revivalism and Separatism in New England, 1740–1800* (New Haven, Conn.: Yale University Press, 1962); Conrad Wright, *The Beginnings of Unitarianism in America* (Boston: Beacon, 1953); Richard L. Bushman, *From Puritan to Yankee: Character and the Social Order in Connecticut, 1690–1765* (Cambridge, Mass.: Harvard University Press, 1967).

26. Leonard J. Trinterud, *The Forming of an American Tradition: A Re-Examination of Colonial Presbyterianism* (Philadelphia: Westminster, 1949); Howard Miller, *The Revolutionary College: American Presbyterian Higher Education, 1707–1837* (New York: New York University Press, 1976).

27. For a good survey of the denominational restructuring, see Sydney E. Ahlstrom, *A Religious History of the American People* (New Haven, Conn.: Yale University Press, 1972), ch. 27, esp. 436–37, on relative Methodist and Baptist strength. See also Gregory Evans Dowd, "Paths of Resistance: American Indian Religion and the Quest for Unity, 1745–1815" (Ph.D. diss., Princeton University, 1986).

28. For a fuller treatment of the issues in this section, see John M. Murrin, "Fundamental Values, the Founding Fathers, and the Constitution," paper read at the Capital Historical Society's March 1989 meeting, Washington, D.C.

29. Perry Miller, *Jonathan Edwards* (New York: Morrow, 1949).

30. John Spurr, "'Latitudinarianism' and the Restoration Church," *Historical Journal* 31 (1988): 61–82; Norman Fiering, "The First American Enlightenment: Tillotson, Leverett, and Philosophical Anglicanism," *New England Quarterly* 54 (1981): 307–44.

31. Of an enormous literature, see especially J. G. A. Pocock, *The Machiavellian Moment: Florentine Political Thought and the Atlantic Republican Tradition* (Princeton, N.J.: Princeton University Press, 1975).

32. For the impact of civic humanism on the evangelical clergy, see Bernard Bailyn, "Religion and Revolution: Three Biographical Studies," *Perspectives in American History* 4 (1970): 85–169; and Nathan O. Hatch, *The Sacred Cause of Liberty: Republican Thought and the Millennium in Revolutionary New England* (New Haven, Conn.: Yale University Press, 1977). No explicit study exists emphasizing the difficulty of moving from committed patriot to reborn Christian, but it is probably no accident that republican convictions reached their peak in America at about the time that church adherence hit its lowest point, in the two decades after independence. The Revolution intensified another trend already evident in American life. Young men aspired to be proud and independent. Young women were socialized to be humble and dependent. The abject humility of the conversion experience raised far fewer difficulties for women than for men. The gender balance among full church members in evangelical denominations, already skewed toward women before the Revolution,

became much more extreme during the following generation. See Richard D. Shiels, "The Feminization of American Congregationalism, 1730–1835," *American Quarterly* 33 (1981): 46–62; and, for the Middle Atlantic, Martha T. Blauvelt, "Society, Religion, and Revivalism: The Second Great Awakening in New Jersey, 1780–1830" (Ph.D. diss., Princeton University, 1974).

33. The fullest argument for the impact of classical liberalism on America is Joyce Appleby, *Capitalism and a New Social Order: The Republican Vision of the 1790s* (New York: New York University Press, 1984).

34. Gary B. Nash, "The American Clergy and the French Revolution," *William and Mary Quarterly*, 3rd ser., 22 (1965): 392–412; Michael Durey, "Thomas Paine's Apostles: Radical Émigrés and the Triumph of Jeffersonian Republicanism," *William and Mary Quarterly*, 3rd ser., 44 (1987): 661–88.

35. Gordon S. Wood, "Interests and Disinterestedness in the Making of the Constitution," in *Beyond Confederation: Origins of the Constitution and American National Identity*, ed. Richard Beeman, Stephen Botein, and Edward C. Carter II (Chapel Hill: University of North Carolina Press, 1987), 69–109.

36. The essays in Istvan Hont and Michael Ignatieff, eds., *Wealth and Virtue: The Shaping of Political Economy in the Scottish Enlightenment* (Cambridge: Cambridge University Press, 1983), provide an outstanding introduction to the main themes of the Scottish Enlightenment. For its impact on America, see David F. Norton, "Francis Hutcheson in America," *Studies on Voltaire and the Eighteenth Century* 154 (1976): 1547–68; Garry Wills, *Inventing America: Jefferson's Declaration of Independence* (Garden City, N.Y.: Doubleday, 1978); Ronald Hamowy, "Jefferson and the Scottish Enlightenment: A Critique of Garry Wills' *Inventing America: Jefferson's Declaration of Independence*," *William and Mary Quarterly*, 3rd ser., 36 (1979): 503–23; Mark A. Noll, "Common Sense Traditions and American Evangelical Thought," *American Quarterly* 37 (1985): 215–38; and Noll, *Princeton and the Republic, 1768–1822: The Search for a Christian Enlightenment in the Era of Samuel Stanhope Smith* (Princeton, N.J.: Princeton University Press, 1989).

37. Thomas E. Buckley, S.J., *Church and State in Revolutionary Virginia, 1776–1787* (Charlottesville: University Press of Virginia, 1977).

38. Benjamin Perley Poore, comp., *The Federal and State Constitutions, Colonial Charters, and Other Organic Laws of the United States*, 2 vols. (Washington, D.C.: U.S. Government Printing Office, 1877), 1:257.

39. Oscar Handlin and Mary F. Handlin, eds., *The Popular Sources of Political Authority: Documents on the Massachusetts Constitution of 1780* (Cambridge, Mass.: Harvard University Press, 1966), 441–42.

40. Poore, *Federal and State Constitutions*, 2:1280–81.

41. Samuel Eliot Morison, ed., *Sources and Documents Illustrating the American Revolution, 1764–1788, and the Formation of the Federal Constitution*, 2nd ed. (Oxford: Clarendon, 1929), 162–63.

42. Handlin and Handlin, *Popular Sources of Political Authority*, 441–42.

43. Poore, *Federal and State Constitutions*, 2:1857.

44. Morison, *Sources and Documents*, 186.

45. Ibid., 151.

46. For New Jersey, see Julian P. Boyd, ed., *Fundamental Laws and Constitutions of New Jersey* (Princeton, N.J.: Van Nostrand, 1964), 161; for Georgia, Maryland, and North Carolina, see Poore, *Federal and State Constitutions*, 1:383, 828; 2:1413.

47. Max Farrand, ed., *The Records of the Federal Convention of 1787*, rev. ed., 4 vols. (New Haven, Conn.: Yale University Press, 1937), 1:450–52; 3:467–73. I discuss this incident more fully in Murrin, "Fundamental Values, the Founding Fathers, and the Constitution."

48. The phrase "secular humanist" was not used in the eighteenth century. It derives, in all probability, from the creation of secular humanist societies in New York City and elsewhere in the early twentieth century. Since the mid-twentieth century, it has become primarily a code word among conservative evangelicals for intellectual forces—in schools and colleges, the media, and government—that they see destroying traditional American values. But even if the term had no currency in the eighteenth century, men of the Enlightenment had their own counterparts that meant nearly the same thing. The "party of humanity" is one example. This phrase usually signified a group of thinkers that derived its ethical values from reason and human experience, not revelation. See Peter Gay, *The Party of Humanity: Essays on the French Enlightenment* (New York: Knopf, 1963).

49. For evidence of Bassett's strong evangelical commitment both before and after the Philadelphia convention, see Francis Asbury, *Journals and Letters*, 3 vols., ed. Elmer E. Clark (Nashville, Tenn.: Abingdon, 1958), 1, 26n, 312–13, 337–38, 345, 449, 674, and passim.

50. Christopher Collier, *Roger Sherman's Connecticut: Yankee Politics and the American Revolution* (Middletown, Conn.: Wesleyan University Press, 1971), 36–37, 325.

51. Mark Noll, "James Madison: From Evangelical Princeton to the Constitutional Convention," *Pro Rege* (Dec. 1987): 2–14; Thomas Jefferson, "The Anas," in *Thomas Jefferson: Writings*, ed. Merrill D. Peterson (New York: Library of America, 1984), 666, 671.

52. Gordon S. Wood, *The Creation of the American Republic, 1776–1787* (Chapel Hill: University of North Carolina Press, 1969); Ruth H. Bloch et al., "*The Creation of the American Republic, 1776–1787*: A Symposium of Views and Reviews," *William and Mary Quarterly*, 3rd ser., 44 (1987): 550–640.

53. John Adams seriously considered a career as a minister but gave it up because it threatened what he called his "liberty to think." Peter Shaw, *The Character of John Adams* (Chapel Hill: University of North Carolina Press, 1976), 9. The best study of Jefferson's religious beliefs is Eugene R. Sheridan, "Introduction," to *Jefferson's Extracts from the Gospels: "The Philosophy of Jesus" and "The Life and Morals of Jesus,"* ed. Dickinson W. Adams and Ruth W. Lester (Princeton, N.J.: Princeton University Press, 1983), 3–42. The two compilations published there represent Jefferson's effort to sort out those parts of scripture that he could accept, versus the remainder that he rejected.

54. After graduating from the College of New Jersey in 1771, Madison spent an extra year at Princeton studying Hebrew under President John Witherspoon, a commitment that suggests he was contemplating the ministry. See also Samuel Stanhope Smith to Madison, Nov. 1777–Aug. 1778, in *The Papers of James Madison*, ed. William T. Hutchinson and William M. E. Rachal, 17 vols. (Chicago and Charlottesville:

University of Chicago Press and University of Virginia Press, 1962–1991), 1:194–212. The Madison letter to which Smith is responding is no longer extant, but Smith's reply shows that Madison still accepted Calvinist orthodoxy on the central question of liberty and necessity. See also Ralph L. Ketcham, "James Madison and Religion: A New Hypothesis," *Journal of the Presbyterian Historical Society* 38 (1960): 65–90; and Ketcham, "James Madison and the Nature of Man," *Journal of the History of Ideas* 19 (1958): 62–76. Ketcham detects a stronger religious influence on the mature Madison than I do.

55. Robert Green McCloskey, ed., *The Works of James Wilson*, 2 vols. (Cambridge, Mass.: Harvard University Press, 1967), 1:144.

56. Jefferson to Peter Carr, 10 Aug. 1787, and to Adams, 11 Apr. 1823, in Peterson, *Thomas Jefferson: Writings*, 900–905, 1466–69, quotation on 1469.

57. For Madison in particular, see especially the *Federalist*, Nos. 10 and 51. See also Michael Kammen, *A Machine That Would Go of Itself: The Constitution in American Culture* (New York: Knopf, 1987).

58. The drafters of the Pennsylvania Constitution of 1776 proclaimed, for example, that God "alone knows to what degree of earthly happiness mankind may attain by perfecting the arts of government." Morison, *Sources and Documents, 163*. For Madison's celebration of radical innovation during the Revolution, see the final paragraph of the *Federalist*, No. 14. See also Jefferson to Dr. Benjamin Waterhouse, 26 June 1822, in Peterson, *Thomas Jefferson: Writings*, 1458–59.

59. See Edmund S. Morgan, *Roger Williams: The Church and the State* (New York: Harcourt, 1967), for the very different seventeenth-century sensibilities on this question. For shifting priorities between civil and religious liberty, see Hatch, *Sacred Cause of Liberty*, ch. 1.

60. Vernon Stauffer, *New England and the Bavarian Illuminati* (New York: Columbia University Press, 1918); Constance B. Schulz, "Of Bigotry in Politics and Religion: Jefferson's Religion, the Federalist Press, and the Syllabus," *Virginia Magazine of History and Biography* 91 (1983): 73–91.

61. Timothy Dwight, *A Discourse in Two Parts, Delivered July 23, 1812, on the Public Fast, in the Chapel of Yale College*, 2nd ed. (Boston: Cummings and Hilliard, 1813), 24. My thanks to Harry S. Stout for bringing this passage to my attention. For Stout's own use of Dwight's comment, see chapter 3 in this volume.

62. Although a slight majority of Congregationalist delegates in state ratifying conventions opposed the Constitution, most Congregational clergy favored it. See Jackson Turner Main, *The Antifederalists: Critics of the Constitution, 1781–1788* (Chapel Hill: University of North Carolina Press, 1961), 208; and Main, *Political Parties before the Constitution* (Chapel Hill: University of North Carolina Press, 1973), 377–79. Presbyterians probably reflected a similar pattern. See James H. Smylie, "Protestant Clergy, the First Amendment, and Beginnings of a Constitutional Debate, 1781–1791," in *The Religion of the Republic*, ed. Elwyn A. Smith (Philadelphia: Fortress, 1971), 116–53. See also William Gribben, *The Churches Militant: The War of 1812 and American Religion* (New Haven, Conn.: Yale University Press, 1973).

63. For the French contrast, see Peter Gay, *The Enlightenment: An Interpretation: The Rise of Modern Paganism* (New York: Knopf, 1966). The tension between orthodoxy and

the Enlightenment in North America resembled the tone already established in Scotland, where even David Hume refrained from overt attacks on the kirk. See, generally, Richard B. Sher, *Church and University in the Scottish Enlightenment* (Princeton, N.J.: Princeton University Press, 1985). See also H. Jefferson Powell, "The Original Understanding of Original Intent," *Harvard Law Review* 98 (1984–1985): 885–948.

64. Farrand, *Records of the Federal Convention*, 470–72.

Religion and Ideological Change
in the American Revolution

Ruth H. Bloch

𝒯HIS CHAPTER ON the American Revolution is meant to address a basic historical question about religion and American politics, a question addressed in various ways by other chapters in this volume as well. How did religious ideas contribute to the development of political ideology? Defining the topic this way necessarily brackets many other interesting questions about the role of religion in the American Revolution that fall more directly into the realms of social and political history—questions involving institutional structures and laws, the extent of clerical and lay activism, regional and denominational comparisons, and so on. To a certain extent, these subjects will inevitably bear upon my discussion, but the central issues I am exploring pertain to intellectual history: What elements of revolutionary thought can be properly described as religious? How did they change over time? To what can we attribute these changes?

In a way, I am addressing an old historiographical problem. Beginning with the revolutionary clergy itself, scholars have endlessly debated the importance of religion to the American Revolution. Some have stressed institutional factors, such as the weakness of the colonial religious establishments or the leadership role of the New England clergy, but most have argued over the interpretation of ideology. Was it best characterized as secular, Enlightened, or Protestant? Were the religious elements of revolutionary thought primary or secondary, radical or conservative?

The main terms of this debate crystallized already in the Progressive generation. Historians such as Vernon Parrington and Carl Becker rejected the Protestant chauvinism of their nineteenth-century forebears and claimed the Revolution for Enlightenment rationalism. Lately, the debate has become more complex. One strong interpretation of revolutionary ideology no longer stresses a monolithic Enlightenment but rather a less rationalistic "republicanism," one derived from a tradition of English political opposition to an expanding royal bureaucracy. This republicanism, it is argued, incorporated both religious and Enlightenment ideas but subsumed them within its own hegemonic framework.[1] Some historians challenging this interpretation have stressed instead the emergence of another, still more fully secular ideology, that of free market liberalism.[2]

On yet a third side of this debate are those, including myself, who have argued for the centrality of religious ideas.[3] While on one level, I intend this chapter to remake this case in a new way, on another level, I want to change the terms of the argument. Most historians now acknowledge the interpenetration of religious and secular themes in the ideology of the Revolution. So much scholarship of the last twenty years has documented the religious symbolism of the revolutionary movement that the debate over the importance of religion is less over the existence and pervasiveness of this language than over its intellectual and social role.

Typically, this debate revolves around conflicting assessments of the relative significance of religious compared to secular ideas. Did religion serve as a vehicle carrying secular political ideas to a Protestant populace?[4] Did American Protestantism itself decisively shape political ideology?[5] Or is the relationship between religious and secular thought best seen as a kind of momentary merger of otherwise distinct intellectual systems?[6] Beneath this dispute lurks yet another issue, which is the one I would like to stress. Virtually all such interpretations, whatever their differences, depict religion as essentially traditional. Thus the role of religion is typically either the dressing of new secular ideas in old, comfortable Protestant garb or, conversely, the ascetic critique of worldly modern fashions. When religion is depicted as a force of revolutionary change, its radical primitivism, not its conceptual creativity, usually receives emphasis.[7] Changing religious ideas appear more often as mirrors reflecting nonreligious intellectual developments than as dynamic components of the process of ideological change itself.[8]

This chapter proposes to survey familiar historical territory from a somewhat different angle of vision. Without seeking to measure the relative importance of other influences upon revolutionary ideology, I wish to highlight a few specifically *religious* contributions to its development between 1763 and 1789. This task requires that I begin by identifying, in very general terms, some basic religious orientations defining early American Protestantism. Drawing such generalizations is admittedly hazardous. Plenty of exceptions can be found—some of these themes are more pronounced in certain regions, social classes, and denominations than in others—yet there was also enough commonality among revolutionary American Protestants to justify a synthetic interpretation. The popular support for the American Revolution came overwhelmingly from Congregationalists, Baptists, Presbyterians, and southern lay Anglicans, almost all of whom can be loosely described as Calvinist. Here I am following David Hall, who has gone so far as to assert that "Calvinism was the common faith of people in America before the Revolution."[9] What Hall claims about colonial Americans is even truer of the revolutionary movement. To be sure, the Revolution also enlisted the support of a number of religious rationalists, particularly among the urban elite and the southern gentry, but, on a more popular level, the religious faith of American revolutionaries was in the main Calvinist. The non-Calvinist Quakers, Methodists, and northern Anglicans drifted disproportionately toward neutrality and loyalism, and typically Calvinist preoccupations underlay much of the development of revolutionary ideology.

Calvinism in early America was, as Hall and others have emphasized, not a rigid system of doctrines as much as an open-ended and ambiguous effort to resolve a series of fundamental tensions posed by the Reformation: grace versus preparation, evangelicalism versus sacerdotalism, sect versus church. The common denominators of American Calvinism that most centrally pertained to the American Revolution were so basic that they can be boiled down to two: first, the experiential approach to salvation, with its uneasy connection to the necessity of righteous behavior in the world; and second, the definition of an elect community—ambiguously visible and invisible, churchlike and sectlike—with a secular history overseen by providence.

These two basic themes weave in and out of the political ideology of the Revolution. Religious concerns about the conditions of salvation helped to shape the understanding of the key revolutionary values of liberty and virtue. The belief in providence underlay the patriots' conviction that the secular history of the Revolution had a higher, transhistorical meaning. And the perennial effort to define the godly community contributed to the formulation of American nationalism. The historical roots of many of these ideological developments can be traced back to the revolutionary Puritanism of the seventeenth century. Indeed, even the Lockean theory of the social contract as the basis of civil society was largely derived from Puritan ideas about the covenanted church. Far from having become secularized by the eighteenth century, the religious preoccupations that had always informed political ideology remained vitally important to Americans of the revolutionary generation.

On the one hand, religion during the American Revolution responded flexibly to a shifting course of events, lending its authoritative vocabulary to legitimate an essentially secular process of change. On the other hand, however, ideological change occurred within a symbolic structure largely defined by the Calvinist experiential approach to salvation and providential understanding of the collective experience of God's people on earth. What happened in the revolutionary period was that the conflict with Britain raised unusually fundamental questions about the justification of political authority and the moral and spiritual basis of collective life—questions so fundamental as to lay bare these religious underpinnings. The interpenetration of religious and political symbolism in patriots' discourse signified neither a newfound politicization of nonpolitical religion nor a newfound sacralization of secular politics, but expressed the very depth and intensity of the crisis. This crisis not only exposed the underlying fusion of preexisting religious and political outlooks but gradually forced these outlooks to change. Neither static nor simply reactive, the religious symbolism of salvation and godly community was both general and problematic enough to allow room for creative reinterpretation over time. The following sketch of three major phases of ideological development during the revolutionary era—roughly characterized by the periods 1763–1774, 1774–1778, and 1778–1789—illustrates the dynamic quality of this religious contribution to revolutionary ideology.

1763–1774

These years of protest against the new British imperial policy have rightly been called a period of "resistance" rather than of "revolution."[10] This characterization points to the limited organization and goals of the early patriot movement as well as to the Americans' repeated declarations of loyalty to king and empire. Despite the momentary display of intercolonial unity during the Stamp Act crisis, American resistance in this period was organized locally, both in the provincial assemblies and in the city streets. The only place that consistently gave widespread popular support to the patriot cause was New England, particularly Boston. Just as the movement remained geographically decentralized, its strategy was for the most part confined to piecemeal responses to a number of different issues.

These issues included not only the legendary taxation-without-representation but efforts to regulate colonial currency, the expansion of the royal bureaucracy, multiple officeholding by appointed officials, and the maintenance of a standing army. There were specifically religious issues as well—most important, the rumors in the early 1760s that the Church of England was planning to install an American bishop and, in 1774, the news that Roman Catholicism would be permitted by the British Crown to remain the official religion of conquered Quebec.[11]

Despite the early and persistent constitutional arguments against British claims that the Americans were "virtually represented" in Parliament, this great variety of issues lacked a specific constitutional focus. What united the protests and gave them an ideological coherence was instead a mythic perception of the violation of a sacred past. Bernard Bailyn and others have argued that the main terms of this myth were borrowed from the ideology of the English political opposition, a radical Whig version of history that featured a virtuous, liberty-loving citizenry under attack by an expanding, corrupt, and tyrannical executive power. Yet, as several other historians have demonstrated, it is clear that early patriot ideology had strong religious components as well.[12] Without seeking precisely to unravel the religious elements from the secular ones, one can identify several ways in which basic American Calvinist concerns about the definition of the godly community and the conditions of grace found immediate expression within early patriot discourse.

Inherited from the Puritans, the language of the covenant spoke directly to the question of an elect community and its protection by providence. Although Perry Miller once argued that a moribund covenant theology was finally buried in the Great Awakening, only to be temporarily brought back to life in the revolutionary period, Harry Stout has shown the enduring vitality of New England's belief in its special, covenanted relationship with God.[13] Just as the polemics of the radical Whigs idealized a mythic past of English liberty within a balanced constitutional order, New England sermons looked backward toward the covenant of early colonial days. In both of these ways, patriots were called to preserve the legacy of an earlier era.

In contrast to the more expansive, imperial framework of radical Whig ideology, the vocabulary of the covenant sharply differentiated America from Great Britain. At this early stage of the patriot movement, however, the concept of the godly community defined by the covenant was still highly provincial, remaining for the most part confined to New England alone.[14] New England patriot ministers spoke in defense of their regional history as a whole, moreover without distinguishing among the social, religious, and political aspects of the past. They simply presumed the New England tradition to be both Christian and free, and their covenant terminology fused together church, state, and society into an undifferentiated godly community set apart from the British forces of sin and tyranny.[15]

Often combined with appeals to the covenant, and likewise involving the Calvinist effort to define the perimeters of God's people, was a Manichaean tendency to polarize the world between the forces of God and the forces of the Antichrist. A dualistic understanding of history as a struggle between good and evil had as long a history in the colonies as covenant theology. By the 1760s, both the conflicts of the Great Awakening and the anti-Catholic crusade of the French and Indian War had reinforced the inclination of American Calvinists to see themselves engaged in a cosmic battle with Satan. Whereas references to the covenant typically appeared in sermons by New England ministers, the Manichaean tendency to conceptualize the imperial conflict in terms of good and evil appeared first within lay political argument and popular patriot ritual as early as the mid-1760s.[16] The symbolic link forging the connection between Great Britain and the Antichrist was typically the pollution of Roman Catholicism. In Boston and elsewhere, traditional anti-Catholic Pope Day celebrations became occasions for dramatizing the patriot cause. Orations, cartoons, and public hangings of effigies depicted the royal ministers as in league alternately with the pope and the devil.[17] Just as these symbols and rituals characterized the royal government as the agent of the Antichrist, other purifying rituals of fasting and abstinence from imported British goods, along with appeals to the covenant, reinforced the connection between American resistance and the legions of God.[18]

In different if occasionally overlapping ways, both the covenant and the Manichaean symbolism of the early patriot movement sought to clarify the relationship between the colonial protests and God's providential plan for the world. Both types of religious symbolism aimed to delineate boundaries that defined the righteous community—either, in the case of the covenant, through identification with New England history or, in the case of Manichaeanism, through detestation of the British Antichrist. Alongside these efforts to specify the godly community, American patriots brought Calvinist preoccupations about salvation into their understanding of imperial politics. These concerns were expressed above all in the religious use of the central revolutionary symbol of liberty.

In New England, especially, historians have found many examples of clergymen endorsing Whig ideas about the importance of constitutional liberty well before the outbreak of the revolutionary conflict. Nathan Hatch has stressed its assimilation into New England religious vocabulary during the French and Indian War, and Harry Stout has offered a detailed account of how the Whig conception of liberty had been incorporated into New England covenant theology by the early eighteenth century.[19] The essentially religious status of the concept of liberty depends, however, only in part on such prerevolutionary endorsements of specifically Whig political ideas. As important was the more diffuse and fecund meaning of the word "liberty" within colonial religious vocabulary. For the term referred not only to the civil liberty of the English constitution but also to the religious liberty craved by religious dissenters and to the spiritual liberty of grace—"the liberty wherewith Christ made us free."[20] When New Englanders fought in the name of liberty against the French Catholics during the Seven Years' War, they had religious and spiritual as much as civil liberty in mind. When colonists in the religiously pluralistic middle colonies engaged in competitive denominational politics, they too demonstrated their commitment to a religious version of liberty.[21]

What was new in the 1760s was not the conflation of religious and political values but the shift of the British government from the side of liberty and Christianity to the side of tyranny and the Antichrist. In the early revolutionary movement, patriots repeatedly associated the Church of England and the royal ministers with papal tyranny. The ease with which so many Americans in the 1760s expanded their definition of Christian liberty to include civil as well as spiritual and religious liberty is comprehensible only when one realizes how these different definitions of liberty were already mixed together. To be sure, some American Protestants, most notably the Baptists, specifically resisted this equation, arguing against the devaluation of spiritual liberty by its association with profane political liberty.[22] They did so, however, well aware that they were seeking to sever the common linkage made within the patriot movement.

By the mid-1770s, then, religion was so deeply intertwined with revolutionary political ideology that it seems virtually impossible to distinguish between them. The overlapping vocabulary of Whig ideology and American Protestantism wielded particular power, of course, in New England, where the fusion of the religious and secular had a long institutional history. Whatever other reasons can be offered to explain the primacy of New England in the early revolutionary movement, the strength of this symbolic association between politics and religious experience must be taken into account. Nor was New England altogether unique. As suggested by the example of a 1765 Philadelphia Presbyterian crowd calling, "No King but King Jesus," or by the Virginian Richard Bland's 1771 description of High Church plans to found a colonial bishopric as "Papal Incroachments upon the Common Law," the overt blurring of religious and political categories was a feature of popular revolutionary politics elsewhere in the early years of resistance as well.[23]

The fact that there were plenty of "secular" political treatises that never referred to the covenant, to the Antichrist, or to the liberty of grace—and, conversely, plenty of "religious" discourses that altogether ignored polities—in no way undercuts this point. Surely there were Americans for whom liberty primarily meant the relative autonomy of the colonial legislatures, and others for whom it primarily meant the salvation provided by grace. The widespread resonance of such terms as "virtue," "corruption," and "liberty" in the early patriot movement depended, however, on their multivalent civil and spiritual references. A connection between what we normally distinguish as religious or secular was embedded in the very meaning of revolutionary language itself.

1774–1778

Religious and political terminology continued to fuse during the next period of open rebellion, warfare, and revolutionary state building. The basic religious orientation expressed in revolutionary ideology from roughly 1775 to 1778 remained essentially the same. The underlying religious issues were still the spiritual quest for salvation and the purification of a godly community on earth. Liberty continued to have a sacred meaning in large part because of its intimate symbolic connection with grace. And revolutionaries persisted in defining their collective experience in providential and morally dichotomous terms: they were the nation under God, the loyalists and the British were the representatives of the Antichrist.

But, for all these fundamental continuities, both the context and the form of much of the specific religious symbolism in patriot ideology changed as America moved from resistance to revolution. The concrete catalysts for this change were several parliamentary measures of 1774—the so-called Coercive (or Intolerable) Acts leveled against intransigent Massachusetts and the Quebec Act protecting Catholicism in French Canada. In response to these events, the colonists mobilized across geographical lines as never before, forming the Continental Congress, extralegal committees, provincial governments, and an army—steps that led within less than two years to national independence. These political developments took place alongside important shifts on the level of religious symbolism. It is possible to identify three particularly significant changes, all involving new efforts to formulate a sacred national identity. These efforts reveal a creative religious interaction with unfolding events. Encompassed within the broader symbolic framework of election and providence, they suggest ways that American religion not only responded to the pressures of circumstances but, through a process of reinterpretation, structured the very meaning of revolutionary change.

One important symbolic change of the mid-1770s was the geographical extension of the definition of God's community. Earlier, the Manichaean, covenant, and providential language describing the virtues and obligations of God's people had been largely embedded within a provincial New England vocabulary. Now this symbolism expanded to cover the entire nation. In the wake of the Quebec Act, especially, the depiction of Great Britain as the Antichrist became frequent throughout the colonies.[24] The New England clergy continued to appeal to its distinctive covenant theory, but, as Harry Stout has argued, even there patriot ministers began in 1775 to stretch the terms of the covenant to include the American colonies as a whole.[25] Covenant imagery appeared prominently elsewhere as well, permeating official proclamations by the Continental Congress, including its calls for fast and thanksgiving days.[26] Jefferson's Declaration of Independence emerged from the drafting committee of the Continental Congress with a reference to the controlling hand of providence.[27] And other secular political leaders in the mid-1770s, ranging from the cool Anglican Alexander Hamilton to the semi-evangelical Patrick Henry, appealed in public to the unity and religious duty of Americans as a Protestant people under God.[28] This rapid redefinition of the righteous community cannot be explained simply as the product of New England influence or as the automatic response to a political situation. The underlying Protestant tendency to conceptualize secular experience in providential, collective terms—a tendency that extended beyond New England and the specific language of the covenant—shaped the emerging expression of American nationalism in the mid-1770s.

A second symbolic shift concerned the location of this righteous community in time. Earlier, New England patriots typically evoked the image of a hallowed past. Beginning in the mid-1770s, however, Congregational ministers instead increasingly stressed the prospects of a millennial future. These millennial hopes, like the image of a national community under God, extended well beyond New England alone, appearing both in sermons and in secular patriot writings in many regions of revolutionary America.[29] A study of my own on the frequency of millennial statements in printed literature suggests that such ideas may well have been as common among Presbyterian and Baptist patriots in the middle and southern regions as they were among New England Congregationalists.[30] Millennial symbolism was a standard feature of much American Protestantism of the late colonial period, weaving in and out of providential theories about the meaning of contemporary events. It was, however, only in the mid-1770s that this symbolism came to pervade revolutionary ideology, enabling Americans to perceive the outbreak of war and the assertion of national independence as steps toward the realization of God's kingdom on earth.

Both in its national scope and in its millennial optimism, then, the providential language of the mid-1770s differed sharply from that of the 1760s and early 1770s. The third important symbolic shift of this period gave a new sacred status to republican government. Earlier, the symbol of liberty had diffusely referred both to the experience of salvation and to the legitimate rights and traditions of the British political order. The term "virtue" likewise ambiguously evoked both Christian moral duties and the self-sacrificial patriotism of the public-spirited citizen. In the early years of the revolutionary movement, however, this was the vocabulary of resistance to, not endorsement of, the state. As the colonists moved toward the establishment of an independent republican system, the symbols of liberty and virtue continued to be imbued with these manifold religious and political meanings, but they acquired a new, positive relationship to conceptions of government. The godly community of the virtuous citizenry became virtually indistinguishable from the republican state.

As Harry Stout has emphasized in his study of New England sermons, ministers now upheld the model of the Jewish republic, a development revealing not only the plasticity of biblical interpretation but the newfound fusion of the state with the godly community.[31] In the millennial literature of these years, the triumph of Christianity and republican government likewise merged together as the joint measure of progress toward the latter days.[32] This symbolic fusion of the state and the Christian community can also be discerned in the *rage militaire* during the beginning of the war, when enlistment in the army became the consummate expression of virtue.[33] Many revolutionary state governments, including constitutionally radical Pennsylvania, sought to institutionalize this connection by passing test acts and other laws limiting inclusion in the republican polity to revolutionary Protestants or, more broadly, Christians, alone. And, of course, in several New England states, the Congregational church remained legally established long after the Revolution.[34]

On one hand, these legal provisions show us the obstacles that the modern principle of religious freedom had yet to overcome.[35] The identification of the secular state with the people of God was scarcely a new theme within the history of providential thought in America, particularly in New England, where the Puritan state had been patterned precisely on this Old Testament model. On the other hand, the forceful symbolic and institutional reassertion of this connection in the years surrounding independence—however retrograde this may seem from a modern perspective—gave powerful religious legitimacy to the new republican system of government.

Together with the national definition of the chosen community and the visionary hopes of a coming new day, this fusion of the religious and the political orders largely defined the ideological shift from resistance to revolution in the mid-1770s. The religious cast of these expressions of revolutionary nationalism, optimism, and loyalty to republican government reveals the continuing allegiance of American Protestants to a concept of providence and to the idea of a righteous community on earth. Similarly, the repeated revolutionary appeals to liberty and virtue spoke to long-standing concerns about the experience and assurance of salvation. Never unproblematic, however, these basic religious orientations were fraught with creative tensions that enabled religion to play a dynamic—not merely either a reactive or a determining—role in the shaping of revolutionary ideology. Inevitably, fundamental religious questions remained unresolved. To what extent could providence be relied on? How closely did the saintly community approximate the secular one? What was the path to salvation? Inasmuch as such questions continued to structure the religious understanding of the Revolution, the ideological answers changed over the course of the Revolution itself.

1778–1789

The third major phase in the development of revolutionary ideology began during the dispirited years of the war after 1778. With a brief respite in the early 1780s, after the welcome news of Yorktown and during the settlement of peace, a mood of anxiety descended over the new nation that lasted at least until the ratification of the Constitution. The increased apprehensiveness during the so-called critical period has been often noted by historians, although they have debated whether or not this anxiety reflected serious political problems subsequently solved by the Constitution.[36] In any case, the crisis of this period was, as Gordon Wood has convincingly argued, moral as much as political.[37] American public spokesmen repeatedly lamented what they perceived to be a decline of virtue, a decline they saw as threatening the very basis of republican liberty.

Several developments underlay this perception. One, emphasized by Wood as most critical, was the outbreak of political conflicts on the state level over both currency policy and the framing of constitutions. A second was the increased consumerism stimulated by postwar access to imported foreign luxuries. These developments exacerbated latent social antagonisms and challenged the republican ideal of a united citizenry willing to sacrifice individual economic interests in the service of the greater public good. According to Wood, the Constitution, with its mechanisms for dividing and balancing power, represented an ideological solution to this moral crisis by divesting the government of the need to rely on popular virtue for the preservation of liberty.[38]

There is, however, another way of looking at the same process, one that emphasizes instead the religious reformulation of republican thought in the 1780s. Clergymen in this period, like secular spokesmen, frequently denounced symptoms of corruption as a threat to the republic, typically in the form of the jeremiad.[39] The millennial zeal of the 1770s abated, replaced by an upsurge of lurid, apocalyptic predictions of doom.[40] The solution advocated by these patriot ministers was neither rededication to public service, financial sacrifice, nor the cessation of factional disputes, but faith. As the Reverend Asa Burton of Vermont explained in his election sermon of 1785, "Political virtue: may serve as a support for a while, but it is not a *lasting* principle." Rather, he insisted, the true basis of free states was a popular spirit of religious benevolence that arose from the fear of God.[41] If national happiness depended on virtue, the religious literature of the 1780s repeatedly proclaimed, virtue depended on piety.[42]

Whereas at the height of the revolutionary excitement of the mid-1770s the religious and political orders were symbolically merged, this connection proved very short-lived. Within less than a decade, religious leaders were urging American Protestants to reconceptualize their relationship to the state. It is possible to understand this development as a logical response to the deflation of high hopes as the new nation turned away from struggles with Great Britain and faced its own inevitable imperfections. The logic of this disillusionment was, however, structured not merely by practical realities but by religious considerations as well. The strong identification of the righteous community with the republican state that characterized the mid-1770s violated an alternative sense of the righteous as an invisible church before God. During the same years, as Virginians moved toward ecclesiastical disestablishment, northern Protestants—including those in the established churches of New England—were on a conceptual level disengaging from the state as well. An emphasis on the legal and institutional differences between Virginians and New Englanders obscures this common development. Although the principle of religious freedom came late and incompletely to most American revolutionaries, the 1780s witnessed a growing insistence on a religious space separate from republican government.

This increased detachment of religion from the state helped to set the stage for what Gordon Wood has called "the end of classical politics."[43] The passage of the U.S. Constitution, with its mechanisms of checks and balances, marks a shift away from a reliance on popular virtue. No longer did the republic depend on extensive public involvement in the military or government. The more limited idea of public virtue that remained in the minds of the proponents of the Constitution hinged instead, as Daniel Howe has argued, on the superior reason of statesmen.[44]

This shift in the definition of public virtue away from popular participation in republican government did not, however, produce an alternatively private or individualistic sense of morality. Despite these developments on the level of political thought, many Americans continued to believe that the future of the republic depended on popular virtue. Far from giving up on the superior righteousness and collective moral imperative of the American people, Protestant leaders in the 1790s redefined the way this popular virtue would be generated and expressed. Instead of being located directly within the institutional perimeters of representative government, public virtue was increasingly defined as a quality of nonpolitical organizational life. Of course, the ministerial jeremiads of the 1780s most typically called the nation back to the churches, but schools and families began to receive greater emphasis as bulwarks of liberty and Christianity as well. In addition, the 1780s and 1790s saw the founding of early voluntary reform associations designed to correct various social ills, ranging from imprisonment for debt to slavery, often also with a religious purpose in mind. What emerged by the end of the revolutionary period was a sense of a virtuous American society distinct from the institutions of government. A major source of this development was, I would like to suggest, the endemic tensions within the American Protestant tradition over the relationship of the godly community to the state. Already by the mid-1770s, the definition of this community had extended to encompass the nation and, with it, republican government. In the 1780s, however, this unstable equation came apart, leaving a strong, religiously informed nationalism that was divested of much of its earlier association with the state.

I HAVE SKETCHED three intellectual stages through which revolutionary American Protestants moved between 1763 and 1789, a movement characterized, first, by a rapidly expanding definition of liberty—one simultaneously embracing spiritual, ecclesiastical, and civil concerns—and, second, by an expanded definition of the righteous community, one encompassing not only the church and the province but the nation. If American Protestantism was not tied to the specific political policies or constitutional structure of the state, it did come to identify itself strongly with the American people and the broad republican values of liberty. This identification drew upon older quests for spiritual redemption, older commitments to religious community, and older struggles against tyrannical, "papist" government, but it was also critically shaped by the successive crises, hopes, and fears of the American revolutionary process itself.

The expanded definitions of liberty and community did not mean that specific spiritual and religious commitments were displaced or subsumed by political ones. The religious involvement in institutionalized political life was, with the brief exception of the mid-1770s, qualified and contingent. Like the framers of the Constitution and unlike the classical republicans whose thought underlay much of the early revolutionary movement, articulate American Protestants resisted the equation of virtue and political participation. As Nathan Hatch has shown, postrevolutionary popular evangelical religious denominations would become more individualistic than their predecessors in their emphasis on personal salvation and scriptural interpretation.[45]

Unlike the founders, however, and unlike subsequent generations of liberty theorists, they and other American Protestants continued to believe that virtue was indispensable to the public good. The rhetorical connections among piety, social happiness, and national destiny lived on, structuring major themes in American ideology. One of the major achievements of the revolutionary era was the birth of a new dimension of American public life, neither church nor state, characterized by voluntary moral and social activism. Typically religiously in-spired and nationalistic, these reform movements emerged as powerful and dis-tinctive features of the American republican way of life. This development was, I would suggest, a direct consequence of the religious experience of the Revolution, an experience that drew upon the basic conceptual materials of the colonial past to forge new ways of thinking about the spiritual significance and moral imperatives of collective life.

NOTES

1. The most comprehensive statement of this position is J. G. A. Pocock, *The Machi-avellian Moment: Florentine Political Thought and the Atlantic Republican Tradition* (Princeton, N.J.: Princeton University Press, 1975). Other key works are Bernard Bailyn, *The Ideological Origins of the American Revolution* (Cambridge, Mass.: Harvard University Press, 1967); and Gordon S. Wood, *The Creation of the American Republic, 1776–1787* (Chapel Hill: University of North Carolina Press, 1969).
2. See especially Joyce Appleby, *Capitalism and a New Social Order: The Republican Vision of the 1790s* (New York: New York University Press, 1984).
3. Ruth H. Bloch, *Visionary Republic: Millennial Themes in American Thought, 1756–1800* (New York: Cambridge University Press, 1985); Nathan O. Hatch, *The Sacred Cause of Liberty: Republican Thought and the Millennium in Revolutionary New England* (New Haven, Conn.: Yale University Press, 1977); Alan Heimert, *Religion and the American Mind from the Great Awakening to the Revolution* (Cambridge, Mass.: Harvard University Press, 1966). Other literature includes Perry Miller, "From the Covenant to the Revival," in his *Nature's Nation* (Cambridge, Mass.: Harvard University Press, 1967); and Edmund S. Morgan, "The Puritan Ethic and the American Revolution," *William and Mary Quarterly*, 3rd ser., 24 (1967): 3–43.

4. This is the main dynamic traced in Hatch, *Sacred Cause*; and Harry S. Stout, *The New England Soul: Preaching and Religious Culture in Colonial New England* (New York: Oxford University Press, 1986).

5. For examples of this way of conceptualizing the issue, see Heimert, *Religion and the American Mind*; Bloch, *Visionary Republic*; and David S. Lovejoy, *Religious Enthusiasm in the New World: Heresy to Revolution* (Cambridge, Mass.: Harvard University Press, 1985).

6. James T. Kloppenberg, "The Virtues of Liberalism: Christianity, Republicanism, and Ethics in Early American Political Discourse," *Journal of American History* 74 (1987): 9–33.

7. For example, Rhys Isaac, *The Transformation of Virginia* (Chapel Hill: University of North Carolina Press, 1982); and Lovejoy, *Religious Enthusiasm*.

8. The assimilation of changing political ideas into older religious forms is the process of intellectual change described, for example, in Hatch, *Sacred Cause*; and Stout, *New England Soul*.

9. David Hall, "Religion and Society," in *Colonial British America*, ed. Jack P. Green and J. R. Pole (Baltimore, Md.: Johns Hopkins University Press, 1984), 323.

10. Pauline Maier, *From Resistance to Revolution: Colonial Radicals and the Development of American Opposition to Britain, 1765–1776* (New York: Knopf, 1972).

11. On the Bishop's Scare, see Carl Bridenbaugh, *Mitre and Sceptre: Transatlantic Faiths, Ideas, Personalities, and Politics* (New York: Oxford University Press, 1962); and Patricia Bonomi, *Under the Cope of Heaven: Religion, Society and Politics in Colonial America* (New York: Oxford University Press, 1987), 199–209. On the Quebec Act, see Bloch, *Visionary Republic*, 58–59; and Stout, *New England Soul*, 261.

12. See the works cited in notes 1–3, above.

13. Miller, "Covenant to Revival"; Stout, *New England Soul*.

14. The extent to which Calvinists in other regions during the early revolutionary movement regarded America as their new Israel deserves more exploration. Only in New England, however, had such a perspective become so hegemonic as to provide an important basis of a regional patriot identity. I thank Patricia Bonomi for raising this issue with me.

15. The localism of the covenant language in this period is stressed by Stout, *New England Soul*, esp. 284. His and other descriptions of the use of New England covenant language in the Revolution illustrates this undifferentiated sense of godly people. See also Miller, "Covenant to Revival"; and Sacvan Bercovitch, *The American Jeremiad* (Madison: University of Wisconsin Press, 1978).

16. Bloch, *Visionary Republic*, 56–57. See also William Pencak, *War, Politics and Revolution in Provincial Massachusetts* (Boston: Northeastern University Press, 1981), 226–27.

17. See, for example, John Hancock, *An Oration Delivered March 5, 1774* (Boston: Edes and Gill, 1774), 9–10; Paul Revere, "A Warm Place—Hell" (1768), in Elbridge H. Goss, *The Life of Colonel Paul Revere*, 5th ed. (Boston: Howard Spurr, 1902), 60. See also Peter Shaw, *American Patriots and the Rituals of Revolution* (Cambridge, Mass.: Harvard University Press, 1981), 15–18, 177–83, 197–99, and 204–26.

18. On the religious significance of the abstinence required by the nonimportation agreements, see Morgan, "The Puritan Ethic."

19. Hatch, *Sacred Cause*, 21–54; and Stout, *New England Soul*, 166–81.

20. Bloch, *Visionary Republic*, 44–45, 61–63, 81–82; Stout, *New England Soul*, 216, 259, 277, 297–99, 307; and Mark Noll, *Christians in the American Revolution* (Grand Rapids, Mich.: Eerdmans, 1977), 56–57.

21. Bonomi, *Cope of Heaven*. On religious pluralism as a basis of American liberty, see also Sidney Mead, *The Lively Experiment* (New York: Harper & Row, 1963).

22. For example, Isaac Backus, "Appeal for Religious Liberty" (1773), in *Isaac Backus on Church, State, and Calvinism*, ed. William G. McLoughlin (Cambridge, Mass.: Harvard University Press, 1968); Nathaniel Niles, *Two Discourses on Liberty* (Newburyport, Mass.: Thomas and Tinges, 1774); and the eloquent anonymous example quoted in Stout, *New England Soul*, 273.

23. As quoted in Eric Foner, *Tom Paine and Revolutionary America* (New York: Oxford University Press, 1976), 115; Isaac, *Transformation of Virginia*, 188.

24. Bloch, *Visionary Republic*, 58–60.

25. Stout, *New England Soul*, esp. 296, 302.

26. For example, *Journals of Congress: Containing Their Proceedings from September 5, 1774, to January 1, 1776*, 3 vols. (Philadelphia: Folwell's, 1800), 1:110, 172; 2:90; 3:370.

27. Carl Becker, *The Declaration of Independence* (New York: Knopf, 1922).

28. Hamilton, *Full Vindication of the Members of Congress*, in *The Papers of Alexander Hamilton*, 27 vols., ed. Harold C. Syrett and Jacob E. Cooke (New York: Columbia University Press, 1961–1987), 1:69. On Patrick Henry, see Isaac, *Transformation of Virginia*, 266–69; and Charles L. Cohen, "The 'Liberty or Death' Speech: A Note on Religion and Revolutionary Rhetoric," *William and Mary Quarterly*, 3rd ser., 38 (1981): 702–17.

29. Bloch, *Visionary Republic*, 75–87.

30. Bloch, "The Social and Political Base of Millennial Literature in Late Eighteenth-Century America," *American Quarterly* 40 (1988): 378–96.

31. Stout, *New England Soul*, 393–96. The chief example is the election sermon by Samuel Langdon, *Government Corrupted by Vice and Recovered by Righteousness* (Watertown, Mass.: Benjamin Edes, 1775), esp. 11–12.

32. Bloch, *Visionary Republic*; and Hatch, *Sacred Cause*.

33. Charles Royster, *A Revolutionary People at War: The Continental Army and American Character, 1775–1783* (Chapel Hill: University of North Carolina Press, 1979), 25–53.

34. Francis N. Thorpe, ed., *The Federal and State Constitutions, Colonial Charters and Other Organic Laws of . . . the United States of America*, 7 vols. (Washington, D.C.: U.S. Government Printing Office, 1909).

35. See the argument of Stephen Botein, "Religious Dimensions of the Early American State," in *Beyond Confederation: Origins of the Constitution and American National Identity*, ed. Richard Beeman, Stephen Botein, and Edwards C. Carter II (Chapel Hill: University of North Carolina Press, 1987).

36. The main lines of this debate can be followed in John Fiske, *The Critical Period* (Boston: Houghton Mifflin, 1888); Charles Beard, *An Economic Interpretation of the Constitution of the United States* (New York: Macmillan, 1913); and Merrill Jensen, *The New Nation* (New York: Knopf, 1950).

37. Wood, *Creation of the American Republic.*
38. Ibid.
39. Ibid.; Hatch, *Sacred Cause*; and Bloch, *Visionary Republic.*
40. Bloch, *Visionary Republic.*
41. Asa Burton, *A Sermon Preached at Windsor . . . on the Day of the Anniversary Election, October, 1785* (Windsor, Vt.: Hough and Spooner, 1786), 22.
42. Salient examples include Charles Backus, *A Sermon Preached at Long Meadow, at the Publick Fast* (Springfield, Mass.: Weld and Thomas, 1788); Samuel Magaw, *A Sermon Delivered at St. Paul's Church* (Philadelphia: Young and M'Culloch, 1786); and Thomas Reese, *An Essay on the Influence of Religion, in Civil Society* (Charleston, S.C.: Markland and M'Iver, 1788).
43. Wood, *Creation of the American Republic*, 606.
44. Daniel Walker Howe, "The Political Psychology of the *Federalist*," *William and Mary Quarterly*, 3rd ser., 44 (1987): 485–509.
45. Nathan O. Hatch, "*Sola Scriptura* and *Novus Ordo Seclorum*," in *The Bible in America: Essays in Cultural History*, ed. Hatch and Mark A. Noll (New York: Oxford University Press, 1982); and Hatch, "The Christian Movement and the Demand for a Theology of the People," *Journal of American History* 67 (1980): 545–66.

3

RHETORIC AND REALITY
IN THE EARLY REPUBLIC
The Case of the Federalist Clergy

Harry S. Stout

TIMOTHY DWIGHT WAS no stranger to the inherited Puritan vocabulary of America as a new Israel. Speaking at a July Fourth oration in 1789, Dwight invited his hearers to "look through the history of your country, [and] you will find scarcely less glorious and wonderful proofs of divine protection and deliverance . . . than that which was shown to the people of Israel in Egypt, in the wilderness, and in Canaan."

But in July 1812, amid ongoing Federalist defeats at the national level and an unpopular war with England, a darker note sounded in Dwight's national assessment, one that he did not often repeat, but that surely loomed large in his and other Federalist clergymen's minds. Speaking at a public fast in Yale College Chapel, Dwight confessed that America's Constitution was non-Christian:

> We formed our Constitution without any acknowledgment *of* God; without any recognition of his mercies to us, as a people, of his gov-ernment, or even of his existence. The [Constitutional] Convention, by which it was formed, never asked, even once, his direction, or his

blessing upon their labours. Thus we commenced our national existence under the present system, without God.[1]

That Dwight and most other Federalist clergy would speak of America both as a Christian nation and, less often but with equal intensity, as a godless republic reveals in graphic fashion the tensions between Christian religion and republican government that lay at the heart of the new republic. These tensions reflected two conflicting realities or points of departure: the one political and constitutional, which explicitly separated church and state and left God out of the formulation; and the other rhetorical and religious, in which "America" inherited New England's colonial covenant and where God orchestrated a sacred union of church and state for his redemptive purposes. These tensions, not to say contradictions, never erupted in violent upheaval, but they did divide American society in profound ways that have persisted throughout American history.[2]

While the contradictions between America as a chosen nation and a godless republic are clear, the reasons for them are not. How could intelligent, honest ministers and statesmen proclaim such opposite sentiments without any sense of impropriety or deception? In what follows, I will suggest that if we are to understand the paradox of conflicting speech over the meaning of America, we must reach through and beyond the early republic to the rhetorical world of the Puritans and see how they bequeathed to their New England descendants an identity as a Christian people that was blind to contrary facts and that quite literally reshaped current realities to fit traditional rhetorical ends.

In speaking of the Puritans' "rhetorical world," I am taking a cue from Gordon Wood's magisterial reconstruction of the mental world of the founding fathers.[3] In that work, Wood asks how the founding fathers, as intelligent and insightful as they were, could both create a democratic republic and, at the same time, remain blind to its radical egalitarian implications. Further, he asks, how could these same wise fathers be so "scientific" about politics and yet be so taken with conspiratorial explanations of history that completely missed the larger economic and demographic forces that were transforming their society? His conclusion is that the founders were neither pathological liars nor paranoids, but intelligent men who, like all peoples, were bounded by the symbols they possessed. Symbols, myths, and language open up and tame reality at the same time that they impose limits on the perceiver. In all symbol systems or rhetorical worlds, some things come clearly into focus, while others remain hidden and inaccessible.

As used in this chapter, the phrase "rhetorical worlds" refers to one particular type of paradigm, or symbol system, that operates in the world of public speech. Just as interpretive paradigms function to shape and mold "reality" in

science, literature, or social theory, so also do they function to supply the operative rules and binding assumptions for communities of discourse. In this sense,
rhetorical worlds are not a form of "propaganda" in which speakers consciously
manipulate symbols to exploit baser ends. Quite the opposite, rhetorical worlds
become shared realities that are as binding on the speaker as they are on the
audience. They represent the master assumptions that speakers and their audiences cannot prove or disprove, but which both accept because, intellectually, they
conform to the community's passionately held assumptions of self, society, and
the cosmos and, socially, because they make the system work.

In the case of the founding fathers, Wood discovers a symbol system whose
reality definitions were largely classical and aristocratic in origin. The rhetorical
world of classical republicanism opened the founders' eyes to the meaning of
liberty at the same time that its aristocratic context closed their eyes to the
possibility of positive social change originating "from beneath," among the ordinary people. Like a gigantic presence from another world, this classical rhetorical world towered over the mundane (and contrary) facts of the Revolution
and shaped "reality" for those founders who shared in its discourse. Try as they
might, the founders could not transcend their world and see the secular and democratic forces that were reshaping their society from the bottom up. Rhetorical
worlds derive their power from the community's shared insistence that its formulations are not rhetorical inventions, but reality as it "really is." At the moment
an individual or community peers around its rhetorical world, it ceases to exist
and the once-gigantic presence dissolves into a mist of dated "fiction" and "mere"
rhetoric.

While the classical rhetorical world described by Wood was central in
shaping the mental universe of the founders, it was not monolithic. Studies have
documented the presence of other, competing rhetorical worlds that held sway
with different speakers and their audiences. Thus, for example, Alfred Young and
Gary Nash have reconstructed a "popular ideology," or "small producer" ideology,
of urban artisans and laborers and subsistence farmers that was organized around
more egalitarian assumptions of popular sovereignty and a "moral economy."[4]
Among elites themselves, Joyce Appleby has described a "liberal" ideology premised less on classical concepts of civic virtue and the sacrifice of self-interest
than on the active promotion of the self-interested pursuit of happiness.[5] Unlike
seventeenth-century New England, which featured one public speaker—the
minister—and entire communities of captive listeners, the early republic encompassed a plurality of rhetorical worlds competing for popular audiences.

In turning to the New England Federalist clergy in the early republic, I
would suggest that we are seeing yet another rhetorical world with a different set

of actors and accompanying symbols. While the clergy shared a common classical education with the founders that supplied some common assumptions, it did not shape their perception of reality at the most formative level. Rather, their reality was shaped by an inherited Puritan rhetorical world that overlapped the founders' world at some points, but diverged dramatically in others. Most important, the inherited Puritan rhetorical world was incapable of seeing the constitutional realities of the First Amendment as "really real." Lying behind the Constitution was another, more important reality of America as a Christian nation.

Before contrasting the rhetorical worlds of the framers and the Federalist clergy more fully, it is important to recognize some convergences between their worlds that allowed for common action and a multilayered republican ideology. On a biographical level, many Federalist clergymen were good republicans, and many republican legislators were good Protestants. When faced with common threats from without or from beneath, they could close ranks in common opposition. Differences that would radically divide "secular humanists" and "evangelicals" in the late nineteenth century were, in 1787, still more potential than real.

One reason that neither the founding fathers nor the Federalist clergy could see the new forces around them was that both shared an elitist sense of history and society. Next to tyranny, the greatest threat these leaders perceived was anarchy, which they defined as any movement whose leadership bypassed them. If the founders could not concede the legitimacy of democratic parties that were led by self-made commoners, neither could the Federalist clergy tolerate the self-trained Methodist itinerants and new "Christian" denominations that were threatening to dominate the nineteenth-century religious scene.[6]

Besides sharing a common elitism, the founders and Federalist clergy shared a common premodern sense of history that was essentially deductive and "personalistic."[7] As statesmen and clergymen surveyed the changes taking place in their society, they did not look for impersonal movements or environmental forces for explanation, but for faces and names. The central question for them was not *what* caused an event, but *who*? Who is responsible for the trials we endure or the blessings we enjoy? Such a view of history was neither modern nor commonsensical. One did not begin with the facts, which would supposedly sort themselves into self-evident patterns, but with the archetypal causes to which the facts were able to adhere. Chief among these archetypal causes was the highly personal and individual confrontations between good and evil men. In this world, there could be no sense of history such as the ironical one described by Reinhold Niebuhr as the dilemma of "moral man and immoral society."[8] Rather, there was a one-to-one correspondence between individual morality and social morality and, in both cases, a "moral tendency" or correlation between personal morality and national well-being.[9]

Yet if the classical and Puritan rhetorical worlds had much in common by virtue of a shared classical education and Protestant ethos, there were also profound differences that made inevitable the ongoing tensions between America as a secular republic and America as a Christian nation. In the early years of the republic, these differences were largely inferential and philosophical—more matters of emphasis and priority than mutually exclusive categories. But in time, as the non-Protestant sector of American society grew ever larger, the possibility for division became greater.

Of all the differences separating the classical and Puritan rhetorical worlds, none was more important than the alternative texts to which each looked for explanation and inspiration. Where the framers derived their sense of the American republic from classical and "Real Whig" political texts, the clergy oriented their speech and commentary around the vernacular Bible—read and internalized by most New England inhabitants for one and a half centuries. For most of the framers, the Bible stood to the side of political oratory as a more or less licit guest that could be brought in to legitimate truths that enlightened reason made clear.[10] Conversely, while the clergy did not ignore enlightened reason and the law of nature—particularly in election sermons and July Fourth orations—those texts were subordinated to the eternal truths of sacred writ. The Bible supplied ministers with most of their metaphors and analogies, both religious and political. It also supplied a self-contained history of redemption that identified the ultimate force behind evil persons—the Antichrist—and that identified the ultimate end of history in the millennial creation of a new world freed from sin.

Beyond textual differences, the two rhetorical worlds differed substantially over the question of what constituted a truly moral, virtuous society. At its core, the Puritan vision of the good society was fixed by an idea—the idea—of a "peculiar" national covenant between God and his sovereignly chosen people. New England was inhabited by such a chosen people and, by virtue of America's support for New England during the Revolution, the nation became grafted onto New England's special destiny.[11]

In Puritan rhetoric, the iron law of God's covenant explained all. This covenant, rather than the science of politics, determined the course of American history and represented the lens through which the nation-state was viewed. Obedience to God's covenant and his prophets was the sole criterion by which America would stand or fall. Where the classical rhetorical world subordinated religion to politics and privatized "conscience" for the public welfare, the Puritan rhetorical world subordinated forms of government to covenant keeping and *imposed* conscience—"rightly informed"—on the members of a public who desperately needed to observe the covenant whether they knew it or not.

CLEARLY, REPUBLICAN REALITIES diverged dramatically from Puritan rhetoric on the level of textual authority and governing assumptions. But, equally clearly, the two did coexist in more or less peaceful harmony. And here we are again confronted with the problem of explanation. How could such rival rhetorics peacefully coexist? The answer is found far back in colonial New England's past, in the Glorious Revolution, when, in circumstances remarkably similar to 1787, the Puritan clergy learned to accept a new, non-Puritan authority without sacrificing their rhetorical identity as a "peculiar" people of the word. When, in 1684, England acted to deprive Massachusetts Bay of its charter, the Puritan state, or "theocracy," came to an official end. Under the new royal charter, government was defined in new terms that made no reference to New England's covenant. The Act of Toleration meant that religion—at least in its Christian manifestations—had become a matter of private conscience beyond the power of the state to control.

Yet, in what surely stands as one of the clearest illustrations of the power of rhetoric to shape and mold contrary realities, New England preachers continued to speak of God's covenant with the "nation" as if nothing had changed. Instead of attacking the new charter as godless and anti-Puritan, most ministers celebrated it enthusiastically, and then went on doing what they had always done.[12] Because the Act of Toleration granted Protestant movements the freedom to use words any way they pleased, ministers were freed to invoke terms like "liberty" in restricted ways that meant simply the liberty to preserve New England's inherited covenant. On the one hand, preachers would praise England's policy of religious toleration, while on the other they continued to address New England audiences as a people still bound in an ancient yet ongoing covenant. Thus, in his 1692 election sermon, Cotton Mather followed up a celebration of the new royal government with the reminder that New England's destiny continued to hang on covenant keeping: "If any one ask, unto what the Sudden and Matchless thriving of *New-England* may be ascribed? It is the Blessing of God upon the *Church-Order*, for the sake whereof . . . this Plantation was first Erected." The new charter did not change the terms of God's covenant with New England, and if the people forgot that, no nation or constitution on earth could protect them from the avenging hand of God: "If we don't go *Leaning* upon God, every step, we shall *go wrong*, and nothing will go *well* in our Hands."[13] As long as speakers and audiences continued to define New England as a peculiar covenanted people, the rhetoric would live on, whatever the contrary realities.

The success of the clergy in bending the new realities to conform to the old covenant hinged on two considerations: intellectual and social. Intellectually, the clergy made their peace with the new regime by exploiting the multiple meanings and studied imprecision of terms like "liberty" and "nation."[14] From the first Puritan settlement, these terms possessed distinct insider and outsider meanings. To outside audiences, whether they be Charles I, William and Mary, or the national Congress, "liberty" would be defined in its fullest meaning as the freedom of all religious groups to worship as they pleased and of speakers to compete for the loyalty of the citizenry. To insiders, however, "liberty" always assumed an instrumental, more restricted meaning as the liberty to create a covenantal society in which the inhabitants voluntarily established public support for their churches, ministers, schools, chaplains, and colleges. In like manner, the word "nation" could mean the broad boundaries of the political state or, to insiders, the "holy nation" of covenanted believers for whose sake God would bless the larger political affiliation.

Socially, the preservation of Puritan rhetoric required a region sufficiently homogeneous for a clear majority of the inhabitants to endorse the rhetorical vision. Rhetorical worlds, after all, are *shared* worlds and require the willing incorporation of speaker and audience in a common script. From colonial origins to the first waves of nineteenth-century Irish immigrants, New England was uniquely such a region.[15] It remained, in Perry Miller's apt characterization, a "laboratory" whose population expanded almost exclusively through a vast natural increase of interconnected families. Thus, as long as the question of religious establishment and support was left to the will of the town majorities, and as long as speakers were free to define terms as they pleased, the Puritans could compete for and win the loyalty of the towns which, in turn, constituted the core of the holy nation.

CLEARLY, MUCH HAD changed in the century separating the royal charter of 1692 from the federal republic of 1787. Constitutional monarchy was replaced by democratic republic, religious tests for office were eliminated at the national level, and New England was no longer several colonies but states integrated in a larger union. Yet, in surveying Federalist preaching in the early republic, one is struck by how little the rhetorical strategy had changed as Federalist preachers unveiled the innermost meaning of America in a number of election, fast, or July Fourth orations. Sermons preached and printed on "national" occasions were remarkably provincial, such that "America" became New England writ large. The new constitutional realities that originated outside of New England and that ignored God did nothing to alter the rhetorical world of the Federalist clergy and their audiences. Constitutional realities were reinterpreted and subordinated to the sacred pretense of a covenanted people. And by shouting the pretense loudly enough over competing voices, the rhetoric prevailed. Liberty remained sacred and instrumental. Because New Englanders utilized their liberty within "gospel bounds," the "nation"—now America—would enjoy the same covenant blessings that New England had enjoyed since first settlement.

In extending the idea of covenant to the nation, the Federalist clergy fastened on three interrelated corollaries that fixed reality for their listeners, even as the neoclassical rhetorical world of the founders pointed in opposite directions. The first, and all-important, corollary to the clergy's Christianization of America was the proposition that America originated ultimately not through social compact but by divine fiat. Arguments from natural law and the consent of the governed were not sufficient explanations for the meaning of America. In the beginning, God created New England. And from that sacred origin the larger nation evolved.

Almost without exception, Federalist clergy in the early republic devoted significant portions of their occasional oratory to a rehearsal of the "great errand" into America inaugurated by the Puritans and their covenant with God. The real America—that is, sacred America—began, David Tappan explained in his 1792 Massachusetts election sermon, not in 1787 or 1776, but in 1620 when "our fathers were led out of the house of bondage in Britain, into the wilderness of America, and planted here, as in the land of promise, by the same divine Shepherd who led ancient Israel from deep oppression and misery, to the joys of freedom and plenty." Here, as elsewhere, speakers grafted New England onto the sacred history of Israel, and then extended that history to America. Such a society, Josiah Bridge explained, was "by no means the result of chance," but of providence.[16]

For the national covenant to endure, individual salvation was not required at all, but corporate morality was. In addressing the national covenant, occasional speakers spent far more time on the subject of "virtue" and "morality" than on personal salvation, while in their Sunday preaching—to insiders—they reminded their hearers that there could be no saving morality without personal faith.[17] Contained in the identification with Israel was far more than regional pride; it was sacred pretense. As far as the founders were concerned, the New England migration was simply one among many competing colonial strains that collectively made up the American mosaic. But for New England speakers and their audiences, the Puritan strain was *the* strain of American history (and destiny), for it represented the covenant around which America must revolve if it were to retain God's blessings. So crucial was New England to American destiny that occasional speakers routinely identified the term "constitution" not with the federal Constitution, but with their state constitution, which, according to Samuel Deane, "approaches so near to perfection...that it can hardly be [revised]."[18]

The second organizing corollary to New England's identification of a Christian America was its millennial destiny.[19] The promise of millennium also appeared in Puritan rhetoric from first settlement, and completed their rhetorical world by moving from a sacred past instituted by divine fiat to a glorious future state ruled by Christ. As a people of providence rather than compact, Americans could expect that the same God who orchestrated New England's beginnings would launch them into a glorious future as a redeemer nation.

Just as Federalist speakers identified America's past with biblical analogies or "types" from the Old Testament, so did they identify the republic's future with millennial texts. The most frequently cited text to fix America's future in the revolutionary era was Isaiah 66:8: "Shall the earth be made to bring forth in one day? or shall a nation be born at once?" This prophecy, speakers argued, was fulfilled on July 4, 1776. That was the day God had in mind when he inspired Isaiah to record his prophecy. With independence, the text continued to resonate with sacred meanings for America. For example, in his 1790 election sermon, Daniel Foster reminded the governor in attendance—John Hancock—that "it was under your presidency and direction, that ancient prophecy was literally accomplished, 'a nation born in a day'—America declared free, sovereign, and independent."[20]

If Americans were to inherit the millennial promise, they must keep the covenant. Along the way, they could be sure there would be evil men and diabolical plots aimed at destroying the covenant. Alongside the promise of Christ was the threat of the Antichrist, defined as anyone opposing the ongoing life of the covenant. The Federalist clergy, like the founders, were attuned to plots and conspiracies in explaining history. But behind evil men, they discovered the even more diabolical presence of Satan. After the Revolution, Federalist clergy continued to discover the plot of the Antichrist in the atheism of the French Revolution and in international conspiracies such as the Bavarian Illuminati.[21] Within America itself, the figure of the Antichrist could be discerned amid domestic unrest and violence and in the failure of America to follow the warnings of New England's prophets regarding war with England. Only by returning to the God of New England and his prophets could America remain in God's favor.

The third corollary to a Christian America was the proposition that religion must be a matter of *both* private conscience and public policy.[22] If the first two corollaries were largely subjective and interpretive, the third was practical and political. America's God was a jealous God who would have no other gods before him. In the Puritan rhetorical world, the greatest threat to republican government was not population expansion, war, or runaway inflation, but infidelity—bad faith. For most of the founders, the greatest enemies to the republic were those who threatened disunity through parties and factions. In the Puritan rhetorical world, however, the greatest enemies were atheists. Such people, Frederick Hotchkiss explained, were "unfit for human society." A nation "habitually irreligious," Samuel Taggart warned, cannot be long free: "Those who are endeavoring to eradicate the principles of religion and virtue, by discarding Christianity, however extensive the benevolence may be which they profess, are our worst enemies." The unforgivable sin of atheism, Timothy Dwight explained, was its "worship of Abstract terms" to the exclusion of a personal deity. Atheists depersonalized the cosmos and, in so doing, denied the possibilities of providential origins, the ongoing covenant, and millennial hope—each of which depended on a transcendent presence in the life of the nation.[23]

The framers could tolerate (if not endorse) the presence of deists and atheists in the national government as long as such citizens were bound to the dictates of reason and civic virtue. Not so the Federalist clergy—and most of their listeners—whose governing assumptions precluded the acceptability of an atheistic leadership. To ensure that atheists and infidelity would not triumph in America, ministers never tired of pointing out that God required his people to elect a "Christian legislature" willing to acknowledge an overseeing deity and committed to supporting such Christian institutions as schools, colleges, churches, chaplains, and biblically derived laws. To ensure such leaders—at least in New England—some form of religious test for office was necessary. Speaking in 1801 at the outset of a new century, Aaron Bancroft conceded that while personal conversion and the covenant of grace were "too sacred for human regulation" (i.e., private), that did not mean there should be no religious establishment. To the contrary, "it clearly falls within the province of a Christian legislature, to support institutions, which facilitate the instruction of people in the truths and duties of religion, which are the means to give efficacy to the precepts of the gospel, and are calculated to instill the spirit of morality and order into the minds of the community."[24]

Having established New England's covenant as the key to America's survival, Bancroft, like other speakers, would appropriate the traditional rhetoric of the jeremiad and apply it to the new nation. In words that echoed almost exactly the colonial threat of "almost" destruction, but not "quite yet," Bancroft openly wondered whether "the period that is now passed, in future [will] be remembered as the golden age of America? [H]ave not too many fallen off from the principles of their ancestors?" If reform were not immediately forthcoming, Bancroft warned, "our nation will be rent by party.... By our vices we shall forfeit the blessings of our God ... and we shall suffer the miseries of impiety and wickedness, of faction and anarchy, of tyranny and oppression." America's only hope was to turn back to the religion of New England's founders, to turn to the "protecting arm of Deity," rather than "become the sport of atheistical chance and accident."[25]

When national policy ran contrary to New England's preference, as in the War of 1812, the Federalist clergy invariably invoked America's "true" constitution (the national covenant) as grounds for dissent and resistance. In nineteenth-century America, as in eighteenth-century New England, there were limits to the fusions of rhetorics. When these boundaries were crossed—in 1776 with George III or in 1812 with "Mr. Madison's war"—the clergy did not hesitate to denounce the outside "nation" and separate themselves from its constitutional pretenses. The blindness to contraries that marked ordinary discourse in times of peace broke down in 1812 into a prophetic New England "we" against a covenant-threatening "them who wanted war." For support, the clergy turned to America's "true" founders—the Puritan founders—who had articulated the "true" standards from which the nation had sadly "declined." Thus, in his July 4, 1812, oration Francis Blake dispensed with the customary paean to America and angrily wondered "how far we have wandered from the landmarks of our political fathers." Those landmarks, it soon became clear, were blazed almost exclusively in New England, and the "fathers" were the fathers of New England. John Fiske concurred in his 1812 address: "For the religious leaders of this land, especially of New England we have reason to believe that war has been commenced on our part, without the approbation of heaven." Consequently, Fiske concluded, Americans must resist their nation's policy or risk a broken covenant.[26]

It is in such moments of tension and disjunction as 1812 that the full variance in republican and Puritan sentiments becomes clear. In fact, all of the corollaries attached to the Puritan notion of a Christian America contradicted the main outlines of the federal Constitution and the republic on which it rested. Yet they continued to define reality for many Americans. In times of dissent, the Federalist clergy condemned the godlessness of America's Constitution and invoked the Puritan founders and their own state constitutions as their true rhetorical standard. That standard enjoyed a longer New World history and, in their view, its genius defined America's true destiny.

WHAT LESSONS CAN we take from the persistence of Puritan rhetoric in the early republic? For one, we are cautioned against completing intellectual revolutions in religious thought too quickly. Habits of speech, like habits of the heart, die hard, and loyal listeners rarely perceive the inner contradictions. The triumph of an individualist, egalitarian evangelicalism with its antihistoricism and commonsense realism was a more gradual transition than historians have generally allowed. In many ways, the transition is still incomplete. Lying beneath the new evangelicalism of nineteenth-century America was an older rhetorical world, one that was corporate, coercive, providential, deductive, and elitist.

As religious historians need to qualify the triumph of an individual evangelicalism, so do constitutional and political historians need to examine the dominance of the secular enlightened naturalism that informed the Constitution. Alongside the celebration of religious liberty, separation of church and state, and the privatization of religious conscience lay a competing rhetorical world, with a longer New World history, that was every bit as real and compelling for its hearers as the language of the Constitution. Logically speaking, the two worlds could not peacefully coexist. But they did, proving once again that America is a disproving ground of logic. It is in the inability of either rhetoric to triumph over the other that we find part of the explanation for the "unstable pluralism" that Michael Kammen sees lurking about the soul of an American "people of paradox."[27] Americans continue to peer through, but never around, their rhetorical worlds, thus leaving perpetually open the question of what is really real: the rhetoric or the reality?

NOTES

1. Timothy Dwight, *The Duty of Americans* (New Haven, Conn.: Green, 1798), 29–30; and Dwight, *A Discourse in Two Parts*, 2nd ed. (Boston: Flagg and Gould, 1813), 24. Sentiments like Dwight's were not uncommon in 1812. In the year following Dwight's address, Chauncey Lee reflected on the republic's godless origins:

   Can we pause, and reflect for a moment, without the mingled emotions of wonder and regret; that that publick instrument, which guarantees our political rights of freedom and independence—our *Constitution* of national government, framed by such an august, learned and able body of men; formally adopted by the solemn resolution of each state; and justly admired and celebrated for its consummate political wisdom; has not the impress of *religion* upon it, not the smallest recognition of the government, or the being of GOD, or of the dependence and accountability of man. Be astonished, O earth!—Nothing, by which a foreigner might with certainty decide, whether we believe in the one true God, or in any God; whether we are a nation of Christians, or—But I forbear. The subject is too delicate, to say more; and it is too interesting to have said less. I leave it with this single reflection, whether, if God be not in the Lamp, we have not reason to tremble for the ark? (*The Government of God* [Hartford, Conn.: Hudson and Goodwin, 1813], 43)

My analysis in this chapter is part of a larger study of preaching in the early republic. It is based on an examination of fifty printed occasional sermons delivered primarily by Congregational clergymen in the period 1787–1813.

2. For an explication of divergent tendencies in Protestant thought, see George M. Marsden, *Fundamentalism and American Culture* (New York: Oxford University Press, 1980).

3. See especially Gordon S. Wood, *The Creation of the American Republic, 1776–1787* (Chapel Hill: University of North Carolina Press, 1969); and Wood, "Rhetoric and Reality in the American Revolution," *William and Mary Quarterly*, 3rd ser., 23 (1966): 3–32.

4. See Gary B. Nash, *The Urban Crucible: Social Change, Political Consciousness, and the Origins of the American Revolution* (Cambridge, Mass.: Harvard University Press, 1979); and Alfred F. Young, ed. *The American Revolution: Explorations in the History of American Radicalism* (DeKalb: Northern Illinois University Press, 1976). The term "moral economy" is taken from E. P. Thompson's pioneering work on English popular ideology, *The Making of the English Working Class* (New York: Pantheon, 1964). For a survey of the extensive literature on social classes and class-linked political dissent, see Gary B. Nash, "Also There at the Creation: Going beyond Gordon S. Wood," *William and Mary Quarterly*, 3rd ser., 41 (1987): 602–11.

5. On the theme of liberalism, see especially Joyce Appleby, *Capitalism and a New Social Order: The Republican Vision of the 1790s* (New York: New York University Press, 1984); J. G. A. Pocock, *The Machiavellian Moment: Florentine Political Thought and the Atlantic Republican Tradition* (Princeton, N.J.: Princeton University Press, 1975); and John P. Diggins, *The Lost Soul of American Politics: Virtue, Self-Interest, and the Foundations of Liberalism* (New York: Basic, 1984).

6. See especially Gordon S. Wood, "The Democratization of Mind in the American Revolution," in *Leadership in the American Revolution* (Washington, D.C.: Library of Congress, 1974), 63–89; Nathan O. Hatch, "The Christian Movement and the Demand for a Theology of the People," *Journal of American History* 67 (1980): 545–76; and Hatch, *The Democratization of American Christianity* (New Haven, Conn.: Yale University Press, 1989).

7. For a description of the "personalistic and rationalistic mode of explanation" that dominated eighteenth-century elite discourse, see Gordon S. Wood, "Conspiracy and the Paranoid Style: Causality and Deceit in the Eighteenth Century," *William and Mary Quarterly*, 3rd ser., 39 (1982): 401–41.

8. Reinhold Niebuhr, *Moral Man and Immoral Society* (New York: Scribner's, 1932). See also Niebuhr's classic statement, *The Irony of American History* (New York: Scribner's, 1952).

9. This theme is developed extensively in J. Earl Thompson, "A Perilous Experiment: New England Clergymen and American Destiny, 1796–1826" (Ph.D. diss., Andover Seminary, 1965).

10. The best description of the Real Whig ideology is Bernard Bailyn, *The Ideological Origins of the American Revolution* (Cambridge, Mass.: Harvard University Press, 1967).

11. On the New England clergy's extension of covenant promise from New England to "America," see Sacvan Bercovitch, "How the Puritans Won the American Revolution," *Massachusetts Review* 17 (1976): 597–630.

12. I have developed this theme in *The New England Soul: Preaching and Religious Character in Colonial New England* (New York: Oxford University Press, 1986).

13. Cotton Mather, *Optanda: Good Men Described and Good Things Propounded* (Boston: Harris, 1692), 77, 83, 51–53. See also Samuel Willard's election sermon, *The Character of the Good Ruler* (Boston: Harris, 1694).

14. The theoretical work of J. G. A. Pocock is useful here in describing the unavoidable "multivalency" of language that grows from the different "social worlds" in which terms and ideas are communicated. See especially Pocock, *Politics, Language and Time: Essays on Political Thought and History* (New York: Cambridge University Press, 1971), 3–41.

15. Nash describes the unique cultural and ethnic homogeneity of colonial Boston in contrast to New York and Philadelphia in *The Urban Crucible*, 361. This homogeneity persisted until undermined in the 1830s by the first waves of Irish immigrants. See Oscar Handlin, *Boston's Immigrants, 1790–1865* (Cambridge, Mass.: Harvard University Press, 1941), 128–55.

16. David Tappan, *A Sermon Preached* (Boston: Adams, 1792), 23; and Josiah Bridge, *A Sermon Preached* (Boston: Adams and Nourse, 1789), 36. See also, for example, William Emerson, *An Oration* (Boston: Manning and Loring, 1802), 7–9.

17. These distinctions were traced in Chandler Robbins's Massachusetts election sermon, *A Sermon Preached* (Boston: Adams, 1791), 32; and in Samuel Parker, *A Sermon Preached* (Boston: Adams, 1793), 21.

18. Samuel Deane, *A Sermon Preached* (Portland, Maine: Wait, 1796), 21.

19. The best discussions of millennialism in the early republic are Nathan O. Hatch, *The Sacred Cause of Liberty: Republican Thought and the Millennium in Revolutionary New England* (New Haven, Conn.: Yale University Press, 1977); and Ruth H. Bloch, *Visionary Republic: Millennial Themes in American Thought, 1756–1800* (New York: Cambridge University Press, 1985).

20. Daniel Foster, *A Sermon Preached* (Boston: Adams, 1790), 28. See also Festus Foster, *An Oration* (Brookfield, Mass.: Merriam, 1812), 5; and Samuel Taggart, *An Oration* (Northampton, Mass.: Butler, 1804), 3.

21. Vernon Stauffer, *New England and the Bavarian Illuminati* (New York: Columbia University Press, 1918).

22. See James Fulton Maclear, "'The True American Union' of Church and State: The Reconstruction of the Theocratic Tradition," *Church History* 28 (1959): 41–59.

23. Frederick Hotchkiss, *On National Greatness* (New Haven, Conn.: Green, 1793), 20; Taggart, *An Oration*, 25. See also John Allyn, *A Sermon Preached* (Boston: Young and Minns, 1805), 20–24, 32.

24. Aaron Bancroft, *A Sermon Preached* (Boston: Young and Minns, 1801), 21.

25. Ibid., 13, 17, 28.

26. Francis Blake, *An Oration* (Worcester, Mass.: Sturtevant, 1812), 3; John Fiske, *A Sermon Delivered* (Brookfield, Mass.: Merriam, 1812), 25. See also Foster, *An Oration*, 14–15; and Samuel Austin, *The Apology of Patriots* (Worcester, Mass.: Sturtevant, 1812), 16.

27. Michael Kammen, *People of Paradox: An Inquiry concerning the Origins of American Civilization* (New York: Oxford University Press, 1972), 57–58.

Religion, Government, and Power
in the New American Nation

John F. Wilson

$\mathcal{W}$HILE THE HISTORICAL discussion of the separation of church and state naturally centers in the founding period, and while I want to focus on the codification given to religion and politics in that period, the subject is, in a sense, always current, and interest in it always derives from contemporary concerns. For this reason, consideration of "church and state" inevitably emphasizes the dialectical relationship between present and past. The present is reflected in concern with a past that gives it legitimacy, and the past is clarified in the present, which is perceived to flow from that past. Accordingly, I propose to develop the discussion in terms of this dialectical relationship, believing it will yield better history and, as a secondary matter, a more adequate understanding of both the possibilities and hazards of our own time.

Two paradigms govern current interpretation of how the Constitution regulates the relationship of religion to the federal regime. Both make claims involving historical perspectives. These are the separationist and the accommodationist. Both are modern positions, worked out within the last seven decades or so, although each grounds its legitimacy on the same texts and supports itself by extensive historical argumentation. Not surprisingly, each reflects modern interests and is advanced in that light. Because contemporary discussion of the broader issue of religion and government in America tends to be polarized according to these paradigms, we need to know their limitations. As a constructive move, I offer a third reading of this topic. While it certainly produces better history, it will not necessarily appeal to the chief interested parties nor encourage them to modify their positions.

The separationist reading of the founding period of our nation was codified in the *Everson* case, which initiated modern interpretation of the First Amendment's establishment clause.[1] It is astonishing to moderns that the two religion clauses of the Bill of Rights went virtually unapplied—and thus unexplored—until well into the twentieth century. This is, of course, because they were an explicit limitation on the powers of Congress only. They were proposed—and adopted—largely at the behest of the Antifederalists, who were antagonistic to the proposed new national government. This opposition was not concerned with rights per se except in the case of states' rights, for it wanted to ensure that the new federal regime would not be strong enough to usurp the powers of the several states. The religion clauses of the First Amendment therefore guaranteed Connecticut, Massachusetts, and New Hampshire, for example, that their statewide provisions for local tax support of settled congregations were secure against federal intervention and reassured the Baptists and Quakers in Rhode Island, for example, that their precious liberty of conscience would be similarly safe. Only as these clauses became limitations upon the states and local governments through application of the due process clause of the Fourteenth Amendment did these provisions become foundational for the separationist paradigm. As already noted, this determination did not take place until the middle of the twentieth century.

The *Everson* case ruled acceptable the reimbursement by the local school board of bus fares paid by parochial school students from Ewing, New Jersey. But Justice Hugo Black's opinion gave voice to a full-blown separationist interpretation of the establishment clause:

> The "establishment of religion" clause of the First Amendment means at least this: Neither a state nor the Federal Government can set up a church. Neither can pass laws which aid one religion, aid all religions, or prefer one religion over another. Neither can force nor influence a person to go to or to remain away from church against his will or force him to profess a belief or disbelief in any religion. No person can be punished for entertaining or professing religious beliefs or disbeliefs, for church attendance or nonattendance. No tax in any amount, large or

small, can be levied to support any religious activities or institutions, whatever they may be called, or whatever form they may adopt to teach or practice religion. Neither a state nor the Federal Government can, openly or secretly, participate in the affairs of any religious organizations or groups and *vice versa*. In the words of Jefferson, the clause against establishment of religion by law was intended to erect "a wall of separation between church and State."[2]

The disjunction between this position and the outcome of the case led Justice Robert H. Jackson to comment in his dissenting opinion: "The case which irresistibly comes to mind as the most fitting precedent is that of Julia, who, according to Byron's reports, 'whispering "I will ne'er consent"—consented.'"[3]

The Black opinion suggests the separationist logic. The First Amendment clauses were interpreted through the metaphor of the wall of separation Thomas Jefferson had used in conveying his political support to the Baptists of Danbury, Connecticut, for their struggle against their Federalist opponents. The image had exercised a powerful hold on the collective imagination before Justice Black appropriated it for the first full explication of the meaning of the establishment clause, but once he had done so, it became virtually an orthodoxy.[4]

In the world of symbols that concerns the legitimation of politics, this step made the struggle in Virginia on behalf of religious liberty—a struggle in which James Madison played a critical role (especially during Jefferson's absence in Europe)—normative for interpreting the First Amendment clauses.[5] Through Virginia's history, the latent meaning of the federal experience could be discovered. Of course, James Madison's role in drafting the Constitution proper, as well as initiating consideration of the amendments we know as the Bill of Rights, provides additional support for this interpretation.[6]

In general, the classic separationist position resolves the vexing question of how the two religion clauses relate to each other by positing a particular version of religious liberty. Religious liberty is understood as the absence of government constraint upon individuals in matters of religion. This is the fulcrum on which issues of church and state turn. Note that emphasis falls on religious liberty as entailing unfettered *individual* action, and then extrapolating that freedom to groups. It is the individual, devoid of participation in society or culture, who engages in the most basic religious action without reference either to others or to an existing tradition. Further, liberty is conceived negatively as the absence of external constraint. This position incorporates an essentially radical Protestant view of faith focused through an Enlightenment emphasis upon the individual that effectively denies the importance of communal dimensions or social categories.

To this point, we have explored the separationist paradigm. Now let us turn to the alternative position, usefully identified as accommodationist. Like separationists, accommodationists see religious liberty as a basic right—but they construe religion less in terms of individual action and give liberty a positive value as something more than the absence of restraint. Thus, they are more concerned with the exercise of religion and are aware of its communal aspects.

Here we do not have the benefit of such a legal *locus classicus* as the *Everson* decision. What we do have is an invitation by former Chief Justice William Rehnquist to rethink the interpretation of the establishment clause on the basis of more adequate history: "Nothing in the Establishment Clause requires government to be strictly neutral between religion and irreligion, nor does that Clause prohibit Congress or the States from pursuing legitimate secular ends through non-discriminatory sectarian means."[7] At its basis, the accommodationist paradigm takes a more catholic position on the nature of religion.

Accordingly, the accommodationist position observes that in narrowly defining religion in terms of the individual, the separationist point of view may lead to a virtual caricature of religion, perhaps vaguely relevant only to the radical Protestant traditions of the modern United States. The accommodationist perspective emphasizes rather that the First Amendment was clearly not intended to be antireligious—indeed, as already suggested, it was drafted precisely to protect the various religious practices of the states, including preferential establishments in some of them. Accommodationists therefore reinterpret the First Amendment to make of religious liberty a positive right, the exercise of which is to be encouraged by government. By the same token, they believe that the First Amendment excludes only the direct establishment of, or preferential treatment for, a particular religion. Indeed, government should facilitate the practice of religion by both individuals and collectivities as essential to the common good.

This position is very different from that of the separationists and leads to markedly different contemporary policies and practices. In addition, as the point of departure for historical interpretation, it focuses attention upon the residual religious quality of this founding period, which was hardly secularist. The same Congress that proposed the First Amendment was opened with prayer and named a chaplain. Indeed, most of the early presidents declared occasional days of thanksgiving—and even of humiliation. Provision was made for support of religion in opening western lands. And, in time, the resources of religious groups were utilized in making government policy for relations with Native Americans. In sum, accommodationists consider that the operative ideal of the early republic was a nonpreferentialist posture of support for religion on the part of government.[8] In turn, that seems to point toward a modern ideal of accommodation of government to religion in ways that secure the greater common civil good as well as serve the spiritual ends of numbers of citizens.

I trust I have made the case that too much interpretation of the First Amendment construes the founding period selectively so as to respond to a modern casting of issues. Instead, can we return to that founding period and understand it in a fuller and more adequate way than is permitted through the separationist and accommodationist viewpoints? Certainly we should make that attempt, only recognizing that selectivity inevitably affects interpretation. This chapter's title, "Religion, Government, and Power," suggests a starting point for such a reconstruction.

The central issue in seeking to understand church and state in the new nation is recognizing that one—and only one—basic objective was held in common by the founding fathers, determining their work in and after the Constitutional Convention. Put bluntly, theirs was an acknowledged conspiracy to frame a government that was adequate to make the infant nation of recently liberated states viable. To that end, the new government had to have sufficient power to give the authority of the nation credibility against the states that constituted it— and which claimed (implicitly, if not explicitly) to represent sovereign jurisdictions. Meeting in camera, delegates from the states framed a scheme of government that, while it would have to be ratified by those states, would then claim to have its own direct relationship to the citizens, who would owe allegiance to both. As the delegates in Philadelphia made their drafts, they found that compromise was the one strategy that worked. In sum, the Constitution represented something of a balancing act or, in a less flattering light, a shell game. The balancing act included calculation of what would work outside and beyond the convention as well as within it. Supporters of the new federal government, despite their differences (like Hamilton and Madison, for example), argued their cases energetically against those who opposed the new polity, the Antifederalists. For everything finally reduced to an essentially political issue: could a viable federal regime be first proposed, then ratified, and finally organized?

Unless we understand that highly political frame of reference, which reduced all other considerations to insignificance, and recognize how deeply and to the exclusion of various other objectives the founders believed in the necessity of a more adequate government for the states as united, I do not think we can understand how the question of religion and regime appeared to them. For the delegates to the convention proper, this question of how to treat religion was not only a diversion from the central issue, it was also among the most divisive issues, if not potentially *the* most divisive issue, facing them. In many of the states represented at the convention, there were traditions of preferential support for one or another religious denomination. The settled churches of Massachusetts, Connecticut, and New Hampshire were an actual form of establishment in those states. Rather mixed patterns of preference for one or several religious bodies characterized some of the other states. Virginia, after a decade of avoiding the issue, had just disestablished the Church of England.[9]

Of greater relevance, however, were the religious tests for office, which were more widespread than the provisions requiring public support of church congregations. The formulations of these tests varied markedly, as did their observance. But the proposed federal government could not include religious tests for office if it were to survive after the convention or succeed in the subsequent ratification process, even though these tests were standard constitutional provisions in the constituent states. At root, while the founding fathers were not antireligious individually or collectively, their overriding and commonly held objective of achieving an adequate federal government would only be frustrated if the issue of religion's relationship to regime were allowed to introduce a dimension of continuing divisiveness into their work.

The outcome is well known to us. The Constitution proper as it emerged from the convention did include a provision regarding religion, but one whose significance is often entirely overlooked—Article VI, section 3: "No religious Test shall ever be required as a Qualification to any Office or public Trust under the United States." This seems to have been taken from Charles Pinkney's early draft proposal and appears to have occasioned no dissent or even significant discussion in the convention. But it did set the federal government on a different course from that of most of the state governments. (Of course, one reason this section is overlooked is because the modern Supreme Court has used the First Amendment establishment clause to rule religious tests for office unconstitutional at other levels of government.)

Occasionally, a counterfactual hypothesis will test the significance of an interpretation. Imagine, if you will, that the convention had proposed a generic religious test for office, or even taken a position in support of a favored church or churches at local option. As we reconstruct the possible alignments of religion and regime in the founding period under this hypothesis, only one conclusion is possible: no version of a proposal to favor one denomination could have contributed to the design and ratification of an adequate federal regime; and had such a scheme been proposed, it would have assured rejection of the document. Similarly, had a religious test for office been put forward, defeat of this desperately sought viable government would have been guaranteed.

I have as yet said nothing of liberty of conscience or religious freedom as a factor.[10] That is deliberate. The point is not that this construct was undervalued or lacked respect—though attitudes and practices varied from state to state. Rather, at the level of accommodation in the states between freedom for the practice of religion or liberty for conscience, effective toleration existed in relationship to widely varying patterns of support for denominations and religious test oaths. In sum, a proposed federal guarantee of religious liberty in opposition to state practices could not have mobilized support for ratification of this new federal venture, for that would have been to expand national authority and power decisively. Once again, the issue of religion had the vast potential to be positively divisive where support for the Constitution was concerned. Accordingly, for this tactical reason alone, it was excluded from the proposed mandate of the new government. To hypothesize again, I am confident that had the religious test oath—or support for one denomination or a particular set of them—been a potentially positive ground for enlisting support for this new government, then so desperate was the need as perceived by the founders that the convention would have proposed such an oath and/or an appropriate pattern of public support for religion.

As it was being reviewed prior to ratification, numerous shortcomings were "discovered" in the proposed Constitution. As I have noted, the Antifederalist opposition, which was scarcely intellectually coherent, centered on the degree of centralization of power the document would legitimate. In response, its proponents acceded to the notion of a series of amendments that would make explicit additional limitations on the power of the federal government. Ratification finally occurred with the presumption, at least in some states, that such amendments would follow, and in the First Congress James Madison took the lead in proposing them. Some further reference to religion had seemed called for beyond that in Article VI. Thus, the First Amendment religion clauses were designed to place explicit limitations upon Congress, assuring those skeptical of federal power that the existing state practices regarding religion—which varied widely—would be protected from federal intervention.

Modern interest in the religion clauses of the First Amendment has resulted in a great deal of scrutiny of both their legislative history and the process of ratification that followed. In capsule form, the story goes like this. Madison's initial proposal was comparatively expansive, doubtless reflecting his own convictions: "The civil rights of none shall be abridged on account of religious belief or worship, nor shall any national religion be established, nor shall the full and equal rights of conscience be in any manner, or on any pretext, infringed."[11] Having revised it several times, and reduced it markedly in scope, the House finally forwarded to the Senate the following language: "Congress shall make no law establishing religion, or to prevent the free exercise thereof, or to infringe the rights of conscience."[12] In turn, the Senate proposed a different, but also reduced, version: "Congress shall make no law establishing articles of faith or a mode of worship, or prohibiting the free exercise of religion."[13]

The reduced language we know was finally worked out in the Committee of Conference between the houses: "Congress shall make no law respecting an establishment of religion, or prohibiting the free exercise thereof."[14] It then went through the process of ratification with numerous other provisions, only by accident of that process becoming part of the First Amendment. We have already noted that the clauses remained virtually unapplied and uninterpreted until the middle decades of the twentieth century, aside from their interpretation in the context of the federal prosecution of polygamy in the Territory of Utah in the late nineteenth century.[15]

Where does this leave us? I suggest that interpretation of the genesis of the religion clauses of the Constitution, including Article VI, section 3, and the two provisions in the Bill of Rights, must start from recognition of the major objective of which they were a secondary expression. This was the overriding preoccupation of the founders with designing and achieving an adequate national government. Their meaning derived from that context. They possessed no independent significance to which, in recent times, both separationist and accommodationist objectives might be related. At root, the outcome the founding generation intended, and sought, was neither pro- nor antireligion in the abstract. The founding fathers' overriding concern was to neutralize religion as a factor that might jeopardize the achievement of a federal government. Here, Jefferson is less helpful than Madison, who suggested strategic or theoretical grounds, beyond the practical ones, for making the government of the United States independent of churches. He recognized that religion provided one basis for a factionalism that could destroy a regime. He did not seek to eliminate the causes of faction (religion being one), because in his view the polity stood the best chance of survival if factions (including those based on religion) counterbalanced each other.[16] We may also view the churches' separation from government as in certain formal respects similar to the deliberate separation of the executive, legislative, and judicial branches of government so as to use to advantage the checks and balances thus constructed among different centers of power. Religion, as one locus of power in the new United States, was to be respected as such and allowed an appropriate role; it was one among many social institutions and cultural activities out of which the new nation would be formed.

In proposing an adequate national government with a reasonable chance of being ratified, the founding fathers did not mention many issues that we might wish they had: provision for education, the status of the family, political parties.

The list is long and the silences of the founders witness to their overriding objective of achieving a limited national government. In consequence, it has fallen to subsequent generations to work out with respect to such issues how the principles that underlie the American polity would in fact apply. And although the Constitution was not in the end silent with regard to religion, I suggest we must approach religion in the same light. To interpret, and finally apply, the religion clauses, we must look for the strategic or theoretical considerations that led to the denial, from the first, of the federal government's competence in the area. What the founding fathers proposed in their minimalist attention to religion was not its wholesale segregation from government—the kind of resolution proposed in the French Revolution—for separationist logic opens the way for radical secularization as a social policy. Nor did they propose that the federal regime should take over (and thus make use of) churches—for an Erastianism of substance (if not form) is the outcome of accommodationist logic. Rather, they proposed that religious institutions should lie beyond the authority or competence of government. Religious activities were a part of the social and cultural life of the new nation which the distinctly limited federal government had no mandate to supervise or to depend upon. Such was appropriate for a religiously plural social order in which religion, left free of regulation, could easily be capable of destructive, as well as highly constructive, roles.[17]

In my own view, this was also a significant step in the resolution of a long-standing issue in Western cultures. This step was not so much a wholly new scheme, an abstract separation of religion and polity, as it was a new status for religions, primarily Christianity—and by implication Judaism as well—that had not been possible for the millennium and a half since the Constantinian revolution had made Christianity the favored religion of empire and religious uniformity under its sponsorship had been mobilized to guarantee social unity.

The framework I would suggest for understanding the genesis not only of the First Amendment religion clauses but also of the religious test clause of the Constitution is that of the broadly political matrix within which the overriding objective was to secure a more adequate federal government for the new nation. This government would necessarily compromise the sovereignty of the constituent states by drawing legitimacy from both them and their constituent citizens. This was a balancing act, requiring that limits be set to those powers the federal regime might exercise. To those skeptical of this polity because it might unduly infringe on the existing state governments, limitations were promised. And among the more prominent was forgoing the authority to require religion to support regime (as in religious test oaths) or to meddle either with existing preferential relationships between the states and particular religious bodies, or with liberty of conscience as it had come to be respected in the various sovereign states. But this balancing act certainly did not exclude government acquiescence in religious ministrations to the members of Congress, or to those in the military, nor did it rule out recognizing that the people as a collectivity—and as one source of federal authority—potentially stood in a relation to higher powers, for example, in exercises of fasting or thanksgiving.[18]

Interpreting the resolution of the church-state question in these contingent terms, seeing it as a product of the political necessities of the new nation rather than as a deduction from philosophical and theological doctrines, however formulated, makes it more comprehensible than accepting either the modern separationist or accommodationist paradigms. On one hand, the separationist paradigm finds it difficult to interpret the ease with which practices like appointing congressional chaplains were adopted, or monies appropriated to make good on relations with the Indian tribes through the agencies of religious communities. Nor does it easily comprehend the recognition accorded to religion and morality in the new territories. On the other hand, the accommodationist paradigm does not readily make sense either of the variety of religious interests in the new nation or the strategic or theoretical grounds for making religion and government, both concerned with power, independent of each other. The denominations themselves had only just begun to organize and in any case had little centralized authority. And the young republic offered fertile ground for numerous new religious movements—to use our modern conception—that immediately took advantage of it and flourished in the next half-century. In sum, the accommodationist version of early American religious culture is too Whiggish, reading more cultural coherence and more thoroughly developed religious institutions back into the late eighteenth and early nineteenth centuries than is warranted.

But the other side of this more contingent reading of the place of religion in the new nation and in the Constitution poses haunting questions. How durable were the formulations embodied in the Constitution? How does the Constitution so read with respect to its religion clauses address our era? More than two hundred years after the founding, a reading of the First Amendment origins such as we have given may be more acceptable history, but does it have any payoff in terms of understanding our contemporary United States or, for that matter, making possible constructive approaches to current issues that will be litigated under the Constitution?

To answer these questions, we must first recognize that the United States has developed in remarkable ways over its history. Without attempting to, or wanting to seem to, preempt the discussion in subsequent chapters, let me simply indicate a few factors that make the context in which church-state issues are faced today rather markedly different from the context of 1789.

First, the authority and power of the federal government now decisively outweigh those of the states. Here the chief circumstance has been the conduct of war, whether international or civil, imperial or cold. It is beyond doubt that the power to conduct war claimed by the new national government—and all that claim entailed—has been basic to this shift in relationships between center and parts. Ours is now a continental society in a way that distances us from the founding era. This factor decisively affects reflection on our questions.

Second, the development of a continental, and now international, economy has had a great influence. Related both positively and negatively to the conduct of war, our dynamic economy has created a national culture which since the mid-twentieth century has reduced significant regional differences to tourist attractions. Ours is now in important respects a common culture. This factor also intersects with our questions.

Third, in spite of this commonality, we also have a variety of new cultural traditions entering the society and constituting vigorous, and not so vigorous, subcultures in tension with the common culture. Ours is a religiously plural nation beyond the powers of the founders' imagination to conceive.

Fourth, religious institutions have progressively expanded their influence beyond the local level so that there has been a pronounced, if changing, religious complexion to the nation. Early in the nineteenth century, a broad hegemony developed, first generally Protestant, then more inclusively Christian, followed by a "Judeo-Christian" axis in the mid-twentieth century. In sum, at least until recently, there has been at least the shadow of a common religion in American society. This factor, too, is not a neutral consideration in relation to our questions.

Fifth, religious innovations (both within the hegemonic tradition and as counterbalances to it) have developed in remarkable ways. In important respects, social deviance, frequently identified in ethnoreligious terms, has represented the rubric under which cultural pluralism has flourished. This factor also intersects with our questions.

By way of parenthesis, neither of the two prevailing paradigms—separationist or accommodationist—seems adequate to do justice to these basic features of our national development. The separationist ideal does not come to terms with the pervasive cultural aspects of religion, especially in relation to this powerful expansion of American society. Nor does the accommodationist paradigm enable us to comprehend either the pluralism of religion in today's culture or the divisive implications of links between government and particular religions. Thus, not only do both paradigms prove inadequate as a basis for interpreting the origin of the United States with respect to religion and regime, but they are also severely flawed as explanations of the place of religion in the contemporary national experience. Does our historical reading offer a better approach to understanding the relationship of religion and government in an America that has developed in this fashion?

By recognizing that religion concerns power as much as government does, and by understanding that making the two of them independent was a tactical but also a strategic commitment, we are positioned to see that the founding fathers' insistence on the independence of religion from the national government was tied to the theoretical foundations of our republic. Ironically, therefore, the thrust of this interpretation is to propose that Article VI, section 3—the neglected clause of the Constitution—provides a better insight into the world of the framers and their intent with respect to religion than do the contested clauses that became the First Amendment of the Bill of Rights. Article VI, section 3, meant that the new national government was accepting a limitation on its own sources of power and authority: religion should not be a category used in the conduct of government. In the eighteenth century, of course, this left the states free to do so. But for the federal side, such a limitation on the central government was a part of the complex of notions—including the division of powers, the strategy of checks and balances, belief in an informed citizenry, the reality of reserved powers, etc.—that provided the theoretical foundation for the new nation. In short, the issue of church and state was securely located within the framework of limited government, thus eliminating for the United States the synergistic relationship between religion and regime typical of other sovereign states and nations.

In this perspective, the role of the two clauses of the First Amendment was to reassure the states and their citizens that the implicit limitations upon the federal government would most explicitly leave each free of interference by the other. By virtue of their incorporation, those clauses now represent guarantees to the citizens against other levels of government—states and municipalities among them.[19] But the theory remains roughly the same though extended down to these other levels. Government shall be conducted without respect to religion. This does not mean society is necessarily rendered free of religious hegemony but that, should such exist, government policies must not be determined on that basis. The other side of this coin, however, is that policies may be determined on bases that accord with such a hegemony. Thus, the religion clauses together form a most explicit constitutional basis, dating from the founding era, for support of at least one class of cultural activities independent of regime. We must think of them as among the best guarantees, along with the rest of the First Amendment, of cultural pluralism.

Ironically, when approached at this level, the insights behind the separationist and accommodationist readings of our history begin to come together. Each grasps a truth that is only part of a more adequate understanding of the American experiment. Put succinctly, separationist logic pertains to linkages between religious institutions and governments, accommodationist logic to the cultural reality of religion. In our political culture, these join as complementary in the context of the undergirding federal theory of limited government. Neither has an independent grounding, however, apart from the contingent achievement of the founding generation, which must be rediscovered, renewed, and reapplied by each successive generation, even our own.

NOTES

1. *Everson v. Board of Education of the Township of Ewing*, 330 U.S. 1 (1947).
2. *Everson* is excerpted in John T. Noonan, Jr., *The Believer and the Powers That Are* (New York: Macmillan, 1987), 370–74, quote 373.
3. Quoted in John F. Wilson and Donald L. Drakeman, eds., *Church and State in American History*, 2nd ed. (Boston: Beacon, 1987), 203.
4. *Reynolds v. United States*, 98 U.S. 145 (1879), makes reference to the metaphor; see Noonan, *Believer*, 197. See also Thomas Jefferson's letter to the Danbury Baptists in Wilson and Drakeman, *Church and State*, 78–79.
5. A good discussion of the events in Virginia is in Thomas J. Curry, *The First Freedoms: Church and State in America to the Passage of the First Amendment* (New York: Oxford University Press, 1986), ch. 6, "Religion and Government in Revolutionary America," part 1, "The Southern States," 134–48.
6. For a general treatment of Madison, see Robert A. Rutland, *James Madison, the Founding Father* (New York: Macmillan, 1987). Chapters 2 and 3, pp. 23–71, delineate his roles in making and implementing, including amending, the Constitution.
7. Justice Rehnquist developed this position in his dissent in *Wallace v. Jaffree*, 105 S. Ct. 2479 (1985). See relevant excerpts in Wilson and Drakeman, *Church and State*, 243–45, quote 245.
8. That this is closer to the original effect of the clauses than the implication of the wall metaphor is clear. What it does not do, however, is to locate the proscription of federal action about religion in its setting of a theory of limited government and, in particular, in relation to strategies for limiting the power of that federal government.
9. The most useful summary overview is Curry, *First Freedoms*, 105–33, in which he emphasizes the variety in understandings of the term.
10. Curry's discussion also summarizes this set of issues in the colonies-become-states; see ibid., 75, 78–104.
11. Wilson and Drakeman, *Church and State*, 75.

12. Ibid., 77.

13. Ibid., 77–78.

14. Ibid., 78.

15. See *Reynolds v. United States*, available (in part) in Noonan, *Believer*, particularly his chapter on Mormon marriage practices as occasioning litigation, 194–207.

16. See Madison in the *Federalist*, No. 10.

17. In a larger sense, this chapter has been written in the context of the discussion of the founding period so brilliantly delineated by Gordon S. Wood in "The Fundamentals and the Constitutions," *New York Review of Books* 25 (18 Feb. 1988): 33–40. While taking seriously the return to texts (in this case of the Constitution) so assiduously cultivated by the disciples of Leo Strauss, Wood argues that the context must govern their interpretation. By implication, their application to another context properly entails understanding both contexts.

18. I have addressed some of these issues in my *Public Religion in American Culture* (Philadelphia: Temple University Press, 1979). See especially the discussion of Thanksgiving on pp. 56–63. See also ch. 4, "Ritualistic Behavior of American Public Life," pp. 67–93.

19. Indeed, *Torcaso v. Watkins*, 367 U.S. 488 (1961), which concerned religious oath taking on the part of local officials, subsumed this issue under the establishment clause as interpreted in *Everson*, thus voiding the question of whether Article VI, section 3, applies to other than federal officeholders.

The Democratization
of Christianity and the Character
# of American Politics

Nathan O. Hatch

 $\mathscr{T}$ HIS CHAPTER WILL argue that at the very inception of the American republic the most dynamic popular movements were expressly religious. However powerful working-class organizations became in cities such as New York and Baltimore, their presence cannot compare with the phenomenal growth, and collective élan, of Methodists, Baptists, Christians, Millerites, and Mormons. It was lay preachers in the early republic who became the most effective agents in constructing new frames of reference for people living through a profoundly transitional age. Religious leaders from the rank and file were phenomenally successful in reaching out to marginal people, in promoting self-education and sheltering participants from the indoctrination of elite orthodoxies, in binding people together in supportive community, and in identifying the aspirations of common people with the will of God.

The vitality of these religious ideologies and mass movements has had a considerable long-term effect upon the character and limits of American politics. Churches, after all, came to serve as competing universes of discourse and action. And the political implications of mass movements that were democratic and religious at the same time are far more profound than merely predisposing members to vote Federalist or Republican, Democrat or Whig. As mass popular movements, churches came to be places in which fundamental political assumptions were forged: ideas about the meaning of America; the priority of the individual conscience; the values of localism, direct democracy, and individualism; and the necessity of dynamic communication, predicated on the identification of speaker or author with an audience.

This chapter will suggest that to understand the democratization of American society, one must look at what happened to Protestant Christianity in the years 1780–1830. In an age when people expected almost everything from religion (and churches) and almost nothing from politics (and the state), the popular churches are essential to comprehending the enduring shape of American democracy. The first half of the chapter will explore the character of these mass religious movements. I will then consider three dimensions of these movements which have long-term implications for American politics: the importance of churches as basic classrooms for molding perceptions about the meaning of America; the competing impulses of democratic dissent and desire for respectability within these movements; and the role of populist forms of Christianity in the forming of a liberal society that is individualistic, competitive, and market driven.

I

The American Revolution is the single most crucial event in American history. The generation overshadowed by it and its counterpart in France stands at the fault line that separates an older world, premised on standards of deference, patronage, and ordered succession, from a newer one to which we are attuned since it continues to shape our values. The American Revolution and the beliefs flowing from it created a cultural ferment over the meaning of freedom, a debate that brought to the fore crucial issues of authority, organization, and leadership.[1]

Above all, the Revolution dramatically expanded the circle of people who considered themselves capable of thinking for themselves about issues of freedom, equality, sovereignty, and representation; and it eroded traditional appeals to the authority of tradition, station, and education. Ordinary people moved toward these new horizons as they gained access to a powerful new vocabulary, a rhetoric of liberty that would not have occurred to people were it not for the Revolution. In time, the well-being of ordinary people edged closer to the center of what it means to be American, public opinion came to assume normative significance, and leaders could not survive who would not, to use Patrick Henry's phrase, "bow with utmost deference to the majesty of the people." The correct solution to any important problem, political, legal, or religious, would have to appear as the people's choice.[2]

The profoundly transitional age between 1776 and 1830 left the same kind of indelible imprint upon the structures of American Christianity as it did upon those of American political life. Only land, Robert Wiebe has noted, could compete with Christianity as the pulse of a new democratic society.[3] The age of the democratic revolutions unfolded with awesome moment for people in every social rank. Amid such acute uncertainty, many humble Christians in America began to redeem a dual legacy. They yoked together strenuous demands for revivals, in the name of Whitefield, and calls for the expansion of popular sovereignty, in the name of the Revolution. It is the linking of these equally potent traditions that sent American Christianity cascading in so many creative directions in the early republic. Church authorities had few resources to restrain these movements fed by the passions of ordinary people. American Methodism, for example, under the tutelage of Francis Asbury, veered sharply from the course of British Methodism from the time of Wesley's death until the end of the Napoleonic Wars. The heavy, centralizing hand of Jabez Bunting kept England's potent evangelical tradition firmly grounded in traditional notions of authority and leadership. After 1800, the leaders of British Methodism were able to bar the eccentric American revivalist Lorenzo Dow from contaminating their meetings. In America, however, Dow took the camp meeting circuit by storm despite periodic censure from bishops and presiding elders. Given his effectiveness and popular support, they were unable to mount a direct challenge to his authority.

A diverse array of evangelical firebrands went about the task of movement building in the generation after the Revolution. While they were intent on bringing evangelical conversion to the mass of ordinary Americans, rarely could they divorce that message from contagious new vocabularies and impulses that swept through American popular cultures in an era of democratic revolution: an appeal to class as the fundamental problem of society, a refusal to recognize the cultural authority of elites, a disdain for the supposed lessons of history and tradition, a call for reform using the rhetoric of the Revolution, a commitment to turn the press into a sword of democracy, and an ardent faith in the future of the American republic.

At the same time, Americans who espoused evangelical and egalitarian convictions, in whatever combination, were left free to experiment with abandon, unopposed by civil or religious authority. Within a few years of Thomas Jefferson's election in 1800, it became anachronistic to speak of dissent in America— as if there were still a commonly recognized center against which new or emerging groups had to define themselves. There was little to restrain a variety of new groups from vying to establish their identity as a counterestablishment. The fundamental history of this period, in fact, may be a story of things left out, as Rowland Berthoff has suggested.[4] Churches and religious movements after 1800 operated in a climate in which ecclesiastical establishments had withered, in which the federal government had almost no internal functions—a "midget institution in a giant land"[5]—and in which a rampant migration of people continued to snap old networks of personal authority. American churches did not face the kind of external social and political pressures which in Great Britain often forced Christianity and liberty to march in opposite directions. Such isolation made it possible for religious "outsiders" to see their own destiny as part and parcel of the meaning of America itself. If the earth did belong to the living, as President Jefferson claimed, why should the successful newcomer defer to the claims of education, status, and longevity?[6]

The reality of a nonrestrictive environment permitted an unexpected and often explosive conjunction of evangelical fervor and popular sovereignty. It was this engine that greatly accelerated the process of Christianization in American popular culture, allowing indigenous expressions of faith to take hold among ordinary people, both white and black. This expansion of evangelical Christianity did not proceed primarily from the nimble response of religious elites meeting the challenge before them. Rather, Christianity was effectively reshaped by ordinary people who molded it in their own image and threw themselves into expanding its influence. Increasingly assertive common people wanted their leaders unpretentious, their doctrines self-evident and down-to-earth, their music lively and sing-able, their churches in local hands. It was this upsurge of democratic hope that characterized so many religious cultures in the early republic and brought Baptists, Methodists, Disciples, and a host of other insurgent groups to the fore. The rise of evangelical Christianity in the early republic is, in some measure, a story of the success of common people in shaping the culture after their own priorities rather than the priorities outlined by gentlemen, such as the founding fathers.[7] A style of religious leadership that the public had deemed "untutored" and "irregular" as late as the First Great Awakening became overwhelmingly successful, even normative, in the first decades of the new nation.

It is easy to miss the profoundly democratic character of the early republic's insurgent religious movements. The Methodists, after all, retained power in a structured hierarchy under the control of bishops; the Mormons reverted to rule by a single religious prophet and revelator; and groups such as the Disciples of Christ, despite professed democratic structures, came to be controlled by powerful individuals such as Alexander Campbell, who had little patience with dissent. As ecclesiastical structures, these movements often turned out to be less democratic than the congregational structure of the New England Standing Order.

The democratization of Christianity, then, has less to do with the specifics of polity and governance and more with the very incarnation of the church into popular culture. In at least three respects the popular religious movements of the early republic articulated a profoundly democratic spirit. First, they denied the age-old distinction that set the clergy apart as a separate order of men, and they refused to defer to learned theologians and received orthodoxies. All were democratic or populist in the way they instinctively associated virtue with ordinary people rather than with elites,[8] exalted the vernacular in word and song as the hallowed channel for communicating with and about God, and freely turned over the reins of power. These groups also shared with the Jeffersonian Republicans an overt rejection of the past as a repository of wisdom.[9] By redefining leadership itself, these movements were instrumental in shattering the centuries-old affinity between Christianity and the norms of high culture. They reconstructed the foundations of religion fully in keeping with the values and priorities of ordinary people.

Second, these movements empowered ordinary people by taking their deepest spiritual impulses at face value rather than subjecting them to the scrutiny of orthodox doctrine and the frowns of respectable clergymen. In the last two decades of the century, preachers from a wide range of new religious movements openly fanned the flames of religious ecstasy. Rejecting in 1775 the Yankee Calvinism of his youth, Henry Alline found that his soul was transported with divine love, "ravished with a divine ecstasy beyond any doubts or fears, or thoughts of being then deceived."[10] What had been defined as "enthusiasm" increasingly became advocated from the pulpit as an essential part of Christianity. Such a shift in emphasis, accompanied by rousing gospel singing rather than formal church music, reflected the success of common people in defining for themselves the nature of faith. In addition, an unprecedented wave of religious leaders in the last quarter of the century expressed their own openness to a variety of signs and wonders—in short, an admission of increased supernatural involvement in everyday life. Scores of preachers' journals, from Methodists and Baptists, from North and South, from white and black, indicated a ready acceptance to interpret dreams and visions as inspired by God, normal manifestations of divine guidance and instruction. "I know the word of God is our infallible guide, and by it we are to try all our dreams and feelings," conceded the Methodist stalwart Freeborn Garrettson. But, he added, "I also know, that both sleeping and waking, things of a divine nature have been revealed to me." Those volatile aspects of popular religion, long held in check by the church, came to be recognized and encouraged from the pulpit. It is no wonder that a dismayed writer in the *Connecticut Evangelical Magazine* countered in 1805: "No person is warranted from the word of God to publish to the world the discoveries of heaven or hell which he supposes he has had in a dream, or trance, or vision."[11]

The early republic was also a democratic moment in a third sense. Religious outsiders were flushed with confidence about their prospects and had little sense of their own limitations. They dreamed that a new age of religious and social harmony would spring up naturally out of their own efforts to overthrow coercive and authoritarian structures.[12] This upsurge of democratic hope, this passion for equality, led to a welter of diverse and competing forms, many of them structured in highly undemocratic ways. The Methodists under Francis Asbury, for instance, used authoritarian means to build a church that would not be a respecter of persons. This church faced the curious paradox of gaining phenomenal influence among laypersons with whom it would not share ecclesiastical authority. Similarly, the Mormons used a virtual religious dictatorship as the means to return power to illiterate men. Yet, despite these authoritarian structures, the fundamental impetus of these movements was to make Christianity a liberating force, giving people the right to think and act for themselves rather than being forced to rely upon the mediations of an educated elite. The most fascinating religious story of the early republic is the signal achievements of these and other populist religious leaders, outsiders who brought to bear the full force of democratic persuasions upon American culture.

The wave of popular religious movements that broke upon the United States in the half-century after independence did more to Christianize American society than anything before or since. Nothing makes that point clearer than the growth of Methodists and Baptists as mass movements among white and black Americans. Starting from scratch just prior to the Revolution, the Methodists in America grew at a rate that terrified other denominations, reaching a quarter of a million members by 1820 and doubling again by 1830. Baptist membership multiplied tenfold in the three decades after the Revolution, the number of churches increasing from 500 to over 2,500. The black church in America was born amid the crusading vigor of these movements and quickly assumed its own distinct character and broad appeal among people of color. By the middle of the nineteenth century, Methodist and Baptist churches had splintered into more different denominational forms than one cares to remember. Yet together these movements came to constitute nearly 70 percent of Protestant church members in the United States and two-thirds of its ministers.[13]

This chapter grows out of research on five distinct traditions or mass movements that came to the fore early in the nineteenth century: the Christian movement, the Methodists, the Baptists, the black churches, and the Mormons. Each was led by young men of relentless energy who went about movement building as self-conscious outsiders. They shared an ethic of unrelenting labor, a passion for expansion, a hostility to orthodox belief and style, a zeal for religious reconstruction, and a systematic plan to labor on behalf of their ideals. However diverse their theologies and church organizations, they were able to offer common people, especially the poor, compelling visions of individual self-respect and collective self-confidence.

II

In his highly suggestive book *The Revolution of the Saints*, Michael Walzer explores the character of the Puritan "saint," the stalwart figure of burning zeal who ignored age-old customs and traditional loyalties to reconstruct the social order of seventeenth-century England. Walzer suggests that the saint's personality itself was his most radical innovation. Hardened and disciplined by a compelling ideology, the saint could offer his own vision and pattern of life as an alternative to traditional social forms. What made the cadre of Puritan saints so formidable, and in Walzer's view so similar to the modern revolutionary, was their extraordinary capacity to mobilize people for a cause and to build organizations sustained by ideological bonds rather than ties of residence, family, and patronage.[14]

This chapter suggests that the social and intellectual ferment of the early republic gave rise to a generation of populist "saints." Their alienation from the established order matched their aptitude for mobilizing people. This set them apart from the generation of George Whitefield and Gilbert Tennent in the mid-eighteenth century, who labored to revive lukewarm establishments but left the creation of new institutional forms to the will of providence and the discretion of those who pursued a New Light call. In the main, the creation of new congregations was an unintended and episodic consequence of the preaching of the earlier Great Awakening.

Dissent in America after the Revolution was characterized by a shift from seeking conversions to movement building from the ground up. A battery of young leaders without elite pedigrees constructed fresh religious ideologies around which new religious movements coalesced. W. R. Ward has noted that Francis Asbury was an entrepreneur in religion, a man who perceived a market to be exploited. The itinerant-based machine which he set in motion was less a church in any traditional sense than a "military mission of short term agents."[15] Similarly, the founder of the Churches of Christ, Barton W. Stone, eschewed normal pastoral duties and dedicated himself utterly to the pursuit of "causes" in religion. Elias

Smith went so far as to define religious liberty as the right to build a movement by itinerating without constraint.[16] All of these leaders eventually defined success not by the sheer number of converts but by the number of those who identified themselves with their fledgling movements. This quest for organization lay at the heart of Methodism's success. One unfriendly critic observed that the movement produced such great results "because it took hold of the doctrines which lay in the minds of all men here, and wrought them with the steam, levers, and pulleys of a new engine."[17]

Above all, these upstarts were radically innovative in reaching and organizing people. Passionate about ferreting out converts in every hamlet and crossroads, they sought to bind them together in local and regional communities. They continued to refashion the sermon as a profoundly popular medium, inviting even the most unlearned and inexperienced to respond to a call to preach. These initiates were charged to proclaim the gospel anywhere and every day of the week—even to the limit of their physical endurance. The resulting creation, the colloquial sermon, employed daring pulpit storytelling, no-holds-barred appeals, overt humor, strident attack, graphic application, and intimate personal experience. These young builders of religious movements also became the most effective purveyors of mass literature in the early republic, confronting people in every section of the new nation with the combined force of the written and spoken word. In addition, this generation launched bold experiments with new forms of religious music, new techniques of protracted meetings, and new Christian ideologies that denied the mediations of religious elites and promised to exalt those of low estate.[18]

The result of these intensive efforts was nothing less than the creation of mass movements that were deeply religious and genuinely democratic at the same time. Lawrence Goodwyn has suggested that the building of significant mass democratic movements involves a sequential process of recruitment, education, and involvement that allows a "movement culture" to develop. This new plateau of social possibility, based on self-confident leadership and widespread methods of internal communication, permits people to conceive of acting in self-generated democratic ways, to develop new ways of looking at things less clouded by inherited assumptions, and to defend themselves in the face of adverse interpretations from the orthodox culture. Like the later Populist movement about which Goodwyn writes, insurgent religious movements such as the Methodists, a variety of Baptists, the Christians and Disciples, the Millerites, and the Mormons dared to aspire grandly, to surmount rigid cultural inheritances, to work together in order to be free individually. If nothing else, these movements were collective expressions of self-respect, instilling hope, purpose, meaning, and identity in thousands upon thousands of persons whom the dominant culture had defined as marginal.[19]

All of these movements challenged common people to take religious destiny into their own hands, to think for themselves, to oppose centralized authority and the elevation of the clergy as a separate order of men. These religious communities could embrace the forlorn and the uprooted far more intensely than any political movement and offer them powerful bonds of acceptance and hope. As one new Methodist convert recalled, "I now found myself associated with those who loved each other with a pure heart fervently, instead of being surrounded by those with whom friendship was a cold commerce of interest."[20] These new movements could also impart to ordinary people, particularly those battered by poverty or infirmity, what Martin Luther King, Jr., called "a sense of somebodiness"—the kind of consolation that another Methodist found so appealing in worship held in the crude environment of a log cabin: "an abiding confidence that he was a subject of that powerful kingdom whose Prince cared for his subjects."[21] These movements also allowed common people to trust their own powerful religious impulses. They were encouraged to express their faith with fervent emotion and bold testimony. In the most democratic gesture of all, some preachers even began to take their cues for evidence of divine power from expressions in the audience. During a camp meeting on an island in the Chesapeake Bay, Lorenzo Dow was interrupted by a woman who began clapping her hands with delight and shouting "Glory! Glory!" In a response that was the opposite of condescension, Dow proclaimed to the audience: "The Lord is here! *He is with that sister.*"[22]

In passing, it is instructive to suggest at least four reasons that historians have failed to explore the dynamics of popular religion in this era. First, in the mid-twentieth century, the quickened interest in religion as a cultural force emerged within a broader historiographical tendency to downplay the social impact of the Revolution. Second, historians have interpreted the Second Great Awakening as an attempt by traditional religious elites to impose social order upon a disordered and secularized society—revivalism as an attempt to salvage Protestant solidarity. A third reason is that church historians from the more popular denominations have had reasons to sanitize their own histories. Modern church historians have chosen to focus on those dimensions of their own heritage that point to cultural enrichment, institutional cohesion, and intellectual respectability. William Warren Sweet, for instance, was committed to a vision of Methodists and Baptists as bearers of civilization to the uncouth and unrestrained society of the frontier. Churches were instruments of order, education, and moral discipline.[23]

A fourth reason that popular religious movements remain unexplored is surprising given the deep commitment by a new generation of social historians to understand the lives of common people in the age of capitalist transformation.

While considerable attention has been focused on the changing nature of markets, on the decline of independent artisans and farmers and the rise of the American working class, surprisingly little energy has gone into exploring the dynamics of insurgent religious movements.[24] This neglect stems both from the neo-Marxist preoccupation with the formation of social classes and the assumption that religion is generally a conservative force and a pernicious one.[25] What these studies fail to take into account is that, for better or worse, the most dynamic popular movements in the early republic were expressly religious.

III

The dissident movements of the early republic championed nothing more than the separation of church and state. Yet they were given to embrace the American republic with as much enthusiasm as had any of the orthodox traditions that still yearned for a Christian nation. These dissidents endowed the republic with the same divine authority as did defenders of the Standing Order such as Timothy Dwight and Noah Webster, but for opposite reasons. The republic became a new city on a hill not because it kept faith with Puritan tradition, but because it sounded the death knell for corporate and hierarchic conceptions of the social order. In sum, a government so enlightened as to tell the churches to go their own way must have also had prophetic power to tell them which way to go.[26]

This is certainly not to suggest that political idioms uniformly colored the thinking of popular preachers in the early republic or that their message was not profoundly religious in purpose and scope. The early Methodist preachers, for instance, were preeminently soul savers and revivalists and saw political involvement as a distraction at best.[27] Their transatlantic connections, furthermore, kept before them the movement of providence abroad as well as at home. Yet even Francis Asbury was given to affectionate reflections on the religious privileges offered in his adopted land. Repeatedly, he made a sharp contrast between the state of Methodism in America and in Great Britain, noting the success of the daughter in outstripping the parent. A Methodist preacher without the slightest interest in politics or in the millennium still had to take note of the phenomenal growth on these shores of a movement that began as "the offscouring of all things."

Even the Mormons, who seemed to have rejected American values and who seemed to impose biblical models upon politics rather than vice versa, developed an eschatology that was explicitly American. Joseph Smith made the garden of Eden a New World paradise, with America becoming the cradle of civilization. In due time, the Book of Mormon recounts, God prevailed upon Columbus "to venture across the sea to the Promised Land, to open it for a new race of free men."[28] A variety of Mormon authors suggest that it was the free institutions of America that prepared the way for the new prophet, Joseph Smith. The early Mormon missionaries to Great Britain made a literal appeal that converts should leave the Old World, bound in tyranny and awaiting destruction, and travel to the New. The contrast is explicit in this early song by John Taylor, which sharply points out the standard which British society does not meet:

O! This is the land of the free!
And this is the home of the brave;
Where rulers and mobbers agree;
'Tis the home of the tyrant and slave.

Here liberty's poles pierce the sky
With her cap gaily hung on the vane;
The gods may its glories espy,
But poor mortals, it's out of your ken.

The eagle sours proudly aloft,
And covers the land with her wings;
But oppression and bloodshed abound,
She can't deign to look down on such things.

All men are born equal and free,
And their rights all nations maintain;
But with millions it would not agree,
They were cradled and brought up in chains.[29]

Not political in any conventional sense, the early Latter-day Saints envisioned a theology of America that was less explicit but far more concrete than any of their rivals. Despite extreme dissent from mainstream America, the Mormons never claimed that the entire stream of American identity, like that of the church, had become polluted. There was a special character to this land and its people that would allow the kingdom of heaven to be restored even if the current generation remained mired in corruption and oppression. This ambivalence allowed Joseph Smith to establish an independent kingdom at Nauvoo while at the same time announcing his candidacy for the presidency of the United States, calling Americans to "rally to the standard of Liberty" and "trample down the tyrant's rod and the oppressor's crown."[30]

Putting this another way, the alienation of insurgent groups in the early republic did not produce "sects" in a traditional European sense. A main reason was that all were convinced that the very meaning of America was bound up with the kind of new beginning which their own movement represented. The kingdom of God could yet be built in America if they were true to their own special calling. The pull was toward providence as much as toward purity, to subdue the culture as much as withdraw from it. The call was to preach, write, convert, to call the nation back to self-evident first principles.

The Latter-day Saints, for instance, were as alienated from mainstream culture as were Roger Williams and the Quakers from the Massachusetts Bay colony. Yet, in withdrawing from society, Smith and his followers did not retreat to modest aims and private ambitions. They were fired with a sense of providential mission of national—even international—scope, a conviction that God's kingdom would yet rise in America, their own endeavors serving as decisive leavening. Much more like Puritan "saints" than Williams or the Quakers, they set their faces to accomplish great and mighty things. Sidney Rigdon's recollections about the charged atmosphere in a log house in 1830 magnificently captures the compelling sense of mission that transformed simple farmers and artisans into thundering prophets intent on shaping the destiny of a nation:

> I met the whole church of Christ in a little log house about 20 feet square . . . and we began to talk about the kingdom of God as if we had the world at our command; we talked with great confidence, and talked big things, although we were not many people, we had big feelings. . . . we began to talk like men in authority and power—we looked upon men of the earth as grasshoppers; if we did not see this people, we saw by vision, the church of God, a thousand times larger. . . . we talked about the people coming as doves to the windows, that all nations should flock unto it . . . and of whole nations being born in one day; we talked such big things that men could not bear them.[31]

A similar hunger for achievement and sense of providential mission propelled other saints to take up different causes, Methodist, Baptist, Universalist, or Christian. One simply cannot underestimate the force of this democratized "errand into the wilderness" in assessing the Christianization of popular culture and the relative weakness of other ideologies of dissent. In all of its diversity, this thundering legion stormed the hinterland of the nation empowered by an incomparable ideology of action: that popular innovation was the handiwork of God and the essential meaning of America.

IV

It is also important to emphasize that popular denominations were socially uniform and thus politically predictable. By the second decade of the nineteenth century, a struggle occurred within the congregations of Baptists and Methodists between those who wanted respectability, centralization, and education and those who valued the tradition of democratic dissent—localism, anti-elitism, and religious experience fed by the passions of ordinary people. The fault line often ran between cosmopolitans and localists, between urban and rural interests. The example of Nathan Bangs superbly captures the tension in popular denominations between democratic dissent and professional respectability.

Although he declined election as bishop of the Methodist church in 1832, Nathan Bangs left an indelible imprint upon the church in the generation after Francis Asbury. Bangs's early career was typical of those called to service in Asbury's missionary band. A largely self-educated young man who spent his youth in Connecticut and his teenage years in rural New York, Bangs moved to Canada at the age of twenty-one and taught school in a Dutch community near Niagara. Troubled by the perplexities of Calvinism, Bangs came under the influence of a Methodist itinerant, James Coleman, experienced a riveting conversion and sanctification, and, conforming to severest Methodist custom, removed the ruffles from his shirts and cut his long hair, which he had worn fashionably in a queue. In 1801, a year after he joined the church and three months after he was approved as an exhorter, he was licensed to preach and given a circuit. Riding circuits from Niagara to Quebec for the next decade, Bangs became the principal force in establishing Methodism in the lower St. Lawrence Valley.[32]

In 1810, the New York Conference presented a charge to Nathan Bangs that would profoundly alter the emphasis of his ministry: he was named "preacher in charge" of the five preachers, five preaching places, and 2,000 members that comprised the single circuit of New York City.[33] Bangs remained a dominant influence in Methodist affairs until the time of the Civil War—when Methodists could boast sixty churches and 17,000 members in the city. Yet despite the Methodist rule of biennial change of appointment, Bangs never managed to leave New York. His career and influence represent the tremendous allure of respectability that faced insurgent religious movements in Jacksonian America as their own constituencies grew in wealth and social standing and it became more difficult to define leaders' pastoral identity as defiant and alienated prophets. Bangs envisioned Methodism as a popular establishment, faithful to the movement's original fire but tempered with virtues of middle-class propriety and urbane congeniality. If Asbury's career represented the triumph of Methodism as a populist movement, with control weighted to the cultural periphery rather than to the center, then Bangs's pointed to the centripetal tug of respectable culture. In America, dissenting paths have often doubled back to lead in the direction of learning, decorum, professionalism, and social standing.

From the time Nathan Bangs arrived in New York City, he set his face to dampen the popular spontaneity that had infused Methodist worship. "I witnessed," he said, "a spirit of pride, presumption, and bigotry, impatience of scriptural restraint and moderation, clapping of the hands, screaming, and even jumping, which marred and disgraced the work of God."[34] Bangs called together the Methodists of New York in the John Street Church and exhorted them to be more orderly in their social meetings. Later, Bangs also went on record as opposed to the spiritual songs of the camp meetings, "ditties" that, in his words, "possessed little of the spirit of poetry and therefore added nothing to true intellectual taste."[35] With a view of his responsibilities not unlike that of his British counterpart, Jabez Bunting, Bangs depicted his role in the church as that of an overseer of a garden beset with the dangerous snake of disorder. Bangs's charge was to strike harder and harder with the whip of the Discipline.[36] One of the consequences of bringing more order and decorum to the John Street Church was that a large faction led by Samuel and William Stillwell, men who opposed centralized control, broke away to set up their own church. The immediate occasion for the split was a plan, backed by Bangs, to rebuild the church in a grand and expensive style, a controversial move at best, given a church whose Discipline instructed that church buildings "be built plain and decent... not more expensive than is absolutely necessary."[37] The expensive style of the building, which even contained a carpeted altar, exacerbated a smoldering tension between what Bangs called "down-town" and "up-town" members. The simpler folk from uptown, led by the Stillwells, rallied against the new building and the heavy-handed tactics of its clerical supporters as a "departure from the primitive simplicity of Methodism."[38]

Nathan Bangs also threw his remarkable energy and political savvy into building powerful central agencies for the expanding Methodist church. After serving for two years as the presiding elder for the New York Conference, he was elected in 1820 the agent of the Methodist Book Concern, a position which would keep him permanently in New York and provide a strategic base from which to promote Methodist publications, missions, Sunday schools, and educational institutions. Under his direction, the Book Concern grew from a struggling agency embarrassed by debt and without premises of its own to a publishing house which was the largest in the world by 1860.[39] Bangs reinvigorated the monthly *Methodist Magazine* and launched, in 1826, the *Christian Advocate and*

Journal, a weekly newspaper that became an official organ of the church in 1828 and rapidly developed the largest circulation of any paper in the country—an estimated 25,000 subscriptions.[40] He was the father of the Missionary Society of the Methodist Episcopal Church and for twenty years its guiding hand. He was also tireless in his efforts for the church's Sunday School Union and was the first to use the powerful agency of the denominational press to push for required ministerial education.[41]

As Methodism's first major polemicist, theological editor, and historian, Nathan Bangs pushed relentlessly for raising the intellectual standards of the church. He was determined to "redeem its character from the foul blot cast upon it, not without some reason, that it had been indifferent to the cause of literature and science."[42] Bangs deplored Asbury's conclusion that the failure of early Methodist schools was a providential sign that Methodists should not attempt to found colleges. Frankly embarrassed and apologetic for the "little progress we have hitherto made in general literature," Bangs set about to make the church "'not be a whit behind the very chiefest' of the Churches in Christendom in the literary and theological eminence of her ministers." In 1830, Bangs transformed the monthly *Methodist Magazine* into the more serious and literary *Methodist Quarterly Review*, a journal to "draw forth the most matured efforts of our best writers . . . and lead others to the cultivation of a similar taste."[43] In his tenure as the doorkeeper of Methodist thinking, Bangs used his considerable resources to accelerate a process by which many Methodists, particularly those in urban settings, shed their populist distinctions and stepped into the ranks of "influential" Christians. By 1844, even the bishops of the church were forced to confess that the church was well on the way to selling out its original birthright: "in some of the Conferences little or nothing remains of the itinerant system."[44]

While there was nothing uniform about this quest for respectability, it was a process powerfully at work among the second-generation leadership of insurgent movements such as the Methodists, the Baptists, and the Disciples. The uneducated Methodist itinerant Hope Hull (1785–1818), for instance, settled permanently in Athens, Georgia, the place selected as the home for the University of Georgia, so that his sons could have the value of a liberal education. One of his sons became a lawyer and eventually Speaker of the Georgia House of Representatives, and the other two were professors at Franklin College.[45] With similar intent, Methodists also came to domesticate the camp meeting, deemphasizing its emotional exercises and restricting its spontaneous exuberance.[46] By the middle of the nineteenth century, Methodists would remove their proscriptions on pew rentals, a move Peter Cartwright lamented as "a Yankee triumph."[47] Most important, in the three decades before the Civil War, the Methodists founded over thirty colleges in nineteen different states; the Baptists, over twenty colleges in sixteen states.[48] By the 1840s, Methodist leadership had shifted firmly into the Whig political camp.[49]

In the long run, basic fault lines of class, education, and social status within a single denomination may have been more significant than sectional tensions, even between northern and southern churches. Despite the regional schisms in their churches, the differences between the Methodist Nathan Bangs or the Baptist Whig Francis Wayland and the "gentlemen theologians" of the South were simply not all that great, as Wayland noted ruefully about the 1845 division in the Baptist church. He argued that the Southern Baptist Convention was led by men representing the very best of enlightened southern life, "governors, judges, congressmen, and other functionaries of the highest dignity."[50] What deserves much greater study are those churches and religious leaders that flourished on the fringes of southern society, those upland whites who defiantly retained their own counsels. Exploring their religious convictions, Bertram Wyatt-Brown has suggested, will reveal the "confused internal cleavage between the folkways of the poor and their social betters, a conflict that belies the notion of a monolithic southern cultural unity in opposition to a northern counterpart."[51]

Similar tensions in the North associated with social status played a key role in the political upheaval within the Methodist church during the 1820s, turmoil that led to the formation of the Methodist Protestant church. In Massachusetts, for example, a local preacher was expelled for clashing with a congregation over the construction of a new chapel. Claiming to speak for the "plain, meek, humble, and old-fashioned Methodist" as opposed to the "gay, assuming, proud, new-fashioned" ones, he thundered against new forms of ostentation that Methodists came to allow.[52] Furthermore, leaders of that movement, such as Nicholas Snethen, employed the rhetoric of democracy with telling effect to stigmatize the hierarchy of Methodism. Similarly, an intense commitment to local autonomy kept Baptists in states like Kentucky, Tennessee, and Missouri absolutely opposed to state, much less national, organization. When infrequent conventions were held, "sovereign and independent" churches would send messengers rather than delegates to ensure that the convention could not claim "a single attribute of power or authority over any church or association."[53] In the American religious economy, moves toward dignity, solemnity, and gentility were sure to bring a swift and strident challenge. New sets of insurgents had ready access to the visions of apostolic simplicity that had inspired their parents and grandparents in the faith. Democratic dissent has been important over the last two centuries not because it has retained control of the major Protestant denominations, but rather because it has served as a residual dynamism unsettling church traditions, breaking out into new and distinctive religious movements, and providing a receptive audience for populist politicians capable of infusing events with moral significance.

V

An additional benefit of piecing together the story of these democratic religious movements is new insight into crucial questions about how America became a liberal society, individualistic, competitive, and market driven. In an age when most ordinary Americans expected almost nothing from government institutions and almost everything from religious ones, popular religious ideologies were perhaps the most important bellwethers of shifting world views. The passion for equality that came to the fore in these years decisively rejected the past as a repository of wisdom. Far from looking backward and clinging to an older moral economy, insurgent religious leaders espoused convictions that were essentially modern and individualistic. These persuasions defied elite privilege and vested interests, and anticipated the dawn of a millennial age of equality and justice. Yet, to achieve these visions of the common good, they espoused means inseparable from the individual pursuit of one's own spiritual and temporal well-being. They assumed that the leveling of aristocracy, root and branch, in all areas of human endeavor would naturally draw people together in harmony and equality. In this way, religious movements fervent about preserving the supernatural in everyday life had the ironic effect of accelerating the breakup of traditional society and the advent of a social order given over to competition, self-expression, and free enterprise. In this moment of fervent democratic aspiration, insurgent religious leaders had no way to foresee that their own assault upon mediating structures could lead to a society in which grasping entrepreneurs could erect new forms of tyranny in religious, political, or economic institutions. The individualization of conscience, which they so greatly prized, moved them to see the hand of providence in a social order of free and independent persons with interests to promote.[54] Nothing better shows this process than the tumultuous career of John Leland, a career illustrating dramatically the ties in the early republic among popular religion, democratic politics, and liberal individualism.

In 1814, Leland was one of the most popular and controversial Baptists in America. He was most famous as a proponent of religious freedom. As a leader among Virginia Baptists in the 1780s, Leland had been influential in petitioning the legislature on behalf of Jefferson's bill for religious freedom and the bill to end the incorporation of the Protestant Episcopal church. There is strong evidence that James Madison personally sought his support for the federal Constitution, which Leland had first opposed. At the same time, Leland also marshaled Baptist opposition to slavery in Virginia. After returning to New England in 1791, he became an outstanding proponent of religious freedom as a preacher, lecturer, and publicist and served two terms in the Massachusetts legislature representing the town of Cheshire.[55]

On a national level, Leland was best known for the 1,235-pound "mammoth cheese" he had presented to President Thomas Jefferson. In New York and Baltimore, crowds flocked to see this phenomenal creation, molded in a cider press supposedly from the milk of 900 cows and bearing the motto "Rebellion to tyrants is obedience to God." Leland made the presentation to Jefferson at the White House on New Year's Day 1802 as a token of esteem from the staunchly republican citizens of Cheshire. Two days later, at the president's invitation, he preached before both houses of Congress on the text "Behold a greater than Solomon is here." One congressman who heard that sermon, Manasseh Cutler, a Massachusetts Federalist and Congregationalist clergyman, had few kind words to say about Leland's politics or his religion, dismissing "the cheesemonger" as a "poor ignorant, illiterate, clownish creature":

> Such a farrago, bawled with stunning voice, horrid tone, frightful grimaces, and extravagant gestures, I believe, was never heard by any decent auditory before. . . . Such an outrage upon religion, the Sabbath, and common decency, was extremely painful to every sober, thinking person present.[56]

Leland's political notoriety has often masked the fact that fundamentally he was a preacher and itinerant evangelist. In 1824, he confessed that he had preached 8,000 times, had baptized over 1,300 persons, had known almost 1,000 Baptist preachers, and had traveled an equivalent of three times around the world.[57] Given Leland's stature and connections, it is not at all surprising that he attended the Baptists' first Triennial Convention in Philadelphia and preached at William Staughton's church the night before the first session. That sermon sounded a sharp alarm for Baptists who were hungry for respectability. Even before any decision had been made about forming a missionary organization, Leland warned against the danger of "Israel" insisting on having a king so that it could be like other nations: "like the people now-a-days; they form societies, and they must have a president and two or three vice-presidents, to be like their neighbors around them."[58] After Baptists joined the Protestant quest for voluntary association, Leland stepped up his attacks upon missionary agencies and the clerical elites who stood behind them. For the next decade and a half, he went on the offensive against the organizational schemes and clerical professionalism at the core of American Protestant denominations. Leland ridiculed the mercenary foundation of foreign and domestic missions,[59] the oppression of "a hierarchical clergy—despotic judiciary—[and] an aristocratic host of lawyers,"[60] the mechanical operations of theological seminaries, the tyranny of formal structures,[61] and the burden of creedalism—"this Virgin Mary between the souls of men and the Scriptures." In a letter to John Taylor, a stalwart foe of mission activity in Kentucky, Leland confessed in 1830 that his calling had been "to watch and check *clerical hierarchy*, which assumes as many shades as a chameleon."[62]

John Leland had every reason to take up the path of order and decorum that appealed to other Baptist leaders. Yet he seemed to come out of revolutionary times with a different set of impulses stirring within. Rather than looking for ways to instill energy in government and to promote vigorous central policies, Leland sought at every step to restrain the accumulation of power. "I would as soon give my vote to a wolf to be a shepherd," he said in an oration celebrating American independence in 1802, "as to a man, who is always contending for the energy of government, to be a ruler."[63] John Leland's dissent flowed out of a passion for religious liberty that exalted the individual conscience over creedal systems, local control over powerful ecclesiastical structures, and popular sensibility over the instincts of the educated and powerful. As a prolific publicist, popular hymn writer, and amusing and satirical preacher, Leland strongly advocated freedom in every sphere of life. Self-reliant to an eccentric degree, Leland is fascinating and important in his own right. He also stands as an important bridge between the revolutionary era and the quest for localism and independence that confounded Baptist history through the Jacksonian period. The importance of this story, played out on the fringes of denominational life, has not been fully appreciated, given its lack of coherence and the orientation of early denominational historians to celebrate the opposite, the growth of respectability and organizational coherence.[64]

Brought up as a fervent New Light, John Leland found the resources to accept, even defend, his own "rusticity of manners."[65] Chief among these was a Jeffersonian view of conscience that championed intellectual self-reliance. In a pamphlet published in 1792 attacking the New England Standing Order, Leland explained how he came to trust his own reasoning rather than the conclusions of great men. Having once had "profound reverence" for leading civic figures, Leland discovered that in reality "not two of them agreed":

What, said I, do *great* men differ? boys, women and little souls do; but can learned, wise patriots disagree so much in judgment? If so, they cannot all be right, but they may all be wrong, and therefore *Jack Nips for himself.*[66]

Leland hammered out his view of conscience as he battled the state-church tradition of Virginia during the 1780s and of New England thereafter. In over thirty pamphlets and regular contributions to Phinehas Allen's staunchly Jeffersonian *Pittsfield Sun*, Leland spelled out a vision of personal autonomy that colored his personal life, his theological views, and his conception of society.

As early as 1790, Leland began to sound his clarion call that conscience should be "free from human control." His passion was to protect the "empire of conscience," the court of judgment in every human soul, from the inevitable encroachments of state-church traditions, oppressive creeds, ambitious and greedy clergymen—and even family tradition. "For a man to contend for religious liberty on the court-house green, and deny his wife, children and servants, the liberty of conscience at home, is a paradox not easily reconciled. . . . each one must give an account of himself to God."[67] Upon returning to New England in 1791, Leland assailed the Standing Order in a pamphlet entitled *The Rights of Conscience Inalienable; . . . or, The High-flying Churchman, Stript of His Legal Robe, Appears a Yaho*. With language borrowed directly from Jefferson's *Notes on the State of Virginia*, he argued that truth can stand on its own without the props of legal or creedal defense. He reiterated the theme that "religion is a matter between God and individuals."[68] In addition to repeating his warning to parents that it was "iniquitous to bind the consciences" of children, Leland clarified his explicitly democratic view of conscience: that the so-called wise and learned were actually less capable of mediating truth than were common people. Leland dismissed the common objection that "the ignorant part of the community are not capacited to judge for themselves":

> Did many of the rulers believe in Christ when he was upon earth? Were not the learned clergy (the scribes) his most inveterate enemies? Do not great men differ as much as little men in judgment? Have not almost all lawless errors crept into the world through the means of wise men (so called)? Is not a simple man, who makes nature and reason his study, a competent judge of things? Is the Bible written (like Caligula's laws) so intricate and high, that none but the letter learned (according to the common phrase) can read it? Is not the vision written so plain that he that runs may read it?[69]

In an 1801 sermon, *A Blow at the Root*, published in five editions in four different states from Vermont to Georgia, Leland continued to project an image of the autonomous person besieged by the coercive forces of state, creed, tradition, and clerical hierarchy. The political triumph of Jefferson, the "*Man of the People*," convinced Leland that the "genius of America," which had been slumbering, had finally "arisen, like a lion, from the swelling of Jordon, and roared like thunder in the states, 'we will be free; we will rule ourselves; our officers shall be honorable servants, but not mean masters.'"[70]

Leland's legacy is an exaggerated opposition to official Christianity. He articulated a twofold persuasion that operated powerfully in the hinterland of Baptist church life: an aversion to central control and a quest for self-reliance. One reason that it is so difficult to write Baptist history in the early republic is that centrifugal forces were so powerfully at work, giving free rein to regional distinctions and take-charge entrepreneurs. Whatever success cosmopolitan leaders like Richard Furman or Francis Wayland had in building central institutions, their way was dogged at every step: by serious defections to the antiformalist appeals of Alexander Campbell and, later, William Miller;[71] by the rise of significant antimission Baptist associations in regions as diverse as New York, Pennsylvania, Illinois, Kentucky, and North Carolina; and by the appearance of charismatic dissenters such as J. R. Graves and his Landmark Baptists.[72] Equally important was the entrenched opposition to central authority among those who remained within the regular Baptist fold. The Triennial Convention, after all, had never represented Baptist churches themselves, but only individuals and societies willing to pay appropriate dues to the organization. After 1826, it was virtually dismembered when its champions from different regions locked horns over issues of authority and control.[73]

John Leland is also important because of the way he turned a quest for self-reliance into a godly crusade. Like Elias Smith, James O'Kelly, Lorenzo Dow, Barton Stone, and William Miller, he fervently believed that individuals had to make a studied effort to prune away natural authorities: church, state, college, seminary, even family. Leland's message carried the combined ideological leverage of evangelical urgency and Jeffersonian promise. Choosing simple language and avoiding doctrinal refinements, he proclaimed a divine economy that was atomistic and competitive rather than holistic and hierarchical. The triumph of liberal individualism, in this form at least, was not something imposed upon the people of America from above. They gladly championed the promise of personal autonomy as a message they could understand and a cause to which they could subscribe—in God's name, no less.

NOTES

1. Two books are superb on these themes: Robert H. Wiebe, *The Opening of American Society* (New York: Knopf, 1984), particularly ch. 8, "Revolution in Choices"; and Sean Wilentz, *Chants Democratic: New York City and the Rise of the American Working Class*,

1788–1850 (New York: Oxford University Press, 1984). See also James A. Henretta, *The Evolution of American Society, 1700–1815* (Lexington, Mass.: Heath, 1973); Robert A. Gross, *The Minute Men and Their World* (New York: Hill and Wang, 1976); Edward Countryman, *A People in Revolution: The American Revolution and Political Society in New York, 1760–1790* (Baltimore, Md.: Johns Hopkins University Press, 1981); and Joyce Appleby, *Capitalism and a New Social Order: The Republican Vision of the 1790s* (New York: New York University Press, 1984). My own book, *The Democratization of American Christianity* (New Haven, Conn.: Yale University Press, 1989), expands on the themes of this chapter in a more general consideration of religion in the early republic.

2. Henry Mayer, *A Son of Thunder: Patrick Henry and the American Republic* (New York: Watts, 1986), 444–45. On the rise of public opinion as an authority, see Gordon S. Wood, "The Democratization of Mind in the American Revolution," in *Leadership in the American Revolution* (Washington, D.C.: Library of Congress, 1974), 63–89.

3. Wiebe, *Opening of American Society*, 142–44. Daniel A. Cohen has provided an insightful interpretation of Charles Brockden Brown's novel *Arthur Mervyn* (1799), as the story of a young man's struggle for survival and success in an age in which it was no longer clear how a young man was supposed to behave. Cohen sees Arthur Mervyn as caught between, on one hand, the conflicting demands of traditional social patterns based on landed property, ascriptive rank, authoritative moral inculcation, household apprenticeship, and ordered general succession and, on the other, a disordered and relentlessly competitive social world—that is, between morality as submission to authority or morality as autonomous enlightened reason. Cohen, "Arthur Mervyn and His Elders," *William and Mary Quarterly*, 3rd ser., 43 (1986): 362–80.

4. Rowland Berthoff suggests about the early nineteenth century that it is difficult to write "a coherent account of so disjunctive a history." "The assumption persists that the history of America can be written without reflecting on what was missing from its unestablished religion, self-made elite, negligible government, discontinuous literary tradition, and loyalty to lofty but impersonal abstractions." See Berthoff, "Writing a History of Things Left Out," *Reviews in American History* 14 (1986): 1–16.

5. The phrase is from John Murrin in "The Great Inversion; or, Court versus Country: A Comparison of the Revolution Settlements in England (1688–1721) and America (1776–1816)," in *Three British Revolutions: 1641, 1688, 1776*, ed. J. G. A. Pocock (Princeton, N.J.: Princeton University Press, 1980), 425.

6. R. Laurence Moore, *Religious Outsiders and the Making of Americans* (New York: Oxford University Press, 1986), 3–24.

7. Gordon S. Wood makes this argument in "Ideology and the Origins of Liberal America," *William and Mary Quarterly*, 3rd ser., 44 (1987): 637.

8. The canonical eighteenth-century distinction between vulgar and refined language denied the possibility of virtuous intelligence in vernacular expression. In the age of democratic revolution, no change was more essential and far-reaching than the act of faith that attributed virtue to the vernacular expression of ordinary people. On this intellectual revolution, see Olivia Smith, *The Politics of Language, 1791–1819* (New York: Oxford University Press, 1984).

9. Appleby, *Capitalism and a New Social Order*, 79.

10. George A. Rawlyk, *Ravished by the Spirit: Religious Revivals, Baptists, and Henry Alline* (Toronto: McGill-Queens University Press, 1984), 14.

11. Quoted in Doris Elizabett Andrews, "Popular Religion and the Revolution in the Middle Atlantic Ports: The Rise of the Methodists, 1770–1800" (Ph.D. diss., Princeton University, 1986), 140; Richard Bushman, *Joseph Smith and the Beginnings of Mormonism* (Urbana: University of Illinois Press, 1984), 59.

12. In a similar sense, Lawrence Goodwyn defines the Populist movement of the late nineteenth century in democratic terms not because of its achievement but because of the intense democratic aspirations and hope that gave it birth. See Goodwyn, *Democratic Promise: The Populist Movement in America* (New York: Oxford University Press, 1976).

13. Richard Carwardine, "Methodist Ministers and the Second Party System," in *Rethinking Methodist History: A Bicentennial Historical Consultation*, ed. Russell E. Richey and Kenneth E. Rowe (Nashville, Tenn.: Abingdon, 1985), 134; David Benedict, *A General History of the Baptist Denomination*, 2 vols. (Boston: Lincoln and Edmonds, 1813), 2:552–53; Timothy L. Smith, *Revivalism and Social Reform: American Protestantism on the Eve of the Civil War* (Nashville, Tenn.: Abingdon, 1957), 22; and C. C. Goss, *Statistical History of the First Century of American Methodism* (New York: Carlton and Porter, 1866), 106.

14. Michael Walzer, *The Revolution of the Saints: A Study in the Origins of Radical Politics* (Cambridge, Mass.: Harvard University Press, 1965), 1–21, and "Puritanism as a Revolutionary Ideology," *History and Theory* 3 (1964): 59–90.

15. W. R. Ward, "The Legacy of John Wesley: The Pastoral Office in Britain and America," in *Statesmen, Scholars and Merchants: Essays in Eighteenth-Century History Presented to Dame Lucy Sutherland*, ed. Anne Whiteman, J. C. Bromley, and P. G. M. Dickson (Oxford: Oxford University Press, 1973), 346–48.

16. Ralph E. Morrow, "The Great Revival, the West, and the Crisis of the Church," in *The Frontier Re-Examined*, ed. John F. McDermott (Urbana: University of Illinois Press, 1967), 72.

17. Parsons Cooke, *A Century of Puritanism and a Century of Its Opposites* (Boston: Whipple, 1855), 258, quoted in Paul G. Faler, *Mechanics and Manufacturers in the Early Industrial Revolution: Lynn, Massachusetts, 1780–1860* (Albany: State University of New York Press, 1981), 47.

18. Richard Carwardine has argued that many of the "new measures" supposedly introduced by Charles Finney (the "anxious bench," women praying in public, colloquial preaching, protracted meetings) had been widely employed by the Methodists before Finney. See Carwardine, "The Second Great Awakening in the Urban Centers: An Examination of Methodism and the 'New Measures,'" *Journal of American History* 59 (1972): 327–40. For the innovative techniques of the Methodists, see Terry D. Bilhartz, *Urban Religion and the Second Great Awakening: Church and Society in Early National Baltimore* (Rutherford, N.J.: Fairleigh Dickinson University Press, 1986).

19. Lawrence Goodwyn, *The Populist Movement: A Short History of the Agrarian Revolt in America* (New York: Oxford University Press, 1978), vii–xxiv, 34–35, 293–96.

20. W. P. Strickland, ed., *Autobiography of Dan Young, a New England Preacher of Olden Time* (New York: Carlton and Porter, 1860), 34.

21. John M'Lean, ed., *Sketch of Rev. Philip Gatch* (Cincinnati, Ohio: Swormstedt and Poe, 1854), 135.

22. The itinerant Methodist Joshua Thomas reported two such incidents with Dow. See Adam Wallace, *The Parson of the Islands: A Biography of the Rev. Joshua Thomas* (Philadelphia: Merrill, 1861), 76, 59.

23. Moore, *Religious Outsiders*, 3–21. Richard Carwardine has also made this point: "Yet later denominational and local church historians often under emphasized or deliberately ignored a side of evangelical life whose emotionalism, disorder, and impropriety were an embarrassment to them." *Transatlantic Revivalism: Popular Evangelicalism in Britain and America, 1790–1865* (Westport, Conn.: Greenwood, 1978), xiv.

24. For examples of the focus on cities and industrial workers, see Faler, *Mechanics and Manufacturers*; Charles G. Steffen, *The Mechanics of Baltimore: Workers and Politics in the Age of the Revolution, 1763–1812* (Urbana: University of Illinois Press, 1984); and Wilentz, *Chants Democratic*. Wilentz is perceptive in treating the role of popular religion in New York City, particularly the role of Methodism, but religion remains only incidental to his work.

25. David Hempton notes this about the work of E. P. Thompson, in *Methodism and Politics in British Society, 1750–1850* (Stanford, Calif.: Stanford University Press, 1984), 75–76.

26. Elias Smith devoted a sermon of 120 pages to the subject of how republican values should be applied to the church. See his *The Whole World Governed by a Jew; or, The Government of the Second Adam, as King and Priest* (Exeter, N.H.: Roulet, 1805).

27. Carwardine, "Methodist Ministers and the Second Party System," 134–47.

28. W. H. Oliver, *Prophets and Millennialists* (Auckland: Oxford University Press, 1978), 235.

29. John Taylor, *Millennial Star* (London, 15 Nov. 1847).

30. These phrases are from a campaign song for Smith written by Parley Pratt. Quoted in Levette J. Davidson, "Mormon Songs," *Journal of American Folklore* 58 (1945): 277.

31. Rigdon's sermon was reported in a Mormon newspaper published by Joseph Smith's brother William. See the *Prophet*, 8 June 1844, p. 2, as quoted in Marvin S. Hill, "The Role of Christian Primitivism in the Origins and Development of the Mormon Kingdom, 1830–1844" (Ph.D. diss., University of Pennsylvania, 1968), 72–73.

32. Abel Stevens, *The Life of Nathan Bangs, D.D.* (New York: Carlton and Porter, 1863), 1–65.

33. Ibid., 182.

34. Ibid., 183.

35. Nathan Bangs, *A History of the Methodist Episcopal Church*, 4 vols. (New York: Methodist Book Concern, 1840–1853), 2:105.

36. Stevens, *Life of Nathan Bangs*, 184–85.

37. *The Doctrines and Discipline of the Methodist Episcopal Church* (New York: Methodist Book Concern, 1820), 165.

38. Samuel A. Seaman, *Annals of New York Methodism* (New York: Hunt and Eaton, 1892), 219, as quoted in Emory Stevens Bucke, ed., *The History of American Methodism*, 3 vols. (New York: Abingdon, 1964), 1:626.

39. Stevens, *Life of Nathan Bangs*, 239–52. By 1860, the Methodist Book Concern, with eastern and western branches and five depositories, employed 4 "book agents," 12 editors for its periodicals, 460 other workers, and between twenty and thirty cylinder and power presses. Its multiple periodicals had an aggregate circulation of over one million copies per month, and its quadrennial sales for the period ending in 1860 were over $1 million (ibid., 248–49).

40. Bangs, *History of the Methodist Church*, 4:434.

41. As early as 1820, Bangs proposed a seminary in New York, a move bitterly opposed by the same people who balked at building a new John Street Church. In 1824, Bangs was also unsuccessful in persuading the General Conference of the Methodist church to establish a central college or university. Stevens, *Life of Nathan Bangs*, 232, 254.

42. Bangs, *History of the Methodist Church*, 4:70.

43. Ibid., 289, 281–82.

44. Robert A. West, *Journal of the General Conference of the Methodist Episcopal Church* (New York: G. Lane and C. B. Tippet, 1844), 157.

45. William B. Sprague, *Annals of the American Pulpit*, vol. 7: *The Methodists* (New York: Carters, 1865), 112–14.

46. For a description of this process in camp meetings around Baltimore, ca. 1820, see Bilhartz, *Urban Religion and the Second Great Awakening*, 93–94.

47. *Autobiography of Peter Cartwright, the Backwoods Preacher*, ed. W. P. Strickland (New York: Methodist Book Concern, 1856), 481.

48. Donald G. Tewksbury, *The Founding of American Colleges and Universities before the Civil War* (New York: Teachers College, Columbia University Press, 1932), 104–6, 115–17.

49. Carwardine, "Methodist Ministers and the Second Party System," 140.

50. Quoted in Bertram Wyatt-Brown, "The Antimission Movement in the Jacksonian South: A Study in Regional Folk Culture," *Journal of Southern History* 36 (1970): 528.

51. Ibid., 503.

52. Alexander M'Lean, *An Appeal to the Public* (Belchertown, Mass.: Warren, 1828), 4, 6, 54–55, as quoted in Steven J. Novak, "The Perils of Respectability: Methodist Schisms of the 1820s," unpublished paper, American Historical Association, 1980.

53. Walter Brownlow Posey, *The Baptist Church in the Lower Mississippi Valley, 1776–1845* (Lexington: University Press of Kentucky, 1957), 115–27.

54. The religious sources on which this chapter depends bear out the contention of Gordon S. Wood that a liberal social order was not simply foisted on the country by merchants and aristocrats, but percolated up from the convictions of the mass of ordinary Americans. See the lively discussion on these issues in the essays on Wood's book, *The Creation of the American Republic, 1776–1787*, in *William and Mary Quarterly*, 3rd ser., 44 (1987): 549–640, particularly the essays by Gary B. Nash, John M. Murrin, and Gordon S. Wood. My own perspective has also been influenced by Appleby, *Capitalism and a New Social Order*.

55. The best assessments of Leland's activities are L. H. Butterfield, "Elder John Leland, Jeffersonian Itinerant," *Proceedings of the American Antiquarian Society* 62 (1953): 155–242; William G. McLoughlin, *New England Dissent, 1630–1833: The Baptists and the Separation of Church and State*, 2 vols. (Cambridge, Mass.: Harvard University Press,

1971), 2:915–38; and Edwin S. Gaustad, "The Backus-Leland Tradition," *Foundations: A Baptist Journal of History and Theology* 2 (1959): 131–52. On Leland's antislavery activity in Virginia, see James D. Essig, *The Bonds of Wickedness: American Evangelicals against Slavery, 1770–1808* (Philadelphia: Temple University Press, 1982), 67–72.

56. W. P. Cutler and J. P. Cutler, *Life, Journals and Correspondence of Rev. Manasseh Cutler*, 2 vols. (Cincinnati, Ohio: Clarke, 1888), 2:66–67. On the creation and presentation of the cheese, see Butterfield, "Elder John Leland," 214–29.

57. L. F. Greene, ed., *The Writings of John Leland* (New York: Wood, 1845), 513–15.

58. Ibid., 377.

59. On Leland's significant role in antimission activities, see Byron Cecil Lambert, *The Rise of the Anti-Mission Baptists: Sources and Leaders, 1800–1840* (New York: Ayer, 1980), 116–52.

60. Leland, "A Little Sermon Sixteen Minutes Long," in Greene, *Writings of John Leland*, 410.

61. Leland's opposition to formal theological education was expressed in a widely circulated poem, "The Modern Priest."

62. Leland, *The Virginia Chronicle* (Fredericksburg, Va.: Prentis and Baxter, 1790), 34; "Extracts from a Letter to Rev. John Taylor of Kentucky, Dated Dec. 10, 1830," in Greene, *Writings of John Leland*, 601.

63. Leland, *An Oration Delivered at Cheshire, July 5, 1802, on the Celebration of Independence* (Hudson, N.Y.: Allen, 1802), 12.

64. Three early historians of the Baptists in America all chronicle the rise of the movement from persecution to respectability. All make an implicit appeal that Baptists be accorded the same respect as were other churches. See Robert B. Semple, *A History of the Rise and Progress of the Baptists in Virginia* (Richmond, Va.: Lynch, 1810); David Benedict, *A General History of the Baptist Denomination* (Boston: Lincoln and Edwards, 1813); and Isaac Backus, *A History of New England with Particular Reference to the Denomination of Christians Called Baptists* (Newton, Mass.: Backus Historical Society, 1871). The same approach is also evident in the writing of Methodist history, as, for example, Nathan Bangs's *History of the Methodist Church*.

65. Leland, "Events in the Life of John Leland Written by Himself," in Greene, *Writings of John Leland*, 10.

66. Leland, "The History of Jack Nips," in ibid., 76–77.

67. See Leland's discussion of "The Right and Bonds of Conscience" in his pamphlet *The Virginia Chronicle*, 45. "Conscience," Leland wrote in 1830:

> is a court of judicature, erected in every breast, to take cognizance of every action in the home department, but has nothing to do with another man's conduct. My best judgment tells me that my neighbor does wrong, but my conscience has nothing to say of it. Were I to do as he does, my conscience would arrest and condemn me, but guilt is not transferable. Every one must give an account of himself. ("Transportation of Mail," in Greene, *Writings of John Leland*, 565)

68. Leland, *The Rights of Conscience Inalienable; . . . or, The High-flying Churchman, Stript of His Legal Robe, Appears a Yahoo* (New London, Conn.: Green, 1791), 8. Elsewhere,

Leland argued explicitly that truth would prevail in a free market of ideas: "Truth is not in the least danger of being lost, when free examination is allowed" (*The Bible-Baptist* [Baltimore, 1789], in Greene, *Writings of John Leland*, 78).

69. Leland, *The Rights of Conscience Inalienable*, 15–16. Three years later, in 1794, the Congregational minister Noah Worcester expressed the very stereotype of common folk that Leland rejected. In Worcester's view, the Baptists succeeded by their ability to engage that "class of persons . . . who possess weak judgments, fickle minds, and quick and tender passions." Worcester explained that such persons "are of such low understanding, that they are incapable of duly examining the force of arguments; and may be confounded by the length and multiplicity of them, while no real conviction is afforded to their minds." Worcester, *Impartial Inquiries Respecting the Progress of the Baptist Denomination* (Worcester, Mass.: Worcester, 1794), 11–12.

70. Leland's *Blow at the Root* was published in New London and Suffield, Connecticut (1801), Bennington, Vermont (1801), Edenton, North Carolina (1803), and Washington, Georgia (1805).

71. Errett Gates, *The Early Relation of Baptists and Disciples* (Chicago: Donnelley, 1904); David L. Rowe, *Thunder and Trumpets: Millerites and Dissenting Religion in Upstate New York, 1800–1850* (Chico, Calif.: Scholars, 1985).

72. Byron C. Lambert, *The Rise of the Anti-Mission Baptists: Sources and Leaders, 1800–1840* (Salem, N.H.: Ayer, 1980); Harold L. Twiss, "Missionary Support by Baptist Churches and Associations in Western Pennsylvania, 1815–45," *Foundations: A Baptist Journal of History and Theology* 10 (1967): 36–49; and James E. Tull, *A History of Southern Baptist Landmarkism in the Light of Historical Baptist Ecclesiology* (New York: Ayer, 1980).

73. Francis Wayland, president of Brown University and editor of the *American Baptist Magazine*, had hoped to transform the Triennial Convention of 1826 into a genuine instrument of Baptist polity. Instead, the convention was virtually dismantled. New England and New York delegates, led by Wayland, were effective in discrediting Luther Rice, whose base of operations was Washington, D.C. They concentrated power in their own hands and moved the headquarters of the missions board to Boston. For a full discussion of these developments, see Winthrop S. Hudson, "Stumbling into Disorder," *Foundations: A Baptist Journal of History and Theology* 1 (1958): 45–71.

Religion and Politics in the Antebellum North

Daniel Walker Howe

Without an understanding of the religion of the middle period, there can be no understanding of the politics of the time. This is the lesson of the historiography of the antebellum republic as it has evolved over the past two generations. Because the North and South display different patterns of political culture, this chapter will deal only with the North. It will address its subject through a sequence of stages. The first step is simply learning to take religion seriously in the study of political history. The second is to comprehend the nature of the great evangelical movement of the age and its consequences for society. Third, I undertake to delineate the basic religious alignments that were reflected in the politics of the second party system. My goal is to reconceptualize the relationship between antebellum politics and religion in such a way as to make the best sense out of existing knowledge. If this goal is attained, it will also help to focus our future inquiries.

TAKING RELIGION SERIOUSLY

The modern historiography of middle-period politics begins with Arthur M. Schlesinger, Jr.'s *The Age of Jackson*, published in 1945. An instant classic, the book reinterpreted its subject for the generation shaped by the New Deal. Today, it remains a readable and engaging account, for Schlesinger took the issues of the second party system seriously and wrote with a narrative verve that still conveys their excitement. It is, of course, a partisan account, and this partisanship is its strength. The book's weakness stems from its failure to take religion seriously as a social and cultural force. Schlesinger's own sympathies lay unashamedly with the anticlericals of the nineteenth century, and his discussions of religious ideas in his book registered nothing except the self-interested apologetics of employers. The transforming power of the great evangelical movement of the nineteenth century utterly escaped him. As a result, his book's ability to command our attention evaporates when its author turns from such economic issues as banking, currency, and the labor movement to the religiously oriented issues of temperance, nativism, Indian policy, and, most significantly, slavery.[1]

A round of criticism of Schlesinger's work reacted against his polarization of the Jacksonians and their Whig adversaries as good and evil, respectively. But this criticism—consensus historiography, as we call it—did not necessarily recognize the importance of religious history. Richard Hofstadter, in his brilliant collection of essays *The American Political Tradition and the Men Who Made It*, scathingly criticized Andrew Jackson as a man-on-the-make but demonstrated the same secularist blind spot as Schlesinger. His admiring and admirable sketch of Wendell Phillips ignored the religious background of antebellum reform, and Hofstadter didn't find Jackson's Whig opponents even worthy of discussion.[2]

Richard P. McCormick, adopting a far more sophisticated methodology, studied the formation of the second party system as a problem of organization and voter turnout. Deliberately avoiding an examination of ideology, he addressed his subject using quantitative techniques.[3] Yet, in the long run, the careful reconstruction of the political system that the elder McCormick did so much to foster has revealed features demanding a reexamination of the hearts and minds of the voters. The parties of the antebellum era commanded extraordinary enthusiasm among the voters, to judge from their high turnout, as well as extraordinary party loyalty, and to judge from the consistency of voting by both electors and elected. The "new political history," as it has come to be called, has borne out the observations of contemporary observers like Tocqueville: politics seems to have been centrally important to the average man in the pre–Civil War North. What was it that so captured the imagination of the public?

Recognition of the important role of religious and moral issues in the second party system begins with Lee Benson's reinterpretation, *The Concept of Jacksonian Democracy*, published in 1961. Benson saw that many of the political issues of the Whig/Jacksonian era involved judgments of moral value. Different ethnocultural or religious communities made these judgments differently, and these communities became the building blocks of party. Benson also made a contribution of lasting worth by defining the role of "negative reference groups." Voters lined up with the party in opposition to the party of their principal negative reference group. Thus, Irish Catholic immigrants voted Democratic while their despised competitors, the free blacks, voted Whig—prompting many Scots-Irish Presbyterian immigrants to vote Whig in reaction against the Irish Catholic Democrats.[4]

We can now say with confidence that issues of morality and religion were built into the second party system from its inception. It has been demonstrated that the moral issues of Sabbatarianism, Antimasonry, and Indian removal all played important parts in the shaping of that system during the 1820s. (The white opposition to Jackson's Indian removal policy was led by Presbyterian missionaries.) As Richard Carwardine has shown, by the time of the classic Whig-Democrat confrontation of 1840, the evangelical community was active and prominent in the Whig campaign.[5]

Out of the approach pioneered by Benson has developed what is sometimes called the "ethnocultural" interpretation of antebellum politics. An outstanding example would be Robert Kelley's fascinating overview, *The Cultural Pattern in American Politics*. This interpretation has not simply replaced the economic interpretation, but has been synthesized with it in such works as Michael Holt's *Forging a Majority: The Formation of the Republican Party in Pittsburgh* and my own *The Political Culture of the American Whigs*. How the synthesis of cultural, moral, and economic elements can be integrated into a powerful narrative history is well displayed in W. R. Brock's *Parties and Political Conscience: 1840–1850*, a work by a leading British historian of the United States that deserves to be better known in this country.[6]

This enrichment of our understanding of antebellum politics has several consequences. In the first place, it underscores the practical effects of ideas and moral values, making American political history seem more ideological than it was once the fashion to admit.[7] Second, it demonstrates more clearly than ever the continuities between the second and third party systems, including those between Whigs and Republicans.[8] This awareness feeds into the third characteristic of still recent scholarship, which is the interest taken in the Whig party. Instead of being simply the conservative opponents of Jacksonian progress, the Whigs now are seen as frequently taking initiatives—evangelical, moral, and economic. Typical of respect for the Whigs is the following quotation from Louise Stevenson's fine book, *Scholarly Means to Evangelical Ends*:

> Whiggery stood for the triumph of the cosmopolitan and national over the provincial and local, of rational order over irrational spontaneity, of school-based learning over traditional folkways and customs, and of self-control over self-expression. Whigs believed that every person had the potential to become moral or good if family, school, and community nurtured the seed of goodness in his moral nature. Richard Jensen identifies Whigs as the party of modernizers who promoted some aspects of the nascent middle-class economy and society while restraining others.[9]

In this vision, party politics are viewed as expressing deep conflicts over cultural values.

In developing this cultural perspective, historians have turned to their sister disciplines in the social sciences. Ironically—in view of the antireligious origins of much modern social science—historians have found in the social sciences tools to help them understand and appreciate the power of religion. Students of the early American republic have been learning much from sociologists like Robert Bellah, Peter Berger, John L. Hammond, and Gerhard Lenski; from political scientists like Michael Walzer, Samuel P. Huntington, and David Greenstone; and from anthropologists like Mary Douglas, Victor Turner, and the oft-quoted Clifford Geertz.[10]

Armed with this understanding, we are better able to appreciate antebellum political culture. From this perspective, we can see that issues of moral value did not arise in American politics only with the debate over slavery expansion and the birth of the Republican party. Moral issues were as characteristic of the second party system as they were of the third. (Therefore, it becomes harder to blame the Civil War on a "blundering generation" of fanatical agitators and irresponsible politicians in the 1850s.)[11] Nor can the *style* of antebellum campaigns be separated from their *substance* and made the explanation for popular involvement. The hullabaloo surrounding the political campaigns of the era—the torchlight parades, the tents pitched outside town, the urgent calls for commitment—was borrowed by political campaigners from the revival preachers. Far from being irrelevant distractions or mere recreation, the evangelical techniques of mass persuasion that we associate with the campaigns of 1840 and after actually provide a clue to the moral meaning of antebellum politics. Even the practice of holding national conventions was borrowed by the parties from the cause-oriented benevolent associations. Anti-Masonry, which held the first presidential nominating convention in 1831, was both an evangelical reform movement (a "blessed spirit" to its supporters) and a political party.[12]

But secular prejudice dies hard. Even though it is now admitted that the voters were interested in religion, it is not universally admitted that religion was a "real" issue. Sometimes historians have offered evidence of ethnoreligious voting as an illustration of how little the ignorant masses really understood politics. Other times, historians have refused to accept the ethnoreligious interpretation because they feel it reflects badly on the rationality of the electorate. And even a respected and thoughtful practitioner of the "new political history" has expressed the fear that it has led us into a blind alley by showing that nineteenth-century American voters were concerned about something so politically irrelevant as religion![13] In my opinion, a proper assessment of antebellum political life has to start by admitting the legitimacy and relevance of religious and moral commitments to the politics of the age. Of course, all political issues didn't have a religious dimension, but the ones that did—antislavery, Indian policy, nativism, temperance, education, penal reform, treatment of the insane—were no less momentous and worthy of attention (from either our point of view or that of nineteenth-century contemporaries) than internal improvements, currency, and the tariff.

REVIVALISM AND AMERICAN POLITICAL CULTURE

The prominence of evangelical piety is one of the major continuities in American life between colonial and national times. Indeed, for all the attention that has been devoted to the so-called Great Awakening and its effects, it seems likely that its nineteenth-century counterparts were even "greater" in their impact on American culture and polities. John Murrin once remarked that the Great Awakening and its legacy probably had even more to do with the Civil War than with the Revolution, and it is a perceptive comment.[14] The later evangelicals became more self-conscious as shapers of society and opinion, for they attached increasing importance to subjecting social institutions and standards to divine judgment and "reforming"—that is, reshaping—them accordingly.

In both the eighteenth and nineteenth centuries, revivalism and democracy were interrelated phenomena. Each asserted popular claims against those of the elite, pluralism against orthodoxy, charisma against rationalism, competitiveness against authority, an innovative Americanism against European tradition. Such is the thrust of a vast body of distinguished scholarship, from William Warren Sweet to Perry Miller, from Richard Bushman to Patricia Bonomi.[15] Indeed, the more active that popular participation in American political life became, the more important moral and religious issues came to be in politics. It is no accident that religion was more potent a political factor in the second party system than it had been at the time of the adoption of the Constitution. It is a natural consequence of the increasingly democratic nature of American politics.[16]

Yet, the popular quality of the evangelical movement was only one side of it. Revivals did not spring forth from the populace spontaneously; they were "worked up." Terry Bilhartz has reminded us (if we needed reminding) that revivals took place not simply because there was a receptive audience, but because evangelists were promoting them.[17] These evangelists had on their agenda a reformation of life and habits, both individual and communal. They were demonstrating a continuation of the historic concern for church discipline so characteristic of the early Protestant Reformers. Voluntary discipline represented Protestantism's alternative to the authoritarianism of traditional society. If popular enthusiasm was the "soft side" of the great evangelical movement, the new discipline was its "hard side."

The new discipline of the evangelical movement had far-reaching consequences. Its reforms did no less than reshape the cultural system of the Victorian middle class in both Britain and America. We remember its morality as strict, and indeed it was—most notably in the novel restraints it imposed on the expression or even mention of sex and the use of alcohol. But even its most punitive severity was redemptive in purpose, as the words "reformatory" and "penitentiary" suggest. Put another way, the converse of Victorian discipline was the proper development of the human faculties. Education and self-improvement went along with discipline. The evangelical reformers characteristically opposed physical violence, campaigning against corporal punishment of children, wives, sailors, and prisoners, for example. They preferred mental coercion like solitary confinement to flogging and hanging. They were didactic modernizers and civilizers who embodied their values in such institutional monuments as schools, universities, hospitals, and insane asylums.[18] Most extreme in their espousal of Victorian modernization were the abolitionists and the feminists. They applied the principles of human self-development, the fulfillment of noble potential and the repression of base passions, to different races and sexes alike.[19]

The usefulness of evangelical moral reform to the new industrial capitalism of the nineteenth century has not escaped the notice of historians, and a vast literature has developed, analyzing it in terms of bourgeois "social control." Pro-southern and anti-Whig historians have been using this approach to discredit abolitionists and other reformers for a long time.[20] But the interpretation took on new vigor with the reception of neo-Marxism and the social thought of Michel Foucault in the American academy during the mid-twentieth century. Its advocates have included Michael Katz, David J. Rothman, Paul Johnson, and—in its most sophisticated and broadly ranging form—David Brion Davis. Davis's monumental volumes on slavery and antislavery in the modern world accord full respect to the moral integrity of the abolitionists and the justice of their cause. But they also portray the abolitionists as inadvertently promoting the hegemony of bourgeois capitalism. Through natural human limitations coupled with a measure of self-deception, the reformers were blind to the full implications of what they were doing. Without their being aware of it, the antislavery crusaders were providing a moral sanction for new capitalist methods of exploitation. Their critique of chattel slavery indirectly legitimated wage slavery. In this interpretation, social control, if no longer a conscious motive, is no less a consequence of the reformers' actions and helps explain their success.[21]

The interpretation of antebellum reform as social control, in both its pre-Marxian and neo-Marxian forms, has provoked an enormous critical reaction. Typically, this criticism has argued that the reformers were motivated by moral principles rather than ambition for worldly power.[22] Many critics of the social control thesis have sought to explain the evangelicals' behavior in psychological, frequently psychoanalytic, categories. In this view, the goal of evangelical commitment was a new personal identity, rather than class interest. The most sophisticated such analysis of antebellum reformers in terms of their quest for identity is Lawrence J. Friedman's *Gregarious Saints: Self and Community in American Abolitionism*.[23] Anthropological categories have also been offered as an alternative to Marxian class analysis, as William G. McLoughlin did when he adapted the "revitalization" theory of A. F. C. Wallace to his study *Revivals, Awakenings, and Reform*. When Wallace himself turned to antebellum history in his community study of Rockdale, Pennsylvania, however, he combined anthropological thick description with a crudely Marxist historical narrative featuring evil Christian businessmen who first destroy their town's harmonious social relationships and then embark on a war of conquest over the South.[24]

The present state of historiography leaves unresolved two different perceptions of evangelical Christianity. The scholarship on the eighteenth century treats evangelical Christianity as a democratic and liberating force, whereas much of the literature on the evangelical movement of the nineteenth century emphasizes its implications for social control. Did some dramatic transformation of the revival impulse come about at the turn of the century? I would argue not; historians have concentrated on the soft and hard sides of evangelicalism in the eighteenth and nineteenth centuries, respectively, but both were consistently present. Evangelical Protestantism did not mysteriously mutate from a democratic and liberating impulse into an elitist and repressive one when it moved from the eighteenth to the nineteenth century. Austerity and self-discipline were present even in eighteenth-century evangelicalism; individual autonomy was asserted even in nineteenth-century evangelicalism. The problem is that our idea of social control, implying *one* person or group imposing constraints on *another*, is appropriate for some aspects of the reform impulse, like the treatment of the insane, but not all. It does not take account of the embrace of *self*-discipline, so typical of evangelicals.

The essence of evangelical commitment to Christ is that it is undertaken voluntarily, consciously, and responsibly by the individual for himself or herself. (That, after all, is why evangelicals, in any century, are not content to let a person's Christianity rest on baptism in infancy.) If we can substitute the more comprehensive category of "discipline" for that of "social control," we will be in a better position to understand the evangelical movement and the continuities between its colonial and antebellum phases. We will also be able to deal with the important psychological issues of personal identity that have been raised by the critics of the social control interpretation. Evangelical Christians were and are people who have consciously decided to take charge of their own lives and identities. The Christian discipline they embrace is at one and the same time liberating and restrictive. Insofar as this discipline is self-imposed, it expresses the popular will; insofar as it is imposed on others, it is social control.

The existing historical literature poses at least one other major problem. Conspicuously absent from the historiography until recently has been an approach that would acknowledge a relationship between evangelical reform and modern capitalism without using this connection to disparage reform. David Brion Davis, as we have seen, took the first step away from this, but he still regarded its connection with capitalism as a tragic limitation of nineteenth-century reform. A significant breakthrough has been achieved in this respect by Thomas Haskell. In a subtle and persuasive pair of articles, Haskell argues that nineteenth-century humanitarianism was the child of the capitalist system and of the market mentality *without* being an instrument of social control, intended or unintended. Haskell links humanitarian reform with the experience of the marketplace and the ideology of possessive individualism in two important ways: (1) the emphasis on covenants, or promise keeping, and (2) the emphasis on causal perception, which encouraged people "to attend to the remote consequences of their actions." These two cultural traits, he argues, expanded the "cognition" of the people living in the new world of capitalism, heightening their moral sensitivity and producing humanitarian reform. Where Davis saw humanitarianism helping capitalism, Haskell sees capitalism fostering humanitarianism. And where Davis linked the two through the mechanism of unconscious motivation, Haskell links them through an expansion of conscious awareness.[25]

Haskell has connected the mentality of nineteenth-century reform to the political economy of capitalism. The moral philosophy of the age, within which political economy was originally a subdivision, also shows the connection between nineteenth-century reform and the disciplined development of human potential.[26] Overall, the new understanding of "cognitive style" supplied by Haskell would appear to supplement but not supplant social control as an aspect of nineteenth-century reform. Haskell looks primarily at abolitionism, but the element of social control is undeniable in movements more closely connected with party politics than abolitionism was, movements like temperance, penal reform, or asylums for the insane. The progression from self-discipline/self-liberation to the benevolent discipline and liberation of others was natural and inevitable; indeed, the progression could also occur the other way around, notably in the case of women.[27] What needs to be found is a way of conceptualizing humanitarian reform that can subsume both social control and personal identity, as well as make profitable use of Haskell's discovery of the positive impact of modern capitalism on moral rationality and cognition. The study of discipline in the Puritan/evangelical religious tradition could provide the answer.

The cultural impulse toward discipline manifested in evangelicalism can be viewed (as its contemporary practitioners did) as a positive and humanizing goal, especially when placed in the context provided by antebellum moral philosophy. The converse of liberating a battered wife in Victorian America might well be imposing discipline on her drunken husband. While compatible with a capitalist system, evangelical moral discipline was by no means equivalent to a desire to strengthen the hand of capitalists within that system. To escape from the dilemma of equating evangelicalism simply with capitalist social control, there is something to be said for looking at nineteenth-century reform as an example of "modernization" rather than of "capitalism." Socialist modernizing societies, after all, found it just as necessary as did capitalist ones to impose new forms of discipline.[28]

Two works on the social history of Victorian Britain can provide models for an understanding of evangelical reform in America as well: Brian Harrison's study of temperance and Thomas Laqueur's study of Sunday schools. Both of them break free of the paradigm of social control by showing how the movements in question transcended class lines. These evangelical reform causes were as much the product of working-class self-help and the voluntary pursuit of order, dignity, and decency as they were of middle-class paternalism.[29] Once the autonomy of evangelical reform and its supporters has been recognized, we can then see how, in the world of the nineteenth century, they would sometimes be found supporting or encouraging capitalism and other times criticizing it or counteracting its consequences.[30]

Haskell has shown that the capitalist rationality of the marketplace fostered humanitarian reform by enhancing the conscious powers of moral perception. The next step, if this conceptual breakthrough is to be properly exploited, will be to see how his analysis of the origins of humanitarianism relates to the Christian tradition. We will never understand nineteenth-century reform in *merely* humanitarian or political terms. We must link humanitarian reform with the Christian tradition and its discipline. For it was the explosive combination of humanitarianism plus Christianity that gave the world the evangelical movement and its attendant reforms. The evangelical emphasis on conscious, voluntary decision and action represents a conjunction of Christianity with modernity. The new personal identity the evangelical attained was both follower of Christ *and* rational, autonomous individual—paradoxical as that may seem to some historians today. And in the America of the nineteenth century, it was the institutional and emotional resources of Christianity that typically empowered humanitarian reform.[31]

ECUMENICISM VERSUS CONFESSIONALISM

The evangelical movement of antebellum America was in many respects the functional equivalent of an established church. Although voluntary rather than compulsory in its basis, the evangelical movement shared with the traditional religious establishments of European countries the goal of a Christian society. For nineteenth-century evangelicals, this goal was defined as something to be achieved rather than something to be maintained. To meet the goal entailed a gigantic effort of organization.[32] The revival established what contemporaries called "a benevolent empire": an interlocking network of voluntary associations, large and small, local, national, and international, to implement its varied purposes. The objectives of these voluntary societies ranged from antislavery to temperance, from opposing dueling to opposing Sunday mails, from the defense of the family to the overthrow of the papacy, from women's self-help support groups to the American Sunday School Union, from the American Bible Society to the National Truss Society for the Relief of the Ruptured Poor.[33]

This organizing process was the religious counterpart of the so-called American system, the political program of Henry Clay and the Whig party. Both wanted to impose a system and direction upon the amorphousness of American society. Whether addressing religious and moral issues, on one hand, or banking, the tariff, internal improvements, and land sales, on the other, the evangelical movement and the American system stood for conscious planning and uniformity rather than laissez-faire and diversity. What is more, both put their trust in the same leadership class of prosperous mercantile laity.[34] One reason that the Whigs may have been slower than the Democrats to accept the legitimacy of political parties is that the Protestant benevolent societies provided Whigs with an alternative mode of organizing in pursuit of their social objectives. Certainly, the Whigs were no less "modern" than the Democrats in their outlook, no less "issue-oriented," and no less willing to make use of the new media of communications.[35] But the rise of political parties could only undercut the influence of the cause-oriented voluntary associations.

One of the features of the evangelical movement suggestive of an established church was its Protestant ecumenicism.[36] Led by laymen and, in a remarkable number of cases, laywomen, the evangelical movement was to a large degree emancipated from control by denominationally organized clergy. The laity was disposed toward interdenominational cooperation by considerations both practical and principled. In practical terms, ecumenicism made for efficiencies of scale. In ideological terms, it reflected a decline of interest in theological distinctions that had often formed the bases for denominational differentiation, accompanied by a rising sense of American nationality and national moral responsibility. For the American evangelical movement, the nation had taken on the character of a Christian community, within which members shared moral responsibility. This ecumenicism, along with much else about the Great Revival, was controversial. The First Awakening had split Americans into New Lights and Old, and the Second was every bit as divisive. Just as there were people who objected to the imposition of political control by the Whigs' American system, there were those who objected to the imposition of the religious and moral discipline of the evangelical movement. If the evangelical movement were the American religious "establishment," its opponents were the American "dissenters." J. C. D. Clark has reinterpreted English politics of the early nineteenth century in terms of religious ideological conflict between Anglicans and Dissenters.[37] There is good reason to believe that a somewhat analogous religious conflict was almost as central to political life in the United States.[38]

The opponents of the revival may be characterized as "confessionalists," people who attached primary importance to hearing witness to the truth as they saw it. They did not share in the declining interest in theological distinctions, and they were unwilling to subsume their differences under the ecumenical banner of the revival. Often their religious loyalties were underscored by ethnic identifications. Among these confessionalists were Roman Catholics, Old School Presbyterians, Missouri Synod Lutherans, Dutch "True" Calvinists, antimission Baptists, Latter-day Saints, and Orthodox Jews. (It is not entirely possible to define the opponents of the revival in denominational terms, since, as we have seen, its support was not defined in denominational terms either.) For our purposes, the handful of avowed freethinkers counts as confessionalists, since they too were critics of the revival. What all of these disparate groups had in common was a grim determination to preserve their independence in the face of the evangelical juggernaut.[39] To them, evangelical ecumenicism looked like religious imperialism. As the Jeffersonian Republicans had rallied deists and sectarians in opposition to the Anglican and Congregational establishments of the late eighteenth century, the Jacksonian Democrats became the party of those opposed to the ecumenical evangelical "establishment" of the antebellum era.[40]

Dedicated as they were to particularism and diversity, the confessional Democrats found doctrines of little government to be congenial. The natural rights philosophy of the Jacksonians asserted the individual's claims to be protected against interference from officious, ecumenical reformers. An emphasis on the separation of church and state was the logical complement of this philosophy, for it removed everything having to do with religion from the potential interference of government. The religious outgroups of the Jacksonian era were the heirs of the Jeffersonian Baptist John Leland. "Leland's legacy is an exaggerated opposition to official Christianity," writes Nathan Hatch. "He articulated a twofold persuasion that operated powerfully in the hinterland of Baptist church life: an aversion to central control and a quest for self-reliance."[41]

On the whole, historians of the Democratic party have found less reason to discuss religion than have historians of the Whig party. The political strategy of the Democrats—indeed, their very raison d'être—dictated a political secularism. Thus, for example, Jean H. Baker's fine study of the political culture of the antebellum northern Democrats scarcely mentions religion. Had she looked into the subject, Baker would probably have been led to a conclusion similar to that of Sean Wilentz, in his study of the New York City Working Men's party. Stressing the diversity of religious opinion among his subjects, Wilentz concludes that "the artisans' disparate religious views provided a rough analogue to their democratic politics, opposed to all men of 'insolent morality' who would ratify their presumed social superiority with the Word of God."[42] When the Working Men's party did not succeed as a separate organization, it merged into the Democratic party. The freedom such people prized was "freedom from," while the goal of the Whigs was "freedom to."

The initiative in the great competition between ecumenicals and confessionals lay with the evangelicals. One of the differences between that America and our own was the dominant culture-shaping power of antebellum evangelical Christianity. It was the evangelicals who then formed what Ronald P. Formisano has termed the "core" of the national culture; the confessionalists occupied the "periphery."[43] The analogy already suggested with the Whig economic program continues to be helpful: Schlesinger interpreted the politics of the Jacksonian age in terms of a conflict between the powerful "business community," on one hand, and all the other interest groups in society, on the other, forced to make common cause to protect themselves. In the cultural interpretation, the evangelicals become the counterparts of Schlesinger's business community, and the confessionalists, the alliance of outgroups. This analogy should not compel us to regard the confessionalists as the heroes of the story. But it should remind us not to focus exclusively on the evangelical core; the religions of the periphery do have a fascinating cultural history (or, rather, histories) of their own. How several such bodies have reinforced their identity by using mainstream American society as a negative reference group is the theme of R. Laurence Moore's book *Religious Outsiders*, a model study that avoids idealizing either side in the cultural conflict it portrays.[44]

The core-periphery metaphor has been applied to many other countries as well and lends itself to comparative study. One of the most interesting of the comparative treatments is Robert Kelley's *The Transatlantic Persuasion: The Liberal-Democratic Mind in the Age of Gladstone*. This work shows how the British Liberals, the Canadian Liberals, and the American Democrats were all parties of the ethnocultural periphery and therefore defenders of pluralism. Kelley's analogy between the American Whigs and the Anglo-Canadian Tory parties is less satisfactory, even though they did indeed all endorse national homogeneity. The difference is that in the British Empire, the evangelicals were part of the cultural periphery and aligned with the Liberal parties, whereas in the United States, the evangelicals defined the cultural core.[45]

The second party system was not based in theological differences, and although the debate between Calvinism and Arminianism was one of the most interesting and sophisticated features of "high" intellectual history in nineteenth-century America, it did not define the distinction between Democrats and Whigs. Certainly, there were Calvinists and Arminians in both political parties. A theological development that was relevant, however, was the emergence of postmillennialism in American Christian thought. This doctrine taught that Christ's Second Coming will occur at the end of the thousand years of peace foretold in scripture. The implication is that human efforts on behalf of social justice form part of the divine plan to bring about the day of the Lord. Postmillennialism became a prominent feature of the nineteenth-century evangelical movement.[46]

Of course, any major party in a two-party political system is bound to be a diverse coalition. The American Whig party included many voters who were not directly involved in the evangelical united front. Some of these Whigs shared in the perfectionist aspirations of the evangelicals but not in their creed—for example, Unitarians and Quakers. Sometimes excluded from evangelical organizations, these groups were particularly prominent in the more radical associations of the benevolent empire, addressing women's rights and antislavery. That such people became Whigs (and, later, Republicans) confirms that it was the perfectionism of the evangelicals rather than their theological orthodoxy that had political implications. Significantly, however, the heterodox perfectionists did not display as high a level of Whig party loyalty as the evangelicals, and they were often drawn into minor reform parties.[47]

The Whig party also included some people who were not evangelical even in a general sense of the term. Contemporaries were aware of this and took account of it; in the end, it became the basis for the important distinction they drew between "Conscience" Whigs and "Cotton" Whigs in the North. Cotton Whigs included groups that identified with the cultural core of bourgeois British-American Protestantism but remained critical of evangelical didacticism, especially the crusade against slavery. Episcopalians and Princeton Old School Presbyterians provide examples of this cultural conservatism. In general, such groups were not identified nearly as strongly with the Whig party as the revivalistic evangelicals were; many Episcopalians and Old School Presbyterians, for example, were Democrats. Some of them switched from Democratic to Whig affiliation only after large-scale Irish Catholic immigration had produced an important negative reference group for them.[48]

In the South, things were different—which is why this chapter can only deal with the North. In the South, the evangelicals had never established themselves as the cultural core. Instead, the core position was occupied by the planters. Their culture, as it has been portrayed by such sensitive historians as Rhys Isaac, Eugene Genovese, Dickson D. Bruce, and Bertram Wyatt-Brown, emphasized premodern values like honor, patriarchalism, generosity, physical violence, and hedonism.[49] Evangelicalism took shape in large part as a critique of these traditional values. Conflict between the two rival value systems of the gentry and their evangelical critics has been a perennial theme of southern cultural history. But the relative marginality of evangelical culture, like the relative marginality of the urban bourgeoisie in southern society, left the Whig party weaker in the South than it was in the North. Furthermore, the increasing identification of the Second Great Awakening with northern ecumenical didacticism in general and antislavery in particular alienated even devout pietists in the South. When secession finally came, it represented (as Joel Silbey has argued) the climax of southern resistance against the threatened cultural hegemony of northern Whig-Republicans.[50]

One of the most ambitious interpretations of the coming of the Civil War in terms of cultural conflict is that of the political scientist Anne Norton. Her book *Alternative Americas: A Reading of Antebellum Political Culture* emphatically affirms the centrality of the evangelical movement to northern Whig-Republican political culture. Norton demonstrates the importance of the Puritan tradition for northern Whig-Republicans and shows the use they made of analogies with the English Civil War and the example of Cromwell. She also properly stresses the difference between North and South over the discipline and subordination of the human "passions." What was wholesome discipline to the northern neo-Puritans represented tyranny to many white southerners. By the time she is finished, Norton has made it very clear why seceding southerners felt threatened by Yankee cultural imperialism.[51]

One of the most striking cultural contrasts between the sections in antebellum America lies in their receptivity to changing gender relationships. The Whig/northern modernizing culture placed a higher value on female self-expression than did the Democratic/southern traditional one. Women played a much more active leadership role in the northern evangelical movement than they did in the southern resistance to it. (Conversely, the southern cult of honor—among both the gentry and the common folk—placed more emphasis on the expression of physical "manliness" than northern culture did.) Northern Whig women like Harriet Beecher Stowe and Sarah Josepha Hale made popular literature an instrument of evangelical didacticism—in their own expression, a "moral influence."[52] The relationship between the evangelical movement and the empowerment of women has been one of the most rewarding areas of historical research since the mid-twentieth century.[53]

CONCLUSION: CULTURE AND PERSONALITY

In the middle period of American history, as today, the goal of the evangelical Christian was to be born again in Christ, to become a new person. The tradition of the Reformation, which the antebellum Whig party carried on, was concerned not only with culture and politics, but also with personality and personal discipline. In this tradition, public policies were frequently reflections of private concerns. Legal prohibition of alcohol as a political issue, for example, was an outgrowth of an evangelical disciplinary impulse that was originally voluntary and individual. The only way we can understand antebellum humanitarian reform, in my judgment, is to approach it through the study of the interaction between culture and personality. In *The Political Culture of the American Whigs,* I tried to show how the private struggles of prominent Whigs to shape their own personalities replicated the public conflicts of their time and the resolutions the Whig party offered for them. The model for this approach was defined originally by Erik Erikson in his classic studies of Luther and Gandhi.[54] It is one more way in which historians of antebellum culture have drawn on the insights of the social sciences.

The values that the evangelical Whig tradition sought to implement in the antebellum North derived from the conjunction of ancient Christianity with the modern market society. As Ruth Bloch also points out in her chapter in this volume, the Puritan/evangelical tradition did not simply adapt to, or borrow from, modernity and democracy; it actively helped to form them. Individualism, voluntarism, and contractualism were features of the Puritan/evangelical religious tradition before they were taken over by the secular political philosophers of possessive individualism. In antebellum America, the evangelical tradition continued to contribute to shaping the culture of the modern world. As a social force, the revival worked largely through the organizations of the "benevolent empire" and party politics, but also through the media of print and lecture circuit.

The political culture formed by the clash between the evangelical movement and its adversaries generated a high level of excitement and participation. Twentieth-century commentators sometimes felt that it generated altogether too much fervor, blaming this for moving the country toward bloody civil war. In other moods, however, present observers sometimes look back nostalgically on a political system that engaged the involvement of the public so much more effectively than does our own. We have learned to attribute the public spirit of antebellum and colonial America to the classical republican tradition.[55] But this secular tradition was complemented in important ways by the Puritan/evangelical religious tradition, which coexisted with it so often in the English-speaking world. Both traditions valued public virtue, private discipline, balanced government, and widespread participation.

As Tocqueville remarked, a host of issue-oriented voluntary associations connected individuals with public participation in antebellum America.[56] The evangelical benevolent empire was by far the largest network of these. It fostered a sense of active purposefulness among groups that had never experienced this before, notably women and free blacks. Whatever its implications for social control, evangelicalism also contributed to social empowerment, and the latter has been less thoroughly studied. Too often, historians have taken it for granted that the Democratic party was the only agency for broadening popular participation in antebellum public life. An innovative essay by Carroll Smith-Rosenberg is an example of how historians are breaking free from this limitation. She uses anthropological theory to describe the ways in which the Great Revival provided religious forms for female self-assertion in early capitalist America.[57]

Today, many people have difficulty accepting the legitimacy of religion in politics. Reflecting this attitude, some historians cannot rid themselves of the feeling that if the politics of the antebellum period were religiously motivated, then it must have been irrational or reactionary. Yet one could argue that American party politics worked at its best during the second party system, when levels of voter participation were the highest in history, when religious issues and organizations were most salient, and when popular interest and involvement were thereby engaged. It was a time of social innovation, and religion was at the cutting edge of this innovation. Far from being reactionary, the religion of the Great Revival was an engine driving rational change, a force of modernization. If there is a special service that historians who are themselves Christians can bring to understanding the American past, if they have in fact a particular responsibility to the scholarly community, it might well be to affirm and explain the political rationality of religious commitment.

NOTES

1. Arthur M. Schlesinger, Jr., *The Age of Jackson* (Boston: Little, Brown, 1945). The same blindness toward the significance of religion is apparent in Robert H. Walker, *Reform in America* (Lexington: University Press of Kentucky, 1985), the failure of which shows the hopelessness of trying to comprehend nineteenth-century reform in terms of twentieth-century liberalism. On the other hand, what is enduringly valid in the Progressive interpretation of the second party system may be seen in John Ashworth, *"Agrarians" and "Aristocrats": Party Political Ideology in the United States, 1837–1846* (London: Royal Historical Society, 1983).

2. Richard Hofstadter, *The American Political Tradition and the Men Who Made It* (New York: Knopf, 1948), esp. chs. 3 and 4. The implications of this "consensus" approach were made explicit by Edward Pessen, who asserted that there was nothing to choose between the Whig and Democratic parties and dismissed their avowed programs as dissimulation. See his *Riches, Class, and Power before the Civil War* (Lexington, Mass.: Heath, 1973) and *Jacksonian America: Society, Personality, and Politics,* rev. ed. (Homewood, Ill.: Dorsey, 1978), 197–260.

3. Richard P. McCormick, *The Second American Party System* (Chapel Hill: University of North Carolina Press, 1966). See also Robert E. Shalhope, "Jacksonian Politics in Missouri: A Comment on the McCormick Thesis," *Civil War History* 15 (1969): 210–25. For the "new political history," see Richard L. McCormick (son of Richard P.), *The Party Period and Public Policy* (New York: Oxford University Press, 1986); and Stephen Maizlish and John Kushma, eds., *Essays on American Antebellum Politics, 1840–1860* (Arlington: Texas A&M University Press, 1982). For a synthesis of the new

political history with an interest in ideology, see Michael Holt, *The Political Crisis of the 1850s* (New York: Wiley, 1978).

4. Lee Benson, *The Concept of Jacksonian Democracy: New York as a Test Case* (Princeton, N.J.: Princeton University Press, 1961). Reference group theory originated with the political scientist Herbert H. Hyman; see his "Reflections on Reference Groups," *Public Opinion Quarterly* 24 (1960): 383–96.

5. See Bertram Wyatt-Brown, "Prelude to Abolitionism: Sabbatarian Politics and the Rise of the Second Party System," *Journal of American History* 58 (1971): 316–41; Kathleen S. Kutolowski, "Antimasonry Re-Examined: The Social Bases of the Grass-Roots Party," *Journal of American History* 71 (1984): 269–93; David J. Russo, "Major Political Issues of the Jacksonian Period and the Development of Party Loyalty in Congress, 1830–1840," *Transactions of the American Philosophical Society* 62:5 (1972): 3–51; Richard Carwardine, "Evangelicals, Whigs and the Election of William Henry Harrison," *Journal of American History* 17 (1983): 47–75.

6. Robert Kelley, *The Cultural Pattern in American Politics: The First Century* (New York: Knopf, 1979); Michael Holt, *Forging a Majority: The Formation of the Republican Party in Pittsburgh* (New Haven, Conn.: Yale University Press, 1969); Daniel Walker Howe, *The Political Culture of the American Whigs* (Chicago: University of Chicago Press, 1979); William R. Brock, *Parties and Political Conscience: American Dilemmas, 1840–1850* (Millwood, N.Y.: KTO, 1979). The ethnocultural interpretation is assessed and contextualized in several of the essays in Robert P. Swierenga, ed., *Beyond the Civil War Synthesis: Political Essays of the Civil War Era* (Westport, Conn.: Greenwood, 1975).

7. Contrast, for example, the recognition of ideology in Samuel P. Huntington, "Paradigms of American Politics," *Political Science Quarterly* 89 (1974): 1–26, with the celebration of the nonideological nature of America in Daniel Boorstin, *The Genius of American Politics* (Chicago: University of Chicago Press, 1953).

8. For example, William Gienapp, *The Origins of the Republican Party* (New York: Oxford University Press, 1986); and Joel Silbey, *The Partisan Imperative: The Dynamics of American Politics before the Civil War* (New York: Oxford University Press, 1985).

9. Louise Stevenson, *Scholarly Means to Evangelical Ends: The New Haven Scholars and the Transformation of Higher Learning in America, 1830–1890* (Baltimore, Md.: Johns Hopkins University Press, 1986), 5–6. She makes reference to Richard Jensen, *The Winning of the Midwest* (Chicago: University of Chicago Press, 1971).

10. For example, Robert Bellah, *Habits of the Heart: Individualism and Commitment in American Life* (Berkeley: University of California Press, 1985); Peter Berger, *The Sacred Canopy: Elements of a Sociological Theory of Religion* (Garden City, N.Y.: Doubleday, 1967); John L. Hammond, *The Politics of Benevolence: Revival Religion and American Voting Behavior* (Norwood, N.J.: Ablex, 1979); Gerhard Lenski, *The Religious Factor: A Sociological Study of Religion's Impact on Politics, Economics, and Family Life*, rev. ed. (Garden City, N.Y.: Doubleday, 1963); Michael Walzer, *The Revolution of the Saints* (Cambridge, Mass.: Harvard University Press, 1965); Samuel P. Huntington, *American Politics: The Promise of Disharmony* (Cambridge, Mass.: Harvard University Press, 1981); J. David Greenstone, "Political Culture and

American Political Development," *Studies in American Political Development: An Annual* 1 (1986): 1–49; Mary Douglas, *Natural Symbols: Explorations in Cosmology* (New York: Pantheon, 1982); Victor Turner, *Image and Pilgrimage in Christian Culture: An Anthropological Perspective* (New York: Columbia University Press, 1978); Clifford Geertz, *The Interpretation of Cultures* (New York: Basic, 1973).

11. As the so-called revisionist historians of Civil War causation claimed; for example, James G. Randall, *Lincoln the Liberal Statesman* (New York: Dodd, Mead, 1947), 36–64.

12. Besides the Kutolowski article cited in note 5, above, writings on Antimasonry include Ronald P. Formisano and Kathleen S. Kutolowski, "Antimasonry and Masonry: The Genesis of Protest," *American Quarterly* 29 (1979): 139–65; William P. Vaughn, *The Anti-Masonic Party in the United States* (Lexington: University Press of Kentucky, 1983): and Paul Goodman, *Towards a Christian Republic: Antimasonry and the Great Transition in New England* (New York: Oxford University Press, 1988).

13. For an example of the first, see Ronald P. Formisano, *The Birth of Mass Political Parties: Michigan, 1827–1861* (Princeton, N.J.: Princeton University Press, 1971), 10–14; for the second, Eric Foner, *Politics and Ideology in the Age of the Civil War* (New York: Oxford University Press, 1980), 17–18. The third view is expressed by Richard L. McCormick in *Party Period and Public Policy*, ch. 1. Much of the secondary literature on the subject is characterized by an anti-Antimasonic bias and/or an unwillingness to consider the Antimasons rational.

14. John M. Murrin, "No Awakening, No Revolution? More Counterfactual Speculations," *Reviews in American History* 11 (1983): 161–71.

15. William Warren Sweet, *Religion in the Development of American Culture, 1765–1840* (New York: Scribner's, 1952); Perry Miller, *The Life of the Mind in America: From the Revolution to the Civil War* (New York: Harcourt, Brace & World, 1965); Richard Bushman, *From Puritan to Yankee: Character and the Social Order in Connecticut, 1690–1765* (Cambridge, Mass.: Harvard University Press, 1967); Patricia Bonomi, *Under the Cope of Heaven: Religion, Society, and Politics in Colonial America* (New York: Oxford University Press, 1986). A somewhat different version of the argument is made in Alan Heimert, *Religion and the American Mind: From the Great Awakening to the Revolution* (Cambridge, Mass.: Harvard University Press, 1966), which interprets revivalism as democratic and communitarian rather than democratic and individualistic.

16. See Stephen Botein, "Religious Dimensions of the Early American State," in *Beyond Confederation: Origins of the Constitution and American National Identity*, ed. Richard Beeman, Stephen Botein, and Edward C. Carter II (Chapel Hill: University of North Carolina Press, 1987), 315–30.

17. Terry Bilhartz, *Urban Religion and the Second Great Awakening* (Rutherford, N.J.: Fairleigh Dickinson University Press, 1986); Richard Carwardine, "The Second Great Awakening in the Urban Centers," *Journal of American History* 52 (1972): 327–40.

18. For themes touched on in this paragraph, see the essays in Daniel Walker Howe, ed., *Victorian America* (Philadelphia: University of Pennsylvania Press, 1976): and Myra Glenn, *Campaigns against Corporal Punishment: Prisoners, Sailors, Women, and Children in Antebellum America* (Albany: State University of New York Press, 1984).

19. On the abolitionists as modernizers opposed by traditionalists, see Leonard Richards, *"Gentlemen of Property and Standing": Anti-Abolition Mobs in Jacksonian America* (New York: Oxford University Press, 1970); on feminism as modernization, see Amy Dru Stanley, "Ideas and Practice of Freedom of Contract: Wage Labor and Marriage in Late 19th-Century America" (Ph.D. diss., Yale University, 1988).

20. For example, Avery Craven, *The Coming of the Civil War* (New York: Scribner's, 1942); Charles C. Cole, *The Social Ideas of the Northern Evangelists* (New York: Columbia University Press, 1954); and Clifford Griffin, "Religious Benevolence as Social Control," *Mississippi Valley Historical Review* 44 (1957): 423–44.

21. Michael Katz, *The Irony of Early School Reform* (Cambridge, Mass.: Harvard University Press, 1968); David J. Rothman, *The Discovery of the Asylum* (Boston: Little, Brown, 1971); Paul Johnson, *A Shopkeeper's Millennium* (New York: Hill and Wang, 1978); David Brion Davis, *The Problem of Slavery in the Age of Revolution* (Ithaca, N.Y.: Cornell University Press, 1975), esp. 251–54 and 346–57. See also Davis, *Slavery and Human Progress* (New York: Oxford University Press, 1984), 109.

22. An excellent introduction to this issue is Martin J. Wiener, ed., "Humanitarianism or Control? A Symposium on Aspects of Nineteenth-Century Social Reform in Britain and America," *Rice University Studies* 67 (1981): 1–84. See also Martin Duberman, ed., *The Antislavery Vanguard* (Princeton, N.J.: Princeton University Press, 1965); Lois Banner, "Religious Benevolence as Social Control: A Critique of an Interpretation," *Journal of American History* 60 (1973): 34–41; and James B. Stewart, *Holy Warriors: The Abolitionists and American Slavery* (New York: Hill and Wang, 1976).

23. Lawrence J. Friedman, *Gregarious Saints: Self and Community in American Abolitionism, 1830–1870* (Cambridge: Cambridge University Press, 1982). Other outstanding studies are Waldo E. Martin, Jr., *The Mind of Frederick Douglass* (Chapel Hill: University of North Carolina Press, 1984); Robert Abzug, *Passionate Liberator: Theodore Dwight Weld and the Dilemma of Reform* (New York: Oxford University Press, 1980); and Lewis Perry, *Radical Abolitionism: Anarchy and the Government of God in Antislavery Thought* (Ithaca, N.Y.: Cornell University Press, 1973).

24. McLoughlin, *Revivals, Awakenings, and Reform* (Chicago: University of Chicago Press, 1978); A. F. C. Wallace, *Rockdale: The Growth of an American Village in the Early Industrial Revolution* (New York: Knopf, 1978).

25. Thomas Haskell, "Capitalism and the Origins of the Humanitarian Sensibility," *American Historical Review* 90 (1985): 339–61 and 547–66. See also the illuminating forum discussion among Haskell, Davis, and John Ashworth, *American Historical Review* 92 (1987): 797–878.

26. See Daniel Walker Howe, *The Unitarian Conscience: Harvard Moral Philosophy, 1805–1861*, rev. ed. (Middletown, Conn.: Wesleyan University Press, 1988). All three participants in the forum discussion cited in n. 25, above, raise issues involving moral philosophy.

27. On the way, evangelical benevolent societies developed women's sense of their own identity; see Nancy F. Cott, *The Bonds of Womanhood: "Woman's Sphere" in New England, 1780–1835* (New Haven, Conn.: Yale University Press, 1977), 126–59; and Mary P. Ryan, *Cradle of the Middle Class: The Family in Oneida County, 1790–1865* (Cambridge: Cambridge University Press, 1981).

28. Notwithstanding the criticism to which modernization theory has been subjected, historians of the nineteenth century continue to salvage and employ to advantage the concept of modernization. See Eric Foner, "The Causes of the Civil War: Recent Interpretations and New Directions," in Swierenga, *Beyond the Civil War Synthesis*, 15–32; James M. McPherson, *Ordeal by Fire: Civil War and Reconstruction* (New York: Knopf, 1982), ch. 1; Daniel Walker Howe, "Victorian Culture in America," in his *Victorian America*, 3–28; and Richard D. Brown, *Modernization: The Transformation of American Life, 1600–1865* (New York: Hill and Wang, 1976).

29. Brian Harrison, *Drink and the Victorians* (London: Faber & Faber, 1971); Thomas Laqueur, *Religion and Respectability: Sunday Schools and Working Class Culture, 1780–1850* (New Haven, Conn.: Yale University Press, 1976).

30. Timothy Smith's classic *Revivalism and Social Reform in Mid-19th-Century America* (New York: Abingdon, 1957) celebrates the autonomy of the evangelicals, though within the framework of a consensus approach to American history that now seems dated.

31. For example, there were virtually no white abolitionists for whom religion was not a central element in their rejection of slavery. Blacks could formulate an antislavery position without invoking religion, but whites could not. On the importance of the evangelical network of voluntary associations for empowering nineteenth-century reformers, see Bellah, *Habits of the Heart*.

32. See Donald G. Mathews, "The Second Great Awakening as an Organizing Process," *American Quarterly* 21 (1969): 23–44; and Robert Wiebe, *The Opening of American Society* (New York: Knopf, 1984), 229–32.

33. Besides works cited earlier, see Charles I. Foster, *An Errand of Mercy: The Evangelical United Front, 1790–1837* (Chapel Hill: University of North Carolina Press, 1960); Richard L. Power, "A Crusade to Extend Yankee Culture," *New England Quarterly* 12 (1940): 638–53; W. J. Rorabaugh, *The Alcoholic Republic* (New York: Oxford University Press, 1979); and Ronald G. Walters, *American Reformers, 1815–1860* (New York: Hill and Wang, 1978).

34. See Bertram Wyatt-Brown, *Lewis Tappan and the Evangelical War against Slavery* (Cleveland, Ohio: Case Western Reserve University Press, 1969); Peter Dobkin Hall, *The Organization of American Culture: Private Institutions, Elites, and the Origins of American Nationality* (New York: New York University Press, 1982); and Robert F. Dalzell, Jr., *Enterprising Elite: The Boston Associates and the World They Made* (Cambridge, Mass.: Harvard University Press, 1987).

35. See, for example, David Paul Nord, "Evangelical Origins of Mass Media in America, 1815–1835," *Journalism Monographs* 88 (1984): 1–30; and Gregory H. Singleton, "Protestant Voluntary Organizations and the Shaping of Victorian America," in Howe, *Victorian America*, 47–58.

36. Sidney Mead, *The Lively Experiment: The Shaping of Christianity in America* (New York: Harper & Row, 1963).

37. J. C. D. Clark, *English Society, 1688–1832: Ideology, Social Structure, and Political Practice during the Ancient Regime* (New York: Cambridge University Press, 1985).

38. Besides the works of Benson and Formisano already cited, see esp. Robert P. Swierenga, "Ethnocultural Political Analysis," *Journal of American Studies* 5 (1971): 59–79; and Kelley, *The Cultural Pattern*.

39. On the distinction between confessionalists and evangelicals, there is a substantial literature. For its origins, see esp. Benton Johnson, "Ascetic Protestantism and Political Preference," *Public Opinion Quarterly* 26 (1962): 35–46; Paul Kleppner, *The Cross of Culture: A Social Analysis of Midwestern Politics* (New York: Free Press, 1970); and Richard Jensen, "Religious and Occupational Roots of Party Identification," *Civil War History* 16 (1970): 325–43.

40. See William G. McLoughlin, *New England Dissent, 1630–1833: The Baptists and the Separation of Church and State*, 2 vols. (Cambridge, Mass.: Harvard University Press, 1970).

41. Nathan Hatch, "The Democratization of Christianity and the Character of American Politics," ch. 5 in this volume.

42. Jean H. Baker, *Affairs of Party: The Political Culture of the Northern Democrats in the Mid-Nineteenth Century* (Ithaca, N.Y.: Cornell University Press, 1983); Sean Wilentz, *Chants Democratic: New York City and the Rise of the American Working Class* (New York: Oxford University Press, 1984), 86.

43. Ronald P. Formisano, *The Transformation of Political Culture: Massachusetts Parties, 1790s–1840s* (New York: Oxford University Press, 1983).

44. R. Laurence Moore, *Religious Outsiders and the Making of Americans* (New York: Oxford University Press, 1986).

45. Robert Kelley, *The Transatlantic Persuasion: The Liberal-Democratic Mind in the Age of Gladstone* (New York: Knopf, 1969). Other important comparative works include Seymour M. Lipset and Stein Rokkan, eds., *Party Systems and Voter Alignments: Cross-National Perspectives* (New York: Free Press, 1967); and Michael Hechter, *Internal Colonialism: The Celtic Fringe in British National Development, 1536–1966* (Berkeley: University of California Press, 1975).

46. See Ernest L. Tuveson, *Millennium and Utopia* (Berkeley: University of California Press, 1949); and James Moorhead, *American Apocalypse: Yankee Protestants and the Civil War* (New Haven, Conn.: Yale University Press, 1978).

47. Some historians use the words "pietism" or "devotionalism" to refer to the religious qualities that have such political implications, but I find these words too vague; as I understand the terms, confessionalists can be pietists and devotionalists too.

48. The writings of Robert Kelley are the best source for information on the politics of Old School Presbyterianism. For the impact of Irish Catholic immigration on Scots-Irish Old School Presbyterian voters, see Kelley, *The Cultural Pattern*, 170–74. See also Paul Kleppner, *The Third Electoral System, 1853–1892: Politics, Voters, and Political Cultures* (Chapel Hill: University of North Carolina Press, 1979), 164, 174, 177, 186.

49. Rhys Isaac, *The Transformation of Virginia, 1740–1790* (Chapel Hill: University of North Carolina Press, 1982); Eugene Genovese, *The Political Economy of Slavery* (New York: Pantheon, 1965); Dickson D. Bruce, *Violence and Culture in the Antebellum South* (Austin: University of Texas Press, 1979); Bertram Wyatt-Brown, *Southern Honor: Ethics and Behavior in the Old South* (New York: Oxford University Press, 1982).

50. See Bertram Wyatt-Brown, "The Antimission Movement in the Jacksonian South," *Journal of Southern History* 36 (1970): 501–29; Wyatt-Brown, *Yankee Saints and Southern Sinners* (Baton Rouge: Louisiana State University Press, 1985); Joel Silbey, "The Surge of Republican Power: Partisan Antipathy, American Social Conflict, and

the Coming of the Civil War," in Maizlish and Kushma, *Essays on American Antebellum Politics.*

51. Anne Norton, *Alternative Americas: A Reading of Antebellum Political Culture* (Chicago: University of Chicago Press, 1986).

52. On women and the moral goals of literary culture, see Jane Tompkins, *Sensational Designs: The Cultural Work of American Fiction* (New York: Oxford University Press, 1985); and William R. Taylor's enduring book, *Cavalier and Yankee: The Old South and American National Character* (New York: Braziller, 1961). Ann Douglas, *The Feminization of American Culture* (New York: Knopf, 1977), argues that the rise of women's cultural power took place at the expense of the clergy.

53. Besides the books of Nancy Cott and Mary Patricia Ryan cited already in n. 27 above, see, for example, Carroll Smith-Rosenberg, *Religion and the Rise of the City* (Ithaca, N.Y.: Cornell University Press, 1971), 97–124; Ross Paulson, *Women's Suffrage and Prohibition* (Glenview, Ill.: Scott, Foresman, 1973); Ellen DuBois, *Feminism and Suffrage: The Emergence of an Independent Women's Movement in America* (Ithaca, N.Y.: Cornell University Press, 1978); and Blanche Hersh, *The Slavery of Sex: Feminist Abolitionists in 19th Century America* (Urbana: University of Illinois Press, 1978).

54. Erik Erikson, *Young Man Luther: A Study in Psychoanalysis and History* (New York: Norton, 1958); Erikson, *Gandhi's Truth* (New York: Norton, 1969).

55. The seminal work is, of course, J. G. A. Pocock, *The Machiavellian Moment: Florentine Political Thought and the Atlantic Republican Tradition* (Princeton, N.J.: Princeton University Press, 1975). Republicanism and its relationship to liberalism have been more thoroughly explored by historians for the period before 1815 than after, but see Michael Holt, *The Political Crisis of the 1850s* (New York: Wiley, 1978); Howe, *Political Culture of the American Whigs*; Steven Watts, *The Republic Reborn: War and the Making of Liberal America, 1790–1820* (Baltimore, Md.: Johns Hopkins University Press, 1987); and Dorothy Ross, "Liberalism," in *Encyclopedia of American Political History*, ed. Jack P. Greene (New York: Scribner's, 1984), 1:750–63.

56. Alexis de Tocqueville, *Democracy in America*, 2 vols. (New York: Knopf, 1945), 1:198–205 and passim.

57. Carroll Smith-Rosenberg, "The Cross and the Pedestal: Women, Anti-Ritualism, and the Emergence of the American Bourgeoisie," in her *Disorderly Conduct: Visions of Gender in Victorian America* (New York: Knopf, 1985), 129–64.

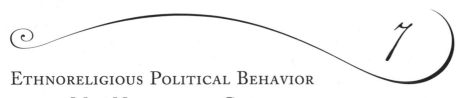

Ethnoreligious Political Behavior in the Mid-Nineteenth Century
Voting, Values, Cultures

Robert P. Swierenga

*T*HE MOST EXCITING development in American political history since the 1960s is the recognition that religion was the key variable in voting behavior until at least the Great Depression. The move to restore religion to political analysis gained momentum slowly in the 1940s and 1950s through the work of the eminent scholars Paul Lazarsfeld, Samuel Lubell, and Seymour Martin Lipset, and it culminated in the 1960s when historians Lee Benson and Samuel Hays brought the new perspective to a generation of graduate students.[1] By the 1970s, this so-called ethnocultural (or ethnoreligious)[2] interpretation of voting behavior had become the reigning orthodoxy, having supplanted the populist-progressive paradigm that "economics explains the mostest," to quote Charles Beard.[3] By the early 1980s, a resurgent neoprogressive, or "new Left," historiography, led by cultural Marxists, had challenged the ethnoreligious interpretation, but the edifice, which stands on solid research at the grassroots, remains largely intact.[4]

This chapter summarizes the accumulated evidence in support of the thesis that religion was the salient factor in nineteenth-century voting behavior. How and why religion was at the center is extremely complex, as are the related issues of

documentation and measurement. There were also regional and temporal variations in the role of religion in politics. Nevertheless, despite its limitations, a
theological interpretation of voting behavior offers a refreshing new angle to our
understanding of political culture in the eras of Andrew Jackson and Abraham
Lincoln.

THE REDISCOVERY OF RELIGION

The revolution in American political history began when Lazarsfeld and his
associates at the Bureau of Applied Social Research at Columbia University
systematically surveyed voters during the 1940 presidential election campaign in
Erie County, Ohio. To their surprise, they found that voters were most influenced
by their churches or, in sociological jargon, their "social reference groups." Protestants and Catholics clearly differed in voting and party identification, even when
controlling for socioeconomic factors.[5] In one giant step, Lazarsfeld and associates
had brought into political analysis the religious variable that had been jettisoned
by the first generation of professional historians and political scientists in the late
nineteenth century. The prevailing wisdom was encapsulated in James Bryce's terse
assertion in 1894: "Religion comes very little into the American party."[6] Sectional
economic rivalries, class conflicts, and melting pot doctrines were the reigning
orthodoxies following the influential historians Frederick Jackson Turner and
Charles Beard. Why the rising professoriate was blind to expressions of religious
values in politics is complex. Put simply, they were highly secularized and believed
religion should be privatized and church and state kept totally separate. The doctrine of the melting pot, then dominant, also held that ethnic and religious differences were narrowing in society and politics.

So strong was this thinking in the twentieth century that political pollsters
of the modern era never considered religious questions when gathering data on voting behavior. George Gallup, the first professional pollster and himself a Protestant churchgoer, did not ask respondents for their church affiliation until after
Lazarsfeld published his 1940 study, *The People's Choice*, in 1944. Indeed, when
Lazarsfeld told Gallup of his startling finding, Gallup expressed disbelief.[7] As late
as 1959, during the Kennedy-Nixon presidential race, Elmo Roper, another leading
pollster, challenged the "myth of the Catholic vote" and denied any connection
between religion and voting.[8] The pollsters' skepticism gave way when Lipset, the
prestigious director of the Institute of International Studies at the University of
California, Berkeley, further documented the place of religion in American culture and politics. But Lipset still deferred to the long-dominant neo-Marxist

paradigm then in its declension. Religion did not "explain everything," he allowed; class position was equally determinative.[9]

The next challenge to the liberal paradigm carried the day. In 1961, Lee Benson, a young historian who had studied nineteenth-century voting patterns at Lazarsfeld's bureau in the mid-1950s, published one of the most significant books in American political history, *The Concept of Jacksonian Democracy: New York as a Test Case.* Benson began his research as a convinced economic determinist, but his analysis of group voting behavior led him to develop a sociological-psychological model based on ethnoreligious conflict. His key conclusion is the now-classic statement: "At least since the 1820s, when manhood suffrage became widespread, ethnic and religious differences have tended to be *relatively* the most important source of political differences in the United States." Benson made no attempt to prove his proposition other than to demonstrate its validity in the 1844 presidential election in New York state. Intuitively, he felt that this theory conformed to common sense. "Since the United States is highly heterogeneous, and has high social mobility," he reasoned, "I assume that men tend to . . . be more influenced by their ethnic and religious group membership than by their membership in economic classes or groups."[10]

Within a decade, a host of historians led by Benson and Hays completed additional research for various northern states that generally confirmed the religious dimension. These publications, which employed quantitative and social science methods and theories, demonstrated that religion and ethnicity were basic to American voting patterns.[11] This finding should not have been surprising. Foreign observers of America in the nineteenth century, such as Alexis de Tocqueville, had remarked often about the high religiosity of American society, especially after the Second Great Awakening filled empty churches with new converts. As Richard Jensen has stated: "The most revolutionary change in nineteenth century America was the conversion of the nation from a largely dechristianized land in 1789 to a stronghold of Protestantism by mid-century. The revivals did it." By 1890, church affiliation was above 70 percent in the Midwest, with the new revivalist sects and churches claiming over half. The revivals sparked confrontation in every denomination. Again quoting Jensen: "Until the mid-1890s the conflict between pietists and liturgicals was not only the noisiest product of American religion, it was also the force which channeled religious enthusiasm and religious conflicts into the political arena."[12] This was all the more true because the militant evangelicals sought to link Christian reform and republicanism into an unofficial Protestant establishment that virtually equated the kingdom of God with the nation.[13]

FROM RELIGION TO POLITICS: VALUES AND CULTURE

The mechanism for translating religion into political preferences is complicated and much disputed. Lazarsfeld, Lipset, Lubell, Benson, and Hays all stressed the socialization process.[14] Individuals learned attitudes and values early in life from family, church, and community, which then shaped their perceptions of the larger world and gave them ethical values to live by. Persons, if you will, absorbed voting habits with their mother's milk, and these subconscious dispositions were later reinforced by the parson's sermons and the wisdom of the brethren. One political party was "right," the other "wrong." Parties were bound to conflict in a society flooded by wave after wave of immigrants. Each ethnoreligious group had its own social character, historical experience, and theological beliefs. Each had its friends and enemies or, in Robert K. Merton's words, its positive and negative reference groups.[15] Irish Catholics, for example, reacted against hostile New England Protestants, who tended to be Whigs, by joining the Democratic party. Then, new British immigrants voted Whig because Irish Catholics voted Democratic, and so on.

The ethnoreligious thesis, on one level, shifted the focus from national to local issues and from elites to the behavior of voters at the grassroots. At a deeper level, it substituted religious culture for class conflict and sectionalism as a significant independent variable in voting choices. As Hays explained simply: "Party differences in voting patterns were cultural, not economic." "Ethnocultural issues were far more important to voters than were tariffs, trusts, and railroads. They touched lives directly and moved people deeply."[16] Instead of battles in Washington and in statehouses over economic benefits and favors, ethnoreligionists stress fights over the prohibition of alcohol, abolition of slavery, Sunday closing laws, parochial-school funding, foreign-language and Bible usage in public schools, anti-Catholic nativism and alien suffrage, sexual conformity and capital punishment, and a host of lesser crusades. The point of the new view is that moral rather than economic issues impelled nineteenth-century voters and produced the major political conflicts. Instead of being assimilated, ethnoreligious groups clung to their customs, beliefs, and identities for generations, and as they clashed over public policy at the polls, their values and attitudes were hardened, reshaped, or mellowed, depending on changing historical circumstances. Nevertheless, these structural differences remained deep-rooted. As Lipset noted, this made "religious variation a matter of political significance in America."[17]

Political socialization of individuals and structural conflict among social groups may explain how voters absorbed their values and prejudices and had them reinforced as groups fought to defend or advance their interests in the political arena; but this does not explain why particular ethnoreligious groups voted as they did. Why were Irish Catholics Democrats and New England Congregationalists Whigs and Republicans?

Ethnoreligionists have offered at least three distinct but often intertwined theories to explain how religious group impulses became political ones. Benson emphasized reference group theory, especially negative reactions. While valid in limited historical settings, such as Boston in the 1840s when Irish Catholic immigrants overran this Anglo-Protestant center, reference group theory is rather limited and simplistic, especially the notion that group members merely "absorb" political ideas and "react" to other groups. Hays added a refinement, that of group hegemonic goals, which he called the "social analysis of politics."[18] Ethnoreligious groups use political means to try to extend the domain of their cultural practices or, conversely, to protect themselves from legal or legislative attacks. As Catholic Irish and German immigrants seemed to inundate the United States, for example, native-born Protestants turned to nativist laws to keep Catholic Sabbath desecration or beer drinking in check. Again, this social approach begs the question of the sources of differing lifestyles. If groups clashed because of historic antagonisms and conflicting cultural traditions, it was because their religious roots differed.[19]

This led to the third theory, that "theology rather than language, customs, or heritage, was the foundation of cultural and political subgroups in America," to quote Richard Jensen.[20] "Political choices were thus derived from beliefs about God, human nature, the family, and government. Citizens were not robots, but reflective beings whose value system had been 'sanctified' by their family, friends, and congregations."[21] Different ways of living and voting derive from different ways of believing. Moral decision making rests on religious values, theological distinctions, or, more broadly, world views.[22]

Paul Kleppner cogently explained the nature of belief. Religion "involves a rationale for existence, a view of the world, a perspective: for the organization of experience; it is a cognitive framework consisting of a matrix within which the human actor perceives his environment." Although it is not the only perspective, it "penetrates all partial and fragmentary social worlds in which men participate; it organizes and defines how they perceive and relate to society in general." Religiosity, Kleppner continued, comprises five core dimensions: belief, knowledge, practice, experience, and consequences. Various denominations emphasize different dimensions and their linkages, and out of these come behavioral differences. Historically, the two broad clusters of denominations are the pietists, who move from belief to experience and consequences, and the liturgicals, who tie belief to knowledge and practice.[23]

It must be admitted that any attempt to explain voting behavior on the basis of Christian theology, liturgy, or lifestyle is a sticky wicket. Voters, because their minds and wills are innately flawed, do not *always* act consistently with their ultimate beliefs. They may be cross-pressured by competing and conflicting religious "oughts." Finney evangelicals, for example, worked to free slaves but not women. Voters may delude themselves and vote their pocketbooks while claiming to follow ethical principles. Churches and historical issues and pressures also changed over time, and generalizations are thus necessarily limited in time and place.[24] Scholars have also struggled with theological typologies that can adequately categorize the many denominations according to their various belief systems.

THE LITURGICAL-PIETIST CONTINUUM

Kleppner and Jensen offered the first sophisticated religious theory of American voting in the nineteenth century. Based on a wide reading in the sociology of religion and the history of individual denominations and groups, they developed the ritualist-pietist, or liturgical-pietist, continuum, which locates ethnoreligious groups and denominations along a single dimension based on the central tendency of their theological orientation.[25] On one side were ecclesiastical, ritualistic, and liturgically oriented groups; and on the other were the sectlike evangelicals or pietists who stress a living, biblical faith and the imminent return and rule of the Messiah. The liturgical churches (such as the Roman Catholic, Episcopal, and various Lutheran synods) were creedally based, sacerdotal, hierarchical, nonmillennial, and particularistic. These ecclesiasticals were ever vigilant against state encroachment on their churches, parochial schools, and the moral lives of their members. God's kingdom was otherworldly, and human programs of conversion or social reform could not usher in the millennium. God would restore this inscrutable, fallen world in his own good time and in his own mighty power.

The pietists (Baptists, Methodists, Disciples, Congregationalists, Quakers) were New Testament–oriented, antiritualist, congregational in governance, active in parachurch organizations, and committed to individual conversion and societal reform in order to usher in the millennial reign of Jesus Christ. Pietists did not compartmentalize religion and civil government. Right belief and right behavior were two sides of the same spiritual coin. The liturgicals excommunicated heretics; the pietists expelled or shunned sinners.

These theological differences directly affected politics in the Jacksonian era because the Yankee pietists launched a crusade to Christianize America, and the liturgicals resisted what they viewed as enforced Anglo conformity.[26] The pietists staged a two-pronged public program. First, they created the "benevolent empire" in the 1810s to spread the gospel and teach the Bible. Then, in the 1820s, they established reform societies to eradicate slavery, saloons, Sabbath desecration, and other social ills. Finally, in the 1830s, they entered the political mainstream by joining the new Whig party coalition against the Jacksonian Democrats. By the 1840s, in fear of the growing Catholic immigrant menace, they added nativist legislation to their agenda, especially by extending the naturalization period from five to fourteen years. As the reform-minded Yankees threatened to gain control of the federal and state governments through the Whig party and, after 1854, the Republican party, the liturgicals, who were mainly immigrants, fought back through the Democratic party.

Why the liturgicals joined the Democrats and the more pietist Christians gravitated to the Whig and Republican parties requires a brief explanation of party ideologies and programs. With Thomas Jefferson as its patron saint and Andrew Jackson as its titular head, the Democratic party from its inception in the 1820s espoused egalitarian, libertarian, and secularist goals.[27] The Democrats were so-cial levelers who believed in a limited, populist government and a society rooted in self-interest and individual autonomy. They sought a secular state that did not try to legislate social behavior and was free of church control.[28] An editorial in an Ohio Democratic newspaper condemned all reform movements that were mo-tivated by "ascetic law, force, terror, or violence," and a Michigan editor declared: "We regard a man's religious belief as concerning only himself and his Mak-er." Government must thus restrain all economic power brokers and promote a laissez-faire society. Democratic theorists like George Bancroft believed that "the voice of the people is the voice of God."[29] The highest good was universal male suffrage, majoritarian rule, a nonexploitative society, and a government that granted no undue favors. The Democrats easily attracted immigrants from the beginning and always stood for cultural and ethnic diversity.[30]

The opposition Whig party was more elitist, paternalistic, cosmopolitan, entrepreneurial, and legalistic.[31] This "Yankee party" viewed government posi-tively, trusted the governors more than the governed, and believed in absolute law based on eternal verities. The goal of the northern Whigs was to enlist all Christians and their clerical leaders who sought collectively to promote moral behavior and social harmony.[32] The Whigs, said Robert Kelley, were "the party of decency and respectability, the guardians of piety, sober living, proper manners, thrift, steady habits, and book learning."[33] The Whig agenda of building a "righ-teous empire" (to use the apt title of a Martin Marty book) received a tremendous boost initially from the Second Great Awakening. Indeed, without the spiritual revivals, the Whig leaders could not have built a viable mass party. Later, in the 1840s, the backlash against mass immigration and the perceived Irish menace further strengthened the Anglo Whig party. When Bishop John Hughes of New York City objected to the reading of the King James Bible in the public schools as an attempt to proselytize Catholic children and tried to obtain public funding for Catholic schools, Protestant leaders became alarmed and worked through the Whig party to enact nativist laws to weaken or contain the Catholic threat.[34] To Yankees, the Irish were English "blacks," social pariahs who were now infesting Protestant America.[35]

Given these opposing ethnoreligious groups, it is not surprising that historians find many links between religion and politics. Liturgicals demanded maximum personal freedom and state neutrality regarding personal behavior. They tended to find a congenial home in the Democratic party. Pietists, who felt an obligation to "reach out and purge the world of sin," found in the Whigs a vehicle to accomplish this.[36] Paul Kleppner's generalization is the standard summary of the ethnoreligious thesis: "The more ritualistic the religious orientation of the group, the more likely it was to support the Democracy; conversely, the more pietist the group's outlook the more intensely Republican its partisan affiliation."[37] In short, "the primary cleavage line of party oppositions . . . pitted evangelical pietistics against ritualistic religious groups."[38]

Was this political and social conflict between religious groups rooted in simple ethnic and religious prejudices and differing lifestyles, or did a theological cleavage underlie the behavioral distinctions? Some scholars (Benson and Formisano, for example) stress the clash of cultures, the historic reference group hatreds and prejudices, the group defenses and hegemonic goals. Although there is no dearth of historical evidence for such a pattern of brokenness in American history, it does not mean that human behavior is usually (or always) unthinking, reactive, and culturally determined. As noted earlier, to explain that German Catholics supported the Democrats because that party opposed prohibition and Quakers voted Whig and Republican because that party favored prohibition is not to explain the behavior at all. To claim that Irish Catholics voted Democratic because they hated Yankee Whigs does not explain the source of the prejudice. The reason that people voted this way ultimately lies deeper than symbols or culture; it is rooted in religious world views.[39] People act politically, economically, and socially in keeping with their ultimate beliefs. Their values, mores, and actions, whether in the polling booth, on the job, or at home, are outgrowths of the god or gods they hold at the center of their being.

In a nation of immigrants, where members of ethnoreligious groups often live out their daily lives together in churches, schools, societies and clubs, work and play, and marriage and family life, group norms are readily passed from parents to children, along with a strong sense of identity and a commitment to their political and social goals. Such groups are understandably ready to promote or defend their beliefs when public policy issues arise that touch their lives directly. Religious issues, more than social class, status, or sectional interests, are at the crux. As Kleppner asserts: "Attachments to ethnoreligious groups were *relatively* more important as determinants of nineteenth-century social-group cohesiveness and party oppositions than were economic attributes or social status." Notice the word *relatively*. Ethnoculturalists have not claimed that their findings *exclusively* explain mass voting patterns, only that differing religious beliefs *best* explain that behavior.[40] They also recognize that in the South the race issue was paramount.

Ethnoculturalists also recognize that cross-pressures and particular historic contexts may change patterns or create unique situations.[41] The Pella (Iowa) Dutch pietists continued to vote Democratic after the Civil War when other Dutch Reformed colonies in the Midwest switched en masse to the Republicans. The nativist attacks on the community in the 1850s had been too strong and bitter to forget.[42]

MEASUREMENT PROBLEMS

Having explained the religious roots of voting behavior, I now turn to the pithy question Lee Benson first posed in 1957: "Who voted for whom, when?"[43] How ethnoreligious group members voted is a factual question that requires an empirical answer.[44] While the question is straightforward, finding the answers has been very difficult. Two basic measurement problems keep cropping up. The first is to determine the religious affiliation of party members and voters, and the second is to measure the extent to which religious values acted in conjunction with socioeconomic and other factors to determine voting behavior.

Identifying the religion of voters is by far the more difficult problem. Federal census publications did not report the number of church members or communicants until the 1890 census. Beginning in 1850, however, the census enumerated church seating capacity per community. Since "sittings" were not directly proportionate with membership, particularly in the Catholic church, some scholars estimated pre-1890 membership by assuming that the 1890 ratio of members to sittings was a reasonable approximation of the earlier ratio.[45] Some scholars simply used sittings or an even cruder measure, the number of church buildings.[46] It is also recognized that church attendance consistently exceeded membership, but nominal and occasional members likely shared the values and world views of full members.[47]

In some areas, local sources such as county biographical directories occasionally stated the religious affiliation of family heads.[48] But one had to pay to be listed in these "mug books," so they did not include all potential voters. Poll books of active voters survive in some counties, and when they are collated with church membership records, it is possible to determine precisely the religion of voters.[49] Such individual-level data are ideal, but rare. One scholar estimated Catholic strength in minor civil divisions by collating the names of fathers and godfathers listed in baptism records with names in federal census records, multiplying by the ratio of births per adult member (15:1 in 1860), and thus determining the Catholic population per ward.[50]

Another common method of estimating religion was to note the state or county of birth in the manuscript censuses (recorded from 1850 on) as a proxy for ethnoreligious identity, and then to locate "homogeneous" counties or preferably townships and wards, that is, communities that were predominantly German Lutheran, Dutch Reformed, Swedish Lutheran, New England Yankee, and so on. The voting behavior in these homogeneous townships is then taken to represent the voting of the entire group in a state or region.[51] Critics have charged that such communities were atypical, because group pressures would be unduly strong there. Would a German Lutheran living in a largely German village in Wisconsin vote differently than a fellow church member who was living among Irish Catholics in Chicago?

The alternative to finding homogeneous areas is to estimate the relative proportion of ethnoreligious groups per county for an entire state or section of the country, either in whole or by sampling. The ideal, which no one has yet attempted, is to draw a random township and ward sample of the northeastern United States, compile township-level aggregate data on religion, ethnicity, occupation, wealth, and other pertinent variables in the period 1850–1900, and then, using multiple regression analysis, determine the relative relationships between religion and voting, taking into account the effects of all of the other variables.[52] Until such a large project is undertaken, we must rely upon the several dozen case studies at the state and local level completed in the mid-twentieth century. These studies cover the years from 1820 to 1900 in the northeastern and midwestern states.[53]

ETHNORELIGIOUS GROUPS

Although regional variations existed, the findings generally agree in the political categorization of the major ethnoreligious groups. The various groups can best be arranged in four categories: strongly Democrat (75+ percent), moderately Democratic (50–75 percent), moderately Whig or Republican (50–75 percent), and strongly Whig or Republican (75+ percent) (see Table 7.1). Strongly

Democratic groups were all Catholics (Irish, German, French, French Canadian, Belgian, Bohemian, etc.), Southern Baptists, and southern Methodists. Moderately Democratic groups were old (i.e., colonial) German Lutheran, old German and old Dutch Reformed, old British Episcopalians, New England Universalists, southern Presbyterians, and southern Disciples of Christ. Moderately Whig and Republican in their voting were the German pietist sects (Brethren, Mennonites, Moravians, Amish), new German and Danish Lutheran, new Dutch Christian Reformed, Old School Presbyterians, regular and missionary Baptists, midwestern Universalists, and the Christian church. Strongly Whig and Republican were northern Methodists (including Irish, Cornish, and Welsh Methodists), Free Will Baptists, Congregationalists, New School Presbyterians, Scots-Irish Presbyterians, Unitarians, Quakers, French Huguenots, Swedish and Norwegian Lutherans, Haugean Norwegians, new Dutch Reformed, Canadian English and New England Episcopalians, and black Protestants. (Groups designated "old" immigrated prior to the American Revolution; "new" arrived afterward.)

The ethnoreligious specialists deserve credit for discovering these group voting patterns. Some distinctions are extremely subtle. For example, among Michigan's Dutch Calvinist immigrants of the mid-nineteenth century, the majority group affiliated with the largely Americanized old Dutch Reformed church in the East in 1850, but a minority opposed the union, seceded, and formed an independent immigrant church, the Christian Reformed church. One of the major doctrinal issues in the split was the conviction of the seceders that the Dutch Reformed espoused a revivalist free-will theology and used evangelical hymns and other "tainted" aspects of Yankee pietism.[54] In their politics, Kleppner found that the Dutch Reformed after the Civil War consistently voted Republican more strongly than did the Christian Reformed (66 percent versus 59 percent).[55] Even among a homogeneous immigrant group like the Dutch Calvinists, the inroads of revivalism strengthened commitments to the Yankee political party.

Religion and Politics

Not only for the Dutch Calvinists but for all ethnoreligious groups, revivalism was the "engine" of political agitation.[56] Evangelist Charles G. Finney began preaching revival in the mid-1820s throughout New England and its Yankee colonies in western New York. By 1831, religious enthusiasm had reached a fever pitch in the area, and mass conversions swept town after town. Church membership doubled and tripled, and large portions of the populace were reclaimed for Protestantism. Finney challenged his followers to pursue "entire sanctification" or perfectionism and to become Christian social activists. The converts first entered

TABLE 7.1. Political Orientation of Major Ethnoreligious Groups, 1830–1890

Strongly Whig/Republican 75–100%	Moderately Whig/Republican 50–75%
Quaker	Christian Church (Disciples)
Scots-Irish Presbyterian	Missionary Baptist
Free Will Baptist	Regular Baptist
Congregationalist	Universalist (midwestern)
New School Presbyterian	Old School Presbyterian
Unitarian	New German Lutheran
Northern Methodist	Danish Lutheran
Irish Methodist	German Pietists
Cornish Methodist	Amish
Welsh Methodist	Brethren
Swedish Lutheran	Mennonite
Norwegian Lutheran	Moravian
Haugean Norwegian	New Dutch Christian Reformed
New England Episcopal	
Canadian English Episcopal	
New Dutch Reformed	
French Huguenot	
Black Protestants	

Strongly Democratic 75–100%	Moderately Democratic 50–75%
Irish Catholic	Old British Episcopal
German Catholic	Southern Presbyterian
French Catholic	Universalist (New England)
Bohemian Catholic	Southern Disciples of Christ
French Canadian Catholic	Old German Lutheran
Southern Baptist	Old German Reformed
Southern Methodist	Old Dutch Reformed

Sources: works cited in note 11, especially Kleppner, *Cross of Culture* and *Third Electoral System*; Jensen, *Winning of the Midwest*; and Formisano, *Birth of Mass Political Parties*.

politics in the anti-Masonic movement in New York in 1826–1827. By the mid-1830s, the evangelicals entered national politics by opposing slavery, alcohol, and other social ills that they believed the Jackson administration condoned. Converts such as Theodore Dwight Weld became leaders in the antislavery movement. And in the 1840s and 1850s, revivalist regions of the country developed strong antislavery societies and voted Liberty, Whig, and later Republican.[57] Ultimately, the allegiance of pietists to the Whig party led to its demise because the pietists put ethical goals, such as abolition of slavery, above party loyalty. The idea of a party system built on patronage and discipline was much stronger in Democrat than in Whig ranks. Evangelicals had a disproportionate share of antiparty men. In their estimation, popery, Masonry, and party were all threats to freedom of conscience and Christian principles.[58]

The disintegration of the Whig party in the early 1850s, followed by the brief appearance of the Know-Nothings and then of the new Republican party, and the fissure of the Democratic party in 1860 were the main components of the political realignment of the decade. The second electoral system gave way to the third system. But "Yankee cultural imperialism," now expressed through the Republican party, continued as the dynamic force, carrying out God's will against racists and other sinners in the Democratic party. Broadly speaking, in the third electoral era, pietist religious groups, both native born and immigrant, led the Republican party against antipietist Democrats.[59]

The 1860 presidential election signaled the future direction of the social bases of partisanship. Catholic groups of all ethnic backgrounds and across all status levels voted more solidly Democratic than ever before. Meanwhile, some former Democrats moved toward the Republicans, notably Yankee Methodists and Baptists and pietistic Norwegians, Dutch Reformed, and Germans.[60] The increasingly Catholic character of the Democrats, as well as that party's presumed responsibility for the Civil War, drove these Protestants away.

The impact of religious conflict on voting behavior in the 1860 Lincoln-Douglas election is illustrated in Cleveland, Ohio, in a study by Thomas Kremm.[61] Although founded by New England Yankees, Cleveland lay astride the immigrant route from New York to points west, and by 1860 the majority of the population was foreign born. Roman Catholic immigrants, mainly German and Irish, comprised 30 percent of the population in 1860. Catholics numbered more than half the population in two wards (out of eleven in the city) and just under half in another ward.

The influx of Catholics in the 1840s and 1850s led to a nativist backlash. To the Protestant majority, Catholics were un-American; they rejected the "public religion" of the republic. Moreover, the Catholic church was an "undemocratic engine of oppression." As the editor of the Cleveland *Express* declared: "Roman Catholics, whose consciences are enslaved, . . . regard the King of Rome—the Pope—as the depository of all authority."[62] Religious tensions were also stirred by Catholic opposition to public-school tax levies, by their "European" use of the Sabbath for recreation, and by their consistent bloc voting for the Democrats. Irish Catholics, charged the editors of the Cleveland *Leader*, "were sots and bums who crawled out of their 'rotten nests of filth' on election days to cast 'ignorant' ballots for the candidates of the 'slavocracy.' These 'cattle' lured to the polls by huge quantities of whisky, worshipped the three deities of the Ruffian Party—the Pope, a whisky barrel, and a nigger driver."[63]

This level of invective suggests that the Cleveland electorate divided along Catholic versus non-Catholic lines, rather than over slavery extension. Voting analysis of the 1860 election proves this. The percentage of Catholic voters per ward and the Douglas vote were almost perfectly correlated. Similarly, the percentage of non-Catholic voters and the Lincoln vote were almost perfectly correlated. Even when removing the effects of ethnicity, occupation, and wealth, religion explains over 80 percent of the variation across wards in the Republican and Democratic percentages. Religion, Kremm concluded, was the "real issue," the "overriding factor determining party preference in 1860." Catholics voted for the Democratic candidate, Stephen Douglas, and non-Catholics, irrespective of other socioeconomic factors, voted for Abraham Lincoln.[64]

The rise of the Republican party in Pittsburgh in the 1850s is similar to the Cleveland story. As Michael Holt discovered, the Republican coalition rose on a wave of anti-Catholic sentiment among native-born Protestants, which flared on issues of Sabbatarian laws and parochial schools. The growing Irish and German Catholic population increasingly voted the Democratic ticket. Holt's careful statistical correlations between voting patterns and the ethnoreligious and economic characteristics of the city's wards revealed:

> [E]conomic issues made no discernible contribution to Republican strength. . . . Instead, social, ethnic, and religious considerations often determined who voted for whom between 1848 and 1861. Divisions between native-born Americans and immigrants and between Protestants and Catholics, rather than differences of opinion about the tariff or the morality of slavery, distinguished Whigs and Republicans from Democrats.[65]

The temperance issue and other social concerns, except the abolition of slavery, lessened during the war years, but in the early 1870s, legal moves against alcohol and saloons resurfaced. The Republicans, who were generally supportive, lost voting support over temperance agitation. The Yankee party also had a negative fallout from the economic depression set off by the financial panic of 1873.[66] The Democrats, meanwhile, benefited from the Catholic fertility "time bomb" that exploded in the 1870s. The relative strength of the ritualists thus grew at the expense of the pietists. In 1860, pietists outnumbered ritualists nationwide by 21 percentage points (50 to 29 percent), but by 1890 pietists led by only 5 percent (40 to 35). The population increase among pietist groups averaged 2.4 percent per year, compared with 5.3 percent among liturgicals (and 6.2 percent among Catholics).[67]

Out of political desperation, as well as concern for the moral decline in American society, the Republican pietists in the 1870s and 1880s revived the "politics of righteousness"—Sabbatarian and temperance laws, anti-Catholic propaganda, and defense of Protestant public schools and English-only language instruction. Despite these efforts, the Democrats, bolstered by the solid South, surged after 1876, winning three of four presidential elections by close margins. In effect, the northern supporting groups held steady in both camps for several decades until the major realignment of the 1890s caused a "cross of culture." In the political upheaval of the nineties, William Jennings Bryan molded the old Democracy into a new "party of reform," and William McKinley redirected the Republicans into a middle-of-the-road position that fought against silver coinage rather than alcoholic beverages.[68]

CONTRIBUTIONS AND CRITIQUE

There are many positive results of the ethnoreligious interpretation of past American voting behavior. Most important is the realization that religious beliefs significantly affected mass voting behavior. Religious groups and political parties had a symbiotic relationship. Churches influenced political agendas by determining that slavery or alcohol or some other moral problem required legislative action.[69] Parties, in turn, built constituencies from various religious groups whose world views jibed with the party's programs and goals. The relationship between religion and politics was so close in the nineteenth century that Kleppner rightly called the parties "political churches" and their ideologies "political confessionalism."[70]

The ethnoreligionists had made their case convincingly, even to the point of "boredom and hostility," in the words of a Marxist reviewer. By 1970, religion had become the new orthodoxy in voting studies. As critic James Wright admitted, members of the new school had "done their work well. It is virtually impossible to avoid their frame of reference."[71] Since the mid-1970s, political historians have had to *disprove* the salience of religion and culture as major explanations of voting patterns. Even the cultural Marxists have factored religious forces into their economic models.[72]

Second, the ethnoreligious research shifted attention from the national to the local level, from political elites to voters at the grassroots. This radically different perspective, working from the bottom up, brought great excitement to the new political history in the 1960s and 1970s and sparked many new studies.[73]

Unfortunately, the momentum slipped in the 1980s. There have been few major research studies since Kleppner's *Third Electoral System* appeared in 1979 and Formisano's *Transformation of Political Culture* in 1983. Must we agree with Jean Baker that "the limits have been reached," or with Richard McCormick that ethnoreligious political analysis "as originally conceived, was at a dead end" by the late 1970s?[74] I think not, and neither does McCormick, who has been a cogent critic. The ethnocultural interpretation received a boost in the 1980s from new scholarship, which blended the political ideology of republicanism and the rising forces of capitalism with the social analysis of politics.[75] Moreover, the best work since the mid-1970s has incorporated more sophisticated statistical techniques (multivariate correlation and regression analysis, partialing, path analysis) that explain the relationship between voting choices and occupation, wealth, status, religion, and ethnicity. These studies proved again that the politics of "Amens and Hallelujahs" determined voting behavior more than did class and status variables.[76]

Critics have leveled against the ethnoreligionists many charges, a few of which are valid but most are not. Unsubstantiated charges are that they are monocausalists who have exaggerated the religious variable to the point of "religious determinism," that they have a "fixation" with vague "symbolic" aspects of politics while ignoring concrete issues, that they are ahistorical in treating religion independently of time and place, that they ignored the unchurched or nominally churched half of the population, that their statistical methods were weak and misguided, and that their case study approach was not representative of the nation at large.[77] The cultural Marxists have also reiterated their a priori assumptions about the centrality of economic factors.[78]

There are, however, two valid criticisms—one relates to the religious model and the other involves research design. Most important is the pietist-liturgical continuum, which predicted how doctrinal beliefs were translated into voting patterns. It is inadequate not because religious beliefs were "seldom dominant" in voting decisions, as one critic charged, but because ultimate values and beliefs, which are always dominant in human decision making, are too complex for a one-dimensional, either-or scale. In his 1979 book, Kleppner offered a more complex model that treated the pietistic and ritualistic perspectives as "more-or-less" characteristic of the various denominations rather than divided into two mutually exclusive types. He also drew distinctions among pietists between northern "evangelicals" and southern "salvationists," and among ritualists between Lutherans and Catholics, centering on the extent to which these groups compartmentalized the sacred from the secular. The sharper the division, the less moral legislation.[79]

But this more sophisticated model still fails to incorporate necessary distinctions among northern evangelical pietists: mainline denominations such as Congregationalists, perfectionist denominations such as Wesleyan Methodists, primitivist denominations such as the Churches of Christ, and separatists such as the Amish.[80] Issues of theology, polity, and praxis separate these groups, and we still need a model that incorporates these complexities and yet is sufficiently simple to be useful in research (the jargon is "operational"). Kleppner's newer model points in the right direction. The relationship of the church to the world is crucial, as H. Richard Niebuhr explained in his book *Christ and Culture*.[81] Niebuhr identified five historic views: Christ *against* culture, Christ in *agreement* with culture, Christ *above* culture, Christ in *tension* with culture, and Christ *transforming* culture. While Niebuhr's categories need revision, especially since the current religious Right has made a shambles of the opposition view which stressed separation from culture, the key issue remains: how do persons of faith relate to the political world? Specialists in American religious history could make a major contribution to political history by developing a usable theological topology.

The other challenge is for energetic political historians with good statistical skills to undertake the massive study for which J. Morgan Kousser called in 1979.[82] This is to validate the ethnoreligious interpretation by drawing random area samples of rural townships and city wards, gathering all relevant socioeconomic facts for several decennial census years in the nineteenth century for these areas, and then making multivariate statistical tests to uncover the key determinants of voting behavior. Such a study might well yield a more generalized model of American voting behavior. It might even convince skeptics that religious institutions and values have counted heavily in American politics and American history generally.

Religion, we now know, was the "stuff of political choice" in the nineteenth century, shaping issues, rhetoric, and party alignments.[83] Churches were primary value-generating institutions, and religious beliefs inevitably affected political choices and goals. Voters responded to the theological outlook toward culture of their particular denominations, encouraged by ingroup pressures and the influence of pastors and teachers. For opening this long-overlooked component of American political history, the ethnoreligious scholars deserve accolades. Until proven otherwise by new research, the legacy of their work stands.

NOTES

1. Joel H. Silbey, Allan G. Bogue, and William H. Flanigan, eds., *The History of American Electoral Behavior* (Princeton, N.J.: Princeton University Press, 1978), 3–27, and references cited therein; Allan G. Bogue, "The New Political History of the 1970s," in Bogue, *Clio and the Bitch Goddess: Quantification in American Political History* (Beverly Hills, Calif.: Sage, 1983), 113–35. See also Bogue, "Inside the 'Iowa School,'" in ibid., 19–50, esp. 22–24; Seymour Martin Lipset, "Religion and Politics in the American Past and Present," in *Religion and Social Conflict*, ed. Robert Lee and Martin E. Marty (New York: Oxford University Press, 1964), 69–126; Samuel Lubell, *The Future of American Politics* (Garden City, N.Y.: Doubleday Anchor, 1956), 129–57; Lee Benson, "Research Problems in American Political Historiography," in *Common Frontiers of the Social* Sciences, ed. Mira Komarovsky (Glencoe, Ill.: Free Press, 1957), 113–83; Benson, *The Concept of Jacksonian Democracy: New York as a Test Case* (Princeton, N.J.: Princeton University Press, 1961); Samuel P. Hays, "History as Human Behavior" (1959) and "New Possibilities for American Political History: The Social Analysis of Political Life" (1964), reprinted in Hays, *American Political History as Social Analysis* (Knoxville: University of Tennessee Press, 1980), 51–65, 87–132; Richard L. McCormick, "Ethnocultural Interpretations of Nineteenth Century American Voting Behavior" (1974), in McCormick, *The Party Period and Public Policy: American Politics from the Age of Jackson to the Progressive Era* (New York: Oxford University Press, 1986), 29–63.

2. Lawrence H. Fuchs coined the term "ethnoreligious" in 1956 because of its "inclusive quality"; it incorporated ethnic groups such as the Irish, religious groups such as Jews and Quakers, and even racial groups such as blacks. See Fuchs, *The Political Behavior of American Jews* (Glencoe, Ill.: Free Press, 1956), 13. Another early analysis of the influence of religion in American voting is Benton Johnson, "Ascetic Protestantism and Political Preference," *Political Science Quarterly* 26 (1962): 35–46.

3. Silbey et al., *American Electoral Behavior*, 20, 253–62; Robert P. Swierenga, "Ethnocultural Political Analysis: A New Approach to American Ethnic Studies," *Journal of American Studies* 5 (1971): 59–79; Samuel T. McSeveney, "Ethnic Groups, Ethnic Conflicts, and Recent Quantitative Research in American Political History," *International Migration Review* 7 (1973): 14–33; McCormick, "Ethnocultural Interpretations." A perceptive analysis of the evolving ethnic component of religion is Harry S. Stout, "Ethnicity: The Vital Center of Religion in America," *Ethnicity* 2 (1975): 204–24.

4. The best summary of the literature is Richard L. McCormick, "The Social Analysis of American Political History—after Twenty Years," in McCormick, *Party Period*, 89–140.

5. Lipset, "Religion and Politics," 70; Silbey et al., *American Electoral Behavior*, 12–13.

6. Quoted in Richard Jensen, "The Religious and Occupational Roots of Party Identification: Illinois and Indiana in the 1870s," *Civil War History* 16 (1970): 325.

7. Lipset, "Religion and Politics," 120n2.

8. Elmo Roper, "The Myth of the Catholic Vote," *Saturday Review of Literature*, 31 Oct. 1959, p. 22.

9. Lipset, "Religion and Politics," 71, 120–21.

10. Benson, *Concept of Jacksonian Democracy*, 165.

11. The core studies are Paul Kleppner, *The Cross of Culture: A Social Analysis of Midwestern Politics, 1850–1900* (New York: Free Press, 1970); Richard J. Jensen, *The Winning of the Midwest: Social and Political Conflict, 1888–96* (Chicago: University of Chicago Press, 1971); and Ronald P. Formisano, *The Birth of Mass Political Parties: Michigan, 1827–1861* (Princeton, N.J.: Princeton University Press, 1971). Other major additions are Paul Kleppner, *The Third Electoral System, 1853–1892: Parties, Voters, and Political Cultures* (Chapel Hill: University of North Carolina Press, 1979); and Ronald P. Formisano, *The Transformation of Political Culture: Massachusetts Parties, 1790s–1840s* (New York: Oxford University Press, 1983). Although omitted in this chapter, Jews also exhibited bloc voting for Jeffersonian Republicans and Jacksonian Democrats in the early republic, and after the 1840s they switched and became solidly Republican until the New Deal. See William Ray Heitzmann, *American Jewish Voting Behavior: A History and Analysis* (San Francisco: R&E Research Associates, 1975).

12. Jensen, *Winning of the Midwest*, 62, 63–64. The exceptional religiosity of American life is also described in Seymour Martin Lipset, *The First New Nation* (New York: Basic, 1963), ch. 4, "Religion and American Values," 140–69.

13. George M. Marsden, *The Evangelical Mind and the New School Experience* (New Haven, Conn.: Yale University Press, 1970), 239–42, relying on Perry Miller.

14. Benson, *Concept of Jacksonian Democracy*, 281–87; Hays, "New Possibilities," 104–16; Hays, *American Political History*, 13–36, 132–56; Lipset, "Religion and Politics," 21, 111–20.

15. Derived from Merton's observation that "men frequently orient themselves to groups *other than their own* in shaping their behavior and evaluations," in *Social Theory and Social Structure* (Glencoe, Ill.: Free Press, 1957), 288.

16. Hays, "History as Human Behavior" (1959), in Hays, *American Political History*, 54; and Hays, "Political Parties and the Community Society Continuum" (1967), in ibid., 300.

17. Lipset, "Religion and Politics," 71.

18. Benson, *Concept of Jacksonian Democracy*, 27, 281–87; Hays, "History as Human Behavior," 66, 87, and passim.

19. McCormick, "Ethnocultural Interpretations," 39–47, perceptively explains that the ethnocultural scholars somewhat carelessly intermixed these three theories.

20. Jensen, *Winning of the Midwest*, 82, 89.

21. Kleppner, *Cross of Culture*, 37, 75; Kleppner, *Third Electoral System*, 183–97; Formisano, *Birth of Mass Political Parties*, 102, 55; Jensen, *Winning of the Midwest*, 58, 88.

22. Kleppner, *Third Electoral System*, 183, following Milton Rokeach, J. Milton Yinger, Rodney Stark, Charles Glock, Peter Berger, and other psychologists and sociologists of religion. While acknowledging religious values, some scholars believe that political parties took shape independently and then they either attracted or repelled religious groups, depending on their platforms and programs. This is only a variant on the interest group interpretation. See John Ashworth, *"Agrarians" and "Aristocrats": Party*

Political Ideology in the United States, 1837–1846 (London: Royal Historical Society, 1983), 219–21. Churches preceded parties in America, and it is also logical to assume that religious preference preceded partisan preference. Jensen, *Winning of the Midwest*, 59.

23. Kleppner, *Third Electoral System*, 183–85.

24. Kleppner makes this point forcefully in ibid., 357–82.

25. Kleppner, *Cross of Culture*, 71–72; Kleppner, *Third Electoral System*, 185–89; Jensen, *Winning of the Midwest*, 63–67. A contemporary scholar, Robert Baird, in *Religion in America* (New York: Harper & Row, 1844), 220, divided all denominations into "evangelical" and "unevangelical." Scholars have struggled with other terms to identify the same distinction: Benson, Puritan/non-Puritan (*Concept of Jacksonian Democracy*, 198); Formisano, evangelical/antievangelical (*Birth of Mass Political Parties*, 138) and center/periphery (*Transformation of Political Culture*, 5–7, passim); Philip R. VanderMeer, church/sect ("Religion, Society, and Politics: A Classification of American Religious Groups," *Social Science History* 5 [1981]: 3–24); Roger D. Peterson, traditionalist/pietist ("The Reaction to a Heterogeneous Society: A Behavioral and Quantitative Analysis of Northern Voting Behavior, 1845–1870, Pennsylvania: A Test Case" [Ph.D. diss., University of Pittsburgh, 1970]); Edward R. Kantowitz, insider/outsider and dogmatist/pietist ("Politics," in *Harvard Encyclopedia of American Ethnic Groups*, ed. Stephan Thernstrom, Ann Orlov, and Oscar Handlin [Cambridge, Mass.: Harvard University Press, 1980], 803–4). Benson and Formisano are more reluctant than the other scholars cited to associate liturgical and pietist values with theology rather than to offer sociological explanations. See McCormick, *Party Period*, 48.

26. Alternatively, some have argued that the Jacksonians were rationalistic, republican nation builders who enlisted Protestant imagery and symbols in order to legitimate and unify the "new experiment in self-government" and create a "public religion," to use Benjamin Franklin's phrase. Sidney Mead argues that in the second half of the nineteenth century, Protestantism was amalgamated with "Americanism" to form an all-encompassing "civil religion," the "Religion of the Republic." See Martin E. Marty, *Pilgrims in Their Own Land: Five Hundred Years of Religion in America* (New York: Viking Penguin, 1984), 154–66; Sidney E. Mead, *The Lively Experiment: The Shaping of Christianity in America* (New York: Harper & Row, 1963), 134–87; and Marsden, *Evangelical Mind*, 239–41.

27. This paragraph and the following rely heavily on Robert Kelley, *The Cultural Patterns in American Politics: The First Century* (New York: Knopf, 1979), chs. 5–8, esp. 160–70, 223–27; and Ashworth, *"Agrarians" and "Aristocrats."*

28. Georgetown *Democratic Standard*, 12 Sept. 1843, as quoted in Stephen C. Fox, "The Bank Wars, the Idea of 'Party,' and the Division of the Electorate in Jacksonian Ohio," *Ohio History* 88 (1979): 257; Ann Arbor *Michigan Argus*, 1 Feb. 1843, quoted in Formisano, *Birth of Mass Political Parties*, 110.

29. See Bancroft, "The Office of the People in Art, Government and Religion," *Literary and Historical Miscellanies* (New York: Harper and Brothers, 1855), 408–35, excerpted in Joseph L. Blau, *Social Theories of Jacksonian Democracy: Representative Writings of the Period, 1825–1850* (Indianapolis, Ind.: Bobbs-Merrill, 1954), 263–73;

and quotes in Arthur M. Schlesinger, Jr., *The Age of Jackson* (Boston: Little, Brown, 1945), 419.

30. Kelley, *Cultural Patterns*, 147; Ashworth, *"Agrarians" and "Aristocrats,"* 178.

31. The best analysis of Whig culture and ideology is Daniel Walker Howe, *The Political Culture of the American Whigs* (Chicago: University of Chicago Press, 1979).

32. The Reverend Ezra Stiles Ely, pastor of Philadelphia's Third Presbyterian Church, was one such cleric who called for a Christian citizens' movement, a loosely organized *"Christian party in politics,"* to influence Christians to vote for avowed Christian candidates. Ezra S. Ely, *The Duty of Christian Freemen to Elect Christian Rulers* (Philadelphia, 1827), cited in John R. Bodo, *The Protestant Clergy and Public Issues, 1812–1848* (Princeton, N.J.: Princeton University Press, 1954). See also Benson, *Concept of Jacksonian Democracy*, 199–200.

33. Kelley, *Cultural Patterns*, 160–69.

34. Sydney E. Ahlstrom, *A Religious History of the American People* (New Haven, Conn.: Yale University Press, 1972), 559–63.

35. Kelley, *Cultural Patterns*, 172.

36. Jensen, *Winning of the Midwest*, 67–68.

37. Kleppner, *Cross of Culture*, 72–75; Kleppner, *Third Electoral System*, 74, 360–63; Jensen, *Winning of the Midwest*, 69; Formisano, *Birth of Mass Political Parties*, 128, 324, 330; and Benson, *Concept of Jacksonian Democracy*, 198–207.

38. Kleppner, *Third Electoral System*, 363.

39. Ibid., 363–64. McCormick allows that religious beliefs explain the political behavior of pietists but not liturgicals, who simply acted in self-defense. Their world view, says McCormick, had "no political significance until they were assaulted by pietists" (*Party Period*, 367). But it is illogical to hold that pietist theology was intrinsically political and liturgical theology was intrinsically apolitical. Liturgicals were on the defensive in the antebellum era because the Great Awakening impelled revivalists toward social activism. In the Progressive Era, however, pietist fundamentalists made the "great reversal" and withdrew from political life, while the liturgicals launched the Social Gospel movement. See David O. Moberg, *The Great Reversal: Evangelicalism versus Social Concern* (Philadelphia: Lippincott, 1972).

40. Kleppner, *Third Electoral System*, 371, 359–61. Kelley, *Cultural Patterns*, 164, speaks of a "marginal preponderance."

41. Kleppner, *Third Electoral System*, 363.

42. Ibid., 363–71, 167–68; Robert P. Swierenga, "The Ethnic Voter and the First Lincoln Election," *Civil War History* 11 (1965): 27–43, reprinted in Frederick C. Luebke, ed., *Ethnic Voters and the Election of Lincoln* (Lincoln: University of Nebraska Press, 1971), 129–50.

43. Benson, "Research Problems," 122.

44. See Kleppner, *Third Electoral System*, 9–15, 322–31, 355–73, and passim for a discussion of the concept of social group.

45. Kleppner, *Third Electoral System*, 204–5; Jensen, *Winning of the Midwest*, 85–87. Dale Baum, "The 'Irish Vote' and Party Politics in Massachusetts, 1860–1876," *Civil War History* 26 (1980): 120, argues that systematic underenumeration in counting "seats," especially for Catholic churches, which served several groups of parishioners,

would "make no difference" in statistical analyses. Formisano is unduly pessimistic when he says: "religion counted for very much in politics, [but] it is almost impossible to measure precisely religious affiliation among the electorate" (*Transformation of Political Culture*, 289–90). Formisano was more favorable earlier. See his "Analyzing American Voting, 1830–1860: Methods," *Historical Methods Newsletter* 2 (Mar. 1969): 1–12. The censuses of "social statistics" from 1850 list each church by denomination in every town and give the number of "accommodations" or "seats" in each building. The percentage of each denomination's seats of the total seats indicates the "religious preferences" of each township.

46. Peterson, "Reaction to a Heterogeneous Society."

47. Lipset, "Religion and Politics," 101–2.

48. Jensen, "Religious and Occupational Roots," 168–69; Jensen, *Winning of the Midwest*, 325; Peterson, "Reaction to a Heterogeneous Society," 263–69.

49. Formisano, *Birth of Mass Political Parties*, 297–98, 318–23, 346–48, found voter lists for Lansing, Detroit, and Ingham County in the 1850s. Melvyn Hammarberg, *The Indiana Voter: The Historical Dynamics of Party Allegiance during the 1870s* (Chicago: University of Chicago Press, 1977), 107–8, found *People's Guides* in Indiana in the 1970s that specified religion. See also Kenneth J. Winkle, "A Social Analysis of Voter Turnout in Ohio, 1850–1860," *Journal of Interdisciplinary History* 13 (1983): 411–35; Paul F. Bourke and Donald A. DeBats, "Individuals and Aggregates: A Note on Historical Data and Assumptions," *Social Science History* 4 (1980): 229–50; John M. Rozett, "Racism and Republican Emergence in Illinois, 1848–1860: A Re-Evaluation of Republican Negrophobia," *Civil War History* 22 (1976): 101–15, based on Rozett, "The Social Bases of Party Conflict in the Age of Jackson: Individual Voting Behavior in Greene County, Illinois, 1838–1848" (Ph.D. diss., University of Michigan, 1974); David H. Bohmer, "The Maryland Electorate and the Concept of a Party System in the Early National Period," in Silbey et al., *History of American Electoral Behavior*, 146–73.

50. Thomas A. Kremm, "Cleveland and the First Lincoln Election: The Ethnic Response to Nativism," *Journal of Interdisciplinary History* 8 (1977): 77–78. This article is based on Kremm, "The Rise of the Republican Party in Cleveland, 1848–1860" (Ph.D. diss., Kent State University, 1974).

51. Lee Benson and Samuel Hays pioneered this technique. See Benson, *Concept of Jacksonian Democracy*, paperback ed. (New York: Atheneum, 1963), ix–x, 165–207; and Hays, *American Political History*, 10–12. J. Morgan Kousser, "The 'New Political History': A Methodological Critique," *Reviews in American History* 4 (Mar. 1976): 1–14, harshly castigates this approach as "gestalt correlation" and "proving correlation by intimidation" (5–6). McCormick is also critical; see "Ethnocultural Interpretations," 41.

52. Kousser, "New Political History," 10–11.

53. In addition to the studies already cited, see Michael F. Holt, *Forging a Majority: The Formation of the Republican Party in Pittsburgh 1848–1860* (New Haven, Conn.: Yale University Press, 1969); William E. Gienapp, *The Origins of the Republican Party, 1852–1856* (New York: Oxford University Press, 1987); William G. Shade, *Banks or No Banks: The Money Issue in Western Politics* (Detroit, Mich.: Wayne State

University Press, 1972); Samuel McSeveney, *The Politics of Depression: Political Behavior in the Northeast, 1893–1896* (New York: Oxford University Press, 1972); John L. Hammond, *The Politics of Benevolence: Revival Religion and American Voting Behavior* (Norwood, N.J.: Abbey, 1979); Frederick C. Luebke, *Immigrants and Politics: The Germans of Nebraska, 1880–1900* (Lincoln: University of Nebraska Press, 1969); Philip R. VanderMeer, *The Hoosier Politician: Officeholding and Political Culture in Indiana 1896–1920* (Urbana: University of Illinois Press, 1985); Dale Baum, *The Civil War Party System: The Case of Massachusetts, 1848–1876* (Chapel Hill: University of North Carolina Press, 1984); Joel H. Silbey, *The Transformation of American Politics* (Englewood Cliffs, N.J.: Prentice-Hall, 1967); Jed Dannenbaum, *Drink and Disorder: Temperance Reform in Cincinnati from the Washingtonian Revival to the WCTU* (Urbana: University of Illinois Press, 1984); Walter D. Kamphoefner, "Dreissiger and Forty-Eighter: The Political Influence of Two Generations of German Political Exiles," in *Germany and America: Essays on Problems of International Relations and Immigration,* ed. Hans L. Trefousse (New York: Brooklyn College Press, 1980), 89–102; Stephen C. Fox, "The Group Bases of Ohio Political Behavior, 1803–1848" (Ph.D. diss., University of Cincinnati, 1973); Fox, "Politicians, Issues, and Voter Preference in Jacksonian Ohio: A Critique of an Interpretation," *Ohio History* 86 (1977): 155–70; Roger E. Wyman, "Wisconsin Ethnic Groups and the Election of 1890," *Wisconsin Magazine of History* 51 (1968): 269–93, reprinted in *Quantification in American History: Theory and Research,* ed. Robert P. Swierenga (New York: Atheneum, 1970), 239–66.

54. The leader of the Dutch colony, Albertus C. Van Raalte, who had led the affiliation with the Reformed Church in the East, was accused of promoting the Arminian theology of the Reverend Richard Baxter, found in his booklet *Call to the Unconverted.* See *Classis Holland Minutes, 1843–1858* (Grand Rapids, Mich.: Eerdmans, 1950), 144–45, 181–82, 227–28, 240–43, 246.

55. Kleppner, *Third Electoral System,* 166–69.

56. Formisano, *Birth of Mass Political Parties,* 104.

57. Hammond, *Politics,* chs. 4–5, esp. 75–76, 124–33.

58. Formisano, *Birth of Mass Political Parties,* 58, 79.

59. Kleppner, *Third Electoral System,* 59, 73, citing Richard L. Power, *Planting Cornbelt Culture* (Indianapolis: Indiana Historical Society, 1953).

60. Kleppner, *Third Electoral System,* 74.

61. Kremm, "Cleveland and the First Lincoln Election," 69–86.

62. Ibid., 82, citing the 30 Jan. 1855 issue of the Cleveland *Express.*

63. Ibid., 83–85, quote on 85, citing various articles of the Cleveland *Leader.*

64. Ibid., Table 6, 76, 80–81.

65. Holt, *Forging a Majority,* 218, quotes 7, 9.

66. Kleppner, *Third Electoral System,* 136–40.

67. Ibid., Table 6.3, 205–6.

68. Kleppner, *Cross of Culture,* 316–68.

69. VanderMeer, "Religion, Society, and Politics," 18. Other positive comments are in VanderMeer, "The New Political History: Progress and Prospects," *Computers and the Humanities* 11 (Sept.–Oct. 1977): 267.

70. Kleppner, *Third Electoral System*, 196.

71. Sean Wilentz, "On Class and Politics in Jacksonian America," *Reviews in American History* 10 (Dec. 1982): 47–48; James E. Wright, "The Ethnocultural Model of Voting: A Behavioral and Historical Critique," in *Emerging Theoretical Models in Social and Political History*, ed. Allan G. Bogue (Beverly Hills, Calif.: Sage, 1973), 40.

72. See, for example, Paul E. Johnson, *A Shopkeeper's Millennium: Society and Revivals in Rochester, New York, 1815–1837* (New York: Hill and Wang, 1978). An excellent review of the Marxist social historians of American politics is McCormick, "Social Analysis," 98–115.

73. Allan G. Bogue, "The New Political History of the 1970s," in Bogue, *Clio and the Bitch Goddess*, 116.

74. Jean H. Baker, *Affairs of Party: The Political Culture of Northern Democrats in the Mid-Nineteenth Century* (Ithaca, N.Y.: Cornell University Press, 1983), 11; McCormick, "Social Analysis," 95.

75. McCormick, "Social Analysis," 96–97.

76. Kleppner, *Third Electoral System*, 326–28, 361–63.

77. Allan G. Bogue, "The New Political History," *American Behavioral Scientist* 21 (Nov.–Dec. 1977), 203 (but Bogue withdraws the charge of monocausality in "New Political History of the 1970s," 122); Richard B. Latner and Peter Levine, "Perspective on Antebellum Pietistic Politics," *Reviews in American History* 4 (Mar. 1976): 19; and Eric Foner, "The Causes of the American Civil War: Recent Interpretations and New Directions," *Civil War History* 20 (1974): 200, make the charge of religious determinism; Edward Pessen, review of Kelley, *Cultural Patterns*, in *Civil War History* 25 (1979): 281, for the fixation charge; Latner and Levine, "Perspective on Antebellum Pietistic Politics," 17; Foner, "Causes of the American Civil War," 200; and Wright, " Ethnocultural Model of Voting," 46, for the ahistorical charge; Hammarberg, *Indiana Voter*, 116, for ignoring the unchurched; Kousser, "New Political History," 1–14, and A. J. Lichtman and L. I. Langhein, "Ecological Regression versus Homogeneous Units: A Specification Analysis," *Social Science History* 2 (1978): 172–93, for methodological critiques (but for a rebuttal, see William G. Shade, "Banner Units and Counties: An Empirical Comparison of Two Approaches," unpublished paper); Bogue, "New Political History," 209, for the case approach comment.

78. Kleppner, *Third Electoral System*, 376; McCormick, "Social Analysis," 98–115. The strongest voting study from an economic perspective is Baum, *The Civil War Party System*.

79. Kleppner, *Third Electoral System*, 186–88.

80. VanderMeer, "Religion, Society, and Politics," 10–16.

81. H. Richard Niebuhr, *Christ and Culture* (New York: Harper, 1951), 39–44.

82. Kousser, "New Political History," 10–11.

83. Silbey et al., *American Political Behavior*, 23.

Methodists, Politics, and the Coming of the American Civil War

Richard Carwardine

*I*n 1868, Ulysses S. Grant remarked that there were three great parties in the United States: the Republican, the Democratic, and the Methodist church. This was an understandable tribute, given the active role of leading Methodists in his presidential campaign, but it was also a realistic judgment, when set in the context of the denomination's growing political authority over the previous half-century. As early as 1819, when, with a quarter of a million members, "the Methodists were becoming quite numerous in the country," the young exhorter Alfred Brunson noted that "politicians ... from policy favoured us, though they might be skeptical as to religion," and they gathered at county seats to listen to the preachers of a denomination whose "votes counted as fast at an election as any others." Ten years later, the newly elected Andrew Jackson stopped at Washington, Pennsylvania, en route from Tennessee to his presidential inauguration. When both Presbyterians and Methodists invited him to attend their services, Old Hickory sought to avoid the political embarrassment of seeming to favor his own church over the fastest-growing religious movement in the country by attending both—the Presbyterians in the morning and the Methodists at night. In Indiana in the early 1840s, the church's growing power had led the Democrats to nominate for governor a known Methodist, while tarring their Whig opponents with the brush of sectarian bigotry. Nationally, as the combined membership of the Methodist Episcopal Church (MEC) and Methodist Episcopal Church, South (MECS) grew to over 1.5 million by the mid-1850s, denominational leaders could be found complaining that the church was so strong that each political party was "eager to make her its tool." Thus, Elijah H. Pilcher, the influential Michigan preacher, found himself in 1856 nominated simultaneously by state Democratic, Republican, and abolition conventions.[1]

Such cases could be multiplied many times over. They indicate that, during the early national and antebellum eras, American Methodists had to confront the political consequences of their burgeoning numerical strength and increasing social influence. Though Methodism secured its early authority by its distance from, not association with, secular power and appealed as a movement to those who were, as Donald Mathews put it, "ill at ease with the way in which institutions and elites . . . affected their lives," clergy and laity had necessarily to fashion a place in America's experimental republican order and the world's first mass democracy.[2] Between the Revolution and the Civil War, Methodists sought to define their political responsibilities and a proper code of political engagement. Their contributions to the forms, functioning, and ideologies of party and electoral politics were substantial but by no means consistent or entirely self-conscious. Their political loyalties were complex, shifting, and shaped by more than simple denominationalism. Most dramatically, the internal stresses of Methodism, the largest religious force in the nation at midcentury, profoundly influenced the course of the Union as it tumbled toward the carnage of the Civil War. Consideration of each of these four themes will remind us of the salient truth that there were many different incarnations of Methodism across time and place, but it will also confirm the essence of Grant's verdict that Methodists exerted a distinctive and potent influence over American political life in the nation's formative years.

METHODISTS AND POLITICAL ENGAGEMENT

Early American Methodists were, in general, apolitical in outlook. Russell Richey describes the period between 1770 and 1810 as one of Edenic innocence for Methodists, whose radical egalitarianism and communalism marked them off from the corrupted secular order. Francis Asbury, echoed by his fellow itinerants, shunned temporal power: "what have we to do with it in this country?" he asked. "Our kingdom is not of this world." Richey argues persuasively that these Methodists, though often intensely patriotic and belonging to the first denomination to organize itself nationally, lacked a concept of the nation as a political entity; rather, they saw America in spatial terms, as a continent to be converted. To a degree, this was functional. Tory legacies within Methodism left political divisions that full-hearted political engagement would expose. But it had more to do with their understanding of being citizens not primarily of the secular state but of "Zion," the church militant. In their response to the secular polity, early Methodists differed profoundly from those churches of the Reformed tradition— Presbyterian, Congregationalist, and Dutch Reformed—that had a strong sense of the political nation and of the need to fashion a new, postrevolutionary relationship between church and state and that were at ease with a "republican language" derived from the Declaration of Independence and the federal Constitution. As Richey puts it, Methodists had access to Reformed "[n]otions of America as God's chosen people, of a covenant between God and the nation, of eternal purposes being worked out through the American experiment . . . of religion as requisite to national prosperity . . . of the millennium as an American affair," but significantly they made no use of these ideas in the earliest days.[3]

By the first and, more evidently, the second decade of the nineteenth century, however, these themes were becoming increasingly apparent in Methodism. The dissident minority of Republican Methodists under James O'Kelly had already, in the 1790s, fused Christian theology and the radical political ideology of the American Revolution, though with an Arminian and democratic outcome that distinguished their view from the conservative republicanism of Reformed theologians more concerned with sustaining Calvinist civic order.[4] Historians have yet to chart the precise intellectual and geographical route by which the majority of Methodists moved to a Reformed understanding of Christian America, but it is clear that by the 1830s and 1840s the church's theologians, especially but by no means exclusively in the northern states, were comfortably speaking the language of Christian republicanism that their predecessors had largely eschewed. When, for example, the nation's clergy addressed the lessons of President William H. Harrison's unexpected death, the chorus of voices on the national fast day in 1841 included a number of Methodists whose analysis embraced the same elements found in the sermons of their Reformed brethren: Christianity as the source of the fundamental ideas and elements of republicanism and political freedom; America as the apotheosis of republican virtue and political freedom; the nation's unique consolidation of "the eternal with the temporal"; America as a model to the world; the vulnerability of republican freedom in the face of selfish individualism, public dishonesty, political corruption, and factional strife; and the harmful consequences of national sins for the country's destiny.[5]

The midcentury convergence of their thought with Reformed public theology was just one expression of Methodists' journey away from Asbury's shunning of temporal power toward a fuller integration into the nation's political life, from an approach to political action that George Marsden has labeled "pietist"—emphasizing the role of the Holy Spirit, holiness, freedom from law, a more private view of Christianity, and an essentially negative view of government and the state—to a "Calvinist" or Puritan vision of politics as a means of introducing God's kingdom.[6] The pietist, or quietist, outlook among some Methodists would remain a significant fact of antebellum life, their early apolitical disposition reinforced by distaste for many of the features of the new mass democratic order that emerged into full maturity during the 1830s. In particular, the violent party battles of the so-called second and third party systems generated an antiparty reaction among those who believed that seemingly endless political contention promoted corrosive social and religious discord in a nation that was, as Chauncey Hobart put it, "really *one at heart*." Methodist critics were repelled by low standards of public morality among those whom Calvin Fletcher called "bagatelle politicians": candidates and officeholders with an eye for the main chance, so often chosen not for their competence or sense of public responsibility but for their "availability." Most debilitating of all was electioneering itself. Campaigns were widely understood to encourage bribery, drunkenness, outrageous slanders, deception, and sheer folly among candidates and the electorate; it was axiomatic among Methodists that religious revivals and vital piety flourished in inverse proportion to political excitement. Thus there continued to be ministers like Thomas B. Miller, who "had but little to say about politics [and] . . . always said they were a bad tick to bite," and Heman Bangs, who consciously shunned politics after becoming a minister. This attitude may help to explain the high proportion of Methodists abstaining from politics in some areas in the Jacksonian period. And it certainly continued to shape the thinking even of those who energetically took part. The young Illinois itinerant Leonard F. Smith, after the Republican campaign of 1860, worried that he had neglected eternal considerations and "indulged in talking politics too freely, also in speaking of the faults of others rather than of their excellencies."[7]

The salient fact, however, was that Smith, whatever his subsequent anxieties, had enthusiastically participated in that campaign in a way that would have appeared quite alien to his late eighteenth-century forebears. By 1860, Methodists had widely absorbed a Calvinist understanding of political responsibilities, viewing the state as a moral being and believing that Christians as active citizens had to take responsibility for ensuring that the highest standards of virtue flourished in civic life. James Watson rebuked those whose piety was "too etherial [*sic*] for the duties of citizenship"; Thomas M. Eddy insisted that those who turned their back on politics demonstrated an apathy toward human progress; Charles Elliott called them "unchristian." They spoke for a denomination that—having shed its countercultural chrysalis—had been unable to resist the forces of a wider culture whose political enthusiasm was ubiquitous and where, as Samuel Patton explained, "there was scarcely any such thing as neutrality" in politics. Methodists joined other evangelicals in seeing that voluntary effort to achieve a godly society might founder on the rock of ungodly secular rule. Electing Christian rulers and effecting a Christian influence in passing and executing laws thus became part of Methodists' obligations.[8]

This would be pursued by a variety of means. It meant bringing men and women to Christ in sufficient numbers to ensure the religious orientation of the nation. It demanded earnest prayer for rulers. It also required regular use of the heaven-sent ballot box, a priceless privilege imbued with profound significance. Though Christians were obliged to avoid personal denigration, on one hand, and "man worship," on the other, they should understand, as Granville Moody explained, that "the folded vote becomes a tongue of justice, a voice of order, a force of imperial law, securing rights, abolishing abuses, and erecting her institutions of truth and love." Even ministers, despite congregational and community pressures encouraging political neutrality, became active, even determined, voters. Wilson Spottswood rode out of Berwick, Pennsylvania, on election day in 1844 to fill an appointment and avoid the ballot; but, he recalled, after wrestling with his conscience and conquering his squeamishness about being seen to be a Democrat by Whig acquaintances, "I turned my horse's head, rode back to town, hitched my horse to a post, got a ticket, marched up to the polls, and exercised the sacred right of an American citizen, by casting my first vote." The pious Methodist had to consider his vote carefully, not automatically sustaining the party ticket, but following conscience and recognizing that at judgment day he would face uncomfortable interrogation over his election choices.[9]

But political engagement did not end at the ballot box. As more and more Methodists came to operate according to the conviction that, in John Inskip's words, "all political questions have a connection, more or less direct, with both morality and religion," so the way was open to lobbying congressmen, circulating and signing petitions, attending political meetings to question candidates and officeholders, and even (in the case of preachers themselves) using their pulpits to address the public issues of the day. The ultimate imperative was to run for office. This was more commonly the course of laymen, who perceived no tension between piety and public service—Ruliff S. Lawrence of New Jersey, for example, ran for the state legislature after his conversion in 1852, believing this was the most effective way of serving his God. But ministers, too, frequently stood for office, often successfully. Many of these had retired from the active ministry, but others managed to combine continuing religious responsibilities with their secular duties. It was said of Walter T. Colquitt, the Georgia judge and U.S. senator, for example, that he could make a stump speech, try a court case and plead another at the bar, christen a child, preach a sermon, and marry a couple "all before dinner."[10]

Methodist political activism reached its climax in the two decades before the Civil War, as two developments converged. First, most Methodists in the first third of the century remained unconvinced that questions of public morality such as drinking alcohol, Sabbath breaking, and dueling were matters for political action as opposed to individual moral regeneration. They feared a return to Puritan "blue laws" and Reformed Protestants using religious legislation to reestablish a Calvinist imperium; but as moral suasion proved demonstrably insufficient, many came to reflect more sympathetically on the utility of legal action. When Luther Lee called for legal prohibition of the drink trade in the mid-1830s, he recognized that he was one of an eccentric Methodist minority, but during the next fifteen years the denomination would experience a significant shift in opinion. "Enlighten the mind of the rum-seller?" scoffed Davis W. Clark in 1847. "You may as well attempt to reason with the midnight assassin, or the pirate on the high seas."[11] Second, the substantive issues that came to dominate the nation's public discourse in the immediate antebellum years were themselves an invitation to Methodist political engagement. As the central questions of political controversy in the early Jacksonian era—banking and economic development—yielded to those of Roman Catholic immigration, territorial expansion, the future of slavery, and the integrity of the Union, more and more Methodists ignored the warnings of their quietist brothers and sisters about political "meddling" and accepted Calvin Kingsley's dictum that evangelicals should "approve what is clearly right, and condemn what is clearly wrong, God's word being the standard, even though the thing condemned or approved may happen to have its political aspects."[12]

METHODISTS' POLITICAL INFLUENCE

When calculating the political influence of Methodism, it is well to estimate cautiously, even though the sheer number of church members and the yet larger population of adherents explain both the eager efforts of politicians to secure their active support and Methodist leaders' strong conviction of their church's unique position. As well as noting the negative influence of Methodist pietists, who continued to disdain political activity, we need to keep in mind that Methodism, like other denominations, was composed disproportionately of women, who lacked the franchise and a position of political equality with men. Furthermore, Methodists, as will become clear, formed no political monolith, but cast their ballots for the full range of political parties, losing electoral leverage as a result. In fact, these qualifications are less crippling to the case for Methodists' political importance than they may seem. The pietists' apolitical stance had more than private significance and, despite itself, became a political fact in a democratic and sectionally polarizing society. Indeed, southern Methodists' claim to moral superiority for avoiding "meddling in politics" (a euphemism for "taking a stand against slavery") was, paradoxically, woven into an argument for their section's political superiority.

Nor should we assume women's entire exclusion from the male world of politics. From the early years of the century, evangelical women, working for benevolent causes and relief organizations, sought to influence local, state, and national governments. They engineered a torrent of petitions demanding action to criminalize seduction, regulate asylums and prisons, alter property laws, prevent Indian removal, restrict slavery, and prohibit liquor sales. They may have lacked the vote, but women did not lack visibility at election times, nor was their influence restricted to decorating the margins of the campaigns with their flag making and handkerchief waving. Some were known to stand outside the polls, handing out voting tickets for temperance candidates. Others, in the free states, attended Liberty, Free Soil, and Republican rallies and exerted themselves for antislavery candidates. The Methodist minister Wilson Spottswood alluded to two cases that implied a generic female political assertiveness: the wife and mother in a Pennsylvania Methodist family who, after James K. Polk's presidential victory in 1844, pointedly sought a "dyed-in-the-wool" Democrat to redeem the pledge of her staunchly Whig Methodist minister that she should have his head "for a foot-ball" if Henry Clay lost the election; and the minister's own wife, who shamed him out of his guilty participation in the clandestine midnight activities of "the dark-lanterned party," the Know-Nothings.[13]

Methodist ministers and leading laymen, even those who lacked education and wealth, did not lack moral authority over their gathered congregations, and while it was relatively rare for preachers openly to advocate support for a particular political party, they helped to set an agenda for moral purpose in public affairs. Editors of the mass-circulation denominational newspapers had to be careful not to alienate readers by party endorsements or an ill-judged remark at election times, but this did not stop them from addressing moral issues— particularly temperance, Roman Catholicism, and slavery—with immediate political significance. When Matthew Simpson took up the issue of the Fugitive

Slave Law in the editorial columns of the *Western Christian Advocate*, it caused "quite a fluttering among the 'smaller fry' politicians," and the paper circulated as widely as any political sheet in Indiana. Methodists successfully sought to gain access to political power at the different levels of government. They increasingly made their mark in the elections for congressional chaplains, as Unitarians and Episcopalians lost influence. Henry Slicer was returned for a unique third term in 1853, while John Durbin, George Cookman, and William Milburn also enjoyed congressional respect. Methodists increasingly won political office, at first reflecting their local status, as in Ohio with Edward Tiffin's election as governor, but later suggesting a growing authority nationally, represented most notably by John McLean's appointment to the Supreme Court and James Harlan's election to the Senate. The Methodist elite also established close friendships with politicians. George F. Pierce, bishop of the MECS, was on excellent terms with Robert Toombs, Alexander Stephens, and Richard Johnson; Augustus B. Longstreet enjoyed a warm friendship with John C. Calhoun; John B. McFerrin's connection with James K. Polk when he was governor of Tennessee and, later, president derived partly from his agency in converting two of Young Hickory's sisters at a Methodist revival.[14]

Methodists' political influence amounted to more than a simple accumulation of the contributions of "great men," significant though these were. At a more profound level, Methodists helped to shape the developing forms and language of politics in the early republic. The arrival of mass participatory politics and the simultaneous flowering of the Second Great Awakening were separate but not wholly independent events. Both derived their energy from ideologies that championed popular participation, individual enterprise, and equality of opportunity: universal white male suffrage in politics was paralleled in religion by the brush-fire spread of Arminianism, principally through the agency of Methodism, at the expense of Calvinist exclusiveness. Moreover, in the generation after the War of 1812, politicians had to devise new organizing strategies by which they could mobilize mass support. The most immediate, indeed the only, models were those proffered by the evangelical churches—it was they who had made the Awakening the most impressive organizing process the nation had yet seen. The Methodist Episcopal church, in particular, with its shrewd and productive balance of central control and local initiative, had drawn men and women with local loyalties into a movement that transcended the immediate community. Party organizers learned much from innovative Methodist preachers about reaching a mass audience, about persevering and dramatic effort, about rotating speakers to maintain and deepen interest, and about channeling mass enthusiasm and consolidating loyalties. It is doubtful if the extraordinary popular engagement in politics at this time—the greatest enthusiasm for politics the republic has ever seen—could have occurred had it not been for the integration of evangelicals and their organizational structures into the new order. To tap into the sources of revivalist excitement, party managers introduced political camp meetings, held over two, three, or four days. During August and September, the season of Methodist camp meetings, huge outdoor gatherings met on sites normally reserved for spiritual assemblies. Introductory prayer preceded sustained political "sermons." The fervent singing of political hymns to familiar tunes reminded listeners of Methodist revivals and the catchy melodies of religious folk music. Political managers invited ministers to offer prayers at party conventions (often held in churches, as the only appropriate buildings available). They spoke of their party as a political church and its activists as "missionaries," "presiding elders," "bishops," and "local preachers," who would "carry the glad tidings of our political salvation to every corner." Learning of Harrison's three-man campaign committee in 1840, one Whig reflected: "Where two or 'three' meet together in my name, there I am in the midst, and that to bless them."[15]

As this suggests, Methodism provided a model for the language as well as the form of political life. Though the perspectives of politicians were necessarily blinkered by the cold realities of the world, day-to-day realism and compromise gave way at election time to a more romantic, millennialist discourse. Campaigning politicians took advantage of the evangelical cast of mind, which saw the whole of history as a continuous conflict between God and Satan. The Methodist revivalist's sermon, with its polarized language of heaven and hell, good and evil, salvation and damnation, grace and sin, Christ and Antichrist, reinforced this framework of thought. This Manichaean perspective—a well-established element in the intellectual framework of the early republic and by no means limited to Methodists[16]—profoundly influenced the way in which evangelical Protestants interpreted politics. Candidates and platforms took on an ethical, even religious, significance. William Gannaway Brownlow, for example, commonly saw presidential elections in apocalyptic terms, as conflicts between "the cause of God and morality" and the devil's legions. This mentality allowed little scope for compromise, complexity, or consensus. Besides encouraging party propagandists to use antithesis and polarization to help induct the electorate into the ways of mass politics, the world of Methodist revivalism also led them to present the election campaign as the means of political redemption. The campaign, like the revival, would turn the community into the ways of righteousness through the multiplying of individual "conversions." Whigs sang lustily of "penitent Locofocos," apostates returning to the fold "like a prodigal son," and "political sinners" groaning on the "anxious seat." Interceding to protect a heckler at a New York meeting in 1856, a Methodist demanded, "let him stay, he came to scoff, he may remain to pray." Presidential candidates were stewards of righteousness, agents of personal and national salvation: Whigs characterized Clay as "the *redeemer* of the country"; Brownlow called him a "Moses" who would help his people "gain the promised land!"[17]

Methodists' influence did not end with their role in shaping the language and forms, the style and institutions, of the nation's novel political order. The church made two further significant contributions to the substance of early national and antebellum politics. First, its members' party loyalties played a part in determining and redetermining the shifting political configurations of successive party systems from the Jeffersonian era to the immediate antebellum years. This was closely related to Methodists' contributions, direct and indirect, to shaping the nation's agenda of issues for political action—in particular, the question of slavery—and to the process of sectional polarization.

METHODISTS' PARTY LOYALTIES

Ethnocultural historians, in emphasizing denominational loyalties and ethnic origins as primary determinants of nineteenth-century voting behavior, have prompted a number of objections about their methods and conclusions, principally from those who consider party alignments to have been based essentially on responses to the rapid socioeconomic changes wrought by the revolution in communications and the concomitant advance of a national market economy.[18] Those objections do not lack substance; yet it is useful to recall that the political managers of the early national era, recognizing the churches' power, consciously aimed to graft religious loyalty onto party loyalties. They were well aware that some of the most profound community conflicts and group loyalties of the early republic could be found between and within the different denominations. It was no accident that politicians wanted to be seen worshiping in churches themselves, played "recognition politics" by choosing candidates who were attached to particular denominations, and exploited issues that they believed would engage the attentions of evangelicals. Individual churches and the larger denomination provided networks of friendship and association whose political potential was well understood. When Trusten Polk, a member of Centenary Methodist Church in St. Louis, ran successfully for governor of Missouri in 1856, he was staunchly supported by his close friend, fellow church member, and Methodist preacher John Hogan; when Hogan conducted a statewide canvass on his friend's behalf, he was in a position to exploit all of his denominational as well as his political connections.[19]

In practice, few Protestant denominations maintained an essentially uniform partisan attachment: of the larger churches, only the Congregationalists presented something approaching a Federalist-Whig-Republican consistency across the three party systems; Primitive Baptists remained loyally Democrat. Methodists certainly presented no uniform picture. "Lord, deliver us from Whiggery!" was the prayer of one preacher at a Tennessee camp meeting. "God forbid!" came a brother's reply. Yet the lack of political consistency within Methodism does not mean that the relationship between church membership and party loyalty was wholly random. While men and women did not generally join churches to advance a political cause, their view of the world, as expressed in their church fellowship, had implications for their political outlook; while Methodist church leaders were careful not to link the institution with a particular political party, the concerns of Methodists *as Methodists* formed one element among the several that shaped their partisanship.[20]

It is possible to hazard some generalizations. We can confidently conclude that, during the first party system, Methodists were very largely drawn into the ranks of Jeffersonian Democracy. Under the succeeding party system, organized around the conflict between Jackson's Democracy and its evolving opposition, the majority of Methodists probably maintained a Democratic outlook, but a substantial body of the church rallied to Whiggery, including quite probably a majority of its ministers. The chipping away at Methodists' attachment to the Democracy continued through the early and mid-1850s as the second party system fragmented under the pressure of new parties—Free Soilers, Know-Nothings, Prohibitionists, and Republicans—each of which attracted sizable support from the denomination. Even so, some Whig Methodists in the South turned to the Democrats as the best sectional defense against Free Soilism, and that party continued to enjoy substantial—probably majority—Methodist support, North and South, in the elections of 1860.

These are broad brushstrokes, however, and they hide the multiplicity of experiences that can be observed locally. Paul Goodman has rightly stressed the importance of community context in explaining patterns of political attachment among New England churches; Harry Watson reflects similarly about Jacksonian politics in general. The advance of the market, the power of the new steam press, and improved transportation all had the power to erode provincialism, but "the intensely local character of American life and politics" remained a salient truth.[21] And among the most important of local influences on party attachment were the kaleidoscopic patterns of interdenominational conflict.

This is not the place to survey the whole range of sectarian rivalry in the early republic and its implications for the ballot box. But it is clear that the pattern of Methodist voting was affected by the absence or presence of particular denominations and by changes in interchurch relationships over time. In New England in the 1790s and early 1800s, the generally poisonous relationships between Methodists and the Calvinist Standing Order, which saw the new movement subject to fines, intimidation, violent attack, and other forms of persecution, understandably drove Methodists into the arms of Jeffersonian Republicans who beckoned with a language of religious toleration and pluralism. Even after disestablishment, the bitterness continued, with the result that many New England Methodists found in Jacksonian Democracy a refuge from Congregationalist bigotry. William Xavier Ninde recalled that in the 1850s Democratic politicians were still able to exploit residual tension between the two denominations in Connecticut: they "went in heart and soul to help the Methodists. It was a sort of 'you tickle me, and I'll tickle you' system, a kind of see-saw arrangement. When the Whigs and the Congregationalists went down, the Democrats and the Methodists went up and *vice versa*."[22]

These conflicts appear to have carried over, for a period at least, in those areas outside New England where Congregationalists and Presbyterians of Yankee extraction were the dominant force and where Methodists initially struggled for recognition, as in the Western Reserve of Ohio. Alfred Brunson, who had seen in Connecticut how Calvinist-Federalist persecution had made staunch Republicans of Methodists, encountered similar disdain from transplanted Yankee "Presbygationalists" when he began work as a licensed preacher in the reserve after the War of 1812. Members of the Methodist minority "were treated as intruders, and with much contempt." Though all settlers united to subscribe to the building of schoolhouses on the understanding that they would be available to all denominations for worship, the informal "standing order" soon took them over, at the expense of excluded Methodists in particular.[23]

Yet even when Methodists' (and, indeed, Baptists') fear of Presbygationalist power dominated their thinking, it did not necessarily drive them into the arms of the Democrats. In the late 1820s and early 1830s, the operations of the interdenominational benevolent agencies that made up the "evangelical united front," which were dominated by Reformed churchmen of the Northeast, increasingly alienated Methodists and Baptists, including those who had lent their support to the reform societies' operations. They were offended not just by a general sense of the presumption and arrogance of the Reformed leadership, but by Presbygationalist efforts to secure a charter of incorporation for the American Sunday School Union. That some leading Methodists, principally Nathan Bangs, saw this as an effort to reunite church and state was unsurprising given the Presbyterian Ezra Stiles Ely's simultaneous call for the creation of a Christian political party to support his favorite, Andrew Jackson, a Presbyterian himself.[24] For some Methodists, Jackson's successful candidacy was the source of acute anxiety about Presbyterian ambitions. It partly explains evidence of considerable antipathy toward Old Hickory among prominent Methodists. Alfred Brunson caustically recalled that when the president-elect attended his church in 1829, "I preached to him as I would to any other sinner."[25]

In some locations, away from the influence of New England Calvinism, aggressive rivalry between the two most successful Protestant denominations of the first half of the century, Methodists and Baptists, dominated the operations of the religious marketplace. Nathan Bangs described the conflict between the two movements in the West, in the early years of the century, as a "sort of warfare," and Peter Cartwright's reminiscences of his early career in Tennessee, Kentucky, and Ohio are seemingly little more than a succession of battles with evangelical rivals, of whom Baptists were the principal foe.[26] This antagonism persisted unrelentingly in some southern and western regions well beyond the heyday of the Second Great Awakening, through to the Civil War. It achieved probably its most dramatic expression in the southern Appalachian highlands during the 1850s, in the conflict between the partisans of two of Tennessee's finest polemicists, the Reverend James Robinson Graves, the editor of the Nashville *Tennessee Baptist*, and the "fighting parson" of Knoxville, William G. Brownlow. Graves's newspaper articles and tracts, which mixed vituperation, ridicule, theological argument over infant baptism, and a critique of Methodists' centralized and "autocratic" church government, were eventually (in 1856) consolidated in *The Great Iron Wheel; or, Republicanism Backward and Christianity Reversed*. Brownlow's venomous response, *The Great Iron Wheel Examined; or, Its False Spokes Extracted, and an Exhibition of Elder Graves, Its Builder*, appeared within the year, blending personal abuse with a sustained attack on Baptists' residual high Calvinist doctrine, their insistence on complete immersion of believers, and their unyielding sectarian exclusiveness. Whole communities were split by this chronic warfare, with clear political consequences. In one town, the two religious groups had their own schools, stores, blacksmiths, taverns, and even ferries to cross the river. In politics, most of the Methodists were Whigs and most of the Baptists Democrats.[27]

Such intense Protestant sectarianism, however, found it hard to survive in urban and northeastern areas, which by midcentury had experienced a reshaping of their traditional religious topography: the huge influx of nonevangelical, principally Roman Catholic, immigrants in the 1840s and 1850s forced those evangelical Protestants in immediate proximity to adopt common strategies of response. The New York *Christian Advocate and Journal* spoke for many readers when it insisted in 1842 that "the times call for unity of spirit and effort among the evangelical churches." That unity demanded a common political front against a Catholic church seemingly shameless in exploiting its own burgeoning power in the political, not just the ecclesiastical, arena. This understanding lay behind the conclusion of a western Methodist in 1841 that "the time is not likely far distant when the political parties will be, not Democratic and Whig, but Popish and Protestant." Given the consistently strong Democratic attachments of the overwhelming majority of Catholic voters through the whole of the period under review, it was understandable that the most deeply anti-Romanist of the Methodists, as of other evangelical denominations, should be drawn to Whiggery and that, when that party's leaders temporized in the face of immigrant voting power, evangelicals should flirt with new political organizations that promised to defend fragile republicanism against the Antichrist. Thus the Know-Nothing party of the early and mid-1850s benefited considerably from a substantial influx of Methodists, including ministers, who now happily rubbed shoulders with Congregationalists, Presbyterians, Baptists, and others who, in other contexts, remained political and religious rivals.[28]

The interdenominational rivalries that shaped political affiliations were not just rooted in differences of theology or religious practice, of course, but were often reinforced by conflict related to class and status and to economic and social aspiration. It is a commonplace that early American Methodism comprised to a very large extent the poor, the powerless, and the socially despised, both black and white. Congregationalists, even where they did not function as the Standing Order, and Presbyterians were commonly the churches of the well-to-do and the sturdily independent. These Reformed critics of Methodism evinced a powerful social condescension toward what they regarded as a movement of the uneducated, the overexcited, and the unwashed. Methodists looked benignly on Jeffersonian Republicanism because it offered a defense against the arrogance of Calvinist social power. But most Methodists were not social levelers or persisting communitarians nor, despite the picture painted by Charles Sellers in his stirring study of Jacksonian America, were they wholly antagonistic to the social and economic opportunities presented by the burgeoning capitalist market. Over the first half of the nineteenth century, Methodists developed into a respected denomination that embraced men and women of social prominence and some wealth, able to mix on equal terms with fellow Protestants. Unsurprisingly, many Methodists—not least, bankers and entrepreneurs like Calvin Fletcher and John Hogan—responded positively to the Whig party's doctrine of economic improvement and its strong tendency to endorse the moral citizen's pursuit of self-control, self-discipline, and respectability. The Democrats' banking and currency policies of the 1830s and 1840s, together with their continuing tolerance toward dissenters from religious orthodoxy, led many Methodists to see them, in William Crane's words, as "the moral dregs, and scurf, and pollution of the land. Atheists, blasphemers, Sabbath-breakers, drunkards and brothel-haunters flocked to this party, because here . . . they were treated as nobility." A similar concern for "improvement"—in both its economic and moral sense—and antipathy to the social values of the Democrats later drew many northern Methodists into the Republican party. After attending a big Democratic meeting in 1860, Leonard F. Smith concluded that Lincoln faced a party "characterized by a noisy dirty ignorant rabble."[29]

The concerns of class and status were sometimes subsumed into the acerbities of ethnicity and regional chauvinism. Antipathy between the English and Scots Irish may have had some influence on Methodists' voting habits. The generally clear picture of Methodist support for the Jeffersonians grew murkier in Delaware, where the denomination drew considerably on former Anglicans of English stock and where the Republicans were perceived as the Scots-Irish, Presbyterian party. Under the second party system, Jackson may have held on more easily to Irish than to English Methodists. More clear-cut was the cultural conflict in much of the lower North and upper South between Yankees and southerners, each side invigorated with a sense of its own superiority. The New Englander Alfred Brunson found in Ohio's Western Reserve that southern-born Methodist preachers were openly contemptuous of Yankees, whom they regarded "as bordering upon the savage state," while Peter Cartwright's experience in the southern part of the same state brought him face to face with superior New Englanders whose learned ministers "were always criticising us poor backwoods preachers." Many of these southern-born settlers in the free states persisted in their dislike of the "meddling Yankee" and the parties that seemed best to represent interventionist attitudes, the Whigs and the Republicans. Men like Cartwright remained Democrats up to the Civil War. "Old Father Gillham," a fellow Illinois Methodist, arrived in Illinois from South Carolina in 1821 and was still a staunch Democrat in 1860.[30]

Significant though sectarian rivalry, class, status, and ethnic chauvinism were as determinants of Methodist voting habits, it is important not to lose sight of the role played by particular issues of social policy in shaping party choice, especially those issues that had a direct bearing on the nation's religious and moral well-being. Methodists were not loyal to party through thick and thin. Like other evangelicals, they expected their political leaders to promote what they understood to be the nation's good and were ready to jettison a party label if betrayed. In the 1830s, it is clear that Jackson's Indian policy, especially the removal of the Cherokee nation from Georgia, was an important element in the decade's political polarization and played its part in cementing the attachment of Methodists like William Winans, William Crane, and Alfred Brunson to the Whig party. Similarly, those Methodists most concerned about the state provision of free schools—Samuel Lewis in Ohio, David R. McAnally in North Carolina, and Colin Dew James in Illinois, for instance—tended to gravitate toward that party, given its greater commitment to free public education as a means of securing a more disciplined population.[31] When, however, Methodists turned from moral suasion toward state intervention as the primary means for effecting an end to the liquor trade, they found both Whigs and Democrats too concerned about alienating voters, especially the newly arrived, to take a prohibitionist stand. Driven by conscience, many of them defected from the two main parties to support the single-issue Maine Law and Prohibition parties in the early 1850s. Similarly anxious about Whigs' and Democrats' wobbles over defending the common school system, sustaining the King James Bible within it, and showing some steel toward Catholics, Methodists flocked in numbers to the American party. Given the denomination's strength, it is no exaggeration to regard Methodists as the single most important agency in the creation and sustenance of a political force that tore apart the vulnerable fabric of the second party system.[32]

No single issue had greater power than slavery to shape Methodists' political responses. Northern Methodists' anxieties over the implications of the annexation of Texas and the Mexican cession for the expansion of the peculiar institution drew some of their number into the Free Soil party, whose crusading stance and revivalist appeal to conscience generated such enthusiasm among its supporters that Matthew Simpson was led to conclude that a fundamental party realignment was not far off. Many more, uneasily mollified by the Compromise of 1850, would help to fulfill that prediction between 1854 and 1856, when the storm of protest over the Kansas-Nebraska Act and subsequent events in Kansas and Washington led them, along with other Free Soil and abolitionist Protestants, into the Know-Nothing and other anti-Nebraska fusion movements, which culminated in the primacy of the Republican party.

William E. Gienapp's detailed study of the origins of that party shows with great clarity the impressive political calculation and manipulation that went into its formation. To win national elections, political parties needed managers, discipline, and professional politicians; coalition building, essential to success, demanded a readiness to compromise and conciliate. Yet much of the Republicans' early energy and the party's continued impetus derived from the energies of zealous evangelicals, impelled by outrage, conscience, and obedience to a higher law. Many of these had been working for years to fuse religion and politics in an effective agency that would provide the route to the kingdom of God. That fusion of sectional alienation and postmillennial aspiration is clear in the diary of Benjamin Adams, a Methodist itinerant in New York, who on the weekend before polling day in 1856 officiated at a Methodist revival at Bridgeport: "The Lord came in power among the people and our souls rejoiced in the Lord. . . . May this work roll on in power and God's name be glorified among his people." Three days later, he was pursuing a complementary means of advancing the kingdom: "Election. Today the battle is to be fought between right & wrong. I went to the polls and did my duty. . . . May God aid the right!" John C. Frémont's defeat in that election seemed to Gilbert Haven a matter both for mourning and for rededication to Christ's work over the next four years, and when Lincoln triumphed in 1860, John Allen of Farmington, Maine, judged it the victory of "the Lord's side." Northern Methodists did not sweep en masse into this crusade, but enough of them stood as candidates, organized locally, raised funds, used their pulpits, and cast their votes, especially in New England and its diaspora (that is, western New York, the Western Reserve of Ohio, the Northern Tier of Pennsylvania, and the northern counties of the midwestern states) that it is easy to understand why some contemporaries believed that the MEC, as "the largest and most influential denomination in the land," exerted "a most controling [sic] power in electing Mr. Lincoln" in 1860.[33] That judgment was no doubt an overstatement of Methodists' role, statistically speaking, in the election itself. When, however, we consider the part played by Methodists in the process of sectional alienation—itself inextricably connected with the Republicans' electoral successes—it encourages the conclusion that the denomination played a significantly more instrumental role than historians have generally recognized.

METHODISTS AND SECTIONAL ALIENATION

There is a sad irony in the fact that Methodism, a major instrument in the process of American national integration in the early republic, became a principal channel of sectional alienation during the middle years of the nineteenth century. When the MEC fractured after the General Conference voted to remove Bishop James O. Andrew for being married to a slave owner, many believed that separation was in the nation's best interests. Southern radicals like William A. Smith regarded efforts to hold together abolitionist and proslavery Methodists within the same national organization as a source of continuing and dangerous tension for church and country. The General Conference, he declared at the organizing convention of the MECS at Louisville in 1845, "had ceased to exert a conservative influence upon the political union." Peaceable separation, by removing southerners from the influence of what Thomas Stringfield called the "reckless fanaticism" of abolitionist Methodists, was "highly important to the union of these states." Conservative evangelicals, on the other hand, North and South, took a far less sanguine view of schism. They believed in what Nathan Bangs called Methodism's "cohesive tendency," not least because of its system of itinerant exchange, which helped "do away with those prejudices which grow out of local circumstances and habits." Rupture would terminate this influence. It would also play into the hands of extremists. A slaveholding Methodist considered denominational unity the best guarantee that moderate northerners would assert their influence on behalf of southern interests, "but let division take place, and . . . [t]he motives to induce moderation [will] no longer exist," and "the excitement of abolition will increase ten-fold." Others feared that ecclesiastical rupture would embolden states' rights radicals inside and outside the churches. Indeed, there were those who speculated that Calhounites had deliberately engineered the Methodist schism as part of a grand design to undermine the American Union. One does not have to adopt their conspiracy theory to see the force of the moderates' argument for circumspection. Hindsight allows us to see that voluntary separation opened the way to new sources of bitterness and sectional stereotyping, which seriously corroded Methodists' sense of belonging to a political and ecclesiastical Union based on common values.[34]

The Plan of Separation, far from providing a basis for the harmonious coexistence of the two branches of a divided church, gave rise instead to a chronic and often ugly conflict that persisted in various guises through to the Civil War. The plan's authors were looking for a way to run a 1,200-mile line through MEC border conferences that embraced both nonslaveholding areas and parts of the slave states of Maryland, Virginia, Kentucky, Arkansas, and Missouri. They decreed that "societies, stations, and conferences" along the line between slave and free states, but not "interior charges," could take a binding vote on their allegiance, which the authorities of both the northern and southern churches would respect; the minority would refrain from forming their own societies. However, antislavery hardliners could see no moral case for limiting their activities in areas where they believed thousands of conscientious men and women would want to continue their membership in the unstained MEC and shun a "slavery church." The plan also left much unclear. If, following a vote, the line separating churches were to be redrawn, was the society newly abutting the border also allowed a vote on allegiance? If the border took on the character of neutral common ground until loyalties were established, what was there to prevent a ceaseless and disruptive campaign of recruitment? This was exactly what vexed one slave-state critic of the proselytizing MECS: "they have declared the border a movable line, so that when they have procured the secession of a society, station, or circuit, from the

Methodist E. Church, the next one north becomes a border, and so on, *ad infinitum.*"[35]

The implementation of the plan consequently generated enormous frustration and anger. Each side came to regard the other as "nullifiers" and predators. Cases of split congregations, irregular voting, political manipulation, and disregard for agreed procedures multiplied. Invective once reserved for the other section's radicals was directed at all of the departed members. Southerners blamed Thomas Bond of the *Christian Advocate and Journal*, Charles Elliott of the *Western Christian Advocate*, and other free-state editors for destroying trust and threatening social order. Their papers were regularly seized and even burned by magistrates at the post offices, whose actions were sustained by a combination of statute, grand jury endorsement, and the demands of vigilance committees.[36]

In many cases anger and fear exploded into physical violence. MEC preachers in Missouri were seized and told to leave. Armed sympathizers of the MECS took over the church at Clarksburg, Maryland, camping in the church at night over several weeks to deny access by MEC loyalists. Probably the worst violence scarred communities in Virginia, especially in the Kanawha Valley and on the eastern shore. In Northampton and Accomac counties, social prestige and judicial power conspired with "mobbism" against the northern church. Valentine Gray, a preacher of the Philadelphia Conference, was forcibly ejected from the church and subsequently hounded from the county court when he turned up for redress. A jeering, missile-throwing mob at Guildford broke up the service of another MEC preacher, James Hargis, without any note of reproof from the *Richmond Christian Advocate* or the local magistrate.[37]

Higher courts, too, offered some comfort to the southern church as it sought to recover meeting places and secure what it considered its share of the property still controlled by the MEC. Litigation kept some premises closed to both parties. The bitter conflict over the status of the church at Maysville, Kentucky, was resolved by the state court in favor of the MECS in a judgment that delighted the South. By ruling that the southern church was not, as many northern Methodists contended, a secession from a continuing MEC, but rather one of two new churches created out of a now-defunct institution, the court gave heart to the South in its attempts to secure a financial share of the two Methodist Book Concerns, in New York and Cincinnati. Not all northern Methodists were implacably opposed to the southern church's securing some part of what had once been considered common funds. Not least, they conceded that superannuated preachers, their wives, and their children had a just claim to the proceeds, regardless of section. But the failure of the northern annual conferences to ratify the Plan of Separation put constitutional doubts into the mind of the MEC General

Conference of 1848, which called for legal arbitration. Incensed at what it considered evasion, the southern church brought suits against the MEC in the U.S. circuit courts in New York and Ohio. Judge Samuel Nelson's 1851 ruling in favor of the MECS in the New York case prompted cries of "southern aggression" from northern Methodists who explained the decision as the inevitable result of cotton influence and the "despotic spirit of slavery." The Cincinnati case went on appeal to the U.S. Supreme Court, which also ruled, under Roger B. Taney, in favor of the MECS. Nelson again wrote the opinion. The decision, described by Granville Moody as "astonishing, unparalleled and unjust," elicited further Methodist denunciations of proslavery bias in the judiciary. Three years later, antislavery forces would exploit the historic Dred Scott ruling to show that the Supreme Court was in the clutches of the slave owners' power, but by then thousands of northern Methodists had already reached that unpalatable conclusion.[38]

The aftermath of the denominational schism thus led Methodists in each section to develop increasingly hostile mutual perceptions, with profound consequences for politics. Southerners increasingly identified all northern churchgoers with irreligious, fanatical abolitionism. They defended separation—constitutional and conservative—as the only option for orthodox believers seeking to defend true religion and the social order in the "war of subjection and extermination" facing the South. "We are compelled to repel invasion and assault," Henry Bascom insisted, "or be overthrown and trodden upon by the assailants." Northern Methodists' attack on slavery turned them into collaborators in a political scheme to deny southerners their constitutional rights. Addressing a southern camp meeting in 1847, William A. Smith aimed to show how the Free Soil attack on southern political interests, as exemplified in the Wilmot Proviso, was a logical sequel to northern aggression in ecclesiastical affairs. Henry Bascom blamed the fracturing of Methodism on the work of "the great Northern Abolition and Antislavery party" in which "the politician, the demagogue, and the religionist all unite." While southern Methodists upheld federal and church law, the MEC had become "a pander[er] to political agitation."[39]

Northern Methodists, too, attached political significance to the traumas associated with separation. Southerners had seceded not to defend doctrine or polity, but "to continue and protect slavery." The MECS had become "a great politico-ecclesiastical party, for the defense and support of the peculiar political institution of the South." Southern Methodists had "practically nullified" the terms of separation by their aggression against the MEC along the border and by their resort to legal action. They had nailed their church's colors to the mast of the slave owners' power by removing the antislavery section from the Methodist Discipline, by tolerating the denial of free speech in the border wars, and by preaching a gospel of ecclesiastical rebellion and secession that had implications for the stability of the political Union.[40]

During the climactic years of political polarization following the passage of the Kansas-Nebraska Act, Methodists continued actively to participate in (as opposed to reactively responding to) the process of sectional alienation. The deterioration in relations between North and South from the mid-1850s was not solely a product of political conflict, narrowly defined. The poison of sectionalism seeped along ecclesiastical channels, too. Indeed, evangelicals' experiences, and especially those of Methodists, help to explain how the issues raised nationally by slavery and the slave owners' power took on meaning in local settings. Methodist and other denominational presses and preachers kept all these aggravations before the widest possible audience.

Not surprisingly, sectional warfare in churches reached unsurpassed levels of drama in Kansas and Missouri. From the outset, missionaries from the free states, determined to win Kansas for liberty and Christ, faced a proslavery party just as committed to driving them away. "Law and order men" intercepted William Moore, a local preacher of the MEC, on his way to Kansas City, forced alcohol down his throat, and threatened to kill him. The presiding elder of the South Kansas mission district lost all his possessions, including his horses, to southern "outlaws."[41] Conflict spilled over into Missouri, where vigilance committees and their supporters broke up quarterly meetings of the Missouri Conference, blocked access to camp-meeting grounds, interrupted sermons, and drove preachers from the state. As free-state Methodists called ever more confidently for the exclusion of slaveholders from the MEC and as Kansas grew bloodier, so the dangers to northern preachers increased. One young minister, C. H. Kelly, was ejected from his pulpit and forced to ride, thinly clad, through bitter December winds to Fort Madison, Iowa. He did not live long. In Rochester, Andrew County, proslavery men set upon the Reverend William Sellers, filled his mouth and smothered his head with tar and left him to fry in the sun, and they shot Benjamin Holland, an elderly class leader. Blaming southern churchmen for creating the climate for these attacks, the *Central Christian Advocate* lamented: "There is an ecclesiastical as well as a political war raging, and we are shamelessly attacked and falsely represented as well by political demagogues and false-hearted slavery-defending preachers."[42]

At the same time, relations between the two branches of Methodism ulcerated in other parts of the border where the MEC maintained an active presence—in Arkansas, Kentucky, and Virginia. In parts of western Virginia, for instance, accusation, counterclaim, and paranoia raised public opinion to fever pitch through the mid-1850s. Charged by MECS leaders with incendiarism, infidelity, and treachery to the Constitution, Wesley Smith and other MEC preachers took their case to the people through press and pulpit. In the West Milford circuit, Smith's four-hour public lecture filled the church to overflowing and halted the harvest and weekday business. He contemptuously dismissed proslavery ministers' efforts "to brand as abolitionists every nonslaveholder in the slave States who will not adopt the nullification doctrines of Drs [William A.] Smith and [Henry] Bascom." Ultras, North and South, sought the same end, he warned—a dissolution of the Union through dissolution of the churches. The result would be "a border war without a figure of speech—a war of bloodshed and carnage." He concluded:

> If any future historian shall be called upon to write the history of the dissolution of the Union, he will trace it to the action of the southern Methodist preachers . . . [since 1844]. We hold them accountable before Heaven and earth for the exasperated state of feeling which exists at present between the North and South, and which is constantly increasing.[43]

Southern Methodists, for their part, perceived the MEC as an even greater threat to sectional harmony and found it hard to remain calm when MEC border preachers described their church as "the most powerful and systematic organization on earth against slavery." The resolutions of various MEC annual conferences throughout 1858 and 1859, calling for resistance to slavery, prompted southern Methodists to assert their right to drive "abolition emissaries" out of their territory. After the volcanic rumblings at Harpers Ferry in October 1859, the operations of the MEC in the border South appeared all the more menacing. "It is a curious fact," ruminated William Brownlow, "that John Brown and his secret advisers selected a portion of Virginia lying within the bounds of the Baltimore Conference, as the most appropriate theatre of their operations." Here the MEC allowed blacks to testify against whites in church trials and refused to ordain slaveholders as local preachers. The church's influence was more dangerous to slavery than a dozen Harpers Ferry insurrections. Not only in western Virginia, but throughout the MEC's areas of operations in the slave states, vigilant southern Methodists stood guard against its provocation and "sedition."[44] Their actions in one of these cases, and the subsequent northern reaction, provide probably the most graphic of all the indications of the destructive power of ecclesiastical alienation and its role in the politics of sectional polarization.

In the summer of 1860, a Texas mob seized and hanged the Reverend Anthony Bewley, an experienced MEC preacher of thirty years' standing and a member of his church's Arkansas Conference since its creation in 1852. Bewley, a southerner who had first served in Tennessee, had been involved in the feeble Texas mission of the MEC for several years. Along with the handful of other preachers attempting to establish a presence in northeastern Texas, he had been regarded as a meddlesome abolitionist. When the Arkansas Conference, with impressive courage but little prudence, had convened under Bishop Edmund S. Janes at Timber Creek, near Bonham, Texas, in March 1859, a crowd of two hundred men armed with revolvers and bowie knives ("a committee of vigilance," in southern parlance) had forced the meeting's suspension and its later adjournment *sine die*. Apart from the region's German Free Soilers, who shunned the MECS because of its positive approbation of slavery, few locally would have demurred from the description of the Arkansas Conference, and of the Texas mission in particular, as "a screen behind which to hide emissaries known as abolitionists, and as dangerous to southern interests." Soon afterward, the Texas District had been discontinued, but Bewley himself had retained a role as superintendent and missionary to Texas, until he fled the state in fear of his life. There are conflicting and ambiguous accounts of what happened next, but it seems that, with a reward of a thousand dollars on his head, he was seized and held at Fayetteville, Arkansas, before being taken forcibly to Fort Worth, where he was subsequently hanged, "having been condemned by a jury of three hundred men."[45]

For northern Methodists, the case confirmed all of their accumulated perceptions about their errant brothers and sisters' sad departure from the paths of righteousness. The murder was a "diabolical deed" of "Turkish cruelty" against a mild Christian of simple, modest character. Southern Methodists, to drive all traces of the MEC from the slave states, had evinced "the pure spirit of a mobocrat," by encouraging a rabble and then defending its appalling actions in their press and pulpit. They seemed blind to the inconsistency of their praising God "for the high privilege of worshiping him according to conscience" while simultaneously repressing republican freedoms. They had lost all capacity for rational judgment, failing to distinguish between radical abolitionists of the school of William Lloyd Garrison or George Barrell Cheever and antislavery constitutionalists who cherished social order. "All who will not bow down to the idol, and acknowledge slavery to be right, and humane, and scriptural, are to be denounced as abolition tories and incendiaries," lamented the *Christian Advocate and Journal*.[46] The MECS had been annexed by an evil proslavery power.

Apart from expressions of alarm in the columns of the *St. Louis Christian Advocate*, most southern Methodist spokesmen either vigorously sustained or resignedly acquiesced in the action against Bewley, dismissing the line between "abolitionism" and "antislavery" as a distinction without a difference. Their logic was clear. The MEC was committed to extirpating slavery, its position all the more assertive since the Buffalo General Conference of May 1860, controlled by "rampant Abolitionism," had altered the chapter on slavery to declare the institution "contrary to the laws of God and nature." The church had become the ecclesiastical arm of William Seward and the Black Republicans: Bewley and all agents of the MEC operating in the slave states were their "advance guard." According to the *New Orleans Christian Advocate*, conspiracy was the natural "fruit of the doctrine taught by the entire Northern Methodist press" of Edward Thomson, Calvin Kingsley, Erastus Haven, and Charles Elliott; "freedom of speech" was one thing, Methodist incendiarism another. For Texans, their minds full of John Brown and, through the summer of 1860, their state consumed by rumors of slave plots, arson, and rebellion, Bewley's death called for no apology. "There are cases in which Lynch law is expedient, necessary, just," explained the editor of the *Texas Christian Advocate*. Bewley had fallen "a victim to a reign of lawlessness, which he and other of his kind have for some time been laboring to inaugurate and promote in Texas." Having ignored several warnings to desist from his antislavery missionary work or be treated "as an aggressor," he had paid the predicted price. A North Carolina editor was in no doubt that Bewley's "complicity with murderous abolition plots of insurrection and bloodshed was clearly proved," while William G. Brownlow, who remembered Bewley from his Tennessee days as "rather a stubborn man," considered the vigilantes' work no more murderous "than the insurrection and burning of towns in Texas, under the direction of those associated with Mr. Bewley." If, as northerners insisted, he really was a pious man, then no harm had been done: "hanging was 'a short cut' to the Kingdom of God."[47]

Bewley's case has scarcely received its historical due in discussions of the political crisis of 1860–1861. It goes unremarked in Clarence Goen's thoughtful study of the fractured antebellum churches, and receives only a single brief mention in Emory Stevens Bucke's multivolume history of American Methodism.[48] Its neglect may have to do with the attention properly afforded the Harpers Ferry raid and John Brown's subsequent "martyrdom," and its occurring within the seemingly parochial world of Methodism. Yet the case did much to aggravate sectional tension at a critical time and in ways that John Brown had failed to do. Northern Methodists were certainly able to respond to Bewley's assassination with a unity of perception that they had failed to muster in Brown's case a year earlier. Where Brown's means seemed to many to have been bloody and dubious, Bewley's were constitutional and Christian. His was the genuine martyrdom of a "modest and peaceful" man, not the death of one whose prior career was stained by suggestions of horse thievery and murder.[49] For southern Methodists, the case confirmed the dangers so fearfully exposed by Brown's raid, but showed the need for even greater vigilance to thwart more cunning assaults on slavery by supposedly Christian missionaries of recognized churches.

The timing of Bewley's death, during the course of a presidential election on which hung the future of the Union, ensured that its lessons were aired well beyond the confines of Methodism, in the political press of both sections. If southerners saw in Bewley's missionary operations the shape of a fiendish future under a Republican presidency, northern critics of the "proslavery" course of national politics treated his lynching as a test of the administration's commitment to defending Americans' fundamental constitutional rights. Among the most insistent of voices was that of Thomas Eddy, the outspoken editor of Chicago's *North western Christian Advocate* and a barely camouflaged Republican. In an open letter to President Buchanan, he pointedly reflected that one million Methodists were asking, "can an Administration be found which will protect the rights of conscience and freedom of worship? . . . A few more such murders as that of Bewley, and the church will ask who will give us an Administration strong enough to uphold the rights dearest of all others? and for that man, be he whom he may, they will cast their united suffrage."[50] It was not long before Eddy's threat was repeated in the columns of the *Chicago Tribune* and other Republican organs across the North, to the acute discomfort of the Democratic press.[51] Such unabashed muscle flexing could leave no doubt that Methodists had reached their political majority.

CONCLUSION

Methodists who voted Republican in 1860 believed they were doing more than casting a ballot for a political party; when Lincoln won, their "flood of ecstasy," as Gilbert Haven expressed it, marked more than a party triumph.[52] Methodists joined with other Protestant evangelicals in a coalition driven not just by political calculation but by a burning sense of Christian duty and moral indignation to realize a multiple vision: freedom for slaves, freedom from the terror unleashed on godly men like hapless Anthony Bewley, release for both black and white from slavery's diabolical grip on both church and state, and a new direction for the Union. Of all Methodists, it was these triumphal Republicans—nourished by a postmillennialist creed that celebrated conscience, obedience to a higher law, and a strong sense of social responsibility—who had traveled furthest from the outlook of their church's first, apolitical generation by identifying the arrival of the kingdom of God with the success of a particular political party.

In rebuking their northern counterparts for this novel fusion of religion and politics, southern Methodists implicitly claimed the role of defenders of the primitive values of their church. Yet they too had drifted from the ground of their apolitical forebears, most pertinently and strikingly over slavery, where they moved from ambivalent hostility to ambivalent defense. Their leaders sustained that defense by maintaining a posture of political nonintervention, but in reality that stance was driven by a fundamental *political* need—the protection of the moral and socioeconomic basis of southern civilization. Moreover, southern Methodists could be as energetically engaged in partisan politics as any of their code-nominationalists in the free states. And though they stopped short of Republican Methodists' linking of the inauguration of God's kingdom with the triumph of a party, they were ready enough to identify the interests of their section, and subsequently the destiny of their Confederate nation, with the purposes of the Almighty. The experience of civil war would, of course, further transform American Methodists' understanding of their country's political mission at home and abroad and of their role in it. But already by 1861 the changes of fifty years had made them philosophically deaf to the language of Francis Asbury and in particular to his insistent prescription, "Our kingdom is not of this world."

Notes

This chapter originally appeared in *Church History* 69:3 (Sept. 2000): 578–609. Reprinted with permission.

1. Walter B. Posey, *The Development of Methodism in the Old Southwest, 1783–1824* (Tuscaloosa, Ala.: Weatherford, 1933), 1; Donald G. Jones, *The Sectional Crisis and Northern Methodism: A Study in Piety, Political Ethics, and Civil Religion* (Metuchen, N.J.: Scarecrow, 1979), 226–27; Alfred Brunson, *A Western Pioneer; or, Incidents in the Life and Times of Rev. Alfred Brunson, A.M., D.D., Embracing a Period of over Seventy Years*, 2 vols. (Cincinnati, Ohio: Hitchchock and Walden, 1872), 1:217–18, 344–45; Robert D. Clark, *The Life of Matthew Simpson* (New York: Macmillan, 1956), 105–11; *Christian Advocate and Journal* (New York; hereafter cited as *CA*), 12 June 1856; James E. Pilcher, *Life and Labors of Elijah H. Pilcher* (New York: Hunt & Eaton, 1892), 115–16.

2. Donald G. Mathews, "Evangelical America: The Methodist Ideology," in *Rethinking Methodist History: A Bicentennial Historical Consultation*, ed. Russell E. Richey and Kenneth E. Rowe (Nashville, Tenn.: Kingswood, 1985), 91. The alternative value system of early Methodists has long been a feature of the movement's historiography. Since the mid-1970s, when Mathews, in *Religion in the Old South* (Chicago: University of Chicago Press, 1977), offered an analysis of the egalitarian elements of southern evangelicalism in the early republic, the countercultural and anti-elitist thrust of early Methodism has been the subject of increasing scrutiny, most notably in William H. Williams, *The Garden of American Methodism: The Delmarva Peninsula, 1769–1820* (Wilmington, Del.: Scholarly Resources, 1984); Nathan O. Hatch, *The Democratization of American Christianity* (New Haven, Conn.: Yale University Press,

1989); Russell E. Richey, *Early American Methodism* (Bloomington: Indiana University Press, 1991); Christine Leigh Heyrman, *Southern Cross: The Beginnings of the Bible Belt* (New York: Knopf, 1997); John H. Wigger, *Taking Heaven by Storm: Methodism and the Rise of Popular Christianity in America* (New York: Oxford University Press, 1998); Cynthia Lynn Lyerly, *Methodism and the Southern Mind, 1770–1810* (New York: Oxford University Press, 1998).

3. Richey, *Early American Methodism*, xii–xiii, xvii–xviii, 33, 35–44, 102; Fred J. Hood, *Reformed America: The Middle and Southern States, 1783–1837* (University: University of Alabama Press, 1980).

4. Richey, *Early American Methodism*, 40–41, 88–91.

5. Benjamin F. Tefft, *The Republican Influence of Christianity: A Discourse* (Bangor, Maine: n.p., 1841), 1–8. See also D. S. Doggett, *A Sermon on the Death of General William Henry Harrison, Late President of the United States, Delivered in the Chapel of Randolph Macon College, April 18, 1841* (Richmond, Va.: Christian Advocate, 1841); George Peck, *National Evils and Their Remedy: A Discourse Delivered on the Occasion of the National Fast, May 14, 1841* (New York: Lane & Sandford, 1841); *Western Christian Advocate* (Cincinnati, Ohio; hereafter *WCA*), 24 and 31 July, 7 Aug. 1840, 24 Sept. 1841 (Leonidas Hamline), 19 and 26 Feb., 9 Apr. 1841 (Rezin Sapp), 21 May 1841 (James B. Finley).

6. George M. Marsden, *Fundamentalism and American Culture: The Shaping of Twentieth-Century Evangelicalism, 1870–1925* (New York: Oxford University Press, 1980), 7, 85–93, 252. Paul Kleppner, *The Third Electoral System, 1853–1892: Parties, Voters, and Political Cultures* (Chapel Hill: University of North Carolina Press, 1979), esp. xix–xx, 185–97, distinguishes between "evangelical pietists," who saw conversion as only part of a broader obligation to sanctify society, and "salvationist pietists," who felt no responsibility to transform the wider culture. His categories correspond respectively to Marsden's "Calvinists" and "pietists," which are less cumbersome and no less theologically nuanced.

7. Chauncey Hobart, *Recollection of My Life: Fifty Years of Itinerancy in the Northwest* (Red Wing, Minn.: Red Wing Printing, 1885), 202–3; Calvin Fletcher, *The Diary of Calvin Fletcher*, 9 vols., ed. Gayle Thornbrough, Dorothy L. Riker, and Paula Corpuz (Indianapolis: Indiana Historical Society, 1972–1983), 3:80; Thomas B. Miller, *Original and Selected Thoughts on the Life and Times of Rev. Thomas Miller, and Rev. Thomas Warburton* (Bethlehem, Pa.: White, 1860), 17; Heman Bangs, *The Autobiography and Journal of Rev. Heman Bangs* (New York: Tibbals & Son, 1872), 316; Leonard F. Smith, "Diary," 29 Aug., 17 Nov. 1860, Illinois State Historical Society, Springfield. Harry L. Watson, *Jacksonian Politics and Community Conflict: The Emergence of the Second American Party System in Cumberland County, North Carolina* (Baton Rouge: University of Louisiana Press, 1981), 240–41, identifies a high proportion of political abstainers among the Methodists of that county.

8. *Northwestern Christian Advocate* (Chicago; hereafter *NWCA*), 12 Nov. 1856; *WCA*, 6 Jan. 1843; D. R. McAnally, *Life and Times of Rev. S. Patton, D.D., and Annals of the Holston Conference* (St. Louis, Mo.: Methodist Book Depository, 1859), 239.

9. Granville Moody, *A Life's Retrospect: Autobiography of Rev. Granville Moody* (Cincinnati, Ohio: Cranston and Stowe, 1890), 311; William G. Lewis, *Biography of*

Samuel Lewis, First Superintendent for Common Schools for the State of Ohio (Cincinnati, Ohio: Methodist Book Concern, 1857), 369; Wilson L. Spottswood, Brief Annals (Harrisburg, Pa.: M. E. Book Room, 1888), 39.

10. William McDonald and John E. Searles, The Life of Rev. John S. Inskip, President of the National Association for the Promotion of Holiness (Chicago: Christian Witness, 1885), 49; WCA, 25 June 1856; William H. Lawrence, The Earnest Minister: A Record of the Life, Labors and Literary Remains of Rev. Ruliff S. Lawrence (Philadelphia: Wallace, 1873), 29; New York Evangelist, 4 Jan. 1844.

11. CA, 5 June 1829; Luther Lee, Autobiography (New York: Phillips & Hunt, 1882), 233; Luther Lee, A Sermon for the Times: Prohibitory Laws (New York: Wesleyan Book Room, 1852); Davis W. Clark, Evils and Remedy of Intemperance: An Address (New York: Osborn, 1847), 11, 13–15; Thomas A. Goodwin, Seventy-Six Years Tussle with the Traffic: Being a Condensation of the Laws Relating to the Liquor Traffic in Indiana from 1807 to 1883 (Indianapolis, Ind.: Carlon & Hollenbeck, 1883), 8–9.

12. McDonald and Searles, The Life of Rev. John S. Inskip, 49; WCA, 25 June 1856.

13. Barbara Berg, The Remembered Gate: Origins of American Feminism: The Woman and the City, 1800–1860 (New York: Oxford University Press, 1978), 167–68; Lori Ginzberg, Women and the Work of Benevolence: Morality, Politics, and Class in the Nineteenth-Century United States (New Haven, Conn.: Yale University Press, 1990), 71–79; Spottswood, Brief Annals, 135–36.

14. J. C. Chambers to M. Simpson, 2 May 1850; J. L. Smith to M. Simpson, 23 May 1850; W. Daily to M. Simpson, 5 Dec. 1850, all in M. Simpson Papers, Library of Congress; Lorenzo D. Johnson, Chaplains of the General Government, with Objections to Their Employment Considered (New York: Sheldon, Blakeman, 1856), 63 and passim; George G. Smith, The Life and Times of George Foster Pierce (Sparta, Ga.: Hancock, 1888), 324; John D. Wade, Augustus Baldwin Longstreet: A Study of the Culture of the South (1924; rpt., Athens: University of Georgia Press, 1969), 123–24; Oscar P. Fitzgerald, John B. McFerrin: A Biography (Nashville, Tenn.: M. E. Church, South, 1888), 91, 116, 168–69, 196–99, 243.

15. Harrison Medal Minstrel: Comprising a Collection of the Most Popular and Patriotic Songs (Philadelphia: Grigg & Elliott, 1840), 3, 21, 65; J. S. Littell, The Clay Minstrel; or, National Songster, 2nd ed. (Philadelphia: Thomas, Cowperthwait, 1844), 235–36; J. Campbell to W. B. Campbell, 4 Feb. 1840, quoted in Thomas B. Alexander, "The Presidential Campaign of 1840 in Tennessee," Tennessee Historical Quarterly 1 (1942): 26–27; George H. Hickman, The Life and Public Services of the Hon. James Knox Polk (Baltimore, Md.: Hickman, 1844), 5; WCA, 7 Aug. 1840; Jonesboro Whig, 9 May 1840.

16. Ruth H. Bloch, Visionary Republic: Millennial Themes in American Thought, 1756–1800 (Cambridge: Cambridge University Press, 1985), 56, 61, 63, 204–5, and passim.

17. New York Tribune, 25 July 1856; Jonesboro Whig, 8 Dec. 1847.

18. For ethnocultural approaches, see Lee Benson, The Concept of Jacksonian Democracy: New York as a Test Case (Princeton, N.J.: Princeton University Press, 1961), esp. 288–328; Ronald P. Formisano, The Birth of Mass Political Parties: Michigan, 1827–1861 (Princeton, N.J.: Princeton University Press, 1971); Michael F. Holt, Forging a Majority: The Formation of the Republican Party in Pittsburgh, 1848–1860 (New Haven,

Conn.: Yale University Press, 1969); Kleppner, *The Third Electoral System.* The classic economic interpretation is Arthur M. Schlesinger, Jr., *The Age of Jackson* (Boston: Little, Brown, 1945). Other influential interpretations, based on the primary importance of a changing economy, include Watson, *Jacksonian Politics and Community Conflict*; John Ashworth, *"Agrarians" and "Aristocrats": Party Political Ideology in the United States, 1837–1846* (London: Royal Historical Society, 1983); Charles Sellers, *The Market Revolution: Jacksonian America, 1815–1846* (New York: Oxford University Press, 1991).

19. Sophia Hogan Boogher, *Recollections of John Hogan by His Daughter* (St. Louis, Mo.: Mound City Press, 1927), 40–41.

20. *CA*, 4 Nov. and 23 Dec. 1840, 17 Nov. 1841; William I. Fee, *Bringing the Sheaves: Gleanings from the Harvest Fields in Ohio, Kentucky and West Virginia* (Cincinnati, Ohio: Cranston & Curts, 1896), 134–37; James D. Anthony, *Life and Times of Rev. J. D. Anthony: An Autobiography* (Atlanta, Ga.: Byrd, 1896), 80–81; Richard H. Rivers, *The Life of Robert Paine, D.D., Bishop of the Methodist Episcopal Church, South* (Nashville, Tenn.: Publishing House of the M. E. Church, South, 1916), 99.

21. Paul Goodman, "The Social Basis of New England Politics in Jacksonian America," *Journal of the Early Republic* 6 (1986): 23–58; Watson, *Jacksonian Politics and Community Conflict*, 23–24.

22. George C. Baker, *An Introduction to the History of Early New England Methodism, 1789–1839* (Durham, N.C.: Duke University Press, 1941), 41–49; Mary L. Ninde, *William Xavier Ninde: A Memorial* (New York: Eaton & Mains, 1902), 50–51.

23. Brunson, *Western Pioneer*, 1:35–43, 172–73.

24. Bangs, however, had his Methodist critics. See Charles I. Foster, *An Errand of Mercy: The Evangelical United Front, 1790–1837* (Chapel Hill: University of North Carolina Press, 1960), 223–48.

25. Brunson, *Western Pioneer*, 1:344–45.

26. Nathan Bangs, *A History of the Methodist Episcopal Church*, 4 vols. (New York: Mason and Lane, 1838–41), 2:351; Peter Cartwright, *Autobiography of Peter Cartwright: The Backwoods Preacher*, ed. W. P. Strickland (New York: Methodist Book Concern, 1856), 64–72 and passim; Richard Carwardine, "Unity, Pluralism and the Spiritual Market-Place: Interdenominational Competition in the Early American Republic," in *Unity and Diversity in the Church: Papers Read at the 1994 Summer Meeting and the 1995 Winter Meeting of the Ecclesiastical History Society*, Studies in Church History, No. 32, ed. R. N. Swanson (Oxford: Blackwell, 1996), 317–35.

27. F. Richardson, *From Sunrise to Sunset: Reminiscence* (Bristol, Tenn.: King, 1890), 107–8.

28. *CA*, 14 Dec. 1842; *WCA*, 18 Nov. 1842; Richard J. Carwardine, *Evangelicals and Politics in Antebellum America* (New Haven, Conn.: Yale University Press, 1993), 199–234.

29. Sellers, *Market Revolution*, 137–38, 157–61, 164–65, 178, 299–300; Fletcher, *Diary*, passim; Boogher, *Recollections of John Hogan*, 18; William W. Crane, *Autobiography and Miscellaneous Writings* (Syracuse, N.Y.: Hall, 1891), 84–85; L. F. Smith, "Diary," 9 Oct. 1860; Richard J. Carwardine, "'Antinomians' and 'Arminians': Methodists and the Market Revolution," in *The Market Revolution in America: Social, Political and*

Religious Expressions, 1800–1880, ed. Melvyn Stokes and Stephen Conway (Charlottesville: University of Virginia Press, 1996), 282–307.

30. Williams, *Garden of American Methodism*, 174–75; Brunson, *Western Pioneer*, 1:173; Cartwright, *Autobiography*, 98; L. F. Smith, "Diary," 3 Sept. 1860.

31. Ray Holder, *William Winans: Methodist Leader in Antebellum Mississippi* (Jackson: University Press of Mississippi, 1977), 103–4; Crane, *Autobiography*, 79; Brunson, *Western Pioneer*, 2:139 and passim; Lewis, *Biography of Samuel Lewis*, 200–202, 211; Robert M. Goodloe, "David Rice McAnally," *Dictionary of American Biography*, ed. Dumas Malone (New York: Charles Scribner's Sons, 1933), 11:549; Edmund J. James, "Reverend Colin Dew James: A Pioneer Methodist Preacher of Early Illinois," *Journal of the Illinois State Historical Society* 9 (1917): 451.

32. For an extended discussion of this theme, see Carwardine, *Evangelicals and Politics*, 199–234.

33. William E. Gienapp, *The Origins of the Republican Party, 1852–1856* (New York: Oxford University Press, 1987), passim; B. Adams, "Diary," 1 and 4 Nov. 1856, Methodist Center, Drew University, Madison, N.J.; Gilbert Haven, "The National Midnight," in Haven, *National Sermons: Sermons, Speeches and Letters on Slavery and Its War* (Boston: Lee and Shepard, 1869), 120–21; Stephen Allen, *The Life of Rev. John Allen, Better Known as "Camp Meeting John"* (Boston: Russell, 1888), 41; William E. Gienapp, "Who Voted for Lincoln?" in *Abraham Lincoln and the American Political Tradition*, ed. John L. Thomas (Amherst: University of Massachusetts Press, 1986), 75; L. F. Smith, "Diary," 8 and 29 Aug., 3 and 10 Sept., 15 Oct. 1860; *Chicago Tribune*, 25 May 1860; W. Hamilton to M. Simpson, 23 Feb. 1861, M. Simpson Papers, Methodist Center, Drew University, Madison, N.J. Cf. Charles Baumer Swaney, *Episcopal Methodism and Slavery: With Sidelights on Ecclesiastical Politics* (Boston: Badger, 1926), 283, which underestimates Methodist support for Lincoln in 1860.

34. Fitzgerald, *McFerrin*, 186; *Pittsburgh Christian Advocate*, 30 Apr. 1840; *CA*, 30 Oct. 1844, 14 May 1845; T. Stringfield to his wife, 4 June 1844, Stringfield Papers, Southern Historical Collection, University of North Carolina, Chapel Hill. For the schism in the MEC in 1844 and its implications for the Union and for sectional alienation, see Clarence C. Goen, *Broken Churches, Broken Nation: Denominational Schisms and the Coming of the Civil War* (Macon, Ga.: Mercer University Press, 1985); Swaney, *Episcopal Methodism and Slavery*.

35. Arthur E. Jones, Jr., "The Years of Disagreement, 1844–61," in *The History of American Methodism*, 3 vols., ed. Emory Stevens Bucke et al. (Nashville, Tenn.: Abingdon, 1964), 2:159–76; Fee, *Bringing the Sheaves*, 242–34; Henry Bascom et al., *Brief Appeal to Public Opinion, in a Series of Exceptions to the Course and Action of the Methodist Episcopal Church, from 1844 to 1848* (Louisville, Ky.: Early, 1848), 93–106, 127–34; *CA*, 12 Jan. and 24 May 1848.

36. Freeborn Garrettson Hibbard, *Biography of Rev. Leonidas L. Hamline, D.D., Late One of the Bishops of the Methodist Episcopal Church* (Cincinnati, Ohio: Hitchcock and Walden, 1880), 192–93, 216; *Knoxville Whig*, 22 July 1846; *CA*, 3 Nov. 1847, 24 May 1848; *WCA*, 27 Sept. and 25 Oct. 1848, 9 Oct. 1850; *Southern Christian Advocate* (Charleston, S.C.), 9 June 1848.

37. Lorenzo Waugh, *A Candid Statement of the Course Pursued by the Preachers of the Methodist Church South, in Trying to Establish Their New Organization in Missouri* (Cincinnati, Ohio: James, 1848), 60–61; Lorenzo Waugh, *Autobiography of Lorenzo Waugh* (San Francisco: Methodist Book Concern, 1896), 164–66; *Knoxville Whig*, 25 Aug. 1849; Hibbard, *Leonidas L. Hamline*, 211–15; J. Thompson to T. Bond, 30 Oct. 1846, P. Twiford to T. Bond, 24 Nov. 1846, both in T. E. Bond Papers, Dickinson College; *CA*, 5 and 12 Oct., 11, 18, and 25 Nov. 1846, 20 and 27 Jan., 3, 10, and 24 Feb. 1847.

38. *WCA*, 11 Feb., 17, 24, and 31 Mar., 7 and 28 Apr., 26 July 1848, 24 Dec. 1851; *CA*, 19 July 1848, 21 Mar. and 13 June 1850; *Southern Christian Advocate*, 28 Mar. 1845, 2 and 16 June 1848, 28 Nov. 1851, 5 and 19 Nov. 1852; *Knoxville Whig*, 24 Jan. and 6 Apr. 1849; Bascom et al., *Brief Appeal*, 5; Hibbard, *Leonidas L. Hamline*, 218–22; Edward H. Myers, *The Disruption of the Methodist Episcopal Church, 1844–46: Comprising a Thirty Years' History of the Relations of the Two Methodisms* (Nashville, Tenn.: Redford, 1875), 151; Jones, "The Years of Disagreement, 1844–61," 177–81; Moody, *Life's Retrospect*, 227.

39. *CA*, 6 Oct. 1847; Bascom et al., *Brief Appeal*, 10, 60, 165–69.

40. Waugh, *Candid Statement*, 70; Waugh, *Autobiography*, 149–71; *CA*, 5 Jan., 15 Mar., 24 May, and 19 July 1848, 17 Oct. 1850; Hibbard, *Leonidas L. Hamline*, 205; Fee, *Bringing the Sheaves*, 239–40; *WCA*, 27 Sept. 1848; John Stewart, *Highways and Hedges; or, Fifty Years of Western Methodism* (Cincinnati, Ohio: Hitchcock and Walden, 1870), 260; Edward Thomson, *Life of Edward Thomson, Late Bishop of the Methodist Episcopal Church* (Cincinnati, Ohio: Cranston & Stowe, 1885), 87–88.

41. *WCA*, 9 July, 17 Sept., 1 Oct. 1856; L. B. Dennis to M. Simpson, 22 Jan. 1856, M. Simpson Papers, Library of Congress.

42. *WCA*, 2 and 23 May, 25 July, 15, 22 (quoting *Central Christian Advocate*), and 29 Aug., 5 and 26 Sept., 10 Oct., 7 Nov. 1855; *NWCA*, 25 May, 29 Oct. 1856; *CA*, 10 July, 7 Aug. 1856.

43. Wesley Smith, A *Defence of the Methodist Episcopal Church against the Charges of Rev. S. Kelly and Others, of the M.E. Church, South* (Fairmont, Va.: True Virginian, 1855), 21, 42, 45, and passim.

44. *Richmond Christian Advocate*, 13 Jan. 1859; *Southern Christian Advocate*, 11 Feb. 1858, 16 June, 21 July, 11 Aug. 1859; *Knoxville Whig*, 15 May 1858, 8 Oct. 1859, 21 Jan., 18 Feb. 1860.

45. Henry B. Ridgaway, *The Life of Edmund S. Janes, D.D., LL.D.* (New York: Phillips & Hunt, 1882), 224–29; *Central Christian Advocate* (St. Louis, Mo.), 26 Sept., 10 Oct. 1860; *CA*, 27 Sept., 22 Nov. 1860.

46. *CA*, 30 Aug., 27 Sept. 1860; *Central Christian Advocate*, 26 Sept. 1860.

47. *CA*, 10–31 May, 7–28 June, 5 July, 27 Sept. 1860 (for *New Orleans Christian Advocate*); *Knoxville Whig*, 30 June, 29 Sept. 1860; *Southern Christian Advocate*, 2 Aug. 1860; *Texas Christian Advocate*, 31 May 1860, quoted in Wesley Norton, *Religious Newspapers in the Old Northwest to 1861: A History, Bibliography and Record of Opinion* (Athens: Ohio University Press, 1977), 122; *Texas Christian Advocate*, 13 Sept. 1860, quoted in *Central Christian Advocate*, 26 Sept. 1860; *North Carolina Christian Advocate* (Raleigh), 6 Nov. 1860.

48. Goen, *Broken Churches, Broken Nation*; Bucke et al., *History of American Methodism*. The Bewley affair is addressed in Wesley Norton, "The Methodist Episcopal Church and the Civil Disturbances in North Texas in 1859 and 1860," *Southwestern Historical Quarterly* 68 (1965): 317–41; and Donald J. Reynolds, "Reluctant Martyr: Anthony Bewley and the Texas Slave Insurrection Panic of 1860," *Southwestern Historical Quarterly* 97 (1993): 345–61.

49. *NWCA*, 13 Sept. 1860.

50. Ibid.

51. See, for example, *Albany Evening Journal*, 19 Sept. 1860.

52. Haven, *National Sermons*, 179.

New Configurations

SLAVERY, RACE, AND POLITICAL IDEOLOGY IN THE WHITE CHRISTIAN SOUTH BEFORE AND AFTER THE CIVIL WAR

Luke E. Harlow

WILLIAM ELLISON BOGGS spoke for many white Christian southerners in 1881 when he addressed a reunited regiment of former South Carolina Confederate soldiers. Boggs, who had served as their chaplain during the Civil War and would later preside over the University of Georgia, brought a message of sectional solidarity. He assured his partisan audience, in the words of the speech's published title, that the South was "vindicated from the charge of treason and rebellion." Boggs knew there might be some southerners who—now sixteen years removed from General Robert E. Lee's surrender at Appomattox Courthouse—thought that the "dead past" should "bury its dead issues." With such thinking on the rise, Boggs wanted to drive home his point: *"questions of principle can never be buried."* The Civil War was a conflict ultimately about "right and wrong," and Boggs saw a long record of northern wrongs. Most recently, his people had lived through the "useless indignities and oppressions" of the so-called Reconstruction era. Before that, there were "the fierce denunciations that for years had poured upon us from the partisan press and from the orators of abolitionism." Southerners—and he meant *white* southerners—were a subjugated people before the war, and as they held strongly to republican constitutional principles, they had been coerced into the conflict. Indeed, Boggs told his listeners, seceding southerners had earned "the inalienable 'right of revolution'" and were on balance no different than those eighteenth-century colonial American patriots who had revolted against Great Britain and established the United States.[1]

Not only were Confederates in the right politically, Boggs claimed, but they were also right religiously. Invoking arguments that dominated white southern religious thought in the late antebellum era, forthrightly Boggs maintained that American slavery was a properly Christian institution. Even if some antebellum northerners "had come to look upon bond-service as an unlawful relation," such an "opinion is totally inconsistent, as anybody with half an eye can see, with the moral standard of the Old Testament, or of the New." Not only was southern slavery biblically sanctioned but, Boggs argued, "the children of Africa . . . were the best servants in the world under the old arrangement." It was not the fault of America's black population that they had been enslaved—that blame fell "chiefly" to "old England and New England" for establishing and sustaining the slave trade. But once slavery was established, it had proved essential to the uplift of Africans as a people. It was true, Boggs believed, that former slaves possessed "simple minds," but their condition had greatly improved since the earliest contact between blacks and whites on American soil. In self-congratulatory and sensationalistic prose, Boggs described the part white southern Christians had played in improving the lives of the "black brother": "They came to us debased savages, the naked worshippers of *fetiches*, the dupes of Obi-men, and of Gre-gre women, some of them being eaters of human flesh. Under our tuition they were taught the habits of order, decency, and industry. Under us they forsook their bestial idolatry." Furthermore, "[h]undreds of thousands of them, more, indeed, than have been won to Christ on heathen ground by all the devoted missionaries of Christendom, have become sincere worshippers of the God in heaven." The white southern religious contribution to American blacks' lives was critical, Boggs argued, and if it were not for the "intermeddling of conceited busy-bodies," white southerners could have done even more.[2]

With the Emancipation Proclamation and the Thirteenth Amendment, the master-slave relationship was legally and permanently severed. Boggs, as a loyal son of the antebellum South, utterly disdained Reconstruction, but he did not blame freedpeople for what he saw as the plight of the white South. Those former slaves—who joined with local "scalawag" white southerners and northern blacks and white "carpetbaggers" to form a dominant Republican coalition during the late 1860s Reconstruction era—"came very near being used by carpet-baggers and other thieves to destroy whatever had been saved from the wreck of the war."

This political development was a most unfortunate one for blacks, Boggs believed, because they did not truly understand what they were doing. African Americans "have been all along used as the '*cat's paw*' to serve the partisan ends of white men." Like "the little child" who, in Boggs's telling, "played with fire" and "burn[ed] down his father's house," freedpeople "were hardly more conscious of the horrible evils wrought by their votes."[3]

Because of Reconstruction, a new set of racial relationships now existed but, because white southerners had reclaimed control of their political destiny—in the period commonly referred to as "redemption"—Boggs argued that his fellow white southerners could exercise new paternalism in a way not altogether different from the old. As a result, whites were still required to practice benevolence toward their racial unequals. While Boggs conceded that his auditors might be "tempted by the fact that [the blacks] once were our bondsmen, and were wrongfully taken from us," he reminded his white southern audience that they had "*consented* to the will of our conquerors." Therefore southern whites should "be kind to the black man in his troubles and afflictions . . . [and] in his sickness and sorrow, as Christ tells you to do." White southerners were still obligated to provide religious instruction for the South's former slaves and, Boggs insisted, whites should take the charge seriously. After all, Boggs argued, whites had provided such teaching under slavery and "know far more than [the former slave] does."[4]

For William Ellison Boggs, as for much of the South's white population after the Civil War, the slavery question might have been resolved legally and by military force, but not ideologically or, above all, socially. In the antebellum era, proslavery ideology had represented a totalizing world view that served to order the lives of white southerners. Central to this ideology was the place of Christian, particularly evangelical Protestant, theology. White southerners in the Old South came to believe that the slavery in their region, and the hierarchy led by white elites that attended it, had been "ordained by God" as a proper mode of social relations.[5] Theological writing on these subjects was so dense, prolific, and intellectually persuasive that it played a central (if not precisely calculable) factor in making hundreds of thousands of southerners, most of whom had never held slaves, willing to face death in the Civil War. Historians have come to know well the idea that Drew Gilpin Faust has stated succinctly: "The most fundamental source of legitimation for the Confederacy was Christianity."[6] White southerners entered the Civil War convinced that God was on their side.

Given the robust nature of southern religious proslavery thought before the Civil War, it is not surprising that white southerners would retain proslavery logic after the conflict. Indeed, historians have long known that many of the ideas associated with proslavery arguments persisted well beyond the immediate years surrounding emancipation and the Confederate defeat.[7] As James L. Roark put it in his classic study of white southern planters in the Civil War era, after the war, "[f]undamental ideas gave way, but old habits lived on."[8] Much the same could be said about southern proslavery religious thought. Theological proslavery rhetoric remained but, in the absence of legal slavery, old arguments had to be deployed in different—though not always new—ways.

For the nation's political history, the lingering force of proslavery ideology exerted a substantial impact. From 1880 through 1916, the Democratic candidate won every presidential race in every one of the eleven states of the former Confederacy (110 out of 110). From 1920 through 1945 (and counting the States' Rights party victories of Strom Thurmond in 1948 as Democratic victories), the Democratic candidate lost only 6 times out of 88 state contests—and 5 of those were in 1928 when voters in the strongly evangelical states of Florida, North Carolina, Tennessee, Texas, and Virginia chose Herbert Hoover over the Roman Catholic Al Smith. The electoral votes of those eleven states represented about one-fourth of the national total during this period (ranging from 94 to 127 and from 23.4 percent to 26.7 percent).[9] Moreover, it is pertinent to note that most African Americans were excluded from the polls for these elections and that white evangelical Protestants were strongly overrepresented in these states as compared to the rest of the country. Given election realities in the South and the influence of the Democratic solid South in the nation, it means that the ideology of southern whites played a larger role in national political history than the simple numbers might suggest. To the extent, therefore, that proslavery ideas remained alive and influential *after* the Civil War, to that extent they were significant for the nation.

This chapter does not pretend to treat the full history of southern religious ideas in connection with the nation's entire political history. It does, however, address a specific issue that bears on these larger matters, but one that has received scant historical attention. The question, which the opinions of William Ellison Boggs show were very much alive in 1881, is: what happened to the white southern religious proslavery argument after the Civil War? In answering that question, this chapter suggests that, once slavery ended, proslavery divines grew increasingly reliant on racist assumptions to hold their intellectual ground. The theological proslavery argument had always been racist, but in the antebellum era, with formal slavery intact, slavery's defenders were not yet a "conquered" people, which is how they saw themselves following the Civil War. After the conflict, defeated Confederates reached for ways to prove the righteousness of their cause. Moreover, because actual slavery no longer existed, white religious southerners faced a social and political landscape that they found uncomfortable and threatening. They could no longer rely on the full force of proslavery ideology to sustain their cause. But, since they were familiar with the contours of the old argument, proslavery Protestants in the postwar South could apply selected aspects of it to make sense of the world that they confronted. Thus the proslavery theology did not disappear, and its racial aspect proved the easiest part to retain.

THE ANTEBELLUM WHITE SOUTHERN ARGUMENT

In the minds of antebellum white southern Protestants, slavery served as shorthand for a much broader range of social concerns. American clergy, both North and South, in the middle decades of the nineteenth century found themselves in an uneasy relationship with the society emerging around them. As historian Mark Hanley has explained, American Protestant ministers—not happy supporters of the values endorsed by the young nation—had a "quarrel" with the American project. These clergy thought the nation had too closely wedded itself to what they called the "new infidelity": a generally liberal outlook on the world that accentuated human ability and accepted that human beings possessed within themselves the capability of leading a healthy march of social and economic progress.[10] In the Old South, as historian Kenneth Startup found, clergy came to believe "that the economic enthusiasm of the day was leading to a deadly indifference toward higher, spiritual things."[11] According to Startup, reservations about materialism were not limited to southern accents. If cultural divisions over regional lines marked many aspects of public culture in late antebellum America, Startup demonstrated that ministerial anxiety about material excess and the pursuit of luxury was surprisingly universal. Leading northern lights like Francis Wayland, the Baptist president of Brown University; Charles G. Finney, the most famous evangelist of the antebellum era; and the New York City Congregationalist minister Henry Ward Beecher all expressed reservations at one time or another about the nature of capitalism.[12]

If reticence about the economic climate of the day was shared above and below the Mason-Dixon Line, opinion diverged between the sections when ministers attempted to explain what a properly Christian social order might look like. For southerners, the common move was to assert the primacy of slavery as a counterweight to the excesses of materialism. The first place they turned for answers, the Bible, provided them with the answers they were looking for. Thus, in the minds of antebellum proslavery divines, religious questions about slavery became tests of religious orthodoxy.

As is the case with any document, let alone a sacred religious text, the words it contains are subject to interpretation. In nineteenth-century America, North and South, the biblical interpretive method that dictated the orthodoxy of the day was what historian Mark Noll has called a "Reformed, literal hermeneutic." Drawing on the Scottish Enlightenment principle of commonsense reasoning and relying on a heavily democratized and individualized understanding of the Christian faith, American evangelicals took the Bible to be the divinely inspired word of God that they could interpret—easily and, many believed, matter-of-factly—for themselves.[13]

Such an interpretive method worked well for southern defenders of slavery. A noted Baptist preacher from Virginia, Thornton Stringfellow, provides the clearest example of the southern proslavery commitment to this form of biblical literalism. In a famous treatise initially published in 1841—it was widely circulated and published in a variety of forms during the late antebellum period—Stringfellow painstakingly mined the biblical text to show the divine imprimatur behind slavery. Canvassing the Old and New Testaments, Stringfellow hoped southerners would "be seen cleaving to the Bible and taking all our decisions about this [slavery] matter from its inspired pages."[14] Undeniably, thinking like Stringfellow's was widespread among southern clergy in the mid-nineteenth century. Passage upon passage, throughout the Old and New Testaments, referred to and endorsed slavery.

Proslavery southerners had all the evidence they believed was required to establish the righteousness of slaveholding. Because the literal letter of the Holy Writ offered no succinct denunciation of slavery, proslavery lights looked upon abolitionist argumentation with derision.[15] Proslavery divines argued that new conceptions about what constituted moral behavior, independent of the aegis of the church, led abolitionists to read too much of their own agenda into the biblical text.[16] South Carolina Presbyterian James Henley Thornwell, the leading proslavery divine of the antebellum era, was dumbfounded by "what may be called *the Christian argument* against slavery." Abolitionists, Thornwell wrote in 1851, created their agenda from "the abstrusest of all speculations upon the vexed question of 'human rights,' and not the obvious teachings of the Scriptures." The only way a biblical case could be made against slavery, Thornwell wrote, was by "strained application of passages, or forced inferences of doctrines, in open violation of the law that Scripture is its own interpreter." By Thornwell's reading, anyone claiming to have a biblical case against slavery violated traditional forms of biblical interpretation and imposed detrimental, novel opinions upon the text.[17] The results of such misreadings of scripture, he argued in an 1850 sermon, was that Yankee abolitionists claimed to be motivated by philanthropic interests, but their "spurious charity" was "dictating the subversion of the cherished institutions of our fathers, and the hopes of the human race." The stakes were high, according to Thornwell. "It is not the narrow question of Abolitionism or Slavery," the minister argued. The matter was "not simply whether we shall emancipate our negroes or not; the real question is the relations of man to society, of States to the individual, and of the individual to the States—a question as broad as the interests of the human race."[18] According to Thornwell and other proslavery southerners, at the heart of the debate over the nature of slavery was a struggle for the primacy of world view.

Thornwell did not survive the Civil War but, for his intellectual heirs who did, it was as if he had been a prophet. Sixteen years after Lee's surrender, George James Atkinson Coulson, a Maryland Presbyterian who also published literary works under the pen name Alcibiades Jones, made just this point in an essay on "The Drift of American Politics" (1881). Recent years had seen the ascendancy of "tramps, negroes, and aliens—many of them ex-convicts" in American political life. Labor unrest marked the urban landscape, "bribery and corruption" abounded in politics, and "the moral character of many of the most prominent men now holding custody of national interests is as bad as that of any score of convicts taken at random from any Penitentiary." The nation was in a sorry state, according to Coulson. It was conceivable that the drift could lead to "Communism," which he styled "positive anarchy."[19]

The problems were myriad, but Coulson knew just whom to hold responsible: abolitionists. Seemingly out of nowhere had come "the sudden triumph of the Abolition party" in the form of organized Republicanism in the 1850s. While abolitionists had existed earlier, until that date they lacked real political power. Coulson argued—drawing a distinction between abolitionists and those who held a more moderate antislavery stance—that abolitionists had forced the South's hand and caused the Civil War. Abolitionists hated the Old South's slaveholding way of life and "published highly distorted caricatures of Southern society" that depicted "slaves universally groaning in chains, or howling under the lash of brutal owners." It was true, Coulson allowed, that there were some oppressive masters. But just the same, "[t]here were multitudes of godly men who owned slaves." Abolitionists may have been genuinely pious in their opposition to slavery, Coulson wrote, but they "were ignorant of the true status of the negro peasantry of the South; while all Southern men who have lived fifty years *know* that this people was the happiest peasantry on the face of the earth, until freedom was thrust upon them." Abolitionists had violated a divine trust and ignored the teachings of the Bible in calling for the end of slavery.[20]

Proslavery Protestants before and after the war believed they held the theological high ground over abolitionists. Yet if the southern clergy scored a cultural victory within their own region as they mastered the biblical interpretive method of the day, it was not an unproblematic victory. Certain southern divines became increasingly aware in the late antebellum period and into the Civil War years that American slavery fell short of Christian standards. The standard Christian pro-slavery move was to assert that slavery was not *malum in se*—evil in and of itself—and that slavery "in the abstract" was a just institution.[21] With this logic in mind, southern clergy proceeded as if the slavery sanctioned in the Bible were one and the same with American slavery.[22]

It was not. Little in the Bible gave a warrant for racism, for slavery in biblical times was not based on race. But racism had much to do with the southern proslavery argument.[23] Proslavery theologians like Thornwell often claimed that their exegesis was not race-based and that whites and blacks shared a "common brotherhood of humanity." In fact, a major inhibitor to just slavery, Thornwell said in an 1860 sermon, "Our National Sins," was that southerners were consumed by racist thinking. At great length, Thornwell laid out an argument that called into question those who justified slavery along racial lines. Biblically considered, Thornwell wrote, all humanity had a common progenitor: "No Christian man, therefore, can give any countenance to speculations which trace the negro to any other parent than Adam." By saying that blacks and whites were of common ancestry, Thornwell was saying that the races had an equal stake in the Christian faith and equally had access to "the redemption of Jesus Christ." In constructing an argument for slavery along racial lines, Thornwell maintained, defenders of slavery undermined the very aspects that made slavery a superior form of social organization to free labor.[24] Thornwell and other proslavery divines believed that slavery held the capacity for benevolence between owner and laborer. They argued the same could not be said about free labor, industrial capitalist arrangements, because the transformative power of the gospel of Jesus Christ, which emphasized charity and benevolence, was checked by the impulse to earn filthy lucre.[25] Yet if the pursuit of mammon bedeviled free labor systems, Thornwell argued that it was racism that undermined white southerners' ability to act as properly Christian masters. "The Saviour requires us to exchange places, in order that we may appreciate what is just and equal," Thornwell wrote. Real mastery, guided by the light of the Christian gospel, commanded masters to actually serve and provide for their slaves. Racial slavery, by definition, did not have within it the capacity for such Christian mastery because it thrived upon an inequitable social relationship.[26]

Thornwell no doubt believed what he said about nonracial slavery. Indeed, roughly a decade prior to his "Our National Sins" sermon, Thornwell preached what has gone down in the historical record as the most famous proslavery sermon of the antebellum era. In "The Christian Doctrine of Slavery"—also published as "The Rights and Duties of Masters" (1850)—Thornwell claimed that the weight of evidence proved that the races belonged to the "same humanity in which we glory as the image of God. We are not ashamed to call him *brother*." The South Carolinian implored his slaveholding audience along the same lines as he would a decade later: his listeners needed to give their slaves access to the gospel, to educate them, and to treat them fairly.[27]

Yet such statements, rather than revealing the possibility of a race-neutral proslavery argument, actually showed how deeply assumptions of racial superiority pervaded white southern culture. Proslavery divines drew upon what Stephen Haynes has called "intuitive racism," which shaped white southerners' attitudes about slavery.[28] Thus even Thornwell—in spite of overtures that called for black-white equality—wrote in 1861, "As long as that race, in its comparative degradation, co-exists side by side with the white, bondage is its normal condition."[29] In the end, even when bending over backward to define a slavery reformed by Christian principles, the Presbyterian leader could not avoid speaking of slavery as an institution solely for blacks. Their race made them fit slaves.

One of Thornwell's top students, Benjamin Morgan Palmer, pastor of New Orleans' First Presbyterian Church and a foremost shaper of postwar racial-religious orthodoxy, revealed even more clearly the extent to which racial concepts of slavery influenced the South's theological elite. In his sermon "Slavery: A Divine Trust" (1860), delivered not long after the election of Abraham Lincoln to the U.S. presidency, Palmer demonstrated that he had absorbed much of his mentor's ideas about the nature of slavery. Yet Palmer extended Thornwell's claims further than Thornwell himself had chosen to take them. Palmer took care to blur the distinction between American and biblical slavery. What, Palmer asked, was "at this time, [the South's] providential trust?" To preserve slavery, he argued. But it was not the slavery that Thornwell had defined, slavery in desperate need of reformation. No, Palmer claimed, southerners were called "*to conserve and to preserve the institution of slavery as now existing*."[30] This claim was a far cry from Thornwell's statement—preached only one week before and subsequently published alongside Palmer's "Slavery: A Divine Trust" in an 1861 collection of sermons on the sectional crisis—that southerners had to "come before the Lord as penitents" to express contrition for their failure to bring American slavery into conformity with a Christian standard.[31]

Persuasive as Thornwell and Palmer may have been among their own people, the southern proslavery argument did not persuade northern coreligionists. In the years leading up to the Civil War, the three most populous and socially prominent Protestant denominations fractured over questions of slavery and sectional loyalty: the Methodists in 1844, the Baptists in 1845, and the Presbyterians—already somewhat geographically divided by the Old School–New School break of

1837, where slavery was an important but secondary issue—in 1861. The Civil War was in many ways a fight about matters of central religious importance. What could not be sorted out by religious argumentation was decided on the field of battle. White southerners joined Confederate ranks to fight for a way of life ordered around the slavery institution that they believed God had provided for his people.[32]

AFTER LOSING THE WAR

If white southerners headed to war convinced that providence supported their cause, Confederate defeat and Reconstruction brought immense challenges to the white Christian South. The Civil War created massive destruction and fomented terror in unanticipated ways. Often with the blessing of religious authorities, northerners and southerners wreaked holy havoc upon their enemies. For the first time, civilian Americans found themselves confronted with warfare that was totalizing in its effects on all aspects of life. As Harry Stout has argued in his moral history of the conflict, it was not a just war; neither side proceeded morally.[33]

The Civil War disrupted routine aspects of American life; it also halted the basic functioning of many essential religious institutions and agencies in the South. Certain denominational newspapers, many of which rivaled the circulation of major secular newspapers even as they maintained the infrastructure for denominations, were brought to a standstill in the early 1860s. State denominational conventions and general assemblies either met irregularly at new locales or stopped meeting altogether. By 1866, church membership numbers had dropped precipitously. Religious colleges often had to shut their doors during the war and incurred huge financial losses. Given the extensive toll of the conflict by 1865, a massive need existed to rebuild the mechanisms and structures that had made religious life possible before 1861.[34]

For white southerners, the effort to reconstruct the South usually meant an effort to restore the antebellum status quo. To some extent they believed that God had used the Civil War to punish them for their sins of pride and arrogance as a section, but they did not think that they had been judged for complicity in slavery or secession. They simply could not believe that God condemned slavery and sought its end. White southerners remained largely convinced that their cause had been right and just. What historian Daniel Stowell called the "Confederate understanding" of the religious significance of the Civil War taught that "God had not deserted the South: the righteousness of the southern cause, the justice of God, and Confederate defeat could and would be reconciled." Thus, starting in the years immediately following defeat, southern clergy began to restate defenses of slavery and secession.[35]

Arnold W. Miller, a southern Presbyterian minister, wrote in an 1870 essay that southern religious whites had "accepted" defeat in only one sense: "The providence of God has sorely smitten them, and humbled them, and they desire to bow in submission to his holy will." Yet such an admission did not "mean that the justice of God has decided against the [Confederate] cause." Miller compared the white South to the biblical Hebrews, a people chosen particularly by God, who were regularly "defeated in battle, and even subjugated, by the more wicked heathen around them!" As was the case in the biblical era, Miller maintained, God's decrees were righteous, but they had to be obeyed by a righteous people. In the course of the war, southerners failed in that regard; they had not "acknowledged and maintained aright their relations to Christ, the great Head of State." No, Miller confessed, Confederates "refused to acknowledge him, in profession and practice; and he refused to acknowledge them." But justice would prevail, Miller argued. As was the case in the biblical record, divine judgment often fell upon "the less guilty people" first. "The heavy blow that has prostrated us, will yet make the North stagger and fall."[36]

Miller ended his essay by lashing out at the Fourteenth Amendment (1869). To Miller, the words of the South's most highly regarded antebellum politician, John C. Calhoun, had come true: the South had experienced "degradation greater than has yet fallen the lot of a free and enlightened people." The amendment, after three years of arduous debate and controversy in Congress, had passed only months before and in spite of unanimous Democratic opposition. It did not extend the vote to freedpeople—that came in 1870 with the Fifteenth Amendment—but did include African Americans as citizens. It also represented a congressional attack on the infamous Black Codes, southern laws passed in the wake of the Thirteenth Amendment, which banned slavery, that greatly hampered freedpeople's legal rights, civil liberties, and geographical mobility (usually these laws sanctioned labor contracts and antivagrancy statutes that bound former slaves to white-owned farms recovering from the devastation of the war). Miller, quoting Calhoun, argued that the result of such political action meant southern whites were "fleeing the homes of our ancestors and . . . abandoning our country to our former slaves." The South was "to become the permanent abode of disorder, anarchy, poverty, misery, and wretchedness." The idea of giving African Americans citizenship rights and political power—"making an inferior race predominant over a superior one," as Miller quoted a northern conservative—was abhorrent.[37]

Not surprisingly, southern African Americans interpreted the end of the war differently. For freedpeople, as for whites, God was in the conflict and providence had moved decisively. Former slaves also believed they were like the biblical Hebrews, but freedpeople read themselves into the Exodus narrative, where God had delivered his chosen people from Egyptian slavery. The Christian religion provided former slaves a means of emphasizing their value as persons, since God loved all people equally. Although before the war blacks and whites had worshiped together in biracial churches—indeed, the church often provided slaves their only outlet for public expression—the end of the war created an opportunity to form racially autonomous denominations, which African Americans seized immediately. Daniel Stowell has mapped out five major tenets of postbellum African-American religion: the belief that former masters had no claim over their religious life; the need for churches outside white influence; the need for black preachers; the acceptance of northern white economic support and education, so long as it did not come with strictures that dictated the shape of black religious life; and the need for schools and colleges to educate the newly freed African-American populace. The implementation of these aims led to the creation of many educational institutions, the abrupt withdrawal of southern blacks from white denominations, and the establishment of separate African-American denominations (or of links to black denominations already existing in the North). Such moves led southern African Americans to "cross Jordan" into their own religious "promised land," but as was the case for the biblical Hebrews, more challenges awaited them on the other side.[38]

Freedpeople's open assertions of autonomy thoroughly frustrated former Confederates. In the proslavery mind, blacks were docile, infantile creatures, certainly not ready for the freedom provided by a federal government under the spell of heterodox abolitionists. In 1868, John Bailey Adger, a noted southern Presbyterian clergyman, joined with George Coulson to claim that emancipation brought an important religious dilemma: how could devout southern whites continue to follow God's command and provide religious education for African Americans who, no doubt, were unable to produce mature religious reflection for themselves? As former slaves,

> suddenly freed, suddenly invested with new and extraordinary privileges, and suddenly inspired with vague apprehensions of their own importance, with indefinite expectations of ease and affluence to be conferred upon them by governmental authority—are thrust upon the hearts and consciences of a Christian nation, the question assumes an aspect both perplexing and threatening.

If southern whites forswore their prior duties as masters—to provide physical and spiritual care for their racial dependents—a "whole race" might "perish in the midst of us" and thereby bring "a lasting curse on the American name." The situation was dire, Adger and Coulson exclaimed: "The slave—may God pity him! Has no friend except his former master." But the former slaveholding class "has been legislated into a condition in which [the slaveholder] is utterly powerless to aid the servant born in his house, or even retard his doom."[39]

Adger and Coulson, like other proslavery southerners, believed former slaves incapable of governing themselves religiously because, as people with dark skin, African Americans could never acquire the same intellectual acumen as whites. Adger and Coulson, like proslavery divines in the antebellum era, did affirm the common ancestry of all humanity and did decry the scientific racism of polygenesis theory—"the pitiful work of Nott and Gliddon"—because the gospel message was given for all. But the "grave discussion of the relative capacities" of the races was a short-circuited one. The main point was clear to Adger and Coulson: "the elevation of the black people to a position of political and social equality with the whites, is simply an impossibility." The difference between the races was so plain, Adger and Coulson argued, that obviously "God has so constituted the two races as to make their equality *forever* impossible." Every true believer knew that it was "[v]ain" to attempt "to resist the decrees of God," a fact that explained why "[i]t is not possible to take an infant from the banks of the Niger, and educate him up to the intellectual status of Newton, because God hath made them to differ." If that image did not resonate with their readers, Adger and Coulson pressed harder, to show just how large the gap between black inferiority and white superiority really was:

> [I]f it were possible for the cultivated and Christianized races of the world to unite and devote all their energies to the elevation of the African race, giving each individual of this multitudinous family a separate and competent preceptor, the result of their labors would not be an intellectual equality, after long years of incessant application.

For that reason, Adger and Coulson argued, blacks lived under the cruel delusion of so-called freedom. The former slaves had to now provide for their own physical and spiritual well-being, which freedpeople simply could not do without the help of good, Christian, paternalistic masters.[40]

In addition to concerns expressed by proslavery white Christians about their section's former slave population, the same individuals also reacted viscerally toward the North. For their part, and as might be expected, northern whites looked at the South as a defeated and conquered land. For them, God was at work in the conflict as he providentially justified the rightness of Yankee ideas about religion and the nation. By the end of the war or the years shortly thereafter, almost all northern denominations issued statements denouncing slavery and secession and demanding an oath of loyalty to the national denomination that paralleled the oath former Confederates were required to take in order to reenter the political sphere. For southerners, such moves pushed too hard and were far too offensive. Rather than seeing a northern olive branch, southerners perceived a Yankee rod of chastisement. There would be no intersectional rapprochement along religious lines, at least not during the Reconstruction years.[41]

One of the prime charges southerners levied against northerners was that they "politicized" religious matters. Southerners in general, but particularly Presbyterians, espoused a doctrine known as the "spirituality of the church." The view maintained that matters of church and state ought to be kept separate. Historian Jack Maddex has argued that the Presbyterian idea of the church's "spirituality" was a particular postbellum innovation. With the rise of aggressive abolitionism prior to the Civil War, and then during the conflict, southern theologians, especially James Henley Thornwell—the divine usually credited with creating the doctrine also known as *jure divino*—had no qualms about offering political opinions. Up until Appomattox, Maddex suggested, southern Presbyterian clergy understood society as a near-theocracy where they exercised immense social influence. The end of the Civil War also ended the preeminence of such southern religious leaders and put southern clerics on the defensive. In Maddex's words, "Smarting under northern accusations that they had formed a 'political alliance' with slavery, Southern Presbyterians assumed an apolitical stance." According to Maddex, the architect of the spirituality-of-the-church doctrine was not Thornwell, a South Carolinian, but the vociferous Stuart Robinson of Louisville, Kentucky. Robinson held a "non-secular" form of Presbyterianism that, though "alien to northern and southern theocrats, suited border-state Presbyterians who were uncertain and divided about slavery and Unionism." Thus, by 1870, southerners had reconceived their understanding of the church's place in society but precisely as a way of maintaining antebellum racial attitudes.[42]

Maddex's claims about the postbellum origins of the spirituality-of-the-church doctrine have not gone without challenge.[43] Yet whether it was an antebellum or postwar creation, the spirituality of the church was never what it appeared. As Drew Gilpin Faust has shown, southern clergy labored mightily to build support for the Confederacy and the war effort.[44] In the years following the Civil War, the "nonsecular" stance was, in fact, always also a political one. Benjamin Morgan Palmer's postwar writings on the church's spiritual nature provide a case in point. On the eve of the establishment of "fraternal relations" between northern and southern Presbyterians in 1883, a move some hoped might smooth the path for a reconciliation and reunification of the denomination,[45] Palmer asked, "why, then, should we not be brought under the same ecclesiastical jurisdiction?" "The true and sufficient answer is," Palmer told his readers, "that the two bodies" differed in their view of the "relations subsisting between the Church and the State. This is the differentiating feature that compels us to separate from one another." Northerners continued to charge southerners with "rebellion" but, as proslavery religious southerners had long maintained, they were not guilty of the charge. If such an accusation could be substantiated, Palmer claimed, "we would repent in sackcloth and ashes all our days."[46]

No white southerners seemed prepared to pursue such repentance. Yet at the same time, not all southerners were so coy about the role of political ideas upon religious opinion. R. C. Reed, a Virginia pastor who would later become an influential professor of church history, argued in 1885 that southern Presbyterians had failed to follow through with their supposed commitment to the religious instruction of the region's African-American population. Reed went so far as to challenge his coreligionists' commitment to white superiority. "If to lift them up religiously it should be necessary to remove the social pressure, will we do it? If to hold them under socially it should be necessary to withdraw the religious uplifting, will we do it?" Reed did not answer those acerbic questions directly; rather, he struck out at the notion that the southern whites practiced nonpolitical religion. In fact, he argued, the current state of racial animosity belied the notion. While it was "True" that "the Church, in her corporate capacity, has nothing to do with politics," it was manifest to anyone who cared to look that "the individual members of the Church have, and are in duty bound to have, something to do with politics. They cannot look on with indifference and see a race of ignorant, degraded, recently manumitted slaves . . . climbing up into political supremacy." Reed, a son of the Confederate South, understood well the source of white anxiety about freedpeople—Reed did not make an egalitarian argument—but white political concerns were trumping the work of the faith for two major reasons. First, Reed asserted, the freedperson "doubts the sincerity of the white brother, who is a political enemy, when he comes to preach him the gospel of love." Second, it required an "unusual amount of grace" for an African American to be "warmly interested in the spiritual welfare of those who are leagued in unrelenting warfare against what he believes to be his political interests."[47]

As Reed's arguments suggest, by seemingly refusing to get involved in political matters, *jure divino* proved an effective religious way to stifle discussions about social action, particularly with regard to racial questions. The death of slavery as a legal institution brought into sharp relief the racial foundations upon which proslavery argumentation had been constructed. With slavery gone, white southern clergy set about shoring up defenses of the cause lost in Confederate defeat and bequeathing vitality to the white supremacist social order. The theological orthodoxy of the antebellum era—which in its defense of slavery and paternalism had allowed for some check on all-out racism—gave way to a new orthodoxy, what H. Shelton Smith called a "racial orthodoxy."[48] Slavery had in effect defined the status of whites and blacks without explicit reference to race but now, with slavery gone, proslavery divines appealed to race as the reason for white-black separation. After the Civil War, southern clerics became all too willing to defend white supremacy simply and for itself.

This racial orthodoxy, when added to southern whites' sense of righteousness about the Confederate effort, gave rise to what Charles Reagan Wilson has termed the "religion of the Lost Cause." The origins of this "southern civil religion" drew in part from, and relied on the language and styles of, historic southern evangelicalism. Postbellum ministers of the religion of the Lost Cause drew upon all sorts of connections to the antebellum proslavery Christian argument in supporting agendas of white supremacy and segregation. Summarizing the centrality of race in the period, Wilson wrote, "racial heresy was more dangerous to a preacher's reputation than was theological speculation"—that is, to defend racial equality was perceived as more threatening than to advance nonorthodox views on ordinary theological questions. Where, in the antebellum period, the slavery question could serve as a test of Christian orthodoxy because classical Christian reflection rooted in scripture was being used to support proslavery argumentation, after the war the racial orthodoxy of whites depended less on straightforward biblical arguments. Its grounding, rather, was found in the white South's civil religion that, by its nature, did not need historic Christian foundations to assure its social influence. Thus, ostensibly Christian terrorist organizations like the Ku Klux Klan, which first appeared in 1866 to fight "Black Reconstruction," benefited from this new racial orthodoxy. No serious observer ever considered the Klan's language densely or precisely theological, but its blend of religious rhetoric and racial animosity reflected the force of the new orthodoxy and also its violent potential.[49] Although it might be an exaggeration to say that the Klan acted on behalf of the entire white South, its tactics and its characterization of blacks as dehumanized beings had much resonance among southern whites in the decades after the Civil War. Somewhat later, the explosion of lynchings in the decades surrounding the turn of the twentieth century was sustained by similarly deep religious roots.[50] Theologians did not support the Klan or lynchings formally; for the most part, they also abandoned the use of scriptural chapter and verse that had sustained antebellum proslavery arguments. But without the strong continuation of the general ideology surrounding the antebellum proslavery position, it is hard to imagine how the racist violence accepted by postbellum white religious society—and not only in the South—could have been maintained.

To be sure, unlike practitioners of the "religion of racial violence," pro-slavery Protestants in the immediate aftermath of the Civil War did not call for black extermination—even if some supported racial separation resembling the colonization schemes of the antebellum period. Instead, as they clung to ideas about blacks and whites sharing a common humanity, proslavery divines instead blamed the postwar order upon their old enemies, the abolitionists. In the best-known defense of slavery after the Civil War, published in 1867, the cantankerous Virginia Presbyterian Robert L. Dabney—former chaplain to the highly memorialized Confederate general Thomas J. "Stonewall" Jackson—opened his argument with a satirical question and answer: "Is not the slavery question dead? . . . Would God it were dead!" For Dabney, the "slavery question" posed a moral dilemma only for those who resided outside the realm of southern religious orthodoxy. And he intended to show that abolitionists were such a people: "in the Church, abolitionism lives, and is more rampant and mischievous than ever, as infidelity."[51]

THE CONFLUENCE OF religious, political, and racial thought that has been traced in this chapter made for a potent ideological amalgam. Clearly, the postbellum longevity of proslavery ideas morphed into a defense of racism that affected later developments in American religious and political history.[52] In a provocative interpretation of the Civil Rights era, which is often called the "Second Reconstruction," historian David Chappell has argued that southern arguments in favor of segregation during the mid-twentieth century lacked a solid theological foundation. White religious people may have lined up in order to preserve social racial separation, but they did not publicly defend their positions with classic sources of Christian reflection, whether the Bible or theology. Rather, as explained differently by historian Paul Harvey, the "folk theology of segregation" was mostly culled from social convention, with a bit of religious language packed on top to give the arguments a sense of moral authority. Thus, in this interpretation, when religious segregationists were finally confronted with an integrationist civil rights agenda that did in fact draw upon biblical injunctions, segregationists could not muster convincing Christian support for their cause.[53]

No one has yet published a thoroughgoing critique of Chappell's argument, and it is too soon to know what the scholarly community will make of what many consider a controversial thesis.[54] Acknowledging that some of Chappell's claims are contested, key aspects of his argument seem quite convincing. For example, Chappell frequently draws comparisons between the religious proslavery argument of the antebellum South and ideological defenses of segregation after World War II. In the earlier era, theological writing on slavery was rigorous and compelling enough to convince a great number of white southerners to give their lives to the Confederacy; it was also strong enough to convince many moderates and conservatives in the North that all-out opposition to slavery was a major theological mistake. According to Chappell, the same cannot be said about the intellectual basis for segregation. No segregationist "seems to have articulated anything equivalent to the 'Positive Good' position of the antebellum slave-holders." Segregation ideology faded quickly and, despite much hotly charged rhetoric in opposition to federally mandated integration, no southern revolt like that of the 1860s occurred a century later. Six hundred thousand Americans died during the Civil War. The forty who died in the name of civil rights are clearly only a fraction of that number.[55]

If, however, careful theological defenses of slavery waned over time, the close tie between religion and race has remained much stronger. It may be the case, as Chappell has argued, that the intellectual vitality of ideological segregationism suffered a relatively quick death. But actions informed by dead ideas did not suffer the same fate. Americans no longer live in a legally segregated nation but, as Darren Dochuk explains later in this volume, southern evangelical political concerns, which are rooted to some degree in postbellum attitudes, remain prominent; moreover, as they have been exported out of the South, they have come to influence the nation at large. In addition, as Michael Emerson and J. Russell Hawkins in this volume show for even more recent decades, the political affinity between socially and racially conservative policy and white evangelical Christianity remains strong even to the present. While it would be a great error to ignore the very important distinction between the cleavages that occurred during the postbellum period and those of the Civil Rights era (and beyond), linkages from more than a century earlier have proved to be persistent and important for later developments. Among the most persistent and most important was the effect of translating the rigorous theological proslavery ideology of the antebellum period into the conventional and folksy religious-racist ideology of the postbellum era.

NOTES

1. William Ellison Boggs, "The South Vindicated from the Charge of Treason and Rebellion," *Southern Presbyterian Review* 32 (Oct. 1881): 745–50, 761. Emphasis in original.
2. Ibid., 759–60, 791–92. Emphasis in original.
3. Ibid., 792. Emphasis in original.

4. Ibid., 792–93.

5. Drew Gilpin Faust, ed., *The Ideology of Slavery: Proslavery Thought in the Antebellum South, 1830–1860* (Baton Rouge: Louisiana State University Press, 1981), 1–20; Elizabeth Fox-Genovese and Eugene D. Genovese, *The Mind of the Master Class: History and Faith in the Southern Slaveholders' Worldview* (New York: Cambridge University Press, 2005), 409–646.

6. Drew Gilpin Faust, *The Creation of Confederate Nationalism: Ideology and Identity in the Civil War South* (Baton Rouge: Louisiana State University Press, 1988), 22.

7. See John David Smith, *An Old Creed for the New South: Proslavery Ideology and Historiography, 1865–1918* (Westport, Conn.: Greenwood, 1985).

8. James L. Roark, *Masters without Slaves: Southern Planters in the Civil War and Reconstruction* (New York: Norton, 1977), 208.

9. All election information is from *Presidential Elections, 1789–2000* (Washington, D.C.: CQ Press, 2002).

10. Mark Hanley, *Beyond a Christian Commonwealth: The Protestant Quarrel with the American Republic, 1830–1860* (Chapel Hill: University of North Carolina Press, 1994), 89–103.

11. Kenneth Startup, "'A Mere Calculation of Profits and Loss': The Southern Clergy and the Economic Culture of the Antebellum North," in *God and Mammon: Protestants, Money, and the Market, 1790–1860*, ed. Mark A. Noll (New York: Oxford University Press, 2001), 217–35, quote 218.

12. Kenneth Moore Startup, *The Root of All Evil: The Protestant Clergy and the Economic Mind of the Old South* (Athens: University of Georgia Press, 1997), 126–39.

13. Mark A. Noll, *America's God: From Jonathan Edwards to Abraham Lincoln* (New York: Oxford University Press, 2002), 367–85.

14. Thornton Stringfellow, "A Brief Examination of Scripture Testimony on the Institution of Slavery," in Faust, *Ideology of Slavery*, 138–67, quote 139.

15. Eugene D. Genovese has cogently summarized the debate: "The God-fearing southern people turned to the Bible to justify slavery, and the Bible did not disappoint them. Their theologians rent the abolitionists, at least on the essentials, in their war of biblical exegesis." Genovese, *The Southern Front: History and Politics in the Culture War* (Columbia: University of Missouri Press, 1995), 34.

16. On the rise of abolitionism as a new moral sensibility connected to the rise of the market, see Thomas L. Haskell, "Capitalism and the Origins of the Humanitarian Sensibility," *American Historical Review* 90 (1985): 339–61 and 547–66. For debate about Haskell's interpretation, which originated as a critique of David Brion Davis's explanation of the rise of abolitionism in *The Problem of Slavery in the Age of Revolution, 1770–1823* (Ithaca, N.Y.: Cornell University Press, 1975), see Thomas Bender, ed., *The Antislavery Debate: Capitalism and Abolitionism as a Problem in Historical Interpretation* (Berkeley: University of California Press, 1992).

17. Thornwell, "Relation of the Church to Slavery," in *The Collected Writings of James Henley Thornwell*, 4 vols., ed. John B. Adger and John L. Girardeau (1873; rpt., Carlisle, Pa.: Banner of Truth, 1974), 4:388. Emphasis in original.

18. Thornwell, "The Christian Doctrine of Slavery," in Adger and Girardeau, *Collected Writings of Thornwell*, 4:401, 405.

19. G. J. A. Coulson, "The Drift of American Politics," *Southern Presbyterian Review* 32 (Apr. 1881): 317–35, quotes 322, 323, 325.

20. Ibid., quotes 319. Emphasis in original.

21. Eugene D. Genovese, *A Consuming Fire: The Fall of the Confederacy in the Mind of the White Christian South* (Athens: University of Georgia Press, 1998), 3–33; and Noll, *America's God*, 386–401.

22. On white religious conservatives in the antebellum South who resisted this pervasive logic, but not ideas about white superiority, see Luke E. Harlow, "Neither Slavery nor Abolitionism: James M. Pendleton and the Problem of Christian Conservative Antislavery in 1840s Kentucky," *Slavery & Abolition* 27 (2006): 367–89; and Harlow, "Religion, Race, and Robert J. Breckinridge: The Ideology of an Antislavery Slaveholder, 1830–1860," *Ohio Valley History* 6 (Fall 2006), 1–24.

23. See E. Brooks Holifield, *Theology in America: Christian Thought from the Age of the Puritans to the Civil War* (New Haven, Conn.: Yale University Press, 2003), 502; Noll, *America's God*, 417; and Stephen R. Haynes, *Noah's Curse: The Biblical Justification of American Slavery* (New York: Oxford University Press, 2002), 125–27. For a different conclusion, see Genovese, *A Consuming Fire*, 4.

24. Thornwell, "Our National Sins," in *Fast Day Sermons; or, The Pulpit on the State of the Country* (New York: Rudd & Carleton, 1861), 49–52, quote 49.

25. See Eugene D. Genovese, *The Slaveholders' Dilemma: Freedom and Progress in Southern Conservative Thought, 1820–1860* (Columbia: University of South Carolina Press, 1992); Genovese, "Introduction to the Wesleyan Edition," in *The World the Slaveholders Made: Two Essays in Interpretation* (Middletown, Conn.: Wesleyan University Press, 1988); and Startup, *The Root of All Evil.*

26. Thornwell, "Our National Sins," 49–52, quote 52.

27. Thornwell, "The Christian Doctrine of Slavery," 402. Emphasis in original.

28. Haynes, *Noah's Curse*, 126.

29. Thornwell, "Address to All Churches of Christ," in Adger and Girardeau, *Collected Writings of Thornwell*, 4:460. On this point in particular, see Mark A. Noll, *The Civil War as a Theological Crisis* (Chapel Hill: University of North Carolina Press, 2006), 51–74.

30. Benjamin Morgan Palmer, "Slavery: A Divine Trust," in *Fast Day Sermons*, 62. Emphasis in original.

31. Thornwell, "Our National Sins," 51.

32. See C. C. Goen, *Broken Churches, Broken Nation: Denominational Schisms and the Coming of the Civil War* (Macon, Ga.: Mercer University Press, 1985); Noll, *The Civil War as a Theological Crisis*; David B. Chesebrough, ed., *"God Ordained This War": Sermons on the Sectional Crisis, 1830–1865* (Columbia: University of South Carolina Press, 1991); and Randall Miller, Harry S. Stout, and Charles Reagan Wilson, eds., *Religion in the American Civil War* (New York: Oxford University Press, 1998).

33. Harry S. Stout, *Upon the Altar of the Nation: A Moral History of the Civil War* (New York: Viking, 2006).

34. Daniel W. Stowell, *Rebuilding Zion: The Religious Reconstruction of the South, 1865–1877* (New York: Oxford University Press, 1998), 15–32.

35. Ibid., 33–48, quote 40.

36. Arnold W. Miller, "Southern Views and Principles Not 'Extinguished' by the War," *Southern Presbyterian Review* 21 (Jan. 1870): 61–62.

37. Ibid., 85.

38. Stowell, *Rebuilding Zion*, 80–99.

39. John Bailey Adger and G. J. A. Coulson, "The Future of the Freedmen," *Southern Presbyterian Review* 19 (Apr. 1868): 281–83, 292.

40. Ibid., 269–70, 276, 279, 280. Emphasis in original.

41. Stowell, *Rebuilding Zion*, 49–64.

42. Jack P. Maddex, "From Theocracy to Spirituality: The Southern Presbyterian Reversal on Church and State," *Journal of Presbyterian History* 54 (1976): 438–57, quote 448.

43. One recent study of Stuart Robinson's Civil War era religious thought argued that "nonsecular" Presbyterianism could be traced to colonial origins and that it always retained a place in southern Presbyterian thought, if not one of the utmost prominence until the late antebellum period. See Preston D. Graham, Jr., *A Kingdom Not of This World: Stuart Robinson's Struggle to Distinguish the Sacred from the Secular during the Civil War* (Macon, Ga.: Mercer University Press, 2002), 169–73. Less critical of Maddex than Graham, James Oscar Farmer, Jr., Thornwell's only recent biographer, subscribes to a nuanced version of Maddex's interpretation. While maintaining that *jure divino* was an element of Thornwell's thought in the late 1850s, Farmer suggests that the doctrine was "not consistently applied" and thus not fully embraced by southern Presbyterians until after the Civil War, when they needed stronger religious defenses to ward off northern attacks. See Farmer, *The Metaphysical Confederacy: James Henley Thornwell and the Synthesis of Southern Values* (Macon, Ga.: Mercer University Press, 1986), 256–60, quote 258.

44. Faust, *Creation of Confederate Nationalism*.

45. See Ernest Trice Thompson, *Presbyterians in the South*, vol. 2: *1861–1890* (Richmond, Va.: Knox, 1973), 223–64.

46. Benjamin Morgan Palmer, "Fraternal Relations," *Southern Presbyterian Review* 34 (Apr. 1883): 328, 330.

47. R. C. Reed, "The Southern Presbyterian Church and the Freedmen," *Southern Presbyterian Review* 36 (Jan. 1885): 93–95. The logic of Reed's arguments led him to make statements that most of his devout white contemporaries in the postwar South would have found objectionable. Reed wrote that he was "not defending slavery" at the present, even if, like his southern coreligionists, he believed that northerners misunderstood how slavery assisted in elevating Africans "far above the low savage state in which [they] had previously existed." Moreover, Reed went so far as to endorse cooperating with northern religious educators who, by his estimation, had done far more to help freedpeople than southern whites. Reed, "Southern Presbyterian Church and the Freedmen," 95–108.

48. H. Shelton Smith, *In His Image, but...: Racism in Southern Religion, 1780–1910* (Durham, N.C.: Duke University Press, 1972), 258–305.

49. Charles Reagan Wilson, *Baptized in Blood: The Religion of the Lost Cause* (Athens: University of Georgia Press, 1980), 1–17, 100–118, quote 101. Several historians, including Gaines Foster, whose *Ghosts of the Confederacy: Defeat, the Lost Cause, and the Emergence of the New South* (New York: Oxford University Press, 1987) stands with

Baptized in Blood as one of the key histories of the cult of the lost cause, finds "civil religion" a slippery term too amorphous to give tangible meaning as an explanatory device. Civil religion, Foster suggests, is an idea that proposes to support too many competing ideas at once. See Foster, *Ghosts of the Confederacy*, 7–8. There is much good sense in what Foster writes, but *Baptized in Blood*, in no small part because of its skillful argumentation and analysis of the relationship between race and nonformal religious ideas in southern culture, remains an important contribution to the subject of religion in the white postbellum South.

50. See Darren E. Grem, "Sam Jones, Sam Hose, and the Theology of Racial Violence," *Georgia Historical Quarterly* 90 (2006): 35–61; and Donald G. Mathews, "Lynching Is Part of the Religion of Our People: Faith in the Christian South," in *Religion in the American South: Protestants and Others in History and Culture*, ed. Beth Barton Schweiger and Mathews (Chapel Hill: University of North Carolina Press, 2004), 153–94. For other discussions of religiously motivated white-on-black violence and white understandings of black inferiority, see Edward J. Blum, *Reforging the White Republic: Race, Religion, and American Nationalism, 1865–1898* (Baton Rouge: Louisiana State University Press, 2005).

51. Robert L. Dabney, *A Defence of Virginia, and through Her, of the South* (New York: Hale & Son, 1867), 6.

52. For a discussion of the persistence of these views among white Baptists in a period slightly later than that discussed in this chapter, see Fred Arthur Bailey, "That Which God Hath Put Asunder: White Baptists, Black Aliens, and the Southern Social Order, 1890–1920," in *Politics and Religion in the White South*, ed. Glenn Feldman (Lexington: University Press of Kentucky, 2005), 11–33.

53. David L. Chappell, *A Stone of Hope: Prophetic Religion and the Death of Jim Crow* (Chapel Hill: University of North Carolina Press, 2004); Paul Harvey, "God and Negroes and Jesus and Sin and Salvation: Racism, Racial Interchange, and Inter-racialism in Southern Religious History," in Schweiger and Mathews, *Religion in the American South*, 283–329.

54. Jane Dailey, "Sex, Segregation, and the Sacred after *Brown*," *Journal of American History* 91 (2004): 119–44, is often considered a serious challenge to Chappell. The crux of Dailey's argument dealt with segregationist fears of sexual integration, where religious language was merely a prop for white southern social fears about interracial sex. Dailey's point here was valid and important, but little in her argument demonstrated that white southern segregationists were any more sophisticated in their theological understanding than Chappell suggested. Thus, while Dailey's argument should not be ignored, it seems that she and Chappell were talking about different, though related, matters.

55. Chappell, *A Stone of Hope*, 2, 5–8, 121–23, quote 122.

10

Protestant Theological Tensions and Political Styles in the Progressive Period

Robert T. Handy

I

THE AMERICAN PROTESTANT world at the dawn of the twentieth century was much smaller and simpler than the one we study in the new millennium. The nation's population, just under seventy-six million, was less than a third of what it is now. Though church statistics are notoriously unreliable, the older, historic, familiar "denominational families" of Protestantism probably then totaled somewhere around sixteen million members. The differences among the major denominational groupings, ranging in overall size from some six million to a half million—Methodist, Baptist, Presbyterian, Lutheran, Disciples, Episcopal, Congregational, Reformed—were deep-rooted in history. Some of these groups traced their origins back to the sixteenth-century Reformation separation from Roman Catholicism, others to religious movements in the centuries since. Some had existed as free churches since their beginnings, others had to learn to carry on without direct governmental assistance when the state establishments of religion disappeared, the last one in the United States voted out in 1833. They all developed somewhat distinctive ways of governing and propagating themselves. Denominational families were internally divided along sectional, national, and racial lines. The examples are familiar, for there were northern and southern branches of Methodist, Baptist, and Presbyterian churches; there were varieties of German and Scandinavian Lutherans; there were Dutch and German Reformed; and there were a number of denominations of African Americans, some of them sizable, for the federal Census of Religious Bodies of 1906 reported that the black Baptists collectively were larger than either of the two major white Baptist conventions.[1]

Not only were there these obvious divisions of Protestantism into denominational families, large and small, but there were also sharp tensions within most of them, sometimes because of different ethnic and racial stocks in a given body, sometimes because of theological disputes between parties within various denominational traditions. Because of the intense bitterness of the fundamentalist/modernist controversies of the 1920s, especially among Baptists and Presbyterians but certainly not only there, it has been easy to look back at the first two decades of the twentieth century through that focus and thus to distort our interpretations of those years, to overlook the actual spectrum of theological parties by picturing an oversimplified dichotomy. Looking back now, after more than a half-century of scholarship in which there have been various attempts to get beyond the clashes of the 1920s between fundamentalism and modernism and perceptive efforts to probe what led up to and followed from those encounters, we can now see that the parties that waved those banners tended to be the extremes of the larger complex movements of conservative and liberal Protestantism.

Those movements were diverse and shifting federations of persons and groups both within and across denominational lines, and they changed over time. In the period of American life that historians have often labeled the Progressive Era, approximately the first two decades of the twentieth century, what came to be called fundamentalism and modernism were deepening currents in a wider theological scene.[2] Most of the denominations that bore the Protestant label defined themselves as trinitarian and evangelical and harbored a range of theological parties across a wide spectrum. The shape and tone of such parties related to the wider history, polity, confessional stance, and liturgical traditions of the denomination of which they were a part. Certainly, there were tensions and debates between them as they faced the intellectual revolutions of their time and sought to come to terms with the rapidly changing and dynamic environing culture. There were indeed many real differences, and age-old debates were renewed in a time of rapid social change, debates over such matters as nature and the supernatural, sacred and secular, immanence and transcendence, revelation and reason, Calvinism and Arminianism, experience and tradition, nurture and revival, postmillennialism and premillennialism, science and religion.

As we look back, we can see that on the organizational level it was not particularly an opportune time for such discussions as they bore on immediate decisions on how a denomination was to fulfill its task. The pace of life was steadily increasing with telegraph and telephone, railroad and motorcar; the population was mounting rapidly, largely as immigrants were arriving in unprecedented numbers, the majority from other than Protestant backgrounds; and the sprawl of vast urban areas was soon to mean the shift of the balance of power to the cities from rural and small-town America where Protestants had made themselves so much at home. Historically divided Protestantism was facing at once unprecedented opportunities and increasing tensions in the Progressive period.

There was, nevertheless, a strong sense of unity in the major Protestant churches of that period, especially among those that were steeped in the British Protestant tradition and/or were grounded in the Calvinist tradition. They had much in common that held in considerable check the centrifugal forces that had divided them and that still persisted as a continual threat. They were well aware of sectarian tendencies that, for example, had led to departures into the Holiness and Pentecostal movements. The major sources of what gave a certain sense of unity and identifiability to the Protestantism they professed are important to note for a full understanding of religion in the Progressive Era. In the following analysis, particular attention is given to matters that may have relevance for understanding political leanings.

- These Protestants shared a common devotion to the Bible, which was evident in their patterns of preaching, worship, and Sunday school education. Familiar biblical phrases and cadences informed the way they spoke and wrote. They could, and often did, disagree over ways of interpreting "the word of God," yet it continued to operate as the central written point of reference for Christian life in church and world.
- Their piety and theology was prevailingly Christocentric in orientation, for they believed that God was in Christ, that God was revealed in the person and work of Jesus Christ as Lord and Savior. When they articulated their Christocentrism in sermonic and theological discourse, differences of interpretation emerged among the various parties. Those attached to historic confessionalism or revivalistic pietism tended to express this in more traditional terms, while the Christocentric liberals, in affirming belief in the unique divinity of Jesus Christ, often

endeavored to ground that divinity in the ontological being of God
and were troubled when some of their number tended to move toward
more naturalistic or humanistic positions, though that rarely became
significant in the Progressive period. As William Hutchison explained,
"Few, if any, Protestant liberals—modernistic or otherwise—denied
normative status to Christ and to the Christian tradition."[3]

- They looked forward to the coming kingdom of God, freely citing
  relevant biblical passages as they expounded this theme. While some
  dwelled on the eschatological aspects of the kingdom's coming, others
  spoke more freely of the "building of the kingdom" on earth, seeking
  a fuller following of God's will in human affairs. Ferenc Szasz has noted
  that the "vagueness of the Kingdom ideal . . . allowed for varying interpretations."[4] But it was effective in encouraging leaders of congregations and denominations to work together as they appealed to their
  people in a time when, as Washington Gladden put it, the kingdom was
  prominent among the ruling ideas of that age.[5]

- Protestantism in the Progressive period was wholeheartedly behind the
  foreign missionary movement, then immensely popular and a principal cause for which the churches, with the help of various voluntary
  agencies, maintained extensive home bases, raised vast sums, and sent
  hundreds of missionaries abroad. Noting that by 1910 the Americans
  had surpassed the hitherto dominant British in the numbers sent out and
  in the financing of missions, in his *Errand to the World* Hutchison observed that Protestant leaders

> spoke with remarkable unanimity across the theological spectrum.
> . . . Opposing forces could collaborate because the principal common
> enterprise, converting the world to Christ, seemed more compelling
> than any differences; but also because they shared a vision of the
> essential rightness of Western civilization and the near-inevitability
> of its triumph.[6]

- The Progressive period was one in which concern for reform was
  widespread, though the scope and purpose of reforming measures were
  quite differently understood among those who advocated them. Within
  Protestantism, concern for social problems had increased noticeably in
  the last decade of the nineteenth century, in part because of the effects
  of the depression of 1893 and the impact of the Populist movement, one
  of the predecessors of Progressivism. In the Progressive Era, many
  Protestants across the religious spectrum spoke and acted on behalf of

social reform. It is surprising to some of us to find that *in those years* persons we now remember as prominent fundamentalists contributed to reform efforts, including Mark A. Matthews, William Bell Riley, and John Roach Straton.[7] The term "Social Gospel" has sometimes been expanded to include all those active in reform movements; it is more clarifying and reflective of the situation then, I believe, to use that term primarily for those reform-minded Protestants who were challenging the individualistic social ethic so dominant at the time and seeking to stress both social and individual salvation, though that balance was not easy to keep. It is also surprising for some to find that many persons now remembered as prominent theological liberals were *not* significantly involved in reform movements or in challenging the dominance of individualistic ethics.[8] They did not align themselves with the social Christian movement, even as broadly defined, while some of the conservative evangelicals at work in the slums did "produce extensive social programs and close identification with the needy," as Norris Magnuson's *Salvation in the Slums* makes very clear.[9] Though the tension between the Social Gospel, which in most cases was rooted in theological liberalism, and the other types of Christian reformers was real, the wider concern for social evils did serve to keep the discussion open and, in some cases, to encourage cooperation.

• A major reforming thrust of the Progressive years was even more clearly unitive, for most evangelical Protestants of various backgrounds and leanings supported the drive for Prohibition. Again, we tend to look back at the prewar crusade for a constitutional amendment through our understandings of the 1920s, when Prohibition had become a matter of law and order, and hence forget that it had been part of the larger temperance movement for social and humanitarian reform, had been a favorite cause of many leaders of the Social Gospel, and with one exception had enlisted the official support of all of the denominations that had been permeated by the Social Gospel.[10] Thousands of congregations participated in the activities of the Anti-Saloon League, which claimed to be the political arm of the churches, "the church in action," though it operated as an independent single-issue group that was instrumental in securing the adoption of the Eighteenth Amendment in 1919. Prohibition was popular among Protestants in the South and was one of the major links between northern and southern evangelicals.[11] In the 1920s, the more negative, even repressive, side of the movement became more conspicuous, though its continuity in holding the loyalty of much of Protestantism was illustrated in that it was one of the factors at work in the defeat of Alfred E. Smith for president in 1928.

- A less dramatic but even more common force for unity among most Protestants was the support for public schools. Protestant backing for the public schools had developed out of the common school movement of the previous century. Few churches found either the will, the need, or the resources to develop their own network of primary and elementary schools; and as Protestantism entered the new century as a dominant cultural force in American life, its leaders believed they could safely entrust the educational task to the public schools. More than that, they believed that such institutions could contribute significantly to the molding of a more homogeneous people, socializing and Americanizing those from many immigrant backgrounds and providing them with a set of moral values. Early in the new century, as Robert W. Lynn has noted, came "the development of a new theme which up until now had been largely implicit in Protestant writings: the school is symbolic of both our national unity and God's handiwork in history. As such it was a sacred cause, worthy of religious devotion."[12] What Protestants were largely unable to see was that what for them was a "common" value system was to other eyes, especially those of Catholics, a specific one rooted in Protestant perspectives. Criticism of public education only heightened the devotion of Protestants of that period to it and strengthened its unitive force among them.   •

- In view of later developments within and against cooperative Chris-tianity, it is not easy now to remember how far it reached across the Protestant spectrum when what became the Foreign Missions Confer-ence of North America was founded in 1893, followed by the Interde-nominational Conference of Women's Boards of Foreign Missions three years later, and, in 1908, the Home Missions Council, the Council of Women for Home Missions, and, climactically, the Federal Council of Churches. The cooperative mission agencies represented many denominational boards, but the FCC was officially sponsored initially by thirty-three denominations. Among its members were many of the larger evangelical denominations, including those from both the North and the South, a major Lutheran synod, and two black Methodist communions. The movement thus reached across racial lines at a time when the trend toward increased segregation was strong and provided one of the few effective links between white and black evangelicals. As the Episcopal Address of 1904 of the African Methodist Episcopal

church put it, "The pronounced tendency to unity of spirit and cooperation in Christian work, and, indeed, to organic union, is hailed with
delight."[13] The FCC had no authority over its members, but encouraged
and provided channels for cooperation in evangelism, missions, education, and social service—the influence of social Christianity and the
Social Gospel was evident from the start. But so was its concern for
missions as it allied itself with the cooperative mission agencies, and in
the Progressive period the FCC succeeded in holding the loyalty of
denominations whose memberships included vast groups—probably
majorities in many cases—of those whose religious sympathies leaned
toward the conservative side. In 1919, William Jennings Bryan, now
remembered as a champion of fundamentalism, called the Federal
Council of Churches "the greatest religious organization in our nation"
and served on its commission on temperance.[14]

- The evangelical world was further linked by a spirit of patriotism.
Though the churches were divided in their attitude toward what to do
about Cuba after the sinking of the battleship *Maine* early in 1898,
majority opinion settled in favor of intervention about the time that the
Spanish-American War was declared. That struggle was short and
precipitated an intense discussion about imperialism, but even most of
those opposed to retaining the Philippines and other islands that were
the fruits of victory accepted a distinction between imperialism and
expansionism and were willing to support missionary work wherever it
was possible. The new century opened with the spirit of patriotism at
a high point, as illustrated, for example, when the General Conference
of the Methodist Episcopal church voted in 1900 permanently to display the American flag on its platform in order that "with our loyalty to
the King eternal may be advanced our love of country and its institutions."[15] American entry into World War I on Good Friday 1917
quickly brought a surge of patriotism to the fore again. Though much of
the literature about the war has tended to overemphasize the jingois-
tic statements in which some Protestant voices indulged, John Piper's
book on the churches and World War I makes clear that there were
other, more moderate statements. The most comprehensive Protestant
agency to guide church war work was under the aegis of the Federal
Council of Churches, which sought a middle ground between pacifists
and militants. A statement prepared by the most representative group
yet gathered by the FCC pledged its support and allegiance to the nation
"in unstinted measure," but insisted that "we owe it to our country to

maintain intact and to transmit unimpaired to our descendants our
heritage of freedom and democracy" and pledged "to be vigilant against
every attempt to arouse the spirit of vengeance and unjust suspicion
toward those of foreign birth or sympathies."[16] Though not all of the
nearly eighteen million persons related to the FCC through their
churches' membership—two-thirds of the total number of Protestants—
abided by that pledge, it was an important leaven. The patriotism expressed did serve as a unifying force toward the end of the Progressive
period and even led to a limited degree of practical cooperation between
Catholic and Protestant leaders.

- The latter was a somewhat new development because anti-Catholicism
  had long been one of the defining characteristics of Protestantism, evident across its divisions and tensions. The contentions between
  Catholics and Protestants went back to the bitter struggles of the Reformation of the sixteenth century and the religious wars and persecutions
  that followed. Many events across several centuries intensified the
  anti-Catholicism of English life. Catholics were a small and persecuted
  minority in the colonial period, and deep into American history they
  were generally considered to be an alien element in an essentially
  Protestant nation. As their numbers dramatically increased during the
  course of the nineteenth century—the Roman Catholic had become the
  single largest church in America by midcentury—fear of the "Romanist
  peril" had important political consequences, as in the nativist Know-
  Nothing movement of the 1850s. As the patterns of European immigration brought in increasing numbers of Catholics—an estimated three
  million between 1870 and 1900, and two million more in the first decade
  of the new century—Protestant reactions intensified. For example, the
  American Protective Association (APA) was founded in 1887 and the
  more moderate National League for the Protection of American Institutions (NLPAI) two years later.[17] The Catholic perception that the
  public schools reflected what to them was a "sectarian" Protestant ethos
  led to the determination in 1884 to extend the parochial school network
  to every parish where that was possible. This infuriated many Protestants and others who were committed to public education; the result was
  the blockage of public funds for private educational institutions.[18]
  Catholics were frequently labeled un-American, and it was said they
  opposed the tradition of religious freedom. Such statements as that of
  the titular head of American Catholicism, James Cardinal Gibbons, that
  "American Catholics rejoice in our separation of Church and State; and I

can conceive of no combination of circumstances likely to arise which would make a union desirable either to Church or State" were dismissed as mere rhetoric.[19] Even a man of ecumenical spirit, Howard B. Grose, called by Martin E. Marty "the least anti-foreign and anti-Catholic among Protestant experts" in the church extension field, could argue for the conversion of Catholics because "the foundation principles of Protestant Americanism and Roman Catholicism are irreconcilable."[20] The awareness of what was conceived as a common enemy served as a unifying force among Protestants of many types.

The preceding analysis has endeavored to illustrate the point that, to many Protestant leaders and followers, the centripetal forces at work seemed to be winning out over the centrifugal ones. It is not intended to minimize the latter but to see them in perspective. Despite certain unitive trends within denominational families and a marked increase in federative movements, boundaries between denominational traditions remained quite clearly marked and various theological tensions remained unresolved.

For the reasons summarized above, however, the Protestant sense of a larger unity despite diversities does allow us to speak of Protestantism in the singular, if we do it with care. The view that in recognizable ways this many-sided movement did have distinguishable common characteristics helped it to enter the twentieth century in a mood of self-confidence, assurance, and glowing optimism. As noted evangelical layman William E. Dodge declared as he helped to prepare for the famous Ecumenical Conference in New York in 1900, "We are going into a century more full of hope, and promise, and opportunity than any period in the world's history."[21] Those present at that gathering could feel they were close to the centers of power as they were addressed by a past, a present, and a future president of the United States—Benjamin Harrison, William McKinley, and Theodore Roosevelt. Protestants shared in and in many ways contributed to the optimistic spirit that was widespread among the nation's opinion makers. In 1901, another future president, then Professor Woodrow Wilson, wrote that "we have become confirmed in energy, in resourcefulness, in practical proficiency, in self-confidence."[22] One who lived through it all was later to write:

> The first fifteen years of the twentieth century may sometimes be remembered in America as the Age of Crusades. There were a superabundance of zeal, a sufficiency of good causes, unusual moral idealism, excessive confidence in mass movements and leaders with rare gifts of popular appeal. The people were ready to cry "God wills it" and set out for world peace, prohibition, the Progressive Party, the "New Freedom"

or "the World for Christ in this Generation." The air was full of banners, and the trumpets called from every camp.[23]

The Protestantism of the Progressive period not only reflected the crusading spirit of the wider culture, but was also a generator and intensifier of it.

II

Political Progressivism is difficult to define, but it set the tone for both major parties in the early twentieth century, which was, as Henry F. May aptly stated, "a time of sureness and unity, at least on the surface of American life."[24] Its roots were diverse as it drew on various reform movements, such as the populism of the 1890s, social scientism, and social Christianity. Those who have attempted to picture it often refer to the many strands it attempted to weave together. Walter Dean Burnham observed that "this movement is a remarkable mixture of contradictory elements: a striving for mass democracy on the one hand and corporatist-technocratic elitism on the other."[25] Dewey Grantham discussed "the paradoxical nature of progressivism: its vitality but its lack of focus; its materialistic emphases but its humanistic achievements; its romanticism but its realism; its particularistic purposes but its nationalistic values."[26]

As a political movement, Progressivism was reformist rather than radically reconstructionist. On one hand, it was a movement that attracted the idealists, the humanitarians, the municipal reformers, and the social Christians: Szasz reported that a 1906 survey discovered that only 15 percent of a large number of social crusaders were not somehow connected with the evangelical Protestantism of that time, and Robert Crunden observed that though Catholics, Jews, and people of no religious affiliation found Progressive goals attractive, "Protestantism provided the chief thrust and defined the perimeters of discourse."[27] In a study of the Progressive intellectuals who were the conspicuous articulators of the movement's ideals, Jean Quandt observed that they used their skills in communication not only as agents of scientific reform and social harmony, but also as "the redemptive agents of the kingdom of God in America."[28] Many of those on that side of the Progressive spectrum, including a number of prominent Social Gospel leaders, wanted to use the powers of the democratic state for the public good, with particular attention to the underprivileged. On the other hand, moving away from interpretations of Progressivism that stem primarily from the rhetoric of leaders of the movement and those who followed their lead, some historians of the late twentieth century who have focused on the actual practices of economic, political, and social groups have gathered a lot of evidence to emphasize another side of Progressivism. In studying in considerable detail the realities of urban reform—one of the jewels in the Progressive crown—Samuel P. Hayes, for example, found that "the leading business groups in each city and the professional men closely allied with them initiated and dominated municipal movements."[29] In a more sweeping interpretation, Gabriel Kolko declared:

> Because of their positive theory of the state, key business elements managed to define the basic form and content of the major federal legislation that was enacted. They provided direction to existing opinion for regulation, but in a number of crucial cases they were the first to initiate that sentiment. They were able to define such sentiment because, in the last analysis, the major political leaders of the Progressive Era—Roosevelt, Taft, and Wilson—were sufficiently conservative to respond to their initiatives.[30]

That Progressivism was indeed a web of many strands can be deduced in that, among its interpreters through the years, some have emphasized its upper-class orientation, others its middle-class nature, and still others its appeal to the lower classes. Yet its accomplishments were considerable as, for example, it secured amendments for a federal income tax, the direct election of senators, Prohibition, and woman suffrage; passed antitrust legislation and provided regulatory commissions in the areas of transportation and manufacturing; advanced the cause of conservation; and in many states instituted the direct primary, the initiative, and the referendum.

Clearly, there was conspicuous support for various Progressive measures across the Protestant spectrum: one has only to mention the reforming role of certain Social Gospel leaders, the Social Creed of the Churches as adopted by the Federal Council of Churches, and the social Christian stance of such a political figure as William Jennings Bryan. But adequate generalizations as to the way elements in the Protestant population actually functioned at the polls are not as readily framed as can be done for some earlier periods. Paul Kleppner, a prolific author in the field of voting behavior, has noted how difficult it is to do that whether one approaches the question from the side of politics or religion. He has said, "No political party has ever wholly conformed to retrospective descriptions of it. . . . Party activities and behaviors have always been sufficiently varied to elude simple descriptive generalizations."[31] He has also emphasized that analysis of voting must deal with the spectrum of ethnocultural values relating to family, religion, education, and community, which implies that it may be difficult to be precise about any one factor, such as religion, in the chain.

It is possible to make more satisfying generalizations about religion and political parties for the period before the political realignments of the 1890s, as we have seen in earlier chapters in this volume. In the latter nineteenth century, the situation was such that the relation of religious allegiance to voting was somewhat clearer than it later became. In his probing book *The Winning of the Midwest: Social and Political Conflict, 1888–1896*, Richard J. Jensen went so far as to declare that then "religion shaped the issues and the rhetoric of politics, and played the critical role in determining the party alignments of the voters." He identified two polar theological positions, the pietistic and the liturgical, which "expressed themselves through the Republican and Democratic parties, respectively." He found these two positions in conflict in every denomination, though he had some trouble fitting both Presbyterians and Lutherans into his schema because of their divisions. The liturgically minded German Lutherans, for example, largely identified themselves with the Democrats, where they were political partners with their religious enemies, the Catholics, while the pietistically oriented ones often gravitated to the Republicans.[32] Despite nuances, however, the evidence points to a fairly clear religiopolitical picture. Jensen's book dealt with the Midwest, but in a later study of the national scene, Kleppner came to a similar conclusion for the late nineteenth century, observing that "as party behaviors began to evoke common meanings for activists, officeholders, and voters, *Democrat* came to represent the outlooks of antipietists, and *Republican* came to resonate emotionally with the dispositions of evangelical pietists." He quoted contemporaries who observed, " 'Catholics . . . think one is not a Catholic if he is a Republican'; or, alternatively, when they pointed to the inconsistency involved in going 'to the Lord's table on Sunday and vot[ing] for Cleveland on Tuesday.' "[33]

The twentieth-century situation was quite different, however, for certain dramatic alterations in that familiar pattern came about in the 1890s. There were many reasons for the change; a major one was clearly economic. A Democratic administration under Grover Cleveland had the misfortune to be inducted in 1893 as a financial panic, followed by mounting unemployment and hard times, was developing. A careful, well-documented book on the political shift that climaxed in 1896 is appropriately titled *The Politics of Depression*. But religious factors were also involved in the political realignment that followed. They contributed not only to the Republican victory of 1896 but to a strengthened party that dominated the political scene for the first three decades of the twentieth century, except for the period when a party split allowed the Democrats to place Wilson in the White House for two terms. The story is complex, but a summary of several aspects of it is relevant here.

As some among the rapidly increasing numbers of Catholics were attracted to the Republicans, the party learned to accommodate that reality. It was reported, for example, that there were some 70,000 Republican Catholics in New

York state by 1894. Nationally, the eloquent Archbishop John Ireland of St. Paul was an ardent Republican who developed considerable influence in party affairs and was among those who absolved the party of anti-Catholic tendencies and deplored Catholic identification with the Democrats.[34] He accepted the concern for temperance that was strong in his chosen party, was a central figure in the Catholic Total Abstinence Union, and even helped to found the Anti-Saloon League.[35] Meanwhile, the party had been broadening its scope by resisting the more extreme, ultra-prohibitionist interpretations of temperance in favor of more moderate stands. Jensen's case study of Iowa in the early 1890s suggested that the GOP there had to draw the line between "responsible temperance and control of the saloon on the one hand, and irresponsible, millenarian prohibition, with its secret dives and bootleggers on the other"; and, having moved toward the softer position, regained control of the state in 1893, thereby laying the groundwork for a critical plurality for McKinley three years later. Similar trends were taking place elsewhere in the Midwest and the North generally; the middle road proved to be politically viable. Ironically, Republican moderation came in part because pragmatic professional politicians were taking a larger role in party affairs, just as the American Anti-Saloon League was founded in 1895. The league eventually attained its goal of Prohibition largely because it also relied on the professionals.[36] In the mid-1890s, Republicans were finding that they could repudiate connections with anti-Catholic organizations such as the American Protective Association without significantly losing the support of traditionally anti-Catholic Protestants—that is, they could advantageously take the middle road. A sign of the new stance was that they chose a rabbi to open their national convention in 1896, so as to avoid offending either their traditional Protestant supporters or their growing Catholic constituency.[37]

According to those who have studied the 1896 returns in depth, the Republicans under McKinley won decisively in what came to be called the urban-industrial heartland of the Northeast and Midwest, where they gained support among Catholics and confessional German Lutherans. The Democrats under Bryan retained strength in the South and West and gathered votes from some who had supported the Populist and Prohibition parties and some who had long espoused the moral integration of society. But Bryan did not go over well among many old-line party regulars, who did not favor strong central government. As Kleppner put it, "Bryan's advocacy of an active and interventionist government, a posture articulated in evangelically toned rhetoric, repelled many of the party's normal ethnic and religious support groups." So, though Bryan did hold the support of many urban native-stock Protestant voters, there was little enthusiasm for him among many Catholics and German Lutherans. Thus, Kleppner concluded, "As a consequence, at its social base, Bryan's Democratic party was more agrarian and evangelical than that party had been at any earlier point in the second half of the nineteenth century."[38] An important but unfortunate result of the election was further steps in the disenfranchisement of southern blacks to ensure that the section remain solidly Democratic, thereby in effect nullifying the Fifteenth Amendment and civil rights legislation. Kleppner has concluded that "the demobilization that occurred in the post-1900 South was the largest, most extensive, and most enduring that this country has ever witnessed."[39] After the realignment, the basic political realities continued to go against the Democrats nationally as they lost the presidential prize in the next three elections, in two of which (1900, 1908) Bryan was again the nominee. The Progressive movement became a powerful political force during the administration of a victorious party that was striving to be open religiously without offending its traditional Protestant supporters, which makes simple generalizations about its religious components somewhat suspect.

The problem of assessing Protestant political leanings in the Progressive period is compounded by the way the separation of church and state has often been understood. Progressivism as an effective force in politics was over long before the flood of Supreme Court cases focused great attention on the religion clauses of the First Amendment, but in 1878 the Court had quoted Jefferson's 1802 interpretation of the establishment clause as "building a wall of separation between church and State."[40] Then, as now, many seemed to assume that this also inhibited political expression by churches and clergy, or at least it often made them hesitate to speak out on partisan matters, though less so on causes understood to be moral—in some cases, very much less so. Some well-known preachers were reluctant to bring political matters to the pulpit, as was the famous Boston pastor of Trinity Church, Phillips Brooks, who remained an influential model long after his death. Though remembered as the leading prophet of the Social Gospel, Walter Rauschenbusch, in the book that made him famous in 1907, was stating prevailing opinion when he declared that the church appropriately cooperates with the state in implanting religious impulses toward righteousness and training moral convictions, "but if it should enter into politics and get funds from the public treasury or police support for its doctrine and ritual, it would inject a divisive and corrosive force into political life," so "the machinery of Church and State must be kept separate."[41] Though this was a time when the missionary crusade was high on the denominational agenda and when missionaries often had visions of a new international order, James Reed observed that, both at home and abroad, with a few exceptions, the missionaries "generally cultivated indifference to the daily realities of power" and "tended to avoid explicitly political questions."[42] They seemed to mirror faithfully the predominant opinion of those who commissioned and sent them.

In part because of the defense of slavery that had explicitly or implicitly been accepted by many southern white Christians, the patterns of excluding political matters from the pulpit in the South had become widespread, and only slowly was there a shift to such nonpartisan matters as supporting Prohibition, upholding Sabbath laws, and opposing gambling. Szasz provided some illustrations of his generalization that "virtually every urban black minister of any standing took positions on such issues as prohibition, black teachers in public schools, and equal rights."[43] There were, of course, Protestant leaders who did engage directly in partisan politics; for example, Bishop Charles Fowler actively campaigned for his fellow Methodist, layman William McKinley, as president in 1900, and the Reverend Alexander J. McKelway, a fiery editor who actively supported fellow southern Presbyterian Woodrow Wilson for president in 1912, was able to get twenty out of twenty-three suggestions incorporated into the Democratic platform in 1916.[44] Such directly partisan activities by clergy seem to have been the exceptions rather than the rule.

As the Progressive movement emerged with growing strength in the twentieth century and pressed for reform to deal with social problems resulting from the unregulated expansion of cities and their new industries, it became a political force that made its way through local and state levels to the national scene. When the ambitious Theodore Roosevelt moved into the presidency after the assassination of McKinley, he shrewdly held the support of business and financial interests while encouraging many Progressive measures. At first under attack from Roman Catholics for some of his Philippine policies, he was concerned to listen to their opinions and to deal fairly with them in appointments to various offices in the islands, working with the civil governor, William Howard Taft. Roosevelt did earn the respect of many Catholics, and then found the razor's edge a little uncomfortable as he was assailed by some Protestants as being too pro-Catholic. But in his victory at the polls in 1904, as Frank T. Reuter's research disclosed, he won in places where there were "large concentrations of Catholic voters, areas that had supported Bryan in 1896 and 1900."[45] Now president in his own right by a sizable plurality, Roosevelt took it as a mandate for Progressivism as he interpreted it, so that some historians date the "era" as beginning in 1905. From then until 1920, leading candidates on both sides waved a Progressive banner. It was Taft versus Bryan in 1908, but as Taft backed away from Roosevelt's policies, the latter bolted the Republicans to form the Progressive party, a split that opened the door for Democrat Woodrow Wilson to carry his Progressive banner to success in 1912. Christians oriented by differing approaches to social reform could therefore find reasons for supporting as progressive their major party of choice throughout the period. The mood of the country was indeed progressive, and it was in that atmosphere that social Christianity flourished. One could be drawn either to its more conservative version or to the liberal Social Gospel, or even to the more radical and reconstructionist socialist camps, and be in tune with the times; one could opt for working directly through a political party, through a denominational or interdenominational agency, or through a voluntary crusade for a given political objective and be relevant to the needs of the age as defined in the Progressive Era.

It was at the height of Progressive enthusiasm and in his most programmatic book that Rauschenbusch made the controversial and oft-criticized claim that political life in America, along with the family, church, and education, had been Christianized, that is, had passed through constitutional changes that made it to some degree part of the organism through which the spirit of Christ can do its work in humanity. "To Americans this may seem a staggering assertion," he wrote in 1912,

> for of all corrupt things surely our politics is the corruptest. I confess to some misgivings in moving that this brother be received among the regenerate, but I plead on his behalf that he is a newly saved sinner. Politics has been on the thorny path of sanctification only about a century and a half, and the tattered clothes and questionable smells of the far country still cling to the prodigal.

His purpose was to emphasize that it was the fifth social institution of society that needed regeneration: business, "the seat and source of our present troubles." He sought to use the channels of government to help correct economic abuses, a familiar Progressive strategy. At the end of his long book, evidently sensing that it might seem to many to pay too little attention to religion and thus sag to the level of mere economic discussion, he insisted that the work's "sole concern is for the kingdom of God and the salvation of men. But the kingdom of God includes the economic life; for it means the progressive transformation of all human affairs by the thought and spirit of Christ."[46]

There were, however, those touched by the enthusiasm of the Social Gospel with its prevailingly liberal theological base who did focus much of their attention on social and economic matters; some took up careers in social work, labor organization, or politics, and some drifted away from the church. Reflecting on the previous three decades, a church historian in 1933 spoke of a type of theological modernism that results from a shift of interest from all these things [rigorous thought, proved scientific facts, philosophical doctrines] as well as from the authorities and the conclusions of the older orthodoxy. Temperamental liberals find in the contemporary social situation both an opportunity and an incentive for a type of liberalism which represents a great deal of human sympathy but very little careful thinking.[47]

Some others were drawn outside of the moderate reformism of the Social Gospel into the social reconstructionism of Christian socialism.[48] In his last book, conscious that the emphasis on social salvation had weaned some away from an emphasis on the personal, Rauschenbusch wrote a chapter entitled "The Social Gospel and Personal Salvation," in which he insisted that "the salvation of the individual is, of course, an essential part of salvation. Every new being is a new problem of salvation. . . . The burden of the individual is as heavy now as ever."[49] Though that was consistent with the tenor of his life and writings, there were representatives of the Social Gospel who let the critique of an individualist ethic so evident then in much church life, liberal and conservative, minimize their attention to the individual in their concern for the social.

By the time Rauschenbusch wrote his last book, the cleavage within evangelical Protestantism, with its range of parties on both sides of the divide, was widening noticeably. Many conservatives who had been active in the wider movement of social Christianity were already pulling away from their concern with reformist thought and action, as George Marsden indicated in his thorough *Fundamentalism and American Culture*. Among the protofundamentalists in the era before World War I, he explained, "progressive political sentiments were still common, even though conservatism prevailed," but he noted "the rather dramatic disappearance of this interest—or at least its severe curtailment—by the 1920s."[50] Reaction to the Social Gospel, its liberal premises, and its attachment to an American culture that was very optimistic and self-confident was among the reasons that conservatives pulled back, so that eventually the centripetal forces at work in Protestantism were weakened because of developments on both sides of the widening cleavage.

At first, American entry into World War I seemed to reinforce some of the motifs of the Progressive period. The crusading spirit was renewed as a "Great Crusade" was launched in support of "the war to make the world safe for democracy." A new surge of patriotism swept across the land, at times with a backlash that left some bitter tastes later. Some Progressive hopes came to fulfillment in transportation, child labor, and conservation, and the Prohibition and woman suffrage amendments were passed. Both Catholic and Protestant churches worked in voluntary cooperation with governmental agencies as they carried out religious and social ministries for soldiers and certain groups of civilians. But Progressivism was a web of many strands, and in an article that summarized the evidence, Arthur S. Link concluded that, under the impact of the stresses of the war, "the Wilsonian coalition gradually disintegrated from 1917 to 1920 and disappeared entirely during the campaign of 1920."[51] But though the movement evaporated as moods of disillusionment dampened earlier idealistic hopes, much that Progressivism had accomplished was not swept away, such as the beginnings of zoning, planning, and social insurance movements; the maturing of factory legislation; and the laying of foundations for the development of hydroelectric power. Some of the weaknesses of the movement lived on after it: immigration restriction was motivated in part by racism, nativism, and anti-Semitism. But certain of its ideas and ideals were carried into the new political era of the 1930s, to contribute to another period of reform.

The last stage of the Progressive period, 1917–1920, however, was marked by a hardening of the theological tensions that had been growing in Protestant life. Probing the "logic of modernism" during and just after the war, Hutchison concluded that one result among some of its thoughtful representatives "was an increasing sense that the progressivist component of modernism, its reverently hopeful interpretation of the immanence of God in culture, had become deeply problematic." But that shift did not seem to extend to the characteristic liberal postmillennialism, while during the war period, fear of the demise of Christian civilization itself led many conservatives to accentuate their premillennialist views emphatically as a key to understanding God's will for the nation.[52] The Progressive period had been one in which the centripetal forces in Protestantism seemed to be winning over divisive centrifugal pressures, but as the era ended in the aftermath of war the latter were becoming resurgent. The social Christian movements had largely opted for a liberal political cast, while various groups that were just gathering around the new term "fundamentalist," though politics was not high on their agendas, were drawn more and more to conservative positions. The changing alignments that can be discerned as the Progressive period drew to its close continued to be of significance in the political turmoil of the 1920s and 1930s.

NOTES

1. Estimates based on the work by Edwin Scott Gaustad, *Historical Atlas of Religion in America*, rev. ed. (New York: Harper & Row, 1976), part II, and on summaries of the

federal Census of Religious Bodies in C. Luther Fry, *The U.S. Looks at Its Churches* (New York: Institute of Social and Religious Research, 1930), appendix, esp. 141.

2. Indispensable works for understanding these movements are Kenneth Canthen, *The Impact of American Religious Liberalism*, 2nd ed. (Washington, D.C.: University Press of America, 1983); William R. Hutchison, *The Modernist Impulse in American Protestantism* (Cambridge, Mass.: Harvard University Press, 1976); George M. Marsden, *Fundamentalism and American Culture: The Shaping of Twentieth-Century Evangelicalism, 1870–1925* (New York: Oxford University Press, 1980); C. Allyn Russell, *Voices of American Fundamentalism* (Philadelphia: Westminster, 1976); Ferenc M. Szasz, *The Divided Mind of Protestant America, 1880–1930* (University: University of Alabama Press, 1982).

3. Hutchison, *Modernist Impulse*, 8. See also H. Shelton Smith's chapter "The Christocentric Liberal Tradition," in *American Christianity: An Historical Interpretation with Representative Documents*, ed. Smith, Robert Handy, and Lefferts Loetscher (New York: Scribner's, 1963), II, 255–308.

4. Szasz, *Divided Mind*, 44.

5. Washington Gladden, *Ruling Ideas of the Present Age* (Boston: Houghton Mifflin, 1895).

6. William R. Hutchison, *Errand to the World: American Protestant Thought and Foreign Missions* (Chicago: University of Chicago Press, 1987), 95.

7. Russell has chapters on Straton and Riley in *Voices of American Fundamentalism*, and an article entitled "Mark Allison Matthews: Seattle Fundamentalist and Civic Reformer," *Journal of Presbyterian History* 57 (1979): 446–66.

8. Hutchison, *Modernist Impulse*, 165. Though his work does not deal with the Progressive period, Henry F. May's treatment of American social Christian movements in the late nineteenth century under the headings of conservative, Progressive (Social Gospel), and radical social Christianity is relevant also to the twentieth: *Protestant Churches and Industrial America* (New York: Harper, 1949), esp. part IV.

9. Norris Magnuson, *Salvation in the Slums: Evangelical Social Work, 1865–1920* (Metuchen, N.J.: Scarecrow, 1977).

10. This point has been strongly made by Paul A. Carter, *The Decline and Revival of the Social Gospel: Social and Political Liberalism in American Protestant Churches, 1920–1940* (Ithaca, N.Y.: Cornell University Press, 1956; 2nd ed., Hamden, Conn.: Archon, 1971), ch. 3. The exception was the Episcopal church. See also K. Austin Kerr, *Organized for Prohibition: A New History of the Anti-Saloon League* (New Haven, Conn.: Yale University Press, 1985).

11. John Lee Eighmy, "Religious Liberalism in the South during the Progressive Era," *Church History* 38 (1969): 363–65.

12. Robert W. Lynn, *Protestant Strategies in Education* (New York: Association Press, 1964), 30.

13. *Journal of the Twenty-second Quadrennial Session of the African Methodist Episcopal Church* (1904), 186–87.

14. Szasz, *Divided Mind*, 113, referring to Bryan's comment in *Commoner* 19 (May 1919).

15. David S. Monroe, ed., *Journal of the General Conference of the Methodist Episcopal Church* (New York: Eaton and Mains, 1900), 186–87.

16. As quoted by John F. Piper, Jr., *The American Churches in World War I* (Athens: Ohio University Press, 1985), 15–16.

17. Donald L. Kinzer, *An Episode in Anti-Catholicism: The American Protective Association* (Seattle: University of Washington Press, 1964), discussed the NLPAI in the course of his treatment of the APA.

18. The literature is vast; for an overall survey, see Lloyd P. Jorgenson, *The State and the Non-Public School, 1825–1925* (Columbia: University of Missouri Press, 1987).

19. Gibbons made this statement in an article in the *North American Review* in 1909, quoted by John Tracy Ellis, *Perspectives on American Catholicism* (Baltimore, Md.: Helicon, 1963), 5.

20. Martin E. Marty, *Modern American Religion*, vol. 1: *The Irony of It All, 1893–1919* (Chicago: University of Chicago Press, 1986), 155. The Grose quotation is from his *The Incoming Millions* (New York: Revell, 1906), 99.

21. *Ecumenical Missionary Conference in New York, 1900*, 2 vols. (New York: American Tract Society, 1900), 1:11.

22. "Democracy and Efficiency," as reprinted in part in *The Issues of the Populist and Progressive Eras, 1892–1912*, ed. Richard M. Abrams (New York: Harper & Row, 1969), 275.

23. Gaius Glenn Atkins, *Religion in Our Times* (New York: Round Table, 1932), 156.

24. Henry F. May, *The End of American Innocence: A Study of the First Years of Our Own Time, 1912–1917* (New York: Knopf, 1963), 18.

25. Walter Dean Burnham, "The System of 1896," in *The Evolution of American: Electoral Systems*, ed. Paul Kleppner et al. (Westport, Conn.: Greenwood, 1981), 166.

26. Dewey Grantham, "The Progressive Era and the Reform Traditions," reprinted in *Progressivism: The Critical Issues*, ed. David M. Kennedy (Boston: Little, Brown, 1971), 118.

27. Szasz, *Divided Mind*, 43; Robert M. Crunden, *Ministers of Reform: The Progressives' Achievement in American Civilization, 1889–1920* (New York: Basic, 1982), ix–x.

28. Jean Quandt, *From the Small Town to the Great Community: The Social Thought of Progressive Intellectuals* (New Brunswick, N.J.: Rutgers University Press, 1970), 75.

29. Samuel P. Hayes, "The Politics of Reform in Municipal Government in the Progressive Era," in Kennedy, *Progressivism*, 91.

30. Gabriel Kolko, *The Triumph of Conservatism* (Glencoe, Ill.: Free Press, 1963), 134.

31. Paul Kleppner, *Who Voted? The Dynamics of Electoral Turnouts, 1870–1980* (New York: Praeger, 1982), 76.

32. Richard J. Jensen, *The Winning of the Midwest: Social and Political Conflict, 1888–1896* (Chicago: University of Chicago Press, 1971), esp. chs. 3 and 7; quotes 58; on the Lutherans, see 67, 83.

33. Kleppner, *Who Voted?* 45, 46.

34. Samuel T. McSeveney, *The Politics of Depression: Political Behavior in the Northeast, 1893–1896* (New York: Oxford University Press, 1972), 76, 105–6.

35. Robert D. Cross, *The Emergence of Liberal Catholicism* (Cambridge, Mass.: Harvard University Press, 1958), 110, 128–29.

36. Jensen, *Winning of the Midwest*, 195–208, quoted words on 202.

37. McSeveney, *Politics of Depression*, 37–38, 85.

38. Kleppner, *Who Voted?* 75. See also John L. Hammond, *The Politics of Benevolence: Revival Religion and American Voting Behavior* (Norwood, N.J.: Ablex, 1979), 152–60.

39. Paul Kleppner, *Continuity and Change in Electoral Politics, 1893–1928* (New York: Greenwood, 1987), 165; see also his *Who Voted?* 56, 65–66.

40. The letter is reprinted in John F. Wilson and Donald L. Drakeford, eds., *Church and State in American History: The Burden of Religious Pluralism*, 2nd ed. (Boston: Beacon, 1987), 78–80; the citation by the Supreme Court is from *Reynolds v. U.S.*, 98 U.S. 145 (1878).

41. Walter Rauschenbusch, *Christianity and the Social Crisis* (New York: Macmillan, 1907), 380.

42. James Reed, *The Missionary Mind and American East Asia Policy, 1911–1915* (Cambridge, Mass.: Harvard University Press, 1983), 96.

43. Szasz, *Divided Mind*, 49.

44. Fowler's role is mentioned by Frederick A. Norwood, *The Story of American Methodism* (Nashville, Tenn.: Abingdon, 1974), 347; on McKelway, see Hugh C. Bailey, *Liberalism in the New South: Southern Social Reformers and the Progressive Movement* (Coral Gables, Fla.: University of Miami Press, 1969), esp. ch. 10, "National Politics."

45. Frank T. Reuter, *Catholic Influence on American Colonial Policies, 1898–1904* (Austin: University of Texas Press, 1967), 135.

46. Walter Rauschenbusch, *Christianizing the Social Order* (New York: Macmillan, 1912), 148–49, 156, 458.

47. Winfred E. Garrison, *The March of Faith: The Story of Religion in America since 1865* (New York: Harper, 1933), 267.

48. See my article "Christianity and Socialism in America, 1900–1920," *Church History* 21 (1952): 39–54.

49. Walter Rauschenbusch, *A Theology for the Social Gospel* (New York: Macmillan, 1917), 944.

50. Marsden, *Fundamentalism and American Culture*, esp. chs. 10, 16, and 23; quotes 207, 85. Also relevant is ch. 5 in Timothy P. Weber, *Living in the Shadow of the Second Coming: American Premillennialism, 1875–1925* (New York: Oxford University Press, 1979).

51. Arthur S. Link, "What Happened to the Progressive Movement in the 1920's?" *American Historical Review* 54 (1959): 839; also reprinted in Kennedy, *Progressivism*, 153.

52. Hutchison, *Modernist Impulse*, 226–56, quote 256; see also Marsden, *Fundamentalism and American Culture*, 141–53.

Roman Catholics and American Politics, 1900–1960
Altered Circumstances, Continuing Patterns

James Hennesey, S.J.

THE CHRONOLOGICAL LIMITS set for this chapter take all the fun out of it. Well, not all, but a great deal. The "Americanism" controversy is over before we begin and, at the other end, John F. Kennedy has been elected but not inaugurated, while the Second Vatican Council is in a preparatory stage little similar to the actual event. Rehearsing the six decades that lie in between is not easy. And while I am committed to the proposition that examining those sixty years will provide some leverage on present concerns, I am not totally sanguine about the outcome of the exercise. The change in the world, and even more in the church, has been so great since 1960 as to give even the most committed historian pause in the enterprise of illuminating the present by reference to the past. That is, nevertheless, the task.

"Politics." What do we mean? In his *Caesar's Coin: Religion and Politics in America*, Richard McBrien writes that "politics has to do with the public forum and with the process of decision making that occurs there."[1] I take that as my ballpark. Roman Catholics in the first sixty years of the twentieth century ran for public office and served in appointive posts at all levels of government. They were involved as commentators upon and occasionally as movers and shakers in some of the major public issues of the time.

Officeholding and public involvement came in two ways, corporate and individual. For Roman Catholics of the period, corporate involvement meant the Holy See—the pope and/or officials of his central administration—or it meant the involvement of American bishops. "The church" in the latter case might be represented by an individual bishop or, from the 1920s on, in the peculiar style of collegial voice harbored in the National Catholic Welfare Conference. Individual priests, sisters, and brothers were likewise often perceived as "the church." The extent to which they might fairly be said to represent the Catholic community was subject to interpretation. The same was true of lay Catholics. The first six decades of the century saw an enormous proliferation in the number of Roman Catholic officeholders at all levels of government. Sheer numbers had a certain sociological importance. The extent to which Roman Catholics running for or holding public office or commenting in a significant way on public affairs reflected well-informed Catholic theological, political, or social thought was something else again.

The twentieth century began for the country's approximately twelve million Roman Catholics amid the shambles of the intramural quarrel which Pope Leo XIII had brought to an end with a sentence in an 1899 encyclical letter: "We cannot approve the opinions which some comprise under the head of Americanism."[2] The pope immediately took pains in the letter *Testem Benevolentiae* to distinguish the religious Americanism he was proscribing from its political cousin, but at the very least his terminology was embarrassing to his American coreligionists, many of whom had already read enough of the widespread newspaper coverage of disagreements among their bishops.[3] At issue was the inclination of some American Catholic bishops, as William Halsey summarized it, to espouse "the activist individualism, self-confident mystique and optimistic idealism" prevalent in American society at the end of the century.[4] William Clebsch thought they were trying to "fit Catholicism into the live-and-let-live pluralism of the American denominations" and singing "the current songs of the middle-class denominations: progress, social reform and shared religious traditions."[5] But the "Americanists" were hardly liberal Protestants, as closer inspection of any of them—Ireland of St. Paul, Gibbons of Baltimore, Keane of the Catholic University, O'Connell of the American College in Rome, and the rest—reveals. In the mid-twentieth century, Robert Cross fixed it in our minds that the Americanists represented a liberal kind of Catholicism.[6] Others preferred the term "progressive." But easy categorization falls apart when confronted by the dynamic progressivism of a "conservative and reactionary" McQuaid of Rochester or the near-nativist obscurantism of "liberal" John Ireland's treatment of eastern-rite Catholics.

Be all that as it may, American Roman Catholics as the new century began faced on the East Coast the "banner immigrational decade" between the years 1900 and 1910, in which nearly one-half of the total net immigration were people religiously Roman Catholic, the great majority of them southern Italians, Hungarians, or Slavs from the Austrian and Russian empires.[7] Across the Pacific and in the Caribbean, tens of thousands of fellow Catholics had come under the American flag, even if President McKinley did seem to think that some of his new empire had yet to hear the gospel.[8] The Americanist episode and its Roman condemnation were followed in Catholicism by a largely European "modernist" crisis that was put down far more severely than had been Americanism. Historical and speculative thought in Roman Catholic theological circles went into a half-century eclipse, particularly in the United States. American Roman Catholics had both the need and the opportunity to devote their energies to the social and political problems of the new century.

Writing in the 1840s of the church that he consigned to the *purgatorio* of "non-evangelical denominations," Robert Baird listed "three things that have occurred to arouse the American people in relation to Rome and her movements":

1. The simultaneous efforts which have been made of late by her hierarchy in many of the States to obtain a portion of the funds destined to the support of public schools, and employ them for the support of their own sectarian schools, in which neither the Sacred Scriptures, nor any portion of them, are read, but avowedly sectarian instruction is given....

2. The efforts made by the hierarchy to bring all the property of the Roman Catholic Church . . . into the possession of the bishops.

3. The disposition, long well known, of some of the leaders of the great political parties, to court the Romanists for their vote at the elections, and the willingness of the hierarchy to be regarded as a "great power in the State," and as, in fact, holding the "balance of power."[9]

Schools, property titles, and politics had been constants in nineteenth-century squabbles, both within the Catholic body in the United States and in Catholics' relationships with the larger society and with the state. Schools and politics remained factors in the twentieth century. In the mainstream American Catholic church, battles between bishops and civil trustees of church property were rare, but flare-ups among newer ethnic groups entering the country helped to keep alive Catholicism's authoritarian image.

Conflict between Roman Catholics and other Americans over the kind of primary schools the nation should have goes back to the early nineteenth century, when Roman Catholics sought a share in the public funds being allocated, first, to

openly denominational schools and, later, as the reform movement associated with the name of Horace Mann took hold, to schools that Catholics and
others saw as Protestant Christian, but most Protestants saw as properly "non-
sectarian."

The first school money disbursed in Chicago went in 1834 to schools located in Presbyterian and Baptist churches; only in 1910 were religious influences
finally eliminated under pressure from an alliance at various times attracting support from Catholics, Jews, Unitarians, Universalists, and liberal Protestants, as
well as atheists and agnostics.[10] In New York City, Bishop John Hughes in 1841
declared open war on the Public School Society. In cooperation with Whig boss
Thurlow Weed, the bishop ran a competing slate in a legislative election that cost
the Democrats seats in the New York Assembly. It is the only such example of
direct political action by a Catholic bishop in our history. The Democrats felt the
sting of the bishop's power, but he got no funds for his schools.[11] Disputes in
Philadelphia during the spring and summer of 1844 over religious observances
and exclusive classroom use of the King James version of the Bible in the common
schools led to rioting, church burning, and confrontations between armed Protestant and Catholic militia units.[12]

The phenomenon was not limited to the East and Midwest. In the newly
minted state of California, a law passed in 1853 to allow funding of church-
controlled schools was repealed in 1855 after Catholic archbishop Alemany of
San Francisco tried to take advantage of it.[13] On the opposite side, thanks to the
efforts of Santa Fe archbishop Lamy, most teachers in the public as well as in the
parochial schools in the New Mexico Territory were in the mid-1870s Roman
Catholic sisters, brothers, or priests, and almost all textbooks used in both private
and public schools were printed by the Jesuits' Rio Grande Press. The Catholic
monopoly was a factor delaying New Mexican statehood. The situation was not
helped when Jesuit Donato Gasparri ("the carpetbagger from Naples," Territorial
Secretary W. G. Ritch called him) sat on the Speaker's bench during legislative
debate on a public education bill he had denounced as a "Cancer which corrodes
and consumes the societies of the United States."[14]

The nineteenth-century Catholic house was not a monolith on the school
question. The "progressionists," or "anti-absolutists," a band of liberal New York
priests, had long opposed parochial schools and other church-sponsored institutions paralleling those of the state.[15] The intramural schools controversy of the
early 1890s revolved around efforts somehow to integrate Catholic and public
education.[16] But as the new century began, the Catholic church in the United
States was officially committed to a policy of separate schools. Where government
aid was available, as it was on Indian reservations after a U.S. Supreme Court

decision in 1908, Catholic missionaries took it; but there was a general policy of suspicion that government control would follow financial aid.

In 1925, the Supreme Court struck down an Oregon law that would have created an educational monopoly for state schools for all children aged eight to sixteen. Religiously affiliated schools were among those that had their status secured. Public debate on another issue was already under way: the question of federal aid to education and the creation of a federal department of education. Cardinal Gibbons of Baltimore, the unofficial but acknowledged leader of the American hierarchy, was not disinclined to deal with "a few intelligent men in Washington" rather than with "so many petty, narrow officials of each state," but the bishops voted in 1919 to oppose any such scheme.[17] A 1922 release explained their opposition to the postwar growth of the federal bureaucracy, which they called "foreign to everything American . . . unconstitutional and undemocratic." "It means officialism," they declared, "red tape and prodigal waste of public money. It spells hordes of so-called experts and self-perpetuating cliques of politicians to regulate every detail of life. It would eventually sovietize our government."[18]

A bishop with a different vision was John Glennon, from 1903 to 1946 archbishop of St. Louis. He had taken a hard line, both with fellow bishops and in his diocese, in the matter of parochial primary and secondary schools, but tight money in the immediate postwar period made him cast about for new sources of funding. Arguing that education must provide moral training, "which must have a religious basis, background and sustenance," he called for tax assistance to Catholic schools such that it would "establish a reasonable equity between the sources and the disposal of taxes."[19] Glennon tried to raise national discussion of state aid to private schools, but it was an issue still two decades away.

The 1950s found America's Catholics embroiled on three interrelated fronts in the schools conflict. Cardinal O'Hara of Philadelphia, a former president of the University of Notre Dame and a bishop who placed great emphasis on diocesan schools, held firmly to the 1920s position of no government aid. Partly, he based his opposition on "the waste of public funds that goes on in public school construction and operation," but his major fear was the control that would inevitably follow government financing.[20] O'Hara was, however, now a minority voice among the bishops. In June 1949, their official representative announced as a new major premise, in testimony before a congressional committee, that "every school to which parents may send their children in compliance with the compulsory education laws of the State is entitled to a fair share of the tax funds."[21] The Glennon view had prevailed.

Bitter controversy soon engulfed the issue. Representative Graham Barden of North Carolina had filed a bill for federal aid that would be based on the total school population in a given state, but restricted in distribution to public schools. Cardinal Spellman of New York, declaring himself in favor of such aid "for needy States and needy children," vehemently protested the exclusion of parochial school children from its benefit. Spellman's vitriolic rhetoric, strewn with references to "bigots" and "unhooded Klansmen," provoked an uproar that attracted attacks from other churches and involved him in an unseemly episode with Mrs. Eleanor Roosevelt, for which he had to apologize.[22] The waters were badly muddied just as the Supreme Court began to hand down the first in a series of decisions, which still continues, interpreting and applying below the federal level the free-exercise and nonestablishment clauses of the First Amendment to the federal Constitution.

Beginning with the Supreme Court's judgment in *Everson v. Board of Education* (1947), jurisprudence in this area has been a complex maze, and I shall not enter that maze. Nonetheless, what I wrote in the early 1980s still seems to be true, that Roman Catholics generally read the Constitution

> as allowing some accommodation between church and state. Advocates of this view appeal to the historical origin of the nonestablishment clause of the First Amendment (designed to prevent a single national state church), to the same amendment's free exercise clause, and to the Fourteenth Amendment's equal protection clause. This approach adopts the philosophical principle of distributive justice.... Historically it accepts the thesis that in America church-state separation was conceived in cooperation and not, as in Europe in the aftermath of the French Revolution, in hostility.[23]

This is a position that, to sum it up in metaphor, does not accept that there is in the Constitution a necessary "wall" of separation between church and state, as that Jeffersonian phrase has been used after its reintroduction in *Everson*.

Catholic schools and their claims on the state were one perduring "Baird" issue. Direct involvement in partisan politics on the part of the hierarchy was another, but there the evidence has been much less clear.

John Carroll, later the first Catholic bishop in the United States, accompanied the new nation's first diplomatic mission, sent by the Continental Congress in the spring of 1776 to Quebec. He did so for patriotic reasons, but with some reluctance because "I have observed that when the ministers of Religion leave the duties of their profession to take a busy part in political matters, they generally fall into contempt; & sometimes even bring discredit to the cause, in whose service they are engaged."[24] The theme is one repeated over and over and over again with other bishops. With few exceptions, they react with near-horror to the suggestion that they be involved in politics. Open partisanship is what they mean.

It is easy in John Carroll's writings to trace his development from enlightened, historically conscious thinker to more cautious Burkean conservative. He also introduced a long tradition of what might be called "a word in your ear" political involvement. When in 1784 he learned that Roman authorities, without consulting the American clergy, were trying to negotiate church affairs with Congress through the agency of the U.S. commissioner in Paris, Benjamin Franklin, he expressed satisfaction at Congress's rejection of the proposal, but added:

> Had I received timely information before Congress sent their answer, I flatter myself it would have been more satisfactory to us, than the one which was sent, tho' a good one. My Brother's triennium in Congress has just expired; and Mr. Fitzsimmons, the only Catholic member beside, had just resigned: these were unfortunate circumstances.[25]

His cousin, Charles Carroll of Carrollton, was president of the Maryland State Convention when John Carroll wrote him about a state law that forbade Roman Catholics to be guardians of Protestant children: "I make no doubt but you will be able to obtain a general repeal of this and all other laws and clauses of laws enacting any partial regards to one denomination to the prejudice of others."[26] On another occasion, he announced opposition to a plan under which the state legislature would impose a compulsory church tax, to be paid to the denomination of one's choice. His opposition was not to the principle, but because

> from certain clauses in [the proposed law], and other circumstances, we, as well as the Presbyterians, Methodists, Quakers and Anabaptists are induced to believe, that it *is* calculated to create a predominant and irresistible influence in favour of the Protestant Episcopal Church.[27]

The coming of the nineteenth-century immigrants brought a different tone. "Irishmen fresh from the bogs of Ireland," a Boston Yankee politician complained, "are led up to vote like dumb brutes."[28] The Irish learned to play machine politics and did it with considerable skill. Occasional bishops like John Hughes indulged openly. But the basic tradition remained that of a quiet word to the political leader when it seemed needed.

There were exceptions. On November 25, 1894, Bishop Bernard McQuaid of Rochester mounted the pulpit of his cathedral. He first announced his own position on bishops in politics. For twenty-seven years, he had not even voted in public elections, "out of anxiety not to put it in any man's power to say that I had voted for one party or the other." "It has been traditional in the Church of the United States," he continued, "for Bishops to hold aloof from politics." But the burden of his pronouncement that day was to pillory Archbishop John Ireland of St. Paul for violating that taboo. Ireland, an unabashed Republican party activist, had openly campaigned in New York state against McQuaid's candidacy for legislative election to the Board of Regents of the University of the State of New York. McQuaid noted the uniqueness of Ireland's activity and declared his un-equivocal opposition:

> I want it understood that it is the policy of the Catholic Church in this country that her bishops and priests should take no active part in po-litical campaigns and contests; that what bishops can do with impunity in political matters priests can also do; that neither have any right to become tools or agents of any political party; that, when they do so, they descend from their high dignity, lay themselves open to censure and bitter remarks from those whom they oppose, remarks which recoil on the sacred office which they hold and expose themselves and [their] office to the vituperation so common in electioneering times.[29]

No doubt, the distinction of what was "political" and what was not was at times more in the mind of the cleric than it was in the logic of the facts, but careful students have noted the generally ambivalent relationships that existed between prominent Catholic prelates and predominantly Catholic city machines. R. Laurence Moore confidently declared, "What bothered Ireland about his New York colleagues . . . was their comfortable acquiescence in the marriage of many Irish Catholics with the very American institution of Tammany Hall." The archbishop's misgivings, Moore thought, "reflected his staunch ties to the Re-publican Party."[30] Perhaps, but more detailed study is needed on when and why Archbishop's House on Madison Avenue became known in New York political circles as "the Powerhouse"—and when and why it lost that sobriquet.

Case studies abound. In San Francisco, Peter Yorke was a priest and the crusading editor of the diocesan newspaper the *Monitor*. His initial focus was on the influence in local politics of the openly anti-Catholic American Protective Association (APA). In 1896, he helped to end the senatorial aspirations of John D. Spreckels on the score of the latter's association with the APA. By 1898, Yorke's field of fire was broader as he attacked Catholic political figures on issues unrelated to religion. One of them was San Francisco mayor James D. Phelan, who at his death would bequeath $10 million to Catholic institutions. But through it all, Archbishop Patrick Riordan serenely proclaimed that, while the clergy were free to make their political views known, "the Catholic Church never dictated a political policy to its clergy and laity." Yorke himself, Riordan biographer James Gaffey states, "genuinely believed that he had never violated the sane tradition that Catholic priests must not interfere in politics." "He belonged," Gaffey explains, "to no political party, viewing Democrats and Republicans, Socialists and Populists, with what was termed 'benevolent neutrality.'"[31] Would-be senator Spreckels and senator-to-be Phelan might have entertained other views.

Many currents that disturbed the West Coast scene flowed also in the East. John Webb Pratt's analysis of the New York state constitutional convention of 1894 is instructive, showing as it does how Archbishop Corrigan of New York, working through lay representatives, accepted a "sectarian amendment" to the state constitution prohibiting public aid to church-related charitable institutions.[32]

The Boston scene had its own dynamics. Cardinal William O'Connell, archbishop from 1907 to 1944, preferred the company of Yankee politicians to that of Irish Catholics, from whom he kept "a studied distance." Asked once for support by James Michael Curley, his reply was negative, because "our religion has nothing to do with it."[33]

Massachusetts had its own battle over a "sectarian amendment" to its constitution in 1917. A difference was that the amendment was supported by two prominent Roman Catholics, the later Speaker of the U.S. House of Representatives, John W. McCormack, and Boston political boss Martin Lomasney, known as "the Mahatma of the West End." Their constitutional amendment struck not only at schools, but at nonpublic institutions of any type. O'Connell declared the proposal a "gratuitous insult" to Catholics; Lomasney's reply was: "Tell His Eminence to mind his own business."[34]

O'Connell lost the 1917 fight. He was not fazed and soon took on bigger fish. Montana Democratic senator Thomas J. Walsh sponsored in 1924 a child labor amendment to the Constitution. Monsignor John A. Ryan of the Catholic University of America had assisted in drafting the document. For Cardinal O'Connell, it was but another example of "overblown government" interference, this time with parental rights. It was, besides, "nefarious and bolshevik."[35] Thirty years later, similar arguments served Cardinal O'Hara of Philadelphia as he argued against federal aid to education.

Catholic governor David I. Walsh brought woman suffrage to a vote in Massachusetts in 1915, and there was a vigorous women's Catholic movement there in its favor. O'Connell and the clergy stayed out of the argument, but opponents of adoption on the state level included Katherine Conway, editor of the archdiocesan newspaper the *Pilot*, and antisocialist crusader Martha Moore Avery, who feared votes for women to be another manifestation of the "red menace" threatening America. The woman suffrage amendment to the federal

Constitution was ratified in 1920. It had drawn opposition from such different Catholics as Cardinal Gibbons of Baltimore and radical labor agitator "Mother" Mary Harris Jones, each playing on some variation of the theme that woman's place was in the home.[36]

Mary Jo Weaver identified Lucy Burns as "the only Catholic woman in the radical wing of the suffragist campaign," bringing "a fierceness and resolution to the American woman suffrage movement that was rarely equalled." She "organized parades, took trainloads of women to campaign against Wilson in western states, gave speeches, lobbied, educated other women, and published a newspaper."[37] Weaver neglected to mention the many women in Massachusetts's Margaret Brent League and the suffragist record of Archbishop Austin Dowling of St. Paul. Most of his peers opposed or were doubtful about suffrage for women, but there is no evidence for Weaver's statement that the "official Catholic position toward suffrage was negative." There was no "official" position.

Friendly persuasion of public officials to carry out Catholic purposes continued into the 1920s. A *New York Times* headline proclaimed in 1921: "Birth Control Raid Made by Police on Archbishop's Orders." The target was the first American Birth Control Conference; the archbishop at whose insistence the New York Police Department shut it down was Patrick J. Hayes, who voiced the extraordinary judgment that, while taking human life "after its inception is a horrible crime, to prevent human life that the Creator is about to bring into being, is satanic."[38] More politic, but as determined to work his will in the public forum, was George W. Mundelein, who arrived from Brooklyn to be archbishop of Chicago in 1915, and stayed until his death in 1939. He passed orders in 1917 to the Speaker of the Illinois House of Representatives to "bury" bills unfavorable to Catholic orphanages, and when ultimately that tactic failed, he took the matter up with Chicago's mayor and the governor of the state. Discovering Roman Catholics to be underrepresented on the Chicago Board of Education (they held five of twenty-one seats), he sent Mayor William Hale Thompson the names of two Catholics for appointment, noting that he had selected them "with a great deal of care."[39] That was in 1917, soon after Mundelein's arrival. His political influence grew with the years and was even symbolized by the license plate on his car: it read "Illinois 1."

The approach in Pennsylvania was more sophisticated. In a move that foreshadowed the lobbyists, who in modern days represent Catholic church concerns in state capitals across the country, Philadelphia archbishop Dennis Dougherty in late 1918 agreed with Bishop McDevitt of Harrisburg that it was time for the Pennsylvania dioceses to hire a lawyer to watch over their interests in the state legislature. For over thirty years, Dougherty dominated the Pennsylvania scene. A biographer summed up his public involvement this way:

> He would move quickly but astutely into the political arena when the welfare of the Church was concerned, and personally followed all legislation involving the welfare of the Church or its institutions. In the best sense he knew how to work behind the scenes, avoiding publicity unless it was necessary as a final measure to procure his goal or alert his subjects.[40]

Finally, there was Cardinal Richard Cushing, archbishop of Boston. He succeeded O'Connell in 1944 and retired in 1970. Cushing reveled in the company of politicians and entered into their world. He gave and demanded favors. When, in 1962, the Kennedys' effort to ransom prisoners taken in Cuba in the Bay of Pigs fiasco was foundering, it was the archbishop who raised, by borrowing, the needed million dollars. Earlier, when the bishops' national education department sought his help during another round in the never-ending battle over aid to church-related schools, he wrote: " 'Holler' if I can do anything more. These men [Congressman Thomas P. O'Neill, Jr., and Senator John F. Kennedy] should be standing by ready to serve me. . . . I have done enough for both of them."[41] In Cushing's world, church and state were co-operators. He disclaimed any right to tell people for whom to vote, but "religious people must be interested in the application of moral and ethical principles to public policy."[42]

In theory, this was hardly different from the thought of William O'Connell. What was different was the close relations between Cushing and political leaders and the unabashed way he organized the Catholic forces for political combat. The 1948 campaign against liberalization of Massachusetts's laws on contraception was an example, complete with voter registration drive, reminders of the citizen's moral obligation to vote, use of an advertising agency to orchestrate radio and newspaper coverage, billboards, flyers and pamphlets, distribution to parish priests of sample sermons, and organization of cadres of responsible adults in each parish to hand out "Vote No" literature near the polling places. The campaign was successful; a new style of active political involvement was born.[43]

Cushing's approach was startlingly like approaches growing out of post–Vatican II "political theology," with its collapse of the dualities that separated and stratified church and world, sacred and secular, clergy and laity. But, in fact, his style owed much to his native environment as a child of "Southie," South Boston, where politics is as natural as air. The substance of his approach was heavily influenced by long-time aide John J. Wright, himself later a cardinal in Rome.

Wright's doctoral dissertation was entitled "National Patriotism in Papal Teaching." His ideas reflected those popular in the time of Pius XI, pope from 1922 to 1939, when identification of the kingdom of God with the Roman Catholic church was very close. Wright urged on Catholics the obligation to establish the kingdom in their homelands ("fatherlands," he called them). Direct and open involvement of the clergy in the political process was not taboo. In Cushing's Boston, it was very real.[44]

World War I was a great turning point in the relationship between American Roman Catholics and their compatriots. The 1920s would be a decade of sharp contrasts. On the domestic front, anti-Catholicism flared in the activities of the Ku Klux Klan and in many of the less savory attacks on the candidacies of New York governor Alfred E. Smith, first for the vice presidency and then for the presidency of the United States. There were also the thoughtful probings of people like Episcopalian attorney Charles G. Marshall, who wondered in print how a conscientious Roman Catholic could reconcile American understanding of church-state relations with the view of Pope Leo XIII in his 1885 encyclical letter, *Immortale Dei*. Al Smith's spontaneous and plaintive "Will somebody please tell me what in hell an encyclical is?" spoke volumes.[45] Historians of religion point to the truism that a religious tradition is passed on through many channels. There is the channel of the theologians, with their precisions and philosophizing; that of the community's public worship, with its delicately nuanced multiple ways of conveying meaning; that of official documents and canonical niceties; and that of the *sensus fidelium*, in this case the instinctive sense of people in the Catholic tradition of who they are and why they are that way. The channels are generally parallel, but they are complementary, not wholly identical. A learned man like Charles Marshall knew about Leo XIII's medieval views on the relationship of church and state. American Catholics in the main did not, although they had been repeated by John A. Ryan and Moorhouse Millar in a 1922 book. Their impact on the thinking of American Catholics was slight, as Smith's reaction suggested, but Marshall and others could hardly be expected to sense that, especially when they put it together with more pedestrian examples of church-state "unionist" thought.

An aspect of 1920s Catholicism highlighted in William Halsey's *The Survival of American Innocence* was its rather confident return from the exile into which conflict with the nineteenth-century world of science, progress, prosperity, and the liberal faith had plunged it. Catholics in the United States found "a new sense of identity, an enthusiasm for ideals, and a rather disconcerting confidence in their beliefs."[46] The approach contrasted with the depression that settled in among heretofore dominant religious groups. It found support in the powerful style of Pius XI. Disdainful of the League of Nations and of the Versailles Treaty, he sought "the peace of Christ in the kingdom of Christ." His world was the church; he was Christ's vicar. Theologically, the church was seen as the kingdom; under his successors, other metaphors would take pride of place: the body of Christ, later the people of God.

Pius XI thought in terms of spiritual conquest. He planned to win Russia from both the Bolsheviks and Orthodoxy; he established a mission to convert Muslims. He shunned ecumenical cooperation, since to participate would admit the presumption that the Church of Christ was not already existent and identical with the Roman Catholic church. Some thought him in the pocket of the Western totalitarians. He was no doubt an autocrat, but Owen Chadwick is also right to see in him "one of the world leaders in the fight against Nazism and Fascism."[47] Important for his impact on American Catholics was the sense he communicated of their church as a proud isolationist world of its own, outside of and superior to other worlds.

The new Catholic spirit found expression philosophically and in literature, in an American version of what German theologian Karl Rahner called the "Pian Monolith."[48] It corresponded with the growing arrival of lay Catholics in business and government circles, a development accelerated during the presidency of Franklin D. Roosevelt. Catholic social doctrine enunciated in Leo XIII's 1891 letter, *Rerum Novarum*, and in Pius XI's 1931 reprise, *Quadragesimo Anno*, found American expression in the 1919 Bishops' Program of Social Reconstruction and in the activities of its author, the "Right Reverend New Dealer," John A. Ryan, and others like him.

How influential Ryan was on the New Deal thinkers, or on the president, is debatable, but the labor movement produced a number of national figures knowledgeable in papal social teachings, while in many cities Catholic labor schools combated communist influence as well as union corruption. FDR courted bishops. He would have liked a favorite, Bernard J. Sheil of Chicago, as archbishop in Washington, and he found Cardinal Mundelein of Chicago sympathetic. But the most public of the bishops was Francis J. Spellman, archbishop of New York from 1939 until his death in 1967. His position as the Catholic church's supervisor of military chaplains and his closeness to Pius XII, pope from 1939 to 1958, founded his influence. He personified the old clerical culture that was dying even as he lived out his final years.[49]

Radicalism growing out of the immigrant segment of American Catholicism was not unknown before the 1960s, but the vast mass of American Catholics has been socially and politically conservative. Until recent years, that did not translate into membership in the Republican party, however, although Catholic Republicans were not unknown. John Ireland was perhaps the most prominent.

Francis C. Kelley, a priest and founder of the Catholic Church Extension Society, was another. A sometimes violent opponent of Woodrow Wilson's Mexican policy, he provoked Secretary of State William Jennings Bryan to the outburst: "When our side of the Mexican story is told, there are some Catholic Republicans who are going to feel very uncomfortable."[50] Political reasons operated: Rhode Island Franco-American Catholics voted Republican because they could not get a look-in with the Irish-controlled Democrats. Sometimes the motivation was economic. My own immigrant grandfather, who had done well as a cotton trader, told his children he voted for the Republicans because he "didn't want the cheap foreign goods following him in." On my mother's side, we were Democrats, in the style of Mayor Frank Hague's Jersey City, surely one of the more conservative baronies in the Roosevelt coalition.

Social historians can probe the American (and European peasant) roots of American Catholic conservatism. It was mightily encouraged by the authoritarian cast that developed in Roman Catholicism during the nineteenth century and the first half of the twentieth. To be sure, not until 1950, and then only in the single matter of the assumption of Mary, did a pope exercise the infallibility defined in 1870 by the First Vatican Council. An aura of authority nonetheless settled over officeholders in the church. Scholarship was discounted. Donna Merwick summed up much of it when she described Archbishop William O'Connell of Boston as "authority's answer to intellectual curiosity." Michael Gannon has documented the "intellectual isolation of the American priest" early in the twentieth century.[51] The situation was ready-made for simplistic single-issue demagoguery. Nineteenth-century Catholicism had known it in immensely influential editors like Louis Veuillot of *L'Univers* and, in the United States, James A. McMaster of the New York *Freeman's Journal.* In France and in America, no journals had greater circulation among Catholic clergy.

Twentieth-century counterparts were the "radio priest," Charles E. Coughlin, and, two decades later, Senator Joseph R. McCarthy. Neither can be dismissed as aberrations in the Catholic community. They spoke to deep-seated fears, prejudices, and insecurities and provided simplistic answers. Coughlin preached voodoo economics long before George H. W. Bush coined the term, supported an abortive third-party movement in the presidential campaign of 1936, degenerated into anti-Semitism, and was finally forced from the air by a combination of church and federal government pressure. During the long night of the Cold War, McCarthy's anticommunist rampage attracted widespread support from Catholics. Both he and Coughlin remain folk heroes in certain circles. An eleven-cassette set of Coughlin's talks is for sale, offering "Fr. Coughlin's predictions of the days to come."

The final decade before the Second Vatican Council opened in October 1962 saw American Catholic political reliability once again under fire. Paul Blanshard's 1949 *American Freedom and Catholic Power* covered, as Barbara Welter remarked, much the same territory as had Maria Monk's *Awful Disclosures* a century earlier. Catholic Americans were pilloried for their un-American servility to the "absolute rule of the clergy," and the parochial school system was denounced as divisive and undemocratic. "Protestants and Other Americans for Separation of Church and State" kept an eagle eye cocked for Catholic miscreancies.[52] President Harry S Truman did not help matters with his nomination in 1951 of General Mark Clark as ambassador to the Holy See. The last U.S. diplomat regularly accredited to the Holy See had left Rome in 1867; the time was not ripe for resuming diplomatic relations. Nor, beyond a small number of bishops, had the idea ever particularly appealed to American Catholics. Proposed in the early 1950s, it stirred a hornets' nest.[53]

Simultaneously, within the American Catholic community, a debate was in progress, unnoticed save by scholars. Joseph Clifford Fenton, professor at the Catholic University in Washington, was vigorously engaged in defending then-standard Catholic positions on relationships between church and state and on religious liberty against the challenge of the Jesuit John Courtney Murray, professor at nearby Woodstock College in Maryland. Fenton argued that the ideal arrangement was one in which the state supported the church. Deviation from that ideal and equality of free exercise of religion might be tolerated in given circumstances, but only as the lesser of two evils. Murray argued that, in the modern world, the state's "care of religion" consisted in assuring the church's ability to operate. He grounded his assertion of the compatibility of Catholicism and American democracy in a natural-law analysis of individual human dignity and its consequences. His defense of the acceptability of the separation of church and state and of religious liberty as a natural right led the way to the Second Vatican Council's declaration on religious liberty in 1965.[54]

Toward the end of the 1950s, in October 1958, Angelo Giuseppe Roncalli became pope. He took the name John XXIII. Under his leadership and that of his successor, Paul VI (1963–1978), a radical shift took place in Roman Catholic thinking that materially affected the approach to the political world both of the official church and of Catholic people. A static and conceptual approach to reality yielded to one more biblically and historically conscious. Sacred and secular, church and world, clergy and laity became less contrasted, less stratified. The council singled out as its primary metaphor for the church that of the people of God. The sense grew throughout the community that "we"—all of us—are the church. Canon lawyer Rose McDermott spelled out some consequences: a sense that "all the faithful enjoy a radical equality prior to any functional diversity ... [and] share in the teaching, sanctifying and governing mission of the Church."[55]

The council's constitution on the church in the modern world charted a new turning to direct concern by church members for the actual needs of the world and the people in it. Moving away from possessive attitudes like that of Pius XI, the document explicitly accepted "the autonomy of many areas of life" and urged Catholics to express their religious belief precisely in and through and by secular activity, penetrating the secular world with a Christian spirit. Involvement in culture, personal and family values, economics, trades, and professions were all seen as ways of participating in the church's mission and apostolate.

Marking in 1981 the ninetieth anniversary of Pope Leo XIII's landmark social encyclical letter, *Rerum Novarum*, Paul VI, in *Octogesima Adveniens*, departed from the deductive approach of his predecessor. He accepted the possibility of a plurality of solutions to problems, given the diversity of human situations and the reality of historical pluralism. The pope had grown up in an Italy where until World War I Catholics were forbidden by papal fiat to participate in the political life of their nation. *Ne eletti ne elettori* was the motto. They were not to stand for office nor to vote. In *Octogesima*, he wrote that politics represents a demanding way, although not the only way, of living a Christian commitment to others.

The sequel has been interesting. Presidential candidates and Supreme Court nominees are no longer questioned on their Catholic beliefs in the way that a Smith or Kennedy was questioned. But neither can they any longer fob off inquirers with inadequate simplicities or the plea of theological ignorance. Throughout most of our history, at least since Charles Carroll of Carrollton retired from active political life, few Catholic politicians have represented a well-informed Catholic point of view, however personally devout they may or may not have been. That is changing, and politicians have emerged who are not only conversant with contemporary philosophical and theological trends and with Catholic thought, but who are unafraid to speak out of that background. The change has not been total. While some bishops produce thoughtful documents on contemporary problems, others remain lineal descendants of those depicted in these pages, and the same is true for laymen and -women and sisters and priests. The actors have changed, and so have many of the lines; large bits of the play remain the same.

NOTES

1. Richard P. McBrien, *Caesar's Coin: Religion and Politics in America* (New York: Macmillan, 1987), 20.

2. John Tracy Ellis, ed., *Documents of America: Catholic History*, 3 vols. (Wilmington, Del.: Glazier, 1987), 2:546.

3. James Hennesey, S.J., *American Catholics: A History of the Roman Catholic Community in the United States* (New York: Oxford University Press, 1981), 196–203.

4. William Halsey, *The Survival of American Innocence: Catholicism in an Era of Disillusionment, 1920–1940* (Notre Dame, Ind.: Notre Dame University Press, 1980), 4.

5. William A. Clebsch, *American Religious Thought: A History* (Chicago: University of Chicago Press, 1973), 114.

6. Robert Cross, *The Emergence of Liberal Catholicism in America* (Cambridge, Mass.: Harvard University Press, 1958).

7. Gerald Shaughnessy, S.M., *Has the Immigrant Kept the Faith?* (New York: Macmillan, 1925), 172.

8. Hennesey, *American Catholics*, 205.

9. Robert Baird, *Religion in America*, ed. Henry Warner Bowden (New York: Harper & Row, 1970), 261–62.

10. James W. Sanders, *The Education of an Urban Minority: Catholics in Chicago 1833–1965* (New York: Oxford University Press, 1977), 20, 25.

11. Diane Ravitch, *The Great School Wars: New York City 1805–1973* (New York: Basic, 1974), 27–76.

12. Hugh J. Nolan, "Francis Patrick Kenrick, First Coadjutor Bishop," in *The History of the Archdiocese of Philadelphia*, ed. James F. Connelly (Philadelphia: The Archdiocese, 1976), 167–86; Michael Feldberg, *The Philadelphia Riots of 1844: A Study of Ethnic Conflict* (Westport, Conn.: Greenwood, 1975).

13. Louis B. Wright, *Culture on the Moving Frontier* (New York: Harper & Row, 1961), 141.

14. Howard Roberts Lamar, *The Far Southwest 1846–1912: A Territorial History* (New York: Norton, 1970), 167–69.

15. Robert Emmett Curran, S.J., "Prelude to 'Americanism': The New York Academia and Clerical Radicalism in the Late Nineteenth Century," *Church History* 47 (1978): 48–65.

16. Daniel F. Reilly, O.P., *The School Controversy 1891–1893* (Washington, D.C.: Catholic University Press, 1943).

17. John Tracy Ellis, *The Life of James Cardinal Gibbons, Archbishop of Baltimore, 1834–1921*, 2 vols. (Milwaukee, Wis.: Bruce, 1952), 2:545.

18. John B. Sheerin, C.S.P., *Never Look Back: The Career and Concerns of John J. Burke* (New York: Paulist, 1975), 66.

19. Nicholas Schneider, *The Life of John Cardinal Glennon, Archbishop of St. Louis* (Liguori, Mo.: Liguori, 1971), 62–63.

20. Thomas J. McAvoy, C.S.C., *Father O'Hara of Notre Dame, the Cardinal-Archbishop of Philadelphia* (Notre Dame, Ind.: Notre Dame University Press, 1967), 401.

21. Hennesey, *American Catholics*, 297.

22. For a pro-Spellman view, see Robert I. Gannon, S.J., *The Cardinal Spellman Story* (Garden City, N.Y.: Doubleday, 1962), 312–22. See also John Tracy Ellis, *Catholic Bishops: A Memoir* (Wilmington, Del.: Glazier, 1983), 93.

23. Hennesey, *American Catholics*, 298–99.

24. Thomas O'Brien Hanley, S.J., ed., *The John Carroll Papers*, 3 vols. (Notre Dame, Ind.: Notre Dame University Press, 1976), 1:46.

25. Ibid., 1:152.

26. Ibid., 1:82.

27. Ibid., 1:168.

28. Carleton Beals, *Brass-Knuckle Crusade: The Great Know-Nothing Conspiracy, 1820–1860* (New York: Hastings House, 1960), 99.

29. Frederick J. Zwierlein, *The Life and Letters of Bishop McQuaid*, 3 vols. (Rochester, N.Y.: Art Printing Shop, 1925–1927), 3:207–10.

30. R. Laurence Moore, *Religious Outsiders and the Making of Americans* (New York: Oxford University Press, 1986), 62. Essays in Robert E. Sullivan and James M. O'Toole, eds., *Catholic Boston: Studies in Religion and Community, 1870–1970* (Boston: The Archdiocese, 1985), are helpful in assessing the relationship of Catholics and church officials to big-city Irish politics. See, particularly, James M. O'Toole, "Prelates and Politics: Catholics and Politics in Massachusetts 1900–1970," 15–65. Also illuminating are Susan S. Walton, "To Preserve the Faith: Catholic Charities in Boston 1870–1930," 67–119; and James W. Sanders, "Catholics and the School Question in Boston: The Cardinal O'Connell Years," 121–69.

31. James P. Gaffey, *Citizen of No Mean City: Archbishop Patrick Riordan of San Francisco (1841–1914)* (Wilmington: Consortium, 1976), 150–55, 162–75.

32. John Webb Pratt, *Religion, Politics, and Diversity: The Church-State Theme in New York History* (Ithaca, N.Y.: Cornell University Press, 1967), 225–56.

33. O'Toole, "Prelates and Politics," 20.

34. Ibid., 25–27, 21.

35. Ibid., 27–31.

36. Hennesey, *American Catholics*, 232–33.

37. Mary Jo Weaver, *New Catholic Women: A Contemporary Challenge to Traditional Religious Authority* (San Francisco: Harper & Row, 1985), 18–20, 38; Hennesey, *American Catholics*, 327.

39. Sanders, *Education of an Urban Minority*, 128–30.

40. Hugh J. Nolan, "Native Son," in Connelly, *Archdiocese of Philadelphia*, 358.

41. O'Toole, "Prelates and Politics," 59–60.

42. Ibid., 46.

43. Ibid., 49–57.

44. Ibid., 48.

45. Hennesey, *American Catholics*, 246–47, 252–58.

46. Halsey, *Survival of American Innocence*, 8.

47. Anthony Rhodes, *The Vatican in the Age of the Dictators, 1922–1945* (New York: Holt, Rinehart & Winston, 1973); Owen Chadwick, *Britain and the Vatican during the Second World War* (Cambridge: Cambridge University Press, 1986), 19.

48. Fergus Kerr, O.P., "Rahner Retrospective: Rupturing Der Pianische Monolithismus," *New Blackfriars* 61 (1980): 226.

49. Gannon's biography, *The Cardinal Spellman Story*, is still the best available.

50. James P. Gaffey, *Francis Clement Kelley and the American Catholic Dream*, 2 vols. (Bensenville, Ill.: Heritage Foundation, 1980), 2:20.

51. Donna Merwick, *Boston's Priests 1848–1910: A Study of Social and Intellectual Change* (Cambridge, Mass.: Harvard University Press, 1973); Michael V. Gannon, "Before and After Modernism: The Intellectual Image of the American Priest," in *The Catholic Priest in the United States: Historical Investigations*, ed. John Tracy Ellis (Collegeville, Minn.: St. John's University Press, 1971), 293–383.

52. Barbara Welter, "From Maria Monk to Paul Blanchard: A Century of Protestant Anti-Catholicism," in *Uncivil Religion: Interreligious Hostility in America*, ed. Robert N. Bellah and Frederick E. Greenspan (New York: Crossroad, 1987), 43–71.

53. James Hennesey, S.J., "Papal Diplomacy and the Contemporary Church," *Thought* 46 (1971): 55–71; James A. Coriden, "Diplomatic Relations between the United States and the Holy See," *Journal of International Law* 19 (1987): 361–73.

54. See Donald E. Pelotte, S.S.S., *John Courtney Murray: Theologian in Conflict* (New York: Paulist, 1976); and, in a scholarly critique, Charles E. Curran, *American Catholic Social Ethics: Twentieth-Century Approaches* (Notre Dame, Ind.: Notre Dame University Press, 1982), 171–232.

55. Rose McDermott, S.S.J., "Women in the New Code," *The Way*, suppl. 50 (1984): 27–28.

Tumults and Realignments

since World War II

FAITH TRANSFORMED
Religion and American Politics from FDR to George W. Bush

Lyman Kellstedt, John Green, Corwin Smidt, and James Guth

$\mathcal{I}$T IS 1936 and FDR and the Democrats are riding high in national politics. Religious communities are key parts of the New Deal coalition. These communities include newly energized Roman Catholics, largely working-class, recent immigrants, and concentrated in northern cities, and Jews, a smaller but vital part of the cosmopolitan culture. Other Democratic allies include the nonreligious, few and mostly unnoticed, and black Protestants, still largely excluded from American political life. Finally, white Protestants in Dixie, the masters of the "solid South" and often from evangelical churches, still constitute an impenetrable Democratic phalanx. The Great Depression has ended the Republican dominance of national politics that began in 1896, but the GOP's chief religious constituency, the Protestant mainline, still dominates national religious life, in both sheer numbers and cultural leadership.

It is now 2006 and religious politics have been transformed, bearing only modest resemblance to the picture seventy years before. George W. Bush and the Republicans are in power, but just barely, having won a series of close elections. As in the case of the New Deal Democrats, religious communities are also key parts of the Republican coalition. Evangelical Protestants, now one of the largest religious traditions in America, have helped to preserve a solid South—but one that is now Republican. The Bush Republicans have maintained strong support from traditionalist mainline Protestants and found a new ally in traditionalist Roman Catholics. The Democrats, beaten but unbowed, are diverse in a new way. Their key supporters still include black Protestants, liberated by the Civil Rights movement of the 1950s and 1960s; a vastly larger secular population; and the small but no less vital Jewish community. But new minorities have joined the Democratic camp: Latino Catholics, Muslims, Buddhists, Hindus, and New Age practitioners. Modernist mainline Protestants have moved into the Democratic camp, joining modernist Catholics and evangelicals who still fly the Democratic flag.

Thus the connections between religion and politics were quite different in 1936 and 2006. One aspect of this change is in the linkage between religious communities and politics, quite strong in 1936 and less so seven decades later. Historians have documented the close connections among religion, ethnicity, and voting behavior in the nineteenth century. This interpretation has been variously labeled as the ethnoreligious or ethnocultural perspective.[1] Before 1896, this perspective posited partisan divisions between "liturgicals" and "pietists," and afterward, this configuration evolved into partisan divisions between Protestant Republicans, on one side, and Catholic and Jewish Democrats, on the other. The major exception to this pattern was the post-Reconstruction South, where the dominant evangelical Protestant churches remained locked into their historic commitment to the Democratic party. Overall, given the numerical dominance of northern Protestants, this lineup favored the GOP.

The Great Depression altered this particular ethnoreligious alignment, as most religious groups moved toward the Democratic party, but with the division between Protestants and other traditions, especially Catholics and Jews, remaining intact. Although some scholars have argued that class divisions were central to this changed landscape favoring the Democrats,[2] the classic early studies of voting behavior showed that religion still mattered. Even when education and income were taken into account, Catholics voted much more Democratic than did Protestants.[3] In other words, the ethnoreligious perspective was still a potent explanatory force: voting and partisan divisions were *between* religious groups.

By the later twentieth century, the linkage between religion and politics had become more complex. No longer were partisan differences simply *between* religious traditions but *within* them—*traditionalists*, on one side, versus *modernists*, on the other.[4] Robert Wuthnow was the first scholar to emphasize this "restructuring" of religion and politics, but James Davison Hunter took the idea a bit further, positing the existence of "culture wars."[5] Certainly, there is plentiful evidence for such wars among religious elites. To cite but two examples, battles within the Southern Baptist Convention and the Episcopal church made front-page news in the late twentieth century, as traditionalists and modernists struggled over a host of theological, social, and practical issues. Nevertheless, it is an open question whether such elite conflicts have penetrated the mass public. We think that the polarization resulting from such conflicts should not be overstated: a sizable *centrist* group frequently stands between the traditionalists and modernists, refusing to take sides or seeking peaceful accommodation. Rather, a *modified culture wars* perspective may be the best way to describe the religious restructuring that has taken place since the 1980s.

The purpose of this chapter is threefold: (1) to document the changes in mass electoral politics since 1936, demonstrating a fundamental transformation in the links between religion and politics; (2) to document the specific alterations in the religious landscape and their implications for voting behavior; and (3) to argue that the ethnoreligious perspective alone no longer provides an adequate account of religious voting behavior today, but requires the addition of new categories based on religious beliefs and practices.

AMERICAN RELIGIOUS GROUPS AND THE PRESIDENTIAL VOTE FROM FDR TO GEORGE W. BUSH

In most presidential elections since 1936, over 90 percent of the ballots have been cast by four religious communities (evangelical, mainline, and black Protestants plus white Roman Catholics) and the religiously unaffiliated, here called the "seculars." As a result, it is useful to focus on the voting behavior of these five groups. Table 12.1 presents the Republican percentage of the two-party presidential vote cast by the five groups from 1936 to 2004. The last column summarizes the GOP's net gain or loss in each group over that period. The data in this table come from a variety of sources: Gallup surveys from the late 1930s and early 1940s; the National Election Study (NES) surveys from 1948 to 2004; and the National Surveys of Religion and Politics, conducted by the authors from 1992 to 2004.[6]

Evangelical Protestants

Evangelical Protestants began the period strongly backing the candidacies of Franklin Roosevelt and Harry Truman, but by the end voted overwhelmingly Republican. Evangelicals cast 36 percent of their votes for Republican Alf

TABLE 12.1. Republican Percentage of Two-Party Vote for President by Religious Tradition, 1936–2004

Religious Tradition	1936	1940	1944	1948	1952	1956	1960	1964	1968
Evangelical Protestant	36	46	48	38	63	60	60	38	69
Mainline Protestant	48	58	60	55	72	71	70	46	72
Black Protestant	35	38	32	6#	20	36	32	0	4
White Catholic	18	28	33	25	49	55	17	22	40
Secular	28	41	39	37	56	53	45	32	46
Nationwide	36	45	48	41	58	60	51	33	54

Sources: for 1936–1944, Gallup polls, AIPO 0149 Forms A and B, AIPO 0208, AIPO 0209, AIPO 0210, AIPO 0211, AIPO 0308, AIPO 0335, and AIPO 0360; for all religious groups in 1948 and for evangelical and mainline Protestants in 1952 and 1956, NES 1956–1960 Panel Study; for 1952–1984, NES Cumulative File; for 1988–2004, National Surveys of Religion and Politics, University of Akron, 1992, 1996, 2000, and 2004.

Landon in 1936, but 78 percent for George W. Bush in 2004. Until 1984, evangelicals were less Republican in presidential voting than were mainline Protestants (except for 1972), but since 1984 evangelicals have become the strongest supporters of GOP candidates, moving 42 percentage points in the Republican direction between 1936 and 2004. Despite party identification that favored the Democrats as late as the 1980s, evangelicals have voted for GOP presidential aspirants at higher rates than the nation as a whole since the 1950s and especially since the 1960s.

Scholars and pundits alike have noted the recent trend that links high church attendance with Republican voting—the so-called attendance gap.[7] Clearly, church attendance among evangelicals has had an impact on their voting behavior. Since the 1960s, those who attend church at least once a week have supported Republican candidates at higher rates than those attending less frequently. This high attendance certainly facilitates political mobilization: those who attend church most frequently are the easiest to find and activate.

1972	1976	1980	1984	1988	1992	1996	2000	2004	Gain/Loss
84	51	65	74	69	69	67	74	78	+42
75	64	70	72	64	57	55	60	50	+2
16	7	7	11	8	10	11	4	17	−18
64	44	58	55	51	46	46	50	53	+35
53	44	59	57	50	34	43	36	28	0
64	49	56	58	53	47	47	50	51	+15

Regional voting differences among evangelicals have disappeared over time. Northern evangelicals have supported the Republicans throughout the past seventy years, with the exception of the Roosevelt era, when they split evenly between the parties.[8] In contrast, southern evangelicals voted Democratic until 1972, but even after that date southerners trailed their northern brethren in support for the GOP. Not until the twenty-first century did southern evangelicals outpace northerners in producing Republican ballots (although the difference between the regions is modest).[9]

Age differences in evangelical voting did not exist during the 1930s and early 1940s. After that, however, older evangelicals gave greater support to Republican candidates than did their younger coreligionists until the 1970s, when the age groups were evenly divided. From the 1980s to the present, however, younger evangelicals have been much more likely to vote Republican than have their older compatriots.[10] This suggests the likelihood of an even more distinctly Republican constituency in the future, as older and

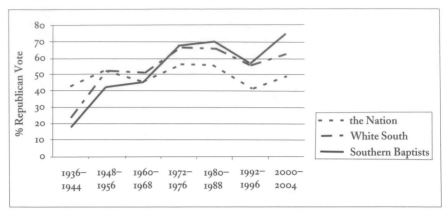

Figure 12.1. The Presidential Vote: Southern Baptists, Other White Southerners, and the Entire Nation. *Sources: for 1936–1944, Gallup polls, AIPO 0149 Forms A and B, AIPO 0208, AIPO 0209, AIPO 0210, AIPO 0211, AIPO 0308, AIPO 0335, and AIPO 0360; for all religious groups in 1948 and for evangelical and mainline Protestants in 1952 and 1956, NES 1956–1960 Panel Study; for 1952–1984, NES Cumulative File; for 1988–2004, National Surveys of Religion and Politics, University of Akron, 1992, 1996, 2000, and 2004.*

more Democratic evangelical voters are gradually replaced by younger, more Republican ones.

Indeed, evangelicals have become the religious centerpiece of the Republican party. And the movement toward the GOP has been dominated by regular church attenders, southerners, and younger evangelicals. Support for the GOP is likely to continue for the foreseeable future, as the issue positions of evangelicals line up with those of the Republican party—not only on the "social" or "moral" issues, but also on foreign policy and domestic economic issues.[11]

The Southern Baptist Convention is the largest Protestant—and largest evangelical—denomination in the United States. As the heart and soul of religion in the South, Southern Baptists set the cultural tone in the region and play a major role in its politics as well. Southern Baptists (and other white southerners) were less supportive of GOP candidates than the nation as a whole until the 1960s, but have been consistently more Republican since then (see Figure 12.1). Both groups of white southerners moved in tandem toward the Republican party from the 1970s until the twenty-first century, when the Southern Baptists became more supportive of GOP candidates than other southern whites.

There is also an attendance gap among Southern Baptists: those who attend church regularly have voted more Republican than the less observant since the 1960s, with the gap largest in the years after 1990. In addition, the GOP vote among Southern Baptists has received strong support from the young. Prior to the 1960s, young Southern Baptists were more likely to vote Democratic than were their older coreligionists, but the pattern has since reversed. For party identification, a somewhat different pattern emerges. Prior to 1970, Southern Baptists were *less* inclined to identify with the GOP than were other white southerners (data not shown). This configuration in party identification continued until the 1990s, when the Southern Baptists finally caught up with other southern whites, and then surpassed the latter in the twenty-first century.

Southern Baptist pastors may be important opinion leaders in this shift, as their partisanship and vote choice are even more Republican than those of younger and regular church attenders in their congregations.[12] All of these findings suggest that the current Southern Baptist attachment to the GOP is not likely to be reversed soon or easily. At present, Southern Baptists are a key component of the Republican party coalition, and their voting behavior looks remarkably like that of other evangelicals.

Mainline Protestants

Historically, mainline Protestants have been the religious bulwark of the Republican party. As Table 12.1 shows, mainline support for GOP candidates was consistently 10 points or more above the national average from 1936 to 1992, falling just below that line in 1996, before rising again in 2000. In 2004, however, the mainline vote for Bush fell to 50 percent, the first time in the history of survey research that it dropped below the nationwide percentage. If one ignores 1936, a banner year for the Democrats, mainline voting for GOP candidates declined 8 percentage points from 1940 to 2004.

As a result, mainline Protestants no longer serve as the cornerstone of the GOP religious coalition. One is tempted to speculate that liberalism among denominational leaders and local clergy has played a part in moving mainline laity from their classic identification with the Republican party.[13] Thus, in sum, the mainline Protestant domination of the GOP is a thing of the past, with declining numbers and less support for Republican candidates reducing their contribution to the GOP electoral coalition.

What role does church attendance play among mainliners? Those who attend church regularly are somewhat more likely to have voted Republican than those who attend irregularly. This has been true since the 1940s and follows the pattern noted above for evangelicals. The finding suggests limits to the influence of the liberal denomination and pastoral leadership noted above. Regional differences have also appeared at times among mainline Protestants. Like other southerners, southern mainliners voted Democratic in elections going back to the

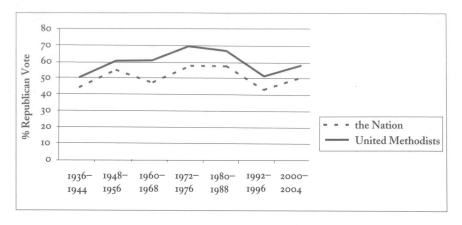

Figure 12.2. The Presidential Vote: United Methodists and the Entire Nation. *Sources: for 1936–1944, Gallup polls, AIPO 0149 Forms A and B, AIPO 0208, AIPO 0209, AIPO 0210, AIPO 0211, AIPO 0308, AIPO 0335, and AIPO 0360; for all religious groups in 1948 and for evangelical and mainline Protestants in 1952 and 1956, NES 1956–1960 Panel Study; for 1952–1984, NES Cumulative File; for 1988–2004, National Surveys of Religion and Politics, University of Akron, 1992, 1996, 2000, and 2004.*

New Deal. While it took southern evangelicals until the twenty-first century to surpass the GOP voting of their northern cousins, this transition occurred earlier for the mainline, where southerners were voting more Republican than were northerners by a small margin in the 1970s, and then by larger ones since 1992. Age differences among mainline Protestants are minimal throughout the period, but older cohorts were slightly more supportive of Republicans than were their younger coreligionists until the 1990s, when the pattern reversed. In sum, the ties among church attendance, region, age, and the vote in the mainline resemble those of evangelicals, but contemporary support for the GOP is much lower.

The United Methodist church (UMC) is the second largest Protestant—and the largest mainline—denomination in the United States. There is hardly a community in the country without a Methodist church. With tongue in cheek, we call the UMC "the church of the large standard deviation," given the theological and political diversity found within its ranks. Despite this diversity, Methodists have voted for Republican candidates for president in every time period but the first (see Figure 12.2) and at higher rates than the nation as a whole. Republican voting among Methodists increased in the 1970s and 1980s to about two-thirds of their votes. Since the mid-1980s, however, some movement toward the Democrats is apparent, led by less-observant, older, and northern Methodists.

In contrast to Southern Baptist pastors, who are more Republican than their parishioners, Methodist ministers are somewhat more Democratic than their congregants, although closely divided in vote choice and partisanship.[14] This suggests that pastoral cues are less likely to point the Methodist laity in a Republican direction than is the case for Southern Baptists. Denominational communications are also much more liberal in their theological and political direction than among Southern Baptists. Yet, despite pastoral and denominational influences, Methodists are somewhat more Republican in vote choice than the mainline laity as a whole.

Black Protestants

Black Protestants' affinity with the GOP ("the party of Lincoln") went back to the Civil War and the end of slavery, but these ties began to erode during the New Deal as the Democratic party came to be identified with assistance to the poor. Table 12.1 shows black Protestants still giving 38 percent of their vote to Willkie in 1940, but by the 1964 National Election Studies survey, not a single black reported voting for Goldwater, and black Protestants have voted overwhelmingly Democratic ever since, largely abandoning the party of Lincoln. Given this monolithic unity, church attendance, region, and age have not influenced black Protestants as they have white Protestant groups.

White Catholics

According to all of the best historical studies, white Catholics voted for the Democrats throughout the nineteenth century.[15] Table 12.1 shows that this tendency persisted until the 1970s, except for a brief flirtation with the candidacy of Dwight Eisenhower in the 1950s. The highpoints of Catholic support for Democrats came in the elections of John Kennedy in 1960 and Lyndon Johnson in 1964. By the 1970s and 1980s, however, Catholic votes were up for grabs. Republicans won on some occasions, while Democrats were victorious in others, with the Catholic vote closely mirroring the national percentages. Since 1992, the white Catholic vote has matched the national vote almost identically.

What accounts for this dramatic change over the past seventy years, a transformation unmatched except by evangelical Protestants? Has church attendance made a difference? Until the 1990s, Catholics who attended mass regularly were more likely to vote Democratic than were those who attended less consistently. This tendency changed in the 1990s, perhaps reflecting the persistent anti-abortion messages from the pulpit that may have moved observant Catholics toward the "pro-life" party, the GOP.

In addition, regional shifts account for some of the movement toward the GOP. The relatively small Catholic population in the South in the 1930s through the 1950s was strongly Democratic, but since the 1960s southern Catholics have voted Republican more consistently than have their northern counterparts, and by larger margins. Southern Catholic support for the GOP does not match that of evangelicals, but it is higher than that from mainline Protestants. Age differences among Catholics in presidential voting were not apparent until the 1970s. Since that time, younger Catholics have been the strongest supporters of Republican candidates. Thus, as older Democratic Catholics die off, they are being replaced by younger Republican voters. Today, all of the large white religious traditions (evangelical and mainline Protestant and Roman Catholic) exhibit the same pattern: regular church attendance, youth, and southern residence are associated with Republican voting.

Some argue that Catholics' movement toward the GOP results from the rise of this historically working-class group aligned with the Democrats toward the upper middle class and its traditional Republican ties. An alternative explanation focuses on a split between traditionalist Catholics, comfortable with the social conservatism of the Republicans, and modernist Catholics, who prefer Democratic liberalism. We will examine this alternative later in this chapter.

The Secular Population

Secular citizens (those with no religious affiliation) are a more significant force in electoral politics today than in the past due to their growing numbers. Unfortunately, the role of this constituency tends to be ignored. Table 12.1 reveals that the religiously unaffiliated began the period voting Democratic, supported Eisenhower in 1952 and 1956, Kennedy in 1960, McGovern in 1972, and Reagan and Bush in the 1980s. As social issues became more prominent in the 1990s, secular voters have cast more ballots for Democratic candidates, especially in 2000 and 2004. As long as gay rights, abortion, and church-state issues are prominent, this trend is likely to continue.

Other Religious Groups

The voting behavior of other religious groups has been less important to election outcomes given their smaller size and, in some cases, their low turnout. However, despite their small national population, Jews are a significant constituency in New York, California, southern Florida, and a few other locations. In addition, they maximize their impact by high turnout and have voted for Democrats in every presidential election since 1936, usually by wide margins.[16] Mormons, on the other hand, are growing in number and are increasingly dispersed across the

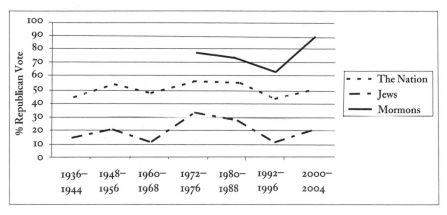

Figure 12.3. The Presidential Vote: Jews, Mormons, and the Entire Nation. *Sources: for 1936–1944, Gallup polls, AIPO 0149 Forms A and B, AIPO 0208, AIPO 0209, AIPO 0210, AIPO 0211, AIPO 0308, AIPO 0335, and AIPO 0360; for all religious groups in 1948 and for evangelical and mainline Protestants in 1952 and 1956, NES 1956–1960 Panel Study; for 1952–1984, NES Cumulative File; for 1988–2004, National Surveys of Religion and Politics, University of Akron, 1992, 1996, 2000, and 2004.*

country from their base in Utah. They vote as strongly for Republicans as Jews do for Democrats (see Figure 12.3).

Latinos were almost absent from surveys conducted before 1970. Now the largest ethnic minority, their votes are being courted by both parties, despite historic low turnout. Few observers, however, have noticed the Catholic-Protestant differences in voting behavior found among Latinos (see Figure 12.4). Latino Catholic support for Democratic candidates is consistently higher than that of Latino Protestants. The latter are theologically conservative and disproportionately Pentecostal or charismatic in their religious orientation, inclining them toward the Republican party. When the GOP takes positions on immigration that displease Latinos, both Protestants and Catholics will vote Democratic; this was the case in 1996. But when immigration is not a key issue and the so-called moral issues are central, one can expect Latino Protestants to vote Republican, as they did in 2004.[17]

Other religious groups are smaller and even less relevant to electoral outcomes. Black Catholics, for example, have never accounted for as much as 1 percent of the electorate. The evidence suggests that they are as reliably Democratic as are black Protestants. There is much speculation about the growth of other religious groups in American society, in particular Muslims.[18] Survey data, however, do not show large numbers of Muslims or, for that matter, Buddhists or

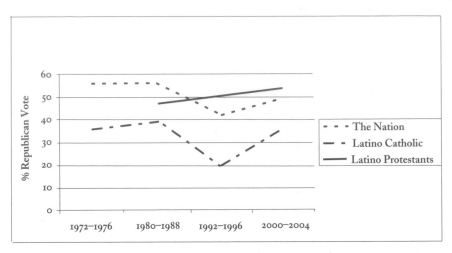

Figure 12.4. The Presidential Vote: Latino Catholics, Latino Protestants, and the Entire Nation. *Sources: for 1952–1984, NES Cumulative File; for 1988–2004, National Surveys of Religion and Politics, University of Akron, 1992, 1996, 2000, and 2004.*

Hindus.[19] These low figures may be due to high survey refusal rates for these groups or, more probably, simply reflect the fact that the numbers are really not that large. When combined into an "other religions" category, they make up over 2 percent of the sample populations since 1990, a slight increase over their numbers in previous decades. In surveys over time, these "other religions" tend to vote Democratic—the historic home of religious minorities.

In sum, data on presidential voting show dramatic changes: evangelical Protestants and white Roman Catholics have realigned, both moving in the direction of the Republican party. Meanwhile, black Protestants and the religiously unaffiliated have gravitated toward the Democrats, the former in the 1960s and the latter since the mid-1990s. Finally, mainline Protestants have lost their key position as a Republican constituency and by 2004 were a swing group in the electorate.

Partisan Voting Coalitions

How important has each major religious group been to party voting coalitions since 1936? Table 12.2 reports the proportion of each party's vote provided by the major religious communities for selected elections, taking into account the size of the group, its turnout rates, and its vote choice. We begin with 1936, turn to the religiously charged election of 1960, then to the Reagan landslide of 1984, and, finally, to the first Clinton victory in 1992 and the two Bush victories in 2000 and 2004.

TABLE 12.2. Presidential Vote Coalitions by Party and Religious Tradition, 1936–2004 (percentage of total party vote)

Religious Tradition	1936 R	1936 D	1960 R	1960 D	1984 R	1984 D	1992 R	1992 D	2000 R	2000 D	2004 R	2004 D	Gain/Loss R	Gain/Loss D
Evangelical Protestant	19	21	24	17	24	12	37	15	38	13	40	12	+21	−9
Mainline Protestant	59	37	58	25	30	16	23	16	22	15	18	19	−41	−18
Black Protestant	1	1	3	6	2	18	2	14	1	18	3	13	+2	+12
White Catholic	9	24	7	36	19	22	23	24	21	20	20	19	+11	−5
All Other Religions	5	8	3	10	7	13	7	18	8	17	11	15	+6	+7
Secular	7	9	5	6	18	19	8	13	10	17	8	22	+1	+13

Legend: R = Republican; D = Democratic

Sources: for 1936–1944, Gallup polls, AIPO 0149 Forms A and B, AIPO 0208, AIPO 0209, AIPO 0210, AIPO 0211, AIPO 0308, AIPO 0335, and AIPO 0360; for all religious groups in 1948 and for evangelical and mainline Protestants in 1952 and 1956, NES 1956–1960 Panel Study; for 1952–1984, NES Cumulative File; for 1988–2004, National Surveys of Religion and Politics, University of Akron, 1992, 1996, 2000, and 2004.

In 1936 and again in 1960, mainline Protestants dominated the Republican coalition, accounting for almost three-fifths of that vote. Indeed, their centrality in American electoral politics is underlined by the fact that mainliners also accounted for over three-eighths of the *Democratic* vote in 1936, the highest percentage for any religious group. Given the size of the mainline, neither party could safely ignore them. But the mainline contribution to the Democratic coalition declined precipitously from 1936 to 1984, though since then it has held steady in the mid-teens. The mainline share of the GOP vote was still at 58 percent in 1960 but declined sharply to 18 percent by 2004.

The evangelical numbers show a very different trajectory. In 1936, evangelicals made a slightly greater contribution to the Democratic total than to the Republican percentage (both around one-fifth), a tendency that persisted until the 1950s. Since 1960, evangelicals have accounted for more of the GOP than the Democratic vote, and by ever-increasing margins. In 1992, evangelicals replaced the mainline as the key GOP religious constituency, and in 2004 four out of ten Bush voters—but only one out of eight Kerry voters—were evangelicals. Indeed, Bush received more than *twice* as many of his votes from evangelicals as from mainline Protestants.

The white Catholic contribution to the party coalitions also changed substantially over the period. In 1936, white Catholics constituted one-quarter of the Democratic electoral coalition, but less than one of ten GOP voters. With Catholic John Kennedy on the ticket in 1960, Catholics provided well over one-third of all Democratic votes, but less than one-twelfth of all GOP ballots. Since 1984, however, both parties have claimed a similar proportion of Catholic voters, with that contribution fluctuating around one-fifth of each party's coalition. Both parties clearly need the Catholic vote.

In some ways, black Protestants have replaced white Catholics as the central Democratic religious constituency. They made only a modest contribution to the voting coalitions of both parties as late as 1960, given their relatively small numbers, exclusion from the voting booth in the South, and low turnout elsewhere. But this changed with the passage of the Voting Rights Act of 1965, which increased turnout among blacks. And with the Democrats' more vigorous espousal of civil rights policies, the African-American vote became overwhelmingly Democratic. By 1984, black Protestants were contributing almost one-fifth of the Democratic vote; they have remained a key Democratic constituency ever since.

Finally, the secular population made only small contributions to either party's vote before the 1960s. By 1984, seculars had increased in number, but their vote remained almost equally divided between the parties. Beginning in 1992, however, growing secular support for the Democrats has been apparent, and by 2004 secular voters provided over one-fifth of all Kerry votes, but less than one-twelfth of Bush ballots.

These changes in the religious composition of each party's voting coalition have been shaped by the realignment of the religious groups noted previously. Also important, however, are the voter turnout rates for the various groups. Throughout the time period, mainline Protestants have voted in higher proportions than other groups except for Jews (data not shown). This has kept the mainline contribution to each party's coalition at a higher level than had their turnout rates been lower. White Catholic voting has also been high throughout the period, trailing only Jews and the mainline (and trumping the latter in 1960). Evangelical Protestant turnout has trailed that of mainline Protestants and white Catholics over the years, but the gap has narrowed in recent elections as the GOP strives to mobilize its expanding base in that community. Meanwhile, turnout rates for black Protestants and seculars, now major blocs in the Democratic party, have fallen below the national average over the past seventy years.

Realignment and turnout are central to the composition of voting coalitions, but group size is also crucial. The most significant development here, of course, is the decline in mainline numbers, documented in great detail by sociologists of religion. Whereas mainline Protestants cast 45 percent of all presidential ballots in 1936, that number fell to 24 percent in 1984 and to 19 percent in 2004. The evangelical component of the electorate rose from 20 to 26 percent over the period, while white Catholic proportions hovered around 20 percent. Black Protestants and seculars have both increased their percentages of the voting public—from 1 to 8 percent and from 8 to 15 percent, respectively. In sum, the data in Tables 12.1 and 12.2 support the hypothesis that a partisan realignment has taken place since 1936: religious traditions have experienced different rates of growth or decline, exhibited changing turnout patterns, and, above all, have modified their electoral choices. Are these changes also apparent in the partisan identifications of these same religious groups?

Partisan Identifications since 1936

Although pollsters and politicians understandably focus on election results, political scientists emphasize the partisan identification of voters, the best single predictor of how people will vote.[20] For many, these identifications are long term in nature—forged early in life, within families, neighborhoods, local communities, and even churches. Once formed, party identifications are highly resistant to change. Voters on occasion may deviate to vote for the other party (or even abstain from voting), especially if they oppose their own party's issue positions or dislike its candidate, but this is not the usual pattern. Given the Democrats' advantage in partisan identification during the decades after the mid-1930s, only such deviations or abstentions permitted Republican victories. Sometimes, however, individuals do change their partisan identification if their perceptions of parties, issues, and candidates change, or if they begin to vote regularly for candidates of the other party.

Table 12.3 examines the partisan identification of religious groups over time. In contrast with Table 12.1, the percentages here represent the average Republican and Democratic identifications by decade rather than by presidential election year, illustrating better the long-term patterns. Evangelicals identified as Democrats in 1940–1944, and they became even more Democratic in the 1948–1958 era, but then moved in a Republican direction in the 1960s and 1970s. Yet, despite some volatility from decade to decade, evangelical partisanship in the late 1970s still closely resembled that of the 1940s. Beginning in the 1980s, however, evangelicals moved dramatically toward the GOP, a trend peaking in 2000–2004. This rather steady progression since 1980 suggests that no one single issue or cause prompted the change, but rather that generational replacement of older Democrats by younger Republicans was an important factor. Whatever the cause, evangelicals have realigned; their partisan identities as well as their votes are now closely linked to the GOP.

In contrast with the steady growth of Republican identity among evangelicals, mainline partisanship has been remarkably stable. Occasionally, there have been slight ups and downs over time, but nothing more. The mainline identified as Republicans in 1940–1944, and they still do, but at a much lower rate than that of evangelicals. Thus, as the twenty-first century began, mainliners were clearly less attached to the GOP than were evangelicals.

In the early 1940s, black Protestants identified as Democrats, but only by a small margin. In the 1960s, black Protestants moved much more closely to the Democrats as that party was identified with support for civil rights, while Republicans embarked on a "southern strategy" to win over the white South. By the 1970s, black Protestants exhibited a greater than a ten-to-one margin of Democratic over Republican partisan identification, and this ratio has mostly held up ever since.

In the 1930s, white Catholics strongly identified as Democrats and retained about a three-to-one ratio of Democrat to Republican until the 1980s, when a movement toward the GOP began. Since then, a gradual abandonment of Democratic ties has occurred, so that by 2004 there was a virtual tie in partisan identities among white Catholics. This remarkable transformation almost matched that of evangelicals.

TABLE 12.3. Partisan Identification of Religious Groups, 1940–2004 (percentage of group in each party)

Religious Tradition	1940–1944		1948–1958		1960–1968		1970–1978		1980–1988		1990–1998		2000–2004		Gain/Loss	
	R	D	R	D	R	D	R	D	R	D	R	D	R	D	R	D
Evangelical Protestant	33	51	26	53	31	59	33	50	44	43	51	31	63	27	+30	−24
Mainline Protestant	49	37	48	39	47	42	50	36	53	36	49	35	49	40	0	+3
Black Protestant	37	44	18	58	11	73	7	81	8	82	10	80	10	80	−27	+36
White Catholic	20	63	25	64	23	66	25	62	35	52	38	45	43	44	+23	−19
Secular	33	44	22	37	29	53	27	51	33	49	33	45	27	51	−6	+7
Nationwide	37	45	31	49	33	55	32	52	37	50	38	44	42	44	+5	−1

Legend: R = strong, not very strong, and independent-leaning Republicans D = strong, not very strong, and independent-leaning Democrats

Sources: for 1936–1944, Gallup polls, AIPO 0149 Forms A and B, AIPO 0208, AIPO 0209, AIPO 0210, AIPO 0211, AIPO 0308, AIPO 0335, and AIPO 0360; for all religious groups in 1948 and for evangelical and mainline Protestants in 1952 and 1956, NES 1956–1960 Panel Study; for 1952–1984, NES Cumulative File; for 1988–2004, National Surveys of Religion and Politics, University of Akron, 1992, 1996, 2000, and 2004.

The changes in the partisanship of religious groups since the mid-1930s are often dramatic. They match the shifts in presidential voting, but usually *follow* rather than *precede* those changes. The importance of these alterations in partisanship, however, should not be minimized. Partisan identities predispose voters to support the candidates of their particular party if those candidates are perceived to be a part of the party's mainstream.

Thus, alterations in both voting behavior and partisan identification provide solid support for the hypothesis that religious alignments in American politics have shifted in vital ways over the past seventy years. The historic ethnoreligious traditions have all changed their alignment in some fashion: evangelicals have moved massively toward the Republicans, as have Catholics, while black Protestants, seculars, and some mainliners have moved toward the Democrats. The result is three traditions that are increasingly one-party (evangelicals, black Protestants, and seculars) and two historic traditions that are more divided (white Catholics and mainline Protestants).

The partisan division of the latter two groups suggests that perhaps the very nature of the linkage between religion and partisanship has undergone an important change. Historically, membership in a major religious tradition predisposed one toward one party or the other. But if there are religious components influencing mainliners and white Catholics in their choice of party, they are certainly not simply membership in that community—or most Catholics would still be Democrats, and mainliners, Republican. Are other religious factors at work?

A MODIFIED CULTURE WARS PERSPECTIVE: IS THERE EVIDENCE FOR A NEW PATTERN?

That high church attendance is now associated with Republican voting in the evangelical, mainline, and Catholic traditions hints that the ethnoreligious perspective on religion and electoral politics may no longer be an adequate explanation for voting behavior. In the past, strong religious involvement in a religious community, if it had any political effect, probably reinforced the dominant partisan orientation of that community, whether Republican or Democratic. Today, church attendance seems to favor the GOP in almost every major religious tradition—and many minor ones. If the arguments of Wuthnow and Hunter are correct, this may be the result of fundamentally new lines of divisions over beliefs and practices—and the associated stances on political issues—that separate more traditionalist believers from the more progressive. Yet, the findings presented thus far provide no evidence that religious beliefs are driving any of the changes noted.[21] And for a good reason: the Gallup and NES surveys upon which we have relied lack extensive religious belief measures. Thus, we are hampered in any effort to test the Wuthnow-Hunter hypothesis.

In a few instances, however, we have enough evidence from Gallup and NES to offer a crude test of the modified culture wars model. Such measures are available in 1944, 1964, 1968, and in each presidential year beginning in 1980. (To increase the sample size and smooth out variations for particular elections, we have combined the cases for 1964–1968, 1980–1984, and 2000–2004.) To test the hypothesis, we have divided the three major white religious traditions into three groups: "traditionalists" are regular church attenders who hold literal or inerrant views of the Bible; "modernists" are defined by infrequent church attendance and views of the Bible as a good book but one that God had nothing to do with; "centrists" fall in the middle on both church attendance and Bible perspective.[22] The Republican vote for each group is reported in Table 12.4.

From the 1940s until the 1980s, the ethnoreligious perspective clearly accounts for religious influence in electoral choice: each religious tradition had a distinctive partisan cast, and internal differences were minimal. Religious traditionalists tended to vote like their modernist compatriots—except among Catholics in 1944 and again in 1964–1968, when they were *less* Republican than the modernists but in keeping with our earlier assumptions. In the 1980s, traditionalist evangelicals (but not others) moved toward the GOP, but the same trend did not occur among mainliners and white Catholics—at least not until the new millennium, when internal differences emerged in all three traditions. As Table 12.4 shows, all evangelical and Catholic groups moved toward the GOP, but traditionalists led the way. For the mainline, most of the partisan shift was among modernists and was toward the Democrats.

A more robust test for the modified culture wars model is found in Table 12.5, using data from the National Surveys of Religion and Politics, conducted by the Survey Research Center at the University of Akron during presidential elections from 1992 to 2004. These data permit the creation of a culture wars classification with much more confidence, given a fuller set of religious belief and practice items and much larger samples.[23] At the same time, the data allow us to see if historic differences between religious traditions persist. (Table 12.5 includes only the three largest white religious traditions.)

The results confirm the cruder results from the NES: there were substantial differences in presidential voting among the three traditions from 1988 to 2004. Evangelicals gave the strongest support to GOP candidates in every election since 1988, and the gap between them and the other two traditions has actually grown over time. Moreover, while evangelicals have grown more Republican, mainline Protestants have become more Democratic. As noted previously, the mainline

TABLE 12.4. Republican Vote for President by Religious Tradition, Controlling for Traditionalism, 1944–2004 (percentages)

Religious Tradition and Group	1944	1964–1968	1980–1984	2000–2004	Gain/Loss
Evangelical Protestant	44	52	70	72	+28
Traditionalist	44	54	74	76	+32
Centrist	44	43	64	69	+25
Modernist	45	58	64	58	+13
Traditionalist/Modernist Difference	−1	−4	+10	+18	+19
Mainline Protestant	58	57	71	54	−4
Traditionalist	58	59	69	60	+2
Centrist	57	52	76	56	−1
Modernist	58	59	71	45	−13
Traditionalist/Modernist Difference	0	0	−2	+15	+15

White Catholic	30	30	56	53	+23
Traditionalist	30	28	56	57	+27
Centrist	32	35	54	50	+18
Modernist	41	33	58	47	+6
Traditionalist/Modernist Difference	−11	−5	−2	+10	+21
Entire Electorate	46	42	57	48	+2

The 46 percent figure for the entire electorate in the 1944 presidential election in this table differs from the 48 percent shown in Table 12.1. Table 12.1 was an average of two surveys that was used to increase the size of the samples upon which to base the percentages. Only one survey had the belief and behavior items needed for Table 12.4, which results in the slight percentage difference between the two tables.

Sources: Gallup poll, AIPO 0335, 1944; National Election Studies Cumulative File, 1964–2000; National Election Studies, 2004 File.

TABLE 12.5. Republican Vote for President by Major Religious Tradition, Controlling for Traditionalism, 1988–2004 (percentages)

Religious Tradition and Group	1988	1992	1996	2000	2004	Gain/Loss
Evangelical Protestant	69	69	67	74	78	+9
Traditionalist	74	83	81	87	88	+14
Centrist	65	68	58	63	70	+5
Modernist	64	44	43	43	56	−8
Traditionalist/Modernist Difference	+10	+39	+38	+44	+32	+22
Mainline Protestant	62	57	54	60	50	−12
Traditionalist	63	64	65	76	65	+2
Centrist	61	59	53	52	49	−12
Modernist	63	50	46	54	39	−34
Traditionalist/Modernist Difference	0	+14	+19	+22	+26	+26
White Catholic	51	46	46	50	53	+2
Traditionalist	51	54	54	61	74	+23
Centrist	48	47	49	49	52	+4
Modernist	54	39	37	39	35	−19
Traditionalist/Modernist Difference	−3	+15	+17	+22	+39	+36
Total Sample	53	47	47	49	51	−2

Source: National Surveys of Religion and Politics, University of Akron, 1988–2004.

was a swing constituency in 2004, giving fewer votes to Bush than did Roman Catholics, a first in the history of survey research. So, religious tradition continues to make a difference, but the lineup in support for each of the parties has changed significantly from the past.

Examining the three traditions as a whole, however, hides the growing differences in vote choice *within* each tradition. Differences between factional groups were already noticeable among evangelicals in 1988, but not among mainline Protestants or white Roman Catholics. By 1992, such differences were apparent in both. Traditionalists were the strongest supporters of the GOP, while modernists were the most Democratic. By 2000 and 2004, these patterns had solidified, and the within-tradition differences were quite large, even larger than those reported in Table 12.4, using the cruder NES measures. The differences among evangelicals peaked in 2000, but among the mainline and white Catholics the largest gaps appeared in 2004. In sum, evangelicals and Roman Catholics have exhibited a similar pattern since 1988. Traditionalists in both religious communities have moved strongly in a Republican direction, while modernists have actually trended toward the Democrats—a countervailing movement not seen in the NES data. Among the mainline, most partisan change since 1988 has been in a Democratic direction, a trend most pronounced among modernists.

At the present time, the gaps between traditionalists and modernists are impressive in all three traditions, suggesting that religion has been restructured in a way that has a significant impact on presidential voting. The new paradigm is apparent, but it is not a full-blown culture wars model, as posited by Hunter; there are large numbers of centrists in each tradition, and ethnoreligious voting continues on the part of black Protestants, Latino Protestants, Catholics, Jews, and Mormons. Instead, we find a *modified* culture wars paradigm superimposed on the remnants of the old ethnoreligious pattern.

CONCLUSIONS

This chapter has documented the changes in the presidential vote of religious communities between 1936 and 2006. Evangelical Protestants began the period as Democrats and ended up as the most important contributors to the Republican coalition. In the 1930s, mainline Protestants were the major players in electoral politics and the bulwark of Republican support. Their declining numbers and movement toward the Democrats left them as a swing constituency at the beginning of the twenty-first century, although still leaning Republican. White Catholics were strong Democrats in voting and partisanship in the 1930s and 1940s; now, they are a swing group as well. Black Protestants have also changed, but primarily in the early 1960s, leaving them as staunch Democrats at the beginning of the twenty-first century. The religiously unaffiliated have tended to be Democratic in party identification since the 1930s. Their voting has been, for the most part, in that direction as well, but since 1990, they have moved in an increasingly Democratic direction, while their growing numbers make them a more important factor in electoral outcomes, limited only by rather modest turnout.

These changes support the conclusion that a partisan realignment has taken place. Changes in group voting and party identification are evidence of such realignment. The analysis also provides some indications of the continuation of the ethnoreligious basis of voting, as members of different religious traditions tend to vote in different fashions. This is particularly the case for smaller groups like Jews and Mormons, as well as Latino Catholics, and even for larger groups like black Protestants. Yet the within-tradition differences found among evangelical and mainline Protestants and white Roman Catholics suggest that a modified culture wars perspective provides an apt description of contemporary electoral politics. This new paradigm puts the centrists in these religious traditions in a critical, swing position in election campaigns. Evangelical centrists have tended to support Republicans, but mainline and Catholic centrists have generally split their votes between the parties. Given the pattern of close presidential contests in the early twenty-first century, centrists may be critical to election results in the near future.

In conclusion, the voting behavior of religious groups has changed dramatically since the mid-1930s. In part, these changes reflect transformations that have occurred within American religion. And, the linkages between religion and politics have, for the largest religious traditions, changed from largely conflicts *between* religious communities to also include conflicts *within* them. At the same time, smaller religious traditions still tend to vote in distinctive ways, consistent with the ethnoreligious description of nineteenth-century electoral alignments. Religion still matters for electoral politics, but it matters in some very different ways.

NOTES

1. See, for example, Paul Kleppner, *The Third Electoral System, 1853–1892* (Chapel Hill: University of North Carolina Press, 1979). The ethnoreligious perspective assumes that members of denominations and religious traditions vote alike based on their religious, ethnic, and racial identities. Religious and ethnic groups cluster in neighborhood settings with the local church serving as a primary cue-giving institution for all areas of life, including the political.

2. See, for example, James Sundquist, *Dynamics of the Party System* (Washington, D.C.: Brookings Institution, 1973).

3. Paul Lazarsfeld, *The People's Choice* (New York: Columbia University Press, 1944); Bernard Berelson, Paul F. Lazarsfeld, and William N. McPhee, *Voting* (Chicago: University of Chicago Press, 1954).

4. Traditionalists hold to historic Judeo-Christian beliefs in God, life after death, the devil, the authority of scripture as inspired by God, and opposition to evolution as the best explanation for the origins of human beings. Modernists have serious doubts concerning the above or reject them out of hand. Centrists fall in between. In addition, traditionalists are very involved in religious practices like attendance at worship services, prayer, reading the Bible, giving money to their places of worship, and involvement in small groups. Centrists do fewer of these things, while modernists do even fewer. These divisions can be found in the largest religious traditions (evangelical, mainline, and black Protestantism, Anglo-Roman Catholicism) and to some extent among smaller faith groups.

5. Robert Wuthnow, *The Restructuring of American Religion* (Princeton, N.J.: Princeton University Press, 1988); James Davison Hunter, *Culture Wars: The Struggle to Define America* (New York: Basic, 1991).

6. The Gallup surveys done in the 1930s and 1940s often lacked denominational specificity and rarely included questions about partisan identification and church attendance. We were able to use two surveys from 1939, two more from 1940, and one each from 1944 and 1945. The National Election Studies (NES) lacked denominational specificity until 1960. Fortunately, NES conducted a panel study from 1956 to 1960, allowing the use of 1960 denominational data for 1956. The 1956 survey asked questions about partisanship and vote choice in 1948 and 1952, as well as 1956, allowing the time series to go back to 1948. The surveys at the University of Akron were conducted by the authors beginning in 1992 and in each presidential year since. The 1992 survey allows us to reconstruct 1988 presidential choices as it asked how respondents voted in that election.

7. Morris Fiorina with Samuel J. Abrams and Jeremy C. Pope, *Culture War? The Myth of a Polarized America* (New York: Pearson Longman, 2005).

8. Northern evangelicals were somewhat more likely to identify as Republican than as Democratic from the beginning time period until the 1960s and 1970s, when they leaned in a Democratic direction. They moved back to the Republicans in the 1980s (from a 39–44 split favoring the Democrats in the 1970s to a 54–43 division in favor of the GOP in the 1980s) and have become increasingly Republican ever since.

9. For details of this regional transformation, see John C. Green, Lyman A. Kellstedt, Corwin E. Smidt, and James L. Guth, "The Soul of the South: Religion and Southern Politics at the Millennium," in *The New Politics of the Old South*, 2nd ed., ed. Charles S. Bullock III and Mark J. Rozell (Lanham, Md.: Rowman & Littlefield, 2003).

10. Younger evangelicals were less Republican in partisan identification than were older evangelicals until the 1970s. The young moved from a 2–1 advantage of Democratic over Republican identification in the 1960s to an over 2–1 advantage for the Republicans in the twenty-first century.

11. James L. Guth, John C. Green, Lyman A. Kellstedt, and Corwin E. Smidt, "Onward Christian Soldiers? Religion and the Bush Doctrine," *Books and Culture* 11 (Aug. 2005), 20–21, and "Religious Influences in the 2004 Presidential Election," *Presidential Studies Quarterly* 36 (2006): 223–42.

12. These results were made available by James Guth, who has conducted surveys of Southern Baptist pastors in each presidential election year since 1980. For results of these surveys done in the twentieth century, see James L. Guth, John C. Green, Corwin E. Smidt, Lyman A. Kellstedt, and Margaret M. Poloma, *The Bully Pulpit: The Politics of Protestant Clergy* (Lawrence: University Press of Kansas, 1997).

13. Ibid.

14. Corwin E. Smidt, ed., *Pulpit and Politics* (Waco, Tex.: Baylor University Press, 2004).

15. Kleppner, *The Third Electoral System*.

16. The Akron surveys show a small segment of Orthodox Jews tending to vote Republican in contrast to other Jews.

17. Protestant-Catholic differences among Latinos are important as are differences based on place or country of origin. Mexican Americans dwarf the small numbers of Puerto Ricans, Cuban Americans, and other Latinos in the NES surveys, making Latino subgroup analysis problematic. The Protestant-Catholic differences are even more impressive when one considers the fact that Cuban Americans are predominantly Republican and less likely to be Protestant than the larger Mexican-American population.

18. Diana Eck, *A New Religious America* (San Francisco: HarperSanFrancisco, 2001).

19. However, in data from a massive survey of over 50,000 respondents conducted in 2001 (Barry A. Kosmin and Seymour P. Lachman, *American Religious Identification Survey: 2001* [New York: Graduate Center of the City University of New York, 2001]), the Muslim population had almost doubled since 1990, while the Buddhist and Hindu populations increased even more. Nonetheless, each of these groups was estimated to be less than 1 percent of the population in 2001. Still, these numbers are larger than the proportions of completed interviews from these groups in the surveys used for this study.

20. Warren Miller and Merrill Shanks, *The New American Voter* (Cambridge, Mass.: Harvard University Press, 1996).

21. Wuthnow, *Restructuring of American Religion*; Hunter, *Culture Wars*. Hunter, in particular, argues that differences in religious beliefs between orthodox and progressive camps account for the changes. His argument ignores the large number of centrists who do not identify with either of the polar positions. His analysis, however, may be an apt description of elite polarization.

22. The traditionalism measure was a bit different in 1944. We did our best to make it comparable to the NES series. Regardless of exact specification, the results were approximately the same. Readers can contact the authors for additional details.

23. The traditionalism measure was constructed by, first, a factor analysis of the belief items, which led to the creation of a belief score. In similar fashion, a behavior factor score was calculated. A secondary factor analysis of these two scores produced a

"traditionalism" factor score. The latter was divided into traditionalist, centrist, modernist, and nominal religionist categories based on responses within religious traditions to a religious salience measure. Modernists and nominal religionists were combined for comparability with the NES traditionalism measure. Details on these procedures are available from the authors.

13

EVANGELICALISM BECOMES SOUTHERN, POLITICS BECOMES EVANGELICAL

From FDR to Ronald Reagan

Darren Dochuk

*S*IGNS OF A monumental shift in American politics were there for all to see in the summer of 1972 when a multitude of evangelical youth flocked to Dallas, Texas, for an event heralded as Explo '72.[1] One only had to look past the religious spectacle to find them. Sponsored by Campus Crusade for Christ, the Great Jesus Rally, or Godstock, as the gathering was alternatively designated, banked its success on an expansive network of prominent religious leaders that included Campus Crusade founder Bill Bright, evangelist Billy Graham, and E. V. Hill, a famed black preacher from Los Angeles's infamous Watts district. Even more remarkable than this legion of evangelical luminaries was the fervent but mannerly display of public religion it invoked. During the course of this weeklong festival, thousands of teens sat reverently while Graham and Hill preached the old-time gospel, listened intently to moving testimonies from celebrities, and danced rapturously to the beat of Christian rock and roll. On the last night alone, 150,000 people jammed a cleared freeway site near the downtown core to take part in a nine-hour music festival headlined by Johnny Cash.[2]

Though partially obscured by such outward displays of Christian devotion, Explo's political dimensions proved no less striking. While the presence of a few Left-leaning evangelical leaders broke the prevailing right-wing consensus, there remained a palpable sense that Explo was a celebration of Sunbelt conservatism and the emerging Republican Right. To be sure, this was a desired effect, for the event's coordinators knew that it came at a propitious time, just months before a critical presidential election; partisanship as much as Christian proclamation thus occupied the minds of those gathered in Texas. And though the favored presidential incumbent, Richard Nixon, was absent from the Christian youth congress, there was no mistaking the presence of his politics. Throughout the week, the *Dallas Morning News* surveyed 500 Explo delegates and found that they favored Nixon by a margin of five to one. As if to confirm this finding, Explo's youth let their opinions be known when they saluted five thousand attending military personnel, applauded at the first glimpse of South Vietnam's banner during a procession of international flags, and voiced agreement with a telegram from Nixon that reminded them that "the way to change the world for the better is to change ourselves for the better" through "deep and abiding commitment to spiritual values."[3]

When all was said and done, it was Explo's political dimension upon which journalists focused when reporting the happenings in Dallas to the rest of the nation. Front-page news in national media outlets like *Life* magazine and the *New York Times*, the picture of a sea of well-behaved teens with arms up and index fingers raised in salute of Jesus, "the one way" to salvation, was one of discipline and order, a fresh portrait of American youth welcomed by middle America.[4] It was left up to southern son and accomplished journalist John Egerton, meanwhile, to parse the political significance of this religious gathering in the language of regional change. He did so in his bestselling book *The Americanization of Dixie: The Southernization of America*. Noting how Explo corresponded neatly with Nixon's strategy to nationalize the politics of Dixie, Egerton concluded that the event's enduring images and sounds served as yet another powerful metaphor for the "southernization of America." Though mostly good-humored in his appraisal of Explo, Egerton's broader assessment of the transformation it reflected oozed with unease. Although he could not help but marvel at the way his once-benighted South had come to represent all that the nation aspired to as a bastion of traditional Christian values and bellwether of the political economy, the young scribe lamented that the South was not exporting its strengths as much as it was selling its sins—racism, redneckism, revivalism, and all—to the rest of the nation. In Egerton's mind, the rise of the South foretold the nation's decline.[5]

Egerton was not the first to discern the southernization of 1970s America or voice his displeasure with it, but he was certainly the most effective in cataloging its many dimensions.[6] It is the provocative nature of his work, in fact, that has helped to restart discussion about the southernization of American politics. Two conversations have figured prominently in this scholarly discourse, both of which follow parallel paths laid by Egerton. The first involves historians who seek to explain the post-1960s political crisis that shattered New Deal liberalism through a reevaluation of the white southern diaspora's impact on labor, race, culture, and party alignment in the North and far West. Constant among these scholars is a common conclusion: since World War II, the expanding reaches of the white South—including its twanging accents and steel guitars, tastes for fast cars and fried food, but especially its strong prejudices for decentralized governance, antilabor and progrowth economics, and white racial superiority—helped to crack the liberal Democratic coalition and chart the "silent majority's" course to the Right side of the political spectrum.[7] The second conversation, meanwhile, centers on transformations within the Sunbelt South after 1970 that led to this makeshift region's shedding of Democratic blue for Republican red. It was in the Sunbelt's burgeoning residential subdivisions especially, environments mapped by the converging forces of capital, consumption, Cold War defense, modernization, and middle-class concern, historians assert, that there emerged a new spatial reality in which political culture could be reimagined and political structures reconstituted along conservative lines.[8] Though driven by a slightly different set of concerns, both groups of discussants thus agree with Egerton that the key to unlocking the mystery of middle America's turn in the 1970s to the Republican Right rests in the southernmost reaches of the country.

As compelling as it is, curiously absent from this burgeoning literature has been sustained examination of a key southernizing force that Explo '72 obliged Egerton to write in the first place: southern evangelicalism.[9] This gap is glaring, on more than one level. No account of the expanding web of southern ideas and institutions that helped to facilitate the rise of conservatism outside the South, after all, is complete without mention of the proliferation of southern churches, preachers, and parishioners. Nor can we expect, on the other hand, to decipher the Republican party's attempts to win the South after 1970 without appreciating the contributions of a politically emboldened Sunbelt evangelical subculture. In short, what Egerton suggested in his journalism during the 1970s historians should take seriously in their scholarship today: when looking for the fulcrum of power from which southern ideas, institutions, language, and priorities gained the momentum necessary to reorient the nation's political landscape in the postwar period, we might begin by engaging those who occupied the pews and pulpits of southern evangelical churches.

To praise Egerton's journalistic savvy, however, is not to ignore his analytical shortcomings. At the time Egerton wrote about Explo '72, he was witness to only one moment in a much longer movement of regional, religious, and political change that had begun decades earlier and would not come to fruition until years later. So to explore more deeply how southern preachers and plain folk southernized American religion and politics, we need to trace a longer and subtler history than Egerton was able to offer, one that moves incrementally from experiences of the southern diaspora during the 1940s through its politicization in the 1950s and 1960s to its regional and national impact on the Republican party's southern strategy in the 1970s.

THE SOUTHERN ERRAND

At a fundamental level, it was the militarization of America during the early 1940s and the outmigration of southerners it precipitated that sparked the southernization of American religion and politics. Because of their deep investment in defense mobilization and the theological significance they attached to it, white southern evangelicals who gathered in the Midwest's and far West's urban "arsenals of democracy" proved especially well equipped to quicken this process. Forced by social realities beyond their control to endure the most intense dimensions of the new economy and the most volatile circumstances of the postwar political climate, these sojourners nevertheless looked to maximize rather than escape the world they were forced to enter. Rejecting the notion of "exile" embraced by their peers, white southern evangelical migrants chose instead to embed their journey in the Puritan motif of the "errand" as if they were a godly vanguard sent off into the wilderness to save themselves and their people. The choice of metaphor was important for it not only empowered them intellectually, but it also made them active participants in (rather than victims of) the seismic transformations that had profoundly altered their lives.[10]

Biblical metaphor, of course, only went so far in convincing southern migrants of their providential role in history. Other, more concrete, evidence of divine potential lent certainty to their beliefs. Providing a basis for their confidence was, in the first place, the sense that they were part of the largest and most profound movement of people in American history, and they were. Between 1910 and 1960, slightly more than 9 million people left the South for the Northeast, Midwest, and Pacific Coast with 5 million of these exiting the region between 1940 and 1960 alone. Easing slightly during the 1960s, southern outmigration nevertheless continued at a staggering rate until 1970, when a total of 11 million southerners were reported to be living outside their home states: 7.5 million whites, 3.5 million blacks. While the Midwest continued, at this date, to represent the region of choice for most transplanted southerners, California far surpassed any other single nonsouthern state in its number of southern-born residents with a total of 2.5 million. By 1970, more white southerners lived in Los Angeles and Orange counties than in Little Rock and Oklahoma City combined.[11]

With this surge of southern migration came a corresponding explosion of southern religious institutions in the Midwest and far West, yet a second reason for southern migrants to feel confident in themselves. At the time of its organization in 1940, for instance, the Southern Baptist General Convention of California could boast no more than a dozen small congregations clustered in the agricultural zones of the state. By 1970, this body numbered over a quarter of a million members, and within another ten years represented the largest Protestant organization in California. In the Midwest, meanwhile, independent Baptist churches operating in southern fundamentalist orbits grew by leaps and bounds. By 1970, nine of the ten largest churches in the United States were southern-based Baptist tabernacles located in Rustbelt centers like Akron and Hammond. No less important in this equation were the thousands of white southern migrants who found their way into Pentecostal and Church of Christ congregations clustered on quiet street corners throughout Detroit's, Chicago's, and Los Angeles's blue-collar neighborhoods, or into other nondenominational "megachurches" that were already flourishing in California's suburbs by the early 1950s.[12]

Whereas momentous demographic change and institutional growth suggested to white southern evangelical sojourners that they were part of something special in history, yet a third factor, their rapid ascent into the middle classes of their new environments, seemed to confirm it was true. Having struggled for much of the twentieth century to bring order to their surroundings, southern California Pentecostal leaders joined other southern denominational heads when, in the early 1950s, they found themselves marveling at the statistical triumphs of their churches. They had much to feel good about. By 1955, the southern California Assemblies of God was dominating the national body in missions giving, church construction, and several other measurements of financial well-being. And when denominational leaders declared a campaign for "1,000 New Assemblies Churches in 1955," southern California Pentecostals responded by far outpacing every other district in the country, a pattern that continued for the rest of the decade. Even more impressive was that congregations once relegated to shacks and garages on unkempt residential streets in Los Angeles now commandeered space on Orange County's palm tree–lined boulevards in concrete buildings rather than cinder block shacks.[13]

Such conspicuous encounters with new wealth drew southern evangelical transplants toward a theology of blessedness that assured them of their divine calling, but the seeds of their confidence also stemmed from deeper-seated values and beliefs rooted in the "burned-over" cultural soil of the outer South.[14] A fourth reason that the southern diaspora saw itself as part of God's unique plan, therefore, is simply because it had always envisioned itself in these terms. Drawn primarily from the outer South; southern frontier states like Texas, Oklahoma, and Arkansas; and the uplands of Tennessee and Kentucky, these migrants drew their sense of providential certainty from denominations that comprised the distended evangelical middle of this region, religious bodies (Cumberland Presbyterian, Campbellite, Pentecostal, Methodist, and especially Baptist) whose doctrinal offerings were distinctive but essentially variants of a central theme of evangelical egalitarianism.[15] "Texas theology" was what some liked to call the social ethic that complemented this emphasis. Certain of the absolute rightness of their doctrine, impassioned with the cause of evangelical democracy, and dedicated to those leaders most willing to flex their muscles on behalf of such sacred causes, evangelicals who were nurtured in this belief system exuded a gritty determination. Unlike mainline liberal Protestants, they possessed little patience for intellectual nuance or social progressiveness; in comparison to northern evangelicals, who turned "serious, quiet, intense, humorless, sacrificial, and patient" in the peak religious experience, they were always "busy, vocal, and promotional" and "task-oriented."[16] Amid the vicissitudes of migration in which a frontier spirit of pragmatism trumped all other concerns, these tendencies molded southern evangelicalism into an aggressive, enterprising force.

They also shaped it into a political force. Indeed, a fifth and final reason that white southern evangelicals in the diaspora exuded confidence in their new environments is because their deep religious convictions were accompanied by clear political imperatives. As it had long been evinced throughout the outer South, evangelicalism served as a medium through which a set of principles rooted in early nineteenth-century American thought continued to rouse the political imagination: pristine capitalism, unbridled optimism about the freedom and power of the individual conscience, a belief in the rightness of government by popular consensus, and, most important, a commitment to the sanctity of the local community.[17] Fully committed to these indelible truths, evangelical leaders and institutions assumed responsibility for protecting society from those who would undermine them. Distinctions between religion and politics ultimately held little meaning in this crusade since a threat to independence in one sphere was considered a threat in both. "Apolitical" in its emphasis on the altering of social and political systems through acts of individual initiative rather than institutional restructuring, southern evangelicalism was, in other words, never unpolitical or antipolitical; quite the contrary.[18] The myth of the spiritual church notwithstanding, proud southerners always knew "how to play political hardball when the prayer meeting let out."[19] Once resettled outside the South, southern evangelicals hesitated little to incorporate politics into their prayer meetings. Here in distant outposts, it seemed, egregious threats to their cherished beliefs and custodial rights in American culture were cause for a more aggressive display of politicization.

Galvanized by the process of migration, emboldened by the freedom of postwar affluence, and determined to carry out its mission of Christianization, southern evangelicalism thus held within itself the impulses to flourish not only as a religious movement but also as a conduit and catalyst for political conservatism. Ensuring that their community of believers realized this political potential were the thousands of preachers who moved out of the South between the 1940s and 1970s to meet the pulpit needs of the diaspora's growing churches. Thanks to the rise in fortunes of their constituents and the impressive breadth of institutional and media support, as well as the growing sense that they could dictate political patterns in the postwar period, these clerics recognized quickly that the future of their ministries could only be enhanced by increased investment in the southern diaspora. Though sometimes at odds with one another over matters of doctrinal emphasis and ecclesiology, with some advocating a firmer separatist brand of fundamentalism and others a more irenic and ecumenical form of evangelicalism, all looked to their southern religious roots fondly as the answer to America's current political problems. Bonded together by this sentiment, these southern clerics brought their heritage to bear on postwar political developments, first at the local level in battles over community, then at the state and regional level in struggles to redefine party lines, and finally at the national level in the quest to gain control of Washington.

RESTORING COMMUNITY

It was amid the exigencies of migration, therefore, that white southern evangelicals embraced a new vision for political involvement that gave notice to the rest of the country that they were determined to act out their convictions. This notice was first delivered in the 1940s and early 1950s when, in accordance with their errand, transplanted southern evangelicals began building churches from which they could provide "collective witness" in their neighborhoods. Although conceived in sacred terms, this powerful imperative carried with it a political mandate to defend communal autonomy and authenticity against coercion from outside. In the early Cold War period, no two threats worried southern migrants more, in this regard, than liberal cosmopolitanism and communism.

The southern diaspora's initial impact on postwar politics came when it first encountered the social chaos created by wartime mobilization and the political initiatives undertaken by an expanded government to remedy this condition. A natural extension of the New Deal state, liberal cosmopolitanism was the political creed that legitimated these initiatives. Conceived by political engineers in Washington and major urban centers throughout the North and West as a way to restore order in a time of great social change and to encourage progressive thinking in matters as far-reaching as public education and organized labor, race relations and urban planning, this program nevertheless struck southern evangelicals as a furtive power grab by a collectivist government. In response, they engineered responses of their own, first by joining grassroots battles over desegregation, then by joining this struggle to a larger crusade against liberalism's national intentions.

Assuming the lead in the fight with liberal cosmopolitanism were southern evangelicals who flocked to the Midwest in search of financial bliss and found there instead a climate of economic insecurity and racial hostility. Unable to avoid these dire conditions, they decided to fight politicians and activists who seemed only to exacerbate them by undermining traditional patterns of community life. Their group size and resoluteness made white southern evangelicals an instant force. One report filed in the aftermath of the Detroit riots of 1943, for example, estimated that over 1,000 "little church communities" of white southerners had been set up in houses and abandoned stores; another survey estimated that between 2,500 and 3,500 southern "Baptist" itinerants had come to Detroit to sell their religious wares.[20] While most of these preachers trumpeted separation from the evils of state and society, many left plenty of room for engagement in local politics. Usually this amounted to aggressive sermonizing on Sunday mornings against the "invidious threats" of racial integration, common themes that found their way into the teachings of E. J. Rollings, the Kentucky-born pastor of the Metropolitan Tabernacle whose supervision of local evangelistic crusades (his greatest success being Billy Graham's Motor City Crusade of 1953) raised his political profile.[21] For some of Rollings's associates, however, political action meant much more. This was the case for the Reverend John Hopkins, Baptist minister and president of the Fenelon-Nevada Improvement Society, a major combative in the Sojourner Truth Housing Project controversy that helped to spark the riots of 1943. Campaigning for city council on a platform that pandered to the "southern vote," Hopkins failed in his attempt to gain a seat, but his showing was respectable. As one observer noted in the wake of the October 1943 election, "Hopkins did fairly well, with 9,000 and 10,000 votes, for a suburban Fundamentalist minister who had no money to spend, and who came to Detroit less than seven years ago from Missouri. This shows that Fundamentalists do turn out for one of their own."[22]

Providing inspiration for all of these preachers was J. Frank Norris, the spiritual sentinel of First Baptist Church in Fort Worth, Texas, who spent the 1940s trying to rally his constituents on behalf of a southern "conservative revolution." It was while living in the diaspora that he was first awakened to this cause. Norris had made his first visit to Detroit in 1934 to close out a citywide evangelistic crusade that had been opened earlier in the summer by Billy Sunday. The overwhelming response to these annual crusades brought the "Texas Tornado" back the following year, at which time he was asked by Rollings, the "directing genius" behind the religious crusades, to consider making Detroit a second home. Norris, quickly realizing the immediate appeal he would have among white southern migrants, accepted the offer and became pastor of Temple Baptist Church.[23] The decision to pastor two churches simultaneously produced national consequences. Throughout the 1940s, Norris not only turned Temple Baptist into the epicenter of southern fundamentalism in the Midwest but also continued to utilize his church home in Fort Worth to train, mobilize, and direct his protégés serving churches scattered along Route 66 all the way to southern California. By offering two models of church growth, plenty of direct mentorship, and weekly print material full of inspiring news from both the frontier and the home front, Norris effectively solidified ties among the Baptist brethren in Dallas, Los Angeles, and Detroit.[24]

His national reputation and grassroots influence during the 1940s further secured these links and helped Norris to fashion his ready-made network of political activists into a movement against cosmopolitan liberalism. During his many well-publicized speaking tours Norris brought the gavel of his religious convictions down hard on Franklin Roosevelt, Harry Truman, and their legacy of government power concentrated in Washington, D.C.[25] While these public proclamations helped to precipitate a southern, antiliberal, anti-Democratic reaction during the presidential elections of 1948 and 1952, it was his influence at the local level that left a lasting mark on the conservative movement.[26] In southern California, Norris-inspired campaigns in the late 1940s against the United Nations, UNESCO, and the CIO (Congress of Industrial Organizations) fueled the fire for more elaborate attempts by southern clerics to undo progress made by the state's powerful liberal Left. By placing himself and his institutions at the center of local politics over issues like open housing and organized labor, Norris thus helped to set the wheels in motion for white southern evangelicals to begin questioning their place in the Democratic party and to embrace the NIMBY (Not in My Backyard) agenda of the Republican Right.[27]

If their adverse reaction to cosmopolitanism nudged transplanted southern evangelicals into the political realm during the 1940s, their confrontation with communism in the early 1950s entrenched them there. Anticommunism was a creed that helped to unite many from a variety of ideological backgrounds and consolidate them into a broad-based conservative movement, but its importance was never as great as for southern evangelical clerics operating in the diaspora, who used this campaign to gain political leverage within an emerging Right.[28] Some who worked in concert with Norris, Carl McIntire, Billy James Hargis, Robert Welch, and their harder-edged brand of southern fundamentalism took full advantage of this cause to construct their own religious empires out of new money and new fears generated by America's Cold War. More effective in its political appeals and therefore more important to the construction of a viable conservative movement, however, was a second cohort of preachers who maximized their southernness to disarm combatants and build unity within wider religious and political circles. Able to deliver a hard-hitting, black-and-white message of traditional Christian values and populist anti-statism in a less threatening, folksy manner that appealed to the domestic yearnings of the new middle class, these crusaders gained a particularly wide audience in southern California. Here, amid the suburban sprawl, their quest to fight communism by shoring up Christian community struck a familiar and heartening chord.

No one was more adept at striking this chord than J. Vernon McGee. Born in Hillsboro, Texas, in 1904, McGee was the product of the Southwest's rugged, frontier economy and religious culture. The son of an alcoholic sharecropper, McGee decided early in life to escape the hardships of his childhood by committing himself to the ministry. Following a short stint as a radio preacher on a country music station and extended pulpit ministries in two country churches, McGee found his way to southern California.[29] In the fall of 1949, at the same moment and in the same city as another southern cleric named Billy Graham was bursting onto the national scene, McGee assumed the pastorate of the Church of the Open Door (COD), the 5,000-member citadel of West Coast evangelicalism.[30] Like Graham, who began his Los Angeles revival by declaring himself a "hillbilly preacher" sent by God to save the City of Angels from communism, McGee opened his tenure at COD by highlighting his credentials as a simple southerner eager to protect his community against modern menaces. Entering COD's pulpit for the first time, McGee introduced himself as but "a plowboy from . . . Texas," then set about transforming his church into a bulwark for anticommunist conservatism.[31]

Indelibly shaped by his southern roots, McGee's unaffected preaching style immediately distinguished him as one of southern California's most effective anticommunist crusaders. Remembered fondly by those who listened regularly to his sermons, either in church or on the radio, as distinctively "folksy" for its nasal timbre and gentle undulations, McGee's voice transported the willing listener back to a simpler time and place.[32] It was this gentle, nostalgic approach that made him an asset for anticommunist conservatism. When speaking out against the "red menace," McGee often guided his reader back through time in a way that demonstrated both his impressive breadth of study and the single-mindedness of his thought.[33] It is in their practical application, however, that McGee's anticommunist lectures assumed a distinctively southern, populist tone. When looking for inspiration and direction in the fight against the red menace, McGee intimated, his congregants would be wise to look to the farms of Georgia and Texas rather than to the grand foyers of Washington and New York; there was where America's foremost anticommunist crusaders—honorable men like John Birch— had been trained in the ways of Christian virtue. If verbal cues failed to drive this point home, McGee regularly turned to his trusty visual aids for help. In many of his sermons, McGee let projected images of his own past reveal the keys to overcoming the communist menace. "Will Russia Destroy the U.S.?" and "A Nation at the Crossroads," two of McGee's more popular anticommunist homilies, for example, were delivered with the help of the pastor's "stereopticon." "I wish I could take you to your home town tonight [but the] best I can do is take you to mine" was how McGee began the second of these sermons before leading his congregation on an elaborate slide show tour of Oklahoma and Texas. Beginning with images of his childhood home in Ardmore, Oklahoma, McGee moved slowly through a repertoire of thirty slides, talking all the while about the values each image portrayed and their potential power in helping to ward off communism.[34]

The simplicity of his preaching, in truth, belied the extent to which McGee intended to train his congregants in the ways of conservative politics. Prior to each of his sermons, McGee spent hours researching his chosen topic by perusing right-wing journals like the *Manion Forum*, *American Mercury*, and *Christian Economics*. Under McGee's watchful eye, meanwhile, COD's weekly routine was adjusted so that afternoon sessions could be held each Sunday during which communism, current events, and other political matters were discussed in open forums.[35] In all of these endeavors, McGee rarely shied away from partisanship. Increasingly agitated in the early 1950s by an "intrusive" government that continued to furnish "no incentive at all even to those who wanted to get out of the poverty level," McGee grew convinced by the last years of the decade that "only an immediate and continuous uprising of conservative thought [could] halt our nation's plunge into socialism." McGee had welcomed the New Deal as a temporary correction to the failings of capitalism. But when evidence began mounting in the postwar years that liberalism had intentions of becoming the established order, he recoiled and reconsidered the New Deal exposed for what it had always been: a collectivist enterprise and a halfway house to communism.[36]

For Norris, McGee, and their cohorts, therefore, personal experiences rooted in migration became the grounds for political action. Constantly referencing their own political awakenings that had caused them to turn away from their Democratic roots, these preachers offered their followers a formula for grassroots political action. Symptoms of the last days were everywhere, they pointed out, from the lack of a national commitment to Christian economics to rampant moral degeneracy in the home to the disappearance of traditional curricula in the classroom. Animated by the very same impulse that operated at the center of cosmopolitan liberalism and communism—a desire to suppress Christian democracy and replace it with a centralized, humanist system—each of these developments, both contended, could be traced to New Deal Democrats. Besides doing all they could to reverse these trends in their neighborhoods, schools, and city halls, Norris and McGee averred, their listeners needed to find ways to make an impact on state and national politics. Their testimonies of faith never left much doubt that political action of this sort would only be effective if carried out on behalf of conservatism and the Republican party.

REVIVING A REGION

Southern preachers involved in the politics of community during the 1940s and 1950s thus helped to create a culture of protest ready to be tapped by a nascent conservative movement in the 1960s. In this decade of partisan realignment, these clerics became major players as political agents who could at once galvanize a critical mass of religious voters in the diaspora, and they began unifying conservatives across regional lines behind the candidacies of George Wallace and Barry Goldwater.

Wallace's succession of third-party campaigns in the 1960s provided the white southern diaspora with its first opportunity to lead the conservative charge. Politicizing race and racial discord was Wallace's greatest weapon, but in the Midwest especially he drew much of his strength from southern religious activists affiliated with the Baptist Bible Fellowship (BBF), the loose coalition of Norris's devotees who broke with their leader before his death in 1952 but never with his brand of Texas theology. By the 1960s, this institutional juggernaut boasted seven of the eight largest Sunday schools in the United States, and only one of these (Jerry Falwell's Thomas Road Baptist Church in Lynchburg, Virginia) was located outside the Midwest. Drawing the most attention within this orb were flagship churches shepherded by high-profile preachers: Temple Baptist in Detroit led by G. B. Vick, Canton Baptist Temple led by Harold Henniger, and Akron Baptist Temple pastored by Dallas Billington.[37] Adding strength to the movement, meanwhile, were churches like First Baptist Church of Hammond, an independent empire led by Texan Jack Hyles that was considered an ally but not an official member of the BBF coalition. By the early 1970s, thanks to its southern flavor and a bus ministry that recruited 10,000 people weekly for Sunday school, First Baptist of Hammond was heralded as the nation's largest church with a recorded weekly attendance of over 30,000.[38]

From the beginning, Wallace support was evident at every level of this Baptist empire.[39] Utilizing the power of the press to affect his readership for political change, editor Noel Smith, for example, ensured that BBF's denominational paper, the *Baptist Bible Tribune*, was unequivocal and unrelenting in its endorsement of the Alabaman; similar approval was garnered in the higher ranks of leadership.[40] For his part, Wallace thrived on the support given him by these notables, but it was his connection to those in the pews that seemed most rewarding. Often a guest in pulpits throughout the South, the candidate nevertheless counted most on his BBF connections when seeking access to displaced southern voters in the upper Midwest. Not uncommon was the gathering in May 1964 that saw five hundred people jam a BBF church in Crawfordsville, Indiana, to hear "the governor" speak about the decline of American society. During this session, like others in subsequent campaigns, congregants internalized a message they heard often from their own pastors, one laced with racist rhetoric and liberal bashing but also consistent with deeper theological precepts of radical egalitarianism and Christian political activism.[41]

As crucial as it was in advancing Wallace's third-party conservatism and serving notice to the nation that the politics of Dixie were moving north, transplanted southern evangelicalism proved to be an even more vital political force on the West Coast. Here, on one hand, southern evangelicals readily softened their theological and racial separatism and actively pursued collective action on behalf of other core conservative principles like free enterprise and Christian morality. By demonstrating this ecumenicism through deployment of their resources—media outlets, parachurch ministries, schools, and churches—southern evangelicals not only proved their mettle in California's vibrant marketplace of religion but also gained legitimacy in the state's political arena. Built on a western progressive tradition of weak parties, strong interest groups, and the ballot initiative, California's distinctive political structure, on the other hand, encouraged consistent and direct involvement in governance. In the 1960s, conservative activists— southern evangelicals included—commandeered these apparatuses to gain control of the state's Republican party. The combination of its entrepreneurial verve and institutional strength coupled with enabling trends within the political system thus politicized southern evangelicals in southern California to a degree not possible elsewhere.[42] And as always, southern California's many outspoken southern preachers set the pace for their constituents. Besides helping to turn their congregants away from the New Deal to the new Right by continuing to preach their message of anticommunism, anti-statism, and morality, these clerics now undertook more formal political functions. While at the grassroots level, they turned their churches into marshaling zones for California's burgeoning Republican Right, at the party level, they acquired leadership positions that guaranteed a hearing with the GOP's top brass.

Bob Wells illustrates the dedication with which southern clerics carried out the first of these tasks. Convinced that he could build an independent church in Orange County that would rival any within the fundamentalist network he operated, the one-time banker and traveling evangelist from Dallas pitched a tent in the middle of an Anaheim orange grove and christened it Central Baptist Church. His personal drive paid collective dividends. Thanks to an aggressive program of evangelism that utilized students from Bob Jones University for door-to-door canvassing, by the time it celebrated its tenth anniversary in 1966, Central proudly boasted a Sunday school attendance of four thousand, making it the largest church in the county, second largest Baptist church west of the Rockies, and another success story for the BBF, its parent organization.[43] Whereas evangelism brought locals into the pews, Wells's politics kept them there.[44] Armed with a theology and political philosophy that emphasized the sanctity of the individual, celebrated the entrepreneurial spirit, and boldly called for a re-Christianization of America, Wells translated the concerns of his congregation into modern political discourse. During Sunday morning services, he accomplished this through subtle references to an idyllic past when Americans were allowed to live free of government constraints. Far less nuanced were Wells's evening sermons. Advertised in bold lettering in local newspapers and attracting audiences that often spilled out of the auditorium into the parking lot, these interpreted current political events through the lens of biblical prophecy and offered explicit, uncompromising calls for political mobilization in the name of Goldwater conservatism. As one can imagine, sermons such as "Be Sure to Vote Right in the Election," "Did Nixon Help or

Hinder," and "Why the John Birch Society Is Right" left little to the political imagination, and that is the way this religious maverick wanted it.[45]

As effective as he was in converting local citizens to his conservative ideology, Wells was equally proficient in turning them into activists. Here he led by example. Determined to reveal "the truth" about American politics by tearing asunder the "feather curtain" of leftist propaganda in the mainstream media, Wells created an intricate web of programs that were consciously designed to counteract the "leftist establishment." So, when the American Civil Liberties Union (ACLU) and the Anti-Defamation League began challenging racialized patterns in housing, Wells formed his own Christian Anti-Defamation League; when news coverage became inundated with pictures of Berkeley radicals and civil rights protestors, Wells started his own magazine, radio, and television programs, all of which conveyed his conservative doctrine to an audience that spanned the entire South. Responding to their pastor's urgings, Central's shock troops, meanwhile, carried out their own political warfare in the trenches. From out of their fundamentalist fortress, Central's legion of concerned citizens infiltrated curricular activities at nearby California State University, Fullerton, to monitor communist influences, protested sex education in Anaheim public schools, lobbied for Proposition 14 (anti–fair housing initiative on the 1964 ballot) and Proposition 16 (antiobscenity initiative on the 1966 ballot), held free enterprise seminars, produced Christian textbooks for distribution throughout the South, completed internal surveillance of local defense industries to ensure the continued production of nuclear arms, then returned home with detailed reports that could be distributed via Central's extensive media. During elections, Central's political activities were even more overt. In the 1964 campaign, Central's parishioners acted out their pastor's cowboy conservatism by setting up Goldwater tables on the sidewalk outside their church and organizing a bus convoy to the Arizona senator's rally at Knott's Berry Farm; Reagan's 1966 gubernatorial campaign received a similar endorsement.[46]

At the same time that southern churchmen like Wells rallied the Republican Right's first wave of "suburban warriors," other southern clerics provided leadership at the party level. During the 1960s, a number of preachers like Wells who operated within the expanding orbits of southern-based denominations like the BBF asserted influence in partisan affiliates like the California Republican Assembly (CRA).[47] It was through their involvement in these organizations that they became liaisons between southern California and southern Republicans. In the heated political climate of the early 1960s, Goldwaterites like John Tower and Strom Thurmond made appearances on the West Coast in hopes of building solidarity across the Southland; it was not uncommon for both senators to rely on the pulpits of transplanted southern preachers for access to the media and the voting public. Other uprooted southern clergy shaped California's GOP more directly by running for office. In the case of southern-based religious institutions like Pepperdine University, the small Christian college located in Malibu, leadership in the California Republican party became almost a rite of passage for its highest executives, all of whom were respected lay preachers within the Church of Christ.[48]

And then there was W. Stuart McBirnie, the itinerant Baptist evangelist who arrived in the Southland during the late 1950s. Once voted by the Sales Executive Club of Texas as the "salesman of the year," McBirnie's smooth delivery quickly made him a star on California's anticommunist lecture circuit. By 1963, McBirnie was pastor of the United Community Church of Glendale, one of the largest congregations in the area, and voice of the Glendale Crusade for Americanism and the popular talk show *The Voice of Americanism*. Each of these enterprises helped to forge McBirnie into a respected consultant for conservative Republican politicians. Even before assuming a leading administrative role in the local Goldwater campaign, McBirnie had gained the ear of Ronald Reagan and soon became one of the politician's close advisors. Struggling to find an appropriate slogan around which he could mobilize conservatives for the 1966 run at the governorship, Reagan turned to McBirnie, who subsequently coined the term "Creative Society" as a phrase that might capture the imagination of voters. Reagan's gubernatorial victory proved his hunch correct.[49]

REDEEMING THE NATION

As crucial as southern clerics were to conservatism's ascent in the California GOP during the 1960s, their political skills proved even more critical in the 1970s when Republicans looked to acquire national power by capturing the South. Striking to these politicians was the potential that religion held as a replacement for race as an organizing principle. Hamstrung in the 1960s by the party's ties to segregationist sympathies, conservative Republicans especially looked for ways to cast off the burden of the lost cause for a more effective "color-blind" ideology of individual entitlement, voluntarism, and moral community that could speak to the new priorities of the Sunbelt's burgeoning white suburban middle class.[50] In southern California's plain folk preachers they found just what they needed for here were individuals who, because of their separation from the embittered racial politics of the South and yet retaining institutional ties to this region, had earlier shed the overt racism of Dixie without surrendering their distinctively southern conservative priorities and cultural power. For their part, southern preachers in the diaspora welcomed Republican overtures as an opportunity to strike a blow against the forces of secular humanism which, in league with liberal Democrats, seemed to have made inroads into their beloved South, the last stronghold of Christian Americanism. Having assumed their errand into the wilderness and succeeded at carving successful lives for themselves, southern émigrés, in other words, spent the 1970s looking for ways to facilitate political revolution in the place they had left behind in hopes of winning the entire nation back to God.

It was Richard Nixon who first saw in southern clerics like Graham a direct line to the hearts of southern voters. Ever since Dwight Eisenhower's successful run at the White House, southern white evangelical leaders like Norris and Graham had been considered important allies for Republican presidential candidates, but Nixon's courting of the evangelical Right raised the bar considerably. Recognizing that white southerners were flustered by the social revolution going on around them and frustrated with the federal government's apparent disregard for their concerns, Nixon hoped that his clerical allies' spectacular appeals to religious virtue and moral conscience would help him to deal a final blow to the solid Democratic South.[51]

Explo '72 not only manifested Nixon's intentions, in this regard, but also demonstrated the extent to which the southern diaspora heeded his call. It is no accident that Explo's leading spokesmen—Graham, Bright, and Hill—were southerners who had already proven their political worth through heavy investment in Nixon's home state.[52] Bright's and Hill's personal profiles were especially relevant to Nixon's political cause. By 1972, three decades after relocating to southern California from Oklahoma and two decades after founding Campus Crusade for Christ, Bright not only commanded one of the largest parachurch ministries in the world but also through his involvement with western Republican activists commanded the attention of Nixon and the national GOP. Raised in the section of Texas that J. Vernon McGee and Jack Hyles called home, Hill, meanwhile, had moved west to Los Angeles with the desire to preach. By 1972, he had not only fulfilled these dreams by becoming pastor of one of Los Angeles's largest black churches, but had also become the great black hope of the Republican party. Recruited by Graham and Bright primarily for his powerful testimony of faith, Hill was coveted also as one who could reconnect white evangelicals with their black brethren and, in bald political terms, confirm to the nation that the Republican party no longer centered on or even impinged its agenda with matters of race. As much as they could, therefore, southern clerics shaped by circumstances in the diaspora threw their weight behind Nixon's southern strategy and, at least in the short term, helped to guarantee the candidate's victory.[53]

For all their public endorsements, however, even Graham, Bright, and Hill could not offer any sufficient solution to the failure of Watergate other than to implore their president to repent and the Republican party to rebuild. On the second count, they proved especially convincing. In the wake of Nixon's collapse, southern preachers at work in the diaspora came to occupy an even more critical place in the Republican party's reworked plans for national power. Whereas Nixon's southern strategy had looked to southern Democratic votes for Republican presidential candidates as the condition for victory, the GOP's second southern strategy sought to transform southern partisanship completely through hard-fought victories in precinct battles. In this quest to dismantle the Democratic South and rebuild the nation "from the bottom up," Republicans turned to single-issue campaigns, media politics, and coalition formation as the key avenues to success.[54] Southern evangelical activists who had already earned their stripes through grassroots and party politics in the diaspora before turning their attention back to the South provided leadership in all three of these crusades.

Top priority for conservative Republican strategists after Watergate was to win and mobilize constituents behind single-issue campaigns galvanized by the "below-the-belt" issues of the decade.[55] Having already fought the culture wars during the 1950s and 1960s on several fronts—including touchstone ballot initiatives first raised in California like school prayer, Bible reading, sex education, pornography, and gay rights—southern evangelicals out west were more than prepared to lead their brethren across the South and the nation in similar moral campaigns.[56] Some, like Louisiana-born and California-trained James Dobson, focused on building specialized organizations that could at once promote moral purity within the evangelical community and guard Christian values in the political arena. Others, like Tim and Beverly LaHaye, meanwhile, formed more explicitly political interest groups. Leaders of California's antiobscenity campaign in the mid-1960s, this husband-wife team from Bob Jones University turned their attention in the 1970s to fights against secular humanism. Besides authoring one of the most important primers for Christian political activism, *The Battle of the Mind*, Tim LaHaye also used his Family Life seminars and private educational system in San Diego to guide evangelicals in their fight against liberal initiatives like gay rights and the Equal Rights Amendment (ERA). An important political player in her own right as founder of Concerned Women for America, Beverly LaHaye joined with her husband in the late 1970s to form Family America, a clearinghouse for profamily groups that would form the backbone of the Christian Right.[57]

A second way in which southern evangelicals in the diaspora stepped up was by proffering their expertise in media politics. In their quest to proselytize their new communities, southern church folk had mastered several different evangelistic tools that were easily translated into the political realm. Following the 1974 ruling that placed limits on individual contributions to political campaigns, Republican strategists looked elsewhere for funds and found them in religious marketing techniques like direct mail and the media. First to recognize this potential was Richard Viguerie, whose personal experience with the Goldwater campaign in California and exposure to southern evangelical marketing prowess convinced him that direct mail was key to future success.[58] Making Republican strategists' jobs easier in getting the conservative message out on the street, meanwhile, was the new electronic church of the late 1970s. Although perfected in Virginia by Pat Robertson's Christian Broadcasting Network, it was the Trinity Broadcasting Network (TBN) in southern California that first demonstrated the political potential of this medium. Started in 1973 by Ralph Wilkerson, Paul and Jan Crouch, and Oral Roberts, all Oklahoman transplants with deep personal ties to the South, TBN quickly became the home of charismatic Christianity and Christian political advocacy.[59] Endorsing this dual emphasis were three of TBN's most famous Republican insiders, McBirnie, Church of Christ crooner Pat Boone, and Robert Grant, heir to McBirnie's pulpit ministry at the United Church of Glendale and founder of Christian Voice, a political precursor to the Moral Majority.[60]

Evangelical involvement in single-issue campaigns and media politics not only galvanized Christian activity in the political realm but also provided the means to build a wider coalition of conservatives. As a broad and still unwieldy alliance of ideas, institutions, and political priorities, the conservative movement that had wrested control of the GOP in California during the 1960s still faced a precarious position at the national level in the late 1970s where moderates like Gerald Ford and Nelson Rockefeller continued to hold sway. Southern evangelicals in the diaspora bolstered attempts to unite right-wing Republicans behind a common agenda that could extend their influence within the party and advance conservative interests at the polls in two ways. In the first place, they worked hard at turning their religious institutions into think tanks and organizational centers in which conservatives from different ideological backgrounds could come together to debate policy and plan strategy. Churches like Central Baptist in Anaheim and its daughter church, Central Baptist, Huntington Beach, home to several Orange County Republican and Christian Right leaders in the 1970s, continued to perform this function on an informal basis by opening up pulpits and foyers to emissaries of the political Right.[61] More substantive was the organizational impetus provided by educational institutions like Pepperdine University. Always a friend to California's GOP, Pepperdine proved especially critical in the 1970s as a place where right-wing thinkers, celebrities, and politicians from around the country could congregate regularly to think of ways to move toward victory in 1980 for their favored local candidate, Ronald Reagan.[62]

Instrumental as they were in strengthening the broader conservative coalition and creating a common language of populist conservatism, southern evangelicals in the diaspora nevertheless were most adept in a second way at constructing political coalitions of their own. By the late 1970s, evangelicals were, of course, already heavily invested in political campaigns across the South that would eventually coalesce in a united Christian Right. Christian activists fighting the ERA in Oklahoma and gay rights in Florida, therefore, hardly needed to be shown what to do.[63] Still, amid this ferment of Christian political activism, the experiences of the southern diaspora became pedagogy for others; indeed, it was the southern evangelical diaspora that would provide instruction on how Christian advocacy groups could work in concert with broader conservative Republican goals. Between 1978 and 1979, for instance, two of the earliest and largest of these organizations—Christian Voice and Religious Roundtable—set a course for the national Christian Right by exploiting the dynamic political potential of Texas theology as it had been witnessed for decades in California politics and by shaping it into a multifaceted movement of political reform that could sweep the nation. Ronald Reagan's 1980 appearance at the Religious Roundtable meeting of southern pastors and laypersons in Dallas, in which he endorsed his audience's contributions to the Republican cause and singled out their special role in his political revolution, was in essence confirmation of a relationship that had been nurtured in California for years.[64]

It was the Moral Majority, however, that fully tapped the leadership potential of the southern diaspora and brought to fruition the process of southern evangelical politicization that had begun in the 1940s. Besides Jerry Falwell, whose leadership at the moment of this organization's founding in 1979 was unquestioned, three other individuals gave shape to this movement: Tim La-Haye, Greg Dixon, and Robert Billings. While LaHaye's political contributions were already well known within evangelical circles at the time of Moral Majority's founding, Dixon's and Billings's were perhaps less so. Yet like LaHaye, both Baptist pastors owed their professional and political livelihoods to the southern fundamentalist frontier folk who had settled the diaspora earlier in the century. Following in the Norris tradition, Dixon built his 8,000-member Indianapolis Baptist Temple into a fortress for Christian fundamentalists, then in the mid-1970s turned his pulpit into a platform for fighting government initiatives that seemed to threaten principles of church autonomy. Even more crucial to Moral Majority's early success was Billings, who brought years of ministry experience working at Hyles's church in Hammond, Indiana, with him into the political sector. After spending years in administration at Hyles-Anderson College and traveling the country teaching strategies for church growth and Christian private education, Billings ran unsuccessfully in 1976 for Congress, then founded the National Christian Action Coalition to defend Christian schools against the Internal Revenue Service. His firsthand knowledge of politics made Billings a natural choice to be Moral Majority's first executive director, religious advisor to the Reagan campaign, and special assistant for nonpublic schools in Reagan's Department of Education.[65]

THE ERRAND FULFILLED

For all intents and purposes, southern evangelicals could feel confident, therefore, that with the election of Ronald Reagan in 1980 their errand had been fulfilled. Although it was not until the 1990s that the Republican party would gain full control of the South by winning both houses of Congress and completely reversing long-standing voting trends, Reagan's victory was the power shift toward which southern evangelicals and conservative Republicans had been working hard for decades.[66] In one respect, it confirmed what pundits had already recognized in the early 1970s: the demographic, economic, and cultural trends responsible for rebuilding the modern South were sure to bring benefit to a conservative Republican coalition best able to talk the new Sunbelt language of individual entitlement and community values. In another respect, it marked the more remarkable culmination of southern evangelicalism's move from the margins into the cultural and political mainstream. Written off in the pre–World War II years by northern liberals as backward and a hindrance to progress, four decades later southern evangelicalism operated as a trendsetting force that could dictate the discourse, priorities, strategies, and policies of the new Right and the new national political reality.

Had John Egerton waited until this moment of victory to write his treatise, then, he would have been able to paint a more vivid portrait of regional, religious, and political change than the one he offered in the wake of Explo '72. The southernization of American politics for which he provided anecdotal evidence was indeed a monumental transformation but one that was triggered much earlier and that carried on much longer than he recognized. And it was a process begun in places distant from the South, in places like Detroit and Los Angeles rather than Dallas. There, southern sojourners took advantage of new social and economic opportunities afforded them by establishing strong churches, schools, missions agencies, and media centers; heralded them through print and from the pulpit as evidence of God's blessing on the diaspora; then turned their attention back to the South in hopes of redeeming it and the nation from the forces of change they had already endured. In their determined quest to protect the intellectual and social underpinnings of their faith and through sustained political involvement to shore up their defense of plain American folk values, they not only succeeded at remaking American religion in their own image but also at significantly remapping the political landscape.

NOTES

1. Some of the central themes discussed in this chapter receive fuller treatment in Darren Dochuk, "From Bible Belt to Sunbelt: Plain Folk Religion, Grassroots Politics, and the Southernization of Southern California, 1939–1969" (Ph.D. diss., University of Notre Dame, 2005). For further documentation, see also Dochuk, "Revival on the Right: Making Sense of the Conservative Moment in American History," *History Compass: An Online Journal* 4 (2006), available online at www.blackwell-compass.com/subject/history/; and Dochuk, " 'Praying for a Wicked City': Congregation, Community, and the Suburbanization of Fundamentalism," *Religion and American Culture: A Journal of Interpretation* 13 (2003): 167–204.

2. For a complete treatment of Explo '72 and the history of Campus Crusade for Christ, see John Turner, "Selling Jesus to Modern America: Campus Crusade for Christ, Evangelical Culture, and Conservative Politics" (Ph.D. diss., University of Notre Dame, 2005).

3. Those in attendance voicing displeasure with Explo's melding of religion and right-wing politics were African-American evangelist Tom Skinner and members of the People's Christian Coalition, a left-wing evangelical student movement led by Jim Wallis and fellow seminarians from Chicago. Only strong opposition from members of his Campus Crusade staff prevented Bright from inviting Richard Nixon to the gathering, a move that the president's handlers would eagerly have welcomed. On ties between the Nixon and Bright camps, see William Martin, *A Prophet with Honor: The Billy Graham Story* (New York: Morrow, 1991), 393–96. On Nixon's speech to the delegates, see Turner, "Selling Jesus to Modern America," 281.

4. See *Dallas Morning News*, 15 and 18 June 1972. See also *New York Times*, 16 June 1972; *Life*, 30 June 1972; Edward Plowman, " 'Godstock' in Big D," *Christianity Today*, 7 July 1972.

5. John Egerton, *The Americanization of Dixie: The Southernization of America* (New York: Harper's Magazine Press, 1974), xx, 24–25, 192–96.

6. Egerton's was one of several installments in a genre of popular literature decrying the loss of southern distinctiveness in the midst of postwar modernization from the North. Others who wrote critically of this political shift included Robert Cole, *Farewell to the South* (Boston: Little, Brown, 1972); Samuel Lubell, *The Hidden Crisis in American Politics* (1970; rpt., New York: Norton, 1971); and Harry S. Ashmore, *An Epitaph for Dixie* (New York: Norton, 1969). Lubell was the first to use the term "souther-

nization" to describe the processes of political change in the late 1960s and early 1970s, in his case to explain George Wallace's popularity in the upper Midwest. See also Peter Applebome, *Dixie Rising: How the South Is Shaping American Values, Politics, and Culture* (New York: Times Books, 1996).

7. See, for example, Dan Carter, *The Politics of Rage: George Wallace, the Origins of the New Conservatism, and the Transformation of American Politics* (New York: Simon and Schuster, 1995); Kenneth Durr, *Behind the Backlash: White Working-Class Politics in Baltimore, 1940–1980* (Chapel Hill: University of North Carolina Press, 2003); James Gregory, *The Southern Diaspora: How the Great Migrations of Black and White Southerners Transformed America* (Chapel Hill: University of North Carolina Press, 2005).

8. Pundits Kevin Phillips and Kirkpatrick Sale were the first to draw attention to the Sunbelt as a distinctive region. See Kevin Phillips, *The Emerging Republican Majority* (New Rochelle, N.Y.: Arlington House, 1969); and Kirkpatrick Sale, *Power Shift: The Rise of the Southern Rim and Its Challenge to the Eastern Establishment* (New York: Random House, 1975). Among the most recent works in this genre, a few stand out: Kevin Kruse, *White Flight: Atlanta and the Making of Modern Conservatism* (Princeton, N.J.: Princeton University Press, 2005); Matthew Lassiter, *The Silent Majority: Suburban Politics in the Sunbelt South* (Princeton, N.J.: Princeton University Press, 2006); Lisa McGirr, *Suburban Warriors: The Origins of the New American Right* (Princeton, N.J.: Princeton University Press, 2001); Robert Self, *American Babylon: Race and the Struggle for Postwar Oakland* (Princeton, N.J.: Princeton University Press, 2003).

9. The exception here is James Gregory's *The Southern Diaspora*, which includes transplanted southern white and black religions in his analysis of political culture in the southern diaspora.

10. Historical works dealing with the white southern diaspora tend to emphasize the dislocating effects of migration. See, for example, Chad Berry, *Southern Migrants, Northern Exiles* (Urbana: University of Illinois Press, 2000). Historians studying black southern migration, on the other hand, emphasize the exodus motif. See, for example, James R. Grossman, *Land of Hope: Black Southerners, Chicago, and the Great Migration* (Chicago: University of Chicago Press, 1989); Nicholas Lemann, *The Promised Land: The Great Black Migration and How It Changed America* (New York: Knopf, 1991).

11. Of the 2.5 million southerners living in California, 1.7 million were white. According to census totals for 1970, the population of Arkansas was 1,923,295 and Oklahoma 2,559,463; Little Rock and Oklahoma City reported populations of 381,123 and 718,737, respectively. These two figures combined fall short of matching the estimated 1.2 million white southerners living in Los Angeles and Orange counties. For full treatment of these census numbers, see James N. Gregory, "The Southern Diaspora and the Urban Dispossessed: Demonstrating the Census: Public Use Microdata Samples," *Journal of American History* 82 (1995): 112; Southern California Research Council, *Migration and the Southern California Economy, Report 12* (Los Angeles: Occidental College, 1964), 16, 21–24.

12. Douglas W. Johnson, Paul R. Picard, and Bernard Quinn, *Churches and Church Membership in the United States* (Washington, D.C.: Glenmary Research Center, 1974), Table 2; Martin B. Bradley, Norman M. Green, Jr., Dale E. Jones, Mac Lynn, and Lou McNeil, *Churches and Church Membership in the United States, 1990* (Atlanta,

Ga.: Glenmary Research Center, 1992), 13–14. Information on the largest independent Baptist congregations in the country can be found in James O. Combs, ed., *Roots and Origins of Baptist Fundamentalism* (Springfield, Mo.: Baptist Bible Tribune Publication, 1984); and George Dollar's *A History of Fundamentalism in America* (Greenville, S.C.: Bob Jones University Press, 1973) and *The Fight for Fundamentalism* (Sarasota, Fla.: Daniels, 1983).

13. See "Interesting Statistics," *Informant*, May 1956; "Where the Evangels Go," *Pentecostal Evangel*, 25 Mar. 1950, 9; "'Go to the Lost . . .': 1,000 New Assemblies of God Churches in 1955," *Pentecostal Evangel*, 30 Jan. 1955.

14. Here, I am borrowing a phrase made famous by Whitney R. Cross, *The Burned-Over District: The Social and Intellectual History of Enthusiastic Religion in Western New York, 1800–1850* (1950; rpt., New York: Octagon, 1981).

15. On the origins of the democratic and egalitarian spirit in popular evangelicalism, see Nathan O. Hatch, *The Democratization of American Christianity* (New Haven, Conn.: Yale University Press, 1989).

16. "Texas theology" was the term used by Baptist moderates at the Southern Baptist Theological Seminary in Louisville to describe their aggressively conservative brethren at the Southwestern Baptist Theological Seminary in Fort Worth. See Paul Harvey, *Redeeming the South: Religious Cultures and Racial Identities among Southern Baptists, 1865–1925* (Chapel Hill: University of North Carolina Press, 1997), 151. The term resonates, however, with evangelical sentiments and styles in other prominent denominations of the outer South. On the comparison between southern and northern evangelicalism, see John Shelton Reed, *The Enduring South: Subculture Persistence in Mass Society* (Chapel Hill: University of North Carolina Press, 1972), 57.

17. James Gregory, *American Exodus: The Dust Bowl Migration and Okie Culture in California* (New York: Oxford University Press, 1989), 142.

18. Samuel Hill, "The Shape and Shapes of Popular Southern Piety," in *Varieties of Southern Evangelicalism*, ed. David E. Harrell, Jr. (Macon, Ga.: Mercer University Press, 1981), 99–102.

19. Grant Wacker, "Uneasy in Zion: Evangelicals in Postmodern Society," in *Evangelicalism and Modern America*, ed. George Marsden (Grand Rapids, Mich.: Eerdmans, 1984), 26.

20. See "Survey of Racial and Religious Conflict Forces in Detroit: Study Made September 10 to September 30, 1943," box 71, Survey of Racial and Religious Conflicts in Detroit—1943 folder, Civil Rights Congress of Michigan Collection (CRCM), Walter Reuther Archives of Labor and Urban Affairs (ALUA), Wayne State University, Detroit, Michigan; and "Interview with Rev. Claude Williams," box 71, Survey of Racial and Religious Conflicts in Detroit—1943 folder, CRCM, ALUA.

21. See "Report on the Metropolitan Tabernacle," box 71, Survey of Racial and Religious Conflicts in Detroit—1943 folder, CRCM, ALUA. On Rollings's ties with Graham, see Correspondence between Rollings and Mr. W. G. Haymaker, Detroit Crusade Director, 2 and 10 Sept. 1953, box 9, folder 11, Collection 1, Billy Graham Evangelistic Association (BGEA), Billy Graham Archives, Wheaton College, Wheaton, Illinois.

22. See "Conversation with Rev. John E. Hopkins," box 71, Survey of Racial and Religious Conflicts in Detroit—1943 folder, CRCM, ALUA; and "Conversation with

Judge Charles Bowles, 22 September and 7 October 1943," box 71, Survey of Racial and Religious Conflicts in Detroit—1943 folder, CRCM, ALUA.

23. See "Visit to Detroit," *Fundamentalist*, 28 Sept. 1934. By 1940, these annual crusades were drawing 40,000 people to Belle Island on a daily basis to hear Norris speak and baptize.

24. The combined membership of Norris's two churches was purported to be over twenty thousand. James Combs, Billy Vick Bartlett, Robert J. Terrey, and Elmer Towns, *The Roots and Origins of Baptist Fundamentalism* (Springfield, Mo.: John the Baptist Press, 1984), 90. The best account of Norris's ministry is by Barry Hankins, *God's Rascal: J. Frank Norris and the Beginnings of Southern Fundamentalism* (Lexington: University Press of Kentucky, 1996).

25. Typical of Norris's activities, in this regard, was the itinerary for 1941 during which he visited with J. Edgar Hoover in Washington, preached in the legislative hall of Texas, and marched through Georgia on a month-long evangelistic crusade. These tours received full coverage in Norris's paper, the *Fundamentalist*. Though supportive of the earliest reform measures advanced by Franklin Roosevelt, Norris grew increasingly disconcerted about a rapidly expanding government which, in his mind, had concentrated power in Washington, D.C., and in the hands of a president seemingly determined to impose the will of a liberal elite on the churches and communities, theologies and traditional values of America's plain folk. Norris authored a pamphlet titled *New Dealism (Russian Communism) Exposed* (n.p., n.d.).

26. Helpful for understanding the southern conservative revolt of which Norris was a part is Kari Frederickson, *The Dixiecrat Revolt and the End of the Solid South, 1932–1968* (Chapel Hill: University of North Carolina Press, 2001).

27. Well into the 1950s, Temple Baptist Church continued to involve itself in local political battles over integrated housing. See, for example, "Report on Second Meeting Held Thursday, October 25, 1956, Temple Baptist Church" and "Organizational Meeting of States-Lawn Civic Association, Temple Baptist Church, February 14, 1957," both in box 43, folder A7-13, Detroit Urban League Collection (DUL), Michigan Historical Collection (MHC), Bentley Library, University of Michigan, Ann Arbor. For a rich analysis of the politics of housing, labor, and race in postwar Detroit and an assessment of their impact on the Democratic coalition, see Thomas Sugrue, *Origins of the Urban Crisis: Race and Inequality in Postwar Detroit* (Princeton, N.J.: Princeton University Press, 1996).

28. Well documented also is the way the politics of anticommunism helped to unite disparate groups of fiscal, social, and religious conservatives for political purposes. See, for example, Richard Gid Powers, *Not without Honor: The History of American Anticommunism* (New York: Free Press, 1995), 252–55.

29. Gertrude Cutler, ed., *The Whole Word for the Whole World: The Life and Ministry of J. Vernon McGee* (Pasadena, Calif.: Thru the Bible Radio Network, 1991), 8.

30. The Church of the Open Door (COD) was founded in 1915 as a supporting ministry of the Bible Institute of Los Angeles (BIOLA) and modeled after the famed Moody Memorial Church in Chicago. Details of this church's history are taken from G. Michael Cocoris, *70 Years on Hope Street: A History of the Church of the Open Door 1915–1985* (Los Angeles: Church of the Open Door, 1985); and G. Ted Martinez, "The

Rise, Decline, and Renewal of a Megachurch: A Case Study of Church of the Open Door (D.Min. diss., Talbot School of Theology, Biola University, 1997).

31. As quoted in Cocoris, *70 Years on Hope Street*, 81. On Graham's Los Angeles crusade, see Martin, *A Prophet with Honor*.

32. See unsigned letters from listeners in J. V. McGee History file, McGee Historical Collection, Thru the Bible (TTB), Pasadena, California.

33. In one of McGee's favorite sermons, titled simply "Origin of Communism," congregants were offered, for example, a history lesson that began with the "Confrerie de la Paix" in the late twelfth century and continued through a who's who list of radicals that included names like Rousseau, Weishaupt, Babeuf, Blanc, Clootz, Paine, Owen, Marx, Engels, and Lenin. "Origin of Communism," McGee Sermon Notes file, TTB.

34. See copy of written notes for "A Nation at the Crossroads," McGee Sermon Notes file, TTB.

35. Frequently, the schedules of these meetings allowed for the viewing of anticommunist films ranging in popularity from the mass-produced *Operation Abolition* to lesser-known documentaries on Iran, Cuba, and the Middle East. On the showing of *Operation Abolition*, see COD Bulletin, 4 Sept. 1960, Bulletin Collection, Church of the Open Door Archival Material (CODA). *Iran, Brittle Ally* was shown the week following; *Castro, Cuba, and Communism* on 26 Apr. 1964.

36. Cutler, *The Whole Word for the Whole World*, 8.

37. See "10 Largest Sunday Schools in the United States Today," reprinted from *Christian Life Report* in "Central Baptist News Letter," 12 Sept. 1968, Newsletters file, Central Baptist Church Archival Material (CBA), Victory Baptist Church, Anaheim, California. Akron Baptist Temple celebrated its twenty-fifth anniversary in 1960 having become a $5 million enterprise. Taking note of this institution's grand celebration were former president Dwight Eisenhower and former vice president Richard Nixon, both of whom sent congratulatory letters to the congregation which were then proudly displayed in the national organ of the BBF. See "Akron Temple Observes 25th Anniversary," *Baptist Bible Tribune*, 13 May 1960, 3.

38. These seemingly exaggerated numbers were verified in a 1975 *Time* magazine article titled "Superchurch," when a skeptical outside observer noted the church's attendance of 30,560 on a Sunday in March of that year; "Superchurch," *Time*, 1 Dec. 1975.

39. Of the 500 BBF pastors surveyed in 1968, nearly 40 percent considered Wallace their candidate while another 40 percent looked to Nixon. See "500 Baptist Pastors Surveyed, Nixon, Wallace Favored by Most," *Baptist Bible Tribune*, 27 Sept. 1968.

40. Editor of the *Baptist Bible Tribune* throughout the 1950s and 1960s, Smith ensured that members of this denomination were always in touch with the political happenings of their day and clear on what their response to these should be. Senator Strom Thurmond was a particular favorite of Smith's, but Wallace, Goldwater, and Governor Ronald Reagan could also count on highly favorable reviews in his paper's news coverage and editorials. In early June 1964, Bob Jones University, unaffiliated but venerated within BBF circles, bestowed an honorary degree on Wallace and, before those gathered in the large auditorium in Greenville, South Carolina, proclaimed him "a David warring against the great Tyranny." For Wallace's appearance at Bob Jones University, see Mark Taylor Dalhouse, *An Island in the Lake of Fire: Bob Jones, Fun-*

damentalism, and the Separatist Movement (Athens: University of Georgia Press, 1996), 99–101.

41. "Gov. George Wallace Speaks in Indiana Baptist Church," *Baptist Bible Tribune*, 29 May 1964. For further insight into Wallace's campaigns in the upper Midwest and the connection to southern religion, see Seymour Lipset and Earl Raab, *The Politics of Unreason: Right-Wing Extremism in America, 1790–1977* (New York: Harper and Row, 1978), esp. ch. 10.

42. On the conservative takeover of the California GOP, see Mary Brennan, *Turning Right in the Sixties: The Conservative Capture of the GOP* (Chapel Hill: University of North Carolina Press, 1995); Kurt Schuparra, *Triumph of the Right: The Rise of the California Conservative Movement, 1945–1966* (Armonk, N.Y.: Sharpe, 1998).

43. During one summer alone, Bob Jones students knocked on 50,000 doors within a thirty-mile radius of the church. See "Bob Wells, an Orange County leader since 1956," *Baptist Bible Tribune*, 24 Oct. 1985, 12.

44. Other than businessman Walter Knott, libertarian newspaper editor R. C. Noiles, and Congressman James Utt, the triumvirate of activists usually credited with transforming Orange County into a hotbed for the political Right, Wells played the most decisive role in handing this constituency over to the conservative wing of the Republican party. See Duff Witman Griffith, "Before the Deluge: An Oral History Examination of Pre-Watergate Conservative Thought in Orange County, California" (M.A. thesis, California State University, 1976), 15–34; Schuparra, *Triumph of the Right*, ch. 3.

45. Sermons available in tape form, CBA.

46. These Central Baptist activities are documented in various church publications, including *Central Baptist Church News Letter, Church Notes,* and *Voice of Truth and Freedom.* Some of the controversies are treated in William C. Martin, *With God on Our Side: The Rise of the Religious Right in America* (New York: Broadway Books, 1996), ch. 4; Sara Diamond, *Spiritual Warfare: The Politics of the Christian Right* (Boston: South End, 1989), ch. 3; Matthew Dallek, *The Right Moment: Ronald Reagan's First Victory and the Decisive Turning Point in American Politics* (New York: Free Press, 2000); and McGirr, *Suburban Warriors*, 226–28.

47. On Wells and the California Republican Assembly, see, for example, "Dr. Wells to Speak on 'Isms,'" *Anaheim Bulletin*, 29 Nov. 1965.

48. On visits by Tower and Thurmond in 1961, see for example, "Coast Cities Freedom Program Presents Senator Strom Thurmond" and "Thurmond Assails Army 'Muzzling,'" both in *Los Angeles Times*, 29 Nov. 1961; "Sen. Tower Hits False Gods in Sermon Here; Assails Worship of Prosperity, Science, from Pulpit of Trinity Methodist Church," *Los Angeles Times*, 4 Dec. 1961. Among those who served in leadership both at Pepperdine and in the GOP were Bill Teague, a school vice president who ran unsuccessfully on the Republican ticket in Orange County, and Bill Banowsky, president of Pepperdine in the early 1970s who assumed several official posts within the California and national Republican parties. Information on Pepperdine's involvement with the California Republican party stems in part from an interview of Bill Banowsky conducted by the author, 2 May 2006, Malibu, California. For a general inside history of Pepperdine, see Bill Henegar and Jerry Rushford, *Forever Young: The*

Life and Times [of] M. Norvel Young and Helen M. Young (Nashville, Tenn.: 21st Century Christian, 1999).

49. For additional background on McBirnie and his activities, consult material in box 34, W. S. McBirnie folders, Radical Right Collection (RRC), Hoover Institution on War, Revolution, and Peace (HIW), Stanford University, Palo Alto, California. The base for these enterprises was McBirnie's congregation, the United Community Church of Glendale. On McBirnie's role in the Goldwater campaign as well as his relationship to Reagan, see Dallek, *The Right Moment*.

50. On the Republican party's Sunbelt strategy, see Lassiter, *Silent Majority*; and Kruse, *White Flight*. Measuring the GOP's success at replacing race with other political issues are Earl Black and Merle Black, *The Rise of Southern Republicans* (Cambridge, Mass.: Belknap Press of Harvard University Press, 2002).

51. On the relationship among Graham, Eisenhower, and Nixon and the Republican party's courting of southern evangelical ministers, see, for example, Steven P. Miller, "The Politics of Decency: Billy Graham, Evangelicalism, and the End of the Solid South, 1950–1980" (Ph.D. diss., Vanderbilt University, 2006).

52. For Graham, the intense ideological warfare of postwar southern California and the support of this region's ardent evangelicals had galvanized his ministry and, in no small way, shaped his understanding of modern American politics.

53. Bright's connections to powerful conservative Republicans like real estate magnate Gerri von Frellick, oilman J. Howard Pew, and political leader John Conlan are explored in Turner, "Selling Jesus to Modern America," 222–23.

54. See Black and Black, *Rise of Southern Republicans*, 24–26.

55. The shift from the politics of race and anticommunism to the politics of morality and sexuality is explored by a number of authors, including Jane DeHart and Donald Matthews, *Sex, Gender, and the Politics of the ERA* (New York: Oxford University Press, 1990). On the shift from race to gender in southern politics, see David L. Chappell, *A Stone of Hope: Prophetic Religion and the Death of Jim Crow* (Chapel Hill: University of North Carolina Press, 2004); Paul Harvey, *Freedom's Coming: Religious Culture and the Shaping of the South from the Civil War through the Civil Rights Era* (Chapel Hill: University of North Carolina Press, 2006); Mark Newman, *Getting Right with God: Southern Baptists and Desegregation, 1945–1995* (Tuscaloosa: University of Alabama Press, 2001).

56. For a brief overview of some of these flashpoints, see Robert Zweir, *Born-Again Politics: The New Christian Right in America* (Downers Grove, Ill.: InterVarsity, 1982), ch. 2.

57. On Dobson and the LaHayes, see John C. Green, Mark J. Rozell, and Clyde Wilcox, eds., *The Christian Right in American Politics: Marching to the Millennium* (Washington, D.C.: Georgetown University Press, 2003), 10; Robert C. Liebman, "Mobilizing the Moral Majority," in *The New Christian Right: Mobilization and Legitimation*, ed. Robert C. Liebman and Robert Wuthnow (New York: Aldine, 1983), 58–60; and Michael Lienesch, *Redeeming America: Piety and Politics in the New Christian Right* (Chapel Hill: University of North Carolina Press, 1993), ch. 7.

58. See Richard A. Viguerie, *The New Right: We're Ready to Lead* (Falls Church, Va.: Viguerie Company, 1981), 20–21, 35.

59. At this time, Oral Roberts was gone from his Tulsa home base and living part of the time in Orange County.

60. Duane Murray Oldfield, *The Right and the Righteous: The Christian Right Confronts the Republican Party* (New York: Rowman and Littlefield, 1996), 96–99; Liebman and Wuthnow, *New Christian Right*, 28–29. For further background on the Trinity Broadcasting Network and its political activities, see Diamond, *Spiritual Warfare*, 23; Richard Quebedeaux, *The New Charismatics: The Origins, Development, and Significance of Neo-Pentecostals* (Garden City, N.Y.: Doubleday, 1976).

61. Central Baptist, Huntington Beach, was formed out of Central Baptist, Anaheim, in the late 1960s. By the 1970s, a number of prominent Republican politicians, including Dana Rohrabacher, attended the church.

62. Information on Pepperdine's role in uniting different conservative activists during the 1970s comes from an interview of Bill Banowsky conducted by the author, 2 May 2006, Malibu, California.

63. For a helpful overview, see Daniel Williams, "From the Pews to the Polls: The Formation of a Southern Christian Right" (Ph.D. diss., Brown University, 2005).

64. On the historical background of Christian Voice and Religious Roundtable, see James L. Guth, "The New Christian Right," in Liebman and Wuthnow, *New Christian Right*, ch. 2.

65. On Dixon's political activities against the Internal Revenue Service and gay rights, see Liebman, "Mobilizing the Moral Majority," in Liebman and Wuthnow, *New Christian Right*, 59. On Billings's political activities, see Liebman, "Mobilizing the Moral Majority," 60–61.

66. See Black and Black, *Rise of Southern Republicans*, ch. 7.

14

Viewed in Black and White
Conservative Protestantism, Racial Issues, and Oppositional Politics

Michael O. Emerson and J. Russell Hawkins

*I*n *Divided by Faith: Evangelical Religion and the Problem of Race in America,* Michael Emerson and Christian Smith explored the history of U.S. evangelicalism and black-white relations.[1] They argued that, in the United States, theologically rooted cultural tools lead black and white conservative Protestants to explain racial inequality, interpret the seriousness of racial problems, and propose solutions to these perceived problems in quite different ways. Analyzing statistical evidence and conducting research interviews, Emerson and Smith found that while most black and white Americans are divided on racial issues, the cultural tools of conservative Protestants, nurtured in racial isolation, serve to create larger divisions in racial understanding than those that exist among other Americans. Black and white conservative Christians, therefore, are divided by faith.

In this chapter, we provide an overview of conservative Protestant racial views and the cultural tools argument. We then seek to extend the cultural tools argument to political attitudes, preferences, and behaviors. Specifically, we seek to understand whether the greater division that exists between black and white conservative Protestants (when compared to other Americans) on racial issues also holds true in the political realm. We find that the cultural tools of black and white conservative Protestants not only affect political attitudes, but have exerted an even stronger influence on political preferences and voting behaviors in elections in the late twentieth and early twenty-first centuries.

Who Are Conservative Protestants?

Many American values—freedom, individualism, independence, equality of opportunity, the value of hard work—derive largely from the confluence of evangelical Protestant Christianity and Enlightenment philosophy, nurtured within the context of New World conditions. Like a smoothly blended soup, the flavors of American values so well combined these traditions that both conservative Protestants and secularists could ladle from the same kettle. This historically rooted fact, as we will see, has implications for both race relations and politics today.

Conservative Protestants now represent about one-quarter of Americans and about one-third of the voting electorate (see Table 12.2 for an indication of their political influence). Before we can begin to analyze this group, we must first define the category of conservative Protestantism by outlining the basic tenets of conservative Protestant theological belief. Though diverse in many ways, conservative Protestants share the view that the Bible is the final and ultimate authority for all things. Conservative Protestants also believe that Jesus Christ died for all humans' sins, and that anyone who accepts Christ as the one way to eternal life will spend eternity in heaven with God. Additionally, conservative Protestants believe it is their responsibility to share this message with others, so no one is condemned to an eternity apart from God for lack of hearing the salvation message. Finally, conservative Protestants believe that their faith should apply to as many areas of their lives as possible, what we might call "engaged orthodoxy."[2]

In addition to these common components, conservative Protestants also have divisions, and, historically, race has figured prominently in the divisions. The clearest division has been between black and white conservative Protestants, due to over one hundred years of separate denominations and congregations (as of this writing, Hispanic, Asian, and Native American conservative Protestants have small or no separate denominations and are much less likely to be in separate congregations).[3] To begin understanding the cultural tools and often separate worlds of white and black conservative Protestants, and the implications these may have for politics, we first explore how conservative Protestants think about racial issues in the United States.

How Evangelicals Think about the Race Problem

"Debbie" (all of the names used here are pseudonyms) is solidly within the white conservative Protestant tradition. She was raised in an evangelical home, is "born again," holds firmly to the authority of the Bible, is active in her church, graduated from an evangelical college, shares the message of Christ with others, and gives money for missions. Raised in a small community in a "wheat belt" state, Debbie, white and twenty-seven years old, has had limited contact with nonwhites.[4]

Sitting down to hot tea on a cold morning, one of the authors interviewed her about a number of subjects. Forthcoming and engaging throughout the interview, she was finally asked about racial issues. When asked if she thought our country has a race problem, she said that we make it a problem. Emerson asked, "How do we make it a problem?"

> Well, to me, people have problems. I mean, two white guys working together are gonna have arguments once in a while. Women are gonna have arguments. It happens between men and women, between two white guys and two white women. It's just people. People are gonna have arguments with people. I feel like once in a while, when an argument happens, say between a black guy and a white guy, instead of saying, "Hey, there's two guys having an argument," we say it's a race issue.

The race problem for Debbie is quite simple and quite unfortunate. It is one of misinterpretation. People disagree, and when they happen to be people of different races, we incorrectly interpret their disagreement as racially based. When asked if she saw a race problem beyond misinterpretation, she said there are cases in which people think or act in negative ways simply because of the race of another person, but such cases are both rare and inexcusable for Christians.

In the interviews conducted for *Divided by Faith*, white evangelicals' focus on the race problem as minimal and caused by relational problems between individuals (or the incorrect interpretation of such) was unremitting. "I think our country has a perceived race relations problem," a Presbyterian man matter-of-factly said. "I think we have individuals still that have race relations problems. I don't think our country has in its current form a race problem." A Baptist woman told us, "Race has very little influence on life in America. It is a shame that there are still some who struggle to get along with each other because of skin color, but such people are a tiny minority."

White conservative Protestants often viewed the race problem in one of two ways: (1) other groups trying to make race problems a group issue when the problems are merely problems among a few individuals, or (2) a creation of the self-interested, such as representative individuals of minority groups, the media, or a liberal government.

For most white evangelicals, the race problem ultimately came down to personal defects of some people in some groups as they, lacking Christlike love and understanding, attempt to relate to one another. To understand the avoidance of the racialized character of the United States in favor of this individual-level assessment of the race problem, we use the concept of cultural tools.

CULTURAL TOOLS AND SEPARATE WORLDS

Culture creates ways for people and groups to organize experiences and evaluate reality. It does so by providing a "tool kit" of ideas, interpretations, skills, and habits.[5] For many Americans, including conservative Protestant Christians, religion plays a major role in shaping people's tool kits. Key to the concept of cultural tools is the understanding that cultural tools are generalizable, that is, they are usable not just in the situation first learned, but also in new, diverse situations.[6] For example, cultural tools may be learned in a religious context, but then used to interpret the race problem or to think about political issues. Accordingly, it is necessary to identify the core cultural tools of white and black conservative Protestants.

White American evangelicalism is rooted in an individualized theology. People are saved "one heart at a time," and the Christian life means a personal relationship with Christ. A maturing Christian nurtures this individual relationship with Christ, usually through Bible study and prayer, but also by relationships with other maturing Christians. This foundational understanding of the Christian life leads to three central cultural tools: accountable individualism, relationalism (attaching core importance to interpersonal relationships), and antistructuralism (the inability to see or unwillingness to accept social structural influences).

Unlike many other Americans, most of whom are individualists to some degree, white evangelicals are accountable individualists. That is, individuals are believed to exist independently of structures and institutions, and are individually accountable for their actions. Individuals are the seat of choice and must account for these choices to themselves, others, and God. The threads of faith, individual choice, and accountability are so tightly woven that they provide a single garment for interpreting life. Individuals are free actors, unfettered by social circumstances, personally responsible for their thoughts and actions.

But human nature is fallen, and so individuals must be made right through a personal relationship with Christ. For conservative Protestants, this is the key biblical story. Individuals are separated from God, and God seeks to reconcile the broken relationship through the atoning work of Christ. Apart from this relationship, individuals will make wrong, destructive, sinful choices and are therefore condemned. Generalizing the fundamental importance and meaning of this person-Christ relationship, evangelicals place strong emphasis on family relationships, friendships, and relationships with other believers. They also place great importance on the state of these one-on-one relationships. Are they healthy or sick? Have they been reconciled or are they in need of reconciliation?

These cultural tools help to account for the phrase commonly heard during interviews for *Divided by Faith*: "The race problem is a sin problem," or as it was sometimes put, "We don't have a race problem, we have a sin problem." An evangelical man attending a Congregational church, when asked why we have a race problem, said, "[I]t is an issue of original sin." Similarly, a Wesleyan man responded, "It's human nature to be a sinner . . . to not be accepting of a black person." As a Baptist woman assessed the root of the race problem, "we don't love our neighbors as ourselves. That is the primary commandment of the Bible, to love our neighbor as our self." The human problem is an individual's broken relationship with God. Generalizing these cultural tools, the race problem consists of broken relationships between individuals.

Absent from white evangelical accounts of the race problem is discussion of the idea that poor relationships and individual actions might be subject to social structural influences, such as laws, the ways in which institutions operate, historical patterns which matter in the contemporary period, or cultural practices. This fact points to the third cultural tool in the white evangelical tool kit. White evangelicals not only interpret the world in individual and relational terms, but also find other types of explanations to be irrelevant or wrongheaded. This antistructuralism—the inability to see or unwillingness to accept alternatives not based on individuals—is thus a corollary to accountable free-will individualism and relationalism. Although much in Christian scripture and tradition suggests the vital influence of social structures on individuals, the stress on individualism and relationalism has been so complete for so long among white American conservative Protestants that such tools are nearly unavailable. To talk about anything beyond individual choice and relationships is interpreted as fallen humans' attempts to pass the buck, to wrongly shift blame away from the responsible individual.

Thus, many white evangelicals interviewed were frustrated with black Americans, especially black Christians, because they viewed them as incorrectly shifting blame from the root problem. One evangelical woman attending a Nazarene church gave a common response: "[Blacks] will attribute any problem to race where it may not be a racial issue at all. It may be a personal conflict and not have anything to do with race." What is more, given their cultural tools, white evangelicals found it difficult to see the race problem as anything other than an individual and relational problem, even when explicitly asked. A Moravian church attender was asked if he saw the race problem as mostly attitudes or whether he also saw it as a structural problem, such as being part of the legal system and job market. "As far as I know," he replied, "I would have to say individual attitude. That would be my experience."

As hinted at, black conservative Protestants have somewhat different cultural tools. As opposed to being free-will accountable individualists, they are limited individualists. By that, we mean that black conservative Protestants believe salvation is an individual decision and that individuals have responsibility, but there are limits to this individualism. Humans are created to be in community, and communities sometimes take precedence over the individual. In this way, individualism is not always at the center of existence. Black churches, for example, often emphasize biblical stories such as God delivering his people from Egypt. The emphasis here is on community, a people, rather than on a collection of accountable individuals.

Black conservative Protestants tend to be structuralists. By that, we mean, in opposition to white conservative Protestants, they believe that the structures of societies and groups matter, influence behavior, and can and do impinge on individual and community freedoms. For example, setting up a society in a way that makes it more difficult for persons defined as black to get loans is acknowledged as real, and can supersede individual initiative. One can have good credit, hold a job, and be debt-free, yet still be denied a loan because of one's race. As such, black conservative Protestants do not have the same overwhelming emphasis on individualism and relationalism that white conservative Protestants do. It also means that black and white conservative Protestants view race issues differently.

Otis, an African-American conservative Protestant who attends a Pentecostal church, presents a contrast to Debbie and the typical white conservative Protestant views about the race problem. Unlike most white conservative Protestants, Otis began bringing race issues and race examples into our interview very early on. Rather than focusing solely on individual initiative and accountability, he said that in his city in order to get a good job or a good promotion, the amount of formal education a person has is not as important as being a part of the "good ol' boy" network. He said he sees people and businesses take advantage of vulnerable people, such as single mothers and racial minorities, because they do not have enough clout. They are outside the system of power. He also sees racial segregation in many forms. As in many places, "in this town the most segregated hour is eleven o'clock on Sunday morning. . . . And not only that, even when five o'clock comes, the people leave their jobs, they pick up the same way of thinking. Like, go home to my little group, my little area." Otis went on to talk about racial inequality in access to quality schooling and about many other structural views that limit individual and community freedom. Ultimately, he saw these systems of oppression as satanic, being used to warp human community. Otis's views were common among the black conservative Protestants we interviewed. The most typical response from black conservative Protestants when asked if the nation has a race problem was a chuckle or a bewildered look that the question was asked, as the answer to them was obvious: "of course."

ACCOUNTING FOR BLACK-WHITE SOCIOECONOMIC INEQUALITY

The different cultural tools of black and white conservative Protestants, nurtured in separate denominations, congregations, and neighborhoods, lead to different views on racial inequality. For most black conservative Protestants to whom we talked, material inequality was a core part of the race problem in the United States. Conversely, for nearly all white evangelicals, the race problem did not include any reference to material inequality. Because inequality is so fundamental to what race means in the United States, we sought to understand how conservative Protestants explained inequality between blacks and whites. What primary factors do they think lead to these divisions?

To do this, we first examined national survey data, using the 1996 General Social Survey.[7] This telephone survey had a special religious identity information section and the following question: "On average blacks have worse jobs, income, and housing than white people. Do you think these differences are:

1. because most blacks have less inborn ability to learn?
2. because most blacks just don't have the motivation or will-power to pull themselves up out of poverty?
3. because most blacks don't have the chance for education that it takes to rise out of poverty?
4. mainly due to discrimination?"

For each of these four options, the person being interviewed could say yes or no. So the respondent could say yes to all of them, none of them, or some number in between.

These options fall into important categories for this chapter. The first explanation—created unequally—should not be one often chosen by contemporary conservative Protestants, as it does not fit their theology that all are created equal and all are equal in Christ. The second explanation—motivation—is an individual explanation, emphasizing that the responsibility for inequality lies with blacks and what they do, or rather, what they do not do. This option aligns well with the cultural tools of white evangelicals, especially accountable individualism. The latter two options are structural explanations, meaning, there is something about the way society is arranged that produces unequal outcomes. Clearly, these latter two options, being structural, do not align well with white conservative Protestant cultural tools, but do align well with black conservative Protestant tools.

If cultural tools are generalized to understand racial issues, we would expect that white conservative Protestants would be more likely to view racial inequality as caused by something inherent in individuals themselves—some people work harder than others, some people are less motivated—rather than by problems with the organization of society itself. Conversely, we would expect black conservative Protestants to be more likely to see the problems as rooted in the structures of society rather than rooted in individual deficiencies or proficiencies.

What is more, if these cultural tools are nurtured within religiously based, race-specific networks and organizations, we would expect that conservative Protestants hold to their race's positions more often. For example, insofar as whites in general will focus on the individual deficiencies of blacks as the main explanation of racial inequality, we would expect white conservative Protestants to hold exaggerated versions of this view. This is because conservative Protestants are the strongest carriers of religiously based American values (core values such as structuralism for African Americans, or individualism for white Americans, for example) compared to others, whether secular or adhering to other religious traditions.

We measured "conservative Protestant" as those who said they are evangelical or fundamentalist and who assent to two hallmarks of these groups: belief in the afterlife and belief that the Bible is the literal or inspired word of God. We then classified the responses to the racial inequality question by both white-black and conservative Protestant–other Americans divisions. The results are reported in Table 14.1.

If conservative Protestants are more individually prejudiced than other whites, as is often believed, they ought to be more likely to say that there is inequality because blacks lack the inborn ability to achieve. This is not the case. The percentages of white conservative Protestants and other whites who agree

TABLE 14.1. Explanations for the Black-White Socioeconomic Gap: White and Black Conservative Protestants Compared to White and Black Other Americans

Explanation	Other Americans			Conservative Protestants			Difference W–B[c]
Individual	White	Black	W–B[a]	White	Black	W–B[b]	
Ability	10%	11%	−1	10%	7%	+3	+2
Motivation	51%	42%	+9	62%	31%	+31	+22
Structural							
Education	46%	53%	+7	32%	54%	+22	+15
Discrimination	36%	63%	+27	27%	72%	+45	+18

[a] Other whites percentage minus other blacks percentage.

[b] White conservative Protestant percentage minus black conservative Protestant percentage.

[c] Conservative Protestant racial difference minus the absolute value of other Americans' racial difference. These figures show how much wider is the gap between conservative Protestant whites and blacks than between other American whites and blacks.

Note: All differences are statistically significant (p < .05, 2-tailed) except for ability explanation.

Source: General Social Survey, machine-readable file, 1996.

with this explanation—10 percent—are identical. For both groups, this is easily the least chosen explanation.

Compared to other whites, are conservative Protestants more likely to explain black-white inequality in individual terms and less likely in structural terms, as suggested by the cultural tools argument? Yes. Compared to other whites, conservative Protestants are more than twice as likely to cite lack of motivation versus discrimination as the reason for inequality (a gap of 35 percentage points for white evangelicals versus a gap of 15 percentage points for other whites). And, compared to other whites, white evangelicals are six times as likely to cite lack of motivation versus unequal access to education (a gap of 30 percentage points versus a gap of 5 percentage points). These large gaps in explanations between conservative Protestants and other whites remain even when we control for other factors, such as educational level and overall prejudice.[8] What is more, the individualist-versus-structural explanation gap is even larger when conservative Protestants are compared to theologically liberal white Protestants.

How do white conservative Protestants compare to black conservative Protestants, and how does the gap between these two groups compare to other whites and blacks? These data suggest that conservative Protestants are divided by their faith. Whereas the gap between other white and black Americans citing lack of motivation by blacks as a reason for black-white inequality is 9 percentage points (51 percent of other whites, 42 percent of other blacks), that gap more than triples to 31 percentage points for conservative Protestants (62 percent of whites, 31 percent of blacks). We find similar gap discrepancies when examining the structural explanations. For the percentages citing lack of access to quality education as a reason for inequality, the other white-black gap is 7 percentage points (46 percent of whites, 53 percent of blacks), but 22 percentage points for conservative Protestants (32 percent of whites, 54 percent of blacks). For the discrimination explanation, the other white-black gap is 27 percentage points (36 percent of whites, 63 percent of blacks), but swells to 45 percentage points for conservative Protestants (27 percent of whites, 72 percent of blacks). In short, blacks and whites holding an evangelical faith are more divided in their explanations of why we have racial inequality than are other American blacks and whites.

These findings are evidence that theologically rooted cultural tools developed in racial isolation are driving the explanations of racial inequality for conservative Protestants. They are also part of the explanation why inequality was not discussed by isolated white evangelicals unless asked (but was discussed by black evangelicals, even when not asked). In short, when perceiving race and explaining racial inequality, conservative religion, when practiced in racially homogeneous social contexts, appears to intensify the different values and experiences of each racial group, sharpening and increasing the racial divide.

CULTURAL TOOLS AND POLITICAL VIEWS, PREFERENCES, AND BEHAVIORS

Does the cultural tools argument help us to understand the political views and behaviors of black and white conservative Protestants? Again, relying on the centrality of faith for conservative Protestants and the principle of generalization, we would expect that it does. Specifically, we would expect white conservative Protestants to adopt political views that appeal to their accountable individualism and relationalism and to avoid those appearing to be structural. Views that hold individuals accountable, that do not support group rights, and that limit government ought to be popular views among white conservative Protestants. At least since the 1970s, the Republican party has appealed to people who emphasize individual freedom, who desire to reduce group rights legislation, and who seek a limited government. As a result, we would expect, given their cultural tools, that white conservative Protestants would be more likely to identify with the Republican party than are other white Americans and more likely to vote Republican.

In contrast, given the different cultural tools of black conservative Protestants, we would expect them to hold political views that work toward equality of groups, that do not overly emphasize individuals, and that recognize the need for federal laws (so that equality of groups can be achieved and discrimination minimized). Given that the Democratic party better aligns with the cultural tools of African Americans, we expect (and already know) that African Americans will both strongly identify with the Democratic party and vote Democratic. But what we expect to find given the cultural tools argument is that black conservative Protestants will be even more likely to identify as Democratic and even more likely to vote for Democrats than other black Americans.

To test these expectations, we used the 1980–2000 cumulative file of the General Social Survey.[9] We examined several variables:

1. Should government reduce income differentials? Measured on a 1 (government should) to 7 (no government action) scale.
2. Should blacks overcome prejudice by working their own way up? Measured on a 1 (strongly agree) to 5 (strongly disagree) scale.
3. Do you favor preferences in hiring blacks to make up for past discrimination? Measured on a 1 (strongly agree) to 5 (strongly disagree) scale.
4. Do you favor or oppose capital punishment?
5. Do you think the government is doing too little to improve the environment?
6. What is your political party preference?
7. Who did you vote for in the 1992 presidential election?
8. Who did you vote for in the 1996 presidential election?
9. Who did you vote for in the 2000 presidential election?

For the voting variables, respondents were asked whom they voted for a few months after each presidential election. For the first and third questions, white conservative Protestants should disagree with or oppose them, as they suggest group-based, structural responses. The second question, however, emphasizes individual effort in overcoming prejudice, a situation with which white evangelicals would likely agree. White conservative Protestants should support capital punishment, as such punishment is justified under accountable individualism and the belief that structures do not influence people's actions. White conservative

Protestants should be unlikely to say the government is doing too little to improve the environment, as that responsibility should rest with individuals and individual companies. And, of course, for the last four variables referring to political party and voting behavior, we would expect white conservative Protestants to be and vote Republican more than other whites.

Black conservative Protestants' responses should differ from white conservative Protestants: more likely to support government efforts to reduce income differentials, less likely to agree that blacks should work their own way up, more likely to support hiring preferences for blacks, less likely to favor capital punishment (from their cultural tools perspective, mitigating factors outside the individual's control may account for part of the person's actions and, even more important, capital punishment is the end of a very long, racially biased system that may not fairly try black people), more likely to think the government is doing too little to improve the environment, and more likely to be and vote Democratic.

RESULTS OF THE ANALYSIS

We classified conservative Protestants in nearly the same way that we did in the above sections, with one difference. Because we did not have a religious identity question except in 1996, we used the denomination with which each person is affiliated. In this case, then, a conservative Protestant is defined as someone who attends at least twice a month a fundamentalist or evangelical congregation, believes in the afterlife, and believes that the Bible is literally true or the inspired word of God.

When asked whether the government should reduce income differentials—with allowed responses ranging from (1) government should to (7) no government action—whites were less supportive of this than were blacks. But as expected, the gap between white and black conservative Protestants was larger than the gap for other Americans; 24 percent larger, to be exact. When asked whether blacks should overcome prejudice by working their own way up, white conservative Protestants were significantly more likely to agree than were other white Americans. For African Americans, there was no difference between black conservative Protestants and others.

The General Social Survey also asked respondents whether they favor preferences in hiring blacks to make up for past discrimination. As expected, African Americans—whether conservative Protestant or not—were significantly more likely to agree than were whites. However, because white conservative Protestants were in greater opposition than other whites, the gap between white and black conservative Protestants was 13 percent larger than the gap between other black and white Americans. We find these same patterns for support for capital punishment—the black-white conservative Protestant gap is 21 percent larger than the gap between other black and white Americans.

When respondents were asked whether they thought the government was doing too little to improve the environment, less than half of white conservative Protestants agreed, compared to about 60 percent of other white Americans. Conversely, while a majority of the other black Americans agreed, an even larger majority of black conservative Protestants agreed that the government was doing too little to improve the environment. As a result, the gap between black and white conservative Protestants is over three times the gap between black and white other Americans.

But perhaps the most important political implications for black and white conservative Protestants' cultural tools are based on their actual party preferences and voting behavior. As chapter 12 shows, at least since the 1960s, African Americans have overwhelmingly identified as Democrats, and voted accordingly. Conversely, as a whole, whites have become more Republican. When we examined the 1980–2000 General Social Survey data for party preferences, we found that for individuals not identified as conservative Protestants, whites on average classified themselves as independents while blacks classified themselves somewhere between weak to strong Democrats (the average was right in between the two categories). When we examined the party preferences of white and black conservative Protestants, we saw that the gap between them was larger than for white and black other Americans. White conservative Protestants, on average, classified themselves as Republicans; black conservative Protestants, on average, classified themselves as strong Democrats. In proportional terms, the party-preference gap between white and black conservative Protestants is 1.4 times greater than for white and black other Americans.

Do all of the differences discussed above translate into different voting patterns? To answer this question, we analyzed data from the 1992, 1996, and 2000 presidential elections. We again classified the responses by black-white and by conservative Protestants–other Americans. The results are presented in Table 14.2. In 1992, when he ran against incumbent George H. W. Bush, Bill Clinton garnered 43 percent of the other white Americans' votes, but only 24 percent of white conservative Protestants' votes. Conversely, Bush received 39 percent of the other white Americans' votes, but a full 60 percent of white conservative Protestants' votes. African-American voting patterns are clear: 91 percent of other black Americans voted for Clinton, and just 5 percent for Bush. With those extreme numbers, it would seem almost impossible for black conservative Protestants to vote at even higher rates for Clinton and lower rates for Bush, but they

Table 14.2. Percentages Voting for Presidential Candidates 1992–2000: White
and Black Conservative Protestants Compared to White and
Black Other Americans

Vote	Other Americans			Conservative Protestants			Difference W–B[c]
1992	(White	Black	W–B[b])	(White	Black	W–B[a])	
Clinton	43%	91%	−48	24%	100%	−76[A]	+28[B]
G. H. W. Bush	39%	5%	+34	60%	0	+60	+26
1996							
Clinton	49%	87%	−38	30%	93%	−63	+25
Dole	33%	6%	+27	57%	4%	+53	+26
2000							
Gore	40%	85%	−45	16%	94%	−78	+33
G. W. Bush	57%	12%	+45	4%	4%	+80	+35

[a] Other whites percentage minus other blacks percentage.

[b] White conservative Protestant percentage minus black conservative Protestant percentage.

[c] Conservative Protestant racial difference minus the absolute value of other Americans' racial difference. These figures show how much wider is the gap between conservative Protestant whites and blacks than between other American whites and blacks.

Note: All differences are statistically significant (p < .05, 2-tailed).

Source: General Social Survey, machine-readable files, 1993, 1997, 2001.

did: in our sample, 100 percent of black conservative Protestants voted for
Clinton and, of course, then 0 percent voted for Bush. Thus we have a familiar
and strong pattern: the 1992 voting gap between white and black conservative
Protestants is larger—28 percentage points larger for Clinton and 26 percentage
points larger for Bush—than for other white and black Americans.

In 1996, although the Republican candidate had changed, we saw almost
identical voting gaps as in 1992. Blacks were much more likely to vote for Clinton
than were whites, but this gap was much larger for conservative Protestants than
for other Americans. Likewise, whites were much more likely to vote for Dole
than were blacks, but this gap was much larger for conservative Protestants than
for other Americans.

In 2000, two new candidates ran for president: Al Gore and George W. Bush. The gaps in voting became even larger. Blacks of all types overwhelmingly supported Gore over G. W. Bush, but black conservative Protestants were even more likely to vote for Gore than were other blacks (94 percent compared to 85 percent). Whites of all types supported Bush over Gore, but white conservative Protestants were even more likely to vote for Bush than other whites (84 percent compared to 57 percent). The gaps between white and black conservative Protestants and white and black other Americans were even larger (33 and 35 percentage points, respectively) than the gaps in 1992 and 1996. Given the limited range of this variable, gaps of 25 percentage points and higher are stunning. Clearly, in presidential voting, black and white conservative Protestants have been deeply divided.

CONCLUSIONS

The United States in the twenty-first century continues to be a highly segregated society. A half-century after Jim Crow's legal abolishment, race is still a prominent factor in determining where people live, work, attend school, and worship. It is in this last institution—places of worship—that Americans have been most racially isolated since the end of the Civil War. Laws can be passed to prohibit racially restrictive housing covenants, outlaw discriminatory employment practices, and desegregate schools, but no legislation or legal rulings can promote racial integration inside places of worship. The freedom of choice in our unregulated religious economy has been a large reason that American religion has flourished.[10] The freedom to choose which church to attend has resulted in multiracial churches being exceedingly rare, and congregations integrated between African Americans and whites are rarer still.[11] Perhaps more so than in any other sector of American life, black and white conservative Protestants are racially isolated in their churches.

Because American churches are so racially segregated, it is little wonder that the theologically rooted cultural tools developed by conservative Protestants have taken different forms in black and white churches. For white evangelicals, individualism is central to theological beliefs. An individual's feelings produce a desire to accept Jesus as "a personal Lord and Savior." Following this conversion, personal piety is touted as key to a deeper relationship with God. The emphasis on individualism in white evangelical theology has resulted in antistructuralism, relationalism, and accountable individualism. As we have seen in this chapter, conservative white Protestants employ these cultural tools beyond their practice of religion. Indeed, these cultural tools affect not only how white evangelicals perceive issues of race, but also help to influence how they fill out their ballots.

African Americans are similarly influenced by theologically rooted cultural tools developed in racial isolation. Although individualism is present in the cultural tools of black conservative Protestants, it is of a more limited variety than that found in white evangelical churches. Community is emphasized more among black conservative Protestants than it is among their white counterparts. Additionally, the idea that social structures impinge upon individual freedom—a view largely rejected by white evangelicals—is taken as truth in black conservative Protestant churches. Not surprisingly, black conservative Protestants' theologically rooted cultural tools help to produce different perspectives on race and different political beliefs and actions than those of their white evangelical brothers and sisters.

As shown by our findings in this chapter, race continues to be a powerful force in American society. Race is strong enough to not only differentiate the political attitudes and behaviors of black and white conservative Protestants, but it also has enough impact to alter what on the surface should be the same universal faith. As long as racial identity continues to shape church demographics, the cultural tools of black and white conservative Protestants will no doubt remain oppositional and will continue to result in political division.

NOTES

1. Michael O. Emerson and Christian Smith, *Divided by Faith: Evangelical Religion and the Problem of Race in America* (Oxford: Oxford University Press, 2000).
2. The definition we are using for conservative Protestants closely mirrors British historian David Bebbington's definition for evangelicals. See D. W. Bebbington, *Evangelicalism in Modern Britain: A History from the 1730s to the 1980s* (London: Routledge, 1989), 4–17. We will occasionally employ the less-cumbersome term "evangelical" in place of "conservative Protestant" throughout this chapter. When using "evangelical," we are referring to an individual who fits the definition of conservative Protestant as we have defined it here.
3. Michael O. Emerson and Rodney M. Woo, *People of the Dream: Multiracial Congregations in the United States* (Princeton, N.J.: Princeton University Press, 2006).
4. For more information about these interviews, see Emerson and Smith, *Divided by Faith*, 18–19. For an expanded discussion about how evangelicals understand the race problem, see Emerson and Smith, *Divided by Faith*, 69–91.
5. Ann Swidler, "Culture in Action: Symbols and Strategies," *American Sociological Review* 51 (1986): 273–86.
6. William H. Sewell, "A Theory of Structure: Duality, Agency, and Transformation," *American Journal of Sociology* 98 (1992): 1–29.

7. James A. Davis, Tom W. Smith, and Peter V. Marsden, *General Social Surveys, 1972–2004 (1996)* (computer file), ICPSR04295-v2 (Chicago: National Opinion Research Center [producer], 2005; Storrs, Conn.: Roper Center for Public Opinion Research, University of Connecticut/Ann Arbor, Mich.: Inter-university Consortium for Political and Social Research [distributors], 2006).

8. Michael O. Emerson, Christian Smith, and David Sikkink, "Equal in Christ, but Not in the World: White Conservative Protestants and Explanations of Black-White Inequality," *Social Problems* 46 (1999): 398–417.

9. James A. Davis, Tom W. Smith, and Peter V. Marsden, *General Social Surveys, 1972–2004 (Cumulative File)* (computer file), ICPSR04295-v2 (Chicago: National Opinion Research Center [producer], 2005; Storrs, Conn.: Roper Center for Public Opinion Research, University of Connecticut/Ann Arbor, Mich.: Inter-university Consortium for Political and Social Research [distributors], 2006).

10. For more on the idea of a religious economy in the United States, see Roger Finke and Rodney Stark, *The Churching of America, 1776–2005: Winners and Losers in Our Religious Economy*, 2nd ed. (New Brunswick, N.J.: Rutgers University Press, 2005).

11. Emerson and Woo, *People of the Dream*.

Roman Catholics and American Politics, 1960–2004

Peter Steinfels

$\mathcal{I}$N 1960, JOHN Fitzgerald Kennedy, the Democratic candidate, was elected the first Roman Catholic president of the United States. Forty-four years later, John Forbes Kerry, the Democratic candidate and the next Catholic nominated by either major party for the presidency, went down in defeat.

In both cases, Catholicism emerged as an obstacle to election. But the differences were dramatic—and they suggested some of the unforeseen twists and turns that the relationship between Catholicism and American politics had taken in the intervening four decades. In Kennedy's case, the opposition arose from non-Catholics' suspicions that he might prove altogether docile toward church teachings and subservient to church authorities. In Kerry's case, the opposition arose, by contrast, from within Catholic ranks, and the complaints were precisely that he had ignored church teachings and defied church authorities. Kennedy was suspect, quite mistakenly it seems, for being a docilely dutiful Catholic. Kerry was suspect, mistakenly or not, for *not* being one. Kennedy won overwhelming support from Catholic voters. Kerry did not; indeed, he lost the Catholic vote to George W. Bush, his Republican Methodist opponent.

Writing in the late 1980s about an earlier period of Catholic involvement in American politics, James Hennesey mused, "The change in the world, and even more in the church, has been so great since 1960 as to give even the most committed historian pause in the enterprise of illuminating the present by reference to the past."[1] The late Father Hennesey certainly had in mind such momentous events as the Second Vatican Council, the political and cultural turmoil of the 1960s and 1970s, the election of the globe-trotting, charismatic Pope John Paul II, and possibly the mobilization of the Catholic church around the issue of abortion following the Supreme Court's 1973 decision in *Roe v. Wade*. But it is doubtful that the Jesuit historian could have imagined such an ironic reversal as the electoral plights of the two JFKs.

I

Consider some of the other moments marking dramatic changes since 1960 in Catholicism's place in American politics.[2]

October 4, 1965: The nightmare of nineteenth-century nativists becomes reality: a pope lands on America's shores. Paul VI's one-day visit to UN headquarters in New York includes the first papal meeting with a U.S. president, Lyndon Johnson, at the Waldorf Astoria Hotel and a papal mass before 90,000 in Yankee Stadium. That whirlwind event proves to be a curtain-raiser for the triumphant tours of John Paul II in 1979, when Southern Baptist president Jimmy Carter welcomes the pope to the White House; in 1987, when President Ronald Reagan, who had established full diplomatic relations with the Vatican three years earlier, meets the pope in Miami; in 1993 and 1995, when President Bill Clinton greets the pope in Denver and in Newark. By the time of John Paul's death in 2005, papal meetings with U.S. presidents are unremarkable, although the photograph of President George W. Bush, his wife, and two former presidents kneeling at John Paul's funeral mass symbolizes a sea change in the relations between Rome and Washington.

May 17, 1968: Two Catholic priests, Daniel and Philip Berrigan, dramatize growing Catholic opposition to the war by raiding a Selective Service office in Catonsville, Maryland, and destroying draft records with homemade napalm. This occurs just three years after Cardinal Francis Spellman of New York represented the fusing of Catholicism and American patriotism, as well as his fervent support of the U.S. war effort in Vietnam, by sending Christmas cards portraying himself standing in front of an American fighter plane.

March 7, 1974: Four cardinals, from Philadelphia, Boston, Chicago, and Los Angeles, testify before a congressional subcommittee on the need for a constitutional amendment that would reverse *Roe v. Wade*, the Supreme Court's 1973 decision striking down laws barring legal access to abortion. Cardinal Terence Cooke of New York will give similar testimony in 1976 and again in 1981, accompanied by the presidents of the bishops' conference.

December 4, 1980: The bodies of four Catholic churchwomen are found in El Salvador. Sometime during the previous two days, the women had been abducted, tortured, and murdered by U.S.-backed security forces. The killing creates new Catholic conflicts over American foreign policy in Central America. Two months later, the new secretary of state, Alexander Haig, a Catholic, will discount the deed in testimony before Congress, and the ambassador to El Salvador, Robert White, also a Catholic, will be promptly dismissed from his post and then from the U.S. Foreign Service after refusing to endorse Haig's stance.

May 4, 1983: The American bishops vote overwhelmingly for a pastoral letter raising serious questions about the morality of the nation's nuclear defense policies. A subsequent letter, approved in November 1986, challenges the justice of the American economy. Both letters provoke sharp and widely publicized opposition from top officials of the government.

September 8, 1984: Archbishop John O'Connor, named earlier in the year to head the New York archdiocese and promptly tangling with Governor Mario Cuomo of New York over abortion, publicly criticizes the Democratic party's vice presidential candidate, Geraldine Ferraro, for misrepresenting Catholic teaching on abortion and holding views on abortion incompatible with the church's.

November 12, 1990: The bishops' conference warns Secretary of State James Baker that American military action to liberate Kuwait from occupation the previous August by Saddam Hussein's Iraq could easily violate just-war principles. The bishops' appeal exemplifies a pattern of moral misgivings, stopping just short of outright condemnation, about American military interventions that will later reemerge in regard to conflicts in Bosnia, Kosovo, and Iraq.

September 9, 1996: President William Clinton bestows a Presidential Medal of Freedom on a terminally ill Cardinal Joseph Bernardin of Chicago, who had been both lauded and criticized for championing a "consistent ethic of life" rather than concentrating Catholic political engagement on abortion. Bernardin nonetheless mentions the "killing of the unborn" in his acceptance remarks. That same month, the cardinal visits a man on death row to signal opposition to capital punishment and, two months later, in his final week of life, sends a letter to the Supreme Court opposing physician-assisted suicide.

February 1, 2004: Just before the Missouri primary, Archbishop Raymond Burke of St. Louis declares that he will refuse to give communion to Massachusetts senator John Kerry, a Catholic and a defender of legal abortion. This rebuke of the eventual Democratic candidate triggers a bitter debate about whether Catholic politicians and voters may diverge from episcopal and papal positions on abortion and whether bishops should take high-profile stances in electoral contests.

January 31, 2006: Samuel A. Alito, Jr., is sworn in as a justice of the Supreme Court, making Catholics a majority on the high court: Chief Justice John G. Roberts, Jr., and Justices Alito, Clarence Thomas, Antonin Scalia, and Anthony Kennedy were all appointed by Republican presidents.[3]

II

The story of Catholics and the Catholic church in American politics since 1960 can be told at two levels, of church leadership and of the great numbers of ordinary adherents.

For church leadership—the bishops, first of all, but also the diocesan clergy serving for the most part in parishes, the priests and sisters belonging to religious orders, and the visible lay activists and thinkers—that story can be usefully divided into three overlapping periods. The years from 1960 to around 1976 were ones of often jarring adjustment, as the church responded both to the Second Vatican Council and to the Civil Rights, antiwar, and countercultural movements of the 1960s and 1970s. Between 1973 and around 1985, the church experienced a period of regained but tense balance between liberal political stances on economic and international issues and conservative stances on cultural ones. From around 1985 to 2004, the church's political emphases shifted steadily, although by no means totally or irreversibly, in a conservative direction.

While church leadership tried to steer American Catholicism this way or that, the mass of American Catholics was steadily moved by large socioeconomic and cultural undercurrents. By 1960, economic and educational upward mobility and the migration to suburbia had already begun to dissolve the distinctive Catholic subcultures, tightly defined by doctrine and devotional practices and often by ethnicity as well, that had long given American Catholicism what one historian called its "prickly apartness."[4] Assimilation had political consequences in two directions. Growing affluence appeared to strengthen economic conservatism or at least reduced the importance that government-provided safety nets had naturally enjoyed for immigrant and working-class Catholics. Weekly churchgoing Catholics, moreover, were drawn to the moral and cultural conservatism that was yoked, however uneasily, with faith in the free market. At the same time, the ranks of these weekly churchgoers were shrinking, and many among the less-devout majority were attracted by the emphasis on individual moral and cultural freedom increasingly eclipsing liberalism's former emphasis on bread-and-butter issues. One way or another, on Left and Right, the Catholic presence in politics seemed to become less distinctive.

III

If the 1960 presidential campaign of John F. Kennedy surfaced historic suspicions of Catholicism's political intentions, the next few years seemed to sweep all that history away. Kennedy did not invite the pope to come by secret passage to the White House, where in any case he would have found the goings-on not at all to his liking. Nuns did not take over the public schools. The government did not censor Hollywood movies to suit the judgments of the Catholic Legion of Decency. And when the young president was assassinated, about the only factor that no conspiracy theorist proposed as a possible cause was his Catholicism. Most important, the ecumenical spirit of the Second Vatican Council (1962–1965) and its rejection, in the Declaration on Religious Liberty, of all state coercion in matters of religious belief and practice finally put to rest the worries of non-Catholic Americans that the commitment of American Catholics to separation of church and state was only a temporary expedient.

The council had other profound effects on the political role of the church. It shifted the church's understanding of its mission. No longer was that mission focused almost exclusively on preparing individuals to attain eternal life. The church had to witness to God's love and compassion by striving for justice and healing in the world here and now. Catholic civic engagement became much more religiously charged than before. The positions of church authorities on social and political questions could no longer be set aside as idiosyncratic opinions irrelevant to sacramental life and salvation. But, ironically, the council also provided a basis for contesting those positions by emphasizing the role and responsibilities of the laity in the church and especially in the world. In fact, the council's simple act of approving major changes in a church that had long boasted of immutability weakened church authority. The erosion was magnified by the protracted battle over rethinking Catholic teachings on contraception and the rejection by many Catholics of Paul VI's 1968 papal encyclical reasserting the official condemnation.

Of equal importance was the council's revision of the church's stance toward contemporary society from one of antagonism and combat to one of critical sympathy and engagement. Dialogue rather than condemnation was the preferred ground for encountering, not only other Christian bodies and world faiths, but modern culture itself. The outcome contrasted dramatically with the period following the early twentieth-century repression of Catholic modernism, when, as

Father Hennesey wrote, "Historical and speculative thought in Roman Catholic theological circles went into a half-century eclipse, particularly in the United States." After Vatican II, making up for lost time, there was a tremendous upsurge of theological thought and debate, much of it with political implications. The council's focus on scripture meant that biblical texts and examples now competed with the natural law and casuistic modes of reasoning that had shaped much Catholic thought on social and political problems. Biblical passages and examples fueled radical social criticism and pacifism. From Europe came political theologies and, of particular importance, from Latin America, liberation theology. The council seemed to underwrite borrowing from previously suspect socialist and Marxist thought: Catholicism's historic minimizing of conflict between the rulers and the ruled now was criticized as implicitly propping up oppression; the church could not avoid taking sides. Theology's agenda should be set by the needs of the oppressed and marginalized, not by the comfortable inhabitants of university classrooms.[5]

Such intellectual currents had their explosive effects because of events, including the civil rights struggle, opposition to the war in Vietnam, and the baby boomers' countercultural rebellion and revels. In an era of marches, assassinations, riots, and campus occupations, explicitly Catholic political leadership fell to charismatic, "prophetic" clergy like the Berrigans or to more pragmatic but often no less confrontational community organizers, many of them priests, like James Groppi in Milwaukee, John Egan in Chicago, Geno Baroni in Washington, or others following the path of Saul Alinsky's Industrial Areas Foundation. Facing off against Catholic war critics and advocates of housing and school integration were other Catholics, often residents of ethnic neighborhoods, and their leaders, like the Boston opponent of busing Louise Day Hicks.[6]

These were years when the pacifist Dorothy Day and the monk Thomas Merton became revered models for Catholic activists, and Cesar Chavez wielded Catholic imagery and sympathies in organizing farm workers. The two Democratic challengers to Lyndon Johnson in 1968, Eugene McCarthy and Robert F. Kennedy, gave their liberal politics a Catholic tinge; so did more conservative members of the party, like Mayor Richard J. Daley of Chicago and Daniel Patrick Moynihan, soon to be senator from New York. Catholicism was a recognizable trait of prominent Republican conservative officials like Patrick Buchanan, President Richard Nixon's advisor, and William J. Casey, director of Central Intelligence for President Reagan.

Where were the bishops? Compared to the past, compared, for example, to the prominence of Cardinal Spellman and Bishop Fulton J. Sheen in rallying the faithful to the anticommunist crusade, the answer can only be "on the sidelines." Not until 1971 did the bishops' conference definitely voice opposition to the war in Vietnam. Not until the mid-1970s did it seem like the episcopacy was ready to play a part in setting a public agenda rather than catching up with one. One sign came with the bishops' contribution to the nation's bicentennial year: a two-year series of regional town-hall meetings where teams of bishops heard both experts and grassroots representatives testify on questions of justice in the church and the world. Local meetings in half of the dioceses supplemented the six major gatherings in Washington, San Antonio, Minneapolis, Atlanta, Sacramento, and Newark. As many as 800,000 Catholics had some input in the process.

For the bishops, experts, and laypeople taking part in the hearings, they proved enlightening, even exhilarating. The denouement was something else. In October 1976, 1,351 Catholic delegates, some elected, the majority appointed by bishops, assembled in Detroit and began voting on proposals synthesized from the earlier hearings. Questions of justice in the church soon overshadowed justice in the world, and positions emerged on issues like contraception, clerical celibacy, women's ordination, and homosexuality that were sure to cause heartburn in Rome. Archbishop Joseph Bernardin, later the hero of liberal Catholics for his openness but at the time archbishop of Cincinnati and the elected president of the bishops' conference, adroitly buried the assembly's recommendations in the nether reaches of the episcopal bureaucracy.[7]

IV

However disappointing this conclusion, the process of consultation turned out to be the vehicle for the bishops to regain the initiative in the church's political engagement. It was the distinctive mark of the two major pastoral letters that the bishops issued in the 1980s. In 1983, "The Challenge of Peace" addressed moral issues surrounding nuclear defense. In 1986, "Economic Justice for All" examined the moral state of the American economy. By holding hearings with secular experts and Catholic activists dealing with questions of international affairs and economic justice and by issuing preliminary drafts of the letters for public reaction as well as further consideration by the whole body of bishops, the episcopal drafters stimulated far more debate, some of it in prime time and on front pages, than if the bishops' conference had worked behind closed doors and simply issued final statements, much like the testimony it was regularly asked to present to congressional committees.

Liberals welcomed the letters on nuclear defense as a careful alternative to the arms buildup favored by the first Reagan administration and its dalliance with notions of nuclear "war fighting." They welcomed the letter on the economy as a respectable alternative to the apparent endorsement of free-market Reaganomics by the president's sweeping reelection in 1984. Entered into the political arena, the letters' contents were sometimes exaggerated.

The letter on nuclear arms, for example, did not condemn nuclear deterrence, let alone call for unilateral nuclear disarmament. Rather, it effectively put deterrence "on notice" if it were not accompanied by serious movement toward negotiated arms limitations. Besides issuing a moral challenge to nuclear war-fighting strategies and expressing moral skepticism about much of the administration's arms buildup, the theological thrust of the letter was twofold. While it affirmed the dominant Catholic just-war tradition applicable to both individuals and states, it gave a new recognition for Catholicism of the Christian refusal to bear arms in resisting evil as a legitimate corrective and complementary tradition, at least for individuals. A kind of post-Vietnam pacifism had evidently become too widespread in the ranks of priests, sisters, lay church workers, and even a minority of bishops to be ignored. But the heart of the letter was its attempt, however much this might require a rather unprecedented grasp for the bishops—of first- and second-strike capacities, targeting policies, throw-weights, and similar technical matters—to subject nuclear weapons and deterrent strategies to evaluation by the traditional moral categories of discrimination and proportionality that in Catholic morality distinguished just from unjust warfare. In these two ways, the bishops modified and extended the church's moral teachings about war, even though more public attention was given to whether their rather nuanced words might be read as supporting the contemporary agitation for a "nuclear freeze" or opposing the installation of a new generation of powerful missiles in Europe.

Likewise, the letter on the American economy was far from the rejection of capitalism or plea for socialism that it was occasionally made out to be; it offered a moral case for something closer to Western Europe's welfare or "social market" economies, with a communitarian stress on the right of all both to a basic level of material goods and to some degree of active participation in economic life.

Besides the unusually broad and open consultation and debate that went into their making, the pastoral letters were path breaking in two other respects. First, they were composed in what has been called a "bilingual" manner. They were meant to instruct the faithful in a language particular to believers: the letters began with, for Catholic texts, very extensive biblical introductions, perhaps in reaction to complaints that Catholic social teaching had relied more on philosophical reasoning than on scripture. But the letters were also meant to contribute to the general public discourse of a pluralist society, so they also argued key points in terms accessible to nonbelievers. Second, the letters made a clear distinction between general moral principles and concrete proposals to apply them. About general principles, like the immunity of civilians from direct, intended military attack or the priority of meeting the basic needs of the poor, the bishops claimed to speak with an authority binding on Catholics. Yet determined not to let their teachings remain abstract and disregarded, the bishops also offered recommendations for the concrete application of those principles, their best judgments after consultation, they said, about weapons systems, deterrence strategy, or economic policies. Such conclusions, they readily stated, reflected prudential judgments about facts and changing circumstances, and about these the bishops recognized the legitimacy of diverse views, asking only that their own be given a serious hearing. This distinction was perfectly clear in the texts, often lost in the media reports, and sometimes willfully ignored by critics who wished to dismiss the bishops as pretending to authority beyond their expertise.

How much impact did these letters have? Even though overtaken in part by the collapse of communism and the nuclear balance of terror, the more narrowly focused and tightly argued letter on nuclear armaments and strategy did much to inject the categories of just-war thinking into the thinking of the armed forces and at least the rhetoric of arguments about foreign policy. The economics letter's impact proved less lasting, except as it blended into a larger Catholic emphasis on economic injustices, the needs of the poor, and the duties of the affluent, voiced most insistently by John Paul II.

Ironically, one lasting effect of the letters was actually to spark the growth of a new conservative opposition, a Catholic neoconservatism that would find common ground with the secular version born in the late 1960s. Led by Michael Novak, once a leading voice of postconciliar radicalism, a group of disillusioned liberal intellectuals joined with affluent and well-connected conservative public figures and think tanks to produce lay letters in opposition to those of the bishops. Until the pastoral letters, post–Vatican II Catholic conservatism had focused mostly on internal church issues, like liturgical changes or catechetics. Now it would take on a strongly political cast, with much more politically sophisticated and well-connected proponents.[8]

Their emergence would prove significant in the future. Meanwhile, the liberal thrust of Catholic leadership from the mid-1970s through much of the 1980s, which included not only the pastoral letters but constant sparring with the White House over U.S. policy in Central and Latin America, was balanced by something else. That was *Roe v. Wade*. The 1973 Supreme Court decision overturning whatever laws limited access to abortion in all fifty states immediately triggered a heavily Catholic grassroots anti-abortion movement. By 1975, the bishops were mobilizing behind a major "Pastoral Plan for Pro-Life Activities." Its provisions for aiding women with problem pregnancies were far less visible than its plans for reversing the High Court's decision. The moral urgency of this objective pushed into the shade matters that had previously been seen as important for winning Catholic support, above all attitudes toward providing assistance for Catholic schools.

Beginning in 1976, every presidential election became the occasion for a delicate episcopal dance. Candidates were pressed on their support for anti-abortion measures like the Human Life Amendment; then individual bishops of varying prominence within the hierarchy signaled degrees of satisfaction or disappointment on this point while either stressing abortion as the all-important issue or rejecting single-issue voting—all the while trying to hew to their traditional position of not endorsing candidates. The dance became harder and harder to execute as the differences between the parties on abortion, relatively narrow in 1976, continued to widen; in these conditions, anything a church official said about abortion took on a partisan cast.

In 1984, the dance almost turned into a brawl. Anticipating the problem, Cardinal Joseph Bernardin (he had been appointed cardinal archbishop of Chicago in 1982 while overseeing the drafting of the pastoral letter on nuclear defense) advocated a "consistent ethic of life" in a late 1983 address at Fordham University. His consistent ethic linked, without equating, questions of genetics, abortion, capital punishment, warfare, care for the dying, and ultimately the needs of "the hungry and the homeless, the undocumented immigrant and the unemployed worker."[9] Cardinal Bernardin did not expect the consistent ethic to eliminate arguments about how the church or Catholic voters should rank such issues. But it was meant to widen the appeal of the Catholic teaching on abortion by linking its underlying concern about protecting life to other issues, while also throwing up a firewall between the church and single-issue politics and between the church and identification with one political party. It accordingly angered Catholics who believed that abortion should be the single decisive issue; they viewed it as a rationale for liberal Catholics to support prochoice politicians.

The consistent ethic of life, even as it remained controversial, became a kind of watchword uniting a host of Catholic political initiatives. But it did not ward off the battle that broke out six months later between Archbishop John O'Connor, the newly appointed archbishop of New York, and Mario Cuomo, New York state's Catholic governor, who had signed legislation providing state funding of abortions. Appalled by Archbishop O'Connor's offhand reply during a televised press conference that he would think about excommunicating Cuomo, the governor fought back, defending his positions in the press and then in a much-publicized address at the University of Notre Dame. The dust had not yet settled when Cardinal O'Connor publicly attacked Geraldine Ferraro, the Democratic party's vice presidential candidate, for having lent her name, two years earlier, to an event where not only church opposition to the legalization of abortion but its teaching on the morality of abortion as well was taken to task.

In a season of speeches by Cuomo, right-to-life Illinois congressman Henry Hyde, O'Connor himself, and again Bernardin, along with statements from other bishops, Bishop James Malone of Youngstown, Ohio, then the elected president of the bishops' conference, had to reassert publicly the hierarchy's existing stance of neutrality in presidential elections.[10]

V

This 1984 wrangling was a sign of a shifting tide. Elected to the papacy in 1978, the cardinal archbishop of Krakow, Karol Wojtyla, embarked on a program of consolidating what he and others believed was a fragmenting postconciliar church. John Paul II and his advisors worried that the American church was slipping out of the bishops' and the Vatican's control. Numbers of priests resigning from the active priesthood and other men and women in religious orders seeking release from their vows; rising marriage annulments; theological questioning of teachings on sex; outspoken feminist theologians, nuns, and advocates for ordaining women; organized conservative complaints about liturgical deviations—although all these developments had counterparts in other parts of the world, in the American case they reinforced the Vatican's impression of the country as a hotbed of permissiveness and hedonism. Where Americans thought that the bishops' new resort to consultation and open debate strengthened the credibility of their public statements, the Vatican feared that these democratic methods weakened the bishops' claim to an authority that was not based on expertise or public opinion. The Vatican, moreover, was disconcerted by the bishops' deep entanglement in the issue of nuclear defense; the Americans, it was felt, were treading on the Vatican's diplomatic turf. Jean Jadot, the apostolic delegate to the United States who had played a key role in the naming and promotion of many of the bishops responsible for initiatives like the pastoral letters, was called back to Rome two years after the election of John Paul and rather unceremoniously put out to pasture.[11]

In 1984, when Boston and New York, two of the nation's most important sees, fell open, Rome named Bernard Law and John O'Connor to fill the posts. The appointments were a surprise—neither man headed a major diocese—but the two were evidently considered reliable Vatican loyalists and doctrinal conservatives. Archbishop O'Connor, a career chaplain in the navy (with the rank of admiral and advanced degrees in both political science and psychology) and ultimately the head of the church's ministry to the armed forces, had represented the military perspective on the small committee drafting "The Challenge of Peace" and had maintained a liaison with the Pentagon. The two men were quickly elevated to the College of Cardinals, as archbishops of Boston and New York inevitably are. They became the basis of Rome's preference, under John Paul II, for making its own handpicked cardinals rather than the elected officials of the bishops' conference the major intermediaries between the Vatican and the American hierarchy.[12]

Official Catholic advocacy of programs for the working poor, immigrants, welfare recipients, the homeless, the medically indigent, and both prisoners and victims of crime continued. Nationally and locally, bishops grew increasingly outspoken in opposition to the death penalty. In international affairs, they continued to pursue a cautious course, wary of American military intervention, generally supportive of international institutions like the United Nations, very active on behalf of banning land mines and forgiving international debt. In the American political context, all of this had a liberal coloration; it was also quite consistent with the politics of John Paul II and in fact often had the active support of Cardinal Law and Cardinal O'Connor.

But in domestic political matters—foreign affairs were somewhat different—the 1986 pastoral letter on the economy was something of a last hurrah. The bishops had also been long at work on a third pastoral letter, addressing issues of special concern to women. As each draft appeared, the proposed letter, under pressure from the Vatican and the growing number of conservative bishops appointed by Rome, became more conservative. Despite eight years of drafting and redrafting, the letter eventually lost the liberal support it had once enjoyed. Unable to garner the necessary two-thirds support, the letter was set aside in 1992. From the late 1980s through the 1990s, cultural issues came to overshadow economic and political ones—and the church's conservative tendencies moved accordingly to the forefront. In 2004, conservative Catholics launched a massive campaign, effectively in support for the Republican ticket, on the basis that five "nonnegotiables" should determine Catholics' voting. The five were abortion, euthanasia or physician-assisted suicide, embryonic stem cell research, human cloning, and same-sex marriage. Abortion set the pace, of course, along with the principle it evoked of not directly taking innocent human lives; but it is worth noting that all the other issues were put on the national agenda since the 1980s, and with at least some liberal support.

VI

Much has been written about the "Catholic vote," especially in advance of each congressional and presidential election. Once seen as reliably Democratic, in the late twentieth and early twenty-first centuries, Catholics have been tagged a crucial swing vote, not only nationally but in key states, including some with large votes in the Electoral College, that are themselves considered swing states.

The general pattern is clear: Catholics were never monolithically bound to the Democratic party. Indeed, competition between Catholic ethnic groups sometimes turned some Republican when others had a stranglehold on advancement within Democratic ranks. But Catholics could be counted on to vote for Democratic candidates, even losing ones, at rates much higher than the rest of the population and for Republican candidates, even winning ones, at rates lower than the general electorate. Since World War II, however, that difference has steadily diminished.

Catholics gave Eisenhower nearly 50 percent of their votes in 1952 and 5 percentage points more in 1956—compared to 35 percent for Dewey in 1948. But this support for Ike was still far less than Protestant support for the popular general. In the 1960 presidential race, Catholics voted Democratic with a vengeance—vengeance, it seemed, for the 1928 defeat of Catholic Al Smith. Almost 80 percent of Catholics voted for Kennedy. Nearly as high a percentage supported Lyndon Johnson in 1964, but this time they were running with the tide: Kennedy had barely squeaked in, while Johnson won in a landslide, so the gap between Catholic Democratic votes and the general electorate was narrower.

By 1968 and 1972, Republican efforts to woo Catholics, along with a reaction, especially in blue-collar Catholic ranks, to the liberalism of the 1960s, began to pay off. Between the close election of 1968 and the landslide of 1972, support for Richard Nixon increased 40 percent in the general electorate—but nearly 60 percent among Catholics, though they still lagged behind Protestants in support for the Republican candidate. Jimmy Carter, the victor in 1976, won a majority of Catholic votes, but Gerald Ford, the Republican opponent, did better among Catholics than Nixon had in 1968. Ronald Reagan did still better in his 1980 victory and better yet in 1984. In 1988, George Herbert Walker Bush hung on to these Reagan gains to finish in a virtual tie with Michael Dukakis for Catholic votes. (Bush won 80 percent of white evangelical and 66 percent of white mainline Protestant votes, by comparison.) Bill Clinton's 1992 and 1996 presidential races temporarily reversed the trend a bit, increasing the margin of Catholic Democratic votes over those in the general electorate, but in 2000 and 2004, that margin slipped back further. George W. Bush went from a slight deficit in the Catholic vote to a distinct majority, a striking majority among weekly mass–attending, non-Latino Catholics.

The trend in congressional voting and party identification lagged behind that of presidential voting, but the pattern was similar. Catholics ceased to be reliably Democratic without becoming reliably Republican. Catholics as a whole remained somewhat more likely than the average voter to vote Democratic than Republican but that "somewhat" got steadily smaller. And by 2004, the likelihood reversed itself for the minority of traditionally minded, non-Latino Catholics who were at church weekly.

Though the overall pattern may be clear, the reasons for it are much less so. Were they primarily socioeconomic: upward mobility making the tax-cutting, small-government stance of the Republicans attractive? Were they primarily religious and cultural: moral opposition to abortion, gay marriage, and explicit sexuality in the media? Were they even ethnic and racial: fears of crime and neighborhood instability associated with school integration and growing minority populations? Undoubtedly, at different times and in different places, the mixture of reasons varied. What was the impact of Catholic leadership in stimulating, in limiting, or in modifying these changes in voting, ideology, and political allegiance? Catholic leaders preferred to think that they exercised some significant influence, but that conviction remained very much an act of faith.[13]

VII

Was the presidential election of 2004 the culmination of this third and steadily more conservative period of the church's political engagement since 1960? Did it possibly open yet another period in that engagement? The contrast between John F. Kerry's electoral fate and John F. Kennedy's has already been noted. Still more striking, perhaps, was the impression that the Catholic hierarchy was departing from what Father Hennesey called its "basic tradition . . . of a quiet word" in the politician's ear, friendly persuasion rather than electoral politicking.

This tendency did not begin with the hierarchy. Consider a picket line outside the Capitol Hill Hotel where, in November 2003, on the eve of the election year, the bishops were holding their annual Washington meeting. The pickets carried large and unusually effective placards, each with two photos on it. One was a photo of a specific bishop or archbishop. The other was a photo of a specific politician, in almost every case a Democrat. The lettered message went something like this: "Bishop So-and-So, have the courage to deny Holy Communion to pro-choice Representative Such-and-Such."

It was Archbishop Raymond Burke, newly appointed to head the St. Louis archdiocese, who first made a national issue of these demands. In his previous position as bishop of La Crosse, Wisconsin, Burke had ordered his priests to refuse communion to two state legislators and to U.S. congressman David Obey, a senior representative, the leading Democrat on the all-important Appropriations

Committee, and a regular supporter of measures advocated by the bishops' conference. Now, on the eve of the Missouri Democratic primary, he declared that he would deny Senator Kerry communion because of his support for abortion rights.

Several more bishops quickly followed where Burke had led. Others, including prominent figures like Cardinal Theodore McCarrick of Washington, Cardinal Roger Mahony of Los Angeles, and Bishop Wilton Gregory, at that time the president of the bishops' conference, disagreed. Indeed, foreseeing a nasty brouhaha over this question, the bishops' conference had established a task force, under Cardinal McCarrick, to formulate a statement on church teaching and Catholic politicians that could be debated in November 2004—after the presidential election. But Archbishop Burke and like-minded bishops felt that they could not wait. They defended their action primarily in terms of their internal church responsibilities. To continue overlooking the prochoice advocacy of Catholic politicians was to leave the faithful uncertain about the seriousness of church teachings. The problem, of course, was that taking such action in the course of an election campaign could not avoid the appearance of a partisan move and the possible accusation of abuse of sacramental power to achieve a political end, especially since the focus was almost entirely on Catholic Democrats like Senator Kerry. No bishop had raised this kind of objection to prochoice Catholic Republican Arnold Schwarzenegger during his upstart race for governor of California.

Obviously, with the news media tracking Senator Kerry on Sundays in what became irreverently known as the "wafer watch," the bishops as a whole could not suspend comment until their postelection meeting. Attempting to forge an "interim statement" at the bishops' June meeting near Denver, the task force reiterated the church's clear position that "[e]very bishop has the right and duty to address these realities in his own diocese." But the task force strongly advised, nonetheless, against "the denial of Communion for Catholic politicians or Catholic voters in these circumstances" and spelled out its reasons in some detail:[14] "[T]he sacred nature of the Eucharist could be trivialized and might be turned into a partisan political battleground." The floodgates would be opened to debates about "what other issues might lead to denial of Holy Communion." Catholics upholding church teachings in public life might be perceived not as representing their own moral convictions but merely "as under pressure from the hierarchy." On the other hand, Catholics "who bend to the political winds" could pose "as courageous resistors of episcopal authority." The lesson of the past was that "such actions have often been counter-productive." They "could push many people farther from the church and its teaching, rather than bringing them closer."[15]

The task force presentations set off a prolonged and intense debate among the bishops. When it was over, a significantly different position emerged. Titled

"Catholics in Political Life," it retained the defense of every bishop's right to do as he chose in his own diocese, but it dropped the advice that this not involve denial of communion and all of the reasoning behind that advice. It retained some of the emphasis on teaching and persuading but moved toward equating the immorality of abortion itself with the immorality of allowing legal access to it or, if such legality were already a fact, failing to reverse it. The *New York Times* headline summing up this June interim statement may not have been entirely accurate, but it was predictable: "Politicians Face Bishops' Censure in Abortion Rift. Said to Cooperate in Evil. Statement Allows Denial of Communion to Those Who Defy Church."[16]

Why did the statement coming out of the meeting differ so much from the stance of the prestigious task force? One reason may have been the task force's presentation, which gave the assembled bishops a mass of information and opinion but no succinct proposal. Linked to that was the desire for brevity, for distilling the task force's material to about the length of an op-ed article. A third reason was episcopal unity and the desire not to be seen as taking sides between those bishops who had made the reception of communion a public marker in their opposition to legalized abortion and the larger number who had publicly disagreed with that approach.[17]

A final reason was simply the long-building frustration at prochoice politicians, especially Catholics. It was not forgotten that the Democrats had begun their primary season in January 2003 at the National Abortion Rights Action League's (NARAL) Pro-Choice America anniversary dinner. Each candidate tried to outdo the next in proclaiming devotion to abortion rights and in some cases recanting any wisp of past anti-abortion sentiment that might be thought to blemish his record. It was the Democrats who, according to the *Times* report of this event, promised to make abortion rights central to the presidential race. It was Senator Kerry who promised that if he should debate Bush, he would make their differences about abortion "one of the first things I'll tell him."[18]

To what extent was the bishops' action shaped by the Vatican? In 2002, the Vatican's Congregation for the Doctrine of the Faith had issued a stern "Doctrinal Note on Some Questions regarding the Participation of Catholics in Political Life." It was a reaction not just to abortion but to the building momentum in the United States, Canada, and Western Europe toward legally authorizing physician-assisted suicide, or euthanasia, and same-sex unions. The latter development produced still another admonition to Catholic political leaders to be faithful to church teachings.

But these and other statements by Vatican sources like Cardinal Joseph Ratzinger, later elected Benedict XVI but then overseeing the integrity of Catholic teachings as head of the Congregation for the Doctrine of the Faith, contained qualifications, ambiguities, and uncertainties large enough to drive a popemobile through. Bishops on all sides could find confirmation for their own positions.

Whatever the factors at play behind closed doors, with the June interim statement, the vocal minority achieved influence in framing Catholicism's public posture far beyond their numbers. The heads of dioceses who, in effect, said that voting for Senator Kerry was not compatible with being a faithful Catholic eventually numbered about a dozen. A much larger number, roughly eighty, urged Catholics to be guided by "Faithful Citizenship," an election-year statement approved by the administrative board of the bishops' conference, stressing that politics involved fundamental moral choices, highlighting those having to do with the protection of life, but also drawing attention to other issues, from warfare and terrorism to world poverty and health care, from marriage ("a lifelong commitment between a man and a woman") and family life to job creation and racial discrimination. But with the help of the media, primed to play up conflicts stirred by Catholic officials over abortion, the minority largely became the face of the church during the campaign.

What were the consequences of this departure from past restraint? Compared to his performance in 2000, President Bush made significant gains among Catholic voters, who continued, however, to support him in numbers far less than those of both mainline and evangelical Protestants. But did those gains arose from anything that the bishops or other Catholic activists did? A postelection poll of 3,000 Catholic voters asked about the impact of conservative claims that issues like abortion and stem cell research were nonnegotiable for Catholics. Just under 19 percent of these Catholic voters said that these appeals had increased the likelihood of voting for Bush, while just under 25 percent said that they had actually increased the likelihood of voting for Kerry. It is possible that the Bush gains among Catholics came despite rather than because of the controversial religious appeals.[19]

The 2004 election raised the possibility of deeper changes, namely, that explicitly Catholic politics may be moving closer in style to evangelical politics. Church officials have traditionally focused on policies rather than persons. Policy has not been absent from evangelical concerns, but there has been, especially at the grassroots, an emphasis on personal identity and connection: "He's a good man"; "he's a Christian"; "he's one of us." By emphasizing whether Catholic politicians were in good standing with their church, 2004 may have shifted Catholic participation in this direction.

And by renouncing any effort to prevent the church's public face from being established by the most outspoken, though not necessarily most representative, bishops, the hierarchy may be abetting a shift in public Catholicism toward an evangelical model, where leadership is often achieved by personality—by charisma, organizational or entrepreneurial skill, or media-captivating militancy.

There is little doubt that the widespread perception of the bishops' political role provoked considerable bitterness among Catholic Kerry voters and Catholic liberals, even as it elated and energized many fervently conservative Catholics, who felt that the hierarchy was finally wielding its authority so as to show that the church really meant what it taught. But what will prove to be lasting and what transient in these reactions? Will the liberal bitterness reinforce an indifference or even cynicism about the bishops as church leaders and as public actors? Will conservatives' enthusiasm turn to disappointment if they find that the bulk of the hierarchy remains centrist and cautious rather than uncompromising and confrontational?

VIII

In the wake of the 2004 election, Democrats mounted a number of initiatives to win back "values voters," in particular among religious American Catholics. Some proposals within Democratic ranks appeared purely cosmetic; others seemed to open room for new policies and candidates. Meanwhile, Republicans struggled to maintain their newly won hold on religious voters, Catholics included, who appeared increasingly disenchanted by the war in Iraq, political scandals, uncertain economic policies, and complaints of torture.

Signals from Pope Benedict XVI, elected in April 2005, have been mixed. If maintaining the clarity of moral principles were to come into conflict with pastoral accommodation, little in his personality or history suggests that he would be any less insistent on the former rather than the latter than he had been as head of the church's office for overseeing Catholic doctrine. On the other hand, among his major appointments have been two Americans known for pastoral flexibility: as his own successor at the Congregation for the Doctrine of the Faith, Archbishop (now Cardinal) William J. Levada of San Francisco; as successor to Cardinal McCarrick in the politically sensitive post of archbishop of Washington, the pope named Bishop Donald W. Wuerl of Pittsburgh.

Finally, active Catholic groups acting independently of the hierarchy have been increasingly mobilized to argue that faith directs them politically in one direction or the other. The voters' guide insisting that Catholics should cast their votes on the basis of "five nonnegotiable issues" was countered in 2004 with one explicitly rejecting "the idea that how Catholics should vote can be answered by applying a simple 'litmus test' of a few selected issues."[20] Among politically and theologically attentive Catholics, the relationship between the church and political life promises to be more volatile than ever during the first decades of the twenty-first century. The underlying question is whether that energy—and discord—will animate or alienate the larger Catholic population in the decades to come.

NOTES

1. Quotations here and below credited to James Hennesey are from ch. 11 of this volume and may be found at pp. 247–65 (quotations 247, 249, 253).
2. General histories and portraits of the Catholic church in the United States providing background or covering parts of this period are James Hennesey, *American Catholics: A History of the Roman Catholic Community in the United States* (New York: Oxford University Press, 1981); Jay P. Dolan, *The American Catholic Experience: A History from Colonial Times to the Present* (Garden City, N.Y.: Doubleday, 1985); Dolan, *In Search of an American Catholicism: A History of Religion and Culture in Tension* (New York: Oxford University Press, 2002); Charles R. Morris, *American Catholic: The Saints and Sinners Who Built America's Most Powerful Church* (New York: Times Books, 1997); William McSweeney, *Roman Catholicism: The Search for Relevance* (New York: St. Martin's, 1980); and Chester Gillis, *Roman Catholicism* (New York: Columbia University Press, 1999). Basic data can be found in Bryan T. Froehle and Mary L. Gautier, *Catholicism USA: A Portrait of the Catholic Church in the United States* (Maryknoll, N.Y.: Orbis, 2000); and James D. Davidson, *Catholicism in Motion: The Church in American Society* (Liguori, Mo.: Liguori/Triumph, 2005), and in annual editions of *The Official Catholic Directory* (New York: Kenedy & Sons). For analytic approaches from generally liberal perspectives, see Peter Steinfels, *A People Adrift: The Crisis of the Roman Catholic Church in America* (New York: Simon & Schuster, 2003); Andrew M. Greeley, *The Catholic Revolution: New Wine, Old Wineskins, and the Second Vatican Council* (Berkeley: University of California Press, 2004); and earlier books by Greeley, including *The Catholic Myth: The Behavior and Beliefs of American Catholics* (New York: Scribner's, 1990), *American Catholics since the Council: An Unauthorized Report* (Chicago: Thomas More Press, 1985), and *The American Catholic: A Social Portrait* (New York: Basic, 1977); and David Gibson, *The Coming Catholic Church: How the Faithful Are Shaping a New American Catholicism* (San Francisco: HarperSanFrancisco, 2003). For conservative analyses, see Richard John Neuhaus, *The Catholic Moment: The Paradox of the Church in the Postmodern World* (San Francisco: Harper & Row, 1987); Neuhaus, *Catholic Matters: Confusion, Controversy, and the Splendor of Truth* (New York: Basic, 2006); George Weigel, *The Courage to Be Catholic: Crisis, Reform, and the Future of the Church* (New York: Basic, 2002); George A. Kelly, *The Second Spring of the Church in America* (South Bend, Ind.: St. Augustine's, 2001); and David Carlin, *The Decline & Fall of the Catholic Church in America* (Manchester, N.H.: Sophia Institute Press, 2003). This chapter draws heavily on my own observations and reporting as an editor at *Commonweal* and senior religion correspondent at the *New York Times* as well as regular reading of five Catholic publications—*Commonweal*, *America*, *National Catholic Reporter*, *National Catholic Register*, and *Our Sunday Visitor*—and perusal of many more,

from *U.S. Catholic* to the *Wanderer*, along with Religion News Service. With only a few exceptions, however, citations are to books.

3. Most details of these events or texts of documents can be found in the archives of the *New York Times* (www.nytimes.com) or on the Web site of the U.S. Conference of Catholic Bishops (www.usccb.org). On the papal visits, see also Peter Hebblethwaite, *Paul VI: The First Modern Pope* (New York: Paulist, 1993); and George Weigel, *Witness to Hope: The Biography of Pope John Paul II* (New York: HarperCollins, 1999). On the Berrigans, see Daniel Berrigan, *To Dwell in Peace: An Autobiography* (San Francisco: Harper & Row, 1987); and Murray Polner and Jim O'Grady, *Disarmed and Dangerous: The Radical Lives and Times of Daniel and Philip Berrigan* (New York: Basic, 1997). On Cardinal Spellman, see John Cooney, *The American Pope: The Life and Times of Francis Cardinal Spellman* (New York: Times Books, 1984). On the killings in El Salvador and the aftermath, see Phyllis Zagano, *Ita Ford: Missionary Martyr* (New York: Paulist, 1996); and Ana Carrigan, *Salvador Witness: The Life and Calling of Jean Donovan* (New York: Simon & Schuster, 1984). On the pastoral letters on nuclear defense and the U.S. economy, see Philip J. Murnion, ed., *Catholics and Nuclear War: A Commentary on "The Challenge of Peace"* (New York: Crossroad, 1983); and R. Bruce Douglass, *The Deeper Meaning of Economic Life: Critical Essays on the U.S. Catholic Bishops' Pastoral Letter on the Economy* (Washington, D.C.: Georgetown University Press, 1986). On Cardinal O'Connor, see Nat Hentoff, *John Cardinal O'Connor: At the Storm Center of a Changing American Catholic Church* (New York: Scribner's, 1988).

4. Morris, *American Catholic*, vii.

5. The literature on the council, its meaning, and its impact is immense, with many dueling interpretations. There is still no accessible single-volume history by an American to replace the contemporary reportage, written for the *New Yorker* and published in several volumes, by Xavier Rynne, the pen name of the Redemptorist priest and scholar Francis X. Murphy. The documents of the council are available in various translations and formats, including *Letters from Vatican City* (New York: Farrar, Straus and Giroux, 1963) and *Vatican Council II* (New York: Farrar, Straus and Giroux, 1968). The most extensive study of the council appears in Giuseppe Alberigo, ed., with Joseph A. Komonchak, ed. for the English editions, *History of Vatican II*, 4 vols. (Maryknoll, N.Y.: Orbis, 1995–2006). For three brief Catholic summaries of the council's work (of many, including those in books already mentioned), see Frans Jozef van Beeck, *Catholic Identity after Vatican II: Three Types of Faith in the One Church* (Chicago: Loyola University Press, 1985); Avery Dulles, *The Reshaping of Catholicism: Current Challenges in the Theology of Church* (San Francisco: Harper & Row, 1988); and John W. O'Malley, *Tradition and Transition: Historical Perspectives on Vatican II* (Wilmington, Del.: Glazier, 1989). Fathers Dulles and O'Malley conducted an enlightening exchange in *America* in 2003, with the former contributing "Vatican II: The Myth and the Reality," 24 Feb. 2003, and "Vatican II: Substantive Teaching," 31 Mar. 2003, while the latter contributed "The Style of Vatican II," 24 Feb. 2003, and "Vatican II: Official Norms," 31 Mar. 2003.

6. The outstanding account of American Catholicism's interaction with 1960s activism is found in John T. McGreevy, *Parish Boundaries: The Catholic Encounter with Race in the Twentieth-Century Urban North* (Chicago: University of Chicago Press, 1996), but

also see David J. O'Brien, *The Renewal of American Catholicism* (New York: Oxford University Press, 1972). Msgr. John Egan's activities are described by Margery Frisbie, *An Alley in Chicago: The Ministry of a City Priest* (Kansas City, Mo.: Sheed & Ward, 1991). Garry Wills, *Bare, Ruined Choirs: Doubt, Prophecy, and Radical Religion* (Garden City, N.Y.: Doubleday, 1972), provides a contemporary impressionist view of this period, as do many essays, collected in various volumes, by Andrew M. Greeley. On grassroots resistance and change among Catholics during this period, see J. Anthony Lukas, *Common Ground: A Turbulent Decade in the Lives of Three American Families* (New York: Knopf, 1985); and Samuel G. Freedman, *The Inheritance: How Three Families and the American Political Majority Moved from Left to Right* (New York: Simon & Schuster, 1996). James J. Farrell, *The Spirit of the Sixties: The Making of Postwar Radicalism* (New York: Routledge, 1997), gives major attention to the role of Catholics.

7. The pivotal place of the hearings organized by the bishops' Committee for the Bicentennial received its due in a special supplement marking Call to Action's (Call to Action is a progressive, lay-organized movement) tenth anniversary that appeared in *Commonweal*, 26 Dec. 1986, with contributions from David J. O'Brien, Cardinal John Dearden, Francis J. Butler, Dolores L. Curran, James Finn, Dennis McCann, Kenneth A. Briggs, and John Tracy Ellis.

8. Michael Novak, "Moral Clarity in the Nuclear Age," *National Review*, 1 Apr. 1983; and Novak, *Toward the Future: Catholic Social Thought and the U.S. Economy: A Lay Letter* (New York: Lay Commission on Catholic Social Thought and the U.S. Economy, 1984).

9. Joseph Cardinal Bernardin, "A Consistent Ethic of Human Life: An American-Catholic Dialogue," Gannon Lecture, Fordham University, 6 Dec. 1983, Archdiocese of Chicago, Joseph Cardinal Bernardin Archives and Records Center, Chicago, Ill. Accessed online at http://archives.archchicago.org/JCBpdfs/JCBaconsistentethic fordhamu.pdf.

10. These events are reported in several of the books already mentioned but see, in addition, William B. Prendergast, *The Catholic Voter in American Politics: The Passing of the Democratic Monolith* (Washington, D.C.: Georgetown University Press, 1999); and Timothy A. Byrnes, *Catholic Bishops in American Politics* (Princeton, N.J.: Princeton, 1991), which also addresses the pastoral letters and the controversies surrounding them, as does Eugene Kennedy, *Cardinal Bernardin: Easing Conflicts—and Battling for the Soul of American Catholicism* (Chicago: Bonus, 1989). See also Patricia Beattie Jung and Thomas A. Shannon, eds., *Abortion & Catholicism: The American Debate* (New York: Crossroad, 1988); Joseph Bernardin, *Consistent Ethic of Life* (Kansas City, Mo.: Sheed & Ward, 1988); and John P. Langan, ed., *A Moral Vision for America* (Washington, D.C.: Georgetown University Press, 1998).

11. On John Paul, see Weigel, *Witness to Hope*, 225–26 and other references to the church in the United States; also see Jonathan Kwitny, *Man of the Century: The Life and Times of Pope John Paul II* (New York: Holt, 1997); and Carl Bernstein and Marco Politi, *His Holiness: John Paul II and the Hidden History of Our Time* (Garden City, N.Y.: Doubleday, 1996), both less informed than Weigel on internal church matters. On differences between American and Vatican views of the consultation process, the

author had personal conversation at a conference in Switzerland with Jan Schotte, then secretary of the Pontifical Justice and Peace Commission, later an archbishop and cardinal, who was vehement on the topic, and also conversations with American participants in discussions with Vatican officials about the pastoral letters. On the role of Archbishop Jadot, see Thomas J. Reese, *Archbishop: Inside the Power Structure of the American Catholic Church* (San Francisco: Harper & Row, 1989); and Kennedy, *Cardinal Bernardin*.

12. On the appointments of Cardinals O'Connor and Law, see Kennedy, *Cardinal Bernardin*. The shift in power from the bishops' conference to the cardinals is based on observation and conversations with individuals with access to the workings of the conference.

13. Prendergast, *Catholic Voter in American Politics*, is a major source for this section. Prendergast was a Republican activist and research director for the Republican National Committee. Andrew Greeley has consistently stressed that the Democratic leanings of Catholics persist when compared to Protestant leanings. See, most recently, Andrew M. Greeley and Michael Hout, *The Truth about Conservative Christians: What They Think and What They Believe* (Chicago: University of Chicago Press, 2006), which does not, however, include the 2004 vote.

14. "Interim Reflections Task Force on Catholic Bishops and Catholic Politicians," U.S. Conference of Catholic Bishops, 15 June 2004. Online at http://www.usccb.org/bishops/intreflections.shtml.

15. Ibid.

16. See Laurie Goodstein, "Politicians Face Bishops' Censure in Abortion Rift," *New York Times*, 19 June 2004.

17. For an expanded discussion of the themes addressed in this paragraph, see Peter Steinfels, "The Bishops' Debate on Roman Catholic Politicians Who Back Abortion Rights Was More Nuanced Than a Statement Suggests," *New York Times*, 26 June 2004.

18. Adam Nagourney, "In Turn, 6 Presidential Hopefuls Back Abortion Rights," *New York Times*, 22 Jan. 2003.

19. For information about a 2004 post-election poll, see Peter Steinfels, "A Compelling Book, an Election, a Study on American Beliefs and a Disaster: Notes from 2004," *New York Times*, 1 Jan. 2005.

20. See Peter Steinfels, "Voters' Guides Define Moral Compromises to Take to Polls," *New York Times*, 14 Oct. 2006.

WOMEN, POLITICS, AND RELIGION

Margaret Bendroth

𝒯HE LATE TWENTIETH-CENTURY story of women, politics, and religion is a complex tangle. To be sure, any two corners of that intriguing triangle offer plenty of room for analysis—a fact easily verified by the rising mountains of scholarly and journalistic literature on women and politics, women and religion, and, of course the perennially fascinating story of religion and politics. But, surprisingly, sustained discussion of all three of those elements—of the ways that both gender and religion shape political behavior—is still much harder to come by.[1]

This is not for lack of subject matter. In recent years, the dramatic confrontation between feminists and religious conservatives has provided endless grist for scholarly analysis. Women like Betty Friedan and Phyllis Schlafly, Hillary Clinton and Beverly LaHaye have come to operate as a kind of convenient shorthand, defining the range of the deepest social and moral polarities of the mid- to late twentieth century. Indeed, since the 1970s, broadly ethical issues like abortion, family planning, and teenage sexuality have become tagged in the political arena as "women's issues," even though they are far from gender-specific problems.

Religion and gender seem to be a combustible political mix, each intensifying the impact of the other. Until the 1970s, women were—much like religious constituencies—a relatively minor factor in political races. Party strategists rarely targeted female voters, except for the wry suggestion that a well-groomed head of hair or a muscular physique could turn a candidate's electoral fortunes. But all that changed with the rise of second-wave feminism. With the campaign for the Equal Rights Amendment, the furor over the *Roe v. Wade* decision legalizing abortion, and the emerging gay rights movement, the politics of gender took center stage in a political era justly famous for moral and religious controversy. In this intensely partisan atmosphere, the "gender gap" became as important a factor as religion. For the first time, politicians openly courted women—increasingly subdivided into interest groups as feminists or traditionalists; as soccer moms, "security moms," or "desperate housewives"; or as full-time professionals—buoyed by the conviction that a well-organized bloc of female voters might provide a critical margin of victory. Since the 1980s, election results have provided a quick and easy gauge of support for feminism, demonstrating its continuing power or declaring its true and final demise.[2]

But the symbolic politics of gender do not necessarily explain the behavior of female voters. Statistical surveys and polling data clearly show, for example, that women do not follow the bifurcated "culture wars" model. According to that now-famous analysis, intense religious belief skews to the conservative side; high levels of church attendance and strongly held beliefs correspond with support for the Republican social agenda, especially opposition to abortion and gay rights. In contrast, liberals are predominantly secular; the less one goes to church or professes religious certainty, the more likely one is to be a Democrat.[3] But for women, the categories do not fit: highly religious women are not necessarily more conservative. Though they are the vast majority of churchgoers in the United States, they tend, as a whole, to vote Democratic, not Republican. In fact, some studies suggest that, in the case of women, higher levels of church attendance and religious belief lower support for conservative Republican causes. But women do not fit a stereotypical liberal mold either: though they are more supportive of welfare state policies and opposed to militarism, they also line up on the conservative side of moral debates over pornography, alcohol and drug use, birth control, and prayer in public schools.[4]

In the case of African-American women, the anomalies are even more pronounced. As late as 1952, only 13 percent of black women had ever cast a ballot in an electoral contest; yet in the 2000 election, they voted at a far higher rate than black men (60 to 53 percent), and higher than any other racial or ethnic group, except for white non-Hispanics (61 percent for men and 63 percent for women).[5] Scholars attribute these high rates of participation to religion, specifically the activist, egalitarian message of black churches, and to encouragement to pursue collective remedies for social evils.[6] As one study has—somewhat cautiously but justifiably—concluded, in the case of women, "religion's influence is much more subtle and much less unidirectional than has been thought."[7]

Nuancing the prevailing assumptions about women, religion, and politics is no simple task, however. The larger narrative of the period from 1945 to the present charts a flow from "margin to mainstream," with women taking dramatic hold of the political process after 1960, and ultimately gaining some real power on the national stage.[8] The basic outlines of this story are secular, framed by the assumption that with the end of the Victorian suffrage crusade in 1920, religion was no longer a major facilitator of women's public role. The chief exception to that rule has been the antifeminist agenda of the religious Right, where women's groups like Phyllis Schlafly's StopERA and Beverly LaHaye's Concerned Women for America mobilized large numbers of conservative Christian churchwomen. But even this episode generally proved the overarching principle, that in the unfolding of women's modern political role, religion itself was now moving from mainstream to margin.

Nuance is fundamental to any discussion of gender and politics. Women in the United States today enter the voting booth as more than half the nation's citizens, bringing with them a broad range of racial and ethnic identities, social class divisions, and, of course, religious commitments. Studies show that, even over the past several decades of feminist consciousness raising, women do not tend to identify themselves as a group, nor do they see themselves in common cause. And in that respect, it is not surprising that women have been so slow to become a distinct factor in electoral races.[9] In response, many theorists argue that because women's political role is so diverse and indirect, traditional definitions of politics, centering on the acquisition and use of public power, are simply inadequate. The usual focus on parties and elections needs to give way to a more open-ended analysis engaging all of the ways that women have sought and exercised different kinds of social power.[10]

Within this broader understanding, women in the United States do share a significant common experience: they were barred from direct political participation until 1920, when the Nineteenth Amendment suddenly made them all full members of the voting public. Until that point, religious institutions—churches, missionary agencies, schools, and social reform groups—provided women's primary access to social power. They achieved leadership and moral authority, and a degree of political leverage, by virtue of their religiosity. And indeed, even in the present day, one of the most significant characteristics of religion in the United

States is its deep and consistent support among women. As long as records have been kept, women have accounted for roughly two-thirds of all church members, a figure that transcends time, geography, and all of the many permutations of theological difference.[11]

In this larger sense, religion offers a revealing framework for understanding women's political role since World War II, particularly their emerging identity as American citizens. In the years immediately after suffrage and up through the 1950s, mainline Protestant religious institutions created a broad platform for inclusion, from which women's organizations campaigned quietly but steadily against racism, poverty, and war. As the reigning religious establishment, these predominantly white, middle-class churches provided an important link between older Victorian forms of female activism and modern political causes—even the early stages of second-wave feminism. "Maternalism," an older nineteenth-century idea that women had a special role in creating and sustaining the common good, was the connecting thread, even when gender itself was not a visible point of contention.[12] Within this context, women's political presence carried with it the presumption of altruism, an assurance that even in the most contentious social debates, they would never advocate for selfish or partisan gain.

The dawn of the political gender gap coincided with the waning of this historic Protestant consensus. During the late 1960s and 1970s, the old order reversed itself, with Roman Catholics and evangelical Protestant denominations carving out new spaces in the public square, vacated by a rapidly declining—and obviously misnamed—mainline.[13] Their rising visibility reflected solid membership gains and a new conviction, especially in the case of conservative Protestants, that the "old-time religion" needed to stay more closely in step with modern society. Despite its well-deserved reputation for moral conservatism, the new traditionalism was very much a product of its time and place. Even solidly conservative religion echoed the individualism and anti-institutionalism of the baby boom generation and the expressive, partisan, and increasingly sectarian character of the surrounding political world. "Religious issues" became a relatively short but explosive list of moral concerns, dealing primarily with sexuality and family relationships.

During those times, old-fashioned maternalism began to change as well, taking on more combative, political overtones; moreover, women's social concern focused increasingly on the welfare of *particular* families, not society as a whole. Thus, even as women began to demand and to receive more public power, their role as citizens often seemed to narrow. As just one interest group among many, their list of "women's issues" was as short and difficult as those bequeathed to religious institutions.

WOMEN, RELIGION, AND CITIZENSHIP, 1920–1970

When the Nineteenth Amendment became law in 1920, American women celebrated over seven decades of dogged effort in a campaign that had begun in a Wesleyan chapel in Seneca Falls, New York. Back in 1848, even to the radical clergymen and social reformers who framed the Declaration of Sentiments and its long list of demands for change, the idea of equal access to the voting booth seemed completely far-fetched. Under the American legal system, women could not own property, sit on juries, or even claim rights to their minor children. Marriage to a foreigner jeopardized their American citizenship. Women had few political rights on their own; according to the principle of "femme covert," fathers and husbands always represented daughters and wives in the public sphere.[14]

But by 1920, suffrage had lost a great deal of its controversial impact, in large part thanks to religion. Its supporters had argued tirelessly that a woman's vote would inject some badly needed moral backbone into the sordid masculine world of politics and government. They needed to do little more than simply point out the powerful contrast between the graft-saturated elections of the Gilded Age and women's long record of work in temperance reform. Even without access to the ballot box, the Woman's Christian Temperance Union had convinced a generation of middle-class Americans that alcohol was a genuine social evil, deserving quick and merciless eradication. By the end of the nineteenth century, thousands of American women were equally convinced that lobbying and petitioning were no less righteous acts than singing temperance hymns or praying on the steps of the local saloon.[15]

Not all suffragists were eager to embrace organized religion as a principal ally, remembering the fierce opposition of conservative clergymen in their movement's early years, but they could not argue with success. The American public accepted the idea of women in the voting booth on essentially conservative grounds, reassured that suffrage would institutionalize the religious and moral qualities long assumed to be essentially feminine attributes. Other less-democratic motives also played a role: as immigration from Europe reached its peak in the World War I era, and racial tensions exploded into riots across many northern cities, the political power of native-born women seemed a critical means of enforcing social stability against the growing political power of Catholics, Jews, and urbanized African Americans.[16]

Yet in spite of all the hopes and fears that greeted the passage of the Nineteenth Amendment, change was slow in coming. In the 1920 presidential election, about 43 percent of women eligible to vote went to the polls, compared with two-thirds of the men in that category. Rates of participation rose gradually over the next several decades, tracking rising levels of education and employment among women, and by 1940 neared 50 percent. But even so, women lagged significantly behind men, on the average by about 10 percent.[17]

Clearly, the suffrage movement left women with a "complex legacy."[18] They were, on one hand, human beings with equal access to the political rights theoretically enjoyed by all American citizens. But they were also, and would always be, female, endowed with special moral sensitivities and an attendant responsibility for the moral tone of American society. In the years ahead, as economic and educational opportunities began to mount, women would still enter the voting booth as gendered American citizens.

In the middle decades of the twentieth century, mainline Protestant institutions provided ample social space for women's activism. As the unofficial religious establishment, leaders of these white, northern denominations assumed a custodial role within American society, advocating for broadly moral causes that they believed represented the general good. As the presumptive leaders of Ivy League colleges and universities, presidential advisors and diplomats, they rarely scrabbled for elected power. The goal was to exercise moral leadership without appearing to be narrowly partisan.[19]

During the 1940s and 1940s, this ambiguity served Protestant women's organizations well. It allowed a generation of well-connected, highly educated, and consistently gracious women to emerge as able advocates for human rights causes. One of the largest of these organizations was United Church Women (UCW), formed in 1941 to unify the work of the many Protestant women's organizations established in the late nineteenth century. In the postwar years, the UCW took the lead in war relief efforts, in lobbying for antilynching laws in the South, and in public opposition to McCarthyism, mostly through public statements, high-level lobbying, and personal example. UCW representatives sat in on high-profile meetings with Eleanor Roosevelt, and in 1953, they hosted President Dwight D. Eisenhower at their national assembly. But, as Virginia Brereton has noted, their power was always indirect and never exercised on their own behalf. "The women met with Eleanor Roosevelt, not Franklin. They dispatched telegrams rather than telephoning senators. They had tea with the Trumans, but they did not confer with the president on matters of state." "In short," Brereton concludes, "they used the means they were familiar with as women."[20]

The same was true for the Young Women's Christian Association (YWCA) and its social agenda in the World War II era. In contrast to the Young Men's Christian Association, which by the mid-twentieth century had become primarily a "gym and swim" club, the YWCA maintained both its gendered and religious identity. Though certainly shed of specific Protestant trappings in language and public piety, the Y's generalized Christian ethic provided a "common language and set of ideals" for a new generation of activists. From its nineteenth-century origins as a moral protection society for young women in the city, the YWCA became steadily more inclusive and more politically attuned by the early twentieth century. During the 1920s and 1930s, it became a major public voice for racial equality; the YWCA was, in fact, the first and, for a long time, the only national organization in the United States to have an integrated leadership and rank and file. YWCA leader Dorothy Height, for example, was an African-American Baptist who served as executive secretary of the National Council of Negro Women during the late 1940s, while she was also secretary of interracial education on the Y's national board. In the late 1950s, she became president of the NCNW and a leader in the Civil Rights movement.[21] But Y leaders rarely pressured political party officials or ran for office themselves. Typically, YWCA techniques included "investigation of social problems, followed by education, publicity, lobbying, and the creation of direct social services through voluntary activities."[22]

Race, rather than gender, was a central concern of Protestant women's organizations in these middle decades. During the 1950s, the Woman's Division of the northern Methodist church played an important role in integrating public schools and housing, largely through "personal moral influence." Methodist women lobbied the federal government to withhold funding to segregated schools and to end discrimination in federal housing policies. In 1954, they issued the first public statement in support of the Supreme Court's *Brown v. the Board of Education of Topeka, Kansas* decision. But their role was not directly partisan. A strong, grassroots movement of nearly 250,000 women, the Woman's Division emphasized education, especially through neighborhood conversations and other forums for racial understanding.[23]

Even within their own church hierarchies, women normally invoked the language of human rights, rather than gender. During the 1950s, both the northern Presbyterian and Methodist denominations granted full ordination rights to women, and other denominations began to visibly loosen the male monopoly on the pulpit. The change had been long in coming: serious agitation for women's ordination had been a regular occurrence in Protestant circles since the early years of the nineteenth century. But the decisions of the 1950s received surprisingly little fanfare. As the *Christian Century* declared in 1957, "a conflict that has long embarrassed groups holding that all Christians are equal members of the body of Christ has been set at rest."[24]

The pronouncement was, of course, badly premature. During the 1960s, within large ecumenical Protestant organizations like the National Council of Churches, a rising generation of sharply political younger women began to challenge the unexamined sexism of male leadership and to take full advantage of the ordination rights that had lain fallow since the 1950s.[25] Although critics of second-wave feminism would later take the movement to task for being far too white, middle class, and secular, religion was in fact an important piece of early consciousness-raising efforts. Interviewed in 2002, veteran activist Charlotte Bunch credited her involvement in the Student Christian Movement and the YWCA at Duke University as the beginning of her forty-year political career. Within these organizational networks, Bunch said, her "vague political ideals" took concrete form. Her growing involvement in civil rights marches and protests gave her "another way of understanding religion" and "a spiritual vision of a politically engaged, interracial, ecumenical community."[26]

Other women, however, demanded more specificity. During the 1950s and 1960s, in communities ranging across the racial divide and along the economic spectrum, religious ideals became a means of organized grassroots protest. In the deep South, where civil rights agitation brought direct retaliation against the persons, homes, and families of leaders like Medgar Evers and Martin Luther King, Jr., black churchwomen were a clear majority of the rank and file. During the voter registration campaigns conducted by the Student Nonviolent Coordinating Committee (SNCC) in the early 1960s, women were three or four times more likely than men to participate, taking workers into their homes for food and shelter, canvassing door to door, and marching down to city hall and attempting to cast ballots. The typical SNCC volunteer was a woman between the ages of thirty and fifty, with older children active in the movement.[27]

During this same time, but for vastly different reasons, conservative Protestants and Catholics felt their homes to be similarly embattled. In the mid-1960s, a series of Supreme Court decisions dismantling school prayer and condoning sex education in public schools appeared to erode not just the moral foundations of society, but the rights of parents to raise their children in the way they believed best. In the growing array of local organizations staffed by suburban housewives and increasingly militant clergy from across the religious spectrum, women again entered the political fray as mothers. But in this case, the old inclusive maternalist paradigm seemed far too vague and far too secular to meet the pressing need of moral crisis.[28]

Women, Religion, and Partisanship

Women in great numbers entered partisan politics in the 1960s. In 1964, for the first time, they outnumbered men at the polls, though in proportional terms they still voted at a lower rate. The relative percentages of male and female voters began to shift measurably during the 1970s, and in 1980 more women voted in the presidential election than did men. Over the next twenty years, the so-called gender gap steadily widened, and by 2000, some 8.4 million more women than men cast ballots, a difference of 3.2 percent.[29]

As a result, women's increased presence at the polls has begun to translate into public power. From 20 members of Congress in 1980, female representation increased to 73 by 2001, from 4 percent to almost 14 percent of the total. On the state level, gains were even larger: in 2001, women accounted for 27.3 percent of executive posts and 22.4 percent of state legislators.[30] Women have also found a seat at the table of party politics—a vivid change from the days when suffragists were forced to negotiate the smoke-filled backrooms of ward heelers and machine politicians. In 2003, women chaired twelve of the Democratic state parties and thirteen of the Republican ones. That same year, the National Federation of Republican Women, an independent organization with a seat on the Republican National Committee's central leadership group, boasted 100,000 members and 1,800 local societies. Among Democrats, the McGovern-Fraser Commission's guidelines, passed in 1972, requires proportional representation of minorities in all state delegations; not surprisingly, the ruling rapidly transformed women's role in the national convention process. From a scant 15 percent in 1948, the proportion of female delegates reached 48 percent in 2000.[31]

But in many ways, women still have a fairly thin purchase on the political landscape—certainly far short of their numerical majority in the American population. Polls and studies show that they do not support female candidates in greater numbers nor appear to vote for shared female interests in equal pay for equal work, childcare subsidies, or access to abortion and birth control. Indeed, despite all of the public discussion since the mid-twentieth century, gender is in many cases less salient than ethnicity, class, region, age, or education in explaining voting patterns.[32] Moreover, women tend to be, as a group, fairly pessimistic about political involvement. The continuing salience of competitive sports metaphors and military references in the popular media suggests that in many ways, the political realm still belongs to men.[33]

Since the 1960s, religion has provided a relatively narrow platform for women's political and social involvement. The undeniable fact of American religious diversity, deepened by a new wave of immigrant faiths and home-grown innovations, instantly negates any denominational claim on common social ground. The overarching metaphor of religion in the late twentieth century, popular among scholars and pundits alike, is of a sprawling, competitive marketplace where no single group may presume to speak for all. In this busy, sectarian world, differences loom larger than commonalities.[34]

There is perhaps no better example of this oppositional process than the career of Phyllis Schlafly. During the 1950s, she rose to prominence in Republican circles by virtue of her cool platform presence and her widely acknowledged expertise in international affairs. Political opponents who dismissed her as a "powder puff" quickly learned otherwise: Schlafly was a trained lawyer with an unusual depth of knowledge about Soviet missile strength and capabilities. In 1957, she and her husband, Fred, coauthored a seminal report on "Communist Tactics, Strategy, and Objectives" for the American Bar Association; the following year, they formed the Cardinal Mindszenty Foundation, an organization designed to educate Catholic laypeople about the dangers of "atheistic communism." In 1964, her memorable campaign biography of Barry Goldwater, *A Choice, Not an Echo*, demonstrated her intellectual skills as well as her deep popularity among the Republican party's rank and file.[35]

During those early years, Schlafly referenced her gender and her religious faith when the occasion called for it. Running for Congress in 1952, she presented herself as a housewife, but only in order to criticize Democratic spending and government waste. She stressed the importance of "virtue" in politics, but talked more about the Korean War and missile defense strategies than about sexual ethics. Similarly, Schlafly commonly invoked religion of a broadly moral sort, not specific Roman Catholic doctrine. When she was ousted from leadership of the National Federation of Republican Women in the mid-1960s, her supporters took to wearing eagle pins, referencing Isaiah 40:31, "They that wait upon the Lord shall renew their strength. They shall mount up with wings, as eagles." In many ways echoing the language of Protestant women reformers from a century before, Schlafly insisted that the core issues of American society were not economic or political, but moral. Without a deep well of civic virtue, grounded in the personal ethics of American citizens, welfare-state solutions had little hope of success. Not surprisingly, the Nixon years were difficult ones for Schlafly and for midwestern Republicans, with the Watergate betrayal only one of a long string of disappointments. In the 1960s, she opposed Nixon primarily because of his policy of détente toward the Soviet Union and China.

Schlafly's political profile would soon change dramatically. When the Equal Rights Amendment was first introduced in 1923 by the National Women's party, it occasioned relatively little controversy. The main opposition came from representatives of women's labor unions, who feared the ERA would dismantle an important web of protective legislation. Momentum gathered slowly, however, and in 1940, Republicans endorsed the ERA, followed by Democrats in 1943; in 1947, Congress reintroduced it with broad bipartisan support. The Senate approved the ERA in 1950, by a vote of 63 to 19. But the measure stalled over a parliamentary dispute until 1967, when it reemerged in vastly different social circumstances. The ERA became a central cause of the National Organization for Women and a political and cultural bellwether of support for feminism. By 1972, it had passed through both houses of Congress and was headed for ratification by three-quarters of the fifty states. Within a year, the campaign was only eight states short of its goal.[36]

Schlafly had paid little sustained attention to the ERA, or to feminism, until she was invited to a debate in Connecticut in 1972. But her preparation for that event proved to be a major turning point in her career, paralleling a sea change in the social agenda of American conservatism. From anticommunism and missile defense, Schlafly turned to the gender-driven politics of abortion, feminism, and protection of the family. She would say little more about missile defense or the SALT treaty; for good or ill, she had become a potent symbol for women and men uncomfortable with the feminist movement's egalitarian ethic. Within months, her StopERA campaign had turned the tide against ratification, and by the late 1970s, the momentum was unstoppable. Despite a thirty-nine-month extension granted by Congress in June 1982, the ERA failed to win the necessary margin.

Schlafly's decision to tackle the ERA began a new era in women's political history. By all accounts, her supporters were religious conservatives; according to some surveys, 98 percent of anti-ERA women were church members. They were primarily evangelical Protestants and Catholics, but also Orthodox Jews and Mormons, and very few had been politically active before.[37] Schlafly's forces readily identified themselves as defenders of women's "traditional" role in the home. Of course, not all of them were stay-at-home moms, nor were they all agreed that women were naturally subordinate to men; despite their opposition to the Equal Rights Amendment, many conservative women took for granted that equal work deserved equal pay. But they believed emphatically in gender differences and insisted that these should be recognized by law. They were convinced that women carried primary responsibility for inculcating moral values through their role in the family.[38]

In other words, maternalism had become sharply partisan. In a wide range of political settings, from school board contests to ERA floor fights, the battle pitted traditionalists against others presumed to care little for the welfare of children and families. The partisan spirit was reminiscent of suffrage rhetoric a century earlier and its claim that female morality would hold the line against politically undesirable immigrants and city dwellers. But it also reflected some old habits among religious outsiders, particularly evangelicals, Mormons, and Roman Catholics. For many decades, from the 1930s through the 1960s, they had viewed the world from a separatist vantage point, a safe distance apart from the secular drift of American society. Direct political involvement was not an option; conservative religious communities understood instinctively that their best protective barrier was a strong network of close-knit families. Thus, for example, the fundamentalist journals of the 1930s, 1940s, and 1950s featured a running conversation, conducted chiefly by women, about ways to keep children "pure" in an actively hostile world. The strategy was defensive, and the tone deeply sectarian.[39]

CONCLUSION

"How is it," one scholar has asked, "that some women, some mothers, use the resources of their kinship networks, communities, and churches to fight for justice for everyone, while others may object to their own subordination but are quite happy to perpetuate and benefit from other people's oppression?" The claim of moral motherhood today spans the spectrum from ecological activists and civil rights crusaders to Aryan Nation racists and anti-busing protesters. While some women "generalize from the needs of their own children to the needs of all children," the evidence is just as strong that others use their "maternal authority to preserve real or imagined privileges."[40]

There are many answers to that question: the role of economic deprivation and relative privilege, the range of available political choices, and of course the deep vagaries of human nature. But religion also provides important clues—as a moral landscape, a source of gendered identity, and a historic platform for women's social and political role. Certainly since the mid-twentieth century, the vast sea change in the nature of religious presence has played no small part in shaping the complex role women play in modern public life.

The intersection of gender, politics, and religion occupies a wide place within the history of the past fifty years and the polarizing moral debates of the present time. And certainly the rapid overview in this chapter leaves out far more than it manages to include; in another time and place, a full accounting would include the growing multitude of women's interfaith, local, and nonwhite grassroots organizations that are closely tied to church support. The full story would no doubt include many other narratives in addition to the one presented here.

There is a lot to tell. Any true accounting of gender and religion in the political world will offer far more than a litany of facts about electoral outcomes or analyses of polling data; in the case of women, the usual focus on voters, parties, and elections obscures as much as it reveals. Women's modern political history goes well beyond debates over abortion, sexual ethics, or family protection, significant as these certainly are. In its fullest sense, it is about an ethic of care in

American society and whether the fate of other people's children will find a permanent spot in the national political marketplace.

NOTES

1. See, for example, Robert Booth Fowler and Allen D. Hertzke, "Women, Religion, and Politics," in their *Religion and Politics in America: Faith, Culture, and Strategic Choices* (Boulder, Colo.: Westview, 1995), 167–83; Sue Tolleson-Rhinehart and Jerry Perkins, "The Intersection of Gender Politics and Religious Beliefs," *Political Behavior* 11 (1989): 33–55; Karen M. Kaufman, "The Partisan Paradox: Religious Commitment and the Gender Gap in Party Identification," *Public Opinion Quarterly* 68 (2004): 491–511; Robert Wuthnow and William Lehrman, "Religion: Inhibitor or Facilitator of Political Involvement among Women?" in *Women, Politics, and Change*, ed. Louise A. Tilly and Patricia Gurin (New York: Russell Sage Foundation, 1990), 300–322.

2. For a good summary of the gender gap, see Barbara Burrell, *Women and Political Participation: A Reference Handbook* (Santa Barbara, Calif.: ABC/CLIO, 2005), 96–98.

3. James D. Hunter, *Culture Wars: The Struggle to Define America* (New York: Basic, 1991); John C. Green, James L. Guth, Corwin Smidt, and Lyman Kellstedt, *Religion and the Culture Wars: Dispatches from the Front* (London: Rowman and Littlefield, 1996); Geoffrey C. Layman, "'Culture Wars' in the American Party System," *American Political Research* 27 (1999): 89–121; David Leege and Lyman Kellstedt, eds., *Rediscovering the Religious Factor in American Politics* (Armonk, N.Y.: Sharpe, 1993).

4. For a summary of findings, see David O. Sears and Leonie Huddy, "On the Origins of Political Disunity among Women," in Tilly and Gurin, *Women, Politics, and Change*, 249–77. See also Virginia Sapiro, *The Political Integration of Women: Roles, Socialization, and Politics* (Urbana: University of Illinois Press, 1983), 143–69.

5. Susan Hartmann, *From Margin to Mainstream: American Women and Politics since 1960* (Philadelphia: Temple University Press, 1989), 6; Burrell, *Women and Political Participation*, 94–95.

6. Allison Calhoun-Brown, "No Respect of Persons? Religion, Churches and Gender Issues in the African American Community," *Women and Politics* 20 (1999): 27–43; Clyde Wilcox and Sue Thomas, "Religion and Feminist Attitudes among African-American Women: A View from the Nation's Capital," *Women and Politics* 12 (1992): 19–35. African-American women are also largely negative on the issue of abortion.

7. Tolleson-Rhinehart and Perkins, "Intersection of Gender Politics and Religious Beliefs," 53.

8. Hartmann, *From Margin to Mainstream*; William H. Chafe, *The Paradox of Change: American Women in the Twentieth Century* (New York: Oxford University Press, 1991); Glenna Matthews, *The Rise of Public Woman: Woman's Power and Woman's Place in the United States, 1630–1970* (New York: Oxford University Press, 1994).

9. Sue Tolleson-Rhinehart, *Gender Consciousness and Politics* (New York: Routledge, 1992), 53, 54.

10. For a useful summary of this conversation, see Estelle D. Freedman, *No Turning Back: The History of Feminism and the Future of Women* (New York: Ballantine, 2002), 327–28.

11. For a summary of findings, see Ann Braude, "Women's History *Is* American Religious History," in *Re-Telling U.S. Religious History*, ed. Thomas Tweed (Berkeley: University of California Press, 1997).

12. See Linda Gordon, *Women, the State, and Welfare* (Madison: University of Wisconsin Press, 1990); Theda Skocpol, *Protecting Soldiers and Mothers: The Political Origins of the Social Policy in the United States* (Cambridge, Mass.: Belknap, 1992); Seth Koven and Sonya Michel, eds., *Mothers of a New World: Maternalist Politics and the Origins of the Welfare States* (New York: Routledge, 1993).

13. The literature is vast; some useful narratives include Robert Wuthnow, *The Restructuring of American Religion* (Princeton, N.J.: Princeton University Press, 1988); and Christian Smith, *American Evangelicalism: Embattled and Thriving* (Chicago: University of Chicago Press, 1998).

14. Linda Kerber, *No Constitutional Right to Be Ladies: Women and the Obligations of Citizenship* (New York: Hill and Wang, 1999).

15. Ruth Bordin, *Women and Temperance: The Quest for Power and Liberty, 1873–1900* (Philadelphia: Temple University Press, 1981).

16. See, for example, Barbara Hilkert Andolson, *"Daughters of Jefferson, Daughters of Bootblacks": Racism and American Feminism* (Macon, Ga.: Mercer University Press, 1986); Philip Cohen, "Nationalism and Suffrage: Gender Struggles in Nation-Building America," *Signs* 3 (1996): 707–27.

17. Hartmann, *From Margin to Mainstream*, 1–22.

18. Nancy Cott, *The Grounding of Modern Feminism* (New Haven, Conn.: Yale University Press, 1987), 13–50.

19. William McGuire King, "The Reform Establishment and the Ambiguities of Influence," in *Between the Times: The Travail of the Protestant Establishment in America, 1900–1960*, ed. William R. Hutchison (Cambridge, Mass.: Harvard University Press, 1989), 122–40.

20. Virginia Brereton, "United and Slighted: Women as Subordinated Insiders," in Hutchison, *Between the Times*, 152–53.

21. Susan Lynn, *Progressive Women in Conservative Times: Racial Justice, Peace, and Feminism, 1945 to the 1960s* (New Brunswick, N.J.: Rutgers University Press, 1992), 27, 28, 29. See also Judith Weisenfeld, *African American Women and Christian Activism: New York's Black YWCA, 1905–1945* (Cambridge, Mass.: Harvard University Press, 1997).

22. Lynn, *Progressive Women in Conservative Times*, 3.

23. Alice G. Knotts, "Methodist Women Integrate Schools and Housing, 1952–1959," in *Women in the Civil Rights Movement: Trailblazers and Torchbearers, 1941–1965*, ed. Vicki L. Crawford, Jacqueline Anne Rouse, and Barbara Woods (Bloomington: Indiana University Press, 1990), 251–58.

24. "Breakthrough for the Woman Minister," *Christian Century*, 23 Jan. 1957, p. 100, quoted in Margaret Bendroth, "An Understated Tale of Epic Social Change:

Women's Ordination 50 Years Ago and Now," *Journal of Presbyterian History* 83 (2005): 105–17.

25. Susan Hartmann, "Expanding Feminism's Field and Focus: Activism in the National Council of Churches in the 1960s and 1970s," in *Women and Twentieth-Century Protestantism*, ed. Margaret Bendroth and Virginia Brereton (Champaign: University of Illinois Press, 2002), 49–69.

26. Quoted in Ann Braude, ed., *Transforming the Faith of Our Fathers: Women Who Changed American Religion* (New York: Palgrave/Macmillan, 2004), 211. Lois Miriam Wilson, president of the World Council of Churches in 1983, tells a similar story. See ibid., 13–14.

27. Charles Payne, "Men Led, but Women Organized: Movement Participation of Women in the Mississippi Delta," in Crawford et al., *Women in the Civil Rights Movement*, 9; Carol Mueller, "Ella Baker and the Origins of 'Participatory Democracy,'" in Crawford et al., *Women in the Civil Rights Movement*, 60.

28. Lisa McGirr, *Suburban Warriors: The Origins of the New American Right* (Princeton, N.J.: Princeton University Press, 2002); and William Martin, *With God on Our Side: The Rise of the Religious Right in America* (New York: Broadway, 1996).

29. Burrell, *Women and Political Participation*, 92–93.

30. Freedman, *No Turning Back*, 378, 379.

31. Burrell, *Women and Political Participation*, 102–5.

32. Sears and Huddy, "On the Origins of Political Disunity among Women," 243–77; Jane S. Jaquette, "Introduction: Women in American Politics," in *Women in Politics*, ed. Jane S. Jaquette (New York: Wiley, 1974), xiv–xxxvii; Sandra Baxter and Marjorie Lansing, *Women and Politics: The Visible Majority*, rev. ed. (Ann Arbor: University of Michigan Press, 1983), 1–3, 28, 38.

33. M. Kent Jennings, "Gender Roles and Inequalities in Political Participation: Results from an Eight-Nation Study," *Western Political Quarterly* 36 (1983): 364–85; Susan J. Carroll and Richard L. Fox, *Gender and Elections: Shaping the Future of American Politics* (Cambridge: Cambridge University Press, 2006), 2, 3.

34. Roger Finke and Rodney Stark, *The Churching of America, 1776–2005: Winners and Losers in our Religious Economy* (New Brunswick, N.J.: Rutgers University Press, 1993).

35. Donald C. Critchlow, *Phyllis Schlafly and Grassroots Conservatism: A Woman's Crusade* (Princeton, N.J.: Princeton University Press, 2005).

36. Jane DeHart and Donald Mathews, *Sex, Gender, and the Politics of ERA: A State and a Nation* (1990; rpt., New York: Oxford University Press, 1992).

37. Critchlow, *Phyllis Schlafly*, 220–27; David W. Brady and Kent L. Tedin, "Ladies in Pink: Religion and Political Ideology in the Anti-ERA Movement," *Social Science Quarterly* 57 (1976): 76–82; Clyde Wilcox, "Religious Attitudes and Anti-Feminism: An Analysis of the Ohio Moral Majority," *Women and Politics* 7 (1987): 59–77.

38. Critchlow, *Phyllis Schlafly*, 220, 222.

39. Margaret Bendroth, *Fundamentalism and Gender, 1875 to the Present* (New Haven, Conn.: Yale University Press, 1993), ch. 5.

40. Kathy E. Ferguson, "Review Essay: Women and Grassroots Organizing," *Women and Politics* 22 (2001): 98, 110. See especially Kathleen Blee, ed., *No Middle Ground: Women and Radical Protest* (New York: New York University Press, 1998); Temma Kaplan, *Crazy for Democracy: Women in Grassroots Movements* (New York: Routledge, 1997); Amy Caiazza, "The Ties That Bind: Women's Public Vision for Politics, Religion, and Civil Society," Research-in-Brief, Institute for Women's Policy Research, June 2005.

Reflections

CONTEMPORARY VIEWS FROM ABROAD

$\mathcal{I}$N LIGHT OF the international attention paid to connections between religion and politics in the United States—especially since the end of the Cold War, the terrorist attacks of September 11, 2001, and the Second Iraq War—it seemed appropriate that this book include a sampling of opinion from outside the United States. Accordingly, Mark Noll sought out individuals whom he knew were knowledgeable about U.S. history as well as current events and asked them to write brief essays, or to adapt what they had already written in their own countries, for this chapter. In every case, the editors knew something about the careful writing these authors had already published on different aspects of U.S. history, but for only one of the five did we know ahead of time what the scholar thought about the wisdom of recent U.S. policy, or the lack thereof.

As it turns out, in these contributions, criticism of recent policy prevails over commendation. It, therefore, becomes relevant to note that at least four of these essayists are associated with evangelical, or evangelical-like, movements in their native lands. They, therefore, illustrate the fact that in other parts of the world, evangelical convictions are not linked to the basically positive stance toward recent

U.S. policy that is widespread among evangelicals in this country itself. In larger perspective, the inclusion of these essays demonstrates once again that there is rarely a simple equation between a religious conviction and a predetermined attitude toward American political values or American political actions. That demonstration, in turn, sustains a major theme of the volume as a whole.

Why It Is Difficult for European Observers to Understand the Relationship between American Politics and Religion in the Twenty-First Century

Manfred Siebald

THAT EUROPEANS HAVE difficulties understanding the relationship between American religion and politics is nothing new, but their difficulties seem to have become greater since the mid-1980s, and their critical questions have been met with more frowns on the American side. Maybe their puzzlement is due to a greater degree of secularization and humanism in the Old World than in the United States. But there are even many conservative Christians in Europe who wonder at the current affiliation of religion and politics in the United States. Why is that so? Is it because they simply do not know enough—or believe the wrong things— about the history of religion in America? Or have American politics and religion indeed coalesced in an unprecedented way? I want to examine two of the tensions perceived by Europeans in the current debates: (1) between American religious diversity and the seeming current uniformity of the religiopolitical sentiment; and (2) the strained relationship between political semiotics and biblical teachings.

I

Why does American political rhetoric so often use religious concepts and vocabulary or draw upon a specifically Christian tradition today—as if there were an undisputed unity among Christians in the United States, let alone a sufficient agreement between American Christianity and the many citizens adhering to non-Christian religions? Since the old Anglocentrist idea of an American identity seems to be a thing of the past and since even the metaphor of the melting pot has given way to an image of the multicultural spicy mix, a religious uniformity in the fight against terror seems strangely out of date. And yet it is invoked again and again in spite of the United States' undeniable religious diversity.

Journalists, politicians, and even some scholars in the Old World have a hard time understanding this apparent contradiction. They cannot really fathom the religious character of a country where, in de Tocqueville's old phrase, religion is "intermingled with all national habits," because they do not understand the forces that shaped this character, forces which never occurred in European countries or were effective to a lesser degree. When my students ask me why at the four corners of some intersections in American towns they see four different Christian churches, I can offer them at least seven factors which throw light on this multifaceted picture (but which, of course are not sufficient to explain everything about Christianity, let alone the other religions in America).

From its very beginning, American religious life has been shaped by the separation of smaller religious bodies from larger bodies—the separatists, and after them the Puritans, leaving the Anglican church, then the dissenters from Puritanism (not quite voluntarily) leaving their communities, New Lights and Old Lights splitting over questions of theology and religious practice, and on and on ad infinitum. The impulse toward separation shaped religious life in America to a greater degree than was possible in Europe during the times when the prince's religion determined the religion of the whole population (*cuius regio eius religio*). A recurrent pattern of schism and church founding can be discerned in almost all subsequent phases of American history.

The various revivals—spontaneous large-scale experiences of divine grace, at first, and later, prepared, organized efforts—were not only responsible for a regeneration of spiritual fervor and for growing churches, but they also caused unrest and dissension in some old denominations which were not able to contain the new leaven. From the Great Awakening of the eighteenth century to the charismatic movement of the twentieth, revivals have consistently produced new churches and denominations. It is also rather obvious that the various waves of immigration have increased the number of church bodies. The Lutherans from Norway, Denmark, Holland, Germany, and other European countries, for example, who quite naturally wanted to live their language and their culture along with their faith, enriched religious diversity during the nineteenth century, even if later mergers diminished that diversity again. And in the context of the westward movement, settlers did not only carry their own distinct brands of faith with them, but the forces that historian Frederick Jackson Turner described in the image of the safety valve allowed some denominations and faiths to be "exported" to the unsettled regions where they were able to survive although they were not liked in the East.

Other denominations emerged through the schisms sparked by the issue of slavery. Abolitionists as well as supporters of slavery did not want to continue spiritual communion with those whose roots and traditions they had shared for a long time. Some such schisms have persisted until today—long after the original source of dissension ceased to exist. Less concentrated in a certain period but not less pronounced were the various splittings of churches over the questions that modernism posed in the field of liberal theology, in the theories of the newly emerged natural sciences that seemed to threaten traditional creeds, and in the perception of social justice or injustice.

The last factor to be mentioned, the division of church and state, can, of course, also be found in European countries. But, for example, in Germany, which is much more secularized than the United States in terms of church attendance, state and church still cooperate in such central affairs as the collection of church taxes. The noninvolvement of the American government in church matters, it has been claimed, supports the principle of free enterprise—with all of the independent denominations competing for members—and thus furthers denominational variety.

This variety is the most puzzling factor to European commentators, who wonder at the curious discrepancy between the First Amendment's separation-of-church-and-state clause and the fact that hardly any important presidential or senatorial speech closes without a "God bless America." They usually have not read Robert Bellah on civil religion and so find it hard to assess the sincerity of such phrases. In Germany, many members of government do not use the phrase "So help me God" when they take their oath of office, and only recently has a German federal president been elected (who, significantly, lived in the United States for some period of time) who is not ashamed to close a speech by saying: "Gott segne unser Land" ("God bless our country").

Together, these factors have all contributed to the creation of a religious landscape which is much more variegated than anything found in Europe. As much as many American Christians wish their nation to be a well-integrated and solidly Christian nation, to outside observers the diversity appears to be greater than the unity, and they wonder whether all Americans really share the conviction that the United States' role of superpower and guardian of the world's freedom is religiously grounded. Some hard-to-erase stereotypical notions help to increase this puzzlement. Let me give one example.

Many German books and articles about the United States start out, with a ritualistic regularity, by recollecting colonial times, in which an alleged Puritan theocracy developed a sense of mission that has been running uninterruptedly through American history and politics ever since. This conception of Puritanism is warped by the 1920s anti-Puritan bias of, for example, an H. L. Mencken, and thus these works easily trespass the fine line between ignorance and arrogance. Usually they begin by misreading John Winthrop's "A Modell of Christian Charity" (1630) as a proud, self-righteous text, a blueprint for American exceptionalism.[1] But such a reading misconstrues a lay sermon of admonition and neglects its New Testament context for the "city upon a hill," while also ignoring Winthrop's warning that a great responsibility lies in being a light to the world—and so it misses the fact that Winthrop was stressing the settlers' obedience to God's law more than any supposed chosenness of the settlers. While the misreading of such an isolated sermon would not do much harm, the decision to define this as *the* seminal text for all of American history is at least highly arbitrary.

Even if one reads the end of Winthrop's sermon as a boastful program for life in the New World, one has to ask how far the thinking of one early American Puritan was representative of the rest of the colonies. Certainly, early New England ministers like John Cotton and Edward Johnson insisted on the notion of the Puritans being a chosen people who built the new Jerusalem; this thought was then gradually secularized by Thomas Jefferson (who called "those who labor in the earth" the chosen people of God), by the nineteenth-century expansionist editor John L. O'Sullivan (who coined the phrase "manifest destiny"), and others; and it is still found, as in Ronald Reagan's articulation of a "divine mission" or Bill Clinton's reference to an "ancient vision of a promised land." But any serious view of early American history has to take into account that by 1660 divisions within the Puritan communities had eroded the movement's unity (if ever there had been any great unity at all). And if indeed Puritan thinking dominated throughout New England, the number of its inhabitants represented just two-fifths of all settlers in the American colonies by 1700. On account of the intellectual potential of its Puritan immigrants, New England may have been the most influential or at least the most vocal part of the colonies, but did the indentured servant or ex-convict who came to Virginia in the early seventeenth century also consider himself the beacon light of the world? In its search for a usable past, America appears to have inscribed a religious sense of mission into its cultural memory that has been somewhat blindly accepted by foreign observers who do not know about the many voices of individuals and groups who over the last two centuries have challenged the religious-patriotic justification of American expansion or military intervention. Americans are much too diverse in their ethnic, cultural, and religious character to allow for such a simplistic overdetermination by individual texts.

II

But should we put the blame for transatlantic misinterpretations on European ignorance alone? Has perhaps the American use of religious rhetoric in political speeches—especially after September 11, 2001, and in political debates before and during the Iraq War—contributed to the confusion through ambiguity, selective reasoning, and the amalgamation of religious and secular values? After the first wave of unprecedented and genuine solidarity following the horrible 9/11 attacks, many people in many parts of the world have increasingly questioned the religious overtones of the arguments heard from the White House. The pronouncements of both politicians and church leaders have increased this effect: the former by claiming divine sanction for their actions and the latter by endorsing such actions with theological arguments.

From a German perspective at least, the way in which, at the beginning of the twenty-first century, American politicians speak of being divinely guided in their decisions when declaring war on terror and on countries harboring terrorists, is a very ambiguous move—and for obvious reasons. It is an uncanny reminder of the time that remains blacker than black in German history, and of the man whose invocation of "providence" helped him to lord it over the German masses in his destructive scheme.

This comparison may sound inappropriate, and indeed it is. The framework of political values and control mechanisms at work in the United States today is totally different from that of Nazi Germany, but phenomenologically the comparison offers itself to modern-day Germans because there is something lodged in our cultural memory which Americans should at least acknowledge as a safeguard against the abuse of political powers. Having been successfully taught by American reeducators after World War II to detest racism, nationalism, and imperialism, Germans remain distrustful of political points of reference that are not accessible to critical inspection.

Apart from such historically rooted misgivings, two kinds of theological doubts also arise about the current American religiopolitical discourse. They are doubts, it is significant to note, that are shared by quite a few evangelical Christians in Germany, among whom I number myself. Seen from a distance, the current conjunction of religious convictions and political practice betrays a good deal of selectivity. No evangelical Christian doubts in theory that one's faith should lead to consequences in one's actions. But should faith in action not include all facets of Christian belief: compassion, for example, and charity, the willingness to share and the readiness to suffer? To put it in ethical terms: recent American politics has all too often been preoccupied with such cardinal virtues as fortitude and justice rather than the theological virtues of faith, hope, and love. One might also say that when American politicians refer to the Bible, they frequently breathe more Old Testament than New Testament.

On the part of American evangelical ministers, the message preached to the individual often sounds different from the message preached to society as a whole, or to the international community. Individually, the evangelical call is to repent, to accept Christ as one's personal savior, and to live a life of sanctification and charity. But collectively, some American evangelicals in leading positions seem to have a markedly different agenda, and this is where I see a problem. A certain kind of politics may be necessary in a fallen world, but then it should not be represented as being the only evangelical solution.

Some sermons preached in the wake of September 11 had a strong taste of "the crown without the cross," of a prematurely triumphant instead of a still-struggling ecclesia. Does the church of Christ, and do Christian politicians, have any right to expect ultimate success and glory on earth? At the Lausanne Conference on World Evangelization, which was held in Switzerland in 1974 under the sponsorship of the Billy Graham Evangelistic Association, a covenant was signed by Christian believers from over 150 countries represented at that remarkably diverse international meeting. As a participant, I signed this covenant, which is still considered one of the leading documents of modern evangelical theology. It insists, on one hand, on "freedom of thought and conscience" but states, on the other hand: "We do not forget the warnings of Jesus that persecution is inevitable." Ignoring this scriptural caveat can lead to an unsound reliance on human strength—as if persecution, injustice, and aggression could be wiped from the face of the earth through the use of military power.

What also troubles some European observers of the relationship between American politics and religion is what, for want of a better term, I would like to call the *amalgamation* of values. This amalgamation refers to the way in which originally secular values have made their way into religious discourse and gradually taken on the character of spiritual values. For example, nobody in Western societies will deny that democracy is the best political system available, that political liberty is one of the basic prerequisites of a well-functioning society, and that civilization is to be preferred to barbarism and brutality. Germany has every reason to be grateful for its liberation from totalitarianism and for a democratic constitution—both having been achieved through the United States' involvement in World War II. But are democracy and liberty and civilization, which are now so freely invoked in American sermons and political speeches alike, really foundational or essential Christian values?

It seems to me that the amalgamation of Enlightenment concepts (as they were formalized in American history) and Christian virtues creates a mélange of values that are hard to distinguish for citizens of non-Christian (or post-Christian) and nondemocratic societies. I am again reminded of the Lausanne covenant, which claims that the church "must not be identified with any particular culture, social or political system, or human ideology." Whether one applies this warning to the current situation or not, it encourages great watchfulness whenever the Christian faith is in danger of being infused with terms that clearly have secular roots.

WHY IS IT so hard—even for well-meaning Europeans—to understand the current relationship between American politics and religion, and for Americans to comprehend European criticism of that relationship? It is not only because Europeans tend to underestimate the complexity of American religious history and cannot make sense of the sometimes contradictory implications of the separation of church and state. It is also because of ambiguous gestures, selective reasoning, and the amalgamation of secular and spiritual values on the part of the Americans. As the noted student of American Puritanism, Samuel Eliot Morison, once observed, "it is always easier to condemn an alien way of life than to understand it"; both Europeans and Americans would be well advised to examine more closely the religious convictions and pronouncements on the other side of the Atlantic—as well as their own—and to anticipate the ways in which their rhetoric will be received elsewhere.

NOTE

1. This sermon is quoted by Massimo Rubboli, p. 402 below.

American Civil Religion and George W. Bush

Sébastien Fath

In the days immediately following the attacks against the World Trade Center and the Pentagon on September 11, 2001, an immense wave of emotion swept over the world, including Europe and specifically France. Jean-Marie Colombani wrote in *Le Monde* on September 13, "We are all Americans," and a poll by Ipsos-LePoint-BFM showed that 70 percent of the French approved "the posture of George Bush after the attacks of September 11." On September 19, Jacques Chirac offered a wreath of flowers at Union Square in New York City in memory of the victims. Along with the flowers, he brought the tribute of the French people who had been "terribly shocked and traumatized by these events." The president of the French republic was thus the first head of a foreign state to meet with George W. Bush after the attacks. In the two weeks that followed that fateful day, 8,000 letters of solidarity arrived at the Peace Memorial in Caen, the principal site for commemorating the battles for the liberation of France in 1944–1945. For a new generation of French citizens, the shocking images of the New York skyline plumed with black smoke reawakened the memory of the GIs' sacrifice on the beaches of Normandy. In those days of trial, the people of France and of the United States once more had found a common community of values.

Three years later, what had become of this sympathy and this almost unlimited solidarity? For nine French citizens out of ten, the White House had come to inspire mistrust about the future unmatched by attitudes toward any European country. In a reversal of 180 degrees, Jean-Marie Colombani now asked, "Is Everyone Non-American?" (*Le Monde*, May 15, 2004). In the intervening years, the Rubicon had been crossed. The Second Iraq War, begun in 2003 at the command of the White House against the advice of the Security Council of the United Nations, has seemed to change things irreversibly. The 10 million demonstrators who on February 15, 2003, marched in different sites around the world in favor of a peaceful solution did not change the course of history. Against the opinion of a majority of the world's states and based on an argument founded on two great mistakes,[1] Uncle Sam invaded a sovereign state, destroyed its administrative infrastructure, privatized its economy, and set up military occupation—and all for the sake of preserving American security (through a preventive war) and for the sake of democracy (by ending the tyranny of Saddam Hussein). With this political fait accompli, the United States in just a few months squandered an immense capital of sympathy; in the process, it also alienated the international community. How did this happen? To read the French and European press, the mutual incomprehension that has developed on both sides of the Atlantic is tied up with one key matter above all: religion. From a European perspective, the White House is thought to be held hostage by a band of religious fanatics for whom today's international realities cannot be understood except as issuing from the Bible.

In the rest of this short essay, I try to show where the common European opinion is based on fact and where it falls short of American reality. I do so by sketching the main themes of America's civil religion as they appear to this one French observer and then by looking more closely at the development of one of those themes in the presidency of George W. Bush. The conclusion to which these comments point is that American religion and politics have moved into new and dangerous territory, but also that close attention must be paid to the character of that religion.

Since 1945, America's civil religion has been visible along five axes, but of course with nearly limitless variations.[2] The first of these themes rests on the mythic events at the foundation of WASP (white Anglo-Saxon Protestant) religious culture. If this theme has become slightly less important since the 1960s, it nonetheless remains an essential component of the imagined community of the United States. The Thanksgiving holiday is its ritual epicenter. For many Americans, Thanksgiving remains *the* family holiday, even more so than Christmas. It is the day of the year when economic activity ceases in favor of festive gathering, in thanksgiving for the blessings that God has lavished upon his children. For many Americans, the contemporary prosperity of the United States remains confusedly associated with the necessity of faithfulness to the religious principles of the first colonists. But Thanksgiving, as a primarily mythic recollection of the foundation of American civil religion, is complemented by several other rituals.

Among these, the Pledge of Allegiance is doubtless most important. When those who recite the pledge refer to the United States as "one nation under God," they evoke a Puritan ideal (though to the fury of atheists who feel discriminated against by this phrase). Another manifestation of this theme is reference to the founders' "old-time religion," a particular emphasis of conservative Protestants of an evangelical and fundamentalist type.

The preacher Billy Graham, chief maestro of American civil religion since the 1950s, has made a specialty of energizing these founding myths—but in his case, usually accompanied by exhortations as well. For example, when in May 1996, Graham received the Congressional Medal of Honor, he said that Americans were wandering on the wrong path and that they needed "to change course," to repent, and to "consecrate our lives to God and to the principles that made this country great." After September 11, 2001, any number of preachers, including Graham, said the same thing in virtually the same words.

A second major theme of American civil religion is the accent on faith and prayer. This is not just a theme, but also a practice, and a practice present in profusion after September 11. When it looks as if the foundations of American society are under threat by an adversary—for whatever reason—American citizens are asked by their presidents to prevail in prayer. The oath which all presidents take upon entering office in the presence of a rabbi, a pastor, and a bishop focuses on faith and prayer. This revered rite of American public life puts politics symbolically very close to transcendence.

It is the same with the national prayer breakfast, which millions of television viewers witness each year. This annual event, held since 1953, gathers the American political aristocracy with a number of invited religious leaders. Its main activity is to pray, publicly, for the United States. The National Day of Prayer, first authorized by Congress in 1952 and fixed by an amendment under President Ronald Reagan for the first Thursday of May, constitutes another event that cannot be missed. Although prayer in the public schools has been banned since a decision by the Supreme Court in 1963, it has never left the political arena.

Even if prayer is often practiced communally, it also illustrates the individualism that constitutes a third key to contemporary American civil religion. This emphasis, which is heard almost as much from politicians and business leaders as from preachers, centers on the role of individuals in fulfilling their responsibilities: prosperity or misery, life eternal or eternal death, hang above all on individual choice. Evangelical preachers like Billy Graham have especially encouraged this individualistic approach since their theological culture is measured above all by conversion, an individual act in and of itself. The larger confluence of political culture and American religion is based on the conviction of the moral autonomy of the individual: the "self-made man" echoes the "self-made saint." It is of course necessary to distinguish among different kinds of individualism. The cultural meaning of evangelical revivalism is not the same as what was practiced during the golden age of Puritan New England, nor is it the same as the consumerist discourse that became so prevalent in the twentieth century. Nonetheless, at the broadest level, American civil religion exalts today the individual decision as a dogma, however far removed from the strictly predestinarian convictions of the first Puritan Calvinists.

A fourth theme of contemporary American civil religion is the providential universalism seen in the old commitment to manifest destiny. Free and Christian America is thought to be supported by a prophetic and messianic special mission. The United States is a beacon for the world and will never be thrust into the darkness. Justice and happiness are at stake in messianism, according to a definition provided by Henri Desroche: it is "the religious belief in the coming of a redeemer who puts an end to the contemporary order of things, whether for all time or for a particular group, and who inaugurates a new order of justice and happiness."[3] For Americans, there has rarely been a doubt about the active role their country can play alongside the divine redeemer. Robert Bellah, for example, has cited a significant statement from President John Kennedy about the work of God being done on earth "by our hands" as a famous, typical example.[4] The choice of the national motto "In God We Trust" registers this messianic conviction. When adopted under President Dwight Eisenhower, it was intended to affirm loudly and clearly the pious confidence of Uncle Sam in the face of the atheistic red menace that threatened, in American understanding, the stability of the world. Alongside Thanksgiving Day, the national celebration of Memorial Day in late May (in memory of those who have died for America) and the national celebration of July 4 (in honor of independence) make up the civic rituals of memory for those who gave themselves so that the messianic ideal would not be defeated.

Finally, optimism constitutes a last constitutive element of contemporary American civil religion. The mission that God has given to the United States is its own guarantee of success, because God is almighty. Will not the one who divided the Red Sea in order to make a way for the elect people not also triumph in the same way against adversaries today? Even in the dark days that followed September 11, this irreducible optimism was still present. At the time of the dramatic national ceremony of September 14, 2001, Billy Graham concluded his sermon by expressing the hope that September 11 would come to be viewed as "a day of victory," if America used the occasion to return to God. This kind of optimism—this determination to rebuild, this belief that *we will prevail*—stands in the great revival tradition of confidence that conversion will lead to a regeneration of the nation. This ineradicable optimism—which is admirable from one angle but insufferable from another—undergirds American society. Its effects can be seen inwardly in the American entrepreneurial ethos, but also outwardly in the conviction (often bordering on naïveté) that no people—in this case, Iraqis at the end of the Saddam years—could remain indifferent to the individualistic and democratic values that the United States wanted to bestow upon them. This universalistic conviction can hardly be perceived as anything but ethnocentric. It is marked by a profound difficulty in grasping the historical conditions of another society and by a tendency to hubris. In his own time, Alexis de Tocqueville already wrote about this optimistic propensity of Americans to push back indefinitely the boundaries of human perfectibility.

In the recent past, one can trace three main stages in the history of American civil religion, which has nonetheless differed substantially depending on the dominant religious emphasis of the times. From the presidency of Woodrow Wilson (1913–1921) through the presidency of Dwight D. Eisenhower (1953–1961), American civil religion was predominately shaped by the mainline Protestant churches—that is, the older, established denominations from the upper classes, who exercised special influence from their centers of cultural power on the East Coast. In the 1950s, in part because of their support for the Cold War, Catholics began to share this public space, especially as illustrated by the presidency of John F. Kennedy (1961–1963).

But from the 1960s, the tone that came to prevail in expressing civil religion arose from Protestants of an evangelical type—that is, from Protestants defined by an emphasis on conversion, marked by a militant biblicism, and stressing a model of the church defined as an elective fraternity. As opposed to mainline Protestantism, this type of evangelicalism comes from the margins of the older established denominations. It favors the individual more than the institution, the local group more than infrastructure, concrete engagement more than theology. Marked by the tradition of the frontier, it has classically valorized the "new birth." On the basis of this sensibility, the preacher Billy Graham, with his exceptional popularity, has remained a major influence in the public sphere for over a half-century. The charisma of the person, his identification with evangelical middle America, and his irenic stance toward politicians help to explain his special influence.

On first appearance, it would seem that with George W. Bush, who has presented himself for many years as sharing evangelical piety, we have an example from this evangelical world. The former governor of Texas and a Methodist by denomination, Bush has never hidden the fact that, following an encounter with Graham in 1985, he experienced a renewed faith that led him to give up alcohol. He practices daily prayer and reading from the Bible. He considers his presidential service as a vocation received from God, leads national prayer breakfasts, and often uses religious or religiously tinged language. And so he is often portrayed in the media as a typical evangelical.

But on closer inspection, even when viewed from France, it seems just as obvious that George W. Bush is driven as much by his pragmatic instincts as by anything distinctly religious. Evidence abounds throughout his career in Texas as well as in Washington that he is motivated by much more than religion. Many commentators at home and abroad have, for instance, spotlighted his intense fixation on results, his proven ability at winning political battles, his demand for loyalty from subordinates, his preference for simple, direct analyses, and even his private use of salty language. These traits point to a disposition that led Bob Woodward of the *Washington Post* to say that the president's "instinct is practically his second religion" and to speak of the president in terms of his "secular faith."[5]

With the Bush presidency, in other words, we come to a third phase of American civil religion which incorporates themes from the mainline Protestant and evangelical Protestant phases, but which tends to project a predominately pragmatic cast.

This pragmatic streak takes on a special form with respect to the messianic theme of civil religion. It is illustrated by the spectacular trajectory in American interventionism from 1917 (World War I) to the period after September 11, 2001. If it is impossible to doubt that a religious element plays a role in the current exercise of American power, it is also impossible to equate that element with what was found in earlier eras. At the time of the First World War, President Wilson proposed an ideal international order in which altruism was to prevail over nationalism. Even for Presidents Jimmy Carter and George H. W. Bush, the religious element was linked to international multilateralism. The movement over the course of the twentieth century, however, was away from the context of Judeo-Christian values in which American messianism originally grew and prospered. This movement justifies the suggestion that a new phase of civil religion has appeared, a more secular phase that is further removed from Christianity itself. Traditionally, viewing life in tension with a transcendent deity encouraged a sense of self-limitation; with greater attention to immanence, the stress shifts to utopian salvation.

In the Western world, the final resolution of the tragic problem of evil has always rested with the one God; it seems now to be taken over by Uncle Sam. In December 2003, Richard Perle, éminence grise of Washington's neoconservatives (and until March 2003 chair of the Defense Policy Board appointed by President Bush), published with his colleague David Frum a work with an eloquent title: *An End to Evil: How to Win the War on Terror.* An end to evil! Compared to the Manichaeanism of this work—its sharp division of the world into powers of good and evil—even Rambo seems like only a nervous nelly.

In 1975, Robert Bellah suggested that American civil religion was becoming an "empty and broken shell" and that spiritual and cultural changes in the United States were giving birth to a new American myth.[6] At the beginning of the twenty-first century, it seems that what Bellah foresaw is becoming reality, though not as he foresaw it. What has happened is the emergence of civil religion in a new shape that tends to identify general worldwide divinity with America itself. But can one still label something as messianism when it is so far removed from its Judeo-Christian roots? Yes, if one follows Henri Desroche, for whom messianisms designate "situations where a founding leader of a historic movement of social-religious liberation is identified with a Supreme Power descending on a particular group or society."[7] The "supreme power" in this perspective is not necessarily the Christian messiah. It can designate a secular form where a nation tries to shock the order of the world for the purpose of emancipation. But in order to identify this model with the Christian messianism of the Puritans, it is necessary to add the prefix *neo-*. Neomessianism describes precisely this contemporary utopian American model that is invested essentially with attributes of the supreme power.

When observing the mutations of the American superpower since 2001, many commentators have leapt to emphasize religious faith. That emphasis seems true and false at the same time. Above all, the pragmatism of the White House, given expression in a pluralistic society, invalidates the hypothesis that American power is held hostage by a missionary-minded belief in God. It is also obvious that influence from denominational or religious lobbies does not determine the essential political agenda of the United States. But it is not wrong to see religious faith as very important, if one understands civil religion as explaining a substitution at the heart of the ideological legitimization of American society. My main argument involves the transition of this civil religion, now substantially decoupled from its traditional Christian anchorage. This new phase—which is therefore an uncertain phase—has been marked by a substitution of Uncle Sam's armed forces for the Christian messiah. The transcendent utopia of the kingdom of God has been secularized into a finite model: contemporary American society itself.

NOTES

This essay is adapted from my book *Dieu bénisse l'Amérique: La religion de la Maison-Blanche* [God Bless America: The Religion of the White House] (Paris: Éditions du Seuil, 2004).

1. See Hans Blix (former head of UN inspections in Iraq), *Irak: Armes introuvables* [Iraq: The Arms That Could Not Be Found] (Paris: Fayard, 2004); and the Carnegie Endowment for International Peace, *WMD in Iraq: Evidence and Implications* (New York: Carnegie Endowment, 2004).
2. For theoretical discussion of the notion of "civil religion," see Fath, *Dieu bénisse l'Amérique*, 47–53.

3. Henri Desroche, *Dieux d'hommes: Dictionnaire des messianismes et millenarismes de l'ere chrétienne* [Gods from Men: Dictionary of Messianisms and Millenarianisms of the Christian Era] (Paris: Mouton/EPHE, 1969), 7.

4. Robert Bellah, "La Religion civile en Amérique," *Archives de Sociologie des Religions* 35 (1975): 10.

5. Bob Woodward, *Bush at War* (New York: Simon and Schuster, 2002).

6. Robert Bellah, *The Broken Covenant: American Civil Religion in Time of Trial* (New York: Seabury, 1973), 139–63.

7. Desroche, *Dieux d'hommes*, 7.

Crusade for Freedom, Exportation of the American Model, and George W. Bush's Second Inaugural Address

Massimo Rubboli

$\mathcal{O}$N JANUARY 20, 2005, despite the protest of those who considered it an insult to the more than 1,360 American soldiers already dead in Iraq, George W. Bush chose to open his second term as president with a sumptuous ceremony of investiture. The triumphal entry of the new president into the capital had been reintroduced by Ronald Reagan in 1981, after a temporary gust of simplicity from 1977 had marked the inauguration of Jimmy Carter, who simply walked down Pennsylvania Avenue with his wife to their new residence in the White House. For President Bush, parades, gala dinners, dances, and fireworks celebrated a world divorced from reality, and the president's address also contributed to this unreal atmosphere.[1]

Forty years before, historian Arthur Schlesinger, Jr., had expressed a quite negative judgment on the speeches delivered by the presidents of the United States on inauguration day: "Even in the field of political oratory, the inaugural address is an inferior art form. It is rarely an occasion for original thought or stimulating reflection. The platitude quotient tends to be high, the rhetoric stately and self-serving, the ritual obsessive, and the surprises few."[2]

Whatever one makes of Schlesinger's judgment, the analysis of inaugural addresses as ritual pronouncements for a ritual occasion can nonetheless be an interesting exercise, not so much for understanding the political strategies of a president as for detecting constitutive elements of American political culture. Under the categories of "permanent" and "transitory,"[3] for instance, it can be observed that presidential inaugurals feature recurring themes that are central to the American cultural and political tradition, and also that these permanent themes are quite significant, whatever one might conclude about the transitory nature of the political program of any single president.

If we consider the speech of investiture as a privileged carrier of American ideology, we can observe how, over the course of American history, it has been used by presidents to solidify national consensus through the reaffirmation of commonplaces, ideals, values, and myths. In their different circumstances, presidential addresses recycle and mix, in variable proportions, reality and myth, and thereby forge a distorted image of reality designed to meet two primary requirements. The first is to legitimate the president at the time of his formal acceptance of office, which is a very important function considering the uncertainties of democratic political representation. The second is to encourage the nation in facing the difficulties of the moment, which may include economic crisis, racial tension, war, and much more.

In this light, it is understandable why in January 2005 Bush did not mention Iraq and the enormous tragedy into which he had dragged the United States. Yet in so doing he was following a well-established precedent. During the Vietnam War, there were four inaugurals, and none of the presidents mentioned the conflict in Southeast Asia. Instead, they chose to concentrate on defending the principles that were most sacred to the national community, which usually meant a concentration on "liberty." In Bush's second inaugural speech, the term occurred fifteen times, while the synonym "freedom" occurred twenty-seven times. The United States, the president solemnly stated, would defend not only its own liberty, but the liberty of others as well. Yet when observers outside the United States look at the way the United States has in recent years carried out the defense of freedom and democracy, the president's promise to promote the cause of freedom everywhere has given rise as much to worldwide fear and anxiety as to hope and security.

Yet Bush was not doing anything new. By choosing the theme of liberty as the guiding thread of his address, the president (and his chief speechwriter, Michael Gerson) was only appealing to one of the foundational concepts of American political discourse. As historian Eric Foner has observed:

[N]o idea is more fundamental to Americans' sense of themselves as individuals and as a nation than freedom. The central term in our political vocabulary, "freedom"—or "liberty," with which it is almost always used interchangeably—is deeply embedded in the documentary record of our history and the language of everyday life.[4]

In the Declaration of Independence, Thomas Jefferson designated liberty, together with life and the search for happiness, as humankind's inalienable rights, and he asserted that these rights were "endowed by [the] Creator." In Jefferson's foundational document, liberty was defined in opposition to tyranny, in fact "the absolute tyranny" of the English monarchy. So it was also in Bush's second inaugural, where he five times contrasted "liberty"—or "freedom"—to "tyranny" and two more times to "oppression."

American political and religious discourse has also been permeated with a concept of the chosen nation, an elect people, to whom a great mission has been entrusted. As many have pointed out, this idea of national election can be traced back to a metaphor used by John Winthrop in a sermon ("A Modell of Christian Charity") preached in 1630 aboard the flagship *Arbella* that was leading the Puritan expedition toward the promised land: "for wee must Consider that wee shall be as a Citty upon a Hill, the eies of all people are uppon us."[5] The biblical metaphor, which originally referred to the individual believer, was applied by Winthrop to a group of believers united by a "covenant," a community of "saints" to whom God had entrusted a historical mission to be "a New Israel in a New Canaan."[6] The Puritans symbolically had "discovered America in the Bible," that is, had found the meaning of America "in the [biblical] promises."[7] Since its origins, the myth of America, which was fully elaborated in 1702 in a book entitled *Magnalia Christi Americana* by the Boston minister Cotton Mather, has come to be applied to the United States. At many times and at different levels of intensity, it has functioned as an identifying model that dissolved old connections while creating new obligations. First in England, then in New England, and finally in the new American nation, the Puritans and their heirs came to perceive themselves as "God's New Israel," a "city upon a hill," and a "people united by a covenant," with a special destiny and mission. The biblical metaphor first employed by Winthrop has been repeated hundreds of times in political addresses, from early in the nation's history to one of Ronald Reagan's last speeches, where he stated that the United States was a "shining city upon a hill."[8]

For my argument, it is relevant to recall that this metaphor has been interpreted in two different ways. In the earliest days of the nation, the concept prevailed in terms of an example for the world of virtue and liberty; thus, the nation was defined by Jefferson as an "empire for liberty" and an "empire of liberty."[9] Later, in the era of Andrew Jackson, the notion of example led to the concept of "manifest destiny" where the United States was held to have been entrusted with a mission of propagating liberty and democracy.[10] Inevitably, warfare came to be viewed in relation to this mission, as was the case with the "war to end all wars," the slogan used by President Woodrow Wilson to justify the United States' intervention in the First World War, or in the "four freedoms," invoked by Franklin D. Roosevelt to support the United States' participation in the Second World War.

More than three-quarters of presidential inaugural addresses have referred to this special mission, starting from the very first, pronounced by George Washington in St. Paul's Chapel in New York on April 30, 1789 (a particularly frigid winter had made it impossible to observe the prescribed date of March 4): "the preservation of the sacred fire of liberty and the destiny of the republican model of government are justly considered, perhaps, as deeply, as finally, staked on the experiment entrusted to the hands of the American people."[11] These same words were quoted by Franklin D. Roosevelt at the beginning of his third term on January 20, 1941.

In 1897, William McKinley declared that the "glorious history" of the nation had "advanced the cause of freedom throughout the world,"[12] before he added that the United States refused to entangle itself in wars of conquest.[13] The fact that, only one year later, the United States declared war on Spain, occupied Cuba, and put down an independence movement in the Philippines—with Filipinos sarcastically chastised by Mark Twain for not thankfully accepting the generous American offering of the "Blessings of Civilization"[14]—does not contradict what McKinley affirmed. Rather, it confirms that he was enunciating a permanent principle of American political culture rather than a transitory element of a particular political moment.

More recently, in 1977, Jimmy Carter inaugurated his presidency by stating, "Because we are free we can never be indifferent to the fate of freedom elsewhere."[15] And Ronald Reagan, in his first inaugural address (January 20, 1981), declared that the United States was "special among the nations of the Earth.... It is time for us to realize that we are too great a nation to limit ourselves to small dreams.... We are a nation under God, and I believe God intended for us to be free."[16]

This enduringly traditional conviction has been repeated by President George W. Bush. For example, at a meeting of the National Endowment for Democracy in November 2003, he affirmed that the United States was trying "to promote liberty around the world" because

liberty is both the plan of Heaven for humanity, and the best hope for
progress here on earth. . . . The advance of freedom is the calling of our
time . . . , the calling of our country. . . . We believe that liberty is the
design of nature; we believe that liberty is the direction of history. . . .
And we believe that freedom . . . is not for us alone, it is the right and the
capacity of all mankind.[17]

This theme Bush reaffirmed in his second inaugural address by speaking of
"the mission that created our Nation." To be sure, he did introduce complexity
into his address by seeming to repudiate the concept of the United States as God's
uniquely elect nation: "Not because we consider ourselves a chosen nation; God
moves and chooses as He wills." But subsequent references in the speech to the
"Author of Liberty," along with the general tone of the whole, partook of the
conviction that the United States, if it were not the "chosen nation," was at least an
almost-chosen nation invested with a divine mission. Not only that. The messianic text of Isaiah 61:1 ("the Lord hath anointed me . . . to proclaim liberty to the
captives"), which in the Gospels Jesus applied to himself (Luke 4:18: "he hath
anointed me . . . to preach deliverance to the captives"), is employed to charge the
United States with a mission that the biblical text assigns to the Messiah, in
particular the liberation of prisoners ("whenever America acts for good . . . the
captives are set free") and the universal proclamation of liberty ("America . . .
proclaims liberty throughout all the world, and to all the inhabitants thereof").

While President Bush should not be charged with using religious language
only for opportunism, and while it should not be denied that some of his personal
decisions are influenced by his own religious beliefs, the fact remains that the
principal choices of his administration, especially in foreign policy, seem to be
dictated by motivations and interests that have more to do with realpolitik (viz.,
balance of power, oil, terrorism) than with religion. Foreign policy guidelines for
the Bush administration have been published in documents like *The National
Security Strategy* of September 2002; *Differentiation and Defense: An Agenda for the
Nuclear Weapons Program* of February 2003; and *Winning the Peace in the 21st
Century* of October 2003. These documents do not contain religious term or
references. However, since the language of political analysis is not suitable for
mass communications like the inaugural address, this president, like his predecessors, has resorted to forms of (religious) language on those occasions more
comprehensible and better able to establish a popular consensus.

Obviously, each president weighs differently the decision about how and
how often to refer to God and also the use of other religious language and imagery. But none has been able completely to avoid it.

In conclusion, as an Italian historian, I refrain from expressing positive or negative political judgments, even if I have no sympathy for America's prophetic interventionist mission. But as an evangelical Protestant, I must register my resentment at the identification of George W. Bush with evangelical Christianity that has become so common in the American and in the Italian mass media. Although I would call his rhetoric more "biblical Americanism" than "biblical Christianity," I find it objectionable that some of his speeches, especially after the terrorist attacks of September 11, 2001, have distorted the meaning of biblical passages and evangelical hymns, for example, "There's power, wonder-working power," which was quoted in the 2003 State of the Union address.

Historically considered, the religious rhetoric of Bush's second inaugural was simply an extension of the long tradition of American civil religion, which has now become inclusive enough to place "the words of the Koran, and the varied faiths of our people" beside "the truths of Sinai" and "the Sermon on the Mount" as sacred scripts of this national religion.

NOTES

1. "President Sworn-In to Second Term," www.whitehouse.gov/news/releases/2005/01 (accessed 5 Feb. 2005).
2. A. M. Schlesinger, Jr., *The Chief Executive: Inaugural Addresses of the Presidents of the United States from George Washington to Lyndon B. Johnson* (New York: Crown, 1965), iv.
3. David F. Erickson, "Presidential Inaugural Addresses and American Political Culture," *Presidential Studies Quarterly* 27 (1997).
4. Eric Foner, *The Story of American Freedom* (New York: Norton, 2000), xiii.
5. John Winthrop, "A Modell of Christian Charity" (1630), in *God's New Israel: Religious Interpretations of American Destiny*, rev. ed., ed. Conrad Cherry (Chapel Hill: University of North Carolina Press, 1998), 40. On historic views of American national election, see William Haller, *Foxe's Book of Martyrs and the Elect Nation* (London: Jonathan Cape, 1963); Ernest Lee Tuveson, *Redeemer Nation: The Idea of America's Millennial Role* (Chicago: University of Chicago Press, 1968); and Cherry, *God's New Israel*.
6. Sacvan Bercovitch, "The Biblical Basis of the American Myth," in *The Bible and American Arts and Letters*, ed. Giles Gunn (Philadelphia: Fortress, 1983), 222.
7. Ibid., 223.
8. Ronald Reagan, *Farewell Address to the Nation*, 11 Jan. 1989. Reagan imprecisely defined Winthrop as "an early Pilgrim," http://www.ronaldreagan.com/sp_21.html (accessed 6 Feb. 2005).
9. The phrase "empire for liberty" is from a letter written by Jefferson to James Madison on 27 Apr. 1809 (*The Writings of Thomas Jefferson*, 20 vols. [Washington, D.C.: Thomas Jefferson Memorial Association, 1904], 12:277), and "empire of liberty" is

from a letter of Jefferson to George R. Clark of 25 Dec. 1780 (*The Papers of Thomas Jefferson*, 31 vols. [Princeton, N.J.: Princeton University Press, 1951], 4:238). Jefferson did not think of "empire" as imperial power but rather as an independent body politick.

10. See, among others, Albert K. Weinberg, *Manifest Destiny: A Study of Nationalist Expansionism in American History* (Baltimore, Md.: Johns Hopkins University Press, 1935); Frederick Merk, *Manifest Destiny and Mission in American History* (New York: Random House, 1963); and Anders Stephanson, *Manifest Destiny: American Expansion and the Empire of Right* (New York: Hill and Wang, 1995).

11. *Inaugural Addresses of the Presidents of the United States: From George Washington, 1789, to George Bush, 1989* (Washington, D.C.: U.S. Government Printing Office, 1989), 3–4.

12. Ibid., 197.

13. Ibid., 200.

14. Mark Twain, *To the Person Sitting in Darkness* (New York: Anti-Imperialist League of New York, 1901).

15. Jimmy Carter, "Inaugural Address," 20 Jan. 1977, www.yale.edu/lawweb/avalon/presiden/inaug/carter.htm (accessed 6 Feb. 2005).

16. Ronald Reagan, "First Inaugural Address," 20 Jan. 1981, www.bartleby.com/124/pres61.html (accessed 6 Feb. 2005).

17. "President Bush Discusses Freedom in Iraq and Middle East," remarks by the president at the 20th Anniversary of the National Endowment for Democracy, 6 Nov. 2003, www.whitehouse.gov/news/releases/2003/11/print/20031106-2.html (accessed 7 Feb. 2005).

For God's Sake? American Religion and Politics Viewed from Denmark

Bente Clausen

THE RELATIONSHIP BETWEEN church and state in Denmark would be unconstitutional from an American point of view. In contrast to the separation outlined in the United States' First Amendment to the Bill of Rights, the Danish Constitution states: "The Evangelical Lutheran Church is the Church of the Danish

People and as such it is supported by the State." Before explaining Danish views on American religion, it is relevant to sketch a simplified explanation of the Danish religious model. Understanding a little bit about this model helps to explain why Danes view American religion as they do, though of course the opinions expressed here are my own; I cannot claim to speak on behalf of 5 million people.

In Denmark, the Lutheran church is the church of the Danish people. Since the year of our constitution in 1849, no majority in Parliament, which legislates on church matters and other religious concerns, has found this church-state relation to be troublesome enough to question.

Parliament and probably a majority of the Danish people find this model the best way to prevent religion from interfering with politics: religion is under control. Religion is also considered a private affair. Most Danes would rather share intimate details of their sex lives than get into a debate about personal faith. Yet since the beginning of the twenty-first century, we have begun to witness a growing interest in questions of religion and society, first and foremost in connection with Islam.

The Danish Lutheran church perceives itself as a tolerant church. In practice, this means that under the same umbrella you find the religious Right (which is usually the political Left) and the religious Left (which is often the political Right) (that is, the church takes in all shades of religious opinion, and, unlike the United States, theologically conservative Danish Lutherans are often politically liberal, and vice versa). Danish church life does not have any representative with influence equaling what Jerry Falwell or James Dobson have exercised in the United States. The majority of pastors are theologically in the middle. The ideal of tolerance is of a broad institution that leaves space for almost everybody baptized in the church; it includes a tradition where no one, including the bishops, presumes to speak on behalf of the church. There is no national church council. Tolerance also means that there are minority rights in the church, which are mainly exercised by those on the Right, since members of the Left do not have the same concerns with socioreligious issues as part of their faith. Pastors can refuse to bless homosexual couples who prior to the blessing have had a civil wedding. Pastors can also refuse to wed divorcees. The religious Right threatened to leave the church in 1948 when female pastors were authorized. But Parliament pushed through the law despite protests and probably will do the same in the future with legislation allowing homosexuals to marry in church. My best guess is that, when this happens, the religious Right, apart from establishing a few free churches, will remain within the historic church family.

Eighty-three percent of Danes are members of the Lutheran church. Most are what we call "four-wheel Christians," who attend church when they are

baptized as infants, at confirmation, to be married, and finally for their funeral. Most find outspoken religiousness embarrassing, perhaps even a sign of
fundamentalism—which explains some of the political and clerical criticism of
Islam. Church attendance stands at less than 2 percent. Pastors are educated at the
universities, which are free. And they are employed by the Ministry of Church.
Financially, most are paid from church taxes, which are drawn at a rate of 1
percent from the tax bills of members. But all Danes, whether church members or
not, support the church financially: 40 percent of the pastors' wages (and their
pensions) plus 100 percent of the bishops' wages and pensions are funded by
everybody, regardless of religion. Danes who are not Lutherans can claim their
contributions to church, temple, mosque, or synagogue as tax-free up to a specified amount.

With this church structure, the Danish system is not too much different
from other European nations. They all believe that theirs is the best system. Danes
believe that their system keeps religion in its proper social and political place.

The original idea that faith is a private matter has not altered, but today, to
be sure, religion is more obvious in the public sphere. Young Muslims born and
raised in Denmark claim religious rights and religious freedom. Their claim is
that how specific questions are answered—like whether head scarves should be
allowed at places of employment, whether there should be a prayer room in
schools and workplaces, or whether there should be isolated showers in gyms—
affects their religious freedom. A group of Catholics has recently gone to court
because they believe some aspects of the historic system discriminate against non-
Lutherans. More generally, it is slowly occurring not only to Danes, but to all
Northern Europeans, that on a world scale the secular approach is the peculiar
one, not the norm. Yet that realization does not change the convictions that the
secular system is the best system for maintaining every citizen's rights and that
religion is best kept out of politics. Since a thorough knowledge of religion and
religious feeling is widely lacking in Parliament and among the public, it means
that debates over religion, including religion and politics, easily become rather
mushy. The cartoon crisis—involving questions of self-censorship concerning
Islam when a newspaper published drawings of the prophet Muhammad, one
with a bomb in his turban—was a wake-up call for Danes. Denmark had never
before faced a situation where the consequences of an internal debate escalated
abroad as it did in February 2006, when embassies around the world were attacked because of the cartoons. Needless to say, this entire crisis greatly increased
the attention to religion.

Until 1989 and the collapse of the Berlin Wall, the United States was
regarded as one of the world's two superpowers; political loyalties dictated love or

hate toward the superpowers. After World War II, Danes in general were grateful for American support. You can still see the odd Ferguson tractor around the countryside, carefully maintained by collectors as remnants of aid from the Marshall Plan. The split in general attitudes toward the United States came with the Vietnam War and the youth revolt, although the latter was, ironically, an indirect import from the United States. It changed Danish society as it also changed American society.

But religion was not a part of it. Nobody noticed the role that faith played in the political actions of Presidents Carter and Reagan. Martin Luther King, Jr., who is well known in Denmark, was and is considered only a civil rights hero; his faith as a driving force behind his actions is not well known. Knowledge of American religion has been more or less limited to the Amish and the Church of Jesus Christ of Latter-day Saints, the Mormons. Danes know about Mormons mainly because of the Osmond family, who were incredibly popular in the 1970s, and because the best-dressed and most visible missionaries in the streets of Danish cities are Mormons. The Danes loved Bill Clinton, whose religion was never an issue. It is against this background that one needs to interpret Danish opinions about President George W. Bush. In Danish eyes, he does not have his predecessor's charisma, charm, and what might be called Europeanness. Bush was originally considered a rich Texas cowboy and, if you knew something about American politics, a throwback to the days of the Monroe Doctrine. His religion did not make the news—until, that is, September 11, 2001, and the president's famous sentence, which he uttered only once, that the war on terrorism was a "crusade." Seen from abroad, the 2004 presidential campaign emphasized faith as an important factor, which also tremendously increased Danish attention to religion in America.

Because of the United States' status as the world's only remaining superpower, because of the impact of September 11, and because of a growing public debate on religion, the older European idea that "Americans are just like us, even on religious matters" has collapsed. Europeans and Americans do watch the same movies, listen to the same music, eat burgers from McDonald's, and believe in democracy as the best form of government. But we are not as much alike culturally as we once took for granted.

I experienced this division for myself when in 2003 I spent three months in the States. During this time, I lived with four different families—Lutheran, Methodist, and two Baptist, including both liberals and conservatives—while I did research for a book on Protestantism and American politics. I saw a much more diverse society than the Danish media portrays. To focus, as Danes often do, only on Bush's presidency and his religious Right supporters, at one end, and filmmaker Michael Moore's *Fahrenheit 9/11*, at the other, is not, in my view, an adequate or a fair portrayal of either America or Americans.

I left the United States convinced that self-understandings were different. Old Europe has developed very different forms of government and very different relations with religion over hundreds and hundreds of years, and through many wars. New America features an ideological understanding of itself in terms of freedom. In addition, the frontier still seems to play an important role in American identity, and with the frontier comes the free churches (and non-Christian faiths equally influenced by the free church ideal), lay preachers, the liberty to interpret the Bible individually, and the conviction that it is dangerous to rely on big government.

The picture probably never was that simple. But it seems to have become muddier than ever because of the so-called culture wars, where every outspoken American has something to say, often about what it means to be a true American. Intellectual confusion is the result. Conservative religious Republicans now salute Washington, D.C., and the Supreme Court when the national government interferes in state matters, at least so long as that interference reinforces their convictions. For instance, religious conservatives support the 1996 law by which the national government defined marriage as an institution for only men and women. In contrast, the same conservatives objected when the Supreme Court allowed the state of Washington the freedom to set its own rules concerning whether scholarships could be denied students pursuing degrees in theology. One might wonder what happened to Republican principles about the autonomy of the states. The only outcry I recall from the 2004 elections was when a group of gay Republicans decided not to recommend a vote for Bush. Protests about governmental entanglement with religion might also have been expected from the neoconservatives, whose belief in exporting democracy seems as devoted as the fundamentalist's faith in God but who otherwise seem more or less secular.

One might also give Supreme Court justice Antonin Scalia the benefit of the doubt in upholding traditional Republican restraints on federal power when he dissented in *Lawrence v. Texas*, the decision that forced Texas to change its laws on sodomy. But would he also be so concerned about resisting federal authority if the case had concerned Texas allowing homosexuals to marry each other? One could also ask if courts are the right place to solve moral issues, though if I were a homosexual in Tennessee, Texas, or Arkansas, I would probably turn to the courts, instead of waiting for my state to come around to a live-and-let-live philosophy.

Especially for American foreign relations, policy seems regularly to trump principles. Americans, for instance, regularly affirm their deep devotion to principles of religious freedom, but the American dependence on Saudi Arabian oil reserves means that the Saudis' daily violation of that principle counts for nothing. As viewed from smaller countries, these contradictions in principle are much more serious because it is the only superpower turning a blind eye.

Another difference that I found striking is the size and behavior of the denominations. From a Danish point of view, the American denominations are huge with, for instance, the Southern Baptist Convention alone almost four times the size of the Danish population. Where in Denmark, Baptists, Methodists, Catholics, and sometimes Muslims are forced to cooperate on various issues—for instance, in securing residential permits for foreign preachers—such cooperation does not appear to happen on a large scale in the United States. Members of different denominations hardly seem to know each other or each others' writings, though leaders of the religious Right have apparently tried to mobilize supporters across denominational lines. As Albert Mohler, president of the Southern Baptist Seminary in Louisville, Kentucky, put it: "When a house is on fire everybody digs in to put it out. Then you discuss differences afterwards." He was talking about cooperation between conservative Protestants and conservative Catholics, but even in that effort he must fight against a long-standing tradition of anti-Catholicism among Southern Baptists.

On the American religious Right, there does seem to be some cooperation in organizing for family values and opposing abortion on demand and stem cell research. The American Left is only just beginning to grasp the importance of such organizing, although because it *is* the Left, this will be a difficult process. In the last presidential campaign, some church liberals did attempt various initiatives, but they could not match the campaigns from religious conservatives.

American denominations, in my experience, tend to isolate themselves from one another. When they became so large as national organizations or as megachurches, they take on a different character. As an example, the political mobilization of the Southern Baptist Convention means that the denomination has exchanged old Baptist traditions that relied on local freedom and lay preachers for efforts at unifying the flock behind the right kind of conservative theology. The result is something that looks suspiciously like hierarchy—which in turn brings the denomination (and the Southern Baptist Convention is probably not the only one) much closer to the European churches from which they fled several hundred years ago in order to establish free churches in America. The Southern Baptist Convention is not in any danger of disappearing in the near future, but migration patterns that move the denomination away from its southern origins might threaten the strength of this denomination, and it might also be threatened by congregations that become fed up with politics. During my stay in the United States, I also met many people—not only in Southern Baptist churches, but also in other centers of the religious Right and Left—who think that it would be good for the churches to concentrate on distinctly religious matters and leave governing to those elected for the job.

The emphasis that Americans put on the personal faith of their presidents never ceases to amaze Danes. The religion of President Bush has become a matter of public interest in Denmark, but very often in a simplistic way: thus, Bush is a fundamentalist who takes his politics raw from the Bible. Among Danes in general that is considered quite strange, but even more, as dangerous, when the president leads the most powerful country in the world. In addition, Danes link American religion to Bush's effort to carry out a worldwide war on terror after September 11. When they see the president and his neoconservative advisors push so hard for the spread of democracy, they conclude that the desire to spread democracy is also religious and that Bush has surrounded himself with religious advisors—even if the neoconservatives do not actively practice any religious faith. It has also been difficult to convince Danes that democracy should be promoted from a gun barrel, or that abuses by American soldiers have helped to promote democracy.

Yet, whether they like him or not, Danes should in my view recognize that Bush is hardly unique, no matter what they or I feel about his politics. They forget that, for American liberals, whose voices they heed, the attack on Bush amounts to payback time for what the religious Right put Clinton through in his second term.

Bush seems to have a genuine faith, but he is not naïve enough to think that he can govern with God's words. I have never encountered a credible report that suggests that he wants to legislate from the Bible. He knows he is not the head of a theocracy. If he prays for advice on a regular basis, he does not go out, as Martin Luther King, Jr., actually did, and tell his "congregation" what God wants them to do. The profusion of "what would Jesus do?" material comes not from the president, but from the religious Right—and now also the Left. In my opinion, Bush is not as literal in his Bible reading as he sometimes implies when he is addressing the religious Right.

In many religious particulars, Jimmy Carter acted much the same as Bush does. The same perhaps goes for Ronald Reagan. For his part, and despite his difficulties with the Sixth Commandment—which prohibits adultery—Bill Clinton was a believer in God. And God help the atheist who wants to run for president. All surveys suggest that faith is an important factor for Americans, Left and Right, who consider it a strength for politicians to claim that they do not rely only on themselves. In the foreseeable future, it is unlikely that any major candidate for president can avoid the faith question. For good reason, Democratic candidates are taking classes in religion, and Hillary Clinton has already announced that she prays daily and is looking for a common ground to help reduce the number of abortions. The Democrats have caught on that many of their fellow citizens see religion as an important factor in politics.

From my experience, the one thing you can rely on with Americans is that they are always arguing with each other. No critics from abroad—whether on Iraq, Abu Ghraib, the war on terror, surveillance, or anything else—can match the vicious language that Americans use among themselves.

To a Dane, faith does not and should not play an active political role. An outspokenly religious candidate would have a difficult time here. Yet Danes probably do need to learn to heed religious arguments and to take them seriously, but not more seriously than other arguments. In Denmark, influential arguments would never be made by someone who claimed that Jesus would have done this, that, or the other.

The greatest influence of the religious Right seems to be not in America itself, apart from local school boards and other forms of local politics. Its major impact is abroad—for example, in shaping Middle East policy that affects Israel or by influencing health delivery programs in developing countries where abortions might be allowed, and so forth. On such values issues, one often finds the United States allied with the Vatican and Muslim interests, as at some UN meetings. Given the tremendous impact and influence of the United States in the world, it is stunning how little the world means to Americans. I think this is the reason that American foreign policy sometimes reflects a religious dimension; it is an easy way of pacifying the religious Right while few other Americans seem to notice.

Will American patterns of religion and politics ever be yet another cultural import to Denmark? Denmark already has culture wars, but in a much more secular form, mainly dealing with immigration (especially Muslim immigrants), cultural canons, and the past activities of present-day politicians. And there are a few, but influential, citizens who claim that one must be Christian to be truly Danish. We have more and more court cases involving religion than just a few years ago. And we certainly do need to learn how to deal with public religious expressions. As President Bush actually showed after September 11, it is possible to distinguish between religious Islam and terrorism. It should also be possible to carry on public debates about issues of faith and religion and to value them as highly as any other arguments, unless they claim that "God commanded" this or that. To learn such lessons, even from Americans, would be helpful for Danes in a globalized world where Lutheranism is no longer the only faith around. It might clarify an otherwise muddy debate on religion in politics to the benefit of the general public, politicians, and minority religions.

Australian Perspectives on American Religion and Politics in the Bush Era

Mark Hutchinson

𝒢AZING ON THE United States from another hemisphere and the other side of the world is always precarious for the observer. What in point of origin may be only a minor matter can loom huge when viewed from afar. Australian visions of American religion are not immune from such forms of intellectual "parallax error." Indeed, given that Australian multiculturalism has produced public divisions much more ideologically charged than have appeared in the American melting pot, one would not expect otherwise.

In rough terms, there are four common Australian positions on contemporary religion in America. They represent categories which, on one plane, follow the public/secular—private/religious division which emerged out of Australia's national history as a post-Christian foundation. On the other plane, they follow the internationalist-nationalist dimensions of its existence as a small, postcolonial, First World country moving uncertainly away from traditional European norms. The first category is a form of astonished silence. Like Australian authors Roger Bell and Philip Bell in their book *Implicated* (a study of Americanization during the 1950s), it is almost as if American religion did not exist, or at least did not project itself in such a way as to impress itself as important for the process of Americanization.[1] And this from a country in which Billy Graham still holds the record for the largest crowd to fill the Melbourne Cricket Ground (which occurred in 1959). America is treated as a wholly secular subject because of the reigning strength of intellectual materialism among Australian intellectual elites. Another reason for the stunned-silence approach is the bewildering diversity of American religions compared to the dominance of the "big four" (Anglicanism, Catholicism, Presbyterianism, Methodism) in Australian religious history. From weird televangelists to American Indian sun dances, religion in America is too various, too lacking in coherence to be taken seriously as a subject. There is a sneaking suspicion that the whole thing is simply Hollywood modalism, John Wayne in various disguises.

A second category is driven by the increasing globalization of Australian politics. A divided and ideological Left committed to socialist secularism recasts the actions of the Australian political Right, which has been ascendant during the Bush years, as the beneficiaries of a vast and shadowy international conspiracy. Partly as a shocked response to the 2004 impact of the nativist Family First party on an Australian political system in which minor parties can have a significant influence, this approach has lumped together Jerry Falwell, Pentecostal mega-churches, and Washington's national prayer breakfast as a baneful yet vaguely unintelligent force cynically being manipulated by conservative political prag-matists. Typical of this view is Marion Maddox's book *God under Howard*,[2] which one reviewer summed up as a "troubling exposé of the unheralded, unholy marriage between religious fundamentalism and political expediency."[3] Religious issues are thus swept up into divisions over the influence of American free marketism on Australian life and values—in particular through the bilateral Free Trade Agreement (FTA) and international military engagements. Faith healers and free trade are perceived as coming together in the impact of the FTA on the national Pharmaceutical Benefits Scheme and the broader national health system. In fact, Maddox's target is not God or religion, but the conservative government of John Howard; his book is a rallying call to the true believers of secular populism to resist American conservative religion as an extension of Australian conservative politics (just as in previous years they were called upon to resist British imperi-alism, Chinese immigration, and other globalizing realities).[4] In doing so, such approaches gloss over the fact that many of the religious subjects discussed are not American in origin, and so ignore the wise counsel of Bell and Bell, who propose that the appropriate model for understanding Americanization in Australia "might be labeled either 'creolization' or 'hybridization' (if you prefer, 'creolisa-tion' or 'hybridisation'). Cultural importation passes through several stages, the end of which is a unique melding of import and native seen by the recipient society as genuinely local."[5]

Representatives of this second category see American religion under Bush as a sort of stupid but powerful giant which, in rolling over, threatens the national identity and moral purity of secularist Australia. Its religious rhetoric—as adopted by the Howard government in Australia—is the conservatism of Decius, that is, the efforts of good postcolonials aimed at restoring the strength of the empire through administrative and moral reform. As such, the picture entails a statist use of religion to unify a fragmenting political entity, rather than a religious use of politics per se. Critics of this practice (Maddox among them) ignore the radical populism and reformism of many Australian subjects (such as Family

First). They find sufficient support for their opinions from selective attention to National Public Radio, the negative press given to neoconservatives in the Bush circle, and visits of American dissidents to Australia.[6] Such critics embrace a typical modernist perception of the homogeneity of Christian expressions wherever they appear, and so they construct Christianity as an enemy of the pluralist, secular state, rather than (in a historically more accurate interpretation) as a major contributor to it.[7] Commentators such as Matthew Ryan, thus, introduce the theme of "religion and Bush" with a dismissive account of technology at Bob Jones University, where Bush spoke prior to the presidential primary in 2000: "it is perhaps strange that a place like BJU should see [the Internet] as useful in their mission to spread the Good News. 'In the beginning there was the word,' and for BJU not much has changed since."[8] For such commentators, the temptation to stereotype is nearly irresistible, particularly given the modernist assumption that religion (any religion) is a major source of violence. It is a short step from discovering that the best predictors for voting behavior in the United States are church attendance and gun ownership to constructing a public view of American conservative religion as largely populated by gun-toting, imperialist rednecks.

The bafflement in the voice of Australian reporter Tony Hassan sums up Australian public puzzlement with American religious exceptionalism: "Is it now understood," he asked American academic historian Philip Goff, "that if you want to win the White House, you must be Christian orientated? Because in Australian politics, that's not the case. One of our most revered Prime Ministers, Gough Whitlam, was a self-declared Agnostic."[9] The iconic figure of Whitlam— a new Labor demagogue who in the 1970s used nationalism to detach Australia from involvement in American-dominated internationalism and whose government was the key architect of Australian multiculturalism—is symbolic of the ambivalence felt by the less-informed Australian population about American international assertiveness. Associating Australia's experience of (British) imperialism with American-Australian bilateralism, Whitlam used federal constitutional powers, including power over immigration, as part of a social engineering program to create a new form of self-confident and multilateral internationalism among Australians.[10] The perceived link in the United States among conservative evangelicalism, conservative politics, and international aggression—with powerful ramifications in the Australian multicultural community (in particular the Middle Eastern community)—thus resonates with the fundamental "causes" that the Whitlam period wrote into Australian society. Negative associations with American life, religious evangelicalism, and political conservatism are thus linked to American interventionism as defined much more by Vietnam than by Iraq. For these Australians, it was the Vietnam conflict that—through moratorium campaigns, street marches, and the rise of the "new knowledge class" in Australia's rapidly expanding baby boomer tertiary institutions—became the touchpoint for a whole generation. (The fact that one of the U.S. presidents during the Vietnam era was a Catholic, John F. Kennedy, and another was only a nominal Protestant, Lyndon B. Johnson, does not seem to register with these Australians.) Whitlam caught the energy of that generational shift and successfully associated the new perspective with a secular, multicultural nationalism that excluded the voice of the churches as well as the voice of conservative politics from the 1950s, represented by the iconic Prime Minister Robert Menzies. Whitlam's secular sainthood among many of Australia's opinion leaders reinforces the Australian tendency to interpret American religion as conservative and backward. The prominence in Australian newspapers of such otherwise obscure topics as intelligent design, faith-based initiatives,[11] and Michael Moore; the Australian preference for the more readily dereligionized Clinton over Bush; and the relative absence of comment in the Australian press on Jimmy Carter's brand of evangelical religion—these are all indicative of a powerful set of cultural filters still firmly in place.[12]

If we understand the second position as replicating the Australia-for-Australians views prominent in the nineteenth century (as opposed to philo-imperialism), it is easy to predict the general stance of a third Australian category that embraces at least some aspects of that earlier philo-imperialism. Religious elements of Australian society that are located in global cities naturally share affinities with other similarly located communities overseas. The notable success in Australia of popular American megachurch authors and pastors, especially Rick Warren and Bill Hybels, indicates the shape of this philo-Americanism. In this view, America is the place where things work, a source of pragmatism, where ideas are tried and proved. Much of religious Australia has seen religious America as a supermarket of workable ideas. The result is mutual regard. From this sector, Australian leaders travel to the United States for inspiration and to be *seen* to be traveling to America. They bring back ideas, increased self-respect, students for their colleges, and money for their projects.

It is important to note, however, that these friends of America are not completely swept away by their positive contact with the United States. Many of them, for example, think they can do better in their own market than any American ever could, in part because they see the invisible edges of American culture that Americans themselves regularly overlook. Both of the largest churches in Sydney, Hillsong and Christian City Church, conduct church-planting operations in the United States, and both accept large numbers of American students into their college programs based largely on the international success of their worship music.[13] The double edge of their perception of religion under George W. Bush is thus visible. "It is," they say, "good to see Christianity strong, and a source of influence in the United States, but . . ." And then the discriminations begin: "But . . . Americans are too caught up in traditional evangelical cultures which restrain their energy. But . . . Americans too closely identify their national priorities with religious identity. But . . . what is this fundamentalism thing?" Even these Australians are antagonized by extreme expressions, except perhaps for politics. As John Carroll has noted concerning the balance between American and Australian attitudes: "Throughout the West there has been rhetoric about a Third Way, one that might combine the efficiency of American capitalism with a broader, more compassionate social perspective, capitalism with a human face. A number of visitors observed that it actually exists, and is called 'Australia.' "[14] In this third perspective, Australian Christians respect American religion as one way—but their own way as another. When in 2003 Ted Haggard, president of the United States' National Association of Evangelicals, spoke at the annual convention of the Australian Assemblies of God and offered rousing support for the American invasion of Iraq, the response from his audience was decidedly muted. In the Southern Hemisphere, it seems that the empire of God and the empire of man can be distinguished fairly easily, even when it comes to the actions of friends in the United States.

A fourth category of opinion about American religion under Bush is represented by the small number of scholars who actually know something about the two cultures and their relative perspectives. Australian views have benefited from the transcultural understanding of Robert D. Linder, a professor of history at Kansas State University, whose work with the Australian historian Stuart Piggin has produced valuable comparative work on the history of Protestants in the two countries.[15] Religious historians—including Grant Wacker from the United States, David Bebbington from Britain, and George Rawlyk from Canada—have visited Australia and taken home useful comparative understandings that have returned to influence Australian understandings of religion in the United States, North America, and the North Atlantic region.[16] A few of the American historians who have visited Australia are now consulted by the Australian press for commentary on American religion, which has provided a more balanced view to that usually provided for Australian audiences by analysts such as Tariq Ali or Gore Vidal.

With respect to international concern about the 2003 American invasion of Iraq, it is also notable that Australian Catholics responded to the religious aspects of the war (typically portrayed in the Australian press as simply Bush's "crusade") as an opportunity to discuss the philosophical bases of "just war."[17] With a longer and more articulate tradition of public theology, with more developed intellectual institutions (such as Australia's Notre Dame University and the Australian Catholic University), with a wide range of well-read publications (such as *Eureka Street* and the *Catholic Weekly*),[18] and backed by Australia's largest Christian constituency, it is not surprising that some of the more nuanced interpretations of American religion in the Bush era have come not from Australian Protestants or secularists, but from Catholic intellectuals. Gerard Henderson, head of a Sydney-based conservative think tank, makes occasional comments on American religion that are informed by his Catholic background. His Sydney Institute is a vector for a more informed understanding of the nature and role of American Christianity.[19] Yet forays by Catholics into this arena are not without controversy: the association of Sydney's conservative Catholic archbishop, George Pell, with many of the positions adopted by the Bush program of "national moral reform" tends to push other Catholics toward opposing conclusions.[20] But, reflecting the same balance observed in some Protestant evangelicals, even Pell is not uncritical of the United States, as in his acknowledgment of dangers in Bush's approach to interreligious and intercultural dialogue.[21]

The emergence in Australia of each of these four responses to "religion under Bush" is inevitably informed by the stance of the one who makes the response. Religion under Bush is never simply an American issue. If the search for a new unity of politics, culture, and faith evident under the Bush presidency has been stimulated by the observable unity of politics, culture, and faith among militantly radical Islamists, that very search affects the public balance of religion and society as it has emerged in other First World countries, including Australia. Responses tend to indicate more about the observers than about the developments themselves. Some continue to hold to the irrelevance of religion for the modern secular endeavor, and their silence is notable. Others defend the fragile secular public sphere in multicultural societies by overplaying the religious factor in the Bush presidency, largely for local application. A third group, made up of Australian people of faith, finds itself targeted by this second group, and so responds with various levels of semipositive ambivalence about the Bush program. It is an ambivalence aimed at maintaining their own identities in the equally fragile set of compromises on which private faith and public action are sustained in Australia. It would be encouraging to think that the fourth group—careful observers of intellectual flows between religious America and religious Australia—might become more prominent in bringing understanding to such matters. Yet with a national conversation still strongly influenced by late nineteenth-century debates about disestablishment and the proper role of religion in a liberal democracy, Australia's preoccupation with its own struggle to maintain a tolerant and stable public sphere may not provide the best position for a measured understanding of what is really going on in the United States of George W. Bush.

Notes

1. Philip Bell and Roger Bell, *Implicated: The United States in Australia* (Melbourne, Australia: Oxford University Press, 1993).
2. Marion Maddox, *God under Howard: The Rise of the Religious Right in Australian Politics* (Crows Nest, N.S.W.: Allen & Unwin, 2005).
3. Muriel Porter, "*God under Howard*: The Religious Right in Australia," review in *The Age*, 26 Feb. 2005.
4. Which is not to say that the wily politician John Howard does not manipulate religious opinion for political purposes. Interestingly, he is willing to fuse concepts of "Christianity" and nation more readily while in the United States than with his own constituency in Australia. See "Remarks by President Bush and Prime Minister Howard of Australia in an Arrival Ceremony," *US Newswire*, 16 May 2006.
5. Jeffery C. Livingston, review of *Americanization in Australia*, ed. Roger Bell and Philip Bell (Sydney: UNSW Press, 1998), in *Journal of American History* 86 (2000): 1877.
6. The irony of the opinion page of the Albury *Border Mail* on 18 Nov. 2005 seems to have been lost on such commentators. Opposite a picture of Family First senator Steve Fielding speaking in opposition to conservative industrial reform legislation is an article outlining a protest against the visit of Donald Rumsfeld to Adelaide.
7. See, for instance, Carole Cusack, "The Future of Australian Secularism: Religion, Civil Society and the American Alliance," *ARPA Digest*, Oct. 2005. Cusack assumes in her *Digest* articles that democracy is incompatible with Christianity and that the goal of the churches is always social dominance.
8. Matthew Ryan, "Click Here for Righteousness: George W. [Bush] Makes the Links to God, Death and Votes," *Arena Magazine*, Apr.–May 2000, pp. 11–12.
9. See http://www.abc.net.au/rn/talks/8.30/relrpt/stories/s1243269.htm. In part, Whitlam's public position was a construct—his sister was the moderator of the Uniting Church, his "welfare state" was so dominated by delivery of welfare through church agencies that the term "the shadow state" has been extended to those agencies, and Whitlam's own language and interest in religion were almost messianic. See Rose Melville and Catherine McDonald, "'Faith-Based' Organisations and Contemporary Welfare," *Australian Journal of Social Issues* 41 (Autumn 2006): 69–86. To the same extent, the strident secularism of Whitlam's devotees is also a construct, developed to protect government involvement (and investment) in the "public" system.
10. "Immigration: Australian Policy and Relations with Lebanon, 1965–75," National Archives of Australia, A1838, 1634/131, part 1. See also Peter McLaren and N. E. Jaramillo, "God's Warriors: The Alliance of Leo Strauss's Philosophy and the US Christian Right Has Implications for Us All," *Arena Magazine*, June 2005, pp. 46–48, where the authors make the slip of referring to evangelicals as "evangelists." As has

been noted, the Howard government's engagement in Iraq caused the "party traditions in Australian foreign policy" to resurface. "These trends illustrated the Coalition Government's preference for bilateral diplomacy with 'great and powerful friends.' In contrast, the Labor opposition emphasized multilateral approaches through forums such as the United Nations." See D. Flitton, "Perspectives on Australian Foreign Policy, 2002," *Australian Journal of International Affairs* 57 (Apr. 2003): 37.

11. As Melville and McDonald point out ("'Faith-Based' Organisations"), the extension of terms like "faith-based initiative" from the American to the Australian context is a form of overgeneralization, and probably a mistake:

> At a minimum, it predisposes Australian users to unreflective engagement with a mode of welfare reform that sits at odds with Australian institutional relations and social conditions. At worst, it has the potential to promote beliefs and myths about the role of the non-government sector that distort our capacity to comprehend the complexities of the Australian mixed economy of welfare.

12. The fact that Australians also get a larger relative input from British news tends to reinforce this perspective. As the major representative of the "coalition of the willing" in Iraq, British prime minister Tony Blair, another public Christian, seems to reconfirm Australian secular presumptions about the violent tendencies of Christianity. See J. Nurick, "Letter from London: Bush's Victory Is Bad News for Tories," *Institute of Public Affairs Review* 56 (Dec. 2004): 35.

13. A DVD advertising the Christian City Church Presence Conference features video footage of senior pastor Phil Pringle apparently prophesying the destruction of the World Trade Center a year before it happened. The role of America as "the place of significant events" is thus emphasized.

14. J. Carroll, "The Blessed Country: Australian Dreaming, 1901–2001," *Alfred Deakin Lectures, 2001*, ABC Radio, 12 May 2001.

15. See, for instance, Robert D. Linder, "The Dry Souls of Christendom: The Challenge of Writing Australian Evangelical History," *Fides et Historia* 32:2 (2000): 33–50; and Linder, "Civil Religion in America and Australia," *Lucas: An Evangelical History Review* (Apr.–May 1988).

16. For examples of these insights, see several essays on Australia in *Evangelicalism: Comparative Studies of Popular Protestantism in North America, the British Isles, and Beyond: 1700–1990*, ed. Mark A. Noll, David W. Bebbington, and George A. Rawlyk (New York: Oxford University Press, 1994); and *Amazing Grace: Evangelicalism in Australia, Britain, and the United States*, ed. George A. Rawlyk and Mark A. Noll (Montreal and Kingston: McGill University Press, 1994).

17. Gary Stone, John Owens, and Bruce Duncan authored three articles on the morality of a just war against Iraq in *Catholic Weekly*, 2 Feb. 2003, p. 11; 9 Feb. 2003, p. 11; 16 Feb. 2003, p. 12.

18. See, for example, Jack Waterford, "Grim Reaping," *Eureka Street*, Apr. 2003, p. 7.

19. See, for example, the address given by Vin Weber at a Sydney Institute function, later published as "The Bush Administration: Prospects and Expectations," *Sydney Papers* 13 (Autumn 2001): 64–74.

20. Compare, for example, Pell's position on intelligent design (George Pell, "Is the Universe Planned?" *Catholic Weekly*, 18 Sept. 2005) with that of Australian Catholic University professor Neil Ormerod ("How Design Supporters Insult God's Intelligence," *Sydney Morning Herald*, 15 Nov. 2005).

21. George Pell, "Islam and Western Democracies," *Quadrant*, May 2006.

Canadian Counterpoint

Mark A. Noll

$\mathcal{C}$ANADA, LIKE THE United States, has since its earliest days experienced close connections between religion and politics, although not in the same way nor for the same reasons.[1] Comparisons between Canadian and American history are especially revealing because of how many political and religious values the two nations share in common. Both are representative democracies. Both are heir to the time-tested legal, political, and cultural traditions of Britain, but also beneficiaries of strong immigrant contributions from the European continent, Asia, and other parts of the world. Both were deeply committed to the Allied side in the twentieth century's great world wars, and both stood solidly with the West during the Cold War (though Canada was not as actively engaged in this latter struggle as was the United States).

In religion as well as politics, contrasts between Canada and the United States are intriguing precisely because they coexist with so many similarities between the two nations.[2] These similarities include an active evangelical voluntarism that in the nineteenth century (outside of Quebec) came close to establishing an informal Protestant establishment in Canada. As a part of Canada's dominant nineteenth-century Christian culture, Catholic as well as Protestant, there was a propensity to use biblical imagery for nationalistic aspirations that mirrored practices south of the border.[3] As an example, when the dominion of Canada was formed in 1867, it seemed only natural for the Methodist Leonard Tilley of New Brunswick to apply the words of Psalm 72:8 to his country ("He shall have dominion also from sea to sea"). Also like the United States, Canada had a dismal record of Protestant-Catholic violence in the nineteenth century, fueled sometimes by Catholic resentment of Protestant missionaries and sometimes by demonstrations of the Irish Protestant Orange Order. Canada has sustained an active revival tradition, indeed, sometimes sharing itinerant evangelicals with the United States.[4] In both nations, the Catholic church and mainline Protestant bodies have acted with proprietary instincts toward the broader society. In both, a variety of liberal-conservative disagreements have divided the churches (although with proportionately more of those divisions in the United States than in Canada). And, in both, there has been ample room for non-Christian religions to flourish. In sum, an awful lot of parallel history—even shared history—joins the United States and Canada. But that shared history makes the contrasts, especially as they affect religion and politics, all the more illuminating.

CONTRASTING CONTEXTS

A good beginning point for comparing Canadian and American national development was provided in 1990 by Seymour Martin Lipset's *Continental Divide*, one of the most thoughtful studies of its kind. Lipset's main argument was that Canada "has been and is a more class-aware, elitist, law-abiding, statist, collectivity-oriented, and . . . group-oriented society than the United States."[5] The anti-statism, individualism, populism, violence, and egalitarianism that characterize American history have been decidedly less prominent in Canada. Where Canada has stressed the state and community values, the United States has featured the individual and laissez faire. In contrast to the American embrace of individualistic liberalism, Canada has fostered a public attitude stressing communalities, whether "Tory/statist" on the Right or "social democratic" on the Left.

According to Lipset, the reasons for these systematic differences are both geographical and historical. Canada's vast space and sparse population have required a more active government and have placed a premium upon cooperation. Historically, the first move was the most important. In the 1770s, Canadians rejected the American Revolution and so were set on a less republican course in both Quebec, where Catholic bishops and laypeople remained loyal to Britain despite American diplomacy and invasion, and the Maritimes and upper Canada, whence many Protestant loyalists fled after being ejected from their former homes.[6] As we will see below, the religious-political effects of that rejection continue to this day. Then, in the War of 1812, when the outmanned Canadians, with late help from Britain, fended off several American invasions, the result was not only a solidification of Canadian loyalty to Britain, but also a significant reduction of cultural influences from the United States, including ecclesiastical influences.[7]

Canada's own would-be republican revolutions in 1837 and 1838, which occurred as one effort in Quebec and a different effort in English Canada, fizzled almost completely. The formal disestablishment of Canada's churches took place in the wake of these failed rebellions. Yet in Canada, disestablishment was not a means of dealing with religious pluralism, as in the United States, but of dealing with two religious monopolies. For Quebec, with a fully functioning state-church system, and the rest of Canada, where Anglicans, Presbyterians, and even Methodists had hoped to re-create church-state systems similar to what they had known in Britain, it meant adjustment rather than, as in the United States, all-out denominational competition. In the words of historian Marguerite Van Die, "A strange paradox happened. In Canada formal disestablishment in reality turned into two informal or shadow establishments, two highly public expressions of religion: Protestantism in English Canada and Roman Catholicism, primarily in Quebec."[8]

The American Civil War frightened Canadians, most of whom abhorred slavery but also feared the North's mobilized military might. Reaction to that war was a prime factor hastening creation in 1867 of the dominion of Canada, which joined together Nova Scotia, New Brunswick, Quebec, and Ontario. Shortly thereafter, Manitoba, British Columbia, and Prince Edward Island joined the confederation, with Saskatchewan and Alberta entering in 1905. The dominion emerged as a free and democratic nation managed by its own responsible government under the imperial surveillance of the British Parliament—in other words, what the thirteen colonies would eventually have become by way of peaceful evolution had not the violent American Revolution intervened. Significantly, the founding motto of the new dominion was simply "peace, order, and good government," which announced a less ambitious set of political goals than the Americans' "life, liberty, and the pursuit of happiness." Again, a contrast is important. American independence took place in the 1770s as a reaction against centralized government; with the exception of the Civil War period, Americans refused to accede power to central federal authority until the Great Depression, World War II, and the Civil Rights movement fundamentally altered historic American localism. In Canada, by contrast, Quebec long remained a society that trusted the centralized leadership of the church and then of business and governmental leaders in league with the church, while "the political culture of Upper Canada [Ontario]," as historian Christopher Adamson has noted, "was statist from its inception."[9] Independence in Canada embraced the centralized authority that independence in America disdained.

In his 1990 volume, Lipset cited a number of social indicators as evidence for his conclusion about American-Canadian differences: Canada's far lower murder rate, its much fewer number of police per capita, its willingness to tolerate higher taxes, its enforcement of nationwide gun control, its general contentment with relatively high levels of governmental regulation, and its single-payer health systems that are funded in significant part by the federal government but administered by the provinces.[10] To this list could now be added the relatively calm acceptance of same-sex marriage that was legislated by Parliament in June 2005. That decision has prompted serious opposition, but, in contrast to the United States, the opposition is spread over Canada's several parties and has been expressed in relatively reserved tones. Such differences manifest deeply ingrained historical patterns.

Of course, it is always also important to remember the many Canadian-American similarities. But the contrasts have been significant—first and foremost, the ongoing presence in Canada of two separate societies of relatively equal political weight (French and Catholic, English and Protestant) united into a single nation. Both the United States and Canada have been free, democratic, and capitalist. But, comparatively speaking, Canada has been more organic, traditional, statist, and hierarchical while the United States has been more free, democratic, local, and individualistic.

In the broad sweep of history, Canadians used forces of cohesion to bind a widely scattered people—indeed, two peoples—into a prosperous, well-ordered, and reasonably stable nation-state. Religious faith and practice were critical in building this nation-state. In the United States, active religion also contributed materially to the construction of American society, but there it was mostly through forms of Christianity expressed in voluntary and individualistic terms, more at home with the operations of a free market than in Canada, where voluntary exertions were always balanced by a reliance upon government and where free-market initiative was matched by respect for received authority and inherited traditions.

REVOLUTION REJECTED

Religion has played a key role in the Canadian rejection of revolution as a means of altering the political system. That rejection has been complemented by a persistent choice against American liberalism as the sole norm for political life (with *liberalism* defined in nineteenth-century terms as a stress on the decisions of individuals, the sphere of civil society separate from government, and the voluntary instead of formal contributions of religion to society). Catholic gratitude for the Quebec Act of 1774, which secured civil rights for Canadian Catholics that their coreligionists in Britain did not gain until 1829, helps to explain Quebec's rejection of American pleas to join the War of Independence. In the Maritimes, a much smaller, more Protestant population also refused to join the patriot cause. In that case, at least part of the reason was the apolitical pietism fostered by the revivalist Henry Alline and other leaders of the "New Light Stir" that began about the same time as the war.[11]

The greatest stimulus to the creation of an anti-American Canadian nationalism, however, was the War of 1812. When undermanned militia and British regulars repelled the attacks of American troops in the Niagara peninsula and on the Great Lakes in 1813 and 1814, Canadian pastors hailed God's providential rescue of his people from American tyranny with the same assurance that American pastors had expressed after their struggle against Britain a generation before. Loyalty to the king and trust in God constituted the Canadian "shield of Achilles" that frustrated the despotic plans of the American democratic mob.[12]

The rejection of revolution remained a political keystone especially among descendants of the fifty thousand loyalists who fled from the revolutionary United States to eventually settle in the Maritimes and Ontario. That rejection, which was sealed decisively by the War of 1812, has contributed much to Canadian politics. It is not as though the individualism, free-market advocacy, and democratic principles that have meant so much in the United States are absent in Canada. Rather, in Canada, liberalism has always been balanced by the corporate visions of the Left and the Right, and often with significant religious support. For example, the fundamentalist preacher William "Bible Bill" Aberhart embodied populist and communitarian principles in Alberta's Social Credit party, which he led to power in the 1930s.[13] A Baptist minister and contemporary of Aberhart, Tommy Douglas, exploited principles from the Social Gospel in organizing the Cooperative Commonwealth Federation in the prairies during the same Great Depression years.[14] That movement eventually was transformed into the New Democratic party (NDP), Canada's socialist alternative to the Liberals and Progressive Conservatives; this party has held power in several western provinces at various times since the 1960s. The NDP is now largely secular, but its roots in a communitarian movement with strong religious connections suggests something about how Canadians have expressed their faith differently than have Americans.

Another example of similar religious overtones informing political positions was provided in the 1960s by the redoubtable Christian thinker George Parkin Grant. In 1963, the federal Conservative government of John Diefenbaker was defeated by the Liberals under Lester Pearson. Almost immediately, the new Liberal government agreed to let the United States install nuclear weapons in the Canadian North. This action precipitated a notable *cri de coeur* from Grant, whose politics combined a great deal of Anglican traditionalism with much social liberalism and moral conservatism. Grant's book *Lament for a Nation* was a widely noticed critique of economic and ethical individualism, the Cold War, and American democracy as corrosive solvents of Canada's historic Christian cultures. It was representative of a right-wing but progovernment kind of conservatism that feared a drift into American economic, political, and intellectual orbits.[15]

Canadian ideals that favor community-oriented, gradualist, and peaceful social change are the product of different political instincts than those that have prevailed in the United States since the nation's beginnings in a republican War for Independence. Sometimes those Canadian ideals have taken shape in leftist or socialist movements, sometimes in rightist or conservative ideologies. Common to both, however, has been a strong religious presence informing these alternatives to the American revolutionary tradition.

Two Societies, Two Languages, Two Religions

Even before North America entered the revolutionary period—with the United States in favor of throwing over British rule and Canada loyally embracing it— Canadian life was being set by the nature of its first European settlements. The fact that those early settlements included a strong Catholic presence—and a Catholic presence linked to France—has meant a great deal for the course of Canadian religion and politics.

The modern history of Canada began in the early seventeenth century with French settlements in what is now the province of Quebec. Unlike the situation in the United States, Catholicism was important politically from the first. Even today, corporate conceptions of civic life that are common in Roman Catholic societies continue to exert an especially strong influence in Quebec, although levels of religious practice in the province have fallen dramatically since the 1970s.

Indeed, the Catholic factor loomed large in almost all major Canadian political developments until recent times. After the Treaty of Paris (1763), which granted Britain control of Quebec, British success at accommodating the province's Catholic establishment prepared the way for Catholic loyalty to the Crown during the American Revolution. When patriots invaded Canada in 1775, Bishop

Briand of Quebec labeled support for the Americans "heresy," and most of his fellow religionists took the message to heart.

For a century and more following the American Revolution, Quebec's Catholic hierarchy mostly aligned itself with Canada's loyalist and conservative political leaders. Within the church, the ultramontane tendency, or the tendency to look "over the mountains" to find direction for religious and social life directly from Rome, prevailed. From the year of confederation, 1867, into the 1890s, Quebec's ultramontane bishops usually succeeded in delivering the province's votes to the Conservative party, which, under the leadership of Canada's first premier, John A. Macdonald, took pains to maintain good relations with the bishops. The church gave the party what it wanted (seats in the Ottawa Parliament); in return, the party gave the church what it wanted (Quebec's control over its own province).[16] Elsewhere in Canada, Conservatives (or Tories) often shared in English Canada's characteristically strong pro-Protestant and anti-Catholic sentiments. But not in Quebec.

The tragic career of Louis Riel played an important role in expanding the influence of Catholicism in Canadian society.[17] Riel, who was a deeply pious individual of mystic tendencies, twice attempted to set up quasi-independent governments in Manitoba for the *metis* (mixed bloods of French Canadian and Indian parentage). Riel's efforts were inspired by his own messianic convictions, but also by a mixture of American democratic views and Catholic social teachings. In the wake of his second failed rebellion in 1885, Riel was executed after a speedy trial. This resolution of the crisis in Manitoba led, however, to bitter conflict in the rest of Canada. The standoff was between British Protestants eager to ensure that Protestant dominance prevailed in the new western provinces and French-speaking Catholics who felt Riel had been wronged. Ill will generated by the Riel episode came to an end only when Wilfrid Laurier, the Liberal party leader in the 1896 national election and a Roman Catholic, successfully assuaged the wounded sensibilities of both sides.

Significantly, Laurier was both the first national premier from Quebec and the first Roman Catholic head of the Canadian government (sixty-four years before the election of Catholic John F. Kennedy as president of the United States). From his time as prime minister (1896–1911) until the last third of the twentieth century, French-speaking Catholics became as strong in their support for the Liberal party as they once had been for the Tories. Only when the institutional Catholic church declined in influence from the 1960s did Quebec break from its earlier pattern of political alliance with one of the major Canadian parties. The rise of Quebec-specific nationalist political parties, which remain strong in the province and in the Quebec delegation to Ottawa to this day, can be considered a negative effect of the Catholic church's loss of influence as a political broker. What Laurier's influential career illustrated—as also Quebec's broader pattern of political allegiance—was the institutional influence of hereditary Roman Catholicism, a permanent feature of Canadian politics that emerged in the United States only from the late nineteenth century.

Yet even with the easing of Catholic-Protestant antagonism since the mid-1960s and the declining rates of church participation, Catholicism still makes a difference in Canadian electoral politics. In the mid-1980s, Richard Johnston found that Catholic or Protestant adherence explained electoral variance more than any other social structural trait and, moreover, that these variances were not just a reflection of Anglophone-Francophone differences.[18] In 1980 and 1995, referenda were held in Quebec to decide whether the province would choose to opt out of Canada. Both times, Francophone Catholics active in their churches were much more likely to vote in favor of the status quo and against Quebec separate sovereignty than were nominally Catholic or secular Quebecois.[19]

SPECIFIC CONTRASTS

The historical background defined by the presence in Canada of two languages and two religions, as well as by the general course of Canadian political development, helps to explain several specific differences from the United States. Most visibly, Catholic corporatism as well as several varieties of Protestant loyalism have together encouraged a more relaxed attitude toward questions of church and state than that allowed by the American ideal of church-state separation. The Catholic establishment in Quebec relinquished control of the school systems, hospitals, and labor organizations of the province only in the decades after the end of the Second World War. In the Maritimes and Ontario, the Anglican and Presbyterian churches never received quite the same levels of governmental support that their established counterparts enjoyed in England and Scotland, but direct forms of aid to the churches did not end until the clergy reserves (land set aside for the use of the churches) were secularized in 1854. Even after that contentious event, indirect government support continued for many religious agencies. Denominational colleges, for example, were folded into several of the major provincial universities so that, to this day, a few such colleges exist as components of the universities. In addition, varying kinds of aid are still provided to at least some church-organized primary and secondary schools in every Canadian province. In Newfoundland, the publicly funded educational system was conducted entirely by the various denominations until the late 1990s, at which time general public schools not connected to the churches appeared for the first time.[20]

Other distinctives that set Canada apart from practices in the United States include stricter enforcement of Sunday closing laws and much stricter restrictions on independent religious broadcasters. By contrast, the religious views of major political leaders have usually been subject to much less public scrutiny than has been customary in the United States. Thus, national political campaigns have been little affected by the fact that Canadian prime ministers Alexander Mackenzie (1873–1878) and John G. Diefenbaker (1957–1963) were practicing Baptists; John Turner (1984) was a serious Catholic; William Lyon Mackenzie King (1921–1926, 1926–1930, 1935–1948) was a Presbyterian spiritualist who enjoyed talking to his long-dead dog and mother; Pierre Elliott Trudeau (1968–1979, 1980–1984) and Brian Mulroney (1984–1993) were more ambiguous Catholics; and John A. Macdonald (1867–1873, 1878–1891) was a casual Presbyterian who (late in life) established a close connection with the evangelists H. T. Crossley and John E. Hunter. As noted below, Canadian public attention to the religious life of candidates has become more frequent in recent years. But for a long time, the parliamentary system and a characteristically British reserve about private religious convictions kept the candidates' religions a private matter in a way that has never been true in the United States.

One of the most important reasons for structural differences in religion and politics between the two nations arises from the varied proportions of religious adherence. A major cross-border survey conducted by the Angus Reid group in October 1996 revealed that although about the same proportions of the two national populations were adherents to mainline churches (15 percent in the United States, 16 percent in Canada), in the United States a much higher proportion of citizens belonged to conservative Protestant churches (26 percent to 10 percent) and to African-American Protestant churches (9 percent to less than 1 percent).[21] This difference is especially important in light of the fact that, as noted in chapter 14, white evangelical Protestants and black Protestants have constituted the United States' most polarized religious-political groupings. Because in Canada these religious groups are not as large, political polarization has not been as sharp.

In addition, a higher proportion of Canadians were adherents of the Roman Catholic church (26 percent to 20 percent), and a much higher proportion were secular or only nominal in religious attachments (40 percent to 20 percent). The fact that each of these large blocs is constituted differently in the two countries—with, for example, the Mennonites and Dutch Reformed relatively more important among Canadian conservative Protestants and the Baptists much more important in the United States—helps further to explain the way that religious constituencies support different political tendencies in the two nations.

The leading student of religious trends in contemporary Canada, Reginald Bibby of Alberta, has noted slight changes in twenty-first-century polls that suggest a weakening of secularizing trends in Canada. Religious beliefs are affirmed by a consistent majority of citizens; distaste for positions labeled as fundamentalist or extremist remains strong; and church attendance is creeping up, especially among Catholics outside of Quebec.[22] Bibby's research, however, only adjusts what has long been understood about the different religious populations in the United States and Canada. Because the makeup of those populations continues to differ, so too do the political implications of religious adherence continue to differ.

THE RECENT PAST

Over the last quarter-century, a number of developments within Canada seems to be pushing in the direction of American patterns on issues of religion and politics. If Seymour Martin Lipset were to write today what he published in 1990 concerning strong social differences between the two countries, he might have a slightly different story to tell.

To be sure, traditional patterns remain discernible. For example, the Angus Reid poll of October 1996 did show that on some issues Canadians and Americans responded virtually alike—for example, in percentages who took a religiously motivated stance on abortion or who reported that their clergy speak out on social issues. But Americans were considerably more likely (by at least 10 percentage points) to say that Christian values should influence politics, to express confidence in organized religion, to belong to a church or a religious group, to say that Christians should get involved in politics to protect their values, and to affirm that religion is important for political thinking. By contrast, Canadians were more likely (again, by at least 10 percentage points) to say that churches and religious organizations should be required to pay taxes, to express confidence in the news media, and to vote for a self-described atheist running for high political office. Such polling results suggest that processes of secularization have moved more rapidly in Canada than in the United States. They also suggest that historical Canadian-American differences in approaching religion and politics continue to make at least something of a difference.

Yet those differences may be receding. One indication is that the personal beliefs of national political figures have recently received the kind of scrutiny in Canada that was once reserved for the United States. It is significant, for instance, that the funeral on October 3, 2000, of former Liberal premier Pierre Elliott Trudeau was conducted as a formal Catholic service in Montreal's Notre Dame

Basilica, and it was probably the most widely noticed religious event in Canadian history. It is also significant that Trudeau's lifelong (but private) Catholic devotional practice has been the subject of significant recent reevaluation.[23]

Even more significant are developments involving evangelical Protestants and the political Right. In recent years, Canadian political conservatism has been rejuvenated through the efforts of effective leaders from the Canadian West, including Preston Manning (head of the Reform party, 1987–2000), Stockwell Day (head of the Canadian Alliance, 2000–2002, which succeeded the Reform party), and Stephen Harper (head from 2002 of a reconstituted Conservative party, which pulled together the Alliance and remnants of the old Progressive Conservative party). In each case, these leaders' evangelical Protestant convictions and their views on issues like abortion and gay marriage received much attention during federal elections, including the January 2006 vote that made Harper the prime minister and head of a minority government.

In the case of Manning and Day, interest in how their personal views might work out in public policy probably helped them throughout much of the Canadian West but undercut their chances in Ontario, Quebec, and the Maritimes. Preston Manning is an especially interesting case, since his father, Ernest Manning, was William Aberhart's successor both as the long-time Social Credit premier of Alberta (1943–1968) and as the pastor cum radio preacher of Aberhart's independent evangelical church. While the combination of evangelicalism and politics is familiar to American observers, the combination of populism and large-government responsibility that Ernest Manning and Preston Manning brought to the public sphere along with their evangelical faith did not fit neatly into the standard American pattern.

Stephen Harper's religious beliefs are similar to those of Manning and Day. Yet he was successful in the 2006 federal election because the Conservatives won some support in Quebec (Harper is a fluent French speaker) and because Harper could keep the campaign fixed on dissatisfaction with the long-standing Liberal government of Jean Chrétien (whose personal Catholicism was never an issue) instead of on the public implications of his personal beliefs. In that respect, the 2006 election was more traditionally Canadian in downplaying the candidates' own religious views. Additionally, although Harper's positions against abortion on demand and against gay marriage were well known, they were not as central as the "values" issues had become in the American presidential election of 2004.

Yet despite the cooling of religious-political issues in the 2006 Canadian election, it did seem as if an American pattern was emerging for voting constituencies. Historically, Canadian mainline Protestants (United Church members, Anglicans, Presbyterians) and members of evangelical denominations had leaned toward the old Progressive Conservative party, while Catholics favored the Liberal party—but as tendencies rather than as the tight adherence witnessed in recent American elections by white evangelicals voting Republican and black Protestants voting Democratic. This general picture prevailed into the 1990s, as indicated by results from the 1996 Angus Reid poll. For example, where in the United States 72 percent of self-identified fundamentalists and evangelicals who regularly went to church voted for the Republican presidential candidate in 1992, only 41 percent of church-attending adherents to conservative Protestant denominations voted for the Reform party in Canada's 1993 parliamentary election. Also, in 1996, the Canadians who showed up as most evangelical in response to questions about religious beliefs and practices were much more likely to support the Liberal party than either the Reform or Progressive Conservative parties (Liberal party support among the "most evangelical" was roughly equal to the total support for the Reform and Progressive Conservative parties). Among Canadian Catholics in 1996, Liberals enjoyed a very large majority of support, and that support increased as church participation increased.

During the Canadian election in 2006, however, the patterns described in chapter 12 of this volume for the United States became more evident. As reported by Andrew Grenville of the Ipsos Reid polling service, two-thirds of Canadian Protestants who regularly attend church voted for the Conservative candidate, which was 25 percent more than in the 2004 Canadian general election.[24] These voters were motivated by conscience issues like abortion and same-sex marriage as well as by their perception of corruption in the Liberal party. Even more dramatic was a shift among Catholic voters. It was, again, a move that paralleled developments in the United States. When Catholics who attend church regularly were separated from nominal Catholics, it turned out that the former delivered more of their votes to the Conservatives than to any other party. This result marks the first time in modern polling history that the Conservatives won a plurality of this Catholic vote. Among regularly attending Catholics, the decline in Liberal support and the rise in voting for Conservatives was considerably stronger in Quebec than in the rest of Canada. So for Catholics, both the party supported and the effect of regular attendance on voting was reversed from only a decade before.

If these patterns are part of a trend, rather than a one-time occurrence, it means that Canadian religious-political connections are coming closer to American patterns. If this is indeed happening, the cause probably involves the mobilization of moral conservatives against the backdrop of structural changes that have made Canadian society more like American society. These changes include a shift away from religious self-identification, a conscious turn to multicultural ideology, and a new climate for judicial activity.

Since the 1960s, Canadian self-identification has shifted massively from what it once had been—language (English or French) plus religion (Protestant or Catholic)—to new markers. For Quebec, those markers still include language, but now in league with nationalist sentiment rather than religion. Cultural heritage is also very important, especially for secular Francophones in Quebec, but also for Chinese Canadians and other newer ethnic communities. Regional identification remains strong for many in the Maritimes and western Canada. Lifestyle choices are increasingly significant, especially in the great urban centers of Montreal, Ottawa-Gatineau, Toronto-Hamilton, Calgary, Edmonton, and Vancouver (which account for almost half of the nation's entire population). And, as in the United States, economic status provides powerful identity for large numbers of people.

Explaining why older religious markers of identity have faded would involve a complicated account of developments from the 1920s through the 1960s that included fateful decisions within the Catholic church and the largest Protestant denominations about how best to adjust historic faiths for new Canadian conditions.[25] But however that process is explained, it was obvious by the 1960s that religion was declining in salience as other factors rose.

For Quebec, the change meant defining provincial identity in cultural and nationalistic terms instead of religious terms. In the rest of Canada, historic markers of Christian civilization seemed to give way almost as rapidly, if not with the same shock as felt in Quebec's once overwhelmingly Catholic society. A study by Gary Miedema has shown how at signal events in 1967—celebrations of Canada's centennial and Expo 67 at Montreal's World Exposition—public symbols and rhetoric moved away from the particulars of Canada's religious history toward a vision of universal multicultural toleration. On these well-publicized occasions, public spokespeople looked to the latter rather than the former to "foster unity, stability, and a common vision in a country perpetually challenged by division, political instability, and multiple and conflicting dreams for the future."[26]

In 1969, Prime Minister Trudeau's Liberal government engineered a declaration that made all of Canada officially bilingual. To Reginald Bibby, this was a key event in the process whereby an ideology of pluralism replaced the traditional Christian ideologies of both French and English Canada. In his view, this declaration revealed that, "since the 1960s, Canada has been encouraging the freedom of groups and individuals without simultaneously laying down cultural expectations." According to Bibby, "colorful collages of mosaics have been forming throughout Canadian life. Our expectation has been that fragments of the mosaic will somehow add up to a healthy and cohesive society. It is not at all clear why we should expect such an outcome."[27]

In 1971, the government began to promote multiculturalism as a national policy. This decision led to government agencies and funds being explicitly devoted to promoting the self-consciousness of ethnic minorities. Equal access and mutual respect were assuming the public place that had once been occupied by recognition of the deity. This process resembled the growing American practice of identity by race, class, and gender. It marked the functional triumph of liberal principles over communal traditions. For the United States, such a triumph merely extended an orientation to freedom and choice rooted in the nation's revolutionary beginnings. For Canada, it represented a reversal of a much more communal past.

The repatriation of the Constitution and the new Charter of Rights and Freedoms, which took place in 1982, reinforced the move of Canadian society in American directions. In typical British fashion, Canada's "constitution" had long been only the actions of Britain's Parliament that created the dominion and regulated its place in the commonwealth, along with the traditions of English common law. After much labor by Trudeau and many others, the British Parliament in 1982 formally handed over all Canadian authority to Canada itself. Significantly, this action also involved the promulgation of a Charter of Rights and Freedoms that was intended, like the much-shorter American Bill of Rights, to guarantee personal liberties, but also, in Canada's case, the liberties of the provinces over against Ottawa. Unlike the American Constitution, the Canadian Charter referred directly to the deity: "Canada is founded upon principles that recognize the supremacy of God and the rule of law."[28] But like the American Bill of Rights, the Canadian Charter has also stimulated great concern for personal liberty and personal choice. The most consequential long-term effect of the new Charter was to push Canadian jurisprudence into an increasingly American pattern where activist judges become the promoters of social change.[29] What Seymour Martin Lipset predicted in 1990 has in fact come to pass:

> [T]he Charter of Rights . . . probably goes further toward taking the country in an American direction than any other enacted structural change, including the Canada–U.S. Free Trade Agreement. The Charter's stress on due process and individual rights, although less stringent than that of the U.S. Bill of Rights, should increase individualism and litigiousness north of the border.[30]

In sum, over the last decades, Canadian society has moved in an American direction by shifting markers of identity away from religious institutions and from inherited status toward identity defined by personal choice, ethnicity, nationalism, lifestyle, and economic status.

Against such a background, it is not surprising that many of Canada's evangelical Protestants and some of its practicing Catholics have borrowed strategies from the United States to promote their morally conservative views. They have begun to do what Americans of all religious persuasions have always done—identify a problem with public dimensions and then immediately mobilize a constituency in order to address that problem head-on.

The controversies these actions have engendered take a peculiarly Canadian shape. Moral conservatives correctly point out how radically and rapidly contemporary cultural change has moved away from Canada's traditional Christian standards for private and public morality; but they make that point by adopting more individualistic, more aggressive—that is to say, more American—means of political activity. Their opponents, who support the recent changes in Canadian society, continue to rely on traditional forms of social corporatism, even though it is now a corporatism in which the Catholic and mainline Protestant churches, which had traditionally played central roles in Canada's corporate life, are marginalized. The general effect on connections between religion and politics is that a mixture of traditional Canadian values and practices has been tinctured by a mixture of traditional American values and practices. The substance of what should constitute public values is contested, as are the means by which public values should be promoted.

To the extent that this account has captured the current moment, it begins to explain why Canadian connections between religion and politics now resemble American connections more than at any other time in Canada's history. Yet because the religious constituencies and religious histories of the two nations remain quite different, it does not mean that adding some American elements has led to an essentially American situation. Nor, even if this account is accurate, does it mean that influences from the past have been extirpated entirely. Where those influences persist, so also do Canadian approaches to religion and politics continue that differ from patterns found in its neighbor to the south.

Notes

This chapter, which compares Canadian and American developments broadly, replaces a chapter in the book's first edition by the late George Rawlyk, which was more tightly focused on specific episodes in Canadian history: "Politics, Religion, and the Canadian Experience: A Preliminary Probe," in *Religion and American Politics*, ed. Mark A. Noll (New York: Oxford University Press, 1990), 253–77. My understanding of things Canadian remains heavily indebted to Rawlyk's publications and his personal tutelage. This chapter draws on Mark A. Noll, "Canada," in *The Encyclopedia of Politics and Religion*, 2nd ed., 2 vols., ed. Robert Wuthnow (Washington, D.C.: Congressional Quarterly Books,

2007), 1:95–99; and Noll, "What Happened to Christian Canada," *Church History* 75 (June 2006): 245–73.

1. The best recent studies of religion and Canadian politics (politics understood in broad terms) are David Lyon and Marguerite Van Die, eds., *Rethinking Church, State, and Modernity: Canada between Europe and America* (Toronto: University of Toronto Press, 2000); and Marguerite Van Die, ed., *Religion and Public Life in Canada: Historical and Comparative Perspectives* (Toronto: University of Toronto Press, 2001).

2. For solid overviews, see Terrence Murphy and Roberto Perin, eds., *A Concise History of Christianity in Canada* (Toronto: Oxford University Press, 1996); and Jean Hamelin and Nicole Gagnon, *Histoire du catholicisme québécois: Le XXe siècle*, vol. 1: *1898–1940*; and Jean Hamelin, *Histoire du catholicisme québécois: Le XXe siècle*, vol. 2: *De 1940 à nos jours*, both ed. Nive Voisine (Montreal: Boréal, 1984).

3. For Catholic employment of that language, see Preston Jones, "Protestants, Catholics, and the Bible in Late-Nineteenth-Century Quebec," *Fides et Historia* 33 (Summer–Fall 2001): 31–38.

4. Kevin B. Kee, *Revivalists: Marketing the Gospel in English Canada, 1884–1957* (Montreal and Kingston: McGill-Queen's University Press, 2006); and Eric R. Crouse, *Revival in the City: The Impact of American Evangelists in Canada, 1884–1914* (Montreal and Kingston: McGill-Queen's University Press, 2005).

5. Seymour Martin Lipset, *Continental Divide: The Values and Institutions of the United States and Canada* (New York: Routledge, 1990), 8.

6. See George A. Rawlyk, *Revolution Rejected* (Scarborough, Ont.: Prentice-Hall, 1967); David Mills, *The Idea of Loyalty in Upper Canada, 1784–1850* (Kingston and Montreal: McGill-Queen's University Press, 1988); and Robert M. Calhoon, Timothy M. Barnes, and George A. Rawlyk, eds., *Loyalists and Community in North America* (Westport, Conn.: Greenwood, 1994).

7. See Neil Semple, *The Lord's Dominion: The History of Canadian Methodism* (Kingston and Montreal: McGill-Queen's University Press, 1996), 40–49; and J. I. Little, *Borderland Religion: The Emergence of an English-Canadian Identity, 1792–1852* (Toronto: University of Toronto Press, 2004).

8. Marguerite Van Die, "The End of Christian Canada: Past Perspectives, Present Opportunities for Faith and Public Life" (unpublished paper delivered at Scarborough United Church, Calgary, Sept. 2002). For Van Die's account of how the informal Protestant establishment worked in a specific part of nineteenth-century English Canada, see *Religion, Family, and Community in Victorian Canada: The Colbys of Carrollcroft* (Montreal and Kingston: McGill-Queen's University Press, 2006).

9. Christopher Adamson, "Necessary Evil or Necessary Good: Christianity, the State, and Political Culture in the Antebellum United States and Pre-Confederation" (unpublished paper, May 2005), 28, 39. For Adamson's fuller discussion of Canadian-American differences, see "God's Continental Divide: Politics and Religion in Upper Canada and the Northern and Western United States, 1775–1841," *Comparative Studies in Society and History* 36 (July 1994): 417–46.

10. Lipset, *Continental Divide*, 92–113.

11. See Maurice Armstrong, "Neutrality and Religion in Revolutionary Nova Scotia," *New England Quarterly* 9 (1946): 50–62; and George A. Rawlyk, *The Canada Fire:*

Radical Evangelicalism in British North America, 1775–1812 (Montreal and Kingston: McGill-Queen's University Press, 1994).

12. A classic account from this perspective is found in the second volume of Egerton Ryerson, *The Loyalists of American and Their Times, from 1620 to 1816*, 2 vols. (Toronto: Briggs, 1880).

13. David R. Elliott and Iris Miller, *Bible Bill: A Biography of William Aberhart* (Edmonton: Reidmore, 1987).

14. Doris French Shackleton, *Tommy Douglas* (Toronto: McClelland and Stewart, 1975).

15. George Parkin Grant, *Lament for a Nation: The Defeat of Canadian Nationalism* (Toronto: McClelland and Stewart, 1965). On the book's impact, see William Christian, *George Grant: A Biography* (Toronto: University of Toronto Press, 1994), 240–55.

16. Rawlyk, "Politics, Religion, and the Canadian Experience," 264–67.

17. Thomas Flanagan, *Riel and the Rebellion 1885 Reconsidered*, 2nd ed. (Toronto: University of Toronto Press, 2000).

18. Richard Johnston, "The Reproduction of the Religious Cleavage in Canadian Elections," *Canadian Journal of Political Science/Revue Canadienne de Science Politique* 18 (1985): 99–114.

19. Andrew Grenville and Angus Reid, "Catholicism and Voting No," *Christian Week*, 30 Jan. 1996, p. 7.

20. Scott Ellis Ferrin et al., "From Sectarian to Secular Control of Education: The Case of Newfoundland," *Journal of Research on Christian Education* 10 (2001): 411–30.

21. Good use of this survey is made in Sam Reimer, *Evangelicals and the Continental Divide: The Conservative Protestant Subculture in Canada and the United States* (Montreal and Kingston: McGill-Queen's University Press, 2003); and Kurt Bowen, *Christians in a Secular World: The Canadian Experience* (Montreal and Kingston: McGill-Queen's University Press, 2004). For my own interpretation of the survey, see Noll, "Religion in the United States and Canada," *Crux* (Regent College, Vancouver) 34 (Dec. 1998): 13–25.

22. Reginald W. Bibby, *Restless Gods: The Renaissance of Religion in Canada* (Toronto: Stoddart, 2002); and for the results of more recent polling supervised by Bibby, see "Macleans Poll 2006," *Macleans*, 1 July 2006, pp. 35–46 (with pp. 42–43 especially on religion).

23. John English, Richard Gwyn, and P. Whitney Lackenbauer, *The Hidden Pierre Elliott Trudeau: The Faith behind the Politics* (Ottawa: Novalis, 2004).

24. Andrew Grenville, "Church, Conscience, Corruption and the Conservatives," *Faith Today*, Mar.–Apr. 2006, pp. 24–27.

25. See, especially, Michael Gauvreau, *The Catholic Origins of Quebec's Quiet Revolution, 1931–1970* (Montreal and Kingston: McGill-Queen's University Press, 2005).

26. I am quoting Gary R. Miedema, "For Canada's Sake: The Re-visioning of Canada and the Re-structuring of Public Religion in the 1960s" (Ph.D. diss., Queen's University, 2000), 27; but see also the book from this dissertation, *For Canada's Sake: Public Religion, Centennial Celebrations, and the Re-making of Canada in the 1960s* (Kingston and Montreal: McGill-Queen's University Press, 2005).

27. Reginald W. Bibby, *Mosaic Madness: The Poverty and Potential of Life in Canada* (Toronto: Stoddart, 1990), 10.

28. An excellent account is George Egerton, "Trudeau, God, and the Canadian Constitution: Religion, Human Rights, and Government Authority in the Making of the 1982 Constitution," in Lyon and Van Die, *Rethinking Church, State, and Modernity*, 99–107.

29. For an argumentative, but still informative, discussion of judicial changes since 1982, see Robert Ivan Martin, *The Most Dangerous Branch: How the Supreme Court of Canada Has Undermined Our Law and Our Democracy* (Montreal and Kingston: McGill-Queen's University Press, 2003).

30. Lipset, *Continental Divide*, 116.

Quid Obscurum

The Changing Terrain of Church-State Relations

Robert Wuthnow

$\mathcal{I}$N HIS HAUNTINGLY memorable description of the Battle of Waterloo, Victor
Hugo makes a startling observation. The opening lines of his narrative are these:

> If it had not rained on the night of June 17, 1815, the future of Eu-
> rope would have been different. A few drops more or less tipped the
> balance against Napoleon. For Waterloo to be the end of Austerlitz,
> Providence needed only a little rain, and an unseasonable cloud crossing
> the sky was enough for the collapse of a world.[1]

What is startling, though, is not the idea that the future of Europe, or even the
outcome of the battle, hinged on something as seemingly trivial as an unexpected
rainstorm. Such explanations fill the annals of military history. Had not the British
expeditionary force been able to evacuate from Dunkirk under cover of heavy fog
during the week of May 26, 1940, the German army might well have gone on to
win the war. Those who tread the battlefields near Gettysburg, Pennsylvania, view
the heights along Culp's Hill and Cemetery Ridge and wonder what the outcome
would have been had Lee's troops—instead of Meade's—occupied those favored

positions. The great turning points of history, it appears, sometimes hinge less on what people do than the conditions under which they have to do it. The flukes of nature—or, as some would maintain, the hand of God—intervene willfully at portentous moments.

And yet, we in contemporary society, schooled as we have been in the complexities of history, know how tenuous these arguments often prove to be. Battles may be won or lost on the basis of a sudden turn of the weather, but wars are not and neither is the course of history. What if, by some chance, Lee's troops had occupied the heights at Gettysburg? Would Meade's then have run the bloody gauntlet that became immortalized as "Pickett's charge"? Or would the federal army have faded away to fight on more opportune terms? Lee, we learn from modern analysts of the battle, was forced to fight, despite the unfavorable terrain, because he desperately needed to win. Supplies were running low and Confederate agents needed to be able to demonstrate to their European creditors that they could win. And the reason supplies were running low lay deep in the South's agrarian economy, compared with the North's industrial economy, and even deeper in the triangular trade that had developed among the South, Great Britain, and West Africa. Lee was forced to fight; Meade could have slipped away.

What startles us as we proceed with Victor Hugo's account is that he succeeds so well in defending his thesis. A soggy battlefield was indeed a decisive factor. But as so often is the case in Hugo's narratives, it was the larger terrain—and the uncertainties inherent in this terrain—that constituted the framework in which the decisions of the two commanders had to be made. An unexpected rainstorm made it impossible for Napoleon to deploy the full force of his artillery. This was a factor that could not have been anticipated, an element of the battle that in essence remained obscure.

The *quid obscurum* in Hugo's account, though, is at once more simple and straightforward than this and more elusive as well. There was, running through the battlefield, interposed directly between the two armies, a ditch. It extended across the entire line that Napoleon's cavalry would have to charge. It was a deep chasm, made by human hands, the result of a road that had been cut as if by a knife through the natural terrain. It was hidden from view. The cavalry charged, and then faced the terror. Hugo recounts:

> There was the ravine, unexpected, gaping right at the horses' feet, twelve feet deep between its banks. The second rank pushed in the first, the third pushed in the second; the horses reared, lurched backward, fell onto their rumps, and struggled writhing with their feet in the air, piling

up and throwing their riders; no means to retreat; the whole column was nothing but a projectile. The momentum to crush the English crushed the French. The inexorable ravine could not yield until it was filled; riders and horses rolled in together helter-skelter, grinding against each other, making common flesh in this dreadful gulf, and when this grave was full of living men, the rest marched over them and went on. Almost a third of Dubois's brigade sank into the abyss.[2]

The *quid obscurum*, quite literally, was a hidden fracture with enormous consequences.

The second, and deeper, meaning of Hugo's reference to the *quid obscurum* is that of the broader uncertainties evoked by the clash of two armies. Only in the heat of battle do the unforeseen contingencies become evident; only then do the plans of the commanding generals prove to have missed important features of the broader terrain. In the struggling line of soldiers engaged in hand-to-hand combat, one begins to realize that the expenditures are greater than expected. The consequences of seemingly unimportant conditions turn out to be incalculable. It is left to the historian to assess, with the advantage of hindsight, what the role of these previously obscured realities was.

My purpose in drawing attention to Hugo's discussion is twofold. At the more literal level, there is a great fracture, like the ravine cutting across the plateau of Mont-Saint-Jean, running through the cultural terrain on which the battles of religion and politics are now being fought. It is a fracture that deserves our attention, for it is of recent creation, a new human construction, unlike the timeless swells of culture through which it has been cut. And it has become a mire of bitter contention, consuming the energies of religious communities and grinding their ideals into the grime of unforeseen animosities. At a broader level, this fracture also symbolizes the unplanned developments in the larger terrain that did not become evident until the battles themselves began to erupt. With the advantage of hindsight, we can now discover the importance of these developments. We can see how the present controversies in American religion were affected by broader changes in the society—the consequences of which remained obscure at the time but have now become painfully transparent.

The ravine running through the culture-scape of American religion is as real as the one made by the road between the two villages on the Belgian border. It differs in one important respect, though. It is not simply a fissure in the physical environment, a ditch that creates the downfall of one of the protagonists. It is to a much greater extent the product of battle itself. The chasm dividing American religion into separate communities has emerged largely from the struggle between these communities. It may have occurred, as we shall suggest shortly, along a fault line already present in the cultural terrain. But it has been dug deeper and wider by the skirmishes that have been launched across it.

Depending on whose lens we use to view it through, any number of ways of describing it can be found. Television evangelist Jimmy Swaggart once described it as a gulf between those who believe in the Judeo-Christian principles on which our country was founded and those who believe in the "vain philosophies of men." On one side are the "old-fashioned" believers in "the word of almighty God," who are often maligned as "poor simpletons"; on the other side are the "so-called intelligentsia," those who believe they are great because they "are more intelligent than anyone else," "socialists," believers in "syphilitic Lenin," and the burdened masses who have nothing better to get excited about than football and baseball games.[3] In contrast, a writer for the *New York Times* depicted it as a battle between "churches and church-allied groups" who favor freedom, democracy, and the rights of minorities, on one hand, and a right-wing fringe interested in setting up a theocracy governed by a "dictatorship of religious values," on the other hand.[4]

Apart from the colors in which the two sides are portrayed, though, one finds general agreement on the following points: (a) the reality of the division between two opposing camps; (b) the predominance of "fundamentalists," "evangelicals," and "religious conservatives" in one and the predominance of "religious liberals," "humanists," and "secularists" in the other; and (c) the presence of deep hostility and misgiving between the two. An official of the National Council of Churches summarized the two positions, and the views of each toward the other, this way:

> Liberals abhor the smugness, the self-righteousness, the absolute certainty, the judgmentalism, the lovelessness of a narrow, dogmatic faith. [Conservatives] scorn the fuzziness, the marshmallow convictions, the inclusiveness that makes membership meaningless—the "anything goes" attitude that views even Scripture as relative. Both often caricature the worst in one another and fail to perceive the best.[5]

To suggest that American religion is divided neatly into two communities with sharply differentiated views is, of course, to ride roughshod over the countless landmarks, signposts, hills, and gullies that actually constitute the religious landscape. Not only do fundamentalists distinguish themselves from evangelicals, but each brand of religious conservatism is divided into dozens of denominational product lines. Similar distinctions can be made on the religious Left. In the popular mind, though, there does seem to be some reality to the cruder, binary way of thinking.

A national survey conducted in 1984 (even before some of the more acrimonious debates over the role of religion in politics had arisen) found both a high level of awareness of the basic divisions between religious liberals and conservatives and a great deal of actual hostility between the two. When asked to classify themselves, 43 percent of those surveyed identified themselves as religious liberals and 41 percent said they were religious conservatives. The public is thus divided almost equally between the two categories, and only one person in six was unable or unwilling to use these labels.[6] Judging from the ways in which self-styled liberals and conservatives answered other questions, the two categories also seem to have had some validity. As one would expect, conservatives were much more likely than liberals to identify themselves as evangelicals, to believe in a literal interpretation of the Bible, to say they had had a "born-again" conversion experience, to indicate that they had tried to convert others to their faith, and to hold conservative views on such issues as abortion and prayer in public schools. Liberals were less likely than conservatives to attend church or synagogue regularly, but a majority affirmed the importance of religion in their lives, tended to regard the Bible as divinely inspired (if not to be taken literally), and held liberal views on a variety of political and moral issues. Some denominations tended to consist of more conservatives than liberals, or vice versa. But, generally, the major denominational families and faith traditions—Methodists, Lutherans, Presbyterians, Catholics, Jews—were all divided about equally between religious conservatives and religious liberals. In other words, the cleavage between conservatives and liberals tends not, for the most part, to fall along denominational lines. It is a cleavage that divides people within the same denominations—to which struggles within the Southern Baptist Convention, the Episcopal church, the Presbyterian Church U.S.A., and the Roman Catholic church all bear witness.

The study also demonstrated the extent to which the relations between religious liberals and religious conservatives have become ridden with conflict. A majority of the public surveyed said the conflict between religious liberals and conservatives is an area of "serious tension." A substantial majority of both groups said they had had unpleasant or, at best, "mixed" relations with the other group. And these relations were said to have taken place in fairly intimate settings: in one's church, among friends and relatives, even within the same Bible study or fellowship groups. Moreover, each side held a number of negative images of the other. Liberals saw conservatives as rigid, intolerant, and fanatical. Conservatives described liberals as shallow, morally loose, unloving, and unsaved. The study also demonstrated that, unlike other kinds of prejudice and hostility, the ill feelings separating religious liberals and religious conservatives *did not mitigate* as the two groups came into greater contact with one another. The more each side came into contact with the other, and the more knowledge it gained about the other, the less it liked the other.

Viewed normatively, it is of course disturbing to find such levels of animosity and tension between religious liberals and conservatives. We might expect nothing better from communists and capitalists or Democrats and Republicans. But deep within the Jewish and Christian traditions lies an ethic of love and forgiveness. In congregation after congregation, prayers are routinely offered for unity among the faithful. Creeds are recited stating belief in the one, holy, Catholic church. And homilies are delivered on Jesus' injunction to love one's neighbor as oneself.

If these findings are disturbing, they are not, however, surprising. They accord with the way in which American religion is portrayed in the media and in pulpits, and with the way in which American religion seems to function. The major newspapers and television networks routinely publicize the bizarre activities of fundamentalists and evangelicals: the conservative governor who prays with his pastor and hears God tell him to run for the presidency, the television preacher who prays (successfully, it turns out) that an impending hurricane will be averted from the Virginia coast, the fundamentalists in Indiana who deny their children proper schooling and medical care, the evangelical counselor in California who is sued by the family of a patient who committed suicide, the deranged member of a fundamentalist church in Maine who mows down his fellow parishioners with a shotgun. Conservative television preachers and conservative religious publications make equally vitriolic comments about their liberal foes: how an Episcopal bishop is condoning sexual permissiveness within his diocese, how Methodist liberals are encouraging homosexuality among the denomination's pastors, how zealous clergy in the nuclear disarmament movement are selling the country out to the Russians, how religious conservatives are being discriminated against in colleges and universities. It is little wonder that the labels begin to stick. Sooner or later, it does begin to appear as if the world of faith is divided into two belligerent superpowers.

But this picture of the religious world is not simply a creation of the sensationalist media. At the grassroots, one can readily find denunciations of liberalism from conservative pulpits and diatribes against fundamentalism from liberal pulpits. One can readily observe the split between liberals and conservatives in church meetings and discussion groups. Liberals freely express doubts about the historical authenticity of the Bible. Conservatives appeal for greater faith in the supernatural, the miraculous, and argue for more emphasis on sin and personal salvation. Beneath the innocent statements of each are deeper feelings about right and wrong, truth and error. Beyond these simple exchanges, the two also isolate themselves in different communities of support and action: liberals in the nurturing environment of local groups promoting peace, worldwide action against AIDS, equitable and affordable housing; conservatives, in the womb of Bible study groups and prayer fellowships. One can also readily observe the polarizing tendencies of national issues on the religious environment. Pick up the latest issue of *Christian Century* or *Christianity Today*. Observe the number of articles that deal with politics. Note the paucity of material on theology or even personal spirituality. Or open the mail. Count the letters from Jerry Falwell, Pat Robertson, James Dobson, People for the American Way, the American Civil Liberties Union. The issues are now national, rather than local or regional. They concern an appointment to the Supreme Court, a constitutional amendment on abortion, a preacher running for president. They are supported by one faction of the religious community and opposed by another. They induce polarization.

But to say that there are many reasons that the chasm between religious liberals and conservatives exists is still only to describe it—to parade the colors of the troops engaged in the great battle of which it consists. It is a chasm deepened and widened by political debate. It is a chasm around which religious communities' participation in public affairs divides. It has become a predictable feature of the contemporary debate over church-state relations. To understand it, though, we must look at broader developments in the social terrain. We must try to discover why this particular fracture line existed in the cultural geography in the first place.

In one sense it is, of course, a fracture line that can be found in the soil of American religion as far back as the years immediately after the Civil War. Even in the eighteenth century and during the first half of the nineteenth, one can identify the beginnings of a division between religious conservatives and religious liberals insofar as one considers the effects of the Enlightenment on elite culture. Skepticism, atheism, anticlericalism, and of course deism constitute identifiable alternatives to the popular piety of Methodists and Baptists and the conservative orthodoxy of Roman Catholics, Jews, Presbyterians, and others during this period. But to an important degree, the potential division between conservatism and liberalism before the Civil War was overshadowed by the deeper tensions to which the society was subject. Nationalism and regionalism, differences between the culture of the eastern seaboard and the expanding western territories, and increasingly the tensions between North and South provided the major divisions affecting the organization of American religion. Not until the termination of these hostilities and the resumption of material progress after the Civil War did it become possible for the gap between religious conservatives and liberals to gain importance. Gradually in these years the discoveries of science, the new ideas of Charles Darwin, and by the end of the nineteenth century the beginnings of a national system of higher education provided the groundwork for a liberal challenge to religious conservatism. The culmination of these changes, of course, came at the turn of the century in the modernist movement and its increasingly vocal opponent, the fundamentalists. In the long view, the present division between religious liberals and religious conservatives can be pictured simply as a continuation or outgrowth of this earlier conflict. The inevitable forces of modernization produced a secular freedom in matters of the spirit and voiced skepticism toward a faith based in divine revelation, and this tendency evoked a reactionary movement in which religious conservatism was preserved.

That, as I say, is the impression gained from taking a long view of American history. If one takes a more limited perspective, though, a rather different impression emerges. One is able to focus more directly on the immediate contours of the religious environment and to see how these contours arc in the short term as shaped by specific events. This, I suppose, is the advantage of taking the perspective of the sociologist—which seldom extends much before World War II.

At the close of that war, the condition of American religion was quite different than it is now. It contained seeds that were to germinate and grow, like weeds in the concrete, widening the cracks that have now become so visible. But the basic divisions ran along other lines. Tensions between Protestants and Catholics had reached new heights as immigration and natural increase contributed to the growth of the Catholic population. Tensions between Christians and Jews also ran deep, even though they were often less visible than the conflicts dividing Protestants and Catholics. There was, as Will Herberg was to describe it a few years later, a "tripartite division" in American religion: to be American was to be Protestant, Catholic, or Jewish.[7] In addition, denominational boundaries also played an important role in giving structure to the Protestant branch of this tripartite arrangement. Ecumenical services were beginning to erode some of these boundaries (often for the explicit purpose of displaying Protestant unity against the threat of papal expansion). But ethnic, national, and geographic divisions—as well as theological and liturgical divisions—continued to reinforce denominational separatism.

In all of this, there was little evidence of any basic split between liberals and conservatives. To be sure, fundamentalism was alive and well, but its very success proved in a deeper sense to be its limitation. By the mid-1930s, fundamentalist spokespeople had largely conceded their defeat in the major Protestant denominations and had withdrawn to form their own organizations. As the Great Depression, and then the rationing imposed by the war, made travel more difficult, these organizations also grew further apart from one another. By the end of the war, they consisted largely of small, isolated splinter groups on the fringes of the mainline denominations. Most of the population that continued to believe in such doctrinal tenets as biblical inerrancy, the divinity of Jesus, and the necessity of personal salvation remained within these larger denominations. And even the official policies of these denominations reflected what would now be considered a strong conservative emphasis. Evangelism, door-to-door canvassing of communities, revivalistic meetings, biblical preaching, missions—all received prominent support. Also of significance was the fact that many of the more outspoken conservative religious leaders were beginning to build their own organizations. As yet, though, these leaders were able to build quietly and were content largely to maintain ties with the major denominations, rather than break away like their fundamentalist counterparts. Certainly, there were differences of opinion about such matters as the literal inspiration of the Bible or the role of churches in political affairs. But these were as yet not the subjects of mass movements or of widely recognized cultural divisions. Only the terms "fundamentalist" and "liberal" suggest continuity between this period and our own; a more careful examination of issues, personalities, and organizations indicates discontinuity.

In the years immediately following World War II, we do find evidence, though, of the conditions that were to predispose American religion to undergo a major restructuring in the decades that followed. Three such predisposing conditions stand out in particular. In the first place, American religion was on the whole extraordinarily strong. The largest churches now counted members in the thousands. Overall, the number of local churches and synagogues ranged in the hundreds of thousands. Some denominations sported budgets in the tens of millions. And collectively, religious organizations took in approximately $800 million annually—a figure, the historian Harold Laski observed, that exceeded the budget of the entire British government.[8] In comparison with Europe, the American churches were especially strong. They had not been subjected to the same limitations on government spending that the churches in England, France, and Germany had faced, nor had they faced the mass withdrawal of the working classes that these churches had experienced; and, of course, they had not been subject to the extensive destruction resulting from the war. They had been weakened by the Depression and by shortages of building materials during the war. But, curiously perhaps, this very weakness turned out to be a strength as well. It prompted major building programs after the war, allowed the churches to relocate in growing neighborhoods, and generally encouraged what was to become known as the religious revival of the 1950s. The critical feature of the churches' massive institutional strength for the coming decades, though, was the fact that religion was able to adjust to a changing environment. Rather than simply wither away—or maintain itself in quiet contemplative seclusion—it adapted to the major social developments of the postwar period. In this sense, we owe much of the present controversy in American religion to the simple fact that it had remained a strong institutional force right up to the second half of the twentieth century.

The second predisposing condition was the strong "this-worldly" orientation of American religion. Not only was it able to adapt to changing circumstances, it also engaged itself actively in the social environment by its own initiative. When the war ended, religious leaders looked to the future with great expectancy. They recognized the opportunities that lay ahead. They were also mindful of the recurrent dangers they faced. Indeed, a prominent theme in their motivational appeals focused on the combination of promise and peril. A resolution passed by the Federal Council of Churches in 1945, for instance, declared: "We are living in a uniquely dangerous and promising time."[9] It was a dangerous time because of the recurrent likelihood of war, the widely anticipated return to a depressed economy after the war-induced boom had ended, and of course the invention of nuclear weapons. It was a promising time because of new opportunities for missionary work and evangelism. The stakes were high, so persistent activism was the desired response. In the words of a Methodist minister, who reminded his audience of the perilous opportunities facing them: "That requires . . . a great godly company of men and women with no axe to grind, desiring only to save, serve, help and heal."[10] The result was that religious organizations deliberately exposed their flanks to the influences of their environment. Programs were initiated, education was encouraged, preaching confronted issues of the day—all of which, like the rain on Napoleon's troops, would reveal the churches' dependence on the conditions of their terrain.

The third predisposing factor was reflected in the relation understood to prevail between religion and the public sphere. This is especially important to understand, because it provides a vivid contrast with the ways in which we now conceive of religion's influence in the political arena. In the 1940s and 1950s, there appears to have been a fairly widespread view among religious leaders, theologians, and even social scientists that values and behavior were closely related. Find out what a person's basic values were, and you could pretty well predict that person's behavior. If persons valued democracy, they could be counted on to uphold it in their behavior. If a person worked hard and struggled to get ahead, you could be pretty sure that person valued success and achievement. More broadly, writers also extended this connection to the society. A nation's culture essentially consisted of values, and these values were arranged in a hierarchy of priority. The society was held together by this hierarchy of values. It generated consensus and caused people to behave in similar ways.

For religious leaders, this was a very convenient way of conceiving things. It meant that the way to shape people's lives was by shaping their values. And this was what the churches did best: they preached and they taught. They influenced the individual's system of values. They shaped the individual's conscience. Their conduit to the public arena was thus through the individual's conscience. Shape a churchperson's values, and you could rest assured that your influence would be carried into the public sphere. That person would vote according to his or her conscience, would manifest high values in his or her work, would behave charitably, ethically, honestly. All the churches needed to do was preach and teach.

This was a view that also gained support from the public arena itself. Public officials spoke frequently and fervently about their commitment to high moral principles. They lauded the work of religious leaders in reinforcing these principles. Truman, Eisenhower, Dulles, and others spoke of their own religious faith and commended this faith as a source of societal cohesion and strength. It was easy for religious leaders to believe their efforts really were having an impact.

Already, though, there were signs that this world view was coming apart. The problem was not that political leaders were suspected of hypocrisy, although this may have been a problem. Nor was the problem, as some have suggested, that this was basically a Protestant view and thus was being undermined by the growing pluralism of the society. Catholic and Jewish leaders in the 1950s articulated it too. The idea was not that religious faith channeled behavior in specifically Protestant or Catholic or Jewish directions. The idea—at least the one expressed in public contexts—was that a deep religious faith gave the individual moral strength, conviction, the will to do what was right. But the premises on which this world view itself was based were beginning to be questioned. Doubts were beginning to be expressed about the basic connection between values and behavior. What if one's basic values did not translate into actual behavior? What if one's behavior did not stem from one's convictions but was influenced by other factors? As yet, these questions were only raised occasionally. But the very fact that they could be raised suggested the presence of a cultural fissure, a fault line along which a more serious fracture could open up. Values constituted one category, behavior another. The two categories were connected and had to be connected closely for arguments about the impact of conscience on public affairs to be credible. But this connection itself was becoming tenuous.

How, then, did these predisposing conditions in the 1950s become transformed to produce the chasm between religious liberals and conservatives that we experience at the present? How did Herberg's tripartite system, in which the basic religious and religiopolitical divisions occurred between Protestants and Catholics and between Christians and Jews, come to be replaced by what some have called a "two-party system"? The answer, of course, is enormously complex because it involves not only the relations among all of the major religious groupings, but also the relations between religion and the forces shaping the broader society. It is, however, enormously important, for it brings together all of the decisive factors that have shaped American religion in the period since World War II. We can, of course, touch only the basic contours.

In picturing the transformation as a tripartite division being replaced by a two-party system, we should not think that the latter simply superimposed itself on the former nor that one led directly to the other. It helps to divide the process in two and seek answers for each of its phases separately. The first phase (not temporally but analytically) amounted to an erosion of the basic divisions comprising the tripartite system. The second phase amounted to developments reinforcing a new, different cleavage between liberals and conservatives. These processes combined to create what many have sensed is a new dynamic in the relations between church and state, or between religion and politics more generally. But they are also analytically separable. It also helps to identify an interim phase between the two. Three categories of religious organization did not simply melt into two. Thinking of it that way causes us to miss the violence associated with any social change as basic as this. Natural communities were torn asunder, their parts flung into the air and scattered in strange configurations, before the subterranean forces at work in the society finally rearranged them in the patterns we see today. We have to recognize the upheaval and displacement associated with this process if we are to tap the wellsprings from which much of the present political fury arises.

The erosion of the divisions separating Protestants and Catholics, Jews and Christians, and members of different denominations came about gradually. It was legitimated from within by norms of love and humility that promoted interfaith cooperation. It was reinforced from without by changes in the larger society. Rising education levels, memories of the Holocaust, and the Civil Rights movement all contributed to an increasing emphasis on tolerance. Regional migration brought Catholics and Protestants, and Christians and Jews, into closer physical proximity with one another. Denominational ghettos, forged by immigration and ethnic ties, were gradually replaced by religiously and ethnically plural communities. Rates of interreligious marriage went up. And it became increasingly common for members of all religious groups to have grown up with other groups, to have friends from other groups, and to have attended other groups. The denominational hierarchies, seminaries, pension plans, and so forth still played a significant role in the organization of American religion. But the ground was in a sense cleared of old demarcations, thereby making it easier for new alliances and cleavages to emerge.

For those who had spent their entire lives within particular denominational ghettos, these changes in themselves represented major disruptions, of course, especially when it was their pastor who began welcoming outsiders, their denomination that lost its identity by merging with another, or their child who married outside the faith. Most of the upheaval, though, came during the 1960s and was closely associated with the upheaval that pervaded the society in general. Young people were particularly subject to this upheaval. Many were the first ever in their families to attend college. For many, attending college meant leaving the ethnoreligious ghetto for the first time. The campuses themselves were growing so rapidly that alienation and social isolation were common experiences. And, of course, the Civil Rights movement and antiwar protests added to the turmoil. Among the many ways in which this upheaval affected religion, two are especially important.

First, the tensions of the 1960s significantly widened the gap between values and behavior that was mentioned earlier. The two major social movements of this period were the Civil Rights movement and the antiwar movement, and significantly, both dramatized the disjuncture between values and behavior. The Civil Rights movement brought into sharp relief what Gunnar Myrdal had called the "American dilemma"—the dilemma of subscribing to egalitarian values in principle, but engaging in racial discrimination in practice.[11] Here was a clear example of values and behavior being out of joint. The antiwar movement pointed up a similar disjuncture. On one hand, Americans supposedly believed deeply in such values as democracy and the right of people to determine their own destiny. On the other hand, the country was engaged in a war in Southeast Asia that to many seemed to deny these principles. Military force was being used, at best, in an effort to determine another people's destiny for them or, at worst, to prop up an ineffective nondemocratic regime. Both movements drove home, often implicitly, the more general point that people of high values and good consciences could not always be counted on to manifest those virtues in their day-to-day behavior.

The wedge that these movements drove into the earlier connection between values and behavior was to prove increasingly important in separating religious liberals from religious conservatives. Although this picture was to be modified somewhat by the 1980s, in the late 1960s it essentially consisted of conservatives grasping the values side of the equation and liberals seizing the behavioral side. That is, conservatives continued to emphasize preaching and teaching, the shaping of high personal moral standards, and above all the personally redemptive experience of salvation. Whether behavior would result that could alleviate racial discrimination or the war in Southeast Asia was not the issue; the issue was what one believed in one's heart and the motives from which one acted. Liberals, in contrast, increasingly attached importance to behavior. Believe what one will, it does not matter, they said, unless one puts one's faith on the line, takes action, helps to bring about change. And changing social institutions was especially important, because institutions provided the reasons that values and behavior did not correspond. People with good intentions were caught up in evil systems that needed to be overthrown. For the time being at least, liberals argued for religious organizations' taking direct action in politics, while conservatives remained aloof from politics entirely, preferring instead to concentrate on matters of personal belief. Indeed, the two often gave lip service to the higher principles held by the other, but expressed disagreement over the tactics being used. Thus, conservatives often expressed sympathy with the ideal of racial equality, but argued against the direct-action techniques in which liberal clergy were becoming involved. Liberals often continued to express sympathy with the ideal of personal salvation, but argued that personal salvation alone was not enough of a witness if churchpeople did not become actively involved in working for social justice as well.

The second consequence of the turmoil of the 1960s that stands out is the increasing role of higher education in differentiating styles of religious commitment. In the 1950s, perhaps surprisingly so in retrospect, those who had been to college and those who had not were remarkably similar on most items of religious belief and practice. By the early 1970s, a considerable education gap had emerged between the two. The college educated were much less likely, even than the college educated of the previous decade, to attend religious services regularly. Their belief in a literal interpretation of the Bible had eroded dramatically. They were more tolerant of other religions. And they were more interested in experimenting with the so-called new religions, such as Zen, transcendental meditation, Hare Krishna, and the human potential movement. Those who had not been to college remained more committed to traditional views of the Bible, were more strongly interested in religion in general, continued to attend religious services regularly, and expressed doubt about other faiths, including the new religions. In short, educational differences were becoming more significant for religion, just as they were being emphasized more generally in the society. Higher education was becoming a more significant basis for creating social and cultural distinctions. And for religion, it was beginning to reinforce the cleavage between religious liberals and religious conservatives.

During the 1970s, it appeared that the gap between religious liberals and conservatives might be bridged by a significant segment of the evangelical community. Many of its leaders had participated in the educational expansion of the previous decade. They were exposed to the current thinking in higher education, had been influenced by their own participation in the Civil Rights and antiwar movements, had come to hold liberal views on many political issues, and yet retained a strong commitment to the biblical tradition, including an emphasis on personal faith. This new evangelical elite was a younger cohort than the evangelicals who had emerged as leaders during and immediately after World War II. Although most were white, they included women as well as men, were more interested in bridging the racial divide, were cosmopolitan in outlook about missions and humanitarian efforts, had emerged with misgivings about the Vietnam War, and were embarrassed by Richard Nixon's involvement in Watergate.

The voice of these moderate-to-progressive evangelicals, however, was largely drowned out in the 1980s by the more strident voices of the religious Right. Television hook-ups and direct-mail solicitations replaced the evangelical periodical, seminary, and scholarly conference as more effective means of forging a large following and extracting revenue from that following. Issues such as abortion, feminism, and homosexuality provided platforms on which the religious Right could organize. Educational differences continued to separate the more conservative from the more liberal. And other issues began to reinforce these differences. Issues arose that also reflected the success of women in gaining higher education and becoming employed in professional careers, or the exposure one gained in college to the social sciences and humanities as opposed to more narrowly technical educations in engineering or business. The religious Right also borrowed the more activist style of political confrontation that had been used by the Left during the 1960s, for instance, in holding rallies at state capitol buildings and on the steps of the Supreme Court. Its interest in personal morality remained strong, but it now urged believers to take political action to advance conservative moral views.

There were, then, deeper features of the social and cultural terrain that underlay the emerging facture between religious liberals and conservatives. Had it simply been, say, the Supreme Court's 1973 decision on abortion that elicited different responses from liberals and conservatives, we might well have seen a temporary flurry of activity followed by a gradual progression of interest to other matters. Instead, the religious environment came increasingly to be characterized by two clearly identified communities. The two were located differently with respect to the basic social division that had been produced by the growth of higher education. Other bases of differentiation, such as regionalism, ethnicity, and denominationalism, that might have mitigated this basic division had subsided in importance. And each side mobilized its resources through special-purpose groups.

The religious Right experienced setbacks during the late 1980s and 1990s, including Pat Robertson's failed run for the presidency in 1988, the so-called telescandals that rocked the ministries of Jimmy Swaggart and Jim and Tammy Faye Baker, little success in advancing legislation against abortion during the Reagan administration, and even less support for its agenda during the Clinton administration. Nevertheless, a national survey in 1999 found the public even more divided along religious lines than had been the case in 1984. Whereas 18 percent had identified themselves as "very conservative" religiously in 1984, that proportion was 26 percent in the 1999 survey, and the proportion saying they were "very liberal" had risen from 19 percent to 28 percent.[12]

There was, then, some empirical support for what pundits increasingly termed a "culture war" in American religion. The church-going public—or at least its most visible spokespersons—were divided about abortion, homosexuality, school prayer, and even such issues as government funding for the arts and social welfare programs. However, several significant factors were also present that contained or reduced the polarization between religious liberals and conservatives. One was the fact that neither side was actually organized as a single party or movement. Each side remained divided into dozens of denominations, represented by dozens of different national leaders, mobilized its political efforts through dozens of special-purpose groups, and at the grassroots consisted of thousands of separate congregations. For either side to operate effectively as a political bloc, it needed to forge coalitions among these various organizations. And, despite the fact that both sides have been able to transcend old divisions, matters of theology, liturgical tradition, and even region remained as formidable barriers. This has been true on the Right, where divisions among Pentecostals and Baptists and between whites and blacks have hindered mobilization. It has been equally true on the Left, where concerns about denominational identities among mainline Protestants and Catholics and divisions between churchgoers and secularists have also prevented a stronger progressive bloc from emerging.

Another mitigating factor is that people on both sides of the religious aisle continue to be ambivalent about government, even when religious leaders sometimes appear eager to use government to achieve their goals. It is true that grassroots mobilization aims to increase voter turnout for favored candidates or embraces religious causes at school board meetings and the like. In the early twenty-first century, the George W. Bush administration appears to have utilized religious rhetoric to its advantage. Yet religious mobilization appears more often to oppose government than to enlist its support. During the Vietnam War, it was those who opposed the government's actions who became most active in politics. Much of the mobilization against abortion and welfare spending has similarly been against government policies. More recently, trade agreements, the invasion of Iraq, and concerns about human rights and torture have all generated more opposition to government from religious groups than support. In surveys, people of faith generally say it is acceptable for political candidates to express religious beliefs and for religious organizations to speak out on political issues, but the public is also skeptical of religious leaders running for office or religious groups endorsing political candidates.

Yet another aspect of contemporary religion that reduces the friction between religious liberals and conservatives is the live-and-let-live attitude that pervades American culture. If half of the public identifies itself with one or the other extreme, the remaining half is firmly in the middle. They weigh particular issues and lean slightly to the Left or Right, but are not ideologues. At times, they appear tolerant of all positions, for instance, holding that abortion is morally wrong, but regarding it as "neat" that their neighbor (or classmate) is a defender of the right to choose. Theirs is an open-ended faith that may regard Christianity as uniquely true and yet regard other religions as equally good ways of knowing God and, for that matter, trust personal experience more than any doctrines or historic religious teachings.

These mitigating factors notwithstanding, we must remember that religion is such a presence in American culture that political operatives are always eager to exploit it. In the late twentieth and early twenty-first centuries, Republicans have been especially clever at framing policy appeals in coded language that evangelical Protestants can recognize as their own. Democrats have wrung their hands, wondering why they cannot find a rhetoric about personal faith and social justice that appeals similarly to mainline Protestants and Catholics. The point is not that public officials should avoid courting religious constituencies. It is rather that religious identities themselves must be understood as political constructions. Such terms as religious Right, conservative Protestant, and even evangelical have connotations now that differ from their historic meanings and have been created by political operatives and the media as much as by church leaders themselves.

We return, then, to the point at which we began. The relations between faith and politics are contingent on the broader terrain on which they occur. Like the Battle of Waterloo, the battle between religious conservatives and religious liberals is subject to its environment. A deep cultural ravine often appears to separate the two communities. Whether this ravine can be bridged depends on raising it from obscurity, bringing it into consciousness, and recognizing the surrounding contours on which these efforts must rest. There is no question that the cultural divide has become more widely recognized in recent years. What has been harder to understand are the complex social conditions underlying this divide.

NOTES

1. Victor Hugo, *Les Miserables* (1862; rpt., New York: New American Library, 1987), 309.
2. Ibid., 328–29.
3. From a broadcast in February 1987 titled "What Is the Foundation for Our Philosophy of Christianity?" I wish to thank Victoria Chapman for the transcription of this sermon.
4. E. J. Dionne, Jr., "Religion and Politics," *New York Times*, 15 Sept. 1987.
5. Peggy L. Shriver, "The Paradox of Inclusiveness-That-Divides," *Christian Century*, 21 Jan. 1984, p. 194.
6. At the extremes, the public was also about equally divided: 19 percent said they were very liberal; 18 percent, very conservative. These figures are from a survey conducted in June 1984 by the Gallup Organization under a grant from the Robert Schuller Ministries. Some of the study's findings were reported in the May and June 1986 issues of *Emerging Trends*, a publication edited by George Gallup, Jr. The results of additional analyses of these data appear in Robert Wuthnow, *The Restructuring of American Religion: Society and Faith since World War II* (Princeton, N.J.: Princeton University Press, 1988).
7. Will Herberg, *Protestant-Catholic-Jew* (Garden City, N.Y.: Anchor, 1955).
8. Harold Laski, *The American Democracy* (New York: Viking, 1948), 283.
9. "The Churches and World Order," reprinted in *Christian Century*, 7 Feb. 1945, pp. 174–77.
10. C. Stanley Lowell, "The Conversion of America," *Christian Century*, 29 Sept. 1949, p. 1134.
11. Gunnar Myrdal, *An American Dilemma* (New York: Harper, 1944).
12. The 1999 survey was one I conducted with assistance from the Gallup Organization; see Robert Wuthnow, *All in Sync: How Music and Art Are Revitalizing American Religion* (Berkeley: University of California Press, 2003).

RELIGION, POLITICS, AND THE SEARCH FOR AN AMERICAN CONSENSUS

George M. Marsden

$\mathcal{R}$ELIGION, ESPECIALLY WHEN combined with ethnicity, has been the best predictor of political behavior throughout most of the history of the United States. From the early colonial settlements through at least the election of 1896, significant correlations existed between religious and political sentiments. This did not mean that religion was always or usually the primary determinant of political behavior, since many other variables came into play, including all those involved with ethnicity. Nonetheless, it is undeniable that, historically, religion has been a major component in American political life. Moreover, it was for centuries a divisive element, or at least a feature of the political scene fitting in with disruption more than harmony.

For our present purposes, it is necessary only to mention the formidable role that religion played during the American colonial era. Throughout the period, a central theme was the extended cold war between Protestants and Catholics. This deep rivalry dominated American thought on international politics in a way not unlike the way the Cold War overshadowed everything after World War II. Anti-Catholicism, of course, was far from the only political consideration for the overwhelmingly Protestant colonies, but for many influential people it was a major concern, one that could elicit their strongest loyalties.

Related was the theme of anti-Anglicanism. For Puritan New England, this was originally the primary religious-political issue, one for which their co-religionists in England went to war and for which the English Puritans experienced bitter suffering after the restoration of the monarchy in 1660. Although eighteenth-century New Englanders accepted the Anglican political establishment for a time, they never reconciled themselves to it.

In the middle colonies and the inland southern settlements of the eighteenth century, anti-Anglicanism was. likewise often a dominating passion for the militant Scots-Irish Presbyterian settlers. They too had a religious-political score to settle. Their anti-English and anti-Anglican sentiments were important ingredients in making the Revolution possible.[1]

Dissenting Protestants in eighteenth-century England also articulated resentments against the Anglican establishments in a respectable enlightened republican form. Such motifs were conspicuous in the Real Whig political writings that shaped much of American revolutionary thought. In the American southern colonies, this tradition was often attractive to those who were by birth Anglicans but who, because of their provincial location, were outsiders to the British and Anglican political-religious establishment. Such leaders, of whom Thomas Jefferson is the prototype, were themselves secularizing, thus giving them an additional reason to oppose the Anglican religious establishment in America.

The American republic was thus shaped by a dissenting Protestant and Enlightenment coalition against Anglican political power in the colonies. Of course, the issue was neither so simple nor so explicit, but religion was still a major feature of the conflict. The animus of many colonials, just before the Revolution, against the possibility of the appointment of an American Anglican bishop was one manifestation of the widespread perception that the Anglican ecclesiastical establishment and political power went hand in hand.

Formally, the new nation was defined in secular terms. The reason for that, as John Wilson suggests in his significant observations on the Constitution in this volume, was not because religion was unimportant to the colonists, but rather because it was too important. Clearly, many of the revolutionaries were not in principle opposed to all church establishments, since several states retained them. Rather, the primary explanation is that which Wilson presents. Only by staying away from the disruptive question of religion could a successful political coalition be forged among these contentious religious-ethnic groups.

Hence, one basis for political consensus in the United States is the recognition that the nation is divided tribally into ethnoreligious groups, which means that it is best to stay away from religion in public life. This tradition emphasizes the acceptance of diversity as a moral duty. It presumes that other ethical principles necessary for the survival of civilization will emerge from nongovernmental sources.

Many within the dominant classes in the new nation, however, shared another heritage that demanded a more integral relationship between Christianity and public life. They were not satisfied with tribal diversity, but were intent on uniting the nation under divinely sanctioned right principles. The revolutionary tradition going back to the Puritan commonwealth included this motif. The mythology that was part of eighteenth-century American revolutionary republicanism contained a version of this theme also. According to this outlook, based in part on the Real Whig republican political thought of eighteenth century English dissenting Protestants, religious authoritarianism and political authoritarianism were related historically and ideologically. On one side of the ledger were Catholicism, Anglicanism, centralized monarchical power, corruption, and tyranny; on the other side were Protestantism, Puritanism, representative government, virtue, and freedom. The American way thus had strong religious and ethical dimensions.

Particularly important in the early nineteenth century was an evangelical version of this outlook with a strong New England component and Puritan heritage. The Great Awakening of the eighteenth century had provided a bridge between Puritanism and democratic revolution. The Second Great Awakening, continuing throughout the first half of the century and longer, expanded the cultural influence of revivalist or evangelical Protestantism. Especially in the North, this heritage furnished the religious rationale for the cultural outlook that became one of the long-standing components in the basic patterns of American political life. Those who adopted this outlook were typically English and religiously evangelical (or Unitarian). Culturally aggressive New England Yankees provided the leadership for this party. Reflecting the Puritan heritage, they sought the conversion of individuals and also strongly favored applying Christian principles to the transformation of society. This transformation would be accomplished by converted individuals who cultivated virtues of industry, thrift, and personal purity, but also by voluntary societies of such individuals who would band together for religious, educational, and political causes.

One of the early political expressions of this impulse was a phenomenon that, outside of this context, would appear as a total anomaly in American political history, the Antimason party. The secret order of the Masons appeared to these evangelicals as an ominous false religion, one that appealed especially to freethinkers. In 1828, Antimasons were numerous enough to deliver nearly half of New York's electoral votes to John Quincy Adams. They soon merged with the new Whig party and became the base for that party's important "conscience" wing, including such strong proponents of antislavery as Thaddeus Stevens and William H. Seward. Evangelist Charles Finney was an ardent Antimason. (After the Civil War, when the antislavery issue was settled, Finney returned to the unfinished business of Antimasonry, allying himself with Jonathan Blanchard, president of Wheaton College in Illinois.)

While the Whig party of the 1830s and 1840s included a substantial New England element, which promoted the effort to regulate society according to evangelical principles,[2] the drive took on a new shape with the demise of the Whig party.

The new factor in the equation was the rise of Catholic political power. Before the mid-nineteenth century, the American rivalries had been intra-Protestant. The Scots Irish, for instance, were pivotal in American politics through the nation's first half-century. Disliking the New Englanders and New England schemes for moral regulation, they allied themselves with the South, which dominated the politics of the early era. In the 1850s, however, the Catholic threat changed the picture. Catholics who also did not like Yankee ideals of a monolithic Protestant moral commonwealth swelled the ranks of the Democrats. The Scots Irish despised the Catholics even more than they disliked the New Englanders and so left the Democratic fold. So did some Baptists and Methodists. As Robert Kelley observes, whereas previously the party of culturally aggressive Protestantism had been *English*, now it was a *British* lineup against the detested Irish Catholics.[3]

Explicit anti-Catholicism emerged as the major political issue of the early 1850s. In 1856, the anti-Catholic, nativist Know-Nothing party won 21 percent of the popular vote for its presidential candidate, Millard Fillmore. Then it merged with the antislavery and purely regional Republican party. The result was that the Republican party had a strong Puritan-evangelical component, bent on regulating the society according to Christian principles. Antislavery was the great achievement of this outlook, but anti-alcohol and anti-Catholicism components were just as much its trademarks.

One thing this party was doing was establishing an insider-versus-outsider mentality toward America and Americanism. Ethnically, it was predominantly British; economically, it was thoroughly allied with the dominant business community. Both these features reinforced its insider view of itself. The Puritan-Methodist ethic of self-help, moral discipline, and social responsibility dominated much of American education and defined its version of Americanism.

In the meantime, the Democratic party after the 1840s was becoming increasingly the party of outsiders. Its two strongest components were Catholics and southerners, two groups that had almost nothing in common except their common disdain of the Republican party, with its self-righteous evangelical penchant to impose its version of Christian morality on the whole nation. Northern evangelicals, such as Methodists, most Baptists, Congregationalists, and New School Presbyterians, usually voted Republican. High Church, liturgical, and confessional Protestants, including some German Lutherans, all groups that had reservations about the evangelical-Puritan version of a Christian America, on the other hand, were more likely to vote Democratic. So were an important group of evangelical Protestants who, in the tradition of Roger Williams, were sufficiently sectarian to question the possibility of ever establishing a Christian political order.[4]

Though the Republican party was a pragmatic coalition and not simply an evangelical voluntary society writ large, a clue to its image of itself as building a Protestant Christian moral consensus is found in the notorious remark by a supporter of James G. Blaine during the presidential campaign of 1884. The Democrats, he said, were the party of "Rum, Romanism, and Rebellion." On one hand, it is revealing of the party's Protestant, nativist, and moral reform heritage that a campaigner in a close race would make such a remark. On the other hand, since the quip was thought to have cost Blaine the election, it may be taken as signaling the end of the era, which began with the Antimason campaigns, when evangelical Protestantism would be an explicitly partisan factor in American political life. Although the symbolic evangelical issue of prohibition remained prominent for another half-century, neither party could afford to be as overtly sectarian as before. The parties were closely enough matched that Republicans had to cultivate some Catholic support and Democrats, some evangelical. This situation was a major change from a period when religion had largely worked against national consensus.

The real turning point in the reorientation of American politics came in 1896, when the Democrats ran the evangelical William Jennings Bryan for president. By the time Bryan had run twice more, in 1900 and 1908, the Democratic party included an interventionist reformist element, much like the Republican party, including even strong sentiments for the archevangelical cause of prohibition.[5] Democrats ended the Progressive Era by electing Woodrow Wilson. Though a southerner, the Presbyterian Wilson was as Puritan as any New Englander who ever held the office.

Just as revealing, however, was what was happening to the Republicans in the meantime. The party of William McKinley and Mark Hanna had toned down its evangelical image and attracted some Catholic constituents. Nonetheless, as Robert Handy shows in this volume, they were still an overwhelmingly Protestant party with strong assimilationist goals. They represented centripetal forces in America attempting to counter centrifugal tendencies accentuated by immigration. Public education became sacrosanct as one means for teaching immigrants the American way and American virtues. The Social Gospel was a program for Christianizing America, but without the offense of the old exclusivist gospel of revivalism. In other words, Republicans were still building a Christian consensus, but were suppressing the exclusivist evangelical Protestant elements so as to be able to absorb the new immigrants within their domain.

In effect, the liberal Protestantism and slightly secularized social reform of the Progressive Era allowed the heirs to accomplish once again what their more explicitly evangelical progenitors had achieved in the 1860s: northern Protestant dominance. As Robert Kelley puts it, the party patterns set in the Progressive Era, from 1894 to 1930, coincided with "the years of Northern WASP ascendancy in all things, including government, literature, scholarship, the arts, and the economy."[6]

So we see an instance of what Martin Marty long ago pointed out as an American pattern of secularization. Secularization in America took place not by a developing hostility between religion and the dominant culture, but by a blending of their goals. So Republican-Protestant hegemony no longer had to be explicitly Protestant. It just represented, as Handy makes clear, a certain concept of civilization. Civilization was equivalent in most minds to Christian civilization. It could be advanced by reforming progressive moral principles that people from all traditions might share. Many Democrats of the era, represented by Bryan and Wilson, adopted this slightly secularized Protestant vision as much as did Republicans. The immense American missionary enthusiasm of this era, sweeping through the country's colleges, reflected this same impulse to help the world by advancing Christian civilization. Wilson's secularized postmillennial vision of the American mission—to make the world safe for democracy—reflected a similar outlook. Religion, in short, had begun to work toward consensus.

Nonetheless, despite this softening of the Protestant hegemony into a melting-pot ideal of citizenship, democracy, and values taught to all in the public schools, the realignment of 1896 did not entirely disrupt the older party patterns.[7] At least through the election of 1960, the strongest bases for the Democratic party were the solid South and Catholic communities. Old-line Protestants still tended to be disproportionately Republican. With the coming of the Depression and the New Deal, however, economic issues dominated party politics. Except when the Democrats ran Catholics in 1928 and 1960, explicit religion was relegated to a ceremonial role.

As James Hennesey's chapter in this volume shows, although there were a number of politicians who were Catholics during this era, there were almost no Catholic politicians in the substantive sense of elected leaders applying Catholic principles to politics. Rather, Catholic politicians were Americanizing. And the price of being an American politician if you were a Catholic was to leave your substantive Catholicism at the church door. Al Smith's remark "What in hell is an encyclical?" perfectly summarizes the stance. Catholics had learned to play the twentieth-century game of appealing to the nation's religious heritage, but in a purely ceremonial way. So John F. Kennedy's public use of religious symbolism qualified him to become Robert Bellah's exhibit number one in his famous characterization of American civil religion.

After the Progressive Era, almost the only place where religion worked against the political consensus was in the Civil Rights movement. Blacks, whose political style had been set by mid-nineteenth-century Republican models and for whom the clergy were traditional community spokespersons in the pattern of Puritan New England, could still challenge the collective conscience of the nation. During the Lyndon Johnson era, they too were finally incorporated into the consensus, although largely in formal and superficial ways.

The wider pattern was a growing ideal of secularized consensus extending from 1896 to about 1968. Despite the persistent ethnoreligious patterns, some differing economic policies, and differing degrees of cold warriorism, the two parties were now much alike. With some significant exceptions, it was difficult to find any difference in principles between them. Rather, the genius of American politics seemed to be that the two parties did not stand for much of anything. George Wallace's campaign slogan of 1968 that there was not "a dime's worth of difference" between the two parties seemed accurate. Supporters of Eugene McCarthy could agree.

Martin Marty has referred to a "four-faith" pluralism that emerged in the consensus America of the 1950s. As Will Herberg showed in 1955, although American Protestants, Catholics, and Jews had differing formal religions, they had much in common in the operative religion of faith in the American way of life.[8] Marty adds the fourth faith of secularism, acceptable as a private option and still fitting within the consensus.[9]

From our retrospective vantage point, one of the striking things about this accurate portrayal of American public life in the consensus era is the lack of any role for explicitly evangelical Protestantism. What had happened was that, as mainline Protestants blended into a secularized consensus, fundamentalists, conservative Protestants, or explicit "evangelicals" were forced out. After the 1920s, they lapsed into political inactivity, or rested quietly on the fringes of American political life, often on the far Right, as quietly conservative Republicans in the North or as birthright Democrats in the South. But in this separation, it is important to note, evangelicals were beginning to nurture dissent that would one day threaten the consensus. They dissented first of all against the liberal theology that made the consensus possible, but also against some of the progressive social policies that grew out of the Social Gospel.

One of the remarkable things that has happened since 1968 is the emergence of this group as an active political force. By 1968, the liberal New Deal consensus had broken down. The Vietnam War, the rioting of blacks, and the counterculture brought down the illusion of a liberal Protestant-Catholic-Jewish-secular, good citizenship, consensus America. While progressives tried to rebuild a more thoroughly secular and more inclusive and pluralistic consensus, conservatives sharply disagreed. Capitalizing at first on what seemed a largely secular backlash, they mobilized around anticommunism and love-it-or-leave-it Americanism. Then, after the Vietnam War and the presidency of Richard Nixon, a new, more-religious coalition began to coalesce around ethical issues, such as anti-abortion, antipornography, and anti-ERA, and symbolic religious issues, such as school prayer.

After 1976, it became clear that a substantial evangelical, fundamentalist, and Pentecostal-charismatic constituency could be mobilized around these issues. Only a portion of theologically conservative evangelicals, however, adopted this stance on the political Right. The evangelical movement itself was a divided coalition that at best maintained a tenuous antiliberal theological unity among a myriad of subgroups and denominations. Although a solid contingent of evangelicals could be organized, as in the Moral Majority or in Pat Robertson's campaigns, evangelicalism was far from unified as a political force.

What those who did mobilize helped to do, however, was very significant for the patterns of American political life. They helped to supply a rhetoric to bring one wing of the Republican party back toward its nineteenth-century heritage. A striking element that was gone, however, was the anti-Catholicism. Evangelicals, conservative Catholics, and Mormons now made common cause on anticommunist and family issues. Such remarkable alliances suggested that, despite the explicitly evangelical stance of much of the leadership of the religious Right, it also was forming a political consensus in which the exclusiveness of evangelicalism would be toned down. At the same time, the new religious Right drew in a conservative white evangelical constituency from the South, which adopted the renewed Christian American ideal with particular fervor.

Despite these realignments, we can see in the rise of the religious Right a revival of a long-standing component in the American religious-political heritage. The war on secular humanism in the 1980s had many precedents, going back to attacks on Jeffersonian "infidelity" by New England's Federalist clergy, the Antimason party, Whig moral agendas, and early Republican reforms.

Responding to a revolution in sexual mores that became linked with the Democratic party, one significant wing of Republicanism recovered the principle of building a coalition around a militant antisecularist agenda and invoking the ideal of establishing a broadly Christian America. Perhaps the most striking thing about this recovery, though, is that so many white conservative evangelical southern Protestants, especially Baptists (who have a tradition of church-state separation) have taken over what were originally New England Puritan and Yankee principles of how religion should guide the state.

Religion continues to be a divisive factor in American politics, but with a new twist. No longer does it primarily accentuate ethnic and regional differences that could be neatly traced along denominational lines. Rather, since the late twentieth century, the religious-political divide more often cuts across denominations. Moderate and liberal Southern Baptists (including a succession of Democratic presidential candidates) deeply oppose conservative Southern Baptists. Moderate and liberal mainline Protestants take strong stands against their conservative counterparts. Conservative Catholics follow the pope on matters of family and sexuality, while progressive Catholics celebrate the Catholic positions on social justice, poverty, and international affairs and vote Democratic.

Robert Wuthnow, in analyzing these realignments in this volume, has pointed out that political conservatives are not the only ones to have a religious-moral vision for the nation. Rather, he observes elsewhere, America has two civil religions:

> The conservative vision offers divine sanction to America, legitimates its form of government and economy, explains its privileged place in the world and justifies a uniquely American standard of luxury and morality. The liberal vision raises questions about the American way of life, scrutinizes its political and economic policies in the light of transcendent concerns and challenges Americans to act on behalf of all humanity rather than their own interests alone.[10]

When the alternatives are stated in this bipolar way, it becomes apparent how much politics shapes religion as much as the reverse. Political parties are coalitions that bring together people of diverse and often opposing interests. The Republican party, like the Whigs before them, is the party of big business as well as being a home for explicit more-or-less evangelical moral visions for the society. Conservative evangelicals, conservative Catholics, and others who in the late twentieth century cast their lot with Republicans because of a moral agenda also tended to adopt something like the "conservative vision" that Wuthnow describes, even though there is nothing inherent in their religious heritage to compel them to adopt that vision as opposed to one that "challenges Americans to act on behalf of all humanity." By the same token, when religious people of all types, including significant minorities of theological conservatives, adopt the Democratic party because of its rhetoric of serving humanity, they become de facto supporters of the self-interests of all the other groups that support that party and of permissive moral agendas that seem contrary to their religious ideals.

Perhaps the most striking example of the way in which American political-religious lineups have been shaped and reshaped by the contingencies of the two-party system is seen in the African-American community. African-American politicians still speak with a bold religious voice, like the nineteenth-century Radical Republicans who were their first political mentors. Yet having long since abandoned a business-oriented Republican party that neglected their racial and economic interests, they find themselves in the party of Jefferson allied with those who normally oppose presenting their moral ideals as a *religious* vision.

Others in the Democratic coalition, which has for the most part argued that explicit religious speech (except the vaguest platitudes) is to be kept out of politics, are put in an awkward position by the conspicuous African-American exception to that rule. Particularly during the administration of George W. Bush, many Democrats deplored the use of religion in politics by the religious Right. At the same time, many white Democratic leaders wondered how they could learn to speak with a more credible religious voice.

The particularity of a substantial religious vision and the generality and the vagueness of the rhetoric necessary to build a viable political coalition in a two-party system in a nation with unprecedented religious diversity makes the task of satisfactorily relating religion to mainstream politics a perilous one. Both party coalitions welcome minority blocs with explicit religious visions, but both demand in return that these visions be compromised in support of essentially secular larger political agendas. Truly prophetic religious voices may exercise real influence on the political system; yet the irony is that those who gain power are likely to be corrupted by the realities of party politics as usual.

Notes

1. Robert Kelley, *The Cultural Pattern of American Politics* (New York: Knopf, 1979), 71–72.
2. Daniel Walker Howe, *The Political Culture of the American Whigs* (Chicago: University of Chicago Press, 1979), provides an excellent discussion of these themes.
3. Kelley, *Cultural Pattern*, 278–79.
4. Howe, *Political Culture*, 17–18, 159–67. A very detailed and sophisticated analysis of these typologies for a later period is offered by Philip R. VanderMeer, *The Hoosier*

Politician: Officeholding and Political Culture in Indiana: 1896–1920 (Urbana: University of Illinois Press, 1985), 96–120.

5. Paul Kleppner, *Who Voted? The Dynamics of Electoral Turnout, 1870–1980* (New York: Praeger, 1982), 77–78. Cf. Kleppner, "From Ethnoreligious Conflict to 'Social Harmony': Coalitional and Party Transformations in the 1890s," in *Emerging Coalitions in American Politics*, ed. Seymour Martin Lipset (San Francisco: Institute for Contemporary Studies, 1978), 41–59.

6. Kelley, *Cultural Pattern*, 285.

7. VanderMeer, *Hoosier Politician*, shows that in general the old patterns held in Indiana during the Progressive Era.

8. Will Herberg, *Protestant-Catholic-Jew* (Garden City, N.Y.: Doubleday, 1955).

9. In *The New Shape of American Religion* (New York: Harper & Row, 1958), 76–80, Marty was already talking about America's fourth faith as "secular humanism" (following John Courtney Murray in the usage). He also remarked that "it has an 'established church' in the field of public education." Presumably, discussions such as Murray's and Marty's were behind Justice Hugo Black's famous reference to secular humanism as a religion in a 1961 Supreme Court decision. Such sober roots for the term run against claims (as by Sean Wilentz, "God and Man at Lynchburg," *New Republic*, 25 Apr. 1988, p. 36) of "the invention of secular humanism as a mass religion" by fundamentalists.

10. Robert Wuthnow, "Divided We Fall: America's Two Civil Religions," *Christian Century*, 20 Apr. 1988, p. 398. Wuthnow's *The Restructuring of American Religion* (Princeton, N.J.: Princeton University Press, 1988) contains an outstanding discussion of political and religious realignments.

Page numbers in bold indicate figures or tables.